Educating Children
with Multiple Disabilities

Educating Children with Multiple Disabilities
A Transdisciplinary Approach
Third Edition

by

Fred P. Orelove, Ph.D.
Virginia Institute for Developmental Disabilities
Virginia Commonwealth University
Richmond

and

Dick Sobsey, R.N., Ed.D.
Developmental Disabilities Centre
University of Alberta
Edmonton, Ontario, Canada

with invited contributions

·PAUL·H·
BROOKES
PUBLISHING CO.

Baltimore • London • Toronto • Sydney

Paul H. Brookes Publishing Co.
Post Office Box 10624
Baltimore, Maryland 21285-0624

Copyright © 1996 by Paul H. Brookes Publishing Co., Inc.
All rights reserved.

Typeset by Signature Typesetting & Design, Baltimore, Maryland.
Manufactured in the United States of America by
Thomson-Shore, Inc., Dexter, Michigan.

Library of Congress Cataloging-in-Publication Data
Orelove, Fred P., 1951–
    Educating children with multiple disabilities: a transdisciplinary approach / by
Fred P. Orelove and Dick Sobsey; with invited contributions. — 3rd ed.
        p.   cm.
    Includes bibliographical references and index.
    ISBN 1-55766-246-0
    1.   Handicapped children—Education.   2.   Handicapped children—Care
I.   Sobsey, Richard. II.   Title.
LC4015.068   1996
371.9—dc20   96-7912
                                                                                                             CIP

British Library Cataloguing-in-Publication data are available from the British Library.

Contents

About the Authors

Fred P. Orelove, Ph.D., Executive Director, Virginia Institute for Developmental Disabilities, Virginia Commonwealth University, Post Office Box 843020, Richmond, Virginia 23284-3020

Dr. Orelove, in addition to being the executive director of the Virginia Institute for Developmental Disabilities, directs Virginia Commonwealth University's Program in Severe Disabilities, where he specializes in children with severe disabilities. Since the 1970s, Dr. Orelove has taught children and has directed numerous training and demonstration projects related to individuals with developmental disabilities. In addition to this book, he has co-authored two books on teamwork.

Dick Sobsey, R.N., Ed.D., Director, Developmental Disabilities Centre, University of Alberta, 6-102 Education North, Edmonton, Alberta, Canada T6G 2G5

Dr. Sobsey is a professor of educational psychology and Director of the Developmental Disabilities Centre at the University of Alberta. He has worked with children and adults with severe and multiple disabilities since 1968. His current research focuses on the relationship between violence and disability. He is the father of two school-age children, one of whom has a severe developmental disability.

CONTRIBUTORS

Irene H. Carney, Ph.D., Director, The Sabot School, 6818 West Grace Street, Richmond, Virginia 23226

Dr. Carney has been active in early intervention; respite care; and family support, policy, and advocacy. She directed the Parent Involvement Project at the University of Virginia and served as Director of Family Support at the Virginia Institute for Developmental Disabilities at Virginia Commonwealth University.

Ann W. Cox, Ph.D., R.N., Director, Preservice Training, Virginia Institute for Developmental Disabilities, Virginia Commonwealth University, Post Office Box 843020, Richmond, Virginia 23284-3020

Dr. Cox, a pediatric nurse by profession, first became involved with team-based collaborative practice in 1974. The needs of children with chronic conditions and disabilities and those of their families are of special interest. Dr. Cox is an advocate for active collaboration between the systems of health care and education and for full participation of individuals and families in decision-making processes at all levels.

Winnie Dunn, Ph.D., OTR, FAOTA, Professor and Chair, Department of Occupational Therapy Education, School of Allied Health, 3033 Robinson, University of Kansas Medical Center, 3901 Rainbow Boulevard, Kansas City, Kansas 66160-7602

Dr. Dunn has worked in community-based programs for children and families since the 1970s. She has conducted research and written about service provision throughout her career. In addition, Dr. Dunn has provided many workshops and seminars with interdisciplinary audiences about recommended practices for children and family services.

Michael Gamel-McCormick, Ph.D., Assistant Professor, Department of Individual and Family Studies, University of Delaware, 117 Alison Hall West, Newark, Delaware 19716

Dr. Gamel-McCormick has worked in the field of early intervention since the early 1980s. He currently assists in preparing early childhood education teachers to work with young children with and without disabilities. His research involves families' perceptions of effective support services, the experiences of families from lower socioeconomic backgrounds regarding Part H services, and the preferences of families who have a child with a disability regarding preservice training programs in early interventions.

Peggy Locke, Ph.D., Director, Education Services, AbleNet, Inc., 1081 Tenth Avenue, SE, Minneapolis, Minnesota 55414

Dr. Locke earned her doctoral degree in special education with an emphasis in augmentative and alternative communication. During her 20-year career, she has spent more than 11 years as a special education teacher of students with severe disabilities in kindergarten through 12th grade and since the mid-1980s has focused on inclusion of children and adults with severe/profound disabilities through simple-to-use technology. In addition, Dr. Locke has provided training and support to thousands of educators and families throughout the world who are interested in expanding the capabilities of their students and children through shared experiences that are accessible and enjoyable for all.

Anne Malatchi, M.A., Director, Together We Can Project, Virginia Institute for Developmental Disabilities, Virginia Commonwealth University, Post Office Box 843020, Richmond, Virginia 23284-3020

Ms. Malatchi has been involved in education in a variety of roles since the 1970s. These roles include general education teacher, special education teacher, inclusion facilitator, education specialist, and behavioral consultant. In addition to being the director of the Together We Can Project, Ms. Malatchi promotes inclusive schools and communities at conferences and workshops in the United States and Canada.

Beverly Rainforth, Ph.D., P.T., Associate Professor, Special Education, School of Education and Human Development, State University of New York at Binghamton, Box 6000, Binghamton, New York 13902-6000

Dr. Rainforth has worked as a physical therapist and special education teacher with infants, children, and adults with developmental disabilities in a variety of settings. She is an associate professor of special education. Dr. Rainforth also chairs the Related Services Interest and Action group for TASH and is Related Services Consultant for the national Consortium on Inclusive School Practices. With Jennifer York and Cathy Macdonald, Dr. Rainforth is the co-author of *Collaborative Teams for Students with Severe Disabilities: Integrating Therapy and Educational Services,* published by Paul H. Brookes Publishing Co.

Madhavan Thuppal, M.B.B.S., D.P.M., M.D., M.Ed., Department of Educational Psychology, University of Alberta, 6-102 Education North, Edmonton, Alberta, Canada T6G 2G5

Dr. Thuppal is a physician and psychiatrist specializing in the needs of individuals with developmental disabilities. He worked for 8 years at the National Institute for the Mentally Handicapped, Secunderabad, India, as an assistant professor. In addition to his medical training, he has completed a master's degree in special education with severe disabilities at the University of Alberta and is working toward a doctoral degree in that area. His primary area of interest is dual diagnosis, and he is completing a residency in psychiatry at the State University of New York at Stony Brook.

Enid Wolf-Schein, Ed.D., CCC-SLP, Independent Consultant, 1703 Andros Isle, Apartment J-2, Coconut Creek, Florida 33066

Dr. Wolf-Schein earned a doctor of education in special education with a major in speech-language pathology from Boston University. She has worked in a series of positions since the 1960s that include speech-language pathologist, special education administrator, research scientist/psychologist, and chief researcher and professor at New York University and the University of Alberta. She has written numerous seminal articles and is writing and consulting in assessment and programming for individuals with severe disabilities.

Jennifer York-Barr, Ph.D., Associate Professor, Department of Educational Policy and Administration, and Preservice Training Coordinator, Institute on Community Integration, University of Minnesota, College of Education, 86 Pleasant Street, SE, Minneapolis, Minnesota 55455

Dr. York-Barr's current program and research interests are in creating learning communities in schools with a specific focus on collaboration among general educators, special educators, and related services personnel to develop more effective learning environments for today's heterogeneous student population. Most of her experience has focused on the inclusion of learners with disabilities. Dr. York-Barr also coordinates the master's of education program in teacher leadership at the University of Minnesota and is the lead member of the doctor of education program in educational leadership at the College of Education and Human Development.

Preface

THE FIRST EDITION OF THIS BOOK was published in 1987. Since that time, the field of severe disabilities has galloped along at a dizzying pace. Our entire world view of what learners need from an education—indeed, what they deserve—has changed in focus. The concept of clustering and teaching students with similar learning abilities, etiologies, and skills has given way to having all students become part of the educational and social fabric of the classroom and the school.

Interestingly, the terms "inclusion" and "inclusive education" have become such accepted parts of our vocabulary that we may forget their recency. Four books published in 1989 explored non-separate instruction for learners with severe disabilities (Gaylord-Ross, 1989; Lipsky & Gartner, 1989; Sailor et al., 1989; Stainback, Stainback, & Forest, 1989). The term "inclusion" does not appear in the index of any one of them.

In the 1990s, both the term "inclusion" and the concept have become inextricably linked. Increasing numbers of students formerly educated in separate classrooms or separate schools are being included in general education classes. Schools are becoming increasingly committed to the philosophy and practice of inclusion and are dealing with the complex issues of curriculum, assessment, scheduling, staffing, professional development, and so forth. As a result, "school restructuring" has become part of our language and culture.

The third edition of *Educating Children with Multiple Disabilities: A Transdisciplinary Approach* was written to embody both the practice and spirit of inclusive education. It is not, however, intended to replace the many fine books and materials on inclusion that have been published over the past several years. Nor is it intended to be a how-to manual for individuals interested in arranging inclusive classes. Rather, the third edition continues to serve the same principal function as the first two editions: to provide current information on individuals with multiple disabilities, strategies for educating them effectively, and a unified framework for doing so.

We believe that this framework, the transdisciplinary model, is more relevant than ever. The practice of inclusive education presents an even greater need for collaboration among school personnel and family members. Inclusion demands continual problem solving, sharing of information, and, above all, a willingness to release control to others—the hallmark of the transdisciplinary approach.

We also believe that children with multiple disabilities are more similar to children without disabilities than they are different. They experience the same range of emotions, have many of the same interests, and have many of the same talents. At the same time, students with significant cognitive, physical, and sensory disabilities require that professionals have the most current information to be effective. Therefore, the third edition provides new or updated materials on facilitated communication, electronic communication boards, instructional adaptations, children with asthma and respiratory conditions, and abuse and neglect. All of the chapters have been updated to reflect new research and philosophy. Chapter 10 has been completely rewritten to be consistent with the literature and practice of inclusion.

Despite these additions and updates, this edition retains the basic format of the previous editions. Chapter 1 examines teamwork models, specifically focusing on transdisciplinary teams. Chapters 2 and 3 present basic terminology and information on the physical and sensorimotor needs of children with multiple disabilities. Because the material on instructional adaptations follows logically from knowledge of handling techniques, it has been moved in this edition to Chapter 4. Readers may find it helpful, however, to read Chapters 4 and 10 together. Chapters 5 and 6 offer information on children's health needs and strategies for transdisciplinary teams to work together toward strategies for prevention and intervention. Chapters 7–10 discuss a process for designing curriculum and instruction and provide specific strategies for teaching communication, mealtime, and self-care skills. Suggestions are provided in each chapter for working on transdisciplinary teams. Chapter 11 focuses on children with sensory disabilities (visual, auditory, or both), and Chapter 12 discusses issues related to understanding and working with families.

As in the first two editions, this book avoids using jargon; where this was not possible or desirable, we have tried to define or describe terms within the text. We hope that this approach will appeal to a broad readership, spanning a wide variety of disciplines.

The ultimate test for this book continues to be whether it contributes to the information and skills of the reader and whether, in turn, this translates into improved education and supports for children. We hope that this book contributes to these outcomes at least in part, and we wish all readers success in meeting their own needs and those of the children whom they work with and whom they love and care for.

REFERENCES

Gaylord-Ross, R. (Ed.). (1989). *Integration strategies for students with handicaps.* Baltimore: Paul H. Brookes Publishing Co.

Lipsky, D.K., & Gartner, A. (Eds.). (1989). *Beyond separate education: Quality education for all.* Baltimore: Paul H. Brookes Publishing Co.

Sailor, W., Anderson, J.L., Halvorsen, A.T., Doering, K., Filler, J., & Goetz, L. (1989). *The comprehensive local school: Regular education for all students with disabilities.* Baltimore: Paul H. Brookes Publishing Co.

Stainback, S., Stainback, W., & Forest, M. (Eds.). (1989). *Educating all students in the mainstream of regular education.* Baltimore: Paul H. Brookes Publishing Co.

Acknowledgments

We wish to thank the following individuals for their help and advice on specific chapters:

Chapter 1: Deana Buck for sharing materials on models of service delivery.

Chapter 3: Amy Atherton and her mother, Linda.

Chapter 4: Lindsay and her teachers and classmates, and Laura Piché, M.A.

Chapter 6: Andy, Carol, and Bill, a special family and valued friends.

Chapter 9: Jayne Shepherd, for generously providing important source materials.

Chapter 10: The many families who have shared themselves and their stories. Special thanks to Harry, Kate, Harry, Jr., and Corrine McCoy, who allowed their personal story to add so much to this chapter. Also to Paula Ropelewski for her contributions to the MAP.

Chapter 11: Jerome D. Schein, Ph.D., for contributions based on his original research.

Thanks also go to many wonderful colleagues at the Virginia Institute for Developmental Disabilities, Virginia Commonwealth University, for their support and understanding during the development of this book. A special thanks to Elaine Ferrell, who provided not only superlative administrative support but also a steady hand and a sense of humor.

We also thank the many students, professionals, and reviewers who responded to the first two editions of this book. Their reinforcement gave us the impetus to work on a third edition, and the critical feedback has, we believe, made for a better book.

A special "thank you" to Melissa Behm, Mary Olofsson, and others at Paul H. Brookes Publishing Company for their patience and unwavering support throughout the development and production of the book.

Finally, we continue to owe a great debt to the families, children, and team members who have provided knowledge, support, and teaching opportunities that were truly transdisciplinary and that have resulted in our personal and professional growth. We hope that this book reflects at least some of their inspiration and strength.

To Edmund E. and Peggy Carney,
devoted to one another and reunited

1

Designing
Transdisciplinary Services

THIS CHAPTER FOCUSES ON A system of providing services to individuals with multiple disabilities that has proved successful—the transdisciplinary model. Major features of the model are discussed, with particular emphasis given to team decision making and implications for providing school-based services. Problems in implementing a transdisciplinary model are also presented. This chapter begins, however, by 1) discussing the needs of children with multiple disabilities, 2) surveying professionals who work with the students, and 3) describing educational teaming approaches.

NEEDS OF CHILDREN WITH MULTIPLE DISABILITIES

As used throughout the book, the phrase "children with multiple disabilities" refers to individuals with 1) mental retardation requiring extensive or pervasive supports, and 2) one or more significant motor or sensory impairments and/or special health care needs. These individuals are an important subgroup of students commonly referred to as "people with severe disabilities" by the federal government and in the professional special education literature. Because of their combinations of physical, medical, educational, and social/emotional needs, children with multiple disabilities present an immense challenge to professionals responsible for their education. The remainder of this section highlights the varied needs these children bring to the educational setting.

1

Physical and Medical Needs

The increased frequency of physical and medical problems in individuals with severe disabilities has been well documented (e.g., Mulligan-Ault, Guess, Struth, & Thompson, 1988; Thompson & Guess, 1989). Within this larger group, the individual with multiple disabilities almost always presents two or more of the characteristics described below.

Restriction of Movement   The most frequently identifiable organic finding in multiple disabilities is cerebral palsy. The hallmark of cerebral palsy (see Chapter 2) is disordered movement and posture. Because of the damage to or improper development of the brain that causes cerebral palsy, the vast majority of children with multiple disabilities are unable to walk. Many of these children, in fact, have voluntary movement that is limited both quantitatively and qualitatively, making it difficult or impossible for them to move freely about their environment or change their positions (Campbell, 1987). Proper positioning and handling (see Chapter 3) are vitally important in facilitating proper movement and posture and in preventing secondary deformities.

Skeletal Deformities   Many children with multiple disabilities are born with or, more commonly, develop physical disabilities secondary to their primary disability as a result of brain damage (Campbell, 1989). Such problems typically include 1) scoliosis (curvature of the spine) and other back and spinal disorders, 2) contractures (permanent shortening of muscles and tendons), 3) partial or total dislocation of the hips, and 4) disorders of the foot and ankle. These and other problems within the bones, joints and connecting muscles, tendons, and ligaments not only cause discomfort and interfere with movement but actually can be life threatening in severe cases.

Sensory Disorders   In addition to experiencing difficulty in movement, students considered to have multiple disabilities are more likely than other people with severe disabilities to have vision and hearing loss. Although the number of children considered to be truly deaf-blind is relatively small (Fredericks & Baldwin, 1987), it is not uncommon to find children with one or more impaired sensory systems.

Seizure Disorders   As is examined further in Chapter 6, the prevalence of seizure disorders is 16% in children with mental retardation and 25% in children with cerebral palsy (Wallace, 1990). Although seizures frequently are controlled with medication, many students with multiple disabilities present a challenge to the physician trying to regulate seizure activity. Moreover, the medication itself can result in adverse physiological and behavioral side effects.

Lung and Breathing Control   Largely because of their muscle and skeletal disorders, children with multiple disabilities are at greater risk of incurring breathing and lung problems. Such problems often occur during mealtimes, when the student may have trouble handling food in the mouth and swallowing. Other children may accumulate excessive amounts of mucus or other secretions in the airway and lungs, obstructing normal breathing. Still others may have an underdeveloped respiratory system, requiring dependence on mechanical respirators.

Other Medical Problems   In general, children with multiple disabilities are less healthy than other children (Thompson & Guess, 1989). Their problems range from ear and bladder infections to skin ulcers and constipation. They are more likely to take a variety of medications, from antibiotics to anticonvulsants to stool softeners. Certainly, proper attention to such matters as physical activity, diet, positioning, and medical referrals can reduce students' discomfort, enhance their education, and improve the overall quality, if not length, of their lives. (Chapter 6 discusses health care issues in greater detail.)

Educational Needs

Many of the educational needs of students with multiple disabilities are similar to those of any individual with severe disabilities. These individuals typically acquire skills slowly, tend to forget skills they do not practice, have trouble generalizing skills from one situation to another, and find it difficult to synthesize skills learned separately (Rainforth, York, & Macdonald, 1992). The loss of or decrease in function within sensory or motor systems, however, makes the demand for organized systematic instruction and management more urgent.

Appropriate Positioning and Handling   It was suggested previously that good positioning and handling of children with multiple disabilities could reduce their pain and prevent further complications of their structural impairments. Because of their possible lack of voluntary control and sensory impairments, it is equally important that these students be positioned to allow them to see, to hear, to reach, and to otherwise become engaged with individuals and materials. Appropriate positioning is essential for efficient movement in all activities.

Appropriate Methods of Communication   Most children with multiple disabilities are unable to communicate through speech. Almost all, however, can express basic wants and needs if given appropriate training and opportunities and if staff are attuned to students' individual behaviors and personalities. Communication is a basic need of any human being, and it certainly is critical for those individuals who are physically unable to retrieve or seek what they want, including food, drink, and companionship.

Means to Choose   Because children with severe disabilities usually cannot say what they want or make the movements necessary to reach it, adults often choose for them. It is important to allow learners to choose and to teach them how to make choices (Guess & Siegel-Causey, 1985). Choice is important for reducing dependence and the sense of "learned helplessness" that can result from lack of control over the environment (Campbell, 1989).

Other Educational Needs   Some of the medical and physical characteristics of children with severe disabilities described previously impinge on their educational programs. Examples include 1) the child whose seizures require restriction from swimming, 2) the child on anticonvulsant medication who sleeps half the day, 3) the student whose lungs must be cleared of secretions before he or she eats lunch, and 4) the student in the body cast to correct scoliosis who needs community instruction. The challenge for the team is to determine how to work with and around the students' medical and physical needs to provide an appropriate education, rather than turning the school day into an extended therapy session. Therapy and specialized health care procedures should facilitate, not replace, instruction.

Social/Emotional Needs

Children with multiple disabilities are more than conglomerations of educational and medical problems. They are, first of all, children; they are the sons and daughters of parents who care about their well-being. Like all other individuals, children with disabilities need affection and attention. They should never become mere passive recipients of services. If you can imagine what it would be like to be trapped physically by your own body and to be unable to tell anyone how you felt or what you wanted, then you can begin to understand how you might interpret and respond to a child's crying or "noncompliant" behavior.

Professionals, no matter how skillful or caring, are unable to provide all of the emotional support children need. Children with multiple disabilities need opportunities to interact with and develop friendships with other children (Forest & Lusthaus, 1989; Strully & Strully, 1989). Professionals can and should facilitate those opportunities, not as a "frill," but as an essential part of a student's educational and emotional life.

IMPORTANCE OF A VARIETY OF DISCIPLINES

It is evident from the preceding description of the needs of children with multiple disabilities that a range of expertise is necessary in educating these children. Skills are needed from fields as diverse as special education, nursing, social work, and physical therapy (and sometimes from fields less traditionally associated with education, such as rehabilitation engineering, dietetics, and respiratory therapy). It should be clear that one or two individuals cannot possibly meet all the needs of these children. Whitehouse recognized the need for interdependence among professionals as far back as 1951:

> We must understand that there are no discrete categories of scientific endeavors. Professions are only cross-sections of the overall continuum of human thought. Fundamentally no treatment is medical, social, psychological, or vocational—all treatment is total. Yet members of each profession within the narrowness of their own training and experience will attempt to treat the whole person. Obviously, no one profession can do this adequately under present conditions. (p. 45)

Although Whitehouse was speaking of the rehabilitation field, his words are equally true for educating students with multiple disabilities in the 1990s.

The remainder of this section briefly explores the nature of the disciplines that work with these children.

This book emphasizes the importance for people representing different disciplines to work together and to share some of their skills. It may seem odd, therefore, to parcel out descriptions of individual fields. Nevertheless, it is essential to recognize that different professions do have distinct training backgrounds, philosophical and theoretical approaches, experiences, and specialized skills. Moreover, the success of an educational team depends in part on the competence of the individual team members and on a mutual understanding and respect for individuals' skills and knowledge.

The roles of people who are typically part of the school-based educational team are described first. The roles of other valuable professionals found less commonly within the school setting are then described.

People on Educational Teams

Special Educator   Gaylord-Ross and Holvoet (1985) summarized five major roles of a teacher of students with severe disabilities: 1) educator of learners with severe disabilities, 2) liaison between the parents and school district, 3) supervisor and teacher of classroom assistants, 4) member and coordinator of a team of professionals who will work with the students, and 5) advocate for the students. The specific skills required in each of those roles are too numerous to be described here. As the profession continues to define itself and to reach a consensus on recommended practices, the teacher's role becomes more complex, encompassing a broad spectrum of concerns. More on the special educator's role appears in the "Transdisciplinary Model of Delivering Services" section of this chapter.

Associate   Sometimes referred to as a teacher's aide or a paraprofessional, the associate frequently plays a vital role in the daily functioning in the classroom. In addition to helping to conduct instructional activities, the associate often is heavily involved in handling and positioning students and in providing for their physical health and comfort.

Physical Therapist   The physical therapist is trained to prescribe and supervise the following types of activities: gross motor activity and weight bearing, positioning, range of motion, relaxation, stimulation, postural drainage, and other physical manipulation and exercise procedures (Fraser, Hensinger, & Phelps, 1987). An essential member of the team, the physical therapist often provides information and direct instruction to team members on appropriate positioning and handling and on the use and construction of adaptive equipment (Copeland & Kimmel, 1989).

Occupational Therapist   Occupational therapy generally is oriented toward the development and maintenance of functions and skills necessary for daily living. Accordingly, occupational therapists in school programs attempt to prevent deterioration of those functions and help remediate limitations that impair performance (Lansing & Carlsen, 1977). These professionals often have special expertise in prescribing and constructing adaptive devices (especially for fine motor activities) and in conducting mealtime activities for individuals with physical involvement.

Communication Therapist   Because a large percentage of students with multiple disabilities not only are nonverbal but also lack any systematic means of communicating, language or communication therapists play a specialized and important role. They are responsible for assessing and training students directly on methods of communicating, teaching other staff these methods, and monitoring students' communication progress (Stremel-Campbell, 1977). Communication therapists also may consult with audiologists when an individual experiences hearing loss. Finally, because of the anatomical and functional relationship between eating and speech, many therapists are trained in assessing and facilitating mealtime skills.

Family Member or Other Caregiver   Although not typically present in the school on a regular basis, a parent or other family member or caregiver should be recognized as a central part of an educational team. Apart from parents' rights to participate in assessment and planning, it simply makes good sense to invite them to participate as the individuals with the most knowledge of their children and the greatest stake in their children's future. The degree to which parents are able to or choose to participate will vary. (Salisbury, 1992; Chapter 12 examines this and other issues concerning families in greater detail.)

Other Professionals Who Serve Students with Multiple Disabilities

The daily contact that individuals described in this section have with children varies with the size and organization of the school division and the degree of specialization of their professions. In some cases, involvement of professionals (e.g., social worker, psychologist, nurse) may be extensive and ongoing. Other people (e.g., audiologist, dietitian) may be consulted on an as-needed basis. Such individuals may be considered to comprise the "support team" (Rainforth et al., (1992). The key principle is to involve those professionals who have the required information and skills *for a particular child*. Thus, a vision specialist may play a more central role for a child with dual sensory impairments than he or she would for a child with average vision.

Psychologist   The role most often associated with school psychologists is that of evaluator of a child's intellectual and adaptive abilities. The child with multiple disabilities, however, presents significant obstacles to traditional psychometric instruments and procedures. Thus, psychologists in some cases have taken increasingly more visible roles in designing strategies for reducing excess behaviors. They could be particularly instrumental in working with teaching staff to develop alternative, long-term adaptive behaviors in students who lack important social or self-regulatory skills (Meyer & Evans, 1989). In addition, psychologists can be helpful in working with families (and professionals) in times of stress and grief, such as following the death of a child.

Social Worker   School social workers serve as facilitators of access to services and advocates for the child and family (West, 1978). They are trained in communicating with and gaining access to community resources. Some programs employ individuals with specialized training to coordinate services among school, home, and community.

Administrator   Administrators include people responsible for policy making, decision making, and implementation in areas such as placement, transition, curriculum development, transportation, related services, equipment, and scheduling. The administrator is also responsible for ensuring compliance with local, state, and federal regulations. It is clear that the administrator (e.g., principal, program director, special education supervisor) is highly influential in the quality of students' educational programs.

Vision Specialist   A large number of children with multiple disabilities experience loss in visual function; therefore, the vision specialist has an important role. These professionals are equipped to assess students' vision and to adapt activities and materials to make full use of each child's residual vision. The orientation and mobility specialist is a professional with specialized training in vision in relation to mobility across environments. Along with the communication, occupational, and physical therapists, the vision specialist provides vital information related to alternative communication systems.

Audiologist   The audiologist is trained to identify different types and degrees of hearing loss and to provide guidelines on equipment and procedures to help students compensate for their impairment (Gaylord-Ross & Holvoet, 1985). The audiologist who works with individuals who experience a combination of cognitive, physical, and sensory impairments must be knowledgeable about a variety of alternative, nontraditional assessment strategies.

Nurse   The school nurse is often the best source of readily available information regarding the physical well-being of children with multiple disabilities. This information covers a range of needs from seizure control to medication to emergency first aid. Nurses also are invaluable for helping students (and teaching staff) who require specialized procedures such as catheterization, suctioning, and nasogastric tube feeding, as well as routine procedures, such as skin care and cast care (Graff, Ault, Guess, Taylor, & Thompson, 1990; see Chapter 6 of this book).

Nutritionist/Dietitian   Nutritionists and dietitians can help with adjusting students' caloric intake, minimizing the side effects and maximizing the effectiveness of medications, and designing special diets for individuals with specific food allergies or health care needs (Crump, 1987; Worthington, Pipes, & Trahms, 1978). Unfortunately, nutritionists and dietitians are not included on most school teams, which is probably attributable to a general lack of information about their skills and about the relevance of diet and nutrition to the physical and instructional needs of students (McCamman & Rues, 1990).

Physician/Pediatrician   The physician can help the school team by revising effects of medications and screening for and treating common medical problems. This professional is most effective when engaged in ongoing communication with school staff.

Other Medical Specialists   School staff and parents are also likely to need the services of one or more of the following specialists: dentist (teeth), ophthalmologist or optometrist (eyes), otorhinolaryngologist (ear, nose, and throat), orthopedist (bones and muscles), neurologist (nervous system), physiatrist (physical medicine and rehabilitation), and urologist (urinary system).

Other Nonmedical Specialists   In interviews with teachers who work effectively with children with the most severe disabilities, Thompson and Guess (1989) reported that numerous disciplines were perceived as critical for team input. Those disciplines not already mentioned above include respiratory therapy, pharmacology, rehabilitation engineering, and computer science. Clearly, teams need to think creatively and across the range of traditional, school-based disciplines when working with individuals with multiple disabilities.

EDUCATIONAL TEAMING MODELS FOR PEOPLE
WHO SERVE CHILDREN WITH MULTIPLE DISABILITIES

The preceding section described the roles of individuals who work directly with children with multiple disabilities or otherwise provide them with services. How well children are served in educational settings depends, of course, on many factors, including the skill and care of each professional. Individual competence itself, however, although essential, is not sufficient to guarantee a good program. Perhaps more than any other group of individuals, students with severe disabilities require a team of professionals who can work together effectively. The manner in which teams are formed and the way in which they operate greatly influence both the process and outcomes of education for children. Although there are numerous ways teams can be designed, this section briefly describes three teaming models: multidisciplinary, interdisciplinary, and transdisciplinary. Most school programs for students with multiple disabilities operate within some variation of one of these models.

Multidisciplinary Team Model

Organization   Through the multidisciplinary model, professionals with expertise in different disciplines work with the child individually. In contrast to more coordinated models, however, individuals within the multidisciplinary model work in isolation from other professionals to evaluate and serve children. Thus, no formal attempt is made to allocate resources by setting priorities for children's needs or to consider the overlap among disciplines (McCormick & Goldman, 1979). Best characterized by coexistence (Sparling, 1980), the multi-disciplinary model was designed to meet the needs of patients within medical settings (Hart, 1977) whose problems are typically isolated within one particular domain. In fact, because individuals work independently of one another, they may not even think of themselves as belonging to a team. Figure 1.1 depicts the model's organization.

Disadvantages The multidisciplinary model has at least two major disadvantages as applied to serving children with multiple disabilities: insufficient assessment and difficult educational planning (Peterson, 1980).

Assessment The more team members work in isolation, the greater the likelihood they will generate information that fails to address the child's needs holistically. As noted previously, students with multiple disabilities often have motor, sensory, and communication impairments, but professionals rarely are trained to be proficient in all areas. When four or five professionals, each representing a different discipline, evaluate a child's needs and submit recommendations, the chance of opposing suggestions is great (Hart, 1977). The likelihood of inaccurate and inconsistent recommendations also increases.

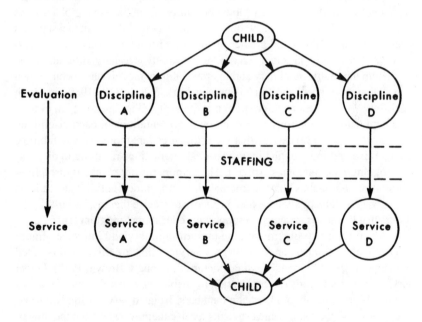

Figure 1.1. Organization of a multidisciplinary model of service delivery. (From McCormick, L., & Goldman, R. [1979]. The transdisciplinary model: Implications for service delivery and personnel preparation for the severely and profoundly handicapped. *AAESPH Review, 4*[2], p. 154; reprinted by permission.)

Educational Planning   Recommendations for educational planning from multidisciplinary teams often are numerous and complicated, making their implementation extremely difficult (Peterson, 1980). As with assessment information, suggestions for educational programs may also result in conflicting ideas. For example, an educator may recommend a specific program to teach a motor skill that the physical therapist believes should be inhibited. Furthermore, team members often end their responsibilities by making recommendations, leaving actual implementation to the classroom teacher (Hart, 1977).

Interdisciplinary Team Model

Organization   Representing a higher order of evolution on the scale of team models, the interdisciplinary model provides a formula structure for interaction and communication among team members that encourages them to share information (Garland, McGonigel, Frank, & Buck, 1989). Although programming decisions are made by group consensus, assessment and implementation remain tied to each discipline (Hart, 1977; McCormick & Goldman, 1979). Thus, although program planning is more collaborative than in the multidisciplinary model, program implementation remains isolated.

Disadvantages   The interdisciplinary model improves on the strict isolationism of the multidisciplinary model but suffers from the same problems. As McCormick and Goldman (1979) observed, the interdisciplinary model supports group decision making and greater opportunity for interactions across disciplines in theory only; in actual practice, responsibility is usually diffused.

Both the multidisciplinary and interdisciplinary models have been termed "discipline-referenced" models (Giangreco, York, & Rainforth, 1989), in which decisions about assessment, program priorities, planning, intervention, evaluation, and team interactions are driven by the orientations of each discipline. Giangreco et al. (1989) caution that such structures "are more likely to promote competitive and individualistic professional interactions resulting in disjointed programmatic outcomes" (p. 57). The authors further note that discipline-referenced approaches "have perpetuated the misguided notion that students with severe handicaps attend school primarily to receive therapy, rather than the notion that therapy is provided to support the educational program" (p. 57).

An additional problem with the multidisciplinary and interdisciplinary models is their total reliance on therapy services that are direct and isolated (Giangreco, 1986; Sternat, Messina, Nietupski, Lyon, & Brown, 1977). Direct services represent hands-on intervention by therapists, rather than the therapists serving as consultants to other team members. Isolated services imply a separate, "pull-out" model, in which students receive therapy away from the flow of ongoing activities, often in separate rooms or even in clinics or hospitals outside the school.

There are several problems with a direct, isolated therapy approach (Albano, Cox, York, & York, 1981; Giangreco, 1986; Giangreco et al., 1989; Sternat et al., 1977; York, Rainforth, & Giangreco, 1990). First, because skills are not assessed in the students' natural environments, the outcomes may not be representative of what the students actually can do in those settings. Second, assessments often test specific, isolated skills instead of clusters of skills used in everyday activities. Third, the assessments frequently result in diagnostic labels and descriptions of students' performances, but fail to include suggestions to help teachers and other professionals to remediate skill impairments. Fourth, when team members work in isolation, it is difficult to collaborate on the performance of individual students in natural situations. Fifth, because of limited staff and time, children may receive small amounts of practice on such vital areas as movement and communication. Sixth, limited resources have led some administrators to create centralized service delivery systems in which students with multiple disabilities are grouped together, preventing or minimizing interactions with peers without disabilities.

Transdisciplinary Team Model

Originally designed to serve infants at high risk for disabilities (Hutchison, 1978; United Cerebral Palsy Associations, 1976), the transdisciplinary model has been embraced by programs serving children with multiple disabilities. The model is characterized by a sharing, or transferring, of information and skills across traditional disciplinary boundaries. In contrast to the multidisciplinary and interdisciplinary approaches, the transdisciplinary model incorporates an indirect model of services, whereby one or two person(s) is the primary facilitator of services and other team members act as consultants (Albano et al., 1981). Figure 1.2 depicts the organization of a transdisciplinary model.

Although simple in concept, implementation of a transdisciplinary model can be initially difficult because it represents a significant departure from most models of service delivery to which professionals are accustomed. The remainder of this chapter examines in greater detail the features of the model.

TRANSDISCIPLINARY MODEL OF DELIVERING SERVICES

The team structure and approach to services known as the transdisciplinary model has gained increasing acceptance by members of many disciplines: occupational therapy (Dunn, 1988; Ottenbacher, 1982, 1983); physical therapy (Giangreco et al., 1989; York et al., 1990); special education (Campbell, 1987); early childhood education (Woodruff & McGonigel, 1988); nursing (Hutchison, 1978); medicine (Bennett, 1982); and rehabilitation counseling (Szymanski, Hanley-Maxwell, & Asselin, 1990). In fact, four professional organizations— the American Physical Therapy Association (1990), the American Occupational Therapy Association (1989), the American Speech-Language-Hearing Association (ASHA) (1991), and The Association for Persons with Severe Handicaps (TASH) (1986)—have issued guidelines on the provision of related services that support the transdisciplinary model.

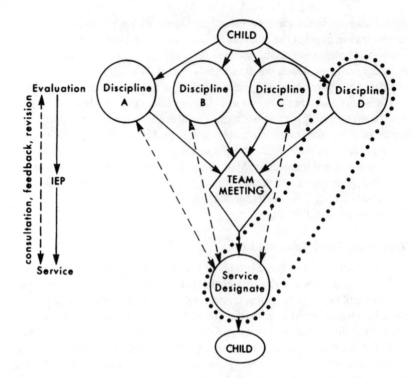

Figure 1.2. Organization of a transdisciplinary model of service delivery. (From McCormick, L., & Goldman, R. [1979]. The transdisciplinary model: Implications for service delivery and personnel preparation for the severely and profoundly handicapped. *AAESPH Review, 4*[2], p. 154; reprinted by permission.)

This section details the 1) major features of a transdisciplinary model, 2) applications of this model, 3) aspects of team dynamics, and 4) challenges to implementing the model and strategies for overcoming these difficulties. Table 1.1 compares the three team models across several dimensions.

Major Features of a Transdisciplinary Model

Indirect Therapy Approach   One of the criticisms of the multidisciplinary and interdisciplinary models is that they rely on a direct service approach; that is, *all* therapy services are provided directly by therapists, often in isolation. York (1984) gave an example of a direct service practice:

> A developmental therapist pushes Mike (a student) in a wheelchair from his classroom to the "therapy" room (or, as is often the case, a classroom staff member delivers him to the therapy room, then picks him up when therapy is completed). In the therapy room, the therapist assists the student to get out of his wheelchair, facilitating the desired weight-bearing, weight-shifting, and trunk rotation movement components. Next, they work on balancing and protective responses in a tall-

Table 1.1. Comparison of three team models

	Multidisciplinary	Interdisciplinary	Transdisciplinary
Assessment	Separate assessments by team members	Separate assessments by team members	Team members and family conduct a comprehensive developmental assessment together
Parent participation	Parents meet with individual team members	Parents meet with team or team representative	Parents are full, active, and participating members of the team
Service plan development	Team members develop separate plans for their discipline	Team members share their separate plans with one another	Team members and the parents develop a service plan based on family priorities, needs, and resources
Service plan responsibility	Team members are responsible for implementing their section of the plan	Team members are responsible for sharing information with one another as well as for implementing their section of the plan	Team members are responsible and accountable for how the primary service provider implements the plan

(continued)

Table 1.1. *(continued)*

	Multidisciplinary	Interdisciplinary	Transdisciplinary
Service plan implementation	Team members implement the part of the service plan related to their discipline	Team members implement their section of the plan and incorporate other sections where possible	A primary service provider is assigned to implement the plan with the family
Line of communication	Informal lines	Periodic case-specific team meetings	Regular team meeting where continuous transfer of information, knowledge, and skills are shared among team members
Guiding philosophy	Team members recognize the importance of contributions from other disciplines	Team members are willing and able to develop, share, and be responsible for providing services that are a part of the total service plan	Team members make a commitment to teach, learn, and work together across discipline boundaries to implement unified service plan
Staff development	Independent and within their discipline	Independent within as well as outside of their discipline	An integral component of team meetings for learning across disciplines and team building

From Woodruff, G., & McGonigel, M.J. (1988). Early intervention team approaches: The transdisciplinary model. In J.B. Jordan, J.J. Gallagher, P.L. Hutinger, & M.B. Karnes (Eds.), *Early childhood special education: Birth to three*, p. 166. Reston, VA: Council for Exceptional Children; reprinted by permission.

kneeling position. Then, they work on improving the way in which Mike walks using the assistance of parallel bars. Finally, he is assisted back into his chair again emphasizing the performance of desirable weight-shifting and rotation movement components. Once in his wheelchair, he is returned to his classroom. (p. 4)

(It should be noted that terms such as "weight bearing" and "protective responses" are part of technical language used by therapists. Concern about use of professional terminology to convey information is raised later in this chapter under "Differences in Philosophy and Orientation.")

Through an *indirect* approach, in contrast, therapists involve themselves to a greater extent as consultants to the teacher and other team members (Giangreco, 1986; Nietupski, Scheutz, & Ockwood, 1980). The transdisciplinary model *does not*, however, presume that therapists cease to provide direct services to children. In fact, therapists who ceased hands-on interactions would become less effective professionals, both to the children as well as to other team members. Moreover, as York et al. (1990) observed,

> There may be circumstances that warrant short-term or long-term frequent and direct services by a therapist. For example, a learner may present such complex movement difficulties that the therapist needs to spend large amounts of individual time with the learner to perform assessment and to determine effective intervention procedures. (p. 76)

Therapists use the analogous terms of *direct therapy, monitoring,* and *consultation* to differentiate among strategies for delivering therapy services (Dunn, 1988, 1991). Clearly, each mode of service delivery has a place in educating children with multiple disabilities. Decisions to use a particular approach at a particular moment need to be made by teams on the basis of appropriate outcomes for the student being served.

To appreciate the differences between direct and indirect therapy approaches, the direct service approach provided to Mike described previously can be contrasted with the following indirect therapy approach:

> The therapist meets Mike and his teacher in his classroom just before it is time to go to the cafeteria for lunch. The therapist explains to the student that he is going to learn to walk part of the way to the cafeteria instead of using his wheelchair for the entire distance. She also explains that she and the teacher will need to determine the best way to assist him and then the teacher will assist him in the same manner every day on their way to lunch. The therapist proceeds to model and give instructions as to how to get Mike out of his wheelchair, transfer to his walker, and walk in therapeutically desirable ways. She is careful to emphasize *where* she holds Mike, *how* she physically assists him, *what* responses she is looking for, the *rate* of the movements involved, and the most efficient sequence to follow. The teacher then assists Mike as the therapist coaches and provides the feedback. After this training session, the therapist writes a detailed task analysis of the steps involved, including both student and trainer behaviors. At a later time, the therapist and teacher go over the sequence together, discuss questions, practice on each other how to physically assist Mike, and decide what data should be taken on his performance to monitor progress. The teacher carries out the program with Mike each

day before lunch. On a weekly, or as needed basis, the therapist participates in the session by observing, providing feedback, or performing the activity to recommend changes in the type of physical assistance provided. (York, 1984, pp. 4–5)

It is important to note in the preceding scenario that the therapist's services were indirect, but the student's educational needs clearly were being addressed directly. In this case, the teacher was acting in a role of facilitator or synthesizer (Bricker, 1976). (In some applications of the transdisciplinary model, teachers also serve at times in a consultative capacity.) The scenario also incorporates four basic assumptions of an indirect therapy model (Sternat et al., 1977):

1. Assessment of motor abilities can be conducted best in natural environments.
2. Students should be taught clusters of motor skills through games and functional activities (those needed in everyday living).
3. Therapy should be provided throughout the day and in all the settings in which the student functions.
4. Skills must be taught and verified in the settings in which they occur naturally.

Three concerns are often raised with regard to an indirect therapy model. The first concern is that therapists have special training and expertise that teachers do not have and cannot (or should not) acquire. A transdisciplinary model does not involve teachers' total takeover of the therapists' role, however (Nietupski et al., 1980; York et al., 1990). In fact, it is because of the need for the therapists' expertise that the model has become so popular.

A second concern about an indirect therapy approach is that students with multiple disabilities are easily distracted and need quiet settings in which to work. Unfortunately, students with multiple disabilities do not remain in quiet, distraction-free settings forever, and it is therefore important to give them the opportunity to cope with real situations whenever possible. In addition, when therapy not only is physically isolated, but also is disconnected from the student's educational goals, one could question whether therapy qualifies as related services under the law (Giangreco et al., 1989).

The third concern is that indirect therapy would cause therapists to lose their professional identity. In reality, however, transdisciplinary models that operate effectively result in *enhanced* professional identity among therapists. There is at least anecdotal evidence that teachers value and understand the importance of therapists to a greater degree after working within a transdisciplinary model and that therapists also feel more valued within the team (Albano, 1983). The rationale for implementing an indirect therapy approach should *not* be to reduce the number of therapist within a given setting, thereby increasing caseloads. As York et al. (1990) noted,

Learners for whom a transdisciplinary model is appropriate usually have intense and comprehensive related service needs.... Caseloads of 60 students across three counties or schedules that allow 1 hour of consultation per student per month are unlikely to be effective in any service delivery model! (p. 78)

Role Release   It is obvious that for staff to serve in consulting positions and for some services to be delivered indirectly, traditional roles of teachers, therapists, and other team members must become more flexible. Role release refers to a sharing and exchange of certain roles and responsibilities across team members (Lyon & Lyon, 1980). The term more specifically implies a *releasing* of some functions of one's primary discipline to other team members (United Cerebral Palsy Associations, 1976).

Woodruff and McGonigel (1988) described a process, *role transition*, through which transdisciplinary teams can teach and learn across disciplinary boundaries. Role transition consists of six separate but related processes, organized sequentially. (Role release, as defined within this model, is one of the six processes.) Table 1.2 briefly describes each of the six processes and provides an example of each process. Table 1.3 lists several practices that can be carried out daily to support some facets of role transition.

Table 1.2.   Role transition processes and examples

ROLE EXTENSION: Self-directed study and other staff development efforts to increase one's depth of understanding, theoretical knowledge, and clinical skills in one's own discipline or area of expertise
Example: An occupational therapist who is an expert on mealtime skills attends a workshop on new feeding techniques.

ROLE ENRICHMENT: Team members being well versed in their own disciplines and developing a general awareness and understanding of the terminology and basic practices of other disciplines
Example: The pediatrician conducts an in-service session on medical terminology.

ROLE EXPANSION: Acquiring sufficient information from disciplines represented on the team to allow a team member to make knowledgeable observations and program recommendations outside his or her own discipline
Example: The special education teacher determines that a child needs her visual acuity tested and makes a referral to the vision specialist.

ROLE EXCHANGE: Learning the theory, methods, and procedures of other disciplines and beginning to implement the techniques learned by practicing them under the observation of the team member from the relevant discipline
Example: A parent demonstrates to the physical therapist an activity to increase a child's capacity to bear weight on his arms.

ROLE RELEASE: Putting newly acquired techniques into practice with consultation from the team member from the discipline that is accountable for those practices
Example: The social worker teaches a father a simple carrying technique for a child for whom he is the primary service provider.

ROLE SUPPORT: Informal encouragement from other team members and, when necessary, backup support and help by the team member from the appropriate discipline
Example: The audiologist tests the child's hearing.

Adapted from Garland, McGonigel, Frank, and Buck (1989).

Table 1.3.   Practices to support role transition

Role extension

    Read current journals and texts.

    Join professional organizations.

    Attend local, regional, and national conferences.

    Request current in-service training and technical assistance.

    Take university courses.

Role enrichment

    Create reference library of conference notes and professional journals.

    Use one-to-one exchange to teach colleagues basic terms and concepts.

Role expansion

    Share information with colleagues during assessment.

    Conduct regular meetings to discuss programming ideas.

Role exchange

    Explore team teaching.

    Engage in regular case consultation.

    Conduct periodic shared home visits.

Adapted from Garland, McGonigel, Frank, and Buck (1989).

It should be noted that sharing or releasing roles occurs in two directions across all team members; each person has unique skills and information to impart. Personnel must keep in mind that parents and other family members should be considered an important part of the team.

Applications of a Transdisciplinary Model

There are three major areas within educational programs upon which the choice of a team model has a direct influence: assessment, development of instructional goals, and delivery of instruction and therapy. This section examines each of these applications.

Assessment   The method an instructional team elects to obtain initial information on a student's performance will directly affect all other aspects of the student's program. It is important, therefore, that team members devote as much attention to assessing skills as they do to teaching those skills. There are at least three different types of assessment information (York et al., 1985).

General Background Information   One or more team member(s) can compile information from the student's family, previous service providers, and the child's cumulative file. This process yields information on past and current educational goals, individuals' preferences for what skills should be taught first, special learning characteristics, medical problems, and so forth. It is particularly important that the parents be consulted. They can provide valuable information on such things as the child's preferences of food, objects, and activities; medical precautions; ways in which the child communicates; and family activities (York, 1984). This general information should be shared among all team members.

Observations of the Student   Traditional assessment is performed individually by each professional on a team. Within a transdisciplinary model, however, several team members jointly plan for and conduct the assessment, in which the student functions in several natural environments and activities. Referred to as an ecological inventory (Brown et al., 1979), this assessment strategy consists of the following steps:

1. Determine the environments in which the student currently functions or is likely to function.
2. Determine the activities necessary to perform in those environments and the skills necessary to engage in those activities.
3. Determine the professionals who should be involved in the assessment. For example, a physical therapist might be called on to help assess a student who has difficulty walking on uneven terrain and negotiating stairs.
4. Conduct the environmental assessment by going to the actual environments with the student, recording the student's responses, and making notes to indicate activities that need further assessment.

Discipline-Specific Information   Sometimes individual team members can obtain useful information through traditional assessment strategies within their own disciplines (e.g., communication, movement). Most of this information, however, can be assessed in the context of naturally occurring situations (Rainforth & York, 1987; York et al., 1990). It is important to remember that the main purpose of assessment is to determine relevant educational goals. As York et al. (1990) observed, the emphasis should be on assessment conducted in priority educational environments on activities identified by the team. This should not imply a decrease in sophistication or quality of assessments conducted by therapists.

Development of Instructional Goals   Once assessment is complete, the team must 1) establish priorities for the skills to be taught to each student and 2) write goals that address those skills deemed appropriate.

Content Priorities   Determining which skills to teach in a given year is a difficult task. The decision takes into account such diverse considerations as the student's preferences, the parents' preferences, the social significance of the skill, the student's age, and so forth. In general, teaching content should be organized around naturally occurring *activities*, rather than isolated skills or tasks (Ford et al., 1989). Moreover, teams should *not* select activities on the basis of whether students will perform them independently; most children with multiple disabilities will require assistance on some or all parts of activities. Rather, activities should be selected based on such criteria as 1) whether performing the activity will make a real difference in the quality of the student's life, and 2) whether performance will increase the student's likelihood of interacting with peers.

Finally, students with the most severe disabilities, who have quite limited repertoires of behaviors, may profit from learning *effective* behaviors, those that produce an effect upon the social environment (Evans & Scotti, 1989). Selecting these behaviors might be done by surveying the caregivers and other significant individuals in the student's life, rather than by relying on an ecological inventory approach (Orelove, 1991).

Writing Educational Goals   The goals and objectives on students' individualized education programs (IEPs) dictate the schedule, the physical organization of the classroom, and the choice of instructional materials and strategies. In short, the IEP drives the flow of the entire day. Therefore, the way in which educational goals are developed is absolutely critical to the success of operating within a transdisciplinary model.

Unfortunately, many people believe that an IEP developed by a team is simply goals and objectives written from individual disciplines and compiled into a single document, with the individual team members responsible for implementing and evaluating progress on their individual goals (York et al., 1990). Having separate sections of IEPs for each discipline, however, is incompatible with the philosophy of a transdisciplinary approach and runs counter to recommended practices for children with multiple disabilities. A separatist approach promotes 1) the development of segregated goals that have no real function in the real world (e.g., "Will increase relaxation," "Will visually track from left to right 180°"); and 2) the exclusion of critical objectives related to movement, communication, and so forth across school and community environments.

An alternative approach is to develop goals that identify educationally relevant priority environments and activities in which performance is desired. The corresponding objectives specify the priority skills for the student to acquire so that participation in each environment is improved. (Chapter 10 provides examples of goals developed in this manner.)

Delivery of Instruction and Therapy   It was stated previously that a key feature of transdisciplinary approach is its incorporation of indirect therapy in which therapists serve in part in consulting roles to other team members. It was also noted that direct therapy is often characterized by delivery of services in isolation; however, the location of services does not in itself determine whether a model is transdisciplinary. A therapist who practices one-to-one therapy in the back of the student's classroom is still engaging in a direct, nonintegrated approach (York et al., 1990).

For a model to be truly transdisciplinary, therapy needs to be *integrated*. An integrated approach is characterized by two features:

> (a) planning is referenced to a common set of goals and needs whereby each team member applies his or her disciplinary skill to the shared goals, and (b) therapeutic techniques are implemented in concert with other instructional methods in the context of functional activities. (Giangreco et al., 1989, p. 61)

Putting a process in place for accomplishing these transdisciplinary goals, however, is not a simple task. Campbell (1987) presented a model for doing so, which she terms an "integrated programming team." These teams, organized around the needs of individual students, consist of professionals (teachers and therapists) who are involved in some form of ongoing service delivery for the students, as well as parents. The administrator acts to support and facilitate team programming. Figure 1.3 presents the steps necessary to implement team programming for an individual student. In Figure 1.3, Step 6 states "Team members train each other in integrated methods (with the student present)." York et al. (1985) described the intricacies of accomplishing such a task:

> When teaching other team members how to perform skills and techniques and how to integrate information from one's own discipline, a variety of teaching strategies may need to be used. For example, when teaching an assistant how to instruct a student to perform a pivot transfer from her wheelchair to the toilet seat in a community restroom stall, the skill sequence may need to be specifically outlined, the assistant may practice the transfer sequence with the physical therapist in a simulated situation at the school, and/or a series of stick figure drawings of the most critical steps may be provided.... The primary point here is that the team member who is teaching *and* the instructor who is learning new information and skills must take equal responsibility for successful transfer of skills from one person to the other... It would behoove those doing the training to recall their first attempts at learning the information they are now expected to teach others. (not paginated)

Dynamics of Teams

As Hutchison (1978) observed, "Calling a small group of people a team does not make them so; team relationships are forged over time" (p. 70). It is particularly easy to see the truth in this statement relative to the transdisciplinary team, whose success depends on close collaboration among members and a relinquishing of individual power. To appreciate the difficulty of organizing truly effective educational teams and to learn how to avoid or overcome some of the common problems teams experience, it is important to understand their dynamics. This section briefly examines the team process and some of the factors influencing teams' effectiveness.

Team Process   Bailey (1984) proposed a triaxial model for understanding the process within teams that work with individuals with disabilities. His model is based on three premises:

1. Team growth is a developmental process; thus, some problems in team functioning can be attributed to the stage a team is in at a given point.
2. Teams are composed of individuals; some problems may result from interpersonal problems or subsystems within the team.
3. Teams themselves are functional units; some problems result from whole team dysfunction.

Examining the first premise, Bailey summarized the model of Lowe and Herranen (1982), who proposed six stages in team development, as shown in Table 1.4. As with any developmental model, each team will not necessarily experience every stage, nor will teams go through each stage in a fixed sequence. It does seem clear, however, that virtually every team experiences growing pains

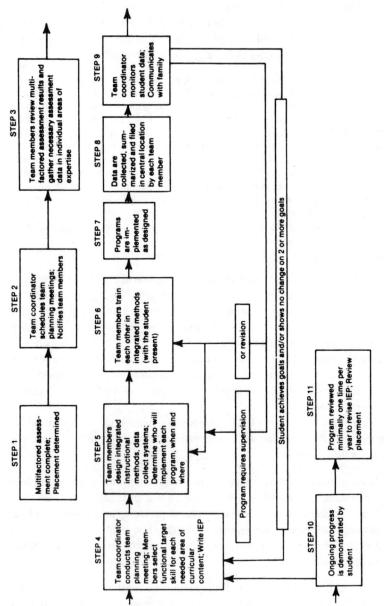

Figure 1.3. Steps to implementing team programming for an individual student. (From Campbell, P.H. [1987]. The integrated programming team: An approach for coordinating professionals of various disciplines in programs for students with severe and multiple handicaps. *Journal of The Association for Persons with Severe Handicaps, 12*[2], p. 114; reprinted by permission.)

Table 1.4. Six-stage process of team development

Stage	Features
I. Becoming acquainted	Hierarchical group structures
	Autocratic leadership
	Polite and impersonal interactions
	Low overall team productivity
II. Trial and error	Begins to work together toward common goal
	Team members align themselves with one or two other team members
	Factions sometimes occur
	Role conflict and ambiguity arise
III. Collective indecision	Attempts to avoid direct conflict and achieve equilibrium
	No group norm for accountability
IV. Crisis	Members realize importance of mission
	Emotion expressed
V. Resolution	Effort to work together as team
	Open communication
	Shared leadership, decision making, and responsibility
VI. Team maintenance	Client's needs major driving force
	Conflict management, client–team relationships important

Source: Lowe and Herranen (1982).

as a normal part of the process of evolving into a smoothly operating unit. In the second premise of the triaxial model, Bailey (1984) asserted that in the ideal team 1) a leader is present but acts as one member of the team, 2) each member is about equal in power and influence, and 3) conflicts and disagreements are based on substantive issues not personality conflicts. Problems that can arise within the team subsystem include dominant leaders, dominant and inferior team members, and specific conflicts between two members or between one member and the others.

The third facet of Bailey's model focuses on the team as a whole. Teams can experience problems of being underproductive, overstructured, or disorganized or having ambiguous roles.

Factors Influencing Team Effectiveness   Group process and decision making have been the subjects of countless theories and research. Despite everything known about communication and working in groups, however, there remains no simple recipe that a team can follow to ensure success. Regardless, the quality of the educational program for children with multiple disabilities depends largely on the degree to which team members can work together and

communicate. This section summarizes several of the factors that typically operate within successful small groups; these factors can be subsumed under three
broad categories: 1) intrapersonal factors, 2) interpersonal factors, and 3) group
identity factors (Fisher, 1980).

Intrapersonal Factors   Because a group is composed of individuals, individual team members must monitor themselves for continued constructive contribution to team functioning. The following are several attitudes and values that
are typical of members of successful groups:

1. Individuals' attitudes toward the group reflect open-mindedness about possible outcomes and a sensitivity toward the feelings and beliefs of other
   group members. The individual is committed to the group and to the
   process. The individual also has a sense of responsibility to the group and is
   willing to expend time and energy for the benefit of the group.
2. Individuals who are committed to a group participate actively, share
   responsibility for the group's decisions, and express feelings and ideas,
   even at the risk of being proved wrong.
3. Individuals demonstrate creativity, proposing numerous ideas, especially
   during the group's early stages.
4. Individuals take stands and defend their beliefs, even if they leave themselves open to criticism. In addition, they constructively criticize others and
   try to do so at appropriate moments in the group process.
5. Individuals express themselves honestly; they say what they mean.

Interpersonal Factors   The ability to understand and relate to others in the
group is a second key area governing success. Some of these specific interpersonal factors follow:

1. All members must participate for group decision making to be effective;
   members who remain forever silent do not contribute.
2. Groups in which members are more skilled at the art of communicating are
   more effective.
3. Members engage in supportive, not defensive, communication. Supportive
   communications evaluate problems or issues, not other members, thus creating a climate of mutual trust.
4. Members make sure they understand one another and they are clearly
   understood by others; they do this by checking others' reactions, being specific in describing an idea, and being descriptive, rather than judgmental, in
   response to others' ideas.

Group Identity Factors   The identity of a group flows directly from the
intrapersonal and interpersonal factors just described. The following are several
of these group identity factors.

1.   Members are sensitive to the group process; they sense *when* to communicate a particular idea.
2.   Members who fail to contribute and, hence, are uncommitted to the group or the task should consider quitting the group. Having uncommitted members reduces the group's effectiveness.
3.   Members who understand the group process exhibit patience at the slowness of change, particularly in the early stages. Allowing time to think through ideas is important to creative and effective decision making.
4.   Successful groups avoid unrealistic formulaic answers to difficult problems.

Carney (1988) has summarized many of the factors described in this section in checklist form. Figures 1.4 and 1.5 present these checklists, which individual team members can use to evaluate their own contributions and reactions to groups in which they participate.

Challenges to Implementing a Transdisciplinary Model

Professionals who try to implement a transdisciplinary model frequently encounter a variety of challenges along the way. None of these obstacles is unsurmountable, and most are grounded in a lack of understanding or a general resistance to change. It is, however, important to appreciate others' views; failing to do so typically results in failure to reach agreed-upon goals, which ultimately harms the students for whom the group is working. Challenges in implementing the model can be divided into three categories: philosophical and professional, personal and interpersonal, and logistical.

Did you contribute more to the task orientation or the emotional orientation of the group?

Did you show enthusiasm and give positive feedback for other members' ideas?

Did you assert your preferences and opinions? If not, why?

Did you paraphrase or ask for clarification when you had a question or felt uncertainty or a strong reaction to another's comments?

Did you identify for the group any concerns you had about the process or outcome of the decision?

Did you feel generally trusting of other group members? If you asked questions, were they open ended or closed ended?

What did your facial expression and body language communicate?

If you had to do it again, would you behave or interact differently?

Figure 1.4. Checklist on personal dynamics related to team performance. (Adapted from Carney, 1988.)

Who assumed responsibility for getting the job done?

Who assumed responsibility for the emotional climate of the group? Did the group have all the information it needed to proceed?

Did group members disagree with one another? How did that feel to the disagreeing member? To other members?

Did the group have a shared frame of reference for how the decision should be reached? Did it help? Would it have?

Did one or two people assume leadership or was leadership shared among all group members?

Did the meeting progress show a balance of permissiveness and control?

Did group members appear to accurately understand one another's questions and comments or did they jump to conclusions?

How would you describe the general atmosphere of the group?

Did you notice any nonverbal communication that influenced communication in the group?

Figure 1.5.   Checklist on group dynamics related to team performance. (Adapted from Carney, 1988.)

Philosophical and Professional Challenges   Philosophical and professional challenges are often encountered when implementing a transdisciplinary model.

Differences in Philosophy and Orientation   A problem that team members confront quickly is the difference in their own training and philosophy (Courtnage & Smith-Davis, 1987; Geiger, Bradley, Rock, & Croce, 1986). Therapists, for example, are usually taught within a medical model, whereby one uncovers the underlying cause of a behavior and then directs therapy toward the presumed cause. Special educators, however, especially those who work with children with multiple disabilities, are taught to emphasize functional assessment and skills. This fundamental difference in orientation can result in significantly different approaches to instruction and therapy. The problem is further exacerbated by the preparation of professionals in isolation, preventing therapists, teachers, nurses, and others in training from learning about and valuing other professionals. In addition, professionals often use jargon, which is appropriate as shorthand and when technical clarity is essential. Unfortunately, other team members, including parents, often do not understand what is being said or written in jargon about a child, which frustrates efforts at solving common problems (Rainforth, 1985; Sears, 1981).

Diminishment of Professional Status   Related to professionals' training and orientation is the status that they acquire or seek. As Bassoff (1976) clearly stated, "The assumption that different disciplines on teams gather together as equals, while an overt statement of a desired state, cloaks the reality that some team members are more equal than others" (p. 224). Releasing part of one's role does threaten the status that some professionals perceive themselves as having. As described previously in this chapter, however, transdisciplinary teams that operate smoothly actually can *enhance* the status of team members by fostering greater respect and interdependence (York et al., 1990).

Professional Ethics and Liability   Some individuals have suggested that a model based heavily on indirect services may foster negligent behavior by not ensuring sufficient supervision by appropriately licensed or certified professionals (Geiger at al., 1986). Moreover, some states have laws governing who can provide therapy (Linder, 1993). These concerns should be taken seriously and appropriate steps taken to ensure the health and safety of all students. As Giangreco (1986) observed, however, "one reason indirect models are necessary is because therapists cannot be available 24 hours a day" (p. 24). Clearly, there are certain highly specialized or potentially risky procedures that only specifically designated, trained individuals should perform. (See Chapter 6 for a description of the development of individualized health care plans.) In all cases, prudence and common sense should prevail.

Isolation of Parents   Some individuals (Bennett, 1982; Holm & McCartin, 1978) have expressed a concern that parents may become confused by a transdisciplinary model because the line between therapy and education becomes blurred. It is essential to explain the model clearly to parents, demonstrating the ways in which integrated therapy services result in better learning for the children. Perhaps more important, an effectively operating transdisciplinary model should provide more opportunities for involving parents at all levels of assessment, program planning and delivery, and evaluation, thereby *reducing* parents' feelings of estrangement.

Personal and Interpersonal Challenges   Personal and interpersonal challenges are also often encountered when implementing a transdisciplinary model.

Threat of Training Others and Threat of Being Trained   At the core of the transdisciplinary model is the need for team members to teach others and to accept other members' skills and information. Meeting this need can be quite threatening because it places the team members' skills under close scrutiny (Peterson, 1980). It calls into question an individual's own competence and confidence, as well as evokes his or her feelings toward fellow team members. In short, a transdisciplinary team, like any other decision-making group, requires its members to trust each other and to risk themselves.

Role Conflict or Ambiguity   A common source of interpersonal problems is a lack of clear differentiation of responsibilities among team members (Butler & Maher, 1981). Because functions often blur within a transdisciplinary approach, it is essential throughout the life of the team to clarify people's roles. It may also be difficult for some professionals to release themselves from traditional service roles (Sparling, 1980).

Misunderstanding of Approach   The transdisciplinary model is complex in its subtleties and logistical demands. As a result, it is often misunderstood and improperly implemented. The model does not advocate that any team member should do anyone else's job, that the amount of therapy services should be reduced, or that the primary interventionist provide all of the services needed by the child (Case-Smith, 1993).

Resistance to Change   Implementing a new service delivery model takes time and concerted effort as well as administrative support and technical assistance. Any significant change will be met with resistance by at least one team member. This resistance must be anticipated and confronted; left unchecked, it can be destructive. It is critical for the team to have jointly developed, common goals that benefit the children.

Logistical Challenges   Although overcoming the challenges described above are central to the successful adoption of the transdisciplinary model, it would be unfair to dismiss real-world problems. These include finding the time to meet, developing processes that are efficient and collaborative, and locating qualified personnel (Orelove, 1994). For specific strategies on how to set up and conduct team meetings (e.g., developing an agenda, establishing a collaborative atmosphere, facilitating accountability), readers are referred to Giangreco (1996), Rainforth et al. (1992), and Thousand and Villa (1992).

School administrators can be especially helpful in supporting the professionals who serve the students. Table 1.5 lists several steps administrators can take to facilitate implementation of a transdisciplinary model in their schools.

CONCLUSION

The challenges described in the preceding section should be viewed as just that—challenges. When professionals act in good faith toward one another and

Table 1.5.   Steps administrators can take to facilitate implementation of a transdisciplinary program

Encourage individuals to view themselves as responsible to the team.

Encourage the team to view itself as responsible to the student and the family.

Encourage involvement of parents at whatever level they choose to participate.

Arrange school schedules to allow for formal, general staff meetings.

Model appropriate behavior in team meetings (e.g., active listening, support).

Arrange the school building to maximize interaction between students with and without disabilities.

Arrange the building and schedule to avoid reliance on separate therapy rooms.

Encourage teachers and related services personnel to work together to assess students strengths and needs and to develop goals and objectives.

Encourage a data-based model of instruction.

Encourage use of clear, simple language in meetings, IEPs, reports, and discussions.

Do not prevent conflict, but help resolve it as it arises.

Give the model time to work.

toward children and families and make a commitment to better educational services for students with multiple disabilities, no barrier is permanent. Teams should not be fooled into believing that implementing the techniques and principles described in this chapter will be easy; although the work is difficult, the outcomes, for both children and professionals, justify the effort.

REFERENCES

Albano, M.L. (1983). *Transdisciplinary teaming in special education: A case study.* Unpublished doctoral dissertation, University of Illinois at Urbana-Champaign.

Albano, M.L., Cox, B., York, J., & York, R. (1981). Educational teams for students with severe and multiple handicaps. In R. York, W. Schofield, D. Donder, D. Ryndak, & B. Reguly (Eds.), *Organizing and implementing services for students with severe and multiple handicaps* (pp. 23–34). Springfield: Illinois State Board of Education.

American Occupational Therapy Association. (1989). *Guidelines for occupational therapy services in the public schools* (2nd ed.). Rockville, MD: Author.

American Physical Therapy Association. (1990). *Physical therapy practice in educational environments.* Alexandria, VA: Author.

American Speech-Language-Hearing Association, Committee on Language Learning Disorders. (1991). A model for collaborative service delivery for students with language-learning disorders in the public schools. *Asha, 3*(33, Suppl.).

Bailey, D.B. (1984). A triaxial model of the interdisciplinary team and group process. *Exceptional Children, 5*(1), 17–25.

Bassoff, B.Z. (1976). Interdisciplinary education for health professionals: Issues and directions. *Social Work in Health Care, 2*(2), 219–228.

Bennett, F.C. (1982). The pediatrician and the interdisciplinary process. *Exceptional Children, 48*(4), 306–314.

Bricker, D.D. (1976). Educational synthesizer. In M.A. Thomas (Ed.), *Hey, don't forget about me!* (pp. 84–97). Reston, VA: Council for Exceptional Children.

Brown, L., Branston-McClean, M., Baumgart, D., Vincent, L., Falvey, M., & Schroeder, J. (1979). Using the characteristics of current and subsequent least restrictive environments in the development of content for severely handicapped students. *AAESPH Review, 4,* 407–424.

Butler, A.S., & Maher, C.A. (1981). Conflict and special service teams: Perspectives and suggestions for school psychologists. *Journal of School Psychology, 19*(1), 62–70.

Campbell, P.H. (1987). The integrated programming team: An approach for coordinating professionals of various disciplines in programs for students with severe and multiple handicaps. *Journal of The Association for Persons with Severe Handicaps, 12*(2), 107–116.

Campbell, P.H. (1989). Dysfunction in posture and movement in individuals with profound disabilities: Issues and practices. In F. Brown & D.H. Lehr (Eds.), *Persons with profound disabilities: Issues and practices* (pp. 163–189). Baltimore: Paul H. Brookes Publishing Co.

Carney, I.H. (1988). *Team membership self-assessment checklist.* Unpublished manuscript, Virginia Commonwealth University, Richmond.

Case-Smith, J. (1993). *Pediatric occupational therapy and early intervention.* Boston: Andover Medical Publishers.

Copeland, M.E., & Kimmel, J.R. (1989). *Evaluation and management of infants and young children with developmental disabilities.* Baltimore: Paul H. Brookes Publishing Co.

Courtnage, L., & Smith-Davis, J. (1987). Interdisciplinary team training: A national survey of special education teacher training programs. *Exceptional Children, 53,* 451–458.

Crump, M. (Ed.). (1987). *Nutrition and feeding of the handicapped child.* Boston: College-Hill.

Dunn, W. (1988). Models of occupational therapy service provision in the school system. *American Journal of Occupational Therapy, 42*(11), 718–723.

Dunn, W. (1991). Integrated related services. In L.H. Meyer, C.A. Peck, & L. Brown (Eds.), *Critical issues in the lives of people with severe disabilities* (pp. 353–377). Baltimore: Paul H. Brookes Publishing Co.

Evans, I.M., & Scotti, J.R. (1989). Defining meaningful outcomes for persons with profound disabilities. In F. Brown & D.H. Lehr (Eds.), *Persons with profound disabilities: Issues and practices* (pp. 83–107). Baltimore: Paul H. Brookes Publishing Co.

Fisher, B.A. (1980). *Small group decision making* (2nd ed.). New York: McGraw-Hill.

Ford, A., Schnorr, R., Meyer, L., Davern, L., Black, J., & Dempsey, P. (Eds.). (1989). *The Syracuse community-referenced curriculum guide for students with moderate and severe disabilities.* Baltimore: Paul H. Brookes Publishing Co.

Forest, M., & Lusthaus, E. (1989). Promoting educational equality for all students: Circles and maps. In S. Stainback, W. Stainback, & M. Forest (Eds.), *Educating all students in the mainstream of regular education* (pp. 43–57). Baltimore: Paul H. Brookes Publishing Co.

Fraser, B.A., Hensinger, R.N., & Phelps, J.A. (1987). *Physical management of multiple handicaps: A professional's guide.* Baltimore: Paul H. Brookes Publishing Co.

Fredericks, H.D.B., & Baldwin, V.L. (1987). Individuals with sensory impairments: Who are they? How are they educated? In L. Goetz, D. Guess, & K. Stremel-Campbell (Eds.), *Innovative program design for individuals with dual sensory impairments* (pp. 3–12). Baltimore: Paul H. Brookes Publishing Co.

Garland, C., McGonigel, M., Frank, A., & Buck, D. (1989). *The transdisciplinary model of service delivery.* Lightfoot, VA: Child Development Resources,

Gaylord-Ross, R.J., & Holvoet, J.F. (1985). *Strategies for educating students with severe handicaps.* Boston: Little, Brown.

Geiger, W.L., Bradley, R.H., Rock, S.L., & Croce, R. (1986). Commentary. *Physical and Occupational Therapy in Pediatrics, 6*(2), 16–21.

Giangreco, M.F. (1986). Delivery of therapeutic services in special education programs for learners with severe handicaps. *Physical and Occupational Therapy in Pediatrics, 6*(2), 5–15.

Giangreco, M.F. (1996). *Vermont interdependent services team approach (VISTA): A guide to coordinating educational support services.* Baltimore: Paul H. Brookes Publishing Co.

Giangreco, M.F., York, J., & Rainforth, B. (1989). Providing related services to learners with severe handicaps in educational settings: Pursuing the least restrictive option. *Pediatric Physical Therapy, 1*(2), 55-63.

Graff, J.C., Ault, M.M., Guess, D., Taylor, M., & Thompson, B. (1990). *Health care for students with disabilities: An illustrated medical guide for the classroom.* Baltimore: Paul H. Brookes Publishing Co.

Guess, D., & Siegel-Causey, E. (1985). Behavioral control and education of severely handicapped students: Who's doing what to whom? And why? In D. Bricker & J. Filler (Eds.), *Severe mental retardation: From theory to practice* (pp. 230–244). Reston, VA: Council for Exceptional Children.

Hart, V. (1977). The use of many disciplines with the severely and profoundly handicapped. In E. Sontag, J. Smith, & N. Certo (Eds.), *Educational programming for the severely and profoundly handicapped* (pp. 391–396). Reston, VA: Council for Exceptional Children.

Holm, V.A., & McCartin, R.E. (1978). Interdisciplinary child development team: Team issues and training in interdisciplinariness. In K.E. Allen, V.A. Holm, & R.L. Schiefelbusch (Eds.), *Early intervention: A team approach* (pp. 97–122). Baltimore: University Park Press.

Hutchison, D.J. (1978). The transdisciplinary approach. In J.B. Curry & K.K. Peppe (Eds.), *Mental retardation: Nursing approaches to care* (pp. 65–74). St. Louis, MO: C.V. Mosby.

Lansing, S.G., & Carlsen, P.N. (1977). Occupational therapy. In P.J. Valletutti & F. Christoplos (Eds.), *Interdisciplinary approaches to human services* (pp. 211–236). Baltimore: University Park Press.

Linder, T.W. (1993). *Transdisciplinary play-based intervention: Guidelines for developing a meaningful curriculum for young children.* Baltimore: Paul H. Brookes Publishing Co.

Lowe, J.I., & Herranen, M. (1982). Understanding teamwork: Another look at the concepts. *Social Work in Health Care, 7*(2), 1–11.

Lyon, S., & Lyon, G. (1980). Team functioning and staff development: A role release approach to providing integrated educational services for severely handicapped students. *Journal of The Association for the Severely Handicapped, 5*(3), 250–263.

McCamman, S., & Rues, J. (1990). Nutrition monitoring and supplementation. In J.C. Graff, M.M. Ault, D. Guess, M. Taylor, & B. Thompson (Eds.), *Health care for students with disabilities: An illustrated medical guide for the classroom* (pp. 79–117). Baltimore: Paul H. Brookes Publishing Co.

McCormick, L., & Goldman, R. (1979). The transdisciplinary model: Implications for service delivery and personnel preparation for the severely and profoundly handicapped. *AAESPH Review, 4*(2), 152–161.

Meyer, L.H., & Evans, I.M. (1989). *Nonaversive intervention for behavior problems: A manual for home and community.* Baltimore: Paul H. Brookes Publishing Co.

Mulligan-Ault, M., Guess, D., Struth, L., & Thompson, B. (1988). The implementation of health-related procedures in classrooms for students with severe multiple impairments. *Journal of The Association for Persons with Severe Handicaps, 13*(2), 100–109.

Nietupski, J., Scheutz, G., & Ockwood, L. (1980). The delivery of communication therapy services to severely handicapped students: A plan for change. *Journal of The Association for the Severely Handicapped, 5*(1), 13–23.

Orelove, F.P. (1991). Educating all students: The future is now. In L.H. Meyer, C.A. Peck, & L. Brown (Eds.), *Critical issues in the lives of people with severe disabilities* (pp. 67–87). Baltimore: Paul H. Brookes Publishing Co.

Orelove, F.P. (1994). Transdisciplinary teamwork. In H.G. Garner & F.P. Orelove (Eds.), *Teamwork in human services: Models and applications across the life span* (pp. 37–59). Boston: Butterworth-Heinemann.

Ottenbacher, K. (1982). Occupational therapy and special education: Some issues and concerns related to PL 94-142. *American Journal of Occupational Therapy, 36*, 81–84.

Ottenbacher, K. (1983). Transdisciplinary service delivery in school environments: Some limitations. *Physical and Occupational Therapy in Pediatrics, 3*(4), 9–16.

Peterson, C.P. (1980). Support services. In B.L. Wilcox & R. York (Eds.), *Quality education for the severely handicapped: The federal investment* (pp. 136–163). Washington, DC: Bureau of Education for the Handicapped.

Rainforth, B. (1985). *Collaborative efforts in the preparation of physical therapists and teachers of students with severe handicaps.* Unpublished doctoral dissertation, University of Illinois at Urbana-Champaign.

Rainforth, B., & York, J. (1987). Integrating related services in community instruction. *Journal of The Association for Persons with Severe Handicaps, 12*(3), 190–198.

Rainforth, B., York, J., & Macdonald, C. (1992). *Collaborative teams for students with severe disabilities: Integrating therapy and educational services.* Baltimore: Paul H. Brookes Publishing Co.

Salisbury, C. (1992). Parents as team members: Inclusive teams, collaborative outcomes. In B. Rainforth, J. York, & C. Macdonald, *Collaborative teams for students with severe disabilities: Integrating therapy and educational services* (pp. 43–66). Baltimore: Paul H. Brookes Publishing Co.

Sears, C.J. (1981). The transdisciplinary approach: A process for compliance with Public Law 94-142. *Journal of The Association for the Severely Handicapped, 6*(1), 22–29.

Sparling, J.W. (1980). The transdisciplinary approach with the developmentally delayed child. *Physical and Occupational Therapy in Pediatrics, 1*(2), 3–16.

Sternat, J., Messina, R., Nietupski, J., Lyon, S., & Brown, L. (1977). Occupational and physical therapy services for severely handicapped students: Toward a naturalized public school service delivery model. In E. Sontag, J. Smith, & N. Certo (Eds.), *Educational programming for the severely and profoundly handicapped* (pp. 263–278). Reston, VA: Council for Exceptional Children.

Stremel-Campbell, K. (1977). Communication skills. In N.G. Haring (Ed.), *Developing effective individualized education programs for severely handicapped children and youth* (pp. 139–182). Washington, DC: U.S. Department of Health, Education, and Welfare, Office of Education, Bureau of Education for the Handicapped.

Strully, J.L., & Strully, C.F. (1989). Friendships as an educational goal. In S. Stainback, W. Stainback, & M. Forest (Eds.), *Educating all students in the mainstream of regular education* (pp. 59–68). Baltimore: Paul H. Brookes Publishing Co.

Szymanski, E.M., Hanley-Maxwell, C., & Asselin, S. (1990). Rehabilitation counseling, special education, and vocational special needs education: Three transition disciplines. *Career Development for Exceptional Individuals, 13*(1), 29–38.

The Association for Persons with Severe Handicaps. (1986). *Position statement on the provision of related services.* Seattle, WA: Author.

Thompson, B., & Guess, D. (1989). Students who experience the most profound disabilities: Teacher perspectives. In F. Brown & D.H. Lehr (Eds.), *Persons with profound disabilities: Issues and practices* (pp. 3–41). Baltimore: Paul H. Brookes Publishing Co.

Thousand, J.S., & Villa, R.A. (1992). Collaborative teams: A powerful tool in school restructuring. In R.A. Villa, J.S. Thousand, W. Stainback, & S. Stainback (Eds.), *Restructuring for caring and effective education: An administrative guide to creating heterogeneous schools* (pp. 73–108). Baltimore: Paul H. Brookes Publishing Co.

United Cerebral Palsy Associations, National Organized Collaborative Project to Provide Comprehensive Services for Atypical Infants and Their Families. (1976). *Staff development handbook: A resource for the transdisciplinary process.* New York: United Cerebral Palsy Associations.

Wallace, S.J. (1990). Risk of seizures [Annotation]. *Developmental Medicine and Child Neurology, 32,* 645–649.

West, M.A. (1978). The social worker specializing in handicapped children. In K.E. Allen, V.A. Holm, & R.L. Schiefelbusch (Eds.), *Early intervention—A team approach* (pp. 269–285). Baltimore: University Park Press.

Whitehouse, F.A. (1951). Teamwork—A democracy of processions. *Exceptional Children, 18*(2), 45–52.

Woodruff, G., & McGonigel, M.J. (1988). Early intervention team approaches: The transdisciplinary model. In J.B. Jordan, J.J. Gallagher, P.L. Hutinger, & M.B. Karnes (Eds.), *Early childhood special education: Birth to three* (pp. 164–181). Reston, VA: Council for Exceptional Children.

Worthington, B.S., Pipes, P.L., & Trahms, C.M. (1978). The pediatric nutritionist. In K.E. Allen, V.A. Holm, & R.L. Schiefelbusch (Eds.), *Early intervention—A team approach* (pp. 199-218). Baltimore: University Park Press.

York, J.L. (1984). *A transdisciplinary model of service delivery for educational teams who serve students with severe and multiple handicaps: Implications for developmental therapists.* Unpublished manuscript, University of Wisconsin–Madison.

York, J., Long, E., Caldwell, N., Brown, L., Zanella Albright, K., Rogan, P., Shiraga, B., & Marks, J. (1985). Teamwork strategies for school and community instruction. In L. Brown, B. Shiraga, J. York, A. Udvari-Solner, K. Zanella Albright, P. Rogan, E. McCarthy, & R. Loomis (Eds.), *Educational programs for students with severe intellectual disabilities* (Vol. 15, pp. 229–276). Madison, WI: Madison Metropolitan School District.

York, J., Rainforth, B., & Giangreco, M.F. (1990). Transdisciplinary teamwork and integrated therapy: Clarifying the misconceptions. *Pediatric Physical Therapy, 2*(2), 73–79.

The Sensorimotor Systems
A Framework for
Assessment and Intervention

Winnie Dunn

THE SENSORY AND MOTOR SYSTEMS form a definitive network through which individuals experience and act on the environment. Information produced through sensory and motor exploration form the foundation for developmental experiences (Rogers & D'Eugenio, 1981; Short-DeGraff, 1988). For example, while learning how to reach and grasp objects in the environment (a motor skill), the young child also acquires cognitive information such as object distance, spatial relationships, and weight. The child who puts on a shirt receives sensory input as the shirt moves across his or her body surface, and the child also uses motor functions to accomplish the task. The sensory input and motor responses necessary for this and other adaptive tasks develop accurate and reliable maps of one's body (called *body scheme*), which a person becomes accustomed to using; this leads to greater independence. When young children are deprived of typical sensory and motor experiences, as a result of either environmental or biological variables, there is a risk that other areas of development may also be affected.

The sensory and motor systems are intimately linked within the nervous system; in fact, many refer to them as the sensorimotor systems (e.g., Moore, 1980; Short-DeGraff, 1988; Weeks & Ewer-Jones, 1983). The sensory systems provide an interface between the environment and the individual for incoming information. Each sensory system receives, transmits, and interprets specific environmental stimuli for the nervous system, creating maps of oneself and one's environment that identify spatial and temporal qualities of body and environment; as more information is gathered from experiences, the maps become more complex (Dunn, 1991c). The motor system uses these maps of the self and the environment to plan, organize, and execute movements in response to environmental demands. The motor response itself then produces sensory feedback regarding the event, which enhances the maps for the next time they need to be used. Figure 2.1 summarizes these relationships.

For example, when a person reaches for a cup, the sensory receptors in the joints and muscles provide information about the arm's location in space; the visual receptors report on the closing distance between the cup and the person's hand; and the tactile system sends information regarding the texture and weight

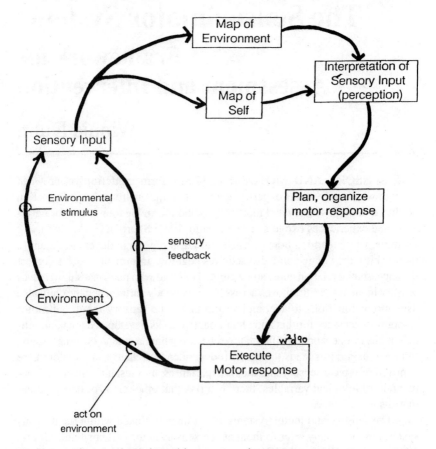

Figure 2.1. The interrelationships of the sensory and motor systems.

of the cup (sensory input). These data are incorporated into maps of the self and the environment, producing accurate current movement (interpretation of sensory input leading to organizing and executing a motor response) and enabling the next reaching task to be more routine. When errors occur in the motor action (as determined by sensory feedback), the nervous system adjusts its maps to improve performance the next time. Therefore, any discussion about motor systems must acknowledge dependence upon sensation for information and guidance.

Knowledge of the operation and interdependence of the sensory and motor systems can be an advantage when planning interventions for children with multiple disabilities. Portions of the sensory and motor systems are involved in all disabilities, and knowledgeable professionals can recognize the variations in performance that indicate both intact and involved systems. Professionals can then facilitate functional performance through intact systems and create strategies that minimize the effects of involved systems.

The first purpose of this chapter is to introduce the basic principles of sensorimotor skill acquisition and use as they apply to students with multiple disabilities. The second purpose is to explore assessment and intervention strategies that incorporate this knowledge to enhance the functional abilities of students with multiple disabilities.

TYPICAL SENSORIMOTOR SKILL ACQUISITION AND USE

The Sensory Systems

Physical stimulation from the environment (e.g., a noise, a light, a tap on the arm) activates the receptors of the sensory systems to create a nervous system impulse. Stimulus thresholds (the strength needed for the stimulus to be noticed) and ranges (upper and lower limits for noticing the stimuli) are specific both to humans as a species and to particular individuals based on their life experiences. For example, dogs hear a range of high-pitched sounds that are inaudible to the human ear. One person may comment on a sound in the environment (e.g., a car driving past the house) that another person does not hear. A person who has never tasted lemonade would have a lower threshold for the tart taste and would therefore have more visible response to it. A person who has drunk lemonade before has developed a higher threshold and responds accordingly.

Sensation arouses and alerts the individual and provides information for discrimination of salient features of the stimuli (Dunn, 1991c). Certain characteristics of each sensory system's input are more likely to produce either alerting or discriminating stimuli. Arousal/alerting stimuli tend to generate noticing behaviors. The individual's attention is at least momentarily drawn toward the stimulus (commonly disrupting ongoing behavior). These stimuli enable the nervous system to become oriented to stimuli that may require a protective response. In some situations, an arousing stimulus can become part of a functional behavior pattern (e.g., when the arousing somatosensory input from putting on a shirt becomes predictable, it becomes a discriminating/mapping characteristic).

Discriminating/mapping stimuli are those that enable the individual to gather information that can be used to support and generate functional behaviors. The information identifies spatial and temporal qualities of body and environment (the content of the maps) that can be used to create purposeful movement. These stimuli are more organizing for the nervous system. Table 2.1 provides examples of the stimuli characteristics that fall into each category. When planning programs for children with multiple disabilities, team members can use this information to create activities that include an optimal combination of sensory inputs. (The "Application of Knowledge of Sensorimotor Systems to the Needs of Children with Multiple Disabilities" section of this chapter describes planning strategies.)

Most milestones associated with the sensory systems occur prior to the preschool period when the child learns to explore the environment and begins building maps of the self and the environment for more complex interactions. The brain combines information from all sensations to build multidimensional maps of the self and the environment. For example, a young child combines movement with visual and tactile information to determine how to retrieve a favorite stuffed animal. Multiple experiences provide the underlying information to facilitate development of motor, perceptual, cognitive, and language relationships (Dunn, 1991c).

The Somatosensory System   The *somatosensory system* responds to touch input through receptors on the surface of the skin. Somatosensory receptors respond to light touch (e.g., tickling), touch-pressure (e.g., firm rubbing or pressing), pain, and temperature. The input from these receptors forms a map of the self; they tell where the individual ends and the world begins (Dunn, 1991c). Somatosensory input triggers many of the early motor reflexes that enable infants to react to environmental stimuli. For example, the rooting reflex occurs when one touches the infant's lower face and results in the child moving his or her head toward the stimulus to suckle; the grasp reflex occurs when one touches the infant's palm, with the result being that the infant grips the object. These early experiences initiate the process of sensory input → motor response → sensory feedback (see Figure 2.1), which will facilitate the development of an accurate body map.

There are many somatosensory receptors on the face and in the mouth, enabling the child to develop a very clear map of the oral-motor structures for eating and talking. Textures and tastes of foods can play an important role in early oral-motor exploration. There are also many receptors on the hand; the information gathered from object manipulation and exploration promotes functional hand use and cognitive development. Children with multiple disabilities cannot generate the volume of independent tactile exploration observed during typical child development. They must rely on skilled care providers to create situations that enable exploration to occur.

Touch also contributes to a psychosocial experience through natural interactions with others. Although a person's cultural experience partially dictates the amount and type of human touch and contact that occurs, touching among humans is critical to survival. Young children who do not receive physical love and contact can "fail to thrive." They do not initiate contact, and they express little interest in eating or interacting with people or the environment.

The Proprioceptive System   The receptors of the *proprioceptive system* are housed in the muscles, joints, and surrounding tissues. They respond to the ongoing repositioning of body parts in space; stretching and compressing the muscles and tendons at the ends of muscles sends information into the nervous system. Proprioceptive input contributes to the map of the body, but through internal mechanisms. Whereas touch input often triggers movement, proprioceptive input occurs *during* the movement to support the movement and to keep the nervous system apprised of body status. Weight-bearing tasks such as kneeling, standing, and walking, activate proprioceptors in the legs; propping on forearms provides that same type of input to the arms. Bouncing, jumping, pushing, pulling, and lifting activate proprioceptors by stretching and compressing joints during a task. Thus, many of the exploratory activities of toddlers and preschoolers stimulate the proprioceptive system and create maps of the body as it moves about in space. Children with multiple disabilities often receive too much (children with high muscle tone) or too little (children with low muscle tone) proprioceptive information from their muscles and tendons, making it difficult for them to modulate muscle actions to support particular movements.

The Vestibular System   The primary task of the *vestibular system* is orientation of the head in space. The vestibular receptor is housed in the inner ear. It is constructed so that any head position or movement can be detected. The eye muscles and the vestibular system are connected to coordinate head and eye movements; body receptors and motor systems are connected to the vestibular system to coordinate head and body movements. The vestibular system forms an interfacing map, one that coordinates the map of the self with the map of the environment, to produce organized, sequenced, and well-timed body adjustments and movements. Balance and equilibrium tasks activate the vestibular receptors; the vestibular system then generates muscle actions to hold the person upright when his or her equilibrium is upset. Because many children with multiple disabilities have a difficult time moving independently, they rely on caregivers to provide movement experiences that produce vestibular information.

Biobehavioral state—the condition of the individual in relation to the ability to notice and respond to information from the environment—is altered with vestibular system input (Guess et al., 1988; Short-DeGraff, 1988). Certain forms of movement stimulate arousal (e.g., spinning, moving the head into the upside-down position), while others are calming and organizing to the nervous system,

Table 2.1. Arousal/alerting and discriminating/mapping descriptors of the sensory system

Sensory system	Arousal/alerting descriptors[a]	Discriminating/mapping descriptors[b]
For all systems	*Unpredictability:* The task is unfamiliar; the child cannot anticipate the sensory experiences that will occur in the task	*Predictability:* Sensory pattern in the task is routine for the child, such as with diaper changing—the child knows what is occurring and what will come next
Somatosensory	*Light touch:* Gentle tapping on skin; tickling (e.g., loose clothing making contact with skin)	*Touch pressure:* Firm contact on skin (e.g., hugging, patting, grasping); occurs both when touching objects or people, or when they touch you
	Pain: Brisk pinching; contact with sharp objects; skin pressed in small surface (e.g., when skin is caught between chair arm and seat)	*Long duration stimuli:* Holding, grasping (e.g., carrying a child in your arms)
	Temperature: Hot or cold stimuli (e.g., iced drinks, hot foods, cold hands, cold metal chairs)	*Large body surface contact:* Includes holding, hugging; also holding a cup with the entire palmar surface of hand
	Variability: Changing characteristics during the task (e.g., putting clothing on requires a combination of tactile experiences)	
	Short duration stimuli: Tapping, touching briefly (e.g., splashing water)	
	Small body surface contact: Using only fingertips to touch something	
Vestibular	*Head position change:* The child's head orientation is altered (e.g., pulling the child up from lying on the back to sitting)	*Linear head movement:* Head moving in a straight line (e.g., bouncing up and down, going down the hall in a wheelchair)
	Speed change: Movements change velocity (e.g., the teacher stops to talk to another teacher when pushing the child to the bathroom in a wheelchair)	*Repetitive head movement:* Movements that repeat in a simple sequence (e.g., rocking in a rocker)
	Direction change: Movements change planes (e.g, bending down to pick up something from the floor while carrying the child down the hall)	
	Rotary head movement: Head moving in an arc (e.g., spinning in a circle, turning head side to side)	

Proprioceptive	*Quick stretch:* Movements that pull on the muscles (e.g., briskly tapping on a belly muscle)	*Sustained tension:* Steady, constant action on the muscles, pressing on or holding the muscle (e.g., using heavy objects during play) *Shifting muscle tension:* Activities that demand constant changes in the muscles (e.g., walking, lifting, and moving objects)
Visual	*High intensity:* Visual stimulus is bright (e.g., looking out the window on a bright day) *High contrast:* Great difference between the visual stimulus and its surrounding environment (e.g, cranberry juice in a white cup) *Variability:* Changing characteristics during the task (e.g., a television program is a variable visual stimulus)	*Low intensity:* Visual stimulus is subdued (e.g., finding objects in the dark closet) *High similarity:* Small difference between the visual stimulus and its surrounding environment (e.g., oatmeal in a beige bowl) *Competitive:* The background is interesting or busy (e.g., the junk drawer, a bulletin board)
Auditory	*Variability:* Changing characteristics during the task (e.g., a person's voice with intonation) *High intensity:* The auditory stimulus is loud (e.g., siren, high volume radio)	*Rhythmic:* Sounds repeat in a simple sequence/beat (e.g., humming, singing nursery songs) *Constant:* The stimulus is always present (e.g., a fan noise) *Competitive:* The environment has a variety of recurring sounds (e.g., the classroom, a party) *Noncompetitive:* The environment is quiet (e.g., the bedroom when all is ready for bedtime) *Low intensity:* The auditory stimulus is subdued (e.g., whispering)
Olfactory/gustatory	*Strong intensity:* The taste/smell has distinct qualities (e.g., spinach)	*Mild intensity:* The taste/smell has nondistinct or familiar qualities (e.g., cream of wheat)

[a]Tend to generate "noticing" behaviors; the individual's attention is momentarily drawn toward the stimulus and away from ongoing behavior. Can become part of a functional behavior sequence. (See text for example.)

[b]Create temporal and spatial qualities of body and environments (maps created) that can be used to create goal-directed movement. (See text for example.)

such as rhythmic movements (e.g., rocking). Knowledge of these effects can aid in the proper structuring of activities for young children. This relationship can easily be seen during a preschooler's bedtime. For example, if a parent begins to roughhouse with a child, bouncing, swinging, and so forth, the child will have a more difficult time going to sleep than if the parent uses rhythmic rocking and cuddling.

Taste   Taste is a response to chemical receptors in the mouth, specifically in the taste buds on the tongue. Descriptions of tastes are derived from four basic qualities: bitterness, sourness, sweetness, and saltiness. Taste is a significant variable to consider when one examines the development of eating skills. Specific oral-motor responses are associated with eating (e.g., sucking, chewing, swallowing) and can be facilitated with the use of taste and texture in the mouth. The movements needed to move food about in the mouth are also needed for the production of language, although language must also be specifically taught. When children with disabilities have been restricted from eating a full range of foods for health reasons (e.g., choking, inability to swallow properly), they may also have limited experiences with tastes. This can sometimes lead to difficulty learning to accept new foods when the medical issues have been resolved.

Smell   Smell is a distance sense that also uses chemical receptors. Researchers have tried unsuccessfully to categorize odors, but the importance of the olfactory system for human behavior is not questioned (Coren, Porac, & Ward, 1984). Smells can signal familiarity of people, places, or things. Potential danger, pleasure, and fear can all be triggered with the introduction of an odor into one's environment. The smell of bread baking or a familiar cologne may remind us of past experiences for which we have feelings. Young children recognize family members by their distinctive odors. Children with multiple disabilities may use their sense of smell to map out their environment, especially when other sensory input is more difficult to obtain.

Hearing   The auditory receptor is housed in the inner ear. The structure of the ear and ear canal facilitates the movement of sound waves into the middle and inner ear for processing. Sound is used to map the environment and is frequently coordinated with movement as the child searches for the source of the sound. As children grow older, the sound of voices directs movement when children give and follow directions. The auditory system also supports the development of communication systems, as one begins to understand and describe sensorimotor experiences.

Vision   The visual system is the last sensory system to mature. The receptors are housed in the eyeball. Some of them react to light and dark and others pick up color stimuli. The receptors identify form by transmitting information about contrasting images and creating a map of the environment. This environmental map must be updated constantly as the child moves about in space and alters the relationships between the self and objects; this requires continuous coordination with the map of the self. As discussed previously, this interface is provided by the vestibular system. Children are often motivated to move and learn by seeing interesting objects and people in the environment.

One specific form of movement, object use, depends heavily on the visual system for refinement. As the child reaches for, grasps, and manipulates objects, visual guidance supports and refines these actions. Gross forms of this sequence can occur with very little visual input, but in order to develop more refined movements, coordination of visual regard of the task and necessary hand movements (which produce somatosensory and proprioceptive feedback as the child manipulates the objects) must occur. Eating with a spoon and using a communication board are examples of visual-motor integration tasks for children with multiple disabilities.

The Motor Systems

The motor systems operate to enable the individual to interact with the environment. Even early movements in infancy, which are random and automatic, are in response to sensory stimuli. When something touches an infant's face, the infant turns toward the stimulus (the rooting reflex); when something is placed into the palm of an infant's hand, the infant grasps the object (grasping reflex); when the infant moves his or her head to the right or left (providing vestibular input), the muscles in the arms and legs move in particular patterns (the asymmetrical tonic neck reflex). Children develop control and organization over these automatic or reflexive movements as they grow. Young children also move in response to visual and auditory stimuli; they turn their heads when they hear their names being called; they reach or move toward interesting objects when they see them.

Approaches to Motor Development Typically, professionals have viewed motor development from a skill-acquisition perspective (Gesell, 1954). This perspective organizes motor skills according to the typical time they emerge in the behavioral repertoire. Although this framework provides a general guideline for the emergence of developmental skills, individual children can vary quite a bit from this standard. Developmental scales do not incorporate a method for recording descriptive information about emerging skills or the level of control over acquired skills (e.g., the length of time the child takes to perform the skill correctly). There is also an implication that skills of an earlier age must be present (i.e., are prerequisites) in order for the later skills to emerge; it is more characteristic for the child to demonstrate interest in and experimentation with several skill components well before mastering the motor skills.

The developmental perspective is not useful for programming with children with multiple disabilities; these children frequently do not have the motor control necessary to explore independently and have a different sensorimotor experience when they do move. Typical children display a great deal of variability in movement patterns; for children with disabilities this variability is frequently a central problem (Scherzer & Tscharnuter, 1982). It is more useful for professionals to describe motor performance in relation to its usefulness for function and its efficiency for present and future performance desires (Campbell, 1990; Dunn, 1991a, 1991c).

A functional approach is more useful when considering children with multiple disabilities. Within a functional skills approach, it is important to identify those motor skills that are *essential* to task performance, particularly tasks that are important for adult life. Campbell (1987a) suggests that looking, vocalization, functional reaching, simple manipulation, and combined manipulation are the essential skills for performing daily life tasks. These simple behavioral forms are useful in themselves but are also necessary components of more complex forms of interaction. The actions that these behavioral forms create can also be built into many opportunities throughout the day, across many types of activities, providing multiple opportunities for practice.

Purposes for Movements   Campbell (1990) delineates three primary purposes for movements. First, movements occur to restore equilibrium when the body has been displaced in relation to gravity. Typically, these movements become automatic during the first years of life, such that people do not need to think about the need to reorient the body when it is displaced. When people are riding in a car and it turns sharply, the passengers readjust their body positions quickly and spontaneously to accommodate themselves to the turn. Second, people combine movements with ideas to create desired actions; this conceptualization and organization process is called *motor planning* or *praxis* (the ability to organize and conceptualize a new motor act) (Ayres, 1980). The child sees a favorite toy in the vicinity and moves in an organized way to obtain the toy. Cognitive and motor systems function together to achieve desired actions. Third, movement is used to increase and refine skills. Although a child may be able to move toward a desired toy, the child may not be able to pick up or explore the toy properly without refined motor skills. Younger children use the same few movements to explore objects (e.g., grasping and releasing objects), while older children can move an object within their hands to discover additional qualities and properties (Exner, 1989).

Component Parts of Movements   Movements have component parts (i.e., the form of the movement) (Campbell, 1989). The components of movement can create an efficient motion, one that expends a great deal of effort, or one that does not produce the desired outcome at all. Skilled observations are used to analyze movement qualities and its effectiveness for desired performance. Young children who are learning to eat with a spoon initially use ineffective movements. For example, a child will dump the contents of the spoon before it reaches the mouth, because the child cannot coordinate the necessary wrist, hand, and arm movements with the utensil position. After practicing, the child discovers a way to keep food on the spoon and get it to the mouth, but movement qualities are poor. The child may miss the mouth, hold the spoon in a primitive manner, or may use excessive head movement to get the food off the spoon.

After experimenting with various patterns of movements, the child creates an efficient method for eating with a spoon and relies on this pattern when eating all meals. This adaptability of form is a hallmark of typical skill acquisition and use but is a significant barrier for many children with multiple disabilities. (See the "Atypical Sensorimotor Skill Acquisition and Use" section of this chapter for a discussion of these barriers.)

Reaching, grasping, manipulating, and releasing objects with the hand are significant components of the exploration process. This sensorimotor sequence enables a person to locate objects within the immediate environment and discover the properties of the objects (Exner, 1989). Most functional tasks require a combination of arm and hand movements to achieve the desired outcome. For example, a child uses simple reaching patterns to put on a shirt, but a complex pattern of arm and hand movements is necessary to button it. Muscle tone and postural control problems inhibit the evolution of this sequence for children with multiple disabilities.

Movement and Cognitive Skill Acquisition It is important to remember the relationship between movement abilities and the acquisition of cognitive skills (Campbell, 1990). Children explore objects and people in their environment to learn their characteristics, qualities, and functions; children must therefore move to explore the environment. Functional movement is a combination of sensorimotor and cognitive systems operations. There must be a reason for the individual to move (a motivating factor), and the child must have sensorimotor capabilities to act on the environment. This is a key focus of attention when working with children who have multiple disabilities. Professionals must acknowledge the potential for sensorimotor impairments to affect cognitive skill acquisition and use and must provide intervention to minimize this possibility.

Acquisition of Postural Control

Postural control is the ability to manage one's body parts with and against the forces of gravity. Postural control begins when an infant can hold the body still to focus on a particular stimulus (Gilfoyle, Grady, & Moore, 1981). The infant proceeds to experiment with many postural control patterns that incorporate combinations of holding one body part still while moving another body part to meet a functional goal. Postural control is observable in all body positions: supine (on the back), prone (on the stomach), sitting, and standing. In each position, the child initially moves toward gravity, and eventually the child can move against the force of gravity.

Young infants depend on adults to provide the stable base for simple movements. For example, the adult commonly holds the child's upper trunk so the child can hold up his or her head without having to manage the whole body. As the child grows and develops better control, the adult provides less external support and the child establishes internal stability to support exploratory movements. Internal support generally occurs within the central trunk—initially to support the head and then to provide a stable base for limb movements (Campbell, 1989). The child also learns to use objects in the environment to provide support when experimenting with new postures and movements. For example, when a child is learning to stand up, the child holds onto furniture for support. The child experiments with movements against gravity by moving only briefly at first, then by increasing the length of time the posture can be maintained, and finally by developing control over the movements (Campbell, 1989). Ultimately the child can move with and against the force of gravity independently. Exploratory movements and postural control for stability become fluid with each other, so that the child can engage in complex motor sequences for problem solving. The child learns to move away from the furniture and walk across the room, and eventually he or she can play with a toy while standing or walking.

Although professionals discuss the emergence of postural control from a head-to-foot and trunk-to-extremities direction, it is clear from watching young children that they experiment with postural control in all directions simultaneously. A child might hold the trunk against the high chair to reach for the fruit chunks on the tray (proximal stability for distal mobility) and later that day might place hands and knees on the floor and rock the shoulders and pelvis back and forth (distal stability for proximal mobility). Children with multiple disabilities frequently lack balance between stability and mobility, which is a significant barrier to the acquisition of postural control for functional performance.

Functional Importance of Typical Sensorimotor System Evolution

The sensorimotor systems support the individual's ability to experience and interact with the environment. The sensory systems transmit information from the environment. This information forms maps of the individual and the surrounding environment. The motor systems use sensory maps to create accurate, smooth, and well-timed movements in response to environmental demands. As the child acquires information, ideas and interests guide sensorimotor experiences; problem-solving activities build the cognitive repertoire but continue to rely on the sensorimotor systems to carry out the intended activities. Typical children acquire and use sensorimotor and cognitive skills systematically through ongoing experimentation with sensory input and movements and their consequences.

The ongoing experimentation processes of young children enable them to learn to socialize, communicate, eat, dress, complete personal hygiene, learn, and play. The sensorimotor systems support these functional life tasks by providing the mechanisms through which the child experiences and acts on the environment in specified ways (Dunn, 1991a). When the sensorimotor systems are disrupted because of disease or trauma, the child has difficulty developing the ability to perform functional life tasks because the experimentation process is disrupted.

ATYPICAL SENSORIMOTOR SKILL ACQUISITION AND USE

Major Features of Atypical Skill Acquisition and Use

Children with multiple disabilities must acquire functional skills even though their sensorimotor systems operate differently. Although each child demonstrates an individual pattern of performance strengths and limitations, several character-istics of atypical sensorimotor skill acquisition and use are commonly observed.

Muscle Tone Is Abnormal   Muscle tone is the underlying tension of mus-cles; as a result of insults to the central nervous system (CNS), it is common for children with multiple disabilities to display abnormal muscle tone (Campbell, 1987a). Tone can be lower or higher than the expected range (see the following section). Because muscle tone underlies the capacity of muscles to act (Camp-bell, 1987a), abnormal tone interferes with task performance.

Primitive Reflexes Persist   Primitive reflexes are those movement pat-terns that occur automatically when a particular stimulus is present. For exam-ple, the asymmetrical tonic neck reflex is generated by movement of the head to the side (chin to shoulder) and causes increased extensor muscle tone in the limbs on the face side and increased flexor tone in the limbs on the skull side. Many reflexes act on the sensorimotor system in the first months of life. The pur-pose of these reflexes is to provide a mechanism through which the infant can begin having experiences in the environment.

It is common for primitive reflexive patterns of movement to continue in children with multiple disabilities (Scherzer & Tscharnuter, 1982). Instead of the child gaining control over his or her movement patterns, these primitive patterns of movement frequently persist. This means that attempts at functional perfor-mance can be interrupted by an obligatory reaction from a primitive reflex pat-tern. For example, a young boy is working to pick up objects and place them in a container in front of him. The influence of the asymmetrical tonic neck reflex may cause the child to knock the materials off the table when he looks to the side to find out who is laughing in the room. Such interruptions in task performance can be difficult to manage because the child may become discouraged or lose interest. When primitive reflexes tend to predominate, tasks can be structured to minimize the interference of these reflexes with task performance.

Postural Control and Movement Are Difficult   Postural control depends on the ability to grade movements across the entire range of joint and muscle capacity. Children with multiple disabilities do not have the sensorimotor resources to experiment with body adaptations to environmental demands. They become fixed in particular positions and are held there either by the force of gravity or by the tension in their muscles. Movement quality is also limited by these same factors, which decrease efficiency or effectiveness of movements. Because postural control underlies the ability to interact with objects and people in the environment, learning experiences may become limited when postural control is poor.

Early Positioning and Handling Problems Can Lead to Orthopedic Changes   The limitations in the repertoire of movements and positions the child can acquire and use independently may also lead to constitutional changes in the child's body. A child's joints and muscles may become stiff, and he or she may ultimately be unable to move in the full range possible. Bony prominences may be present because of the lack of muscle and tissue bulk and can themselves become sources of skin breakdown and infection. Many of the intervention techniques that facilitate postural control for functional movement also serve to prevent or limit the effects of these orthopedic changes on the child's ability to function.

Functional Skill Development Is Interrupted   The most important global characteristic of children with multiple disabilities is their difficulty acquiring and using functional life skills. They require specific and individually designed strategies to learn to use their sensorimotor and cognitive systems for functional performance. The goals set for other children are equally applicable to these children and include participation in daily care routines (e.g., attention to personal hygiene, dressing, eating) and in interactional activities (e.g., those related to socialization and communication).

Classification Systems for Children with Disabilities

There are several ways to classify the problems of children with multiple disabilities. They may be classified by the particular systems that are affected, by medical diagnoses, by intellectual status, or by functional limitations. When considering a sensorimotor perspective, classifications are most frequently based on particular diagnoses and functional issues.

Classification of Cerebral Palsy   Cerebral palsy is the most common medical diagnosis for children with multiple disabilities. Cerebral palsy is a nonprogressive CNS disorder that affects motor performance. Specific patterns of motor performance have characteristic behavioral manifestations and are associated with particular areas of the brain. Other disabilities are frequently present with cerebral palsy, including visual abnormalities, hearing and speech difficulties, seizures, mental retardation, learning disabilities, and socioemotional problems (Scherzer & Tscharnuter, 1982).

Historically, cerebral palsy has been categorized by motor characteristics and by involved body parts (Scherzer & Tscharnuter, 1982). Table 2.2 presents general definitions of the terms for each. Motor characteristics include spasticity, athetosis, ataxia, rigidity, and hypotonia (Campbell, 1990). Spastic cerebral palsy is the most common type of motor dysfunction; *spasticity* can be defined as increased muscle tone or stiffness in the muscles, sometimes referred to as *hypertonus* (*hyper* means high; *tonus* means tone). *Athetosis* is characterized by continuous, uncontrolled movements of the limbs, hands, and feet. Athetoid movements have a writhing quality and are usually visible both during activity and at rest. *Ataxia* refers to movements characterized by poor balance and coor-

Table 2.2.   Terms used in the diagnosis of cerebral palsy

Term	Definition
Muscle status	
Spasticity	Stiffness or constant tension in the muscles; sometimes called hypertonus
Athetosis	Writhing movements within the muscles; movements can be seen during tasks and at rest
Ataxia	Uncoordinated movements, especially during activities requiring balance and equilibrium; most noticeable during task performance
Rigidity	Extremely high muscle tone (hypertonicity); it is even difficult for caregivers to move body parts
Hypotonia	Low muscle tone; difficulty moving body parts against the force of gravity
Limb involvement	
Quadriplegia	Involvement of all four extremities
Hemiplegia	Involvement of the arm and leg on one body side
Diplegia	More serious involvement of the legs than the arms

dination. The individual with ataxia has more pronounced difficulty when trying to perform a specific movement (e.g., taking a step, reaching for a glass) than when at rest. An individual might also display *rigidity,* in which muscle tone is severely rigid (i.e., hypertonic), which interferes with any movement by the individual or by a caregiver. *Hypotonia* is characterized by decreased muscle tension, which interferes with postural alignment; the joints are excessively mobile (i.e., hypermobile in range of motion); and it is difficult for the individual to move against gravity because the weight of the body part is much greater than the power of the muscle.

Professionals also refer to particular patterns of limb involvement in cerebral palsy. The term *plegia* means paralysis, or loss of functional ability. *Quadriplegia* refers to involvement of all four limbs. *Hemiplegia* refers to involvement of the arm and leg on one side of the body; hence, a child can have a right or left hemiplegia. *Diplegia* applies to more serious involvement in the lower extremities than in the upper extremities. Because the motor involvement and the body part involvement refer to different characteristics of the same disorder, a child's diagnosis typically includes both references (e.g., a child has spastic quadriplegic cerebral palsy).

Classification for Intervention Planning   Campbell and Forsyth (1990) have created a system for classifying posture and movement skill acquisition delays and impairments, and they use this system in young children with CNS dysfunction. Rather than relying on particular medical diagnoses, their system addresses problems that are the focus of the intervention planning process. They considered the following factors when creating their classification system:

integrity of muscle tone, the relationship between body alignment and performance of motor skills, patterns of delayed skill acquisition, and atypical performance of posture and movement skills. Three of the classifications (Type 1: hypotonia present in combination with genetic disorders, prematurity, or other medical complications; Type V: spastic diplegia; and Type VI: hemiplegia) describe children who are *not* candidates for programs serving individuals with severe and multiple disabilities. The other four classifications include children who *are* likely candidates for these programs.

Type II includes children with severe hypotonia. These children have a very difficult time moving any body parts against the force of gravity and therefore are unable to move with any frequency. Lack of movement leads to significant delays in skill acquisition and eventually can contribute to other problems such as contractures (the tissues surrounding the joints become shortened and inflexible, preventing movement or change in position). Professionals who work in the area of multiple disabilities will have children with severe hypotonia in their programs. It is important to create intervention strategies that compensate for the child's inability to move body parts (e.g., through good positioning; see Chapter 3) so that the child can engage in cognitive and language tasks.

Children who have disabilities that are characteristic of Type III classification have decreased muscle tone in the trunk and increased muscle tone in the extremities. Because of the increased muscle tone in the extremities, these children can position themselves, but their positioning prohibits other interactions (e.g., if the child uses his or her arms to hold up in sitting, then the child cannot play with a toy or eat because the arms and hands are occupied). Children in this category may display ataxia, athetosis, or overall spasticity as they grow older. These children are also likely to develop deformities from lack of functional movement patterns. Intervention planning for this group facilitates functional performance by providing external support for certain body parts so that other body parts can be used to engage people and objects in the environment. For example, a seat can be designed to support the trunk and head so the child can reach for a communication board.

Type IV includes children who have hypertonia throughout the body (spastic quadriplegia). It is difficult for these children to move; when they do move, spasticity is involved in the movement, which results in their condition affecting both the rate and the quality of movement. Skill acquisition is delayed and these children frequently develop compensatory patterns of movement. They can develop contractures and deformities as they grow older. Children with spastic quadriplegia can also have other complications. Intervention addresses the ability to move body parts in functional patterns. As these children grow, intervention also includes compensatory strategies to minimize the interference of spasticity so they can use acquired movements to interact with the environment.

Type VII includes children with severe and multiple disabilities. They may have significantly increased or decreased tone and have additional visual and/or

auditory problems (see Chapter 4) or other disabilities. These children have difficulty with producing and using movement to engage the environment, which
results in poor rates of performance, additionally affecting skill acquisition.
Because these children are unable to engage the environment with even simple
movement schemata (e.g., looking, reaching), cognitive and language areas can
also be affected due to lack of experiences. Intervention planning must be multifaceted and must address functional performance within naturally occurring
opportunities; this facilitates skill acquisition, which is supported by environmental cues.

Functional Manifestations of Atypical
Sensorimotor Skill Acquisition and Use

When serving children with multiple disabilities, caregivers must focus attention
on the many factors that contribute to the pattern of their performances. The children's difficulties with sensorimotor functions interfere with both caregiver routines and their abilities to participate in daily life tasks, including handling,
diaper changing, bathing, eating, dressing, and personal hygiene. Each of these
activities requires variability and adaptability of movement in response to environmental demands, which is the central problem for children with multiple disabilities. Team members recognize the components of these tasks and create
interventions that maximize functional performance and minimize the interference of the sensorimotor problems. The cognitive components of the above tasks
are also a factor in successful performance. Socialization and communication are
cognitive processes that rely heavily on the sensorimotor systems for both information and mechanisms to respond. As with other daily life tasks, plans are created to address all aspects of the activity and the children's skills and limitations.

APPLICATION OF KNOWLEDGE OF SENSORIMOTOR SYSTEMS
TO THE NEEDS OF CHILDREN WITH MULTIPLE DISABILITIES

Service Provision Models and Approaches Used by Therapists

Service Provision Models   Educationally related and early intervention
services require a range of service provision options to meet the divergent needs
of children and their families (Dunn, 1988, 1989, 1991b). Historically, occupational and physical therapists have employed a *direct service* model of providing
services to address sensorimotor needs. In this situation, the therapist creates an
individualized intervention plan and carries out the programming with the individual in a one-to-one interaction. In addition to a direct service model, therapists can provide monitoring and consultation (American Occupational Therapy
Association, 1990).

In a *monitoring* model of service provision, the therapist creates an intervention plan to meet the child's needs and supervises someone else in the rou-

tine implementation of the plan (Dunn & Campbell, 1991). The therapist remains responsible for the plan, the necessary adaptations, and the program outcomes. The therapist and the teacher meet regularly to ensure that procedures are carried out in a safe, consistent manner and to answer questions. This is a useful service provision option because many therapeutic opportunities occur throughout the week, and therapists are not available to be with a specific child at all times to take advantage of these opportunities. It is most common for monitored (or supervised) programs to address positioning, handling, carrying, eating, adaptive, and other activities of daily living. For example, a team has determined that eating independently is a goal for a particular student. The occupational therapist determines that a physical guidance procedure will enable the child to move the spoon to the mouth and that oral-motor activities will improve the child's ability to eat the food off the spoon. The therapist and teacher meet during mealtime so that the teacher can learn the procedures, and then they meet twice a month to adjust programming strategies and refine procedures as the child acquires eating skills.

Consultation   Consultation occurs when the therapist uses discipline expertise to address the needs of another adult on the intervention team (e.g., a teacher) (American Occupational Therapy Association, 1990). The therapist and the teacher create intervention plans using their collective knowledge of the child and the situation. The therapist provides consultative services when he or she adjusts task demands to enable task performance, adapts environmental conditions to improve integration, alters materials to address specific strengths and areas of concern, creates optimal postural conditions, establishes movement parameters within the educational environment, and instructs the classroom personnel about specific methods that can be used to improve learning (Dunn & Campbell, 1991).

When teachers work on teams with occupational therapists and physical therapists, they can expect to see all service provision models in operation within their classrooms. Children with multiple disabilities require multifaceted strategies to produce successful outcomes; this includes the expertise of many disciplines. A wider range of service provision options ensures that the child's entire environment is therapeutic, instead of providing therapy during only isolated portions of the day. Many of the services provided by therapists will be incorporated into the curriculum routine; this provides opportunities for practice and reinforcement in naturally occurring situations. It is sometimes necessary to isolate children from the natural environment (e.g., when a child needs to concentrate on acquiring a new skill, when the procedure is disruptive to ongoing classroom activities). In these situations, therapists provide a specific rationale for isolating children from the natural environment for services (Dunn & Campbell, 1991).

Service Provision Approaches   A therapist may also choose various service provision approaches (Dunn, Campbell, Oetter, Hall, & Berger, 1989). Dunn, Brown, and McGuigan (1994) have outlined five therapeutic approaches that are available to providers, including *establishing* or *restoring* function, *adapting* to enable function, *altering* environments to support function, *preventing* disruptions to function, and *creating* environments that facilitate optimal functional performance. The therapist considers the child's status, environmental conditions, and team priorities when selecting an approach to a particular problem.

The therapist selects an establishment/restoration approach (i.e., remediation) when the problem can be at least partially corrected, and the intervention results in improved functional performance. Therapists have chosen a remediation approach in working with children to develop head control, trunk control, reach, and grasp. These basic motor skills underlie all functional activities. If they can be at least partially corrected, the child will have increased independence. Therapists have particular expertise to address sensorimotor skill acquisition and use, and they contribute this knowledge to team strategies.

Children with multiple disabilities also have problems that persist and interfere with functional performance. In these cases, an adaptive (i.e., compensatory) approach is appropriate. The therapist designs strategies that neutralize the effects of the problem, and therefore enable the child to engage in activities. For example, a child with severe hypotonia is unable to hold his or her body up against gravity; this problem interferes with the child's ability to interact with people and objects in the environment. The therapist creates strategies that provide external support for the head and trunk (to compensate for excessively low muscle tone) so the child can see others easily for communication and so the arms and hands are in a proper position to play with toys on the table.

Providers implement an alteration approach when they study various environments and select the one that is the best match for the child. An alteration approach does not expect providers to change the environment and does not expect the child to have to drastically change skills or behaviors to work in that environment. This approach addresses the possibility that certain environments may be more manageable and supportive for certain people. For example, if a child has a high need for structure, the school personnel can place the child either in a more casual classroom and ask the teacher to provide additional structure (i.e., adapt the environment) or in a classroom that is inherently more structured. There are many opportunities in education to find better matches for children, rather than making the children and the teachers work harder to try to be compatible.

A prevention approach is used when the team wishes to intervene to prevent problems that may arise in the future. For children with multiple disabilities, a prevention intervention approach might be used to prevent the occurrence of later orthopedic deformities. The therapist might design positioning strategies to be implemented throughout the day and teach the classroom staff to work on range of motion prior to particular activities.

As inclusion is implemented more in schools, it is sometimes useful to consider interventions within the system to make school environments more

enriching for all students, not just those who have disabilities. In these circumstances, a creation approach is appropriate. When providers design an environment or activity to enhance the development of *all* children they are using a
creation approach. The creation approach does not presume any disability, but
rather addresses the needs of a group of children in a particular setting. For
example, teachers may design activities to encourage cooperation because it is in
all the children's interest and is not focused on a particular child or disability.

Therapists may select all the service provision approaches within a comprehensive program for a child with multiple disabilities. It is important for the team
to discuss these possibilities so that everyone is working toward the same outcomes. Approaches that are at cross-purposes are not in the child's best interests.
Table 2.3 presents examples of activities using these service provision models
and approaches.

Typical Intervention Strategies Used by Therapists

Occupational therapists and physical therapists employ many strategies when
they create interventions for children with multiple disabilities. These strategies
are based on theories and frames of reference developed within their respective
fields, knowledge from other fields, and interventions originally designed for
different groups of people that are adapted to meet particular needs. It is useful
for all team members to understand the bases for these intervention choices, so
that more collaborative strategies can be created. The primary tenets of the most
common intervention strategies are introduced below, with a discussion of their
application to the needs of children with multiple disabilities.

Neurodevelopmental Treatment (NDT)   Neurodevelopmental treatment
(NDT) addresses the movement problems of children with neurological dysfunction. The therapist identifies the posture and movement problems and imple-
ments procedures to decrease the effects of abnormal muscle tone and to
increase the normal, balanced actions of muscles for functional movement
(Bobath, 1963; Campbell, 1990). Campbell (1990) summarizes the goals of
NDT:

- To analyze dysfunction in order to identify primary problems with posture
  and movement
- To implement facilitation and inhibition procedures to establish postural stability and functional movement
- To teach sensorimotor procedures to others so problems are managed across
  situations
- To select and use equipment that will support postural control and functional
  movement
- To prevent abnormal patterns from persisting and creating secondary changes
  (e.g., tightness, deformities)

The therapist identifies posture and movement problems by observing the
child in various situations. Stern and Gorga (1988) suggest that one should

Table 2.3. Examples of service provision approaches and models

Service provision models	Service provision approaches				
	Establish/restore (remediate)	Adapt (compensate)	Alter	Prevent	Create (promote)
Direct	Facilitate neck extensor muscles so child can look at friends when playing.	Fabricate a splint to enable the child to hold the cup at snack time.	Select a community preschool based on the level of noise the child can manage.	Facilitate weight bearing during infancy to prevent possible delays in walking.	Provide a play program for the community for all children to attend.
Monitoring	Supervise the teacher's aide to facilitate tone for reaching during a game.	Supervise a feeding program that minimizes the time for eating and enables socialization.	Work with parents to identify the community locations that will be best for their family outings.	Create a "positions alternatives" chart for the aides to prevent skin breakdowns.	Oversee the development of a morning preschool routine that optimizes early development possibilities.
Consultation	Teach classroom staff how to incorporate enhanced sensory input into play routines during free time.	Show teachers how to change the pieces of a game so all children can handle the pieces.	Provide the team with information from skilled observations that enables them to select the best play partner for a child.	Teach parents a range-of-motion sequence to prevent deformities.	Assist the child care provider to develop a comprehensive curriculum.

From Dunn, W. (1996). Occupational therapy. In R. McWilliam (Ed.), *Rethinking pull-out services in early intervention: A professional resource*, p. 282. Baltimore: Paul H. Brookes Publishing Co.; reprinted by permission.

observe a child with a critical eye to determine the child's response to dynamic interactions (e.g., Is the child frightened? Does the child stiffen with movements?) and the child's ability to change. The therapist records the motor characteristics, paying particular attention to the postural stability patterns used and the form and function of the movements (Campbell, 1990). For example, a child with hypertonicity may sit without support, but the therapist may notice that the pelvis is poorly positioned to support an aligned trunk and head. Proper alignment of the trunk and head enables the child to see objects and people in front of him or her and facilitates interactions. This child might also reach for food on the plate (movement with a function), but may take a long time and have poor wrist and hand position for picking up the food (form of the movement). In this example, the child has the functional aspects of the movement but lacks the form to succeed. Proper form within functional movement might be obtained with the application of NDT techniques. Therapists guard against the attainment of proper form without corresponding functional application of the movement.

The therapist uses a range of facilitation and inhibition techniques when working from an NDT frame of reference. These techniques are applied to affect muscle tone and improve patterns of postural control and movement. The sequence begins with preparation (Campbell, 1990) to establish body alignment and to decrease interfering muscle tension (i.e., hypertonicity). During this phase, the therapist applies deep pressure to the child's body surfaces, either with hands or via the supporting surface (pushing the body into the mat, floor, or chair also produces pressure on the body part touching the surface), to obtain and maintain proper relationship of each part of the body. This provides an optimal base of support for functional movements.

Next, the therapist provides intervention to facilitate desired muscle actions and inhibit unwanted patterns (Campbell, 1990). Because children who are the primary focus of NDT cannot move independently, the therapist moves the child through small, subtle movement patterns (e.g., body rotation) to facilitate adaptations to postural demands. The therapist then incorporates these patterns into functional routines. For example, if the child has achieved rotational postural shifts with the arms forward, the team then uses this skill to begin using an augmentative communication board.

Therapists have primarily used NDT within a direct service model; however, NDT contains many useful principles that can be applied to all aspects of the child's life. It is important that children with multiple disabilities be positioned, handled, and moved in consistent ways to minimize the effects of their sensorimotor problems on their ability to function. Therapists who are trained in the use of NDT principles can apply these principles to school routines. A therapist might supervise the classroom staff as they facilitate an upright, aligned posture before a cognitive task. The therapist could also consult with classroom staff to create functional positioning and handling strategies for the child throughout the school day (see Chapter 3 for examples).

Although therapists have reported clinically that NDT produces positive changes in children's performance, research has not supported these claims (e.g., Harris, 1988; Parette, Hendricks, & Rock, 1991; Stern & Gorga, 1988). Research is needed that includes both adequate amounts of intervention and appropriate outcome measures to document the clinical reports of therapists.

Sensory Integration Sensory integration is a neurobiologically based theoretical model used by occupational therapists and physical therapists. Sensory integration theory hypothesizes that individuals develop skills through a process of receiving and interpreting sensory stimuli from the environment and creating adaptive responses to those stimuli (Ayres, 1980). An adaptive response is an appropriate action toward or reaction to an environmental stimulus. Adaptive responses themselves create additional sensory information (feedback) that the CNS assimilates for future task performance. When occupational therapists and physical therapists use a sensory integrative approach to problem solving, they consider the sensory qualities of the tasks, the environment, and the child's interactions with others and objects. They examine those sensory qualities that are enabling or blocking the production of an adaptive response.

Most of the research that has been completed on sensory integration has involved children with learning and behavior impairments. Some researchers have reported that carefully designed sensory integrative procedures enable children to respond to environmental demands (e.g., Ayres, 1977; Ayres & Mailloux, 1981; Horowitz, Oosterveld, & Adrichem, 1993; Humphries, Snider, & McDougall, 1993; Ottenbacher, 1982; Polatajko, Kaplan, & Wilson, 1992; Polatajko, Law, Miller, & Schaffer, 1991; Revelj, 1987; Tew, 1984; VanBenschoten, 1975; Wilson, Kaplan, Fellowes, & Gruchy, 1992). Other authors have questioned the efficacy of sensory integration (e.g., Arendt, MacLean, & Baumeister, 1988; Ayres & Mailloux, 1983; Carte, Morrison, Sublett, Uemura, & Setrakian, 1984; Cummins, 1991; Densem, Nuthall, Bushnell, & Horn, 1989; Jenkins, Fewell, & Harris, 1983; Kaplan, Polatajko, Wilson, & Faris, 1993; Morrison & Sublett, 1986; Werry, Scaletti, & Mills, 1990). Research is needed to demonstrate the applicability of sensory integration to the needs of children with severe and multiple disabilities.

Intervention using a sensory integrative approach can incorporate all of the service provision models listed previously. In a consultative model, the therapist and the consultee (usually the teacher) create environmental conditions and intervention strategies that increase the chances that an adaptive response will occur. The therapist and the teacher may collaborate to design a learning activity that incorporates sensory integrative knowledge into the task. For example, the therapist has learned from assessment that a certain child pays attention to tasks longer when receiving a more intense form of vestibular input. The teacher and therapist decide to place the child in a prone position during a small group activity because this will increase vestibular input (and the new head position will provide additional input).

The therapist can address the sensory aspects of movement and interaction with the environment when using a direct service model of intervention. For example, the team has determined that functional performance will be enhanced if the child can sit independently. The therapist places the child in prone (face down), supine (face up), and sitting positions on a large inflated ball. The child works on looking and reaching to the front and sides while the therapist slowly rocks the ball in various directions. These activities enhance vestibular, proprioceptive, and tactile input for body scheme and improved postural control. As the child acquires particular skills, the therapist incorporates these skills into classroom routines.

In some cases, the child may benefit from consistent implementation of a specific intervention strategy, but the therapist cannot be present consistently to provide the intervention. In these cases, the therapist may need to use a monitoring model of intervention to ensure that the process of intervention is carried out in a consistent manner. For example, the team determines that a child who has hypersensitivity to textures in and around the mouth, which interferes with eating, can learn to eat independently. The therapist can contribute to the daily eating routine of the child by designing an intervention strategy to decrease the child's sensitivity (e.g., by using firm touch pressure around the mouth) and to increase oral-motor control simultaneously. The therapist shows the teacher and aide how to implement the procedure and observes during lunchtime to ensure that the procedures are carried out safely and consistently. The classroom staff carry out the program daily as part of the child's routine. The therapist might also teach parents the same technique to make mealtimes at home less stressful.

Sensory integrative approaches were originally designed for children with educational disabilities such as learning disabilities. Because its core principles are based on nervous system functions that are well documented in the neuroscience literature (Cool, 1987; Dunn, 1988, 1991a, 1991c), many professionals have clinically extended the use of this theory to people with other disabilities, including children with multiple disabilities. Because the need for nervous system information is universal to all human beings, there is face validity to this practice. Studies are needed to clearly validate that it is acceptable to apply sensory integration principles to the needs of people with clearly documented CNS problems. For example, it is still unknown whether significant insults to the CNS change the operation of the sensorimotor processes in some primary way such that the application of these principles to people with these needs becomes inappropriate.

Developmental Frame of Reference   Professionals understand the typical evolution of skills from a developmental perspective (Rogers & D'Eugenio, 1981). People who use a developmental frame of reference operate under the assumption that skill acquisition occurs similarly in children with and without disabilities. Interventions are designed to facilitate the acquisition of the predetermined set of skills found in developmental tests and curriculum materials. Skills at earlier levels in development are considered general prerequisites to skills at later levels. Interventions address the mastery of earlier skills for the ability to then acquire the later skills.

It is difficult to employ a developmental perspective with children who have multiple disabilities. These children do not have the abilities of typical children to interact with the environment and, therefore, cannot acquire skills in the same manner. If one were to work with a child with multiple disabilities on a skill, remaining at one developmental level until the child used the skill in a typical manner, this child would never learn functional skills. Other approaches are better suited to the needs of children with multiple disabilities. Significant adaptations in tasks and performance standards are necessary to enable children to engage in functional tasks.

Adaptive Approaches   It is also common for therapists to select adaptive strategies in intervention planning for children with multiple disabilities. Adaptation occurs when the professionals identify the child's limitations and create alternative strategies that will support successful task performance (see Chapters 3 and 4). Baumgart et al. (1982) suggest that there are four types of adaptations: 1) personal help, 2) skill/activity modification, 3) use of an adaptive device, and 4) environmental modification.

Teachers and therapists participate in adaptive approaches when they create programs for children with multiple disabilities. It is important for people with divergent expertise to join forces, because one frame of reference will not provide adequate information to create the range of adaptations necessary to facilitate participation. Chapter 8 discusses the adaptive strategies in detail.

Joint Mobilization Techniques   Joint mobilization techniques have been documented in the literature for many centuries. They include passive movements applied to the joint and surrounding soft tissues in a specific manner to restore active range of motion to the joint (Saunders, 1985). Therapists apply joint mobilization techniques to those joints that are hypomobile (i.e., the joint is tight, unable to move through the normal range of motion). The intimate connection between the joint space and the muscles makes it important to consider intervention to both structures (Cyriax & Cyriax, 1983; Saunders, 1985; Wadsworth, 1988). Saunders (1985) states "a muscle cannot be fully rehabilitated if its joint is not free to move, and conversely, a muscle cannot move a joint which is not free to move" (p. 196). The therapist employs a combined mechanical and neurophysiological approach to relieve pain, produce relaxation, increase joint range, and gain muscle control when reflexive activity predominates.

These techniques have most commonly been applied to acute injuries, but some therapists will use joint mobilization in their overall programs for children with multiple disabilities. Because the techniques require special knowledge and skills, they are generally incorporated into the direct service components of the programs. As with any of the traditional therapeutic interventions, therapists also design strategies to incorporate the improved joint integrity into functional daily tasks.

Myofascial Release Techniques   Myofascial release is a therapeutic technique that relies on the therapist's skills to stimulate the muscles and related tissues in a specified manner (Manheim & Lavett, 1989; Travell & Simons, 1983). The techniques and mechanisms of myofascial release are not completely understood, but clinical trials have shown improvements in specific cases (Travell & Simons, 1983). Proponents suggest that myofascial release is safer and more comfortable for the individual than traditional stretching techniques used by therapists in the past (Manheim & Lavett, 1989). The goal of myofascial release is to remove restrictions to movement and enable effective postural alignment.

The therapist trained in myofascial release techniques palpates (feels the integrity of muscles, skin, and joint tissues) the body areas to determine where restricted movements may be occurring. Then the therapist gently stretches the area of the body along the lines of the muscle fibers and, through this process, the muscles and related tissues (i.e., fascia-tissue that surrounds body structures) let go or relax (Manheim & Lavett, 1989). Application of the techniques looks like massage. This then allows the therapist to align or realign body parts for better postural positioning and control.

Myofascial release techniques are applied by therapists who have had special training. The therapist selects a direct service provision model and a remedial approach. It is important to remember, however, that myofascial release only prepares the system. The therapists and teachers must always incorporate this preparedness into functional life tasks for children with multiple disabilities. Postural alignment alone is not an adequate goal for a child's program; it does, however, enable the child to have opportunities to interact and to develop basic movement sequences.

Craniosacral Therapy   The craniosacral system is described as a physiological system of membranes that connects the bones and related structures (Upledger & Vredevoogd, 1983). Proponents of craniosacral therapy believe that these structures form an internal hydraulic system that either supports or prohibits movements. Typically there is thought to be a craniosacral rhythm affecting the entire body; when this rhythm is disrupted, restricted physiological motion is said to be present (Upledger & Vredevoogd, 1983).

Upledger and Vredevoogd (1983) describe the typical craniosacral therapy techniques as "non-intrusive and indirect" (p. 21). They are not referring to service provision models as described previously. They use the terms direct and indirect to describe the particular methods used to address the craniosacral problem. The therapist uses light touch to assist the hydraulic system and therefore improve the body's internal environment. It is most common for the application of this technique to occur in the neck or pelvis regions. This approach is much less frequently used in pediatric practice, but increasingly therapists are pursuing training in this specialized set of techniques. They are applied in a direct service model of service provision, most often with a remediation approach. As with myofascial release, this is a preparatory technique and must be used in combination with functional skill acquisition and use.

APPRECIATION FOR ALTERNATIVE FRAMES OF REFERENCE IN INTERVENTION

It is sometimes confusing to other professionals that therapists have a variety of frames of reference for assessment and intervention; however, this range of viewpoints is comparable to the approaches used in education. Some educators advocate the use of behavioral approaches to address children's needs, whereas others prefer cognitive or developmental approaches. As in education, multiple viewpoints are not incompatible with each other. They offer alternative ways of solving problems and frequently can be combined to create integrated assessment and intervention strategies (Campbell, 1987a; Dunn, 1991b). When educators and therapists combine their viewpoints, many more options present themselves. Therapists have expertise that enables the student to perform the skills properly, and teachers contribute knowledge about the functional use of the skills in selected activities (Campbell, 1987a).

For example, a child may need to learn to grasp a cup, bring it to his or her mouth, and take a drink. There are several ways of viewing this situation to determine an effective strategy. Table 2.4 provides an example of the issues that team members with various perspectives might raise when assessing this child. Although none of these perspectives addresses the situation completely, each contributes vital information for the intervention planning process. Team members would consider all of these issues in light of multiple observations and data sources to determine the best approach for the particular child.

Team members can use a hypothesis-testing approach to program planning for children with multiple disabilities. In this approach, the team members analyze the problem situation, determine all possible barriers to successful performance, and then create a plan based on only one factor at a time. This process enables the team members to discover successful and unsuccessful adaptations, which is useful for future intervention planning and environmental design.

A teacher observes that a particular child is more successful scooping chocolate pudding than vanilla pudding onto the spoon. The teacher and the therapist hypothesize that either the chocolate pudding is easier to see on the beige plate, or the child may prefer chocolate. To test their hypotheses, they serve vanilla pudding on a red plate at the next meal and discover that the child scoops the vanilla pudding easily. In this example, the team members created a plan based on one characteristic of the activity—the contrast between the colors of the food item and the plate. If they had changed both the visual contrast and the flavor at the same time, they still would not have known which variable was

Table 2.4.   Parameters considered by various team members for a child who needs to learn to drink from a cup independently

Frame of reference/ perspective	Factors considered within the various perspectives
Neurodevelopmental	What is the status of muscle tone (e.g., hypertonus, hypotonus)?
	Does muscle tone interfere with movement (e.g., tightness restricts movement, low tone prohibits child from moving)?
	What is the base of support (e.g., legs, pelvis, back supporting body weight when sitting)?
	How is the trunk aligned for the task?
	How can I support functional movement (e.g., use facilitation or inhibition)?
Sensory integrative	Does the child notice the stimulus (e.g., voice command, cup of liquid)?
	How does the child respond to positioning (e.g., light touch, touch pressure)?
	What are the characteristics of the cup surface?
	How does the child respond to the surface (on hand, on lips)?
	Will the grasping pattern further enable adaptive responses or will it interfere with movement (e.g., the tension for gripping may enhance extensor muscle tone; then the child cannot get the cup to the mouth)?
Behavioral	Is the child interested in drinking from cup?
	Does the child like the liquid being used?
	Is the child thirsty?
	How does the child know it is time to drink (e.g., what cues are used—verbal prompt, physical prompt)?
Cognitive	Does the child understand what he or she is supposed to do?
	Does the child have the perceptual skills to accomplish the task (e.g., can he or she find the cup on the table with other eating utensils)?
	Can the child generalize skills from one cup to another, from one setting to another?

causing the problem, nor would they have been able to generalize their knowledge about this student to other situations. Having tested their hypotheses systematically, however, they have discovered information that can be used in future program plans. For example, the teacher now selects brightly colored objects to place on the child's white lap tray when they practice reaching and grasping, and other team members have designed highly contrasting plates for the child's augmentative communication board.

ANALYZING LEARNING SITUATIONS
FROM A SENSORIMOTOR PERSPECTIVE

A sensorimotor perspective expands the problem-solving possibilities for educational tasks. Therapists and teachers can collaborate to enrich the life experiences of children with multiple disabilities. This section provides examples of how to apply sensorimotor knowledge to children's needs within natural environments. (See also Chapters 3 and 8 for additional information, especially in regard to motor issues.)

Creating Interventions Based on Sensory Qualities

Therapists and other team members can use several methods to identify the child's sensory-processing abilities. When children have multiple disabilities, it is best to rely on skilled observations to obtain information. Professionals infer the integrity of the sensory systems by observing and recording motor behaviors (Dunn, 1991a). Professionals identify the child's tolerance, preference, and need for particular sensory experiences during daily life tasks and interactions with the child. For example, while lifting and moving a child across the room for a new activity, the teacher has a natural opportunity to determine the child's response to vestibular stimulation (the child's head will be changing position, direction of movement, and speed of movement during this experience) and tactile stimulation (the teacher will be touching the child's skin with his or her hands and body as he or she carries the child). The teacher can note the child's response to these experiences; the child may smile when being moved, indicating pleasure, or may become irritable when touched. Table 2.5 provides examples of observations that can be made during daily life tasks that may indicate the integrity of the sensory system.

The professionals accumulate information across many activities to confirm the meaning of the responses. In the previous example, the child who smiles may be responding to the movement, may be happy to be held by the teacher, or may have been bored with the past activity and is anticipating a new task. Irritability may indicate fear of change of any sort, displeasure with movement rather than touch, or unhappiness about being interrupted from an interesting task. Professionals must make multiple observations to determine the relationship between responses and situational characteristics. The team can then systematically test the hypotheses in additional situations.

Sensory processing can also be inferred by examining the sensory qualities of tasks and environments. Figure 2.2 provides a worksheet to assist professionals in examining the sensory properties of functional tasks. Each sensory system is listed in the first column; the second column contains key descriptors for each sensory system. Refer to Table 2.1 for additional information about these descriptors.

When using the worksheet in Figure 2.2, select a task or routine and write the selection in the upper left section. Next, consider how a typical individual

Table 2.5. Examples of observable behaviors that indicate difficulty with sensory processing during daily life tasks

Sensory system	Personal hygiene	Dressing	Eating	Homemaking	School/work	Play
Somatosensory	Withdraws from splashing water Pushes washcloth/towel away Cries when hair is washed and dried Makes face when toothpaste gets on lips, tongue Tenses when bottom is wiped after toileting	Tolerates a narrow range of clothing items Prefers tight clothing More irritable with loose textured clothing Cries during dressing Pulls at hats, head gear, accessories	Tolerates food at only one temperature Gags with textured food or utensils in mouth Winces when face is wiped Hand extends and avoids objects and surfaces (finger food, utensils)	Avoids participation in tasks that are wet, dirty Seeks to remove batter that falls on arms	Cries when tape or glue gets on skin Overreacts to pats, hugs; avoids these actions Tolerates only one pencil, one type of paper, only wooden objects Hands extend when attempting to type	Selects a narrow range of toys, textures similar Cannot hold on to toys/objects Rubs toys on face, arms Mouths objects
Proprioceptive	Cannot lift objects that are heavier (a new bar of soap) Cannot change head position to use sink and mirror in same task	Cannot support heavier items (belt with buckle, shoes) Fatigues prior to task completion Misses when placing arm or leg in clothing	Uses external support to eat (propping) Tires before completing meal Cannot provide force to cut meat Tires before completely eating foods that need to be chewed	Drops equipment (broom) Uses external support (leaning on counter to stir batter) Difficulty pouring a glass of milk	Drops books Becomes uncomfortable in a particular position Hooks limbs on furniture to obtain support Moves arm, hand in repetitive patterns (self-stimulatory)	Unable to sustain movements during play Tires before game is complete Drops heavy parts of a toy/game

Vestibular	Becomes disoriented when bending over the sink Falls when trying to participate in washing lower extremities	Gets overly excited/distracted after bending down to assist in putting on socks Cries when moved around a lot during dressing	Holds head stiffly in one position during mealtime Gets distracted from meal after several head position changes	Avoids leaning to obtain cooking utensil Becomes overly excited after moving around the room to dust	Avoids turning head to look at people; to find source of a sound After being transported in a wheelchair, more difficult to get on task Moves head in repetitive pattern (self-stimulatory)	Avoids play that includes movement Becomes overly excited or anxious when moving during play Rocks excessively Craves movement activities
Visual	Cannot find utensils on the sink Difficulty spotting desired item in drawer Misses when applying paste to toothbrush	Cannot find buttons on patterned or solid clothing Overlooks desired shirt in closet or drawer Misses armhole when donning shirt	Misses utensils on the table Has trouble getting foods onto spoon when they are a similar color to the plate	Cannot locate correct canned item in the pantry Has difficulty finding cooking utensils in the drawer	Cannot keep place on the page Cannot locate desired item on communication board Attends excessively to bright or flashing objects	Trouble with matching, sorting activities Trouble locating desired toy on cluttered shelf

(continued)

Table 2.5. (continued)

Sensory system	Personal hygiene	Dressing	Eating	Homemaking	School/work	Play
Auditory	Cries when hair dryer is turned on Becomes upset by running water Jerks when toilet flushes	Distracted by clothing that makes noise (crisp cloth, accessories)	Distracted by noise of utensils against each other (spoon in bowl, knife on plate) Cannot keep eating when someone talks	Distracted by vacuum cleaner sound Distracted by television or radio during tasks	Distracted by squeaky wheelchair Intolerant of noise others make in the room Overreacts to door closing Notices toilet flushing down the hall	Play is disrupted by sounds Makes sounds constantly
Olfactory/gustatory	Gags at taste of toothpaste Jerks away at smell of soap	Overreacts to clothing when it has been washed in a new detergent	Tolerates a narrow range of foods Becomes upset when certain foods are cooking	Becomes upset when house is being cleaned (odors of cleaners)	Overreacts to new person (new smells) Intolerant of scratch-n-sniff stickers Smells everything	Tastes or smells all objects before playing

ROUTINE/TASK SENSORY CHARACTERISTICS		WHAT DOES THE TASK ROUTINE HOLD?			WHAT DOES THE PARTICULAR ENVIRONMENT HOLD?	WHAT ADAPTATIONS ARE LIKELY TO IMPROVE FUNCTIONAL OUTCOME?
		A	B	C		
Somatosensory	light touch (tap, tickle)					
	pain					
	temperature (hot, cold)					
	touch, pressure (hug, pat, grasp)					
	variable					
	duration of stimulus (short, long)					
	body surface contact (small, large)					
	predictable					
	unpredictable					
Vestibular	head position change					
	speed change					
	direction change					
	rotary head movement					
	linear head movement					
	repetitive head movement -rhythmic					
	predictable					
	unpredictable					
Proprioceptive	quick stretch stimulus					
	sustained tension stimulus					
	shifting muscle tension					
Visual	high intensity					
	low intensity					
	high contrast					
	high similarity (low contrast)					
	competitive					
	variable					
	predictable					
	unpredictable					
Auditory	rhythmic					
	variable					
	constant					
	competitive					
	noncompetitive					
	loud					
	soft					
	predictable					
	unpredictable					
Olfactory/ Gustatory	mild					
	strong					
	predictable					
	unpredictable					

Task
Components:

A =
B =
C =

Figure 2.2. Form for analyzing sensory characteristics of task performance.

under typical circumstances would perform the task in a routine manner. Mark the sensory qualities that would be activated during task performance in the third column of the worksheet. If the task or routine is more complex, it is helpful to break it down into components. Three columns (A, B, C) are provided for this possibility; the task components can be listed at the bottom left of the worksheet.

One then considers the specific environment in which the task will take place in the next column of the worksheet. Although typical performance of face washing occurs in one's bathroom at home, a child who is learning to wash his or her face at school frequently performs this task in the classroom or school bathroom with other children and adults present. These changes can affect particular children, and therefore must be considered in the analysis. If the environment is a familiar one, the boxes can simply be marked, and brief descriptions can be written for those less familiar environments. Figure 2.3 displays a completed form for face washing.

The last column is used to create intervention planning strategies for children who have been unable to engage in the task or routine successfully. Team members consider alterations in task qualities that may facilitate the child's ability to perform the task. For example, a child may react negatively to the terry cloth washcloth because the terry cloth texture may be providing too much arousal/alerting input, which causes disruption in task performance. The team may consider other fabrics that would elicit a better discrimination/mapping response during face washing (e.g., cotton cloth or cotton knit).

Table 2.6 summarizes the reasons for targeting various sensory qualities during the intervention process and provides examples to illustrate their coverage in integrated programming. There is a strong interrelationship among the various sensory qualities. A certain level of arousal is necessary for a child to engage in a functional task, and arousing stimuli can be used to generate an appropriate level of alertness for activities. However, arousal/alerting stimuli can also be disruptive to ongoing task performance. For example, a child who is intent on placing an object into a container can lose postural and movement control when distracted by a slamming door. Discriminating/mapping stimuli are very useful both for facilitating the child's ongoing involvement in a task, and for calming the child who has been overstimulated. Too much calming input can lead to lethargy and listlessness, however, prohibiting the child from interacting with others and the environment. Team members collaborate to determine the optimal balance for particular children.

After considering all possible modifications, the team initiates one change at a time (hypothesis testing) to determine which change is most effective. This hypothesis testing model is important for future planning as well. As the child begins to demonstrate a pattern of preferences across activities that facilitate function, those preferences can systematically be built into all classroom tasks and routines to support the child's learning. In the face washing example, team members may generalize their knowledge about textures to clothing selection.

ROUTINE/TASK SENSORY CHARACTERISTICS	WHAT DOES THE TASK ROUTINE HOLD? A	B	C	WHAT DOES THE PARTICULAR ENVIRONMENT HOLD? (classroom sink)	WHAT ADAPTATIONS ARE LIKELY TO IMPROVE FUNCTIONAL OUTCOME?
Somatosensory light touch (tap, tickle)	X				Turn water off to decrease splashing
pain					
temperature (hot, cold)	X				Try alternative water temperatures
touch-pressure (hug, pat, grasp)	X				Pat face instead of rubbing cloth on face
variable	X				Pat large face area
duration of stimulus (short, long)	L				
body surface contact (small, large)	L				Try washing one part only; begin with chin area
predictable	X				
unpredictable					(NOTE: make sure routine is consistent day to day)
Vestibular head position change	X				Alter water source so don't have to bend head down
speed change					(e.g., in a pan or tub)
direction change	X				Keep head up so don't have the down-up pattern
rotary head movement					
linear head movement	X				Keep head up: if need arousal, place items on
repetitive head movement -rhythmic					counter to encourage more head turning
predictable					
unpredictable					
Proprioceptive quick stretch stimulus					
sustained tension stimulus	X				Move objects to decrease head control requirements
shifting muscle tension	X				
Visual high intensity					
low intensity					
high contrast					
high similarity (low contrast)	X			X Other objects	Use dark wash cloths & light soap; use dark containers on
competitive	X			X on sink	light counter; remove extra items from counter
variable				X Counter changes day to day	If arousal is needed, vary placement of items
predictable	X			X	
unpredictable					
Auditory rhythmic	X				Prepare wet cloth; don't have running tap water
variable	X				Use tub of water instead of running water
constant					
competitive				X Other students	Move child to the bathroom alone
noncompetitive	X				
loud				X Teacher's voice	Provide physical prompts and decrease talking
soft					
predictable	X				
unpredictable				X Unplanned	
Olfactory/ Gustatory mild	X				If arousal is needed, use strong smelling soap
strong	X				
predictable					
unpredictable					

Routine/Task: Washing face

Task _____
Components: A = _____
            B = _____
            C = _____

Figure 2.3. Sample completed form for analyzing sensory characteristics of face washing.

69

Table 2.6. Reasons for incorporating various sensory qualities into integrated intervention programs

Sensory system	Arousal/alerting descriptors	Discriminating/mapping descriptors
For all systems	*Unpredictability:* To develop an increasing level of attention to keep the child interested in the task/activity (e.g., change the position of the objects on the child's lap tray during the task).	*Predictability:* To establish the child's ability to anticipate a programming sequence or a salient cue; to decrease possibility to be distracted from a functional task sequence (e.g., use the same routine for diaper changing every time).
Somatosensory	*Light touch:* To increase alertness in a child who is lethargic (e.g., pull cloth from child's face during peekaboo). *Pain:* To raise from unconsciousness; to determine ability to respond to noxious stimuli when unconscious (e.g., flick palm of hand or sole of foot briskly). *Temperature:* To establish awareness of stimuli; to maintain attentiveness to task (e.g., uses hot foods for spoon eating and cold drink for sucking through a straw). *Variability:* To maintain attention to or interest in the task (e.g., place new texture on cup surface each day so child notices the cup). *Short duration:* To increase arousal for task performance (e.g., tap child on chest before giving directions). *Small body surface contact:* To generate and focus attention on a particular body part (e.g., tap around lips with fingertips before eating task)	*Touch pressure:* To establish and maintain awareness of body parts and body position; to calm a child who has been overstimulated (e.g., provide a firm bear hug). *Long duration:* To enable the child to become familiar, comfortable with the stimulus; to incorporate stimulus into functional skill (e.g., grasping the container to pick it up and pour out contents). *Large body surface contact:* To establish and maintain awareness of body parts and body position; to calm a child who has been overstimulated (e.g., wrap child tightly in a blanket).

Vestibular	*Head position change:* To increase arousal for an activity (e.g., position child prone over a wedge). *Speed change:* To maintain adequate alertness for functional task (e.g., vary pace while carrying the child to a new task). *Direction change:* To elevate level of alertness for a functional task (e.g., swing child back and forth in arms prior to positioning him or her at the table for a task). *Rotary head movement:* To increase arousal prior to functional task (e.g., pick child up from prone [on stomach] facing away to upright facing toward you to position for a new task).	*Linear head movement:* To support establishment of body awareness in space (e.g., carry child around the room in fixed position to explore its features). *Repetitive head movement:* To provide predictable and organizing information; to calm a child who has been overstimulated (e.g., rock the child).
Proprioception	*Quick stretch:* To generate additional muscle tension to support functional tasks (e.g., tap belly muscle of hypotonic muscle while providing physical guidance to grasp).	*Sustained tension:* To enable the muscle to relax, elongate, so body part can be in better position for function (e.g., press firmly across belly muscle while guiding a reaching pattern; add weight to objects being manipulated). *Shifting muscle tension:* To establish functional movement patterns that contain stability and mobility (e.g., prop and reach for a toy; reach, fill, and lift spoon to mouth).
Visual	*High intensity:* To increase opportunity to notice object; to generate arousal for task (e.g., cover blocks with foil for manipulation task). *High contrast:* To enhance possibility of locating the object and maintaining attention to it (e.g., place raisins on a piece of typing paper for prehension activity). *Variability:* To maintain attention to or interest in the task (e.g., play rolling catch with a clear ball that has moveable pieces inside).	*Low intensity:* To allow the visual stimulus to blend with other salient features; to generate searching behaviors because characteristics are less obvious (e.g., find own cubby hole in back of the room). *High similarity:* To establish more discerning abilities; to develop skills for naturally occurring tasks (e.g., scoop applesauce from beige plate). *Competitive:* To facilitate searching; to increase tolerance for natural life circumstances (e.g., obtain correct tools from equipment bin).

(continued)

Table 2.6. *(continued)*

Sensory system	Arousal/alerting descriptors	Discriminating/mapping descriptors
Auditory	*Variability:* To maintain attention to or interest in the task (e.g., play radio station after activating a switch). *High intensity:* To stimulate noticing the person or object; to create proper alerting for task performance (e.g., ring a bell to encourage the child to locate the stimulus).	*Rhythmic:* To provide predictable and organizing information for environmental orientation (e.g., sing a nursery rhyme while physically guiding motions). *Constant:* To provide a foundational stimulus for environmental orientation; especially important when other sensory systems (e.g., vision, vestibular) do not provide orientation (e.g., child recognizes own classroom by fan noise and calms down). *Competitive:* To facilitate differentiation of salient stimuli; to increase tolerance for natural life circumstances (e.g., after child learns to look when her name is called, conduct activity within busy classroom). *Noncompetitive:* To facilitate focused attention for acquiring a new and difficult skill; to calm a child who has been overstimulated (e.g., move child to quiet room to establish vocalizations). *Low intensity:* To allow the auditory stimulus to blend with other salient features; to generate searching behaviors since stimulus is less obvious (e.g., give child a direction in a normal volume).
Olfactory/ gustatory	*Strong intensity:* To stimulate arousal for task (e.g., child smells spaghetti sauce at lunch).	*Mild intensity:* To facilitate exploratory behaviors; to stimulate naturally occurring activities (e.g., smell of lunch food is less distinct, so child is encouraged to notice texture, color).

Creating Interventions Based on Motor Qualities

Campbell (1990) suggests that observations of movement qualities include an assessment of muscle tone, postural alignment, the use of compensatory strategies, and identification of present deformities and limitations related to the sensorimotor systems. Although the therapists may evaluate the child for specific motor involvement, observations within naturally occurring situations are also important. For example, it is only partially useful to know that a child has hypertonia, has poor ability to sit up independently, and can hold his or her head up when supported in sitting. The picture is more complete when the team knows that the hypertonia interferes with the child's attempts to crawl across the room (e.g., the legs become very stiff and extended). It is also helpful to know that positioning adaptations significantly reduce the effects of poor trunk and head control and hypertonus in the arms, enabling the child to both see and reach for objects in front. Figure 2.4 provides a framework for analyzing the motor components of the performance, which will then facilitate effective program planning.

Motor problems are best addressed within the context of daily activities and with the combined expertise of multiple disciplines (see Chapters 3 and 4; Campbell, 1987a). There are several important considerations in creating integrated programs (Campbell, 1987a). First, the child should be positioned so that the best possible postural alignment is attained. This enables the child to have access to environmental cues and opportunities. Second, the level of support or interference provided by muscle tone should be determined. Both low and high muscle tone can interfere with task performance, as discussed previously. Team members must also consider the effects of the child's tone during the activity, because muscle tone can change as the child intends to accomplish a goal. Therapists provide specialized expertise for this consideration (Campbell, 1987a). Third, physical guidance and therapeutic facilitation of the proper movement should be provided (Campbell, 1987b). The first two considerations provide information that is helpful in creating these facilitation strategies. The goal is to provide input to the muscles, joints, and limbs so the child experiences the sensorimotor sequence and can rely on this information to perform the action with decreasing assistance over time. This is an important step because children with multiple disabilities do not know what it feels like to move in and interact with the environment and therefore may not be motivated to move or may not understand what the verbal prompt means.

Finally, team members must consider the environmental variables and the context of the task. Children with multiple disabilities may also have visual and/or auditory problems and therefore may require objects with a bright color or with a unique sound (refer to Table 2.1 to review the characteristics of each sensory system). Children with very low vision may rely more heavily on the somatosensory aspects of objects. When a particular reaching or manipulation pattern is desired, the target objects can be placed in regions in front of or to the side of the child to encourage the optimal motor pattern (see Campbell, 1987a,

Routine/Task Motor Characteristics		General Status of Individual	Status During This Task	What adaptations are likely to improve functional outcome?
Muscle Tone	Hypertonic			
	Hypotonic			
	Other pattern			
	Reflexive patterns			
Physical Capacity	Strength			
	Endurance			
	Range of motion			
	Structural limitations			
Postural Control	Accomplishes alignment			
	Maintains alignment			
	Adaptability (e.g., restore equilibrium)			
Movement Characteristics	Efficient			
	Effortful but functional			
	Ineffective			
	Use of compensatory actions			
Essential Skills	Looking			
	Vocalizing			
	Reaching			
	Manipulating			
Cognition Requirements				

Figure 2.4. Form for analyzing motor characteristics or task performance.

for good examples). The context also includes knowledge about the child's interests to ensure that selected activities not only are therapeutic from a sensorimotor and cognitive perspective but also will keep the child's attention to persisting in acquiring and using the desired skills. There is a delicate balance in programming between therapeutic benefit and the child's interest in the task. A well-designed intervention in which the child will not participate is not going to yield effective outcomes. The final aspect of the context is the reinforcement the child receives for engaging in the task. Activities are graded both to provide an adequate challenge and to ensure success to encourage the child to continue.

Because some of the problems of children with multiple disabilities will prohibit performance of functional tasks or even the essential skills necessary for functional task performance, adaptations can be constructed to minimize the interference of the particular problems. Chapters 3 and 8 provide excellent examples of positioning, handling, and environmental adaptations that acknowledge and accommodate for motor problems and therefore will not be elaborated upon here.

CONCLUSION

The sensorimotor systems provide a vital link between the individual and the environment. Environmental conditions are noticed and observed via sensory system input. Responses to environmental demands are carried out by the motor systems. The sensorimotor systems are an interdependent network that enable the individual to acquire increasingly complex skills and use them in functional tasks. Children with multiple disabilities have difficulty with certain aspects of the sensorimotor systems. These problems interfere with the acquisition and use of sensorimotor skills for functional performance. When the sensorimotor problems diminish the adaptability, frequency, and form of interactions, the child can also miss the cognitive opportunities that facilitate growth in problem-solving skills. Effective intervention acknowledges these relationships and serves to minimize the effects of the disability while maximizing function.

REFERENCES

American Occupational Therapy Association. (1990). *Guidelines for occupational therapy services in the schools* (2nd ed.). Rockville, MD: Author.

Arendt, R., MacLean, W., Jr., & Baumeister, A. (1988). Critique of sensory integration therapy and its application in mental retardation. *American Journal of Mental Retardation, 92*(5), 401–411.

Ayres, A., & Mailloux, Z. (1981). Influence of sensory integration procedures on language development. *American Journal of Occupational Therapy, 35*(6), 383–390.

Ayres, A., & Mailloux, Z. (1983). Possible pubertal effect on therapeutic gains in an autistic girl. *American Journal of Occupational Therapy, 37*(8), 535–540.

Ayres, A.J. (1977). Effect of sensory integrative therapy on the coordination of children with choreoathetoid movements. *American Journal of Occupational Therapy, 31*(5), 291–293.

Ayres, A.J. (1980). *Sensory integration and the child.* Los Angeles: Western Psychological Services.

Baumgart, D., Brown, L., Pumpian, I., Nisbet, J., Ford, A., Sweet, M., Messina, R., & Schroeder, J. (1982). Principle of partial participation and individualized adaptations in educational programs for severely handicapped students. *Journal of The Association for the Severely Handicapped, 7*(2), 17–27.

Bobath, B. (1963). A neurodevelopmental treatment of cerebral palsy. *Physiotherapy, 49*(8), 242–244.

Campbell, P.H. (1987a). Integrated programming for students with multiple handicaps. In L. Goetz, D. Guess, & K. Stremel-Campbell (Eds.), *Innovative program design for individuals with dual sensory impairments* (pp. 159–188). Baltimore: Paul H. Brookes Publishing Co.

Campbell, P.H. (1987b). Programming for students with dysfunction in posture and movement. In M. Snell (Ed.), *Systematic instruction of persons with severe handicaps* (3rd ed., pp. 188–211). Columbus, OH: Charles E. Merrill.

Campbell, P.H. (1989). Posture and movement. In C. Tingey (Ed.), *Implementing early intervention* (pp. 189–208). Baltimore: Paul H. Brookes Publishing Co.

Campbell, P.H. (1990). *A guide to neurodevelopmental treatment with infants centered approach: A family-centered approach.* Unpublished manuscript. Akron, OH: Family and Child Learning Center, Children's Hospital Medical Center of Akron.

Campbell, P.H., & Forsyth, S. (1990). *A system for classifying impaired or delayed posture and movement skill development.* Unpublished manuscript, Akron, OH: Family and Child Learning Center, Children's Hospital Medical Center of Akron.

Carte, E., Morrison, D., Sublett, J., Uemura, A., & Setrakian, W. (1984). Sensory integration therapy: A trial of a specific neurodevelopmental therapy for the remediation of learning disabilities. *Journal of Developmental Behavioral Pediatrics, 5*(4), 189–194.

Cool, S.J. (1987). A view from the "outside": Sensory integration and developmental neurobiology. *Sensory Integration Specialty Section Newsletter, 10*(2), 2–3.

Coren, S., Porac, C., & Ward, L.M. (1984). *Sensation and perception* (2nd ed.). Orlando, FL: Academic Press.

Cummins, R.A. (1991). Sensory integration and learning disabilities: Ayres' factor analyses reappraised. *Journal of Learning Disabilities, 24*(3), 160–168.

Cyriax, J.H., & Cyriax, P.J. (1983). *Illustrated manual of orthopaedic medicine.* London: Butterworths, OM Publications.

Densem, J., Nuthall, G., Bushnell, J., & Horn, J. (1989). Effectiveness of a sensory integrative therapy program for children with perceptual-motor deficits. *Journal of Learning Disabilities, 22*(4), 221–229.

Dunn, W. (1988). Basic and applied neuroscience research provides a basis for sensory integration theory. *American Journal of Mental Retardation, 92*(5), 420–422.

Dunn, W. (1989). Occupational therapy in early intervention: New perspectives create greater possibilities. *American Journal of Occupational Therapy, 43*(11), 717–721.

Dunn, W. (1991a). Assessing sensory performance enablers. In C. Christiansen & C. Baum (Eds.), *Occupational therapy: Overcoming human performance deficits* (pp. 470–505). Thorofare, NJ: Slack.

Dunn, W. (1991b). Integrated related services. In L.H. Meyer, C.A. Peck, & L. Brown (Eds.), *Critical issues in the lives of people with severe disabilities* (pp. 353–377). Baltimore: Paul H. Brookes Publishing Co.

Dunn, W. (1991c). Sensory dimensions of performance. In C. Christiansen & C. Baum (Eds.), *Occupational therapy: Overcoming human performance deficits* (pp. 230–257). Thorofare, NJ: Slack.

Dunn, W. (1996). Occupational therapy. In R. McWilliam (Ed.), *Rethinking pull-out services in early intervention: A professional resource* (pp. 267–313). Baltimore: Paul H. Brookes Publishing Co.

Dunn, W., Brown, C., & McGuigan, A. (1994). The ecology of human performance: A framework for considering the effect of context. *American Journal of Occupational Therapy, 48*(7), 595–607.

Dunn, W., & Campbell, P.H. (1991). Designing pediatric service provision. In W. Dunn (Ed.), *Pediatric occupational therapy: Facilitating effective service provision* (pp. 140–159). Thorofare, NJ: Slack.

Dunn, W., Campbell, P., Oetter, P., Hall, S., & Berger, E. (1989). *Guidelines for occupational therapy services in early intervention and preschool services.* Rockville, MD: American Occupational Therapy Association.

Exner, C.E. (1989). Development of hand functions. In P.N. Pratt & A.S. Allen (Eds.), *Occupational therapy for children* (2nd ed., pp. 235–259). St. Louis, MO: C.V. Mosby.

Gesell, A. (1954). The ontogenesis of infant behavior. In L. Carmichael (Ed.), *Manual of child psychology* (pp. 335–373). New York: John Wiley & Sons.

Gilfolyle, E.M., Grady, A.P., & Moore, J.C. (1981). *Children adapt.* Thorofare, NJ: Slack.

Guess, D., Mulligan-Ault, M., Roberts, S., Struth, J., Siegel-Causey, E., Thompson, B., Bronicki, G.J.B., & Guy, B. (1988). Implications of biobehavioral states for the education and treatment of students with the most profoundly handicapping conditions. *Journal of The Association for Persons with Severe Handicaps, 13*(3), 163–174.

Harris, S. (1988). Early intervention: Does developmental therapy make a difference? *Topics in Early Childhood Special Education, 7*(4), 20–32.

Horowitz, L., Oosterveld, W., & Adrichem, R. (1993). Effectiveness of sensory integration therapy on smooth pursuits and organization time in children. *Patiatr-Grenzgeb, 31*(5), 331–344.

Humphries, T., Snider, L., & McDougall, B. (1993). Clinical evaluation of the effectiveness of sensory integrative and perceptual motor therapy in improving sensory integrative function in children with learning disabilities. *Occupational Therapy Journal of Research, 13*(3), 163–182.

Jenkins, J., Fewell, R., & Harris, S. (1983). Comparison of sensory integrative therapy and motor programming. *American Journal of Mental Deficiency, 88*(2), 221–224.

Kaplan, B., Polatajko, H., Wilson, B., & Faris, P. (1993). Reexamination of sensory integration treatment: A combination of two efficacy studies. *Journal of Learning Disabilities, 26*(5), 342–347.

Manheim, C.J., & Lavett, D.K. (1989). *The myofascial release manual.* Thorofare, NJ: Slack.

Moore, J. (1980). Neuroanatomical considerations relating to recovery of function following brain lesions. In P. Bach-y-Rita (Ed.), *Recovery of function: Theoretical considerations for brain injury rehabilitation* (pp. 9–90). Baltimore: University Park Press.

Morrison, D., & Sublett, J. (1986). The effects of sensory integration therapy on nystagmus duration, equilibrium reactions and visual-motor integration in reading retarded children. *Child Care Health Development, 12*(2), 99–110.

Ottenbacher, K. (1982). Sensory integration therapy: Affect or effect. *American Journal of Occupational Therapy, 36*(9), 571–578.

Parette, H., Hendricks, M., & Rock, S. (1991). Efficacy of therapeutic intervention intensity with infants and young children with cerebral palsy. *Infants and Young Children, 4*(2), 1–19.

Polatajko, H., Kaplan, B., & Wilson, B. (1992). Sensory integration treatment for children with learning disabilities: Its status 20 years later. *Occupational Therapy Journal of Research, 12*(6), 323–341.

Polatajko, H., Law, M., Miller, J., & Schaffer, R. (1991). The effect of a sensory integration program on academic achievement, motor performance, and self-esteem in children identified as learning disabled: Results of a clinical trial. *Occupational Therapy Journal of Research, 11*(3), 155–176.

Revelj, E. (1987). Improving learning of minimally handicapped preschoolers using sensorimotor integration therapy. *Practicum II Report,* Nova University, Ft. Lauderdale, FL.

Rogers, S.J., & D'Eugenio, D.B. (1981). *Developmental programming for infants and young children: Assessment and application.* Ann Arbor: University of Michigan Press.

Saunders, H.D. (1985). *Evaluation, treatment and prevention of musculoskeletal disorders.* Minneapolis, MN: H. Duane Saunders.

Scherzer, A.L., & Tscharnuter, I. (Eds.). (1982). *Early diagnosis and therapy in cerebral palsy: A primer on infant development programs.* New York: Marcel Dekker.

Short-DeGraff, M.A. (1988). *Human development for occupational and physical therapists.* Baltimore: Williams & Wilkins.

Stern, E.M., & Gorga, D. (1988). Neurodevelopmental treatment (NDT): Therapeutic intervention and its efficacy. *Infants and Young Children, 1*(1), 22–32.

Tew, B. (1984). *Language therapy and sensory integration therapy in maximizing language gains in developmentally delayed preschool children. Report of Results, May 1983 through April 1984.* Lafayette, IN: Wabash Center, Inc.

Travell, J.G., & Simons, D.G. (1983). *Myofascial pain and dysfunction: The trigger point manual.* Baltimore: Williams & Wilkins.

Upledger, J.E., & Vredevoogd, J.D. (1983). *Craniosacral therapy.* Seattle, WA: Eastland Press.

VanBenschoten, R. (1975). A sensory-integration program for blind campers. *American Journal of Occupational Therapy, 29*(10), 615–617.

Wadsworth, C.T. (1988). *Manual examination and treatment of the spine and extremities.* Baltimore: Williams & Wilkins.

Weeks, Z.R., & Ewer-Jones, B. (1983). Assessment of perceptual-motor and fine motor functioning. In K. Paget & B. Bracken (Eds.), *A psychoeducational assessment of preschool children* (pp. 261–291). Orlando, FL: Grune & Stratton.

Werry, J., Scaletti, R., & Mills, F. (1990). Sensory integration and teacher-judged learning problems: A controlled intervention trial. *Journal of Pediatric Child Health, 26*(1), 31–35.

Wilson, B., Kaplan, B., Fellowes, S., & Gruchy, C. (1992). The efficacy of sensory integration treatment compared to tutoring. *Physical and Occupational Therapy in Pediatrics, 12*(1), 1–36.

Handling and Positioning

Beverly Rainforth and Jennifer York-Barr

THROUGHOUT DAILY ACTIVITIES PEOPLE SKILLFULLY position and move their bodies to perform a variety of functions. Even the simple task of face washing, which most people can perform without being fully awake, requires a series of complex motor actions. By practicing this task thousands of times, however, people increase proficiency to the extent that they can execute the motor components of face washing on a subconscious level. Analysis of this task discloses several forms of positioning and movement activities that are essential to all types of independent functioning. These positioning and movement components include the following:

1. Selecting a position that matches the practical and movement demands of the task
2. Assuming and balancing the body in that position
3. Coordinating the movements required to engage in the task

Each component is discussed below.

Prior to performing any task, a person selects a position in which the task can be performed easily. For example, standing at a sink is ideal for face washing. When a person is standing, both hands are free to perform the task. One can also shift forward, backward, and sideways to look in the mirror, reach the washcloth or towel, adjust the faucets, confine drips to the sink basin, and so forth. In turn, one has constructed the environment so that the sink, towel bar, and mirror are easily accessible when standing. Other positions (e.g., sitting) usually are not chosen for face washing because they restrict reaching and body shifting, which interferes with the practical and movement demands of the activity. Once an efficient position is selected, balance and comfort must be achieved before the task can be performed. For face washing, people generally stand at the sink with their feet and legs separated and the muscles throughout their legs and back contracted slightly to maintain a stable, upright position. Some people also might lean their hips against the front of the sink or rest one hand on top of the sink to increase balance or support (stability). Throughout the activity, one makes minor postural adjustments in the ankles, knees, hips, and back to maintain balance.

Once balance and comfort are achieved, the arm movements required for the task of face washing can begin. One must coordinate the muscles around the various joints to provide adequate support and to execute efficient movements. For example, simply bringing a washcloth to the face requires complex coordination between joint stability and mobility. First the shoulder blade is stabilized on the back to provide a base of support for moving the arm. Then, simultaneously, one rotates the forearm so the palm of the hand faces upward, straightens the wrist and fingers, bends the elbow, and brings the elbow slightly forward and out to the side (see Figure 3.1). For this movement to be coordinated, however, there also must be some motion at the shoulder blade and shoulder joint (mobilization) and some stabilization at the other joints. Each step of the face-washing task requires one to combine joint stability and mobility in a similar manner to produce efficient patterns of arm movement.

In summary, in order to accomplish even the simplest daily activity, a sophisticated combination of positioning and movement skills is required. It is important for educational team members, including family members, to recognize the complex motor demands of such simple tasks. These positioning and movement activities often present challenges for children with physical disabilities such as cerebral palsy. For example, a child who is unable to stand at a sink may sit in a wheelchair, but this position restricts access to the sink and face-washing materials. Another child might be capable of standing at the sink, but only when using both hands for support. Efforts to use either hand for face washing reduce the child's balance, and in turn, eliminate the stable foundation needed to use the hands. Another child may have adequate balance but still may be unable to coordinate arm movement sufficiently to perform the task. Efforts to flex (bend) the elbow may elicit uncontrolled muscle contractions (spasticity) through the arm causing 1) the child's arm to pull close to the body; 2) the elbow, wrist, and fingers to bend excessively; and 3) the palm of the hand to turn downward (see Figure 3.2). The arm position prevents the child from completing the task.

Because children with neuromotor disabilities often encounter the types of problems described previously, they may find it difficult or impossible to participate in tasks such as face washing. When they do perform such tasks, these children often develop postures and movement patterns that appear abnormal and limit skill development. Continued practice of such abnormal patterns can

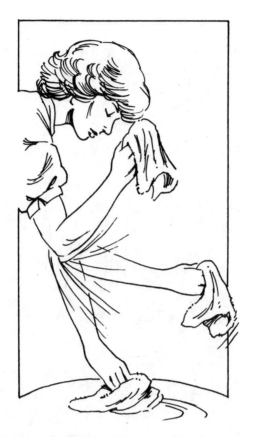

Figure 3.1.   Arm position when bringing a washcloth to the face.

decrease rather than increase proficiency in task performance (Bobath, 1980). To minimize the influence of these abnormal postures and movement patterns, educational team members can apply a variety of handling and positioning techniques (Bergen, Presperin, & Tallman, 1990; Bobath & Bobath, 1972; Connor, Williamson, & Siepp, 1978; Finnie, 1975; Fraser, Hensinger, & Phelps, 1990; Jaeger, 1987; Levitt, 1982; Morris & Klein, 1987). Because occupational therapists and physical therapists have developed and used them extensively, handling and positioning techniques are sometimes considered specialized treatment provided by therapists. Episodic intervention is inadequate, however, because 1) children need extensive practice to learn new movement patterns (Kottke, Halpern, Easton, Ozel, & Burrill, 1978); and 2) poor positioning generally has a deleterious effect on performance, even among children who do not have motor impairments (Sents & Marks, 1989). Furthermore, most children with disabilities are handled, moved, and positioned each day by numerous people, including parents, teachers, and assistants, regardless of whether these people know appro-

Figure 3.2. A child with cerebral palsy attempting to bring a washcloth to his face.

priate methods. When therapists delineate methods and provide systematic instruction, other team members can learn to use handling and positioning methods effectively (see, e.g., Inge & Snell, 1985).

It is essential that all team members provide consistent handling for children with neuromotor disorders. Successful implementation of a transdisciplinary approach to service provision (see Chapter 1; Rainforth, York, & Macdonald, 1992) promotes this consistency. Within the transdisciplinary model, therapists teach the principles of handling and positioning to other team members. Parents, teachers, and therapists also share information about the methods each has found effective with individual children. Finally, the entire team works together to establish a complete set of handling and positioning procedures for each student. Within this model, handling and positioning become integral components of the daily routine for children with multiple disabilities. To enhance a transdisciplinary approach, this chapter discusses theory, research, and practices relevant to handling and positioning children with cerebral palsy and similar neuromotor impairments.

HANDLING CHILDREN WITH CEREBRAL PALSY

Children with cerebral palsy display a variety of posture and movement problems, which are discussed thoroughly in Chapter 2. It may be recalled that these children typically have too much or too little tension (tone) in their muscles, resulting in problems with positioning and movement. The term *handling*, as used in this chapter, applies to techniques intended to improve these impairments. The following are the goals of handling:

1. To elicit more normal muscle tone
2. To facilitate upright positions with normal posture
3. To facilitate normal movement patterns, including
   a. Automatic movements that maintain balance
   b. Locomotion for independent mobility
   c. Arm and hand movements for task performance
   d. Oral movements for eating and speech

Methods to achieve each goal are discussed below. Teachers are encouraged to confer with an occupational therapist or physical therapist regarding which methods are appropriate for individual children.

Normalizing Tone

The presence of too much, too little, or fluctuating muscle tone is symptomatic of damage to the child's brain. Although the damage itself cannot be repaired, there are a variety of ways to influence muscle tone. One way to normalize muscle tone is through the postural and movement strategies that compose handling. For handling techniques to be effective, however, certain health, emotional, and environmental factors may require attention.

Health, Emotional, and Environmental Factors   When children become excited or irritated, their muscle tone tends to increase. These responses may result from 1) physical conditions such as pain, 2) personal interactions producing overenthusiasm or apprehension, or 3) stimulating environments with high levels of noise and activity. In contrast, children who are subdued tend to have lower muscle tone. This situation may result from 1) conditions such as fatigue or illness, 2) personal interactions producing complacency or depression, or 3) environments that are quiet or languid. Medications often have side effects of irritability or lethargy, with a corresponding influence on muscle tone (Gadow, 1986). Theoretically then, children with excessive tone (spasticity or hypertonia) would benefit from being somewhat subdued, whereas children with very low tone (hypotonia or floppiness) would benefit from greater stimulation and excitement. Children's responses to various health conditions, personal interactions, and environmental stimuli vary tremendously, however, and each child must be assessed as an individual. For example, children with severe spasticity have demonstrated the ability to eat as well in a bustling cafeteria as in a quiet classroom, whereas children with hypotonia sometimes withdraw when they encounter stimulating environments.

Educational team members should be cognizant of how health, emotional, and environmental factors might influence a child's muscle tone. Of course, health care problems and unsatisfactory relationships need resolution, regardless of their effect on the child's muscle tone. Furthermore, when a child shows strong negative responses to the varied levels of stimulation encountered in natural environments, conscious efforts must be made to control the type and amount of stimulation. A balance must be sought, however, between protecting the child from undesirable stimulation and systematically teaching the child to develop the tolerance required for successful participation in typical life activities.

Posture and Movement Factors   Rapid or jerky movements tend to stimulate muscle contractions, much like when a physician taps the patellar tendon at a person's knee joint. Conversely, slow, smooth, rhythmic movement, like rocking in a rocking chair, promotes relaxation. These principles apply as much to children with cerebral palsy as they do to other people. Therefore, spasticity often can be reduced by an adult slowly rocking the child in a rocking chair, slowly rotating the child's hips and shoulders in opposite directions, or slowly bending or straightening a limb while gently moving the limb side to side. A child who is floppy often can have his or her low tone increased by an adult bouncing the child on the lap, applying vibration to a group of muscles, or quickly tapping a body part in the direction of a desired movement.

Children with ataxic and athetoid cerebral palsy have muscle tone that fluctuates between high and low. For these children, the procedures described previously are alternated as necessary to reduce or increase the tone demonstrated at a particular moment. As noted previously, each child with cerebral palsy must be handled individually, with the particular type and intensity of motion determined by its effectiveness for that particular child. For some children, it may be necessary to experiment with numerous techniques before finding one that is effective to normalize tone. Many children with cerebral palsy also have primitive reflexes, which result in obligatory postures and movement patterns and concurrently interfere with normal muscle tone. When these reflexes are present, avoidance of reflex stimulating positions is essential to normalize tone.

Unfortunately, hypotonia often prevents children from experiencing the positions that stimulate postural control. In addition, spasticity increases as children attempt to move, preventing adequate movement experience. These situations illustrate that normal muscle tone is both the prerequisite for and the result of normal postural control and movement. For this reason, children with cerebral palsy derive the greatest benefit from relaxation and facilitation procedures when the procedures are applied to posture and movement activities in which the children are active participants (e.g., sitting, reaching, rolling). Although some children with spasticity are able to reduce their own muscle tone using biofeedback, there is no evidence that this alone leads to more normal movement (O'Dwyer, Neilson, & Nash, 1994).

Facilitating Normal Postures and Movement Patterns

Although the specific methods to achieve various positions and movements vary, three general principles remain the same: normalizing tone (discussed previously), "breaking up" atypical postures, and using "key points of control" (Bobath & Bobath, 1972). Children with cerebral palsy often become "locked" into abnormal postures that interfere with or completely prevent functional movement. For example, a child with flexor spasticity would tend to hold many or all joints in flexion, as depicted in Figure 3.3a. To break up this flexed posture, an opposite posture of greater extension must be achieved. It is not sufficient, however, simply to extend the hip, knee, and elbow joints, where flexion is most obvious. A closer look at Figure 3.3a reveals that there is not just an abnormal degree of flexion at many joints, but that the hips, shoulders, and other joints are also rotated into abnormal positions. Therefore, breaking up the flexed posture requires the child's arms and legs to be both extended and rotated in the opposite direction (see Figure 3.3b), while using the relaxation techniques described in

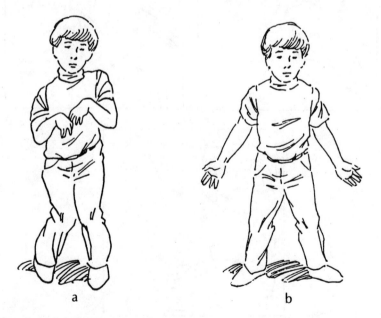

a   b

Figure 3.3.   A child with increased muscle tone: a) standing with excessive flexion and internal rotation, and b) standing with the pattern reversed to increase extension and external rotation.

the preceding section. Frequently, rotation is more influential than either flexion or extension alone to break up abnormal postures.

The key points of control are those parts of the child's body where the facilitator can most effectively break up abnormal postures and elicit more normal postures and movement patterns. These key points of control are usually at the head, trunk, shoulders, and hips, with preference for the area of the body closest to the trunk where normal patterns can be elicited most effectively. The principles and methods of normalizing tone, breaking up abnormal postures, and using key points of control cannot be isolated from one another. Examples of how these principles are integrated and applied to achieve the goals of therapeutic handling are presented below.

Facilitating Upright Positions and Normal Posture   The child depicted in Figure 3.4a has severe spasticity and cannot assume or maintain a sitting position independently. Note that the child's neck is extended and rotated, the shoul-

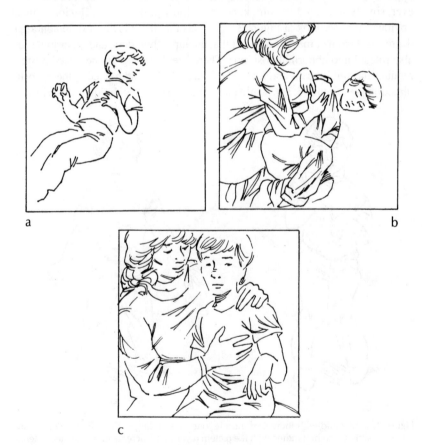

a

b

c

Figure 3.4.   A child with spasticity: a) in an undesirable resting posture, b) relaxed and positioned on his side, and c) seated on the teacher's lap with his muscle tone controlled.

ders are extended, and the elbows, wrists, and fingers are flexed. The hips and knees are flexed slightly and pulled together (adducted). To position the child for instruction, the teacher first rolls the student from his back to his side, a position that is less likely to stimulate extension. The teacher uses the student's head, shoulders, and hips as key points of control, flexing and rotating his neck, bringing his arms together, and further flexing his hips and knees. At the same time the teacher gently rocks the student and rolls him onto his side (see Figure 3.4b). With the student in this position, the teacher lifts the student and seats him on her lap. The teacher keeps one hand behind the student's head and around his shoulders to keep his shoulders and arms forward and neck slightly flexed. When the student begins to extend his neck and push his head backward, the teacher tips his head forward with her elbow while pressing in and down on his breast bone and gently rocking the student side to side (see Figure 3.4c). Because the student continues to push into extension periodically, this *dynamic* positioning offered by the teacher is somewhat more effective in maintaining normal sitting posture than the *static* positioning offered by the student's adapted chair. Every effort is made to adapt the student's chair to provide the same type of control at the head, shoulders, and hips as the teacher provides, because sitting in a chair has both social and instructional advantages for the student.

The child in Figure 3.5a has low muscle tone (hypotonia) and cannot assume or maintain sitting independently. To position this student for instruction, the teacher will help him roll to the side and then push up to sitting. Using the student's shoulders as the key point of control, the teacher slowly turns the student's shoulders toward sidelying. The teacher uses a series of short, quick pushes to the shoulder to stimulate muscle tone in the student's trunk and to elicit his participation in rolling (see Figure 3.5b). With the student on his side, the teacher helps him use his arms to push upward (Figure 3.5c) to sidesitting, resting on his hands (Figure 3.5d), and finally, to longsitting (Figure 3.5e). The teacher continues to use short, quick, upward pushes to stimulate muscle tone in the student's arms and trunk and to elicit his participation in pushing up to sit. In sitting, the student's legs are positioned to give him a wide base of support, and his arms are positioned so he can continue to lean on them. The teacher keeps her hands on the student's shoulders to prevent falling and to give more quick pushes down through the back and arms, which increases the student's awareness of his position and stimulates his muscle tone (Figure 3.5e).

Although the previous two examples use therapeutic handling to achieve and maintain normal upright sitting postures for instruction, numerous positions (e.g., sidelying, kneeling, standing) have therapeutic and instructional value for students with multiple impairments. Table 3.1 presents the advantages and disadvantages of various positions that might be used in educational programs for students with severe and multiple disabilities. In addition to the immediate benefits of using upright positions, retrospective studies confirm that early development of head and trunk control is associated with later achievement of walking (da Paz, Burnett, & Braga, 1994; Trahan & Marcoux, 1994).

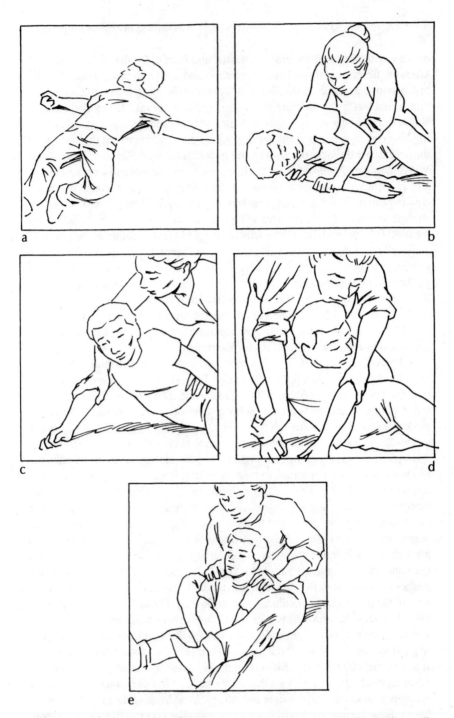

Figure 3.5. A child with hypotonia: a) unable to sit without assistance, b) being taught to roll to his side, c) pushing up to semisitting, d) then sidesitting, e) with pressure applied through the spine and shoulders to increase muscle tone and position awareness in the trunk and arms.

Table 3.1.   Positions for students with physical disabilities

Position	Advantages	Disadvantages
Prone	Normal resting position; requires no motor control; promotes trunk and hip extension	Possibility of suffocation; stimulates asymmetry if head turned to side; may stimulate flexor tone; functional activities limited
Supine	Normal resting position; requires little motor control; no danger of suffocation; symmetry can be maintained	May stimulate extensor tone; prolonged position inhibits respiration; possibility of aspiration; ceiling view; functional activities limited
Prone on elbows	Encourages head, arm, and trunk control; allows improved view	May stimulate flexor tone; may stimulate excessive extension; tiring position; limits hand use
Sidelying	Normal resting position; usually does not stimulate abnormal tone; improves alignment, brings hands together at midline	May require bulky equipment; sideward view; few functional activities; pressure on bony prominences (hips)
Sidesitting	Easy to assume from lying, hands and knees, kneeling; promotes trunk rotation, range of motion in hips, trunk if sides alternated	May reinforce asymmetry; may require one or both hands for support; difficult with tight hips or trunk
Tailor- or ring sitting	Wide base of support; symmetrical position; easier to free hands	Difficult transition to/from other positions; may reinforce flexed posture
Long sitting	May provide wide base of support; may prevent hamstring contractures	Impossible with tight hamstrings; may stimulate trunk flexion, flexor spasticity
Heel or W-sitting	Easy transition to/from other positions; stable base of support; frees hands	Reinforces hip, knee, and ankle deformity; reduces reciprocal movement, weight shifting, and trunk rotation
Chair sitting— standard chair	Normal position and equipment; easy transition to/from other positions; minor adaptations can be added to improve position	May not provide adequate position for feet, trunk, hips; may be overused
Chair sitting— bolster chair	Reduces scissoring at hips; may increase anterior pelvic tilt	Bulky equipment; difficult transition to/from other positions

(continued)

Table 3.1.   *(continued)*

Position	Advantages	Disadvantages
Chair sitting—corner chair	Inhibits extensor tone in trunk and shoulders	May encourage excessive flexion; may rotate trunk and pelvis
Chair sitting—wheelchair	Allows for positioning and mobility simultaneously; adaptations can control most postural problems	Chairs may be expensive, complicated, easily maladjusted; may become over-reliant on chair
Kneeling	Promotes trunk and hip control; improves hip joint; possible despite knee flexion contractures; stabilizes hip joint	May cause bursitis at knees
Standing prone	Promotes trunk and hip control; standing stabilizes hip joint; allows access to normal work surfaces (e.g., counters)	May stimulate flexor tone; may stimulate excessive extension; may need hands for support; requires bulky equipment
Standing supine	Promotes trunk and hip control; stabilizes hip joint; hands free for work; head supported	May stimulate flexor tone; may not reach work surfaces; requires bulky equipment
Standing upright	Promotes greater trunk and hip control and balance	May require bulky equipment

Facilitating Automatic Movements that Maintain Balance   When children learn to sit, kneel, or stand, they maintain their upright positions using automatic reactions such as protective reactions and righting reactions (Fiorentino, 1963). These automatic reactions are described in Chapter 2. *Righting reactions,* in which a person positions and maintains the head and trunk upright in space, are first seen when an infant lifts his or her wobbling head off a parent's shoulder. For children with multiple disabilities, experiencing upright positions is an important aspect of developing righting reactions. These reactions can be strengthened further by seating the child on an adult's lap, a stool, or the floor and gently tipping the child from the upright position. The key point of control might be at the child's head, shoulders, trunk, hips, or even the thighs, depending on the child's head and trunk control. *Protective reactions,* in which a person extends the arms to break a fall, start developing when a child bears weight on the arms in sitting and hands-and-knees positions (see Figure 3.6a). When a child with cerebral palsy can use the arms for the basic function of propping, facilitating more advanced protective reactions can involve holding the child's arm with wrist and elbow extended, gently pulling the child off balance, and positioning the arm to break the fall (see Figure 3.6b). In this example, the

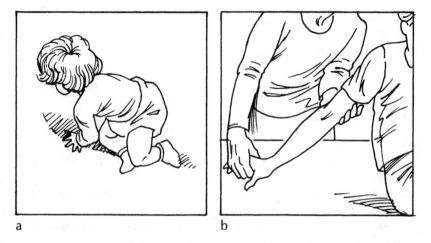

a   b

Figure 3.6.   a) A young child using his arms to break a fall and resume sitting, b) assisting a child with cerebral palsy to extend and bear weight on his arm as part of a sequence for teaching protective reactions.

child's hand and elbow are the key points of control. There is some evidence that, in addition to improving balance, weight bearing on the hands and arms helps develop hand control among children with cerebral palsy (Chakerian & Larson, 1993).

Facilitating Locomotion for Independent Mobility   Children move around their environments by rolling, crawling on their stomachs, creeping on hands and knees, knee walking, and walking. Children may also move by driving a wheelchair or by riding a tricycle or bicycle. Teaching any means of mobility to children with cerebral palsy requires them to maintain relatively normal postures while coordinating smooth movements of the arms, legs, and trunk. Although commando crawling and creeping on hands and knees are considered basic locomotor patterns, encouraging their use is counterproductive for many children with cerebral palsy. The prone position and the movements themselves may stimulate so much flexor tone in the trunk and limbs that effective movement is impossible. Rolling, riding an adapted tricycle, or driving an electric wheelchair are more successful alternatives for children with severe cerebral palsy. Mobility equipment that improves a child's positioning, like posterior walkers, also tends to improve the quality and efficiency of movement (Greiner, Czerniecki, & Deitz, 1993).

The movement requirements for independent mobility can be analyzed much like those of any task. (This type of analysis requires the teacher's skills in task analysis to be combined with the therapist's knowledge of normal movement patterns and offers an excellent opportunity for collaboration between teacher and therapist.) Table 3.2 presents a task analysis for rolling, showing both the movements to be performed by the student and the key points for facili-

Table 3.2.   Task analysis for rolling

Student movements	Staff key points[a]
Supine lying, extend right arm over-head	Move at right upper arm
Rotate head and shoulders to face right	Stabilize at right upper arm; move at left shoulder
Swing left leg over and forward	Stabilize at left shoulder; move at left thigh (prevent trunk, hip, and knee flexor pattern)
Extend left arm over head and roll to prone	Move at left upper arm (prevent pushing up on elbows)
Plant right hand next to right shoulder	Stabilize at left upper arm; move at right elbow
Rotate head and push right shoulder up to face right	Stabilize at left upper arm; move at right upper arm
Swing right leg over and backward	Stabilize at left upper arm; move at right thigh (prevent trunk, hip, and knee flexor pattern)
Roll supine, bring head to midline, and bring left arm down to side	Move at left forehead and left upper arm

[a]Parenthetical notations indicate postures the student tends to assume during rolling, which the staff must be prepared to inhibit if necessary.

tation by the teacher. The task analysis for another student might have different components depending on the type and extent of that student's independent movement and atypical postures. The movements required for other forms of independent mobility can be analyzed in the same way.

   Facilitating Arm and Hand Movements for Task Performance   The previous sections have offered examples of facilitating arm movement for weight-bearing functions. Although it had been believed that proximal control and weight bearing were prerequisites for skillful hand use, research on typically developing children suggests that these abilities evolve simultaneously with distal control and reach, grasp, and object manipulation skills (Case-Smith, Fisher, & Bauer, 1989; Loria, 1980). Furthermore, children with cerebral palsy tend to use total patterns of movement (e.g., they are unable to isolate elbow or finger movement), so it is useful to facilitate patterns of movement that involve the entire upper limb: shoulder, elbow, wrist, and fingers. Arm and hand movements required to perform functional activities can be analyzed, as was done for rolling in Table 3.2 (see, e.g., Safaee-Rad, Shwedyk, Quanbury, & Cooper, 1990). The only essential prerequisites for trying to facilitate functional arm and hand movement (e.g., for reach, grasp, and manipulation) are 1) that the student be positioned with sufficient support so the hands are not needed to stabilize the body, and 2) that the student's position promotes normalization of tone throughout the trunk and limbs.

The student depicted in Figures 3.7a and 3.7b has flexor spasticity, which interferes with reaching for the washcloth, grasping it, or bringing it to his face. To facilitate these movements, the teacher provides control at the student's upper arm, forearm, and hand. The teacher first normalizes the student's tone by slowly rotating his arm inward while moving his arm down and away from his body. When the teacher feels the student participating in these movements, she repeats the same pattern, helping the student pick up the washcloth and bring it to his face (see Figures 3.7c and 3.7d). If the student's tone starts to increase, the teacher resumes the rhythmic pattern of arm movement. The student is encouraged to participate in the activity to the greatest extent possible while maintaining functional movement. Using the principle of key points of control, the teacher facilitates at the part of the arm closest to the trunk where normal move-

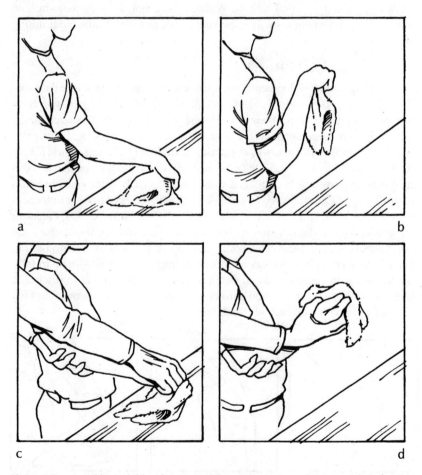

a

b

c

d

Figure 3.7.   a) and b) A child with increased flexor tone trying to bring a washcloth to his face, c) and d) a teacher facilitating more typical and efficient movement for picking up and bringing the washcloth to his face.

ment patterns can be elicited. Generally, the key point is at or just below the joint to be moved. One exception to this rule occurs when opening a fisted hand. The anatomy of the hand makes it possible (and easier) to open a fisted hand by flexing the wrist joint, which automatically extends the fingers. Then the teacher can hold the student's fingers extended while gently extending the wrist (see Figure 3.8) and proceed with the activity. It must be noted, however, that efforts to open the student's hand and facilitate hand use will not be successful if the student's entire posture is not addressed.

Facilitating Oral Movements for Eating and Speech   The methods used to facilitate oral movement are discussed thoroughly in Chapter 4. It is appropriate to emphasize here the importance of normalizing overall postural tone and positioning the student upright with sufficient support to the trunk and head to allow concentration on oral activity. Without addressing these prerequisites, no oral facilitation techniques will be powerful enough to overcome the resulting abnormalities.

Validity of Therapeutic Handling

According to neurodevelopmental treatment theory, handling provides the experience with normal postures and movement through which children with cerebral palsy learn to control their muscle tone (Bobath, 1980). Research on the effects of neurodevelopmental treatment, however, has demonstrated no significant improvement for many of the children studied (DeGangi, Hurley, Linscheid, 1983; Lilly & Powell, 1990; Noonan, 1984). Whereas Noonan noted that treatment effectiveness is correlated with (not necessarily determined by) children's intelligence, others have concluded that intelligence strongly influences treatment outcomes for children with cerebral palsy (Goldkamp, 1984; Parette & Hourcade, 1984). The interaction, however, between treatment outcomes and other variables (e.g., frequency, duration, context, goals of treatment) has not been studied enough to draw conclusions (Campbell, 1990). With up to 60% of children with cerebral palsy thought to have mental retardation (Eicher & Batshaw, 1993), greater attention must be given to methods to improve treatment results for children with multiple disabilities.

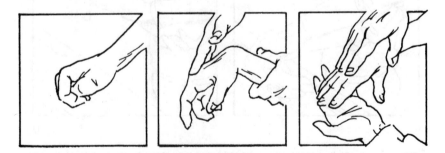

Figure 3.8.   Opening a fisted hand by changing the wrist position.

Demonstrating the effectiveness of intervention is also influenced by the method of measuring change. Efficacy research typically has used standardized assessment tools that are insensitive to small increments of change. DeGangi (1994a, 1994b) has demonstrated the effectiveness of neurodevelopmental treatment for four young children through a case study approach, which supplemented standardized motor assessment with individualized checklists of both movement quality and specific motor skills assessed by parents and therapists. Although research is limited, encouraging results have been reported when aspects of systematic instruction and neurodevelopmental treatment have been combined. In studies by Campbell, McInerney, and Cooper (1984) and Giangreco (1986), four children with multiple disabilities all improved significantly when therapeutic handling techniques were combined with frequent practice in meaningful contexts (e.g., reaching for microwave oven door) and when movement immediately elicited desirable consequences (e.g., lunch from the microwave oven). In these applications, handling might be viewed as a specialized form of physical prompting that applies to posture and movement disorders. Such an integration of handling and systematic instruction procedures concurrently addresses the cognitive, movement, and motivational needs of children with multiple disabilities. Other research concludes that children can help their siblings with cerebral palsy achieve a variety of treatment goals, affirming the importance of involving all people in the child's environment (Craft, Lakin, Oppliger, Clancy, & Vanderlinden, 1990). This comprehensive approach offers the greatest possibilities to evaluate therapeutic handling techniques adequately and to teach children with multiple disabilities effectively.

POSITIONING STUDENTS WITH CEREBRAL PALSY

Therapeutic positioning is the placement of body parts in postures to achieve the following goals:

1. To maintain normalized muscle tone
2. To maintain alignment of body parts
3. To maintain stabilization of body parts
4. To promote active participation in meaningful activity

Although the first three goals are critical, they are not ends in themselves; rather, they are means to achieve the ultimate goal of preparing a person to perform functional activities. Proper positioning is an essential prerequisite for effective instruction of students with multiple disabilities.

Positioning can be either *static* or *dynamic*. Dynamic positioning is achieved and maintained entirely through therapeutic handling; static positioning is maintained through use of adapted equipment. Static positioning is considered a supplement to, rather than a substitute for, dynamic positioning. Prior to positioning a child in an adapted chair, for example, therapeutic handling techniques are applied to place the child in a sitting position with tone normalized and the body properly aligned. Without performing this dynamic positioning first, it becomes difficult to achieve any of the four goals listed above through static positioning. There are advantages, however, to providing static positioning with adapted equipment. These include 1) making the student more mobile, 2) freeing the student from a one-to-one relationship with parents or educational staff, 3) freeing staff from positioning to provide instruction and to facilitate other types of student performance, and 4) enabling students with disabilities to participate in activities with peers without disabilities without constant adult presence.

In addition to the therapeutic benefits of positioning, researchers have identified several functional benefits for providing children with physical disabilities with adapted equipment for positioning. Benefits include the following:

1.   Children at school maintained upright postures longer, attended to and participated in more instruction, and learned to perform academic and self-care tasks more quickly and more independently (Trefler, Nickey, & Hobson, 1983).
2.   Children at home spent less time lying in their bedrooms, spent more time sitting and less time lying down, maintained better alignment in upright postures, improved their abilities to eat and drink, increased their abilities to grasp objects and feed themselves, and spent more time interacting with others (Hulme, Poor, Schulein, & Pezzino, 1983; Hulme, Shaver, Acher, Mullette, & Eggert, 1987).

When positioning equipment also provided a means of mobility (e.g., wheelchair), the following additional benefits were demonstrated:

1.   Children went more places outside of their homes (Hulme et al., 1983).
2.   Children (and their families) engaged in more social activities, had more contact with peers outside of school, increased their participation in activities in school, and had greater independence in all environments (Kohn, Enders, Preston, & Motloch, 1983).
3.   Children engaged in more positive social interactions, became more curious about the environment, and became interested in other activities involving movement (e.g., playing baseball, going hiking) (Butler, 1986; Butler, Okamoto, & McKay, 1983).

To achieve therapeutic positioning for children with multiple disabilities, team members should understand the purpose of the various types of equipment and procedures for effective positioning. The following sections provide information on positioning with chairs; braces, splints, and casts; and other pieces of equipment.

Positioning in Adapted Chairs

Sitting is a traditional position and therefore a "normal" position for children in educational settings. Sitting in adapted chairs allows children with physical disabilities to be in the same upright position, to be at the same eye level, and to use the same work surfaces as their peers without disabilities. Sitting in wheelchairs has the added benefit of providing children with a means of mobility that is a commonplace alternative to walking. Studies of the use of wheelchairs and other adapted seating reveal that children with physical disabilities spent 2–4 hours per day in wheelchairs at the ages of 2 and 3 years (Butler et al., 1983) and 4–6 hours per day at a somewhat older age (Hulme et al., 1983), increasing to an average of 9 hours per day by adolescence (Kohn et al., 1983). Despite such extensive use and ongoing technological developments, adapted chairs do not always meet the needs of children with neuromuscular disabilities. Problems may result from poor selection (design and/or measurement) by rehabilitation professionals, poor acceptance by the child or family, or poor placement of the child in the seat by caregivers (Hundertmark, 1985; Kohn et al., 1983). Considering the amount of time many children spend in adapted chairs, it is essential that educators understand and execute principles of effective seating to minimize the problems resulting from the situations identified previously and to maximize therapeutic and functional benefits. Figure 3.9 is a checklist for assessing the

PELVIS AND HIPS
_____ Hips flexed to 90°
_____ Pelvis tilted slightly forward
_____ Pelvis centered in the back edge of seat
_____ Pelvis not rotated forward on one side

THIGHS AND LEGS
_____ Thighs equal in length
_____ Thighs slightly abducted (apart)
_____ Knees flexed to 90°

FEET AND ANKLES
_____ Aligned directly below or slightly posterior to knees
_____ Ankles flexed to 90°
_____ Feet supported on footrest
_____ Heel and ball of feet bearing weight
_____ Feet and toes facing forward

TRUNK
_____ Symmetrical, not curved to the side
_____ Slight curve at low back
_____ Erect upper back, slight extension

SHOULDERS, ARMS, AND HANDS
_____ Relaxed, neutral position (not hunched up or hanging low)
_____ Upper arm flexed slightly forward
_____ Elbows flexed in midrange (about 90°)
_____ Forearms resting on tray to support arms and shoulders if necessary to maintain alignment
_____ Forearms neutral or rotated downward slightly
_____ Wrists neutral or slightly extended
_____ Hand relaxed, fingers and thumb opened

HEAD AND NECK
_____ Midline orientation
_____ Slight chin tuck (back of neck elongated)

Figure 3.9. Checklist for seated positioning. (From York, J., & Weimann, G. [1991]. Accommodating severe physical disabilities. In J. Reichle, J. York, & J. Sigafoos, *Implementing augmentative and alternative communication: Strategies for learners with severe disabilities,* p. 247. Baltimore: Paul H. Brookes Publishing Co.; reprinted by permission.)

application of these principles to seating students with physical disabilities. The items on the checklist were derived from an analysis of efficient seated positioning of individuals who do not have physical disabilities. The principles outlined previously for positioning children in adapted chairs apply directly to positioning in other types of equipment. Similar checklists can be developed to guide positioning in other equipment. The checklist is meant to serve only as a guide, however, and there may be individuals for whom specific items on the checklist are inappropriate.

Positioning the Pelvis   When a child with physical disabilities is positioned in an adapted seat, the pelvis becomes the key point of control. The pelvic bones in the lower trunk are attached to the backbone, the thigh bones (femurs), and the trunk and leg muscles. The hips provide the base of support for the trunk and therefore influence trunk alignment and posture, head position, and arm use. To provide the proper base of support, the right and left side of the pelvis must be level so the child sits evenly on both hips (see Figure 3.10). When the pelvis is not level, lateral pelvic tilt and curvature of the spine (scoliosis) interfere with normal digestive and respiratory functions and may contribute to dislocation of the hip (Kalen & Bleck, 1985). The top of the pelvis should also be tipped forward slightly to maintain the normal arch in the low back (lumbar lordosis) and to prevent spasticity in the low back muscles (Hundertmark, 1985). A lumbar roll in the low back area of the seat may help produce this position (see Figure 3.11).

Therapists have observed that seating children upright with hips and knees flexed to 90° often minimizes the influence of primitive reflexes and spasticity, while providing a functional work position. Bringing the trunk forward an additional 15°, with or without additional hip flexion, reduces spasticity in the low back extensors of children with cerebral palsy (Myhr & von Wendt, 1991;

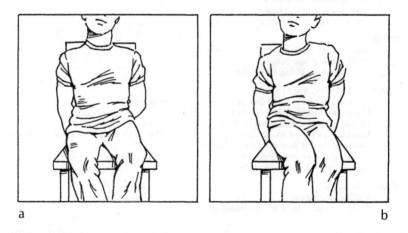

a   b

Figure 3.10.   Alignment of the hips in a seated position: a) with the pelvis symmetrical, and b) with the pelvis tilted, causing poor alignment of the trunk, shoulders, head, and legs.

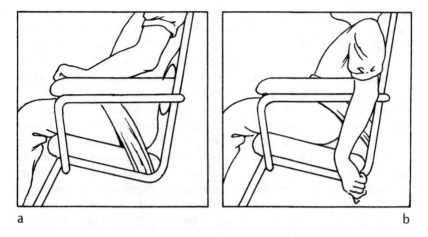

a   b

Figure 3.11. Sitting in a chair: a) with a seat belt keeping hips flexed and lumbar roll supporting the low back, and b) with the seat belt improperly positioned across the abdomen.

Nwaobi, Brubaker, Cusick, & Sussman, 1983; Nwaobi, Hobson, Eng, & Taylor, 1988). The appropriate hip angle generally is determined at the time the child is fitted with a chair and then is built into the chair. This therapeutic angle in the chair is effective, however, only when the child's hips are properly flexed prior to placement in the chair. With some children, it is helpful to tip the chair backward during positioning so gravity aids, rather than interferes, with placing the hips back in the chair. Tipping a chair 30° has been found to increase tone in low back extensors, hip adductors, knee flexors, and ankle plantar flexors (Myhr & von Wendt, 1993; Nwaobi, 1986), so the benefit of tipping the chair needs to be assessed for each child. Once the child's hips are well aligned and positioned in the chair, a seat belt maintains the position. The seat belt crosses the bend in the hip joint (see Figure 3.11) and is tightened as needed to allow the child freedom of movement in the hips while still holding the therapeutic position of the pelvis. The seat belt should not be placed across the child's abdomen because it will put pressure on internal organs and tip the top of the pelvis backward, both upsetting the base of support and increasing spasticity (Myhr & von Wendt, 1993). Figures 3.10a and 3.11a illustrate the correct positions, and Figures 3.10b and 3.11b illustrate the incorrect positions for the pelvis and seat belt. Seat belts and other positioning aids that restrict mobility and cannot be easily removed by the individuals who are wearing them may be considered to be restraints. The use of restraints is rarely ethically justified and is subject to strict legal regulation. Any team member considering the use of a positioning device that might be considered a restraint should consult fully with the team and seek legal advice if necessary before application.

Positioning the Thighs With the hips stabilized in the chair, the child's base of support is improved further by positioning the thighs. The preferred position is with the legs symmetrical and the thighs slightly separated. If the student's thighs pull together, a wedge may be necessary to position them (see Figure 3.12). An abduction orthosis, two connected thigh cuffs worn just above the knees, has been shown to decrease spasticity and improve positioning (Myhr & von Wendt, 1993). Less frequently, children pull their thighs far apart, which requires pads to push them closer together. If one or both hips are dislocated, it may be difficult to keep the thighs in a symmetrical position. In this event, first consideration is given to the position of the pelvis in relation to the child's back and the back of the wheelchair. (Positioning the trunk is discussed in a later section.) The thighs are positioned the best way possible without disturbing the position of the pelvis. Some older children have such serious deformity of the hips and back that they develop a difference in leg length or a deviation of both legs to one side in a "windblown" deformity. When this occurs, the chair seat might be extended forward on one side so that the full length of both thighs is supported (see Figure 3.13). To provide good support for the thighs, the seat should extend to approximately 1 inch from the back of the calf. A deeper seat puts pressure on the blood and nerve supply behind the knee and pulls the hips forward in the chair.

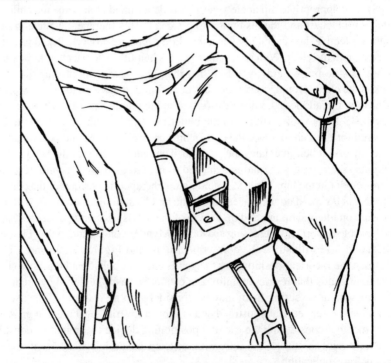

Figure 3.12. A wedge positioned between the thighs to keep them separated and aligned for a stable seating base. (Note that the wedge is not placed against the pelvis. It must not be used to keep the child from sliding forward.)

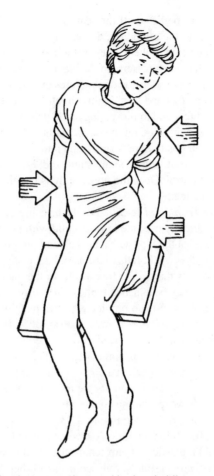

Figure 3.13. A child with severe scoliosis and leg length difference, resulting from hip dislocation. The seat is lengthened on the right side to support the right leg without putting pressure on the back of the left knee. The arrows indicate where lateral supports would be placed to provide counterpressures to achieve optimal alignment.

Positioning the Feet Once the hips and thighs have been positioned, they can be stabilized further by positioning the feet. The feet are supported by a footrest directly below the knees, or behind the knees if the child has flexor spasticity or contractures (Myhr & von Wendt, 1991). If the child has a severe "windblown" deformity, it may be necessary to adjust the foot position to one side. The footrest can have straps or built-up sides to keep the feet positioned and to prevent them from being bumped or entangled in the chair. The feet are positioned flat with the toes straight forward to prevent ankle deformity. The footrest should be low enough so the thighs rest comfortably on the chair seat and high enough so the child's weight is distributed between the seat and footrest. If the footrest is too high, the thighs will be lifted off the seat, decreasing stability, shifting the child's weight back onto the hip bones, decreasing comfort, and increasing the possibility of pressure sores. If the footrest is too low, the feet will hang and the weight of the legs will create pressure on the blood and nerve supply behind the knees. If the child has knee extension contractures or poor circulation, it may be necessary to elevate the feet and legs. In this situation, attention is given to supporting the calves and feet and to preventing ankle deformity, excessive rotation of the legs, or localized pressure on the heels. Although the foot position reinforces the hip and thigh position, only quick and temporary foot placement may be possible before the trunk and head are stabilized, especially if the child has poor trunk and head control. Once the upper body is positioned properly, attention is redirected to the feet.

Positioning the Trunk and Head   For the best alignment of the trunk, the shoulders should be directly over the hips. A child with poor trunk control may wear a harness, secured at the hips with a lap belt and secured at the shoulders to the back of the chair. If the child falls to the side, lateral supports may be necessary. The lateral supports may come forward from the back of the chair at the level of the rib cage or may be attached to the child's tray. A molded support for the front and sides of the chest can provide effective positioning when the chair tips the child's trunk forward (Pope, Bowes, & Booth, 1994). Children with scoliosis or other back deformity may require more specialized adaptations. The back of the chair may be built up in some areas and cut out in others to provide support to areas of the child's back that curve inward and relieve pressure from areas that curve outward. Lateral supports are most effective when placed at the extreme points of the curve, providing counterpressure to straighten the curve or to prevent increased deformity (see Figure 3.13). To provide comfortable and effective positioning for children with very severe back and hip deformity, it may be necessary to mold a plastic or foam seat to the child's body. Some children move about independently despite severe scoliosis or other deformity. For these children, scoliosis pads and other types of chair adaptations are not as effective for long-term positioning as braces, which are discussed later.

The stable and well-aligned trunk provides a good base of support for the student's head. Achieving and maintaining an appropriate head position, with the head erect and chin tucked, remains one of the greatest challenges when positioning children with equipment. Children with poor head control may benefit from pads placed behind and/or beside the head. In some situations, it may be necessary to use a "halo," which surrounds the head and provides anterior as well as lateral support. Even more control can be gained with an overhead sling that provides support under the chin, at the base of the skull, and on both sides of the head. Although simply having the child in an upright position tends to stimulate head control (Trefler et al., 1983), positioning combined with sensory feedback and contingent reinforcement (Domaracki, Sisson, Robinson-Dassel, Hamilton, & Goldstone, 1990; Murphy, Doughty, & Nunes, 1979) can further improve head control and decrease the need for head supports.

Positioning the Arms   Students with adapted chairs often have trays, used to provide a work surface and to provide additional support. The tray should be high enough to allow the student to rest both elbows and forearms on the tray without bending the trunk forward. For children with poor head and trunk control, leaning on the tray provides greater voluntary control of the shoulders, and in turn, more stability for the trunk and head. As noted previously, lateral trunk supports can be mounted on the tray. Other pads, straps, or pegs also can be attached to the tray to facilitate arm positioning. Naturally, the tray must be large enough to accommodate the various adaptations and the student's work materials, while remaining small enough to fit through doorways. If the only purpose of the tray is to provide a work surface, it may be preferable to dispense with the tray and position the student at a table. This alternative would provide the students with a more typical work situation and opportunities for more interactions with teachers and peers. Students who do not need extensive chair adaptations can transfer from their wheelchairs to regular classroom chairs for table work, increasing their normalization. With regular furniture, students still need their feet positioned flat on the floor or on a footrest; the table should be just high enough to allow the students to rest their elbows and forearms (Sents & Marks, 1989).

Determining the Need for Positioning Adaptations   When positioning children with physical impairments, the dangers of providing too much or too little control must be considered. The obvious danger of providing too little control is that proper positioning is not maintained, and therefore fails to offer experience in aligned and upright postures, allows deformity, and hampers participation in instructional activities. In fact, research conducted with preschoolers showed that poor positioning lowered performances on IQ tests, both for children with cerebral palsy (Miedaner & Finuf, 1993) and for children who had no motor impairments (Sents & Marks, 1989). Providing too much support is also potentially dangerous, however, because some children will rely on whatever support they are given, using their own motor skills as little as possible and eventually losing rather than gaining abilities. Maintaining too much external control also limits opportunities to improve motor skills and to develop internal control. Maintaining adaptations and monitoring their use is a time-consuming responsibility that should be eliminated if the adaptations are not necessary. Furthermore, chair adaptations increase the time and difficulty of seating the child for work or transportation and removing the child for repositioning or emergencies. Finally, the presence of numerous adaptations on a chair may elicit undesirable reactions, such as pity or apprehension, that should be minimized. Although unnecessary adaptations can be completely eliminated from chairs, even essential controls or supports might be removed at certain times of the day. For example, a student might need a headrest during transportation but not when listening to a story. During eating, the static positioning offered by the headrest might be less beneficial than dynamic positioning, in which the teacher puts one hand on the student's head only when stabilization is needed.

When positioning children with multiple disabilities in adapted chairs or other equipment, it is necessary to view each child as an individual. An adaptation that is necessary or effective for one child may be neither for another child. Many minute adjustments may be necessary before a chair adaptation has the desired effect. Once the desired effect is attained, change in the child's size or condition may necessitate more modifications. These warnings are not meant to be discouraging; they emphasize that positioning equipment is not a quick cure but a tool to be used skillfully. In the same way, chair positioning has many advantages for children with multiple disabilities, but it cannot meet all the positioning needs of any child. Therefore, a variety of positioning options should be considered for each child. Selecting the proper pieces of equipment requires knowledge of what equipment is available or technologically feasible and how that matches therapeutic, functional, and social needs and goals of the individual child and family (Taylor, 1987). *Exceptional Parent* magazine regularly provides resource guides to commercially available adapted equipment. To ensure access to the full range of positioning apparatus, rehabilitation equipment specialists as consultants are now essential members of teams for children with multiple disabilities (Hedman, 1990).

Alternative Positions

In selecting a variety of positions for a student with physical disabilities, the educational team addresses each of the following questions:

- What postures should be reinforced?
- What postures should be avoided?
- What functions must be performed?
- What are the social contexts?
- What positioning alternatives are possible in the course of the day?

The postures to be reinforced may be any in which the child is currently developing greater control. The postures to be avoided are those that reinforce primitive reflexes, deformities, abnormal postures, or abnormal movement patterns. (These considerations are outlined in Table 3.1.) An analysis of the function to be performed requires an evaluation of the postural and movement demands of the tasks involved. A good frame of reference for this analysis is to consider how people without disabilities perform the task. To perform the task of face washing, discussed previously in this chapter, a student must be able to see the task area and reach the materials (e.g., water, soap). Although a basin of water might be placed on a table or tray where the student sits, it is awkward to put both hands in a basin at chest height, and it may be difficult to see to perform the task. Removing the child from the sink also eliminates the possibility of performing important steps in the task, such as turning the water on and off. Children with physical disabilities may be unable to use the "normal" position of standing unsupported at the sink for face washing. Many children can perform the task while standing in a prone stander or parapodium stander, either of which gives postural support, frees the hands sufficiently to perform the task, provides a clear view and good access to the necessary materials, and approximates the normal position for the activity. Figures 3.14 and 3.15 show a child washing dishes at home while standing at the sink in a prone stander. This child is also pictured lying on her side to watch television (see Figure 3.16) and, with her sister, prone over a wedge strumming a guitar (see Figure 3.17). These positions accommodate the performance demands of the activities and simultaneously facilitate normal postures and movements. Of equal importance, the child's daily routine provides natural opportunities to use a variety of therapeutic positions.

Another consideration in determining appropriate positions is the social context in which activities will be performed, both currently and in the future. The child in Figures 3.14 and 3.15 is engaged in activities at home, using positions that are suitable for the social context of her home. Within a self-contained special education classroom, these positions might still meet the social norm. If this child is included in general education classes, however, sitting may be preferable to enhance social interactions because other students sit in chairs for many of their classes. Experiences in inclusive elementary and secondary schools have shown that typical students are extremely accepting of less traditional positioning, especially when they understand the reason for alternative positions.

Figure 3.14.   Therapeutic positions are matched with normal daily living activities for this girl with cerebral palsy. In this picture she stands in a prone stander to wash her lunch dishes.

Figure 3.15.   Here is another view of the girl using a prone stander to assume the common position for dishwashing.

Finally, the educational team must consider the various positions available to the students over the course of the day. Medical professionals have long recognized that immobility has adverse effects on motor, cardiovascular, respiratory, gastrointestinal, urinary, and metabolic functions (Olson, 1967). Prolonged sitting invites hip and knee flexion contractures and other deformities, particularly for children who cannot independently assume other positions (Fulford & Brown, 1976). Some muscles will develop contractures unless they are in a lengthened position for a minimum of 5 hours per day (Tardieu, Lespargot, Tabary, & Bret, 1988). Once deformities develop, the best positioning does not reverse contractures of muscles and tendons (Kunkel et al., 1993; Lespargot, Renaudin, Khouri, & Robert, 1994). Sitting motionless creates circulatory problems underneath the hip bones, with noticeable changes occurring after just 30 minutes and pressure sores developing in as little as 1–2 hours (Garber, 1985). Intense pressure, friction on the skin, or irritation from urine all increase the possibility of skin breakdown over bony areas when children with severe physi-

Figure 3.16. Recumbent positions are natural for leisure activities at home. The girl lies on her side to watch television.

Figure 3.17. For leisure activity, the girl lies on her stomach over a small wedge to strum her guitar.

cal disabilities remain in the same position for long periods. Immobility and lack of weight bearing on the legs contribute severely to osteoporosis (Kaplan, 1983), which is irreversible (Kunkel et al., 1993). Immobility and poor positioning interfere with pulmonary function and are directly related to shortened life expectancy for people with profound disabilities (Eyman, Grossman, Chaney, & Call, 1990; Nwaobi & Smith, 1986). For these reasons, it is important that children experience a variety of positions. A good rule of thumb is for students to have at least two different positions between which they can alternate, and for these positions to be changed at least once an hour, preferably every 30 minutes. Table 3.3 presents a list of positions, equipment that might be used to achieve positions, and activities that typically would be performed in those positions. It is useful to develop a positioning plan to ensure that each student's positioning matches daily activities while alternating between positions in which 1) the head and trunk are upright, then reclined; 2) the hips and knees are flexed, then extended; and 3) weight bearing is on the hips and thighs, then on other body parts (preferably on the feet). The relative importance of each consideration depends on the student's risk for the health and therapeutic concerns identified previously. A positioning plan is presented in Figure 3.18 for a 14-year-old boy with severe physical disabilities who attends an inclusive middle school program.

Braces, Splints, and Casts

Braces and splints are prescribed when 1) other positioning is not effective to maintain normal posture or alignment, 2) children are too active to remain in sta-

Table 3.3.   Activities and equipment for alternative positions

Position	Typical activities	Standard equipment
Lying prone or supine	Resting, sunbathing	Mat or bed, pillow, wedges, rolls, sandbags
Sidelying	Resting, looking at books, listening to music or stories	Sidelying board, pillow
Prone on elbows	Watching television, looking at books	Wedge, roll, sandbags
Kneeling	Playing at low table, gardening, washing tub, cleaning cupboards	Kneeling box, adapted prone stander, tray or table
Sitting	Eating, playing board games, watching television, clerical work, needlework, toileting, riding in car	Wheelchair, corner chair, standard chair, stool, adapted toilet seat, carseat, tray or table
Standing	Grooming at sink or mirror, washing dishes, cooking, ironing, house cleaning, sports, locomotion	Prone stander, supine stander, parapodium stander, standing box, tray or table, walkers
Miscellaneous		Small cushions, belts

Period	Activity	Position
Homeroom	Arrival routine (inclusive)	Sitting in adaptive wheelchair
1	Work in cafeteria	Standing in supine stander
2	Science (inclusive)	Sitting in adapted wheelchair
3	Hygiene and break (grooming, changed in nurse's office, then rest)	Sitting, then supine lying with legs positioned
4	Lunch	Sitting in adapted wheelchair
5	Art (inclusive) (M–Th)	Sidelying
	Music (inclusive) (T–F)	Prone over wedge
	Community-based instruction (CBI) (W)	Sitting in adapted wheelchair
6	Language arts (inclusive) (CBI) (continued) (W)	Sitting in adapted wheelchair
7	Technology (inclusive) (M–Th)	Standing in supine stander
	Home and careers (inclusive) (T–F)	
	CBI (continued) (W)	
8	Hygiene and break (same as third period)	Sitting, then supine lying
Homeroom	Departure routine (inclusive)	Sitting in adapted wheelchair

Figure 3.18. Positioning plan for a middle school student with multiple disabilities.

tic positions, and 3) external control of a particular joint enhances more normal posture or movement patterns for the entire limb. A brace or splint may be worn on the trunk, leg, or arm. One type of brace, a plastic corset, has been used successfully in the treatment of scoliosis (Laurnen, Tupper, & Mullen, 1983), preventing further curvature of the spine but not necessarily reversing the process. For children with cerebral palsy, scoliosis, and poor head control, plastic corsets with chin and skull supports have controlled the scoliosis, increased the ease of handling and positioning the children, and simultaneously facilitated development of head control (Fulford, Cains, & Sloan, 1982). Although problems can arise when children have sensitive skin, corsets are worn in warm climates, and fit is not adjusted during growth, children with scoliosis typically wear corsets 23 hours per day with no detrimental effects (Keim, 1983).

For the leg and foot, splinting and casting have been used to reduce deformity, reduce spasticity, maintain stable joint positions during rest and standing, and ultimately reduce the need for surgery (Barnard et al., 1984; Booth, Doyle, & Montgomery, 1983; Sankey, Anderson, & Young, 1989; Sussman, 1983; Zachazewski, Eberle, & Jeffries, 1982). When children with cerebral palsy wear ankle-foot orthoses while walking, they typically increase their speed and decrease their energy consumption (Mossberg, Linton, & Friske, 1990).

Although plastic splints have almost replaced metal braces, some children with severe spasticity or excessive weight require the more traditional high-top shoe and short leg brace. There is little evidence that orthopedic shoes alone prevent flat feet or deformities associated with physical disabilities. Nevertheless, all children should enjoy the safety and cosmetic benefits of wearing shoes.

Splinting and casting have also been used to reduce deformity, reduce spasticity, and increase stabilization during functional use of the arm and hand. Although some practitioners believe that splinting masks spasticity in the hand and increases the abnormal tone in the rest of the arm, studies of electrical activity in the arm muscles do not support this contention (Mills, 1984). In fact, children with cerebral palsy have developed and maintained better bilateral hand use, grasp, and arm–hand posture after treatment with hand splints (Exner & Bonder, 1983). Range of motion and movement quality improve even more significantly when upper limb casting is continued for at least 6 months and is combined with neurodevelopmental treatment (Law et al., 1991). There are numerous types of orthokinetic, functional, and resting arm splints, however, and the attributes of each type must be understood for use to be effective (Exner & Bonder, 1983; McPherson, Kreimeyer, Aalderks, & Gallagher, 1982).

The majority of splints are made of heat-molded plastics. Therapists have started experimenting with soft splints, made of polyurethane and neoprene (Anderson, Snow, Dorey, & Kabo, 1988; Casey & Kratz, 1988). Soft splints hold promise for greater comfort, function, and decreases in deformity than rigid splints.

No matter what type of splint is used, splinting one's arms or legs can be expected to improve function *only* when muscle tone, posture, and movement in other parts of the body are normalized using therapeutic handling and positioning methods.

BODY MECHANICS

A discussion of handling and positioning would not be complete without attention to the body mechanics used by team members. The term *body mechanics* refers to the way caregivers position themselves and move when lifting and positioning children. Although adults have sustained back strain or more serious injuries when moving children with multiple disabilities, these problems usually can be avoided by using principles of body mechanics. Employing these principles also ensures greater safety and security for the children being moved.

Planning the Transfer

Prior to actually lifting the child, the adult arranges the environment, determines the extent to which the child can assist in the transfer, considers the position in which the child will be lifted, and determines whether assistance is needed to lift the child. The environment is arranged to minimize the distance the adult must carry the child. When positioning equipment can be moved easily, it is brought to the child rather than the child being carried to the equipment. Belts and other equipment needed for positioning are collected and placed nearby for quick application. The path between the child and positioning device is cleared to ensure a safe transfer.

Children are lifted and carried only when other more independent transfers and mobility cannot be facilitated. Most children with physical disabilities can roll, crawl on hands and knees, or walk within their home and classroom. Often they can be taught to climb in and out of their chairs as well. Although it is easy to lift young children, it is important that they learn to participate actively in transfers while they are small. Waiting until the child is older means the child will have to manage increased size, weight, and, possibly, contractures while working to develop the coordination needed for transfers and mobility. Even when children must be lifted and carried, their participation is enlisted. For one child, participation may be reaching for and holding the adult's shoulders. For another child, it may be staying relaxed or moving the head forward slightly when the adult reaches toward the child. The practice of soliciting the child's participation serves to maximize opportunities to teach children with multiple impairments and to further protect adults from unnecessary physical strain.

The next consideration is the position in which the child will be lifted. Children with extensor spasticity, flexor spasticity, and hypotonia (floppiness) are handled differently to normalize their tone. Therefore, they are positioned, lifted, and carried in somewhat different ways. It is helpful to physically orient the child to the next position prior to lifting. This protects the adult from having to change the child's position during the transfer, when adult and child are most precarious.

The final consideration in planning the transfer is how many adults are needed to lift the child. Although adults frequently lift small children independently, assistance should be enlisted to lift larger children. A good rule of thumb is to seek assistance when a child's weight is more than one fourth of one's own. To lift heavier children it may be necessary to have a third or even a fourth person. Although these guidelines may seem unnecessarily restrictive and, therefore, impractical, they serve to protect both children and adults from injury.

Lifting the Child

When all aspects of the lift have been planned, the adult prepares to lift the child. If the child is on the floor, the adult will squat or kneel on the floor facing the child and as close as possible. If the child is not on the floor, the adult will stand facing the child, with weight evenly distributed over both legs. If it is necessary to reach downward for the child, the adult will squat slightly by bending the knees. The trunk is not bent or twisted because these positions tend to cause back injuries. The adult then informs the child of the move to be made and requests the child's assistance. The adult takes hold of the child and brings the child close to the trunk to keep the child's weight over the adult's hips. When the child is positioned securely in the adult's arms, the adult can proceed to lift or lower the child. The essential rules for lifting and lowering are 1) position the feet to provide a stable base of support, 2) keep a slight arch in the low back, 3) tighten and hold the abdominal muscles (but continue breathing), and 4) bend and straighten the hips and knees rather than the trunk. McKenzie (1985) recommends arching the back five or six times immediately before and after lifting to relieve pressure on the disks in the spine, thereby decreasing the chance of injury. Figure 3.19 illustrates the proper body position for lifting a small child. When two people lift a child, the same principles apply. Usually one adult holds the child's arms while the other adult holds the child's legs. One adult coordinates the lift, verbally rehearses the plan for the transfer, informs the child, and signals the other adult when to lift or lower the child. Figure 3.20 illustrates one way to hold a large child for lifting. Although the adults shown are handling the child securely, their own positions are precarious. Note that their backs are rounded, making them

Figure 3.19.   Correct handling and body mechanics for lifting a small child.

Figure 3.20. The correct handling for two people to lift a large child, but *incorrect* body mechanics.

prone to back injury, and their foot position is unstable, increasing the chance of falling off balance. These poor body mechanics also increase the probability of injury to the child. Preventing injuries and ensuring safety requires that team members consistently apply the principles listed previously.

DEVELOPING AND IMPLEMENTING HANDLING AND POSITIONING PROGRAMS IN EDUCATIONAL SETTINGS

All members of the educational team can provide important information about handling and positioning techniques that enhance the performance of students with multiple disabilities. For this reason, decisions on these matters are *team* decisions. Occupational therapists and physical therapists offer the team particular expertise in therapeutic handling and positioning, current technological developments, and fitting equipment. Therefore, an occupational or physical therapist on each student's team takes primary responsibility for developing procedures for normalization of tone, dynamic positioning, and positioning in equipment. Therapists also develop procedures to facilitate normal movement patterns and sequences, such as rolling, rising to stand, or walking. Once these procedures are developed, therapists create task analyses or checklists that become the basis for staff training. Therapists have used these tools successfully to train teachers in handling and positioning (Inge & Snell, 1985), and to monitor positioning, application of splints, and functions of various pieces of adapted equipment (Stephens & Lattimore, 1983; Venn, Morganstern, & Dykes, 1979). Checklists, pictures of proper positioning, and schedules of positioning and mobility for each activity and transition can be posted on bulletin boards and adapted equipment as reminders for educational team members. Using these simple systems to train staff and promote proper ongoing implementation of procedures, educational team members can ensure that each student derives the greatest benefit from therapeutic handling and positioning.

REFERENCES

Anderson, J., Snow, B., Dorey, F., & Kabo, J.M. (1988). Efficacy of soft splints in reducing severe flexion contractures. *Developmental Medicine and Child Neurology, 30*(4), 502–508.

Barnard, P., Dill, H., Eldredge, P., Held, J., Judd, D., & Nalette, E. (1984). Reduction of hypertonicity by early casting of a comatose, head-injured individual: A case report. *Physical Therapy, 64*(10), 1540–1542.

Bergen, A., Presperin, J., & Tallman, T. (1990). *Positioning for function: Wheelchairs and other assistive technologies.* Valhalla, NY: Valhalla Rehabilitation Publications, Ltd.

Bobath, K. (1980). *The neurophysiological basis for the treatment of cerebral palsy* (2nd ed.). Philadelphia: J.B. Lippincott.

Bobath, K., & Bobath, B. (1972). Cerebral palsy. In P. Pearson & C. Williams (Eds.), *Physical therapy services in the developmental disabilities* (pp. 31–185). Springfield, IL: Charles C Thomas.

Booth, B., Doyle, M., & Montgomery, J. (1983). Serial casting for the management of spasticity in the head injured adult. *Physical Therapy, 63*(12), 1960–1966.

Butler, C. (1986). Effects of powered mobility on self-initiated behaviors of very young children with locomotor disability. *Developmental Medicine and Child Neurology, 28*(3), 325–332.

Butler, C., Okamoto, G., & McKay, T. (1983). Powered mobility for very young disabled children. *Developmental Medicine and Child Neurology, 25*(4), 472–474.

Campbell, P., McInerney, W., & Cooper, M. (1984). Therapeutic programming for students with severe handicaps. *American Journal of Occupational Therapy, 38*(9), 594–602.

Campbell, S.K. (Ed.). (1990). Consensus conference on efficacy of physical therapy in the management of cerebral palsy. *Pediatric Physical Therapy, 2*(3), 123–176.

Case-Smith, J., Fisher, A., & Bauer, D. (1989). An analysis of the relationship between proximal and distal motor control. *American Journal of Occupational Therapy, 43*(10), 657–663.

Casey, C., & Kratz, E. (1988). Soft splinting with neoprene: The thumb abduction supinator splint. *American Journal of Occupational Therapy, 42*(6), 395–398.

Chakerian, D.L., & Larson, M.A. (1993). Effects of upper extremity weightbearing on hand opening and prehension patterns in children with cerebral palsy. *Developmental Medicine and Child Neurology, 35*(3), 216–229.

Connor, F., Williamson, G., & Siepp, J. (1978). *Program guide for infants and toddlers with neuromotor and other developmental disabilities.* New York: Teachers College Press.

Craft, M.J., Lakin, J.A., Oppliger, R.A., Clancy, G.M., & Vanderlinden, D.W. (1990). Siblings as change agents of function of children with cerebral palsy. *Developmental Medicine and Child Neurology, 32*(12), 1049–1057.

da Paz, A.C., Burnett, S.M., & Braga, L.W. (1994). Walking prognosis in cerebral palsy: A 22 year retrospective analysis. *Developmental Medicine and Child Neurology, 36*(2), 130–134 .

DeGangi, G.A. (1994a). Examining the efficacy of short-term NDT intervention using a case study design: Part 1. *Physical and Occupational Therapy in Pediatrics, 14*(1), 71–78.

DeGangi, G.A. (1994b). Examining the efficacy of short-term NDT intervention using a case study design: Part 2. *Physical and Occupational Therapy in Pediatrics, 14*(2), 21–61.

DeGangi, G.A., Hurley, L., & Linscheid, T. (1983). Toward a methodology of short term effects of neurodevelopmental treatment. *American Journal of Occupational Therapy, 37*(7), 479–484.

Domaracki, L.S., Sisson, L.A., Robinson-Dassel, K., Hamilton, D.W., & Goldstone, F. (1990). Evaluation of biofeedback for improving head and trunk position in children with multiple, severe disabilities. *Pediatric Physical Therapy, 2*(4), 192–195.

Eicher, P.S., & Batshaw, M.L. (1993). Cerebral palsy. *Pediatric Clinics of North America, 40*(3), 537–551.

Exner, C., & Bonder, B. (1983). Comparative effects of three hand splints on bilateral use, grasp, and arm-hand posture in hemiplegic children: A pilot study. *Occupational Therapy Journal of Research, 3*(2), 75–92.

Eyman, R., Grossman, H., Chaney, R., & Call, T. (1990). The life expectancy of profoundly handicapped people with mental retardation. *New England Journal of Medicine, 323*(9), 584–589.

Finnie, N. (1975). *Handling the young cerebral palsied child at home.* New York: E.P. Dutton.

Fiorentino, M. (1963). *Reflex testing methods for evaluating CNS development.* Springfield, IL: Charles C Thomas.

Fraser, B.A., Hensinger, R.N., & Phelps, J.A. (1990). *Physical management of multiple handicaps: A professional's guide* (2nd ed.). Baltimore: Paul H. Brookes Publishing Co.

Fulford, G., & Brown, J. (1976). Position as a cause of deformity in children with cerebral palsy. *Developmental Medicine and Child Neurology, 18*(3), 305–314.

Fulford, G., Cains, T., & Sloan, Y. (1982). Sitting problems of children with cerebral palsy. *Developmental Medicine and Child Neurology, 24*(1), 48–53.

Gadow, K. (1986). *Children on medication: Vol. II. Epilepsy, emotional disturbance, and adolescent disorders.* San Diego, CA: College-Hill Press.

Garber, S. (1985). Wheelchair cushions: A historical review. *American Journal of Occupational Therapy, 39*(7), 453–459.

Giangreco, M. (1986). Effects of integrated therapy: A pilot study. *Journal of The Association for Persons with Severe Handicaps, 11*(3), 205–208.

Goldkamp, O. (1984). Treatment effectiveness in cerebral palsy. *Archives of Physical Medicine and Rehabilitation, 65*(5), 232–234.

Greiner, B.M., Czerniecki, J.M., & Deitz, J.C. (1993). Gait parameters of children with spastic diplegia: A comparison of effects of posterior and anterior walkers. *Archives of Physical Medicine and Rehabilitation, 74*(4), 381–385.

Hedman, G. (Ed.) (1990). Rehabilitation technology. *Physical and Occupational Therapy in Pediatrics, 10*(2), 1–173.

Hulme, J., Poor, R., Schulein, M., & Pezzino, J. (1983). Perceived behavioral changes observed with adaptive seating devices and training programs for multihandicapped, developmentally disabled individuals. *Physical Therapy, 63*(2), 204–208.

Hulme, J., Shaver, J., Acher, S., Mullette, L., & Eggert, C. (1987). Effects of adaptive seating devices on the eating and drinking of children with multiple handicaps. *American Journal of Occupational Therapy, 41*(2), 81–89.

Hundertmark, L. (1985). Evaluating the adult with cerebral palsy for specialized adaptive seating. *Physical Therapy, 65*(2), 209–212.

Inge, K.J., & Snell, M.E. (1985). Teaching positioning and handling techniques to public school personnel through inservice training. *Journal of The Association for Persons with Severe Handicaps, 10*(2), 105–110.

Jaeger, L. (1987). *Home program instruction sheets for infants and young children.* Tucson, AZ: Therapy Skill Builders.

Kalen, V., & Bleck, E. (1985). Prevention of spastic paralytic dislocation of the hip. *Developmental Medicine and Child Neurology, 27*(1), 17–24.

Kaplan, F. (1983). Osteoporosis. *Clinical Symposia, 35*(5), 1–32.

Keim, H. (1983). Fundamentals and basic principles of scoliosis. *Orthopedic Review, 12*(3), 31–40.

Kohn, J., Enders, S., Preston, J., & Motloch, W. (1983). Provision of assistive equipment for handicapped persons. *Archives of Physical Medicine and Rehabilitation, 64*(8), 378–381.

Kottke, F., Halpern, D., Easton, J., Ozel, A., & Burrill, C. (1978). The training of coordination. *Archives of Physical Medicine and Rehabilitation, 59*(11), 567–572.

Kunkel, C.F., Scremin, A.M.E., Eisenberg, B., Garcia, J.F., Roberts, S., & Martinez, S. (1993). Effects of "standing" on spasticity, contracture, and osteoporosis in paralyzed males. *Archives of Physical Medicine and Rehabilitation, 74*(1), 73–78.

Laurnen, E., Tupper, J., & Mullen, M. (1983). The Boston brace in thoracic scoliosis: A preliminary report. *Spine, 8*(4), 388–395.

Law, M., Cadman, D., Rosenbaum, P., Walter, S., Russell, D., & DeMatteo, C. (1991). Neurodevelopmental therapy and upper extremity inhibitive casting for children with cerebral palsy. *Developmental Medicine and Child Neurology, 33*(5), 379–387.

Lespargot, A., Renaudin, E., Khouri, N., & Robert, M. (1994). Extensibility of hip adductors in children with cerebral palsy. *Developmental Medicine and Child Neurology, 36*(11), 980–988.

Levitt, S. (1982). *Treatment of cerebral palsy and motor delay* (2nd ed.). Boston: Blackwell Scientific.

Lilly, L., & Powell, N. (1990). Measuring the effects of neurodevelopmental treatment on the daily living skills of two children with cerebral palsy. *American Journal of Occupational Therapy, 44*(2), 139–145.

Loria, C. (1980). Relationship of proximal and distal function in motor development. *Physical Therapy, 60*(2), 167–172.

McKenzie, R. (1985). *Treat your own back.* Lower Hutt, New Zealand: Spinal Publications Ltd.

McPherson, J., Kreimeyer, D., Aalderks, M., & Gallagher, T. (1982). A comparison of dorsal and volar resting hand splints in the reduction of hypertonus. *American Journal of Occupational Therapy, 36*(10), 664–670.

Miedaner, J., & Finuf, L. (1993). Effects of adaptive positioning on psychological test scores for preschool children with cerebral palsy. *Pediatric Physical Therapy, 5*(4), 177–182.

Mills, Y. (1984). Electromyographic results of inhibitory splinting. *Physical Therapy, 64*(2), 190–193.

Morris, S., & Klein, M. (1987). *Pre-feeding skills: A comprehensive resource for feeding development.* Tucson, AZ: Therapy Skill Builders.

Mossberg, K., Linton, K., & Friske, K. (1990). Ankle-foot orthoses: Effect on energy expenditure of gait in spastic diplegic children. *Archives of Physical Medicine and Rehabilitation, 71*(7), 490–494.

Murphy, R., Doughty, N., & Nunes, D. (1979). Multielement designs: An alternative to reversal and multiple baseline evaluation strategies. *Mental Retardation, 17*(1), 23–28.

Myhr, U., & von Wendt, L. (1991). Improvement of functional sitting position for children with cerebral palsy. *Developmental Medicine and Child Neurology, 33*(3), 246–256.

Myhr, U., & von Wendt, L. (1993). Influence of different sitting positions and adduction orthoses on leg muscle activity in children with cerebral palsy. *Developmental Medicine and Child Neurology, 35*(10), 870–880.

Noonan, M. (1984). Teaching postural reactions to students with severe cerebral palsy. *Journal of The Association for Persons with Severe Handicaps, 9*(2), 111–122.

Nwaobi, O. (1986). Effects of body orientation in space on tonic muscle activity of patients with cerebral palsy. *Developmental Medicine and Child Neurology, 28*(1), 41–44.

Nwaobi, O., Brubaker, C., Cusick, B., & Sussman, M. (1983). Electromyographic investigation of extensor activity in cerebral palsied children in different seating positions. *Developmental Medicine and Child Neurology, 25*(2), 175–183.

Nwaobi, O., Hobson, D., Eng, P., & Taylor, S. (1988). Mechanical and anatomical hip flexion angles on seating children with cerebral palsy. *Archives of Physical Medicine and Rehabilitation, 69*(4), 265–267.

Nwaobi, O., & Smith, P.D. (1986). Effect of adaptive seating on pulmonary function of children with cerebral palsy. *Developmental Medicine and Child Neurology, 28*(3), 351–354.

O'Dwyer, N., Neilson, P., & Nash, J. (1994). Reduction of spasticity in cerebral palsy using feedback of the tonic stretch reflex. *Developmental Medicine and Child Neurology, 36*(9), 770–786.

Olson, E. (1967). The hazards of immobility. *American Journal of Nursing, 67*(4), 780–797.

Parette, H., & Hourcade, J. (1984). How effective are physiotherapeutic programs with young mentally retarded children who have cerebral palsy? *Journal of Mental Deficiency Research, 28*(3), 167–175.

Pope, P.M., Bowes, C.E., & Booth, E. (1994). Postural control in sitting. The SAM system: Evaluation of use over three years. *Developmental Medicine and Child Neurology, 36*(3), 241–252.

Rainforth, B., York, J., & Macdonald, C. (1992). *Collaborative teams for students with severe disabilities: Integrating therapy and educational services.* Baltimore: Paul H. Brookes Publishing Co.

Safaee-Rad, R., Shwedyk, E., Quanbury, A.O., & Cooper, J.E. (1990). Normal functional range of motion of upper limb joints during performance of three feeding activities. *Archives of Physical Medicine and Rehabilitation, 71*(7), 505–509.

Sankey, R., Anderson, D., & Young, J. (1989). Characteristics of ankle-foot orthoses for management of the spastic lower limb. *Developmental Medicine and Child Neurology, 31*(4), 466–470.

Sents, B., & Marks, H. (1989). Changes in preschool children's IQ scores as a function of positioning. *American Journal of Occupational Therapy, 43*(10), 685–688.

Stephens, T., & Lattimore, J. (1983). Prescriptive checklist for positioning multihandicapped residential clients: A clinical report. *Physical Therapy, 63*(7), 1113–1115.

Sussman, M. (1983). Casting as an adjunct to neurodevelopmental therapy for cerebral palsy. *Developmental Medicine and Child Neurology, 25*(6), 804–805.

Tardieu, C., Lespargot, A., Tabary, C., & Bret, M. (1988). For how long must the soleus muscle be stretched each day to prevent contracture? *Developmental Medicine and Child Neurology, 30*(1), 3–10.

Taylor, S. (1987). Evaluating the client with physical disabilities for wheelchair seating. *American Journal of Occupational Therapy, 41*(11), 711–716.

Trahan, J., & Marcoux, S. (1994). Factors associated with inability of children with cerebral palsy to walk at six years: A retrospective study. *Developmental Medicine and Child Neurology, 36*(9), 787–795.

Trefler, E., Nickey, J., & Hobson, D. (1983). Technology in the education of multiply handicapped children. *American Journal of Occupational Therapy, 37*(6), 381–387.

Venn, J., Morganstern, L., & Dykes, M. (1979). Checklists for evaluating the fit and function of orthoses, prostheses, and wheelchairs in the classroom. *Teaching Exceptional Children, 11*(2), 51–56.

York, J., & Weimann, G. (1991). Accommodating severe physical disabilities. In J. Reichle, J. York, & J. Sigafoos, *Implementing augmentative and alternative communication: Strategies for learners with severe disabilities* (pp. 239–255). Baltimore: Paul H. Brookes Publishing Co.

Zachazewski, J., Eberle, E., & Jeffries, M. (1982). Effect of tone inhibiting casts and orthoses on gait: A case report. *Physical Therapy, 62*(4), 453–455.

4

Developing Instructional Adaptations

Jennifer York-Barr, Beverly Rainforth, and Peggy Locke

AN ADAPTATION CAN BE THOUGHT of as any device or material that is used to accomplish a task more efficiently. Most people use a variety of adaptations in everyday living. For example, datebooks and calendars are used for recording appointments, birthdays, holidays, and deadlines for various projects and commitments. Timers are used to indicate when food should be removed from the oven. Lists are used to remind shoppers of groceries or other items to be purchased. Each of these examples is an adaptation to assist with memory. Other adaptations simplify physical demands. Common examples are using an electric mixer instead of stirring batter by hand or using an electric garage door opener instead of lifting open the door by hand. Another type of adaptation is used to serve as a model. A picture of a pineapple upside-down cake illustrates how the pineapple and cherries should be arranged; a picture of a completed needlework project shows the colors of thread to use and how various stitches should be made. An analysis of the daily activities performed by most people undoubtedly would reveal the use of numerous other adaptations.

The business world is replete with adaptations, many of which enhance the efficiency, accuracy, and speed of one's performance of various tasks. Automatic coin counters at banks are used to sort and stack coins. Cash register keys at fast-food restaurants are color coded by food category (e.g., beverages, sandwiches, side orders) to make locating keys easier for clerks. Frequently, the keys also have specific food or drink labels that, when pushed, automatically enter the price of the item to be purchased. This eliminates the need for clerks to remember the different prices and decreases the time required to complete food purchases. Many businesses invest enormous amounts of money to research and develop adaptations that will increase productivity and efficiency while maintaining a high degree of quality.

Not surprisingly, the value of adaptations also has been recognized in the field of education, particularly for assisting students with severe physical and multiple disabilities to participate more fully in home, school, and community activities (Falvey, 1995; Knight & Wadsworth, 1993). Parents and professionals have found that motor, sensory, and intellectual disabilities presented by some students require creative approaches in which systematic instruction is augmented by the development and use of individualized adaptations. The "principle of partial participation" asserts that when systematic instruction and adaptation strategies are integrated and applied, "all students can acquire skills that allow them to function in a wide variety of least restrictive environments" (Baumgart et al., 1982, p. 19). Certainly, this presents a significant challenge to educators, therapists, parents, and others involved in educational programming. Meeting the challenge of making adaptations to attain meaningful participation, however, is a cornerstone in educational service provision and, more broadly, community integration for people with multiple and often complex learning needs.

This chapter presents a process for developing and using individualized adaptations to increase the participation of students with multiple disabilities in educational activities. Application of the strategy draws from experiences a high school student has using a community library. Following presentation of the strategy, one specific elementary student is profiled to illustrate how creative use of simple adaptive technology can promote meaningful participation and contributions in general education settings. Next, a variety of adaptive devices that have been used to enhance participation in school, home, and community environments is described. This chapter finishes with a discussion of considerations, precautions, and resources related to effective use of adaptations as a complement to instruction.

A PROCESS FOR DEVELOPING INDIVIDUALIZED ADAPTATIONS

The need for adaptations is determined by an ecological analysis of individual student abilities and needs. That is, the process starts by identifying individually relevant contexts in which a particular student needs to learn to participate. Meaningful, individualized instructional objectives and effective strategies are then determined. Use of adaptations may be one important component of an instructional strategy. Figure 4.1 presents a flowchart of the steps involved in an ecological approach for developing adaptations. This process originated with

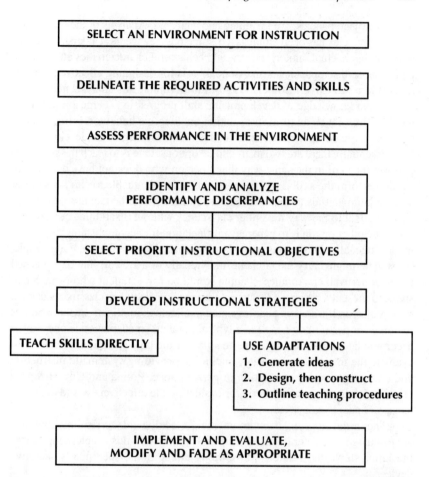

Figure 4.1.   Flowchart of an environmentally referenced individualized adaptation process. (*Source:* Baumgart et al., 1982.)

Brown and his colleagues (Baumgart et al., 1982; Brown et al., 1979; Brown et al., 1980; Brown, Shiraga, York, Zanella, & Rogan, 1984a, 1984b). In recent years, the process has been expanded to reflect knowledge gained through experience using an ecological approach over the past 10 or so years (Falvey, 1995; Ferguson & Baumgart, 1991; Piuma & Udvari-Solner, 1993b).

The first step in the process is to identify the actual school, home, and community (including vocational for secondary students) environments in which a given student should learn to function. Second, the activities and skills necessary to participate in the selected environments are delineated. Third, the ability of the student with disabilities to engage in the required activities and skills is assessed in the actual environments. Fourth, difficulty areas, referred to as performance discrepancies, are identified and analyzed. Analysis of the reasons for the discrepancies has been emphasized in the past few years. Understanding the potential intellectual, motor, sensory, and behavioral characteristics attributed to performance discrepancies is an essential basis for designing effective interventions (Piuma & Udvari-Solner, 1993b). Furthermore, this analysis necessarily draws from knowledge of developmental skill progression (Ferguson & Baumgart, 1991), as well as from information on adaptive behavior. Fifth, priority skills are targeted for instruction. Sixth, instruction strategies are developed.

Essentially there are two instructional options. One is to teach the student to perform the skill in the same way that a person who does not have a disability would perform the skill. For example, if a student is unable to carry his or her science lab materials to the lab table, the student would be taught to do so in a way identical to the way his or her classmates without disabilities perform the skill. The other option is to generate an adaptation for accomplishing the task by modifying skill requirements or by developing an adaptive device. For example, the student might carry the lab items individually or use a carrying bag attached to his or her walker. Another example would be for a student who is unable to speak to present a report on leisure interests to social studies classmates using a slide projector. If a student lacks essential intellectual, motor, or sensory abilities required for performing a skill in a typical manner, an adaptation is one way to accommodate the difficulties. The final part of the process is to implement and evaluate the instructional strategy, including providing systematic instruction and engaging ongoing evaluation of performance. Piuma and Udvari-Solner (1993b) delineate specific criteria for evaluating the effectiveness and appropriateness of adaptive devices.

The initial steps in an environmental, or ecological, curriculum approach are discussed in greater detail in Chapter 10; therefore, this chapter emphasizes the latter steps that relate to developing adaptations, specifically adaptive devices.

Application of the process is illustrated through an example of a student using a public library for recreation/leisure purposes. The student, George, was 19 years old and had been diagnosed as having mental retardation requiring extensive to pervasive supports. He enjoyed community activities immensely and was beginning to be included in such activities with some of his senior classmates in high school. He had fair control over turning his head to each side when provided with a headrest for support. He could extend one elbow and exert pressure downward with the side of his hand. George's primary method of mobility was being pushed in a wheelchair by another person. He was not able to speak but readily communicated likes and dislikes through facial expressions, and he could indicate choices or direction with his eyes.

Select an Environment for Instruction

The first phase of an ecological approach to curriculum development is to select the "real world" environments in which the student must learn to function. Environments must be determined individually for each student. Some of the reasons for selecting the public library as a recreation/leisure environment for George included the following: 1) he enjoyed listening to music and looking at magazines, both of which activities were available at the library; 2) the activities were age appropriate; 3) George's family used the particular branch of the library in which instruction would take place; 4) the library was located close to George's home; 5) the library was located near other community environments in which George might learn to function (e.g., a grocery store, clothing store); 6) use of the library required little or no money; and 7) the library was open much of the week, including weeknights and weekends. Although use of the library was not a preferred activity of peers without disabilities, current and future use of the library was determined to be a priority for George.

Delineate the Activities and Skills Required in the Environment

After selection of an environment, a skills inventory is completed; this involves delineation of activities performed and skills required, by a person without a disability, for functioning within the selected environments (Brown et al., 1984a; Falvey, 1995). A detailed breakdown of some of the activities and skills required at the public library is presented as the skills inventory of a person without disabilities in the first column of Figure 4.2. For example, the activity of choosing an audiotape at the library required the following skills: locate the audiotape section, browse through the audiotapes, and select one audiotape. An inventory of a person without a disability that specifies skills is used as the assessment tool for determining student abilities in a natural environment.

Assess the Performance of the Student with Disabilities

Next, current participation of the student with disabilities is assessed in the designated environment (Brown et al., 1984b; Falvey, 1995). Assessment requires taking the student to the specific environment and using the inventory as the assessment tool for recording performance. First, the response of the student to the natural conditions that should ultimately cue performance of specific skills within the environment is recorded. Independent and acceptable performance and the type and degree of any assistance required should be recorded also. An example of assessment information on George's performance at the library is provided in the second column of Figure 4.2. There were four skills performed independently: looked at one tape, scanned then located one tape, looked at one magazine, and looked at pictures in magazine. Acceptable performance of all other skills required teacher assistance.

Identify and Analyze Performance Discrepancies

After the assessment is conducted in the actual environment, student performance discrepancies, or problem areas, are identified in relation to how a person without disabilities would function in the environment. In this way, specific activities and skills in which the student requires instruction are identified. The

Person without disabilities inventory	Student with disabilities inventory (assessment)	Instructional solutions (teach directly or adapt)
Activity: Choosing an audiotape		
Skills:		
Locate audiotape section.	– T pointed to audio-visual section, then to audiotapes.	D: S will look in direction of audiotape area once in visual field. (T/peer will push wheelchair.)
Browse through audiotapes.	– T located age-appropriate section then selected four.	A: S will look at audiotapes pulled from stack by T/peer.
Select one audiotape.	+ S looked at one audiotape after T presented four.	
Activity: Listening to audiotape		
Skills:		
Locate audiotape.	+ S scanned, then located after T pointed to picture of audiotape player on communication board.	A: S will be pushed by T/peer to audiotape section.
Position self.	– T wheeled and positioned S.	A: S will push on lever extended from eject button; T/peer will position audiotape player.
Open audiotape player lid.	– S initiated move toward eject button; T relaxed S's arm, then primed reaching for and pushing button.	A: S will push in audiotape after T/peer places audiotape player close to S's wrist and aligns tape.
Insert audiotape.	– S pushed audiotape into place with back of wrist after T aligned audiotape in track.	D: S will push lid closed with forearm after T/peer places tape player near forearm.
Close lid	– S initiated move toward lid; T relaxed S's arm, then assisted to reach down and push closed.	A: T/peer will perform.
Put on headphones.	– T placed earphones on S's head.	A: S will turn on audiotape with hand/head using microswitch.
Turn on audiotape	– S was unable to reach and exert enough pressure; T turned on.	

Skill	Observation	Teaching note
Adjust volume.	– T moved volume dial; S frowned then smiled.	A: S will smile when appropriate volume dialed by T/peer.

Activity: Choosing a magazine
Skills:

Skill	Observation	Teaching note
Locate magazine section.	– T pointed to magazine section.	D: S will look in direction of magazines once in visual field (eventually S will choose between audiotapes and magazines).
Locate preferred magazines.	– T located age-appropriate and preferred content magazines.	A: S will scan magazine section with T/peer guiding by pointing.
Select one magazine.	+ S looked at one magazine and smiled after T presented three.	

Activity: Browsing through magazine
Skills:

Skill	Observation	Teaching note
Locate an area to sit.	– T pointed out several open spots, then decided to go near window.	D: S will choose where to sit by looking at one area (window or lounge) pointed out by T/peer.
Position self.	– T wheeled and positioned S.	A: S will be positioned by T/peer (consider getting S out of chair to sit on carpet).
Hold magazine.	– T positioned and held magazine on wheelchair tray.	A: T will place magazine in magazine/book holder adaptation.
Read articles/look at pictures.	+ S looked at pictures.	
Turn pages.	– S initiated reaching to page but required T's assistance to relax, reach, and turn pages.	A: S will turn pages with hand/mouth using dowel rod with Plasti-Tac end.

Figure 4.2. Example of a partial assessment conducted at a public library. (T = teacher; S = student; + indicates independent and acceptable performance; – indicates assistance was required to achieve acceptable performance; D = teach directly; A = adapt.)

skills for which George required assistance in the audiotape-playing activity were locate the audiotape section, browse through the audiotapes, position self, open the audiotape player lid, insert the audiotape, close the audiotape player lid, put on the headphones, turn on the audiotape, and adjust the volume. Discrepant skills in the magazine activity were locate the magazine section, locate the preferred magazines, locate an area to sit, position self, hold magazine, and turn the pages.

Research by Piuma and Udvari-Solner (1993b) provides insight into team members' thought processes related to analysis of discrepancies. "When examined more closely, these professionals engaged in a complex discourse of discriminating questions, in a sense theorizing, making educated guesses about the source of the discrepancy, engaging in a delicate process of elimination, and ultimately acting on these 'hunches'" (p. 16). Piuma and Udvari-Solner go on to state that "this element [in the adaptation process] is central in determining the original or cause of the discrepancy and consequently leading the instructor to systematic selection of adaptations" (p. 16). Four categories of causal factors were identified: 1) instructional/student learning characteristics, 2) environmental, 3) physical/motor, and 4) motivation (behavioral). In the case of George, most of the discrepancies were considered to result from his physical and intellectual disabilities.

Select Priority Instructional Objectives

Drawing from the analysis of the identified discrepancies, instructional priorities are selected, and corresponding objectives written. Considerations in selecting priorities are discussed in greater detail in Chapter 10 and typically include such variables as maintains health and vitality, enhances participation in current and future integrated environments, increases social inclusion and interactions with peers, has frequent and multiple applications across environments and activities, is essential for further development, is a preference or interest of the student, is a family priority, and is a priority for a significant person in that specific environment (Rainforth, York, & Macdonald, 1992).

Develop Instructional Strategies

The next step is for team members to decide how each of the priority skills will be addressed instructionally. Designing inclusive instructional methods involves drawing upon the expertise of all team members. The decision is made whether to teach the skill directly (i.e., the way that a person without disabilities would perform the skill) or to generate adaptations that will enable greater and more independent participation. When students are unable to engage in individually appropriate activities by typical means because of motor, sensory, and/or intellectual disabilities, it is necessary to develop individualized adaptations that involve modifying the environment or teaching strategies to enhance participation.

Given the performance discrepancies of George at the library noted previously, the following instructional strategies were selected. The team decided on direct instruction for the following skills: locate the audiotape section, close the audiotape player lid, locate the magazine section, and locate an area to sit. It was decided that George would be taught to scan the library, then to indicate the appropriate locations by looking in one direction for a few seconds, and also to push the audiotape player lid closed with his forearm. The remaining discrepant skills required various adaptations.

Baumgart et al. (1982) presented four categories of adaptations: 1) providing personal assistance, 2) modifying skills or activities, 3) using an adaptive device, and 4) modifying the physical and social environments. In the following sections these adaptation strategies are described, and examples specific to George are provided. The third column in Figure 4.2 summarizes the instructional strategies decided upon for George.

Providing Personal Assistance   Providing personal assistance is a familiar adaptation. Occasionally, educational team members decide to provide personal assistance on a long-term basis for skills that a student is very unlikely to learn using direct instruction or other adaptations. For example, a student who has not been successful learning to move between high school classes independently may require the assistance of a peer on a long-term basis. In the library example, it was decided that personal assistance would be provided; specifically, a peer without disabilities would accompany George and assist him with mobility between areas of the library and with appropriate positioning for particular activities.

Modifying Skills or Activities   The second type of adaptation, modifying skills or activities, involves changing typical skill sequences. A student who has difficulty managing his or her belongings and his or her dine-in meal at a fast-food restaurant may be taught first to deposit belongings at a table, then proceed to the counter to order and obtain a meal. Another example involves a student with severe disabilities in a middle-school reading class. This student's primary reading class objectives were selecting a magazine from the school library, checking it out, browsing, and returning the magazine. Although most of the students in the class used the library on a biweekly basis, this student used the library three times a week. In yet another reading class example, this time for an elementary school student with multiple disabilities, the student's reading routine deviated from that of her classmates because she remained in the quiet reading area of the room for all of the three reading periods. Her classmates rotated between the quiet reading area, independent seated work, and small group instruction.

In George's library example, use of an activity adaptation was an appropriate instructional strategy for him to learn to locate a set of audiotapes and magazines from which to select one. Because of inefficient arm use, George was not able to secure and browse independently through the magazines and audiotapes prior to making a selection. It was decided that a peer without disabilities would choose several age-appropriate audiotapes and magazines that were interesting, and George would then make a final selection by looking at or touching one of the options presented.

Using an Adaptive Device   The third type of an adaptation, using an adaptive device, was also employed in the library example. George was unable to depress the play button on the audiotape player using a controlled, desirable arm movement. Using a microswitch as an adaptation was considered appropriate. The switch was to be positioned for activation either by controlled arm or head movement. Another difficulty area indicated in the assessment was turning pages of a magazine. To adapt the physical skills required for holding a magazine and turning the pages, the magazine/book holder illustrated in Figure 4.3 was made. This allowed George to browse independently through a magazine after a peer (or teacher) secured the magazine in the device.

Modifying the Physical and Social Environments   The final category of adaptations, modifying the physical and social environments, includes changes such as making entryways to buildings accessible, rearranging furniture to create space for maneuvering a wheelchair, modifying public transportation vehicles, and creating space for wheelchairs to be positioned in movie theaters. An inventory of environmental modifications and examples can be found in Nordic Committee on Disability (1985) and Orelove and Hanley (1979). Such adaptations are encountered frequently in general education classes and vocational and domestic situations. Some examples include rearranging desks so that wheel-

Figure 4.3.   Magazine or book holder. (Developed by Jennifer York-Barr and Jo-Ann Schaidle.)

chairs can be maneuvered around them, rearranging bedroom furniture so that a wheelchair can be maneuvered close to at least one side of the bed, installing a sink that does not have a cabinet underneath so that a person who uses a wheelchair can be close enough to use the sink, and lowering a work surface so that a person seated in a wheelchair can work at a comfortable height.

Adapting the social environment to promote positive interdependence among classmates is being used to an increasing degree in classrooms that include students with multiple disabilities. A variety of peer support strategies for facilitating interactions among classmates with and without disabilities is presented in Stainback and Stainback (1990) and Thousand, Villa, and Nevin (1994).

Implement and Evaluate the Effectiveness of Instruction

Whether teaching skills directly or using an adaptive device, it is important to remember that direct instruction is necessary. Use of an adaptive device serves only to simplify the task in some way—it does not teach the student. In fact, criticism of the principle of partial participation and use of adaptations has arisen from the not uncommon practice of adaptive devices substituting for skill development and sometimes resulting in passive involvement (Ferguson & Baumgart, 1991). Instructional programs that delineate systematic cuing and fading strategies should be designed, implemented, and evaluated as described in Chapter 10. In addition, Piuma and Udvari-Solner (1993b) offer evaluation criteria for determining the effectiveness of vocational adaptive devices, many of which would apply to all adaptations. The criteria include that the adaptation 1) performs its intended functions, 2) is integrated into the instructional sequence, 3) is accompanied by sufficient instruction to learn the adaptation, 4) facilitates independence, 5) results in the least intrusive assistance, 6) is attractive and safe, 7) "fits" in the specific context, 8) results in acceptable rate and quality of performance, and 9) does not interfere with interactions.

MARGITA'S PARTICIPATION IN FIFTH GRADE

A relatively new context for use of adaptations by students with multiple disabilities is in general education classrooms. For Margita, a 10-year-old girl who has spent many of her school years in self-contained classrooms for students with severe disabilities, participation and contribution in her fifth-grade classroom has become a reality. Her labels of cerebral palsy, nonambulatory, and severe developmental disabilities have not stood in the way of her full-time membership in Mr. Peterson's fifth-grade class at Graniteville Elementary School in Graniteville, Minnesota. Giving classmates their weekly spelling test, alerting fellow students when it is time for lunch, running a slide projector, and communicating the refrain of a poem during reading time are all part of Margita's life in general education. All of her school work and goals are written for implementation in the general classroom, just like those of her peers.

Adaptive devices, specifically simple technologies, have been an integral part of Margita becoming "just one of the kids." Another facilitator of her participation in a general education classroom has, of course, been the people around her—supportive school personnel and classmates who view her as a full-fledged participating member of the class. Following are some examples of how simple technology, people, and Margita herself have joined together to create meaningful participation in fifth grade.

During language arts, Margita's partner records the weekly spelling words on an audiotape. This occurs sometime early in the week before the Friday test date. On Friday, the audiotape recorder is connected to Margita's PowerLink 2 Control Unit and Big Red Switch (Figures 4.4a and 4.4b). Using her hand to touch her switch, the tape recorder is activated and the spelling test is underway. During the spelling test, Margita's PowerLink is set in a timed mode of control for about 8 seconds. That means that each time Margita activates her switch, the audiotape recorder turns off for 8 seconds, long enough for the student who recorded the test to say the spelling word, use it in a sentence, and repeat the word one more time. At the end of the 8 seconds, the control unit automatically

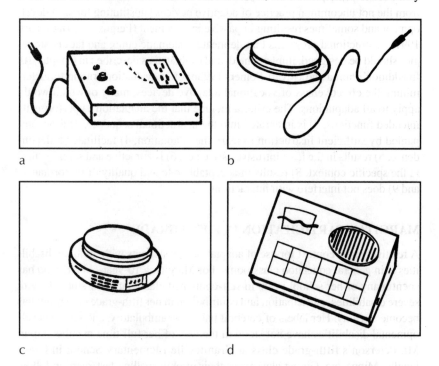

a   b

c   d

Figure 4.4. Examples of AbleNet's adapted devices used by Margita in fifth-grade general education classes. (a) PowerLink 2 Control Unit, (b) Big Red Switch, (c) BIGmack Single Message Communication Aid, and (d) SpeakEasy Voice Output Communication Aid. (Reproduced by permission of AbleNet.)

turns off the audiotape recorder until Margita activates her switch again to "tell" her fellow classmates the next word.

Mr. Peterson reports that he and the students appreciate Margita's lead in this classroom activity. Margita has a different but valued role in the test-taking activity. This reinforces an overall theme of different but equally important roles and contributions by members of a classroom community. Students also are attentive to Margita's pronouncements and provide positive reinforcement for her efforts. A specific advantage for the teacher is the flexibility afforded to walk around the room and carefully monitor student behavior. Rarely are teachers freed from direct instruction responsibilities to check in with individual students. Margita, in essence, joins Mr. Peterson as a partner in a teaching team.

Margita's participation is evidenced in other classes as well. During physical education, her classmates have affectionately labeled the workout she facilitates as "Sweatin' with Margita." Margita uses her microswitch to activate the audiotape player so that music plays while her classmates do their warm-up exercises. When the teacher announces the name of an exercise, such as "Jumping Jacks," Margita turns on the background music. Because exercising continues until the music stops, classmates always prod her to let them rest, especially when their least favorite exercises are announced.

Throughout the gym, classmates will shout out a variety of verbal prompts for Margita to lift her hand and therefore stop the music. These range from subtle suggestions like, "Margita, feel free to stop any time," to very direct pleas, "Margita, take your hand off the switch, now!" Like any child who thrives on the bonds of friendship, Margita laughs and typically responds quickly to her peers' cries for a break. At the end of "Sweatin' with Margita," Margita's classmates will spontaneously line up and file by her wheelchair to give "high fives" for a job well done.

Literacy activities also bring Margita and her peers together. During reading time, Margita uses AbleNet's BIGmack Single Message Communication Aid (Figure 4.4c) to repeat a word or phrase from a book she and her classmates read together. With Margita appropriately supported in a beanbag chair and her classmates seated on either side of her, Margita shares her part of a story or poem that was recorded by her friends into her BIGmack. It took only 2 minutes to teach Margita's classmates to program her BIGmack. They can quickly program and reprogram the communication device with each new phrase or word for each new story. Also during reading time, Margita uses a switch to activate an audiotape player to play stories to her peers during reading time. A classmate assists her by holding up the book and turning the pages when appropriate.

There are many opportunities throughout the school day for Margita to use her SpeakEasy Voice Output Communication Aid (Figure 4.4d). With the touch of an appropriate switch, Margita can inform her friends of specific choices and needs. For example, during morning break, she indicates whether she wants white or chocolate milk. She is also learning the sequence of the daily activities at school and can announce what is happening next during the day (e.g., "It's time to go to music class") by selecting one of the items programmed into her SpeakEasy.

Last year as a fourth grader, Margita helped her teacher in having the students pay closer attention to their lessons and respond to questions. She accomplished this using the slide projector control and a slide carousel that contained two slides of each student, one serious and one silly pose. Each time the teacher asked a question in class, Margita would activate her switch connected to the slide projector control. With each switch activation, Margita advanced the carousel one slide to picture the student who now had to answer the question. The teacher found that students listened better because they never knew when they would be called upon to answer a question. Anticipating whether a serious or silly photograph would appear on screen also kept the students involved and attentive, as well as entertained.

"Margita is a very accepted member of the classroom," said Mr. Peterson who, like other educators in the school, understands the importance of opportunities for students like Margita to be active participants in everyday activities alongside same-age peers. Mr. Peterson believes that Margita's peers have benefited as well, learning both the value of differences and the remarkable similarities regardless of apparent differences as a result of shared experiences and friendship.

The students do almost everything together and Margita's classmates take note when she is absent, inquiring as to why she is absent and when she will return. One of Margita's friends, Derrick, says "She is fun to have around." In particular, he enjoys the humor she introduces in the classroom. "One time Mr. Peterson was discussing something really boring and Margita knew it," he said. "She started talking [with her communication aid] and making noise. It was pretty fun." Another friend, Karen, says she loves talking to Margita because "she never tells my secrets." The two are often seen together, Karen speaking close to Margita's ear, confident that she will not be judged because she is communicating with her trusted friend, Margita.

Margita's experiences in fifth grade illustrate key elements of the individualized adaptation process presented previously in this chapter. Careful consideration of the individual, the specific context in which she functions (i.e., fifth grade), knowledge of adaptations, and creativity resulted in enhanced participation and valued membership in an inclusive school community.

EXAMPLES OF DOMESTIC, RECREATION/LEISURE, AND VOCATIONAL ADAPTATIONS

This section of the chapter provides examples of adaptations, specifically low-tech adaptive devices. The devices were developed by public school personnel in educational programs serving students with severe disabilities in Urbana, Illinois; Madison, Wisconsin; and Mansfield, Connecticut. Most were designed for use by specific students. The examples are simple and are intended to illustrate that, with a bit of creativity and not much expense, participation of students with disabilities can be enhanced. Appropriate use of these adaptations, however, requires individual consideration of student needs and environmental demands. Most of the adaptive devices were developed to compensate for motor and intellectual difficulties. The examples are categorized as domestic, recreation/ leisure, and vocational adaptive devices, but they could be used in a variety of school, home, and community environments.

Domestic Adaptive Devices

Pouring Device   The pouring device shown in Figure 4.5 was constructed with Plexiglas, a plastic pitcher, a wire hanger for the handle, and a metal band. It was made for a high school student to use during meal preparation. The student was able to flex and extend his left elbow slightly, approximately 30°. The pouring adaptation was placed on his wheelchair tray so that the extended handle of the pitcher hooked around his forearm. After a peer placed a glass on the plastic base of the adaptation, the student bent his arm, thereby pushing up on the handle, tipping the pitcher, and causing liquid to pour into the glass. He learned to judge when the glass was full and then relaxed his arm to right the pitcher.

Plate and Glass Holder   The plate and glass holder shown in Figure 4.6 was made from wood and is covered with nonslip material. It was made for a high school student to enable independent eating. The student demonstrated large, sweeping arm movement but had difficulty coordinating hand-to-mouth movement and bilateral hand use. The square surface of the adaptation was covered with a nonslip mat, and the student learned to scoop his food independently and bring it to his mouth. The student's glass was placed in the cutout hole. The

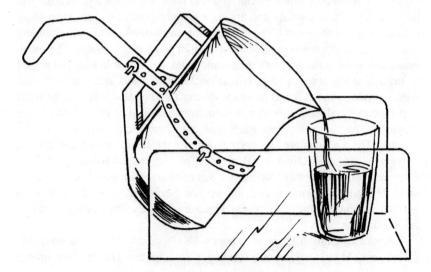

Figure 4.5.   Pouring adaptation. (Developed by Nancy Caldwell.)

Figure 4.6.   Plate and glass holder. (Developed by Nancy Caldwell.)

straw extended far enough that the student could lean his head and trunk forward, then close his mouth around the straw to drink. Previous attempts to teach bringing the glass to his mouth with his hand were unsuccessful and frustrating. The adaptation compensated for inadequate upper extremity and head coordination. Independence increased dramatically.

Spoon Splint and Plate Wedge Adaptations   The spoon splint and plate wedge shown in Figure 4.7 were used by a 4-year-old boy who demonstrated only fair control of full elbow flexion and near full extension. Range of motion at his shoulders, elbows, wrists, and fingers was limited because of slight webbing (i.e., tight skin at the joints). The spoon splint was formed with plastic splinting material, and a spoon was molded into the splint under the palm area. The spoon protruded between the student's thumb and index finger. It was bent and angled to maximize the amount of food that could be scooped independently and remain on the spoon as it was moved to the mouth. The splint was secured at the upper forearm and wrist with narrow foam straps attached to Velcro fasteners on the splint. The plate wedge was made from cardboard and covered with nonslip material. The wedge angle was steep enough for the student to use vertical arm movement almost exclusively. Horizontal movement toward the body was extremely difficult for this student and was minimized by use of these adaptations. The student learned to combine vertical forearm movement and forward head movement to achieve success and greater efficiency with placing food into his mouth.

Sandwich Clip   Illustrated in Figure 4.8 is a sandwich clip that was made for a 4-year-old girl who had only one finger on each hand. The child was unable

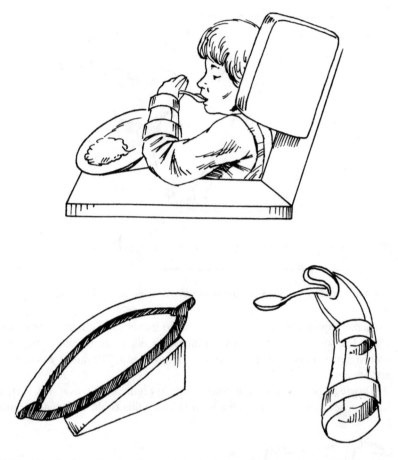

Figure 4.7.   Spoon splint and plate wedge adaptations. (Developed by Jennifer York-Barr.)

to hold a sandwich, cookie, or other finger foods in her hand. Commercial sandwich clips proved unsatisfactory. Devising an alternative involved securing a large tension binder clip to a wooden platform. A butterfly barrette (hair clip) was held in the jaws of the binder clip and functioned as the sandwich clip or holder for other food. The sandwich clip was made removable for washing. An adult continued to provide assistance by placing the food item in the clip, but the child could eat the food independently by leaning forward to take a bite.

Extended-Handle Duster Mounted to Wheelchair   The extended-handle duster shown in Figure 4.9 was mounted on the abductor of the wheelchair of a high school student. To extend the handle, a dowel rod was secured to the handle of an ordinary duster. (The student who used this duster also used the pouring adaptation described previously.) After positioning the student in the wheelchair and in front of a hard, flat surface (e.g., table, counter, shelf) in need of dusting,

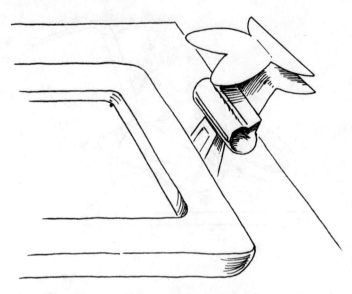

Figure 4.8.   Sandwich clip. (Developed by Barbara Williams and Debra Kohrs.)

the teacher adjusted the angle of the duster so it exerted slight pressure on the surface. The student then alternated pushing each side of the handle, causing the duster to move laterally over the surface to remove dust. The duster was used in home environments.

Dusting Mitt   The dusting mitt shown in Figure 4.10 was a very simple adaptation sewn of soft cloth with a Velcro closure that could be fastened across

Figure 4.9.   Extended-handle duster mounted to wheelchair. (Developed by Nancy Cald-well.)

Figure 4.10. Dusting mitt. (Developed by Nancy Caldwell.)

the palm or wrist. The dusting mitt was used by several high school students who had difficulty simultaneously holding on to a dust cloth and moving their arms in a dusting motion. Prior to use of the mitt, common problems were scrunching the dust cloth into a ball in the hand, leaving insufficient cloth protruding to dust with, and excessive muscle tension throughout the arm as a result of maintaining a fisted hand.

Toothpaste and Toothbrush Holder Illustrated in Figure 4.11 is a toothpaste and toothbrush holder that was used by a high school student who had functional use of one arm only. The muscles in her other arm were contracted in a totally flexed position, and she could not use that arm to assist in daily activities. The holder rested on the side of a sink. On the board was a rubber band that crossed over and secured a tube of toothpaste and a toothbrush. With the toothpaste tube secured, the student unscrewed the cap and pushed on the tube until a small amount of toothpaste protruded. Next, she removed the toothbrush and brushed its bristles over the protruding toothpaste. After brushing her teeth, the student rinsed her toothbrush and replaced it under the rubber band; she then screwed the cap back onto the toothpaste tube. Using this adaptation required use of only one arm for the entire toothbrushing sequence.

Toothpaste Pump Adaptation The introduction of toothpaste pumps to the general public has unintentionally assisted people who have difficulty with fine movements of their hands. Figure 4.12 shows one such toothpaste pump that was screwed onto a piece of wood to prevent tipping. In addition, a thin piece of wood with a notch cut at one end was attached so that depressing the lever would

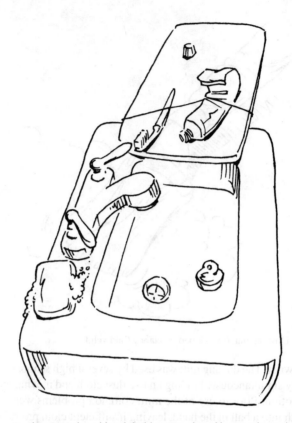

Figure 4.11.   Toothpaste and toothbrush holder. (Developed by Jennifer York-Barr.)

place pressure on the push knob, thereby dispensing toothpaste. This adaptation was used by people who demonstrated only gross arm movement.

Hinged Tray   The hinged tray is an adaptation attached to one armrest of a wheelchair (Figure 4.13). With the assistance of a local metalworking expert, a Plexiglas tray was mounted along one armrest using heavy piano hinges. The piano hinges allowed the tray to be lifted up from a horizontal position across the armrests and moved in a 270° arc to rest against the rim of one wheel. Prior to the development of this particular hinged tray, the only skill that prevented a high school student from total independence using restrooms was his inability to remove, then replace, this wheelchair tray. His tray was necessary for positioning purposes and because it held his communication board. Prolonged removal of the tray, therefore, was not a reasonable option. The student required only a few weeks of instruction on removing and replacing the hinged tray. Most of the instruction was directed at teaching controlled lowering of the tray to the side of the wheelchair, instead of the student releasing the tray from its highest point and watching it crash into the side of the wheelchair.

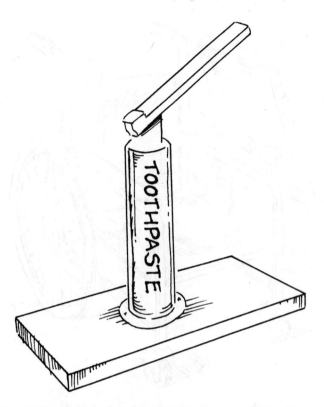

Figure 4.12.   Toothpaste pump adaptation. (Developed by Nancy Caldwell.)

Recreation/Leisure Adaptive Devices

Needlework Holder   The needlework holder illustrated in Figure 4.14 was made of wood. Its width was adjustable to accommodate varying canvas or mesh dimensions. The mounting angle for the needlework was adjustable also. It was constructed for a junior high school student who demonstrated some functional use of her left arm but whose fine motor skills and rate were poor. The right arm could be relaxed and the elbow and forearm positioned on the wheelchair tray or table, allowing the student to lean on the arm to increase support. The student learned to keep her trunk forward and to lean on her right forearm independently. This placed her body in an efficient and stable position in which she could use the needle with her left arm with reasonable control and efficiency. Initially, a mesh with large holes and rug yarn were used. Most of the resulting needlework projects were abstract and unique (i.e., wherever the student managed to place the needle through the mesh, the yarn was pulled through). When supervised closely, however, the student could place the needle more accurately in accordance with the colors on a mesh with a printed design.

Figure 4.13.   Hinged tray. (Developed by Jane Barry and Jennifer York-Barr.)

Magazine/Book Holder   The magazine/book holder illustrated in Figure 4.3 and briefly discussed previously was initially made for a 5-year-old girl who loved books. It was made of cardboard and ½-inch-wide elastic straps to hold the books. The girl enjoyed looking through books and listening to the stories read by her peers, parents, or a teacher. She demonstrated full range, but uncontrolled, rigid, sweeping movements of both arms. There was no functional arm use. To use the holder, she was positioned in her wheelchair with her head totally supported in a neck collar support and her wheelchair tray raised to give support to both arms. The magazine/book holder was made to hold books upright so that the student could see the material without looking down and losing control of her head position. She was taught to reach toward and push the right side of the book with her left hand. Then, she pushed against the book to achieve stability of her arm and turned pages by sliding her hand to the left, pulling a page along with this arm movement.

Card Holder   The card holder illustrated in Figure 4.15 was simply a 12-inch piece of 2 x 4 wood with a deep groove cut down the middle. With the same design but a wider groove, this adaptation was also used to hold needlework projects that were purchased with the frames already in place.

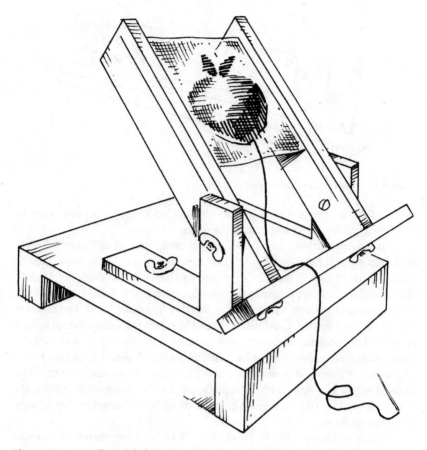

Figure 4.14. Needlework holder. (Developed by Jennifer York-Barr and Rod Ivey.)

Remote Control Car Adaptation The remote control car and its control unit illustrated in Figure 4.16 were adapted for use by a 4-year-old boy who was able to fully flex and partially extend his left elbow. (This is the same student who used the spoon splint and plate wedge adaptation described previously.) The control unit lever was simply extended with a ¼-inch dowel rod attached with plastic splinting material. The student was positioned in a kneeler that was made for his body dimensions. The control unit was placed on a low and narrow table in front of him. In this stable, upright kneeling position, the student demonstrated an adequate amount of controlled elbow flexion and extension to push the lever. A particularly nice feature of this control unit was that it could be locked into one of three operating modes. One mode allowed the car to go only straight (forward or backward). Another mode allowed the car to go around in circles only. The third mode freed the car to go in whatever direction the lever was pushed. The straight or circle modes enabled the child to play independently for a longer time because the area in which the car could run had definite bound-

Figure 4.15.   Card holder. (Developed by Rod Ivey.)

aries; in the free direction mode, it was not long before a peer needed to rescue the trapped car from a remote area of the room.

Pulley Adaptation   The pulley adaptation illustrated in Figure 4.17 was made of a wooden base, metal rod, plastic cup, rope, pulley, and cotton straps to attach the adaptation to the user's forearm and hand. It was made for a junior high school student who learned to isolate controlled elbow flexion, then to relax back to a natural position without her entire body becoming tense. The cuff was attached around her wrist and palm. When she flexed her elbow the string was pulled and the contents of the cup were dumped. Initially, the student used the pulley adaptation to throw dice. Over time, the student was able to use the pulley adaptation for many different skills. During cooking, the standard cup could be replaced with a measuring cup, so that after appropriate amounts of ingredients were measured into the cup, pulling on the string would dump the ingredients into a mixing bowl.

Grasping Mitten   Illustrated in Figure 4.18 is a grasping mitten that was made for a 4-year-old boy to use during a music class. Tracing the boy's hand produced a pattern for the mitten. A heavy-weight cotton fabric was used to construct the mitten, and a T-shaped strap was sewn into the tip of the mitten. The mitten was placed on the student's hand, in which there was an item to be held. The fingers, inside the mitten, were passively flexed around the item and then maintained in a whole hand grasp by the strap being secured around the wrist. This particular student demonstrated no active muscle control for grasping. Use of this adaptation allowed him to participate in a general kindergarten music class. He also used this adaptation to maintain a grasp on a joystick during initial training to operate a power wheelchair.

Microswitch Mounts for Sidelying and Sitting   A common difficulty with the use of microswitches is both mounting them securely and also in such a way that daily variability in a child's ability to control movement can be accommodated. Figure 4.19 shows two ways that microswitches were positioned to enable independent access to and control of a microswitch by two students. Figure 4.19a shows a 6-year-old boy who had very low underlying muscle tone and

Figure 4.16. Remote control car adaptation. (Developed by Jennifer York-Barr.)

whose only arm movement was uncontrolled, rigid crossed extension with hands fisted. In a sidelying position, however, the student learned to control elbow flexion and extension of his lower arm (i.e., the arm that was very stable because of bearing the weight through the shoulder girdle). The microswitch that was used by this student required only slight pressure to push. It was mounted on its edge so that the push panel was perpendicular to the surface of the sidelyer. Mounted in this way, the student had only to slide his arm along the surface of the sidelyer to push the switch; no lifting the arm against gravity was necessary. During free time, the student could choose a switch-operated toy he wished to operate by looking at the preferred item; he then proceeded to manipulate the toy through the switch as described above.

Figure 4.19b shows a microswitch that was mounted from the back of a chair made for a 4-year-old boy. Standard microphone equipment (i.e., gooseneck, counting flange, and microphone holders; all available at local radio equipment stores) was used. The microswitch was placed into the microphone holder

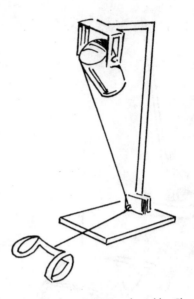

Figure 4.17. Pulley adaptation for dumping. (Developed by Cheryl Moran-Behrens and Rod Ivey.)

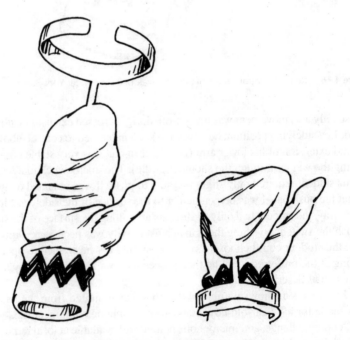

Figure 4.18. Grasping mitten. (Developed by Jennifer York-Barr.)

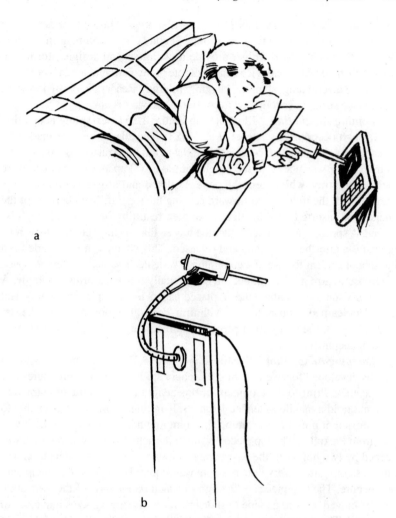

Figure 4.19.   Microswitch mounting for (a) sidelying and (b) sitting positions. (Developed by Jennifer York-Barr.)

and, because of the flexibility of the gooseneck, could be placed to the left or the right of the student's head. The student was placed in a supported sitting position with a neck collar supporting his head. He learned to drop his head slightly to the side to push the switch.

Vocational Adaptations

Since the last edition of this volume, two new resources have been published of particular relevance to use of adaptive devices for increasing participation of students with severe and multiple disabilities in integrated work environments.

First, Piuma and Udvari-Solner (1993b) articulate a detailed process for the development of vocational adaptations. Second, in a companion manual (1993a), Piuma and Udari-Solner provide illustrations and design information for more than 40 adaptive devices that promote participation in a variety of work functions (e.g., collating, stapling, bagging, folding). Readers interested in work inclusion are strongly encouraged to consult these two resources.

Stapling Adaptation   Illustrated in Figure 4.20 is a stapling adaptation that was first described by Nisbet et al. (1983). The adaptation was made of a moveable tray that held letter-size paper and was mounted on a wooden base. An electric stapler was placed at the far end of the tray. Papers to be stapled were placed in the tray, which kept the pages collated and aligned appropriately. When pushed, the tray moved forward causing the top, left-hand corners of the papers to be inserted into the electric stapler, resulting in a staple being discharged. A spring was mounted under the tray so that the tray returned to its resting position after being pushed and released. This adaptation was made for a high school student for use at a community worksite. The student demonstrated no purposeful arm movement but did occasionally move her arms randomly. A teacher, assistant, or another student placed papers to be stapled in the tray, and the student learned to push the tray with firm, controlled movement. As the staple discharged, the adaptation provided immediate feedback to the student regarding the movement.

Stamping Adaptation   Illustrated in Figure 4.21 is a stamping adaptation that was developed for use by a middle school student to stamp brochures at a travel agency. Prior to development of this adaptation, the student learned to reach and hold a handle extended from a self-inking stamp but was unable to apply sufficient pressure to stamp. The stamping adaptation shown here was made from Plexiglas. The top piece, to which the actual stamp was secured, was attached by two hinges to the base. The resting position for the adaptation was with the stamp raised. Very little pressure was required to depress the stamp onto the brochure. The two pieces of Plexiglas located on the base of the adaptation could be moved to form a guide to slide brochures of varying sizes into place to be stamped. The stamp position was adjustable also.

Collating Adaptation   The collating adaptation illustrated in Figure 4.22 employed the use of two microswitches. It was made from Plexiglas, two lever microswitches, a metal track, and a control unit. The top part consisted of one

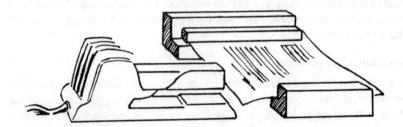

Figure 4.20.   Stapling adaptation. (Developed by Alice Udvari-Solner.)

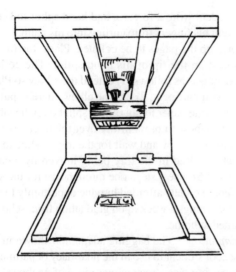

Figure 4.21.   Stamping adaptation. (Developed by Kathy Zanella Albright.)

tray divided into two compartments. The left compartment held the first page to be collated; the right compartment contained the second page. The top tray was mounted onto the base in two horizontal tracks. The tray could slide laterally in these tracks. One lever microswitch was placed under each compartment of the top tray and each was wired to the control unit located behind the device.

The collating adaptation was designed by a vocational teacher who was responsible for developing a community worksite for a 21-year-old student with severe intellectual and physical disabilities. The student had to remain lying on his back in a reclined wheelchair for health reasons. His one reliable movement (besides that of opening and closing his mouth) was extension and flexion of his

Figure 4.22.   Collating adaptation. (Developed by Alice Udvari-Solner.)

right elbow. The student wore a forearm and hand splint to keep his wrist near neutral and to prevent his fingers from curling into his palm.

In order to pick up the pages to be collated, Plasti-Tac (a sticky, putty-type material) was placed on the tip of his hand splint. The collating procedure learned by the student was as follows: 1) extend the elbow so Plasti-Tac lands on the paper in the left compartment; 2) flex the elbow, thereby pulling the top page off the pile; 3) wait for the paper to fall off the splint onto the table in front of the device; 4) extend the elbow to press firmly over the microswitch under the left compartment; 5) flex the elbow and wait for the tray to slide to the left (pushing of the microswitch resulted in the tray being moved by a chain through the horizontal tracks); and 6) repeat steps one through five for the second page. The ability of this student to collate afforded him the opportunity to work in the community for several mornings a week upon graduation from school. Otherwise, he would have remained at home.

Bagging Adaptation The bagging adaptation shown in Figure 4.23 was made for a high school student to use in the pharmacy department of a local hospital. The bottom section was a rectangular piece of pegboard with solid wood sides. Mounted on the pegboard were three sets of vertical metal rods with alligator clips welded at the top of each (only one pair of rods is illustrated in the figure). A plastic bag was clipped open between each pair of rods. A funnel

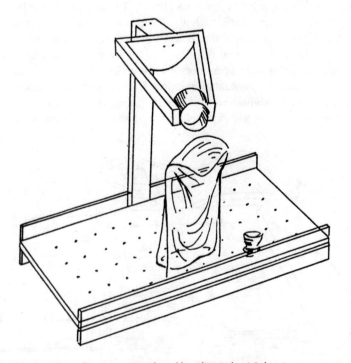

Figure 4.23.   Bagging adaptation. (Developed by Alice Udvari-Solner.)

attachment extended vertically from the end of the top section as illustrated. An open bag was aligned under the funnel in a position to receive items that fell through the funnel. Metal drawer glides were mounted in the base to allow the pegboard section to slide laterally. The black handle was used to move the pegboard laterally to position the bags under the funnel.

The student who learned the bagging activity demonstrated gross arm movements and unrefined grasp and release. A variety of items were bagged (e.g., sodium chloride packets, plastic syringes). Each was bagged in groups of 30. (Another student with disabilities arranged the item in groups of 10 by placing one item in each compartment of a cardboard adaptation that had 10 divisions. Once this cardboard container was filled, all of the items were removed and placed in one box. The student filled three of these boxes, making 30 items that were then bagged by the student using the bagging adaptation.) The student using the bagging adaptation grabbed a handful of items from the first box of 10 and placed them in the funnel. The items then fell into the opened bag. This continued until all three boxes of 10 items were bagged. The student then pulled on the black handle until the next open bag was moved into place under the funnel. The bagging procedure continued until all three bags were full. The teacher then removed and sealed the bags and placed three more empty bags in the clips for filling.

Coffee-Bagging Adaptation   The coffee-bagging adaptation shown in Figure 4.24 is a funnel made of flexible sheet metal to which a hook was attached to the back and a clip attached to the bottom. The funnel was hooked onto the coffee bin as illustrated. A plastic bag was clipped open under the funnel. This adaptation was used by a junior high school student at a local bakery and health food store. She was not able to hold open the plastic bag and simultaneously scoop coffee, so the adaptation was made to require scooping only. The student stood in front of the coffee bin and scooped coffee beans into the funnel. She learned to stop scooping when the funnel began backing up. This indicated that the bag was full, at which point she was assisted in removing and closing the bag.

Plant-Watering Adaptation   The plant-watering adaptation illustrated in Figure 4.25 was made of wood, various pieces of hardware, a plastic watering can, and cord. The base of the adaptation extended the width of a wheelchair to clamp to the armrests. The same clamps used to secure trays to armrests were used here. A small triangular platform was added to the right side of the base to provide a place for the student using the device to stabilize her right elbow. A piece of wood extended vertically from the base and another piece extended horizontally from the top of this piece, forming an inverted "L" off the base. To this extension, the watering can was attached in such a way that it was allowed to swing. A cord was attached to the front part of the watering can. On the other end of the rope was a 2-inch-wide cuff that was secured with Velcro fasteners around the wrist of the student using the device.

A student in junior high school used the device to water plants at the public library two afternoons each week. The student sat in the wheelchair with her

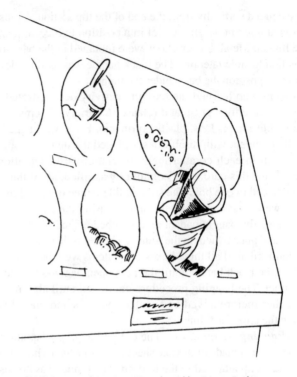

Figure 4.24.   Coffee-bagging adaptation. (Developed by Renee Reif.)

right elbow supported on the triangle base and the cuff secured on her wrist. She was pushed through the library and learned to turn her head to identify the plants that she was responsible for watering. Once the plants were identified, the student's instructor would place the plant under the watering can. The student then pulled back on the rope by flexing her right elbow. This caused the can to tip and water to be poured onto the plant.

After the suggestions from the student's mother, use of a water meter to determine whether plants, in fact, needed to be watered was initiated. Although this student had never learned colors or numbers previously, she learned through this job that when the meter needle was on black, she pulled back the rope and held momentarily. This resulted in a large amount of water being poured. When the meter needle was on red, she pulled back then relaxed immediately, resulting in a small amount of water being poured. When the meter needle was on green, she did not water the plant. These were discriminations previously thought too difficult for the student to learn.

CONSIDERATIONS FOR USING ADAPTATIONS

There are numerous factors that team members should consider carefully before determining which adaptations should actually be used by individual

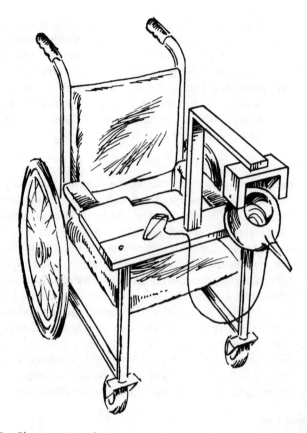

Figure 4.25.   Plant-watering adaptation. (Developed by Jennifer York-Barr and Rod Ivey.)

students (Baumgart et al., 1982; Nisbet et al., 1983; York, Nietupski, & Hamre-Nietupski, 1985).

Active Participation

First, use of an adaptation should increase active participation in an activity. This is important for many reasons. Active participation can increase responsibility, foster development of age-appropriate attitudes, and increase self-esteem. Increased active participation also can change the perceptions of students with disabilities that are held by people without disabilities. For example, active participation of students with disabilities in general education classroom routines and activities fosters the perception of the students as doing the best they can do and making a contribution. Using an adaptation to achieve active participation without assistance from an adult can increase the opportunity for interaction with classmates. Adults assigned to support students in general education classrooms sometimes inhibit interactions between the student and classmates or even the classroom teacher (York, Vandercook, Heise-Neff, & Caughey, 1990).

Postschool functioning in inclusive community environments may occur more frequently if students learn partial participation and positive interdependence during their school years. If the goal of community inclusion for all people with disabilities is to be achieved, the responsibility cannot rest solely on paid human services support personnel. During the school years, therefore, educational teams must systematically plan for more interdependent participation of students with disabilities with peers who do not have identified disabilities. Use of adaptations can be a tool for promoting interdependence.

Preference

A second consideration when contemplating use of an adaptation is preference. Would use of an adaptation allow a student to engage in an activity that he or she enjoys or finds interesting? Would use of an adaptation increase participation in activities that are preferred, enjoyed, or highly valued by family members and peers? Research suggests that some students have distinct opinions regarding use of classroom and instructional adaptations (Vaughn, Schumm, Niarhos, & Daugherty, 1993). Student willingness or preference for accommodations would certainly increase the likelihood of successful implementation. Every effort should be made to facilitate participation in preferred, age-appropriate, and family activities. Students who have opportunities to indicate and engage in preferred activities sometimes enter into the learning process with greater enthusiasm. For example, for one student who was taught to choose preferred audiotapes and to activate the tapes with a microswitch, sharing this preferred musical activity with classmates was the highlight of her school day.

Longitudinal Use

A third consideration is the anticipated longitudinal use of an adaptation. Will it be used in future as well as in current environments? Will the adaptation remain age appropriate? For example, using the magazine/book holder described previously in this chapter could remain appropriate throughout life if reading or browsing materials were changed in accordance with changing interests and age. However, an adaptation designed to assist a 2-year-old child in stacking blocks would not remain age appropriate.

Instructional Time

A fourth consideration concerns the amount of instructional time required for teaching the student to use the adaptation compared to the amount of time that might be required to teach participation *without* the use of an adaptation. Sometimes team members resort to the use of an adaptation before carefully considering or systematically implementing unadapted participation options. If, within a reasonable period of time, a student could learn to engage in an activity without using an adaptation, then the student should be taught to engage in the activity directly, and no adaptation should be used. Failure in direct approaches, however, would indicate the need to consider use of adaptations.

Design and Construction

Fifth, design and construction characteristics are another consideration. Some adaptation ideas require more technical expertise than the team has. Is the design of an adaptation so complex or are the construction requirements so time consuming that months will pass before the adaptation is developed? Will frequent repairs be likely? Complex adaptations have a greater likelihood of breakdown. Broken equipment can delay teaching students the skills that will enhance participation in home, school, and community environments.

Related to design and construction concerns *who* will develop the adaptations. Given the movement toward inclusion of students in general education classrooms, it is relevant to note that generally speaking, classroom teachers (i.e., general educators) do not assume responsibility for creating most individualized adaptations required to accommodate students with unique learning needs (Schumm & Vaughn, 1991). Practically speaking, therefore, the responsibility for creating the adaptations is likely to be that of special educators, related services personnel, family members, and others who comprise an instructional support team.

Physical Movement Demands

A sixth consideration must be the physical movement demands required to use an adaptation. Some physical movements (e.g., excessive, rigid extension of the arm), if used to activate adaptions, can ultimately result in more restricted movement and loss of function. However, if using an adaptation promotes more efficient movement patterns, the likelihood of developing contractures and deformities is reduced, and long-term functional maintenance is increased. Use of an adaptation sometimes can reduce the physical demands of an activity and enable the individual to move with greater ease and efficiency.

Given the characteristics and abilities of each individual student and the range of instructional priorities, the influence of each of the above-discussed considerations in the adaptation decision-making process will vary. Discussions regarding appropriate use of adaptations require active participation from parents, teachers, therapists, classmates, and others to ensure careful consideration of many factors. Appropriate decisions result from the expertise of all educational team members.

PRECAUTIONS FOR USING ADAPTATIONS

Precautions for the use of adaptations have been suggested by several authors (Baumgart et al., 1982; Davis, 1981; Ferguson & Baumgart, 1991; York et al., 1985) and are summarized here. First, perhaps the most common misuse of adaptations results from their mere existence. That is, because a particular adaptation exists or because it was successful and appropriate for one student, team members overgeneralize its use to other students for whom use is inappropriate. For example, the introduction of microswitches as valuable instructional tools has resulted in the overuse of microswitches to activate, for example, audiotape players. Many children can learn to operate audiotape players using a finger, toe, or pencil to depress the buttons, or pushing a tongue depressor that is extended from the buttons (York et al., 1985). Microswitches are unnecessary and, therefore, inappropriate in such cases. Furthermore, when microswitches are necessary, team members should consider that not all children need or can use the same type. There are many different microswitches, each requiring a different type of movement for activation. Also, not all children enjoy music or the same music as their peers, or listening to the same songs throughout a week of instruction. During leisure time, some children may prefer listening to a talking book, watching battery-powered games and toys, or operating a slide projector to view slides of the family vacation. The use of any adaptation must be considered individually, based on the abilities of the student, preferences for activities, and specific demands of the activity.

A second precaution concerns the critical need for systematic instruction when using adaptations. As mentioned previously, implementation of adaptive devices for some students has resulted in no direct instruction and passive participation (Ferguson & Baumgart, 1991). Individualized adaptations do not replace the need for instruction. Just as placing a student in a sidelyer is not instruction, neither is providing a student with an adaptive device. One student for whom use of the magazine/book holder adaptation was appropriate required months of instruction using a mouthstick to become efficient at turning pages. Similarly, Maloney and Kurtz (1982) and Walmsey, Crichton, and Droog (1981) reported that proficiency in activating a microswitch to play music using efficient movement patterns required ongoing instruction. Adaptations are one means by which performance is enhanced and dependence is decreased. However, most students will require direct instruction to learn appropriate use of an adaptation.

A third precaution is to engage in ongoing evaluation of student performance with and without an adaptation. This will help ensure that appropriate decisions regarding the long-term use of an adaptation are made. Adaptations may be required for only short periods of time until student abilities improve. For example, if a student's arm and hand movement improves so that direct activation (i.e., without use of a microswitch) of an audiotape player is possible, the microswitch should be removed. Similarly, if a student learns to turn magazine pages independently, demonstrating controlled arm movement, the magazine/book holder adaptation should be removed. Adaptations must be modified, replaced, or eliminated based on changes in student abilities and/or task requirements.

A final precaution aimed at reducing frustration for team members and students is to expect that adaptations will require several modifications before an efficient match of student abilities and task demands is attained. Very rarely does the initial adaptation prove most functional. An example is the plant-watering adaptation illustrated in Figure 4.25, which underwent more than 10 modifications over at least a 6-month period of time before optimal efficiency was attained.

ADAPTATION RESOURCES

Local Community Resources

Numerous local community resources can be invaluable in the design and construction of adaptive devices. Most average-size towns have professionals with expertise in the use of plastic, metal, wood, electronics, and upholstery. Frequently, these individuals can construct adaptive devices at a fraction of commercial cost and much more efficiently than educational team members. A situation involving one of the authors illustrates this point well. A 20-year-old man required a wheelchair tray hinged to one armrest that he could remove by lifting up the tray from one side, then lowering it alongside the wheelchair. (This hinged tray, illustrated in Figure 4.13, is discussed briefly previously in this chapter.) Commercially available hinge-mounting equipment was expensive and not durable enough to withstand the repeated tray removal and twisting that occurred when the student was upset. This harsh use of the tray resulted in the metal being bent and the joint weakened. After many months of attempts at modification by several team members, a local metal-working company was contacted. The problem was described and the existing equipment was shown to one of the metal experts, who recommended that heavyweight metal piano hinges that extended the entire length of the tray be used. The expert reconstructed and mounted the hinge joint, which resulted in a more durable and functional tray. The process took about 2 hours, and a nominal fee was charged. In the process of working with this metal expert, school staff learned that he had been involved previously with modifying wheelchairs. He designed and constructed fenders to prevent mud, rain, or snow from spraying onto the clothes of people using the wheelchairs. He was a creative individual, quite willing and interested in providing expertise and, of course, developing a new clientele.

The time involved in the construction of devices can be minimized greatly if appropriate expertise and tools are available. In many situations it is more time and cost efficient to contract with local experts instead of purchasing all of the necessary equipment required for construction and spending countless hours learning to use it proficiently.

A material that is very useful in adaptation development, particularly for constructing initial models, is Tri-wall cardboard. Tri-wall is a very sturdy material made of three layers of cardboard. It can be purchased in large sheets, approximately 3×4 feet. It is much less expensive than wood, and working with it requires only basic design knowledge and the skills of using an Exacto knife, a saw, and glue. Tri-wall can be obtained through the central supply stores in many school districts. Workshops in the design and construction of devices and equipment using Tri-wall cardboard are available. In addition, several written resources are available on this subject (see Bergen & Colangelo, 1982).

One more resource possibility available in some communities is school district and university students or staff. Occasionally, students from industrial arts, architecture, and other design curricula can be recruited to assist with adaptive devices to fulfill one of their design project requirements. In addition, some universities, clinics, or businesses devote a percentage of time to providing various services to the community at large. For example, one university-based center was developed primarily to provide service and support to university students with physical or sensory disabilities. This center was expected to allocate 10% of its time for community service as well. People working at this center provided repair and maintenance service of wheelchairs for some school-age students and also allowed school personnel to borrow various equipment to use on a trial basis.

Educational service providers are encouraged to develop cooperative working relationships with local community resource personnel. The time expended doing so will yield benefits for students and staff. These interactions also provide an opportunity to educate community members about school programs.

Written Resources

In addition to local human resources, numerous written resources are available that provide useful information regarding adaptations. Davis (1981), Finnie (1975), and Robinault (1973) are sources for ideas on relatively simple adaptations for daily living, house-care, and leisure activities. They also include lists of local and national resources. Campbell (1977, 1982) provides specific teaching and adaptation strategies for mealtime and dressing activities; she also includes a list of local and national resources. Clothing adaptations to make dressing easier for people with limited postural and movement abilities are described by Bowar (1978) and Hoffman (1979). Bigge (1991) presents communication, self-care, house-care, and recreation/leisure strategies and adaptations useful for people whose primary disabilities are motor in nature. Vocational adaptations are described and illustrated in Nisbet et al. (1983). Kangas (1988) developed an excellent bibliography of seating, positioning, mounting, and physical access resources. Additional resources for obtaining positioning and communication adaptations are presented in this book (Chapters 3 and 7, respectively). Also, the reference list for each chapter contains resources.

In the area of electronic devices, Webster, Cook, Tompkins, and Vanderheiden (1985) provide an overview of current technology available to assist people with motor, visual, and hearing difficulties. Adaptations to assist with mobility, conversation, writing, manipulation, and work are covered particularly well. Specifically related to the use of microswitches, Burkhart (1980, 1982) and Campbell, McInerney, and Middleton (1982) provide information about construction and related hardware. They also present guidelines for using the equipment in instructional situations. York et al. (1985) present a step-by-step decision-making process for use of microswitches as an adjunct to educational programming for students with multiple disabilities.

One more resource for adaptations is equipment companies and manufacturers. One can obtain catalogs that illustrate a variety of products by writing to each company or manufacturer. People interested are warned that in order to obtain products it may be necessary to order through a local medical supplier, because some companies do not accept orders directly from individual consumers or will not provide small orders. Although many useful ideas can be gleaned from these resources, more economical, individualized versions often can meet the particular needs of an individual student in a specific situation.

CONCLUSION

The use of individualized adaptations provides a creative and useful tool in educational programming for students with multiple disabilities. Adaptations present a means for increasing the interdependence and ease with which students engage in age-appropriate and functional activities in general school, domestic, community, vocational, and recreation/leisure environments. Central to an adaptive instructional approach is an affirmative, problem-solving, and nonexclusionary orientation to educational service provision for all students. Team members are encouraged to adopt enthusiastically the philosophy inherent in the principle of partial participation and to be optimistic about the possibilities afforded to students through use of individualized adaptations. Appropriate use of adaptations can allow all children, regardless of their disabilities, to participate and be fully included in typical family, school, and community life. The degree of participation is limited only by the bounds of the collective creativity of members of the educational team.

REFERENCES

Baumgart, D., Brown, L., Pumpian, I., Nisbet, J., Ford, A., Sweet, M., Messina, R., & Schroeder, J. (1982). Principle of partial participation and individualized adaptations in educational programs for severely handicapped students. *Journal of The Association for the Severely Handicapped, 7*(2), 17–27.

Bergen, A., & Colangelo, C. (1982). *Positioning the client with central nervous system deficits.* Valhalla, NY: Valhalla Rehabilitation Publications.

Bigge, J.L. (1991). *Teaching individuals with physical and multiple disabilities* (3rd ed.). Columbus, OH: Charles E. Merrill.

Bowar, M.T. (1978). *Clothing for the handicapped: Fashion adaptations for adults and children.* Minneapolis, MN: Sister Kenny Institute.

Brown, L., Branston-McLean, M., Baumgart, D., Vincent, L., Falvey, M., & Schroeder, J. (1979). Utilizing the characteristics of current and subsequent least restrictive environments as factors in the development of curricular content for severely handicapped students. *AAESPH Review, 4*(4), 407–424.

Brown, L., Falvey, M., Vincent, L., Kaye, N., Johnson, F., Ferrara-Parrish, P., & Gruenewald, L. (1980). Strategies for generating comprehensive, longitudinal, and chronological age appropriate individualized education programs for adolescent and young adult severely handicapped students. *Journal of Special Education,14*(2), 199–215.

Brown, L., Shiraga, B., York, J., Zanella, K., & Rogan, P. (1984a). Ecological inventory strategies for students with severe handicaps. In L. Brown, M. Sweet, B. Shiraga, J. York, K. Zanella, P. Rogan, & R. Loomis (Eds.), *Educational programs for students with severe handicaps* (Vol. XIV, pp. 33–41). Madison, WI: Madison Metropolitan School District.

Brown, L., Shiraga, B., York, J., Zanella, K., & Rogan, P. (1984b). The discrepancy analysis technique in programs for students with severe handicaps. In L. Brown, M. Sweet, B. Shiraga, J. York, K. Zanella, P. Rogan, & R. Loomis (Eds.), *Educational programs for students with severe handicaps* (Vol. XIV, pp. 43–47). Madison, WI: Madison Metropolitan School District.

Burkhart, L. (1980). *Homemade battery powered toys and educational devices for severely handicapped children.* Millville, PA: Author.

Burkhart, L. (1982). *More homemade battery devices for severely handicapped children with suggested activities.* Millville, PA: Author.

Campbell, P. (1977). Daily living skills. In N. Haring (Ed.), *Developing effective individualized education programs for severely handicapped children and youth* (pp. 115–138). Washington, DC: Department of Health, Education and Welfare.

Campbell, P. (1982). *Problem oriented approaches to feeding the handicapped child* (2nd ed.). Akron, OH: Children's Hospital Medical Center of Akron.

Campbell, P., McInerny, W., & Middleton, M. (1982). *A manual of augmentative sensory feedback devices for training severely handicapped students.* Akron, OH: Children's Hospital Medical Center of Akron.

Davis, W.M. (1981). *Aids to make you able: Self help devices for the disabled.* New York: Beaufort Books.

Falvey, M.A. (Ed.). (1995). *Inclusive and heterogeneous schooling: Assessment, curriculum, and instruction.* Baltimore: Paul H. Brookes Publishing Co.

Ferguson, D.L., & Baumgart, D. (1991). Partial participation revisited. *Journal of The Association for Persons with Severe Handicaps, 16*(4), 218–227.

Finnie, N.R. (1975). *Handling the young cerebral palsied child at home.* New York: E.P. Dutton.

Hoffman, A.M. (1979). *Clothing for the handicapped, the aged and other people with special needs.* Springfield, IL: Charles C Thomas.

Kangas, K. (1988). *Bibliography: Seating, positioning, mounting and physical access.* Harrisburg: Pennsylvania Assistive Device Center.

Knight, D., & Wadsworth, D. (1993). Physically challenged student. *Childhood Education, 69*(4), 211–215.

Maloney, F.P., & Kurtz, P.A. (1982). The use of a mercury switch head control device in profoundly retarded, multiply handicapped children. *Physical and Occupational Therapy in Pediatrics, 2*(4), 11–17.

Nisbet, J., Sweet, M., Ford, A., Shiraga, B., Udvari, A., York, J., Messina, R., & Schroeder, J. (1983). Utilizing adaptive devices with severely handicapped students. In L. Brown, A. Ford, J. Nisbet, M. Sweet, B. Shiraga, J. York, R. Loomis, & P. Van-Deventer (Eds.), *Educational programs for severely handicapped students* (Vol. XIII, pp. 101–146). Madison, WI: Madison Metropolitan School District.

Nordic Committee on Disability. (1985). *The more we do together: Adapting the environment for children with disabilities.* New York: World Rehabilitation Fund.

Orelove, F.P., & Hanley, C.D. (1979). Modifying school buildings for the severely handicapped: A school accessibility survey. *AAESPH Review, 4*(3), 219–236.

Piuma, C., & Udvari-Solner, A. (1993a). *A catalog of vocational assistive devices for individuals with severe intellectual disabilities*. Madison: Madison Metropolitan School District and University of Wisconsin–Madison.

Piuma, C., & Udvari-Solner, A. (1993b). *Materials and processes for developing low cost vocational adaptations for individuals with severe disabilities*. Madison: Madison Metropolitan School District and University of Wisconsin–Madison.

Rainforth, B., York, J., & Macdonald, C. (1992). *Collaborative teams for students with severe disabilities: Integrating therapy and educational services*. Baltimore: Paul H. Brookes Publishing Co.

Robinault, I.P. (Ed.). (1973). *Functional aids for the multiply handicapped*. New York: United Cerebral Palsy Associations.

Schumm, J.S., & Vaughn, S. (1991). Making adaptations for mainstreamed students: General classroom teachers' perspectives. *Remedial and Special Education, 12*(4), 18–27.

Stainback, W., & Stainback, S. (Eds.). (1990). *Support networks for inclusive schooling: Interdependent integrated education*. Baltimore: Paul H. Brookes Publishing Co.

Thousand, J.S., Villa, R., & Nevin, A.I. (Eds.). (1994). *Creativity and collaborative learning: A practical guide to empowering students and teachers*. Baltimore: Paul H. Brookes Publishing Co.

Vaughn, S., Schumm, J.S., Niarhos, F.J., & Daugherty, T. (1993). What do students think when teachers make adaptations? *Teaching and Teacher Education, 9*(1), 107–118.

Walmsey, R.E., Crichton, L., & Droog, D. (1981). Music as feedback for teaching head control to severely handicapped children: A pilot study. *Developmental Medicine and Child Neurology, 23*, 739–746.

Webster, J.G., Cook, A.M., Tompkins, W.J., & Vanderheiden, G.C. (1985). *Electronic devices for rehabilitation*. New York: John Wiley & Sons.

York, J., Nietupski, J., & Hamre-Nietupski, S. (1985). A decision making process for using microswitches. *Journal of The Association for Persons with Severe Handicaps, 10*(4), 214–223.

York, J., Vandercook, T., Heise-Neff, C., & Caughey, E. (June, 1990). Does an "integration facilitator" facilitate integration? *TASH Newsletter*, p. 4.

5

Children with Special Health Care Needs

Dick Sobsey and Madhavan Thuppal

ALL CHILDREN CAN EXPERIENCE ILLNESS and injury. Sometimes they may require special care and treatment. Occasionally, their illness or injury can be life threatening. Children with multiple disabilities are typically more susceptible to illness, and many experience more injuries than children without disabilities. Illness and injury make many aspects of life generally more difficult. They can interfere with learning and place additional demands on resources. This chapter describes some of the more common health care problems that often affect children with multiple disabilities. It also suggests some strategies for intervention and, perhaps more important, for prevention of these problems.

This chapter includes some practical suggestions for responding to emergencies. These are presented with two important cautions. First, this book is not intended to provide training in first aid. All teachers, especially those working with students with multiple disabilities, should take a practical course in first aid. Second, individualization is a fundamental principle of quality in health care and education. The general rules discussed here will not always be the best for every individual or every situation. When the health care team has made individual plans based on a particular student's needs, those plans, rather than more general rules, should be carried out for that individual. For example, having more than one seizure in any single day is typically considered to be a sign of a potentially serious problem and would require immediate notification of the family or the physician. For some individuals, however, two or more seizures in a day may be common and not associated with any serious problem. Although the greater frequency of seizures does not indicate the need for special concern about these individuals, a change in the frequency, duration or pattern of the seizures may be cause for legitimate concern, and individualized warning criteria need to be identified for these children.

Children with multiple disabilities have unique health care needs as a result of varied amounts of damage to the neuromuscular and other systems. Some of the medical problems routinely encountered in these children are seizures, gastrointestinal motility disorders, inadequate ventilation of lungs, renal and cardiac disorders, sensory problems, and susceptibility to frequent infections (MacFaul, 1986). Some of the most common medical problems faced by people with multiple disabilities and their caregivers are managing infectious diseases, controlling and monitoring seizures, administering medications, minimizing mealtime concerns (e.g., gagging; choking; aspiration of foods or fluids; problems with chewing, sucking, and swallowing), managing chronic constipation, and maintaining mobility and range of motion. In a study of health care needs of people with multiple disabilities in a residential facility, Thuppal (1994) reported seizures (77.7%) as *the* greatest health care concern. Gastrointestinal problems (63.8%) included reflux esophagitis and gastrostomy tube insertions. Chronic constipation (97.2%) required use of stool softeners and laxatives on a regular basis. Aspiration and choking were also major concerns for all the residents. Wheezing and other respiratory conditions required nebulizers in 27.7% of residents. The individuals in this study were nonambulatory and thus were predisposed to fractures, dislocations, and skin problems. Nevertheless, analysis of records revealed an average of only 2.2 visits by a physician per individual per year.

COMMUNICABLE DISEASE

Communicable disease is a general term that includes all the illnesses that can be transmitted directly or indirectly from person to person.

Susceptibility and Effects

Communicable disease may be caused by viruses, bacteria, protozoans, and fungi. Some diseases, like colds, are extremely common and usually not serious. Other diseases may be much less common and some are much more dangerous. Communicable diseases are a particular concern for many children with multiple disabilities for two reasons. First, many children with multiple disabilities are more likely to contract some communicable diseases than are children without multiple disabilities. Second, once infected, these children are likely to experience more severe symptoms and to be ill longer than people who do not have disabilities.

Although not every child with disabilities exhibits an increased risk for contracting communicable diseases or for experiencing serious effects from illness, many appear to be more vulnerable because of one or more factors. Some of these children have genetic and metabolic anomalies that reduce their resistance to infection. For example, children with Down syndrome often have such severe problems with respiratory infections that survival until adulthood was considered to be exceptional before antibiotics became available. Reduced levels of physical activity and nutritional problems also contribute to the vulnerability of children with multiple disabilities. In addition, many medications that are frequently used by children with disabilities can inhibit the body's natural defenses against infection. Some of these children have not learned sanitary adaptive (i.e., self-care) skills, a situation that might contribute to their risk of contracting a communicable disease (e.g., by putting soiled objects in their mouths). The crowded conditions often found in institutions certainly contribute to increased illness among people with disabilities who live in group residences. For example, delta hepatitis, which is commonly found in some developing countries, is also found in institutions for individuals with developmental disabilities (Benenson, 1990). Although crowded conditions have become less common as there have been improvements in service provision, many children and adults with multiple disabilities continue to live under such conditions. Children with multiple disabilities also are more likely than children without disabilities to experience severe illness because diagnosis is often delayed until the illness becomes more serious. Although changes in behavior, lethargy, or irritability might be early signs of illness, they may not be recognized as such by caregivers in the absence of more specific signs because of the child's inability to communicate the nature of the distress. Finally, some children with multiple disabilities acquired their disabilities as a result of an ongoing illness. For example, 20%–40% of children born to mothers who carry the human immunodeficiency virus (HIV) will be infected before, during, or shortly after birth (United Nations International Children's Emergency Fund, 1991). The rate of transmission of HIV from infected mothers to their offspring depends on maternal virological and immunological status as well as the infected status of the placenta (McIntosh, Avery, & First, 1994). In some African countries, as many as 40% of all infants born to mothers who are HIV positive contract the virus. Approximately 20% of infected children develop disease quickly with a rapid progression to the end stage within the first year of life, while the remaining 80% of infected children have a slow progression. Many of these latter children may not develop symptoms of acquired immunodeficiency syndrome (AIDS) until they are in school or even in adolescence. Although sporadic reports suggest that some children infected with HIV recover fully and appear to have completely eliminated the virus, these cases appear to be exceedingly rare.

Some of the factors that contribute to increased risk for contracting communicable diseases are beyond the control of caregivers, and even if as many sources of increased risk as possible were controlled, communicable diseases would occur among children with multiple disabilities as frequently as they are found in other children. Therefore, it is important to minimize the risk for students and staff whenever possible, to detect illness as soon as possible, and to take appropriate action when illness occurs.

Controlling Communicable Diseases

The control of communicable diseases has been an ongoing challenge throughout the history of civilization. Although the challenge remains, much progress has been made. Most of this progress is the result of improvements in personal hygiene and sanitation, new and better immunization agents, more effective treatment of infected individuals, epidemic control measures (e.g., quarantines), and improved living conditions. Because of these measures, polio, smallpox, rubella (German measles), pertussis (whooping cough), and many other diseases have been eliminated or significantly reduced in occurrence. The United Nations reports that "after smallpox eradication in the 1970s, polio is likely to be the next major disease to be eliminated" (United Nations International Children's Emergency Fund, 1991, p. 14) and points out that more than 1.5 million cases of polio have been prevented in developing countries during the 1980s. The World Health Organization has targeted the year 2000 for final elimination of polio.

Professionals working with children with multiple disabilities have a responsibility to do their part in protecting the children they serve (and themselves) from the spread of communicable diseases. The children they serve typically experience the same risks as all other children, and generally, they require the same precautions. Some children with multiple disabilities, however, experience greater risk because they have poor resistance to infection, their own behavior puts them at risk, or environmental factors increase their risk. Table 5.1 lists a few examples of communicable diseases that can be found among children with multiple disabilities along with their modes of transmission and some control measures. (For more complete information about the control of communicable diseases, see *Control of Communicable Diseases in Man* [Benenson, 1990]. This book should be available in every school, child care center, and other facility serving significant numbers of children.)

Sanitation and Hygiene   Arguably, clean food and water, sanitary sewers, and modern cooking and hygiene practices have done more to extend the lives of people in contemporary society than all other developments in science and medicine. Children with disabilities usually benefit from these developments in public health to the same extent as all members of society; however, in some cases, they may not receive the full benefit from these developments because they live in substandard environments or because they have not adequately learned personal hygiene skills.

Children with multiple disabilities who live in institutions or crowded group residences almost always have a greater risk of contracting a communicable disease (Benenson, 1990). Many diseases that are exceptional in community settings are endemic to institutions housing people with developmental disabilities. The best remedy for this problem is moving people out of these facilities to more typical community living arrangements. Until this goal is realized, increased emphasis on sanitation and immunization programs may help to control the excessive risk associated with institutional living.

Children who pick up discarded food, soiled items, or even body wastes and put them in their mouths obviously experience an increased risk of infection. The best method for eliminating this source of excess risk is teaching improved personal hygiene skills. These skills should be reflected in the goals of all students who require them and be among the highest priorities for training. Extra emphasis on environmental cleanliness is essential. Keeping the environment free of potentially contaminated materials can prevent the cycle of transmission even if students do not exhibit good personal hygiene skills.

Immunizations   Vaccines can provide immunity against some infections. The devastating effect of smallpox, polio, rubella, and whooping cough seen in previous generations has been greatly reduced through the introduction of vaccinations. The risk of contracting serum hepatitis, influenza, some forms of meningitis, and a number of other diseases can also be substantially reduced by vaccination. Nevertheless, vaccinations also involve some risk (though typically much less risk than contracting the disease) and discomfort; therefore, the decision regarding whether to vaccinate any individual against any specific disease requires evaluation of potential risks and benefits. For example, influenza vaccination is typically not recommended for most healthy children, but it may be advisable for a child with complex medical needs because a respiratory infection would be more dangerous to this child. Also, children living in group residences with active cases or known carriers of hepatitis B should be considered for vaccination.

Many schools require proof of vaccination against some diseases for all students as a method of preventing the spread of disease. School personnel should have current immunization records for each student and work with public health agencies to provide parents with accurate information about the benefits and risks of immunization. Parents should be told to inform teachers when a child is vaccinated because adverse reactions to a vaccination may develop at any time for several days after a vaccination. In some cases, these reactions can develop rapidly, and immediate detection and treatment can be important.

Classroom staff should work closely with parents, physicians, the school health team, and public health staff to determine which immunizations are appropriate for each child. These decisions should consider the needs and welfare of both the individual and the group because each child who is not immunized increases the risk for others.

Diagnosis and Treatment of Communicable Diseases   The primary responsibility for the diagnosis and treatment of communicable diseases rests with the family and their physician. Nevertheless, teachers and other program staff can play an important role in the detection and treatment of communi-

Table 5.1. Some communicable diseases found among children with multiple disabilities

Communicable disease	Type	Source	Control measures
AIDS Acquired immunodeficiency syndrome	HIV-1 virus HIV-2 virus	Blood Sexual contact Contaminated needles	Report to public health; careful handling of blood and body fluids that may contain blood (e.g., saliva); control sexual contact and biting
Hepatitis A[a] Infectious hepatitis	Hepatitis A virus	Feces Fecal contamination	Prevent fecal contamination of food, hands, and any other objects that may be put in mouth.
Hepatitis B[b] Serum hepatitis	Hepatitis B virus	Blood, saliva, semen, and vaginal fluid	Vaccination recommended if exposure risk is high; report to public health; careful handling of blood and body fluids that may contain blood
Scabies Sarcoptic itch	Sarcoptes scabiei (a parasite mite)	Skin, less frequently undergarments or bedding	Identify and treat cases quickly; avoid contact with infected skin, launder undergarments and bedding, thorough washing; treat all cases in cohort group concurrently

Pediculosis Lice	Pediculus capitis (head), humanus (body), or pubis (pubic area)	Physical contact, under-garments or bedding	Identify and treat cases quickly; avoid contact with infected skin, launder undergarments and bedding, thorough washing; treat all cases in cohort group concurrently
Common cold Acute viral rhinitis	Various rhinoviruses	Airborne droplets, conta-minated hands	Handwashing, proper disposal of contami-nated materials, keeping fingers out of nose
Influenza	Influenza virus (Type A, B, or C)	Airborne droplets, conta-minated hands	Handwashing, proper disposal of contami-nated materials, keeping fingers out of nose; immunization of those most vulner-able

[a]Exposed individuals may transmit the disease from several weeks before symptoms appear usually until several days after the onset of jaundice. Incubation period is 15–50 days. Most cases are probably not infectious after the first week of jaundice.

[b]Exposed individuals may transmit the disease from many weeks before symptoms appear and throughout the acute stage. Incubation period is 45–180 days. Some individuals can be asymptomatic carriers of hepatitis B. Certain syndromes (e.g., Down syndrome) increase the risk of being an asymptomatic carrier.

cable diseases, and they have a specific responsibility to their students to fulfill this role.

The symptoms of a communicable disease may be noticed first in the classroom for at least two reasons. First, many infectious diseases are cyclical. This means that the symptoms may be more apparent at certain times of day, and in some cases, they may be more obvious during school hours. Second, program staff have the opportunity to observe all their students. This can provide additional information unavailable to parents. For example, a particular child may be predisposed to noncommunicable rashes, but if several children in close contact with this child begin developing similar rashes, more careful evaluation is required. When communicable diseases are discovered among students, efforts to treat the child and to protect other students and staff from exposure should be coordinated among the school, the family, and health professionals. In most cases, treating the individual who has the illness as soon as possible is essential not only for his or her recovery, but also for protecting others from being infected.

Information regarding how and when illness may be spread is essential in determining other appropriate precautions (Holvoet & Helmstetter, 1989). For example, chickenpox is infectious for no more than 5 days after the appearance of the first outbreak of a rash. Thus, children returning to school after this time who still have visible signs of a rash cannot give chickenpox to other children. However, children who have never had chickenpox but have been exposed should be considered potentially infectious 10–21 days after exposure. Therefore, requiring these children to stay home from school for more than 5 days will provide little or no extra protection for classmates. Careful handling of items that are soiled with nasal and respiratory secretions from children who are potentially infectious can help provide additional protection. Because 95% of all people contract chickenpox before they reach adulthood, and because chickenpox during pregnancy creates serious risks for babies born with the infection, exposure in childhood may be difficult to prevent but less risky than entering adulthood without being exposed. Nevertheless, children with leukemia or other health problems that compromise their abilities to fight the disease may experience prolonged and sometimes fatal effects and need special protection. A vaccine has been used successfully in Japan to protect children with leukemia or other special health care needs (Benenson, 1990), and it is beginning to be introduced in North America on a limited basis. Although individual factors must be considered in each case, students and staff fall into three basic categories of risk, requiring three different approaches to immunization. First, those who have already had an infectious illness are typically immune to reinfection and therefore are at little or no risk and probably need no prevention plans. Second, those who have not yet had the disease are at greater risk and require moderate precautions. Third, children with leukemia, AIDS, or other conditions that increase the risk of contracting the disease and women who are pregnant and have not yet had chickenpox require a much more complete protection plan because of their greater risk. As this example of chickenpox suggests, accurate information is vital to the development of any plan to limit the spread of communicable diseases.

Occasionally, classrooms serving children with multiple disabilities, like any other classroom, may experience epidemics of parasites or other infectious diseases. The term *epidemic* simply refers to the occurrence of more than the usual number of cases among a particular group of individuals. Often, the control of epidemics in the school requires careful coordination of home- and school-based efforts to eliminate the problem. Concurrent disinfection is typically a key element in controlling these outbreaks. *Concurrent disinfection* requires simultaneous treatment of all members of the group and simultaneous eradication of other sources of infection from the environment. Head lice (Pediculus capitis), for example, are a fairly common problem among children and adults and are transmitted directly from person to person through direct, typically prolonged contact. Head lice can also be spread through clothing and bedding. Although medicated shampoo is generally effective in treating the problem, failure to eliminate sources of reinfection often leads to recurrence. If several children in a classroom have head lice, it may be important to identify all of them and coordinate the treatment in order to prevent a recurrence. Often, however, nonsymptomatic adults (who may be classroom staff or family members), siblings or other children in close contact outside of school, or even clothing may lead to reinfection, even if every child in the classroom is successfully treated. Laundering in hot water or dry cleaning possibly contaminated clothing at the same time that all infected individuals are treated is essential to the successful eradication of lice. Successful treatment may be possible only with careful coordination of home and school efforts.

Children with Increased Vulnerability   All children are vulnerable to communicable diseases, but some children may be more likely to become infected and develop more severe symptoms. Many factors can contribute to increased vulnerability, and the degree of risk varies. Genetically transmitted immunodeficiency syndromes, leukemia and some other forms of cancer, AIDS, Down syndrome, certain medications, nutritional imbalances, and several other factors can greatly increase the risk associated with communicable diseases for some children. These children will require enhanced protection from exposure and special treatment if they become infected. For example, children with HIV infections served in school settings require special protection.

Individuals infected with HIV go through several phases (Watkins, Klotman, & Gallo, 1995). The first phase is the preseroconversion or the primary infection phase (indeterminate infection). The second phase is the asymptomatic seropositive phase, and the final stage is the clinical disease manifestation phase. The preseroconversion or the primary infection phase lasts a few weeks and is accompanied by flooding of blood with HIV viruses, constitutional symptoms, and swelling of lymph glands. In the second phase, there is a decline in symptoms and a decline in the viral counts in the blood. This asymptomatic phase can last for as long as 5–10 years. During the third phase, the disease manifests itself as recurrent infections, pneumonia, progressive neurological disease, and secondary cancers.

AIDS is not diagnosed until the third phase, but the virus is present and may be transmitted long before a diagnosis of AIDS. For this reason, attention must be given to preventing the spread of AIDS during the earlier stages (McCormick, 1989). Ironically, although children with AIDS experience a much greater risk of being fatally infected by their schoolmates with a common childhood disease, more attention has been given to protecting their schoolmates from them. A well-designed program considers both of these concerns rationally when making team decisions about the best health care and educational program components for each child. Because blood and other body fluids from an infected child could infect others, attention to preventing exposure of these fluids is essential (Caldwell, Todaro, & Gates, 1991). It is important to recognize that sexual contact, sharing contaminated needles, transfusions (especially prior to 1985 testing procedures), and congenital infection of newborns account for the greatest majority of transmissions. "Routine social or community contact with an HIV infected person carries no risk of transmission" (Benenson, 1990, p. 3). Although the virus occasionally has been found in saliva, tears, urine, and other body secretions, there is no record of HIV being transmitted through these fluids (Benenson, 1990). Children with AIDS are very vulnerable to viral and bacterial infections. Efforts to minimize exposure to infections are important. The educational and social advantages of inclusion, however, must be balanced against potential health advantages of isolation. Because it is almost impossible to fully protect the susceptible individual from every source of infection, isolation may be justified only when an unusual risk is present. Special precautions with vaccinations are also essential. It is important that children with HIV receive all relevant vaccinations, but live virus vaccines should be avoided because they may actually cause infections in children with weakened immune systems. Careful consultation with the physician and public health officials is essential to ensure that decisions regarding immunization are made on the basis of the most current research. However, health specialists cannot make the best decisions in all cases without information from parents and the educational team regarding the environment and potential risks for exposure.

Summary   Because all children encounter communicable diseases, they require the best protection and treatment available. Some children with multiple disabilities have increased risk for contracting communicable diseases and are likely to experience more severe consequences if infected. The education team and the health care team must join forces to determine and implement appropriate prevention and treatment strategies. The adequate control of communicable diseases is an important component of health care that improves the quality of life for students and provides a better environment for educating children with multiple disabilities. Management of other health-related concerns can also contribute to an improved context for learning.

SEIZURE DISORDERS

Epilepsy is not a specific disease. Seizures are a symptom of many different disorders that affect the brain (Devinsky, 1994). The terms epilepsy and seizures are used interchangeably. Some prefer to restrict the term *epilepsy* to those instances in which a specific cause is not established, whereas the term *seizures* is used to refer to a broad group of convulsive disorders that result from various causes; these include a low glucose level in blood, infections, a brain tumor, brain injury, and so forth. No single term, such as epilepsy, can adequately cover the broad spectrum of clinical presentations or the innumerable possible patterns of seizures (Aicardi, 1994). Several definitions of epilepsy have been proposed, and to date, no single definition has been accepted uniformly. In spite of minor differences in definitions, however, most authorities agree that epilepsy is a condition characterized by recurrent episodes of excessive and simultaneous discharge of neurons in one or more areas of the brain and manifested in disturbances of consciousness, sensation, or motor function (Batshaw & Perret, 1992; Lishman, 1987; Vining & Freeman, 1996).

During an epileptic attack, there is a sudden, excessive, and disorderly discharge of neurons in the brain accompanied by an abrupt alteration in movement, sensory function, or consciousness. Because these episodes of abnormal electrical discharge in the brain can vary greatly, and the frequency of recurrence required for diagnosis of epilepsy is not uniformly specified, individual diagnosis depends greatly on the physician's judgment. Statistics on incidence and prevalence vary greatly, depending on the diagnostic criteria used for inclusion. In general, estimates of the prevalence of epilepsy in the American population range from 0.5% to 2.0% (Vining & Freeman, 1996; Yousef, 1985). The prevalence of epilepsy seems to be uniform across the globe. The prevalence rate of chronic epilepsy is about 4–6 per 1,000 people. It is estimated that 1 in 10–20 people (i.e., 5%–10% of the world population) will have an epileptic attack of some type at some point in their lives. About 150,000 new cases of seizures occur each year in the United States (National Institutes of Health, 1990). Shorvon (1990) estimated that 1 in 200 people has epilepsy. The overall incidence is the same in males and females, and onset most frequently occurs in the first year of life.

Epilepsy occurs much more frequently among children with multiple disabilities, and as many as 31% of people with severe disabilities have been reported to have epilepsy (Vining & Freeman, 1996). Mental retardation is often accompanied by epilepsy, and the more severe an individual's disability, the greater the chance of epilepsy (Richardson, Koller, & Katz, 1981). The occurrence of epilepsy varies with the syndromes associated with mental disabilities. For example, in people with Down syndrome, epilepsy is relatively rare for young children, but as the children become older adults (in their 30s and 40s), its frequency increases along with changes in the brain (O'Donohoe, 1994). In tuberous sclerosis, however, epilepsy is very common at younger ages and often increases in severity over the years. Cerebral palsy is also commonly associated with epilepsy. Keats (1965) suggested that about 35% of children with cerebral palsy will develop seizures. Although epilepsy can first manifest itself at any time during a person's lifetime, 75% of cases first occur before age 20 (Sands & Minters, 1977). When epilepsy begins early in a child's life, it often becomes more difficult to control later in life (Aicardi, 1994). Structural brain lesions or additional neurological symptoms also can be negative predictors for seizure management. Symptomatic epilepsy (epilepsy for which a specific cause has been identified) accounts for only 30% of cases, whereas idiopathic epilepsy (epilepsy or which no underlying cause has been identified) accounts for the remaining 70% (Yousef, 1985).

Etiology

Many of the known causes of epilepsy also are causes of cerebral palsy and mental retardation, and many children have more than one of these disabilities. Typically, these causes are divided into three major categories: 1) prenatal (occurring before the child's birth), 2) perinatal (occurring during or very close to birth), and 3) postnatal (occurring later in life).

Prenatal Causes   A number of events before a child's birth can result in epilepsy. Exposure to radiation, toxic substances (alcohol and cocaine), or infectious diseases (toxoplasmosis, herpes simplex, German measles) during pregnancy can damage the developing nervous system of the fetus (Sands & Minters, 1977). Fetal anoxia (lack of sufficient oxygen) can occur for a variety of reasons (e.g., improperly attached placenta, compression of the umbilical cord) and damage the child's brain. Despite the excellent natural protection provided in utero, trauma can occur as a result of an accident or violence before birth. The widespread belief that epilepsy was always inherited was controversial because it contributed to stigma and repressive laws. Nevertheless, genetic factors do contribute to epilepsy. Siblings and children of individuals with epilepsy appear to be about twice as likely to be affected as other people (Gumnit, 1983), but the risk remains low (4%–5%) in this group. When two or more family members are affected, this risk increases to 6%–8% (Gumnit, 1983). Except where specific inherited syndromes have been identified, these differences probably have little practical predictive value (Newmark, 1983a).

There are at least 140 single-gene disorders, mostly autosomal recessive in nature, in which epilepsy is an important feature. At least two thirds of these disorders also produce mental retardation (Shorvon, 1990). Research suggests that some individuals have a genetic predisposition to an increased susceptibility to epilepsy as a result of trauma. A genetic factor appears more clearly for generalized seizures than for partial seizures (Newmark, 1983a). Researchers continue to work on mapping human "epilepsy genes" and chromosomal loci; at least seven epilepsy genes have been identified (Delgado-Escueta et al., 1994). The resistance of epilepsy to treatment in some individuals appears to result from the presence of a multiple drug resistance gene, MDR-1. This gene influences the way that drugs pass in and out of the capillaries of the brain (Tishler et al., 1995).

Perinatal Causes   Epilepsy may occur as a result of trauma or oxygen deficit during the birth process (Sands & Minters, 1977). A fetal head too large for the maternal pelvis (cephalopelvic disproportion), premature separation of the placenta, abnormal uterine contractions, interrupted labor, or excessive loss of blood can produce damage to the brain that results in epilepsy. Incompatible blood types (most often Rh factor) between mother and baby may result in erythroblastosis neonatorum (i.e., clumping and breakdown of red blood cells) shortly after birth, but the frequency of this problem has decreased dramatically since the advent of preventive medication and the trend toward having fewer children. There is little risk of Rh problems with a first pregnancy, but the risk increases with subsequent pregnancies. When erythroblastosis neonatorum does occur, brain damage and epilepsy can occur if exchange transfusions do not bring the effects of antibodies rapidly under control (Sands & Minters, 1977).

Postnatal Causes   Brain injuries and childhood infections that cause encephalitis or meningitis (e.g., measles, tuberculosis, viral infections) also can cause epilepsy (Yousef, 1985). Brain tumors and strokes are also implicated (Sands & Minters, 1977). Both accidents and violence are major causes of brain injury in children. Child abuse, the major source of serious acquired brain injury in children, must also be considered a major postnatal cause of epilepsy. It should be pointed out that the occurrence of seizures may not immediately follow a causal event; therefore, certainty regarding the cause for any individual's seizures generally is not possible. Regardless of the cause, however, the physiological process that produces seizures remains the same.

Seizure Mechanisms   The brain is a complex network of approximately 10 billion individual neurons. Nerve impulses are transmitted when the electrical potential across a nerve cell membrane increases. This electrical charge is brought about by exchange of ions (e.g., sodium, potassium, calcium, chloride) across the cell membrane. A charge is transmitted to the neighboring neurons across junctions called *synapses* by chemicals called *neurotransmitters*. Some neurotransmitters excite the neurons they reach, whereas others inhibit the firing of neighboring neurons. Usually, there is a balance between the neurotransmitters that excite and the neurotransmitters that inhibit the firing of neurons. This balance results in rhythmic electrical activity in the nervous system. The reticular activating system, a network of neurons in the core of the brain that includes the brain stem, hypothalamus, and certain nuclei of the thalamus, controls the balance of neurotransmitters and the pace of the brain's electrical rhythm. The balance changes in various biobehavioral states (e.g., sleep, drowsiness, relaxation, alertness, attention). When the balance is disturbed, abnormal electrical activity is produced, and if it cannot be restored, the abnormal electrical activity spreads to the surrounding neurons and seizures occur. For example, if too little glucose in the blood reaches the brain, the metabolic environment of the brain will be disturbed and seizure activity is likely to occur. Abnormal electrical discharges also may be produced by pressure from a tumor on neighboring normal neurons. Normal neurons around a scar in the brain, left by a lack of oxygen, infection, or trauma, may become hypersensitive and start discharging abnormal impulses. With 3% of children having convulsions during a fever, there seems to be genetic susceptibility to this condition (O'Donohoe, 1994). Thus, a variety of factors can result in the abnormal electrical activity of a group of neurons, which tends to spread to neighboring areas.

Normal neurons around damaged brain tissue tend to contain the spread of the abnormal electrical activity. Depending on where the abnormal electrical activity starts and how far it spreads, seizures take different forms associated with the various types of epilepsy. If the abnormal electrical activity reaches the reticular activating system, loss of consciousness occurs. In some instances, neurons discharge too easily and the repetitive neuronal firing, which is not contained by surrounding neurons, leads to seizures. The abnormal electrical activity can be detected as spikes on an electroencephalogram (EEG). A single area of abnormal discharge makes a sharp spike on the EEG. Multiple spikes indicate more than one area of abnormal discharge.

International Classification System

Seizures can be classified on the basis of their cause or etiology, the location of the responsible lesion, or on presumed mechanisms (Aicardi, 1994). Classification is important because, to be effective, medication should be prescribed according to the type of seizure. The International League Against Epilepsy (ILAE) introduced a classification in 1969, which was revised in 1981, that is based on clinical seizure type and EEG findings. Despite some disagreement about details, it is used by virtually all clinicians. According to the 1981 ILAE classification, seizures are grouped into partial, generalized, and unclassified categories. Table 5.2 summarizes this classification system. For additional details, readers may refer to Aicardi (1994). An accurate diagnosis of some of the epileptic syndromes requires the individual's participation, and this may be impossible in young children or individuals with severe communication impairments. For example, those with sensory as well as psychiatric manifestations of epilepsy need to describe the phenomena vividly so that the clinician can make a proper diagnosis. Level of consciousness is taken as an important indicator to diagnose seizures. People with mental retardation requiring extensive supports and people with multiple disabilities are known to show fluctuations in their level of consciousness as confirmed in studies of biobehavioral states (Guess et

Table 5.2. International classification system of seizures

1. Partial (focal, local) seizures
   Simple partial seizures
      –with motor signs
      –with autonomic symptoms and signs
      –with somatosensory or special sensory symptoms
      –with psychic symptoms
   Complex partial seizures (with impairment of consciousness)
      –simple partial onset followed by impairment of consciousness
      –with impairment of consciousness at onset
   Partial seizures evolving to secondarily generalized tonic-clonic seizures (GTC)
2. Generalized seizures (convulsive or nonconvulsive)
   Absence seizures
   Atypical absences
   Myoclonic seizures
   Clonic seizures
   Tonic seizures
   Tonic-clonic seizures
   Atonic seizures
3. Unclassified epileptic seizures

al., 1993). Many people with multiple disabilities are also unable to fully describe the sensations and experiences associated with seizures. As a result, it is sometimes difficult to make appropriate diagnoses of seizures in this group of people.

Diagnostic Procedures

Epilepsy is diagnosed primarily on the basis of the history, the clinical picture, and the EEG. The diagnosis of epilepsy is straightforward in most cases, although in certain instances the presenting complaint is vague and the history is incomplete, resulting in an inaccurate diagnosis. Some other medical, neurological, and psychiatric conditions may mimic seizures. A thorough clinical examination, detailed laboratory investigations, and an inpatient observation may be necessary to confirm the diagnosis and start appropriate treatment. In some cases, response to trial treatment may be considered in arriving at a diagnosis. For example, a physician may suspect that the frequent sudden changes in an individual's behavior result from epileptic seizures, but inadequate data may be available to confirm this diagnosis. If episodes of atypical behavior clearly decrease during a trial period of antiepileptic medication, a diagnosis of epilepsy is more likely to be correct. The conditions most often confused with seizures are fainting spells, hypoglycemic attacks (glucose level in blood falls suddenly), sleep attacks, breath-holding spells, acute psychiatric manifestations, panic attacks, and hysterical convulsions (Devinsky, 1994). Because a host of conditions mimic epilepsy, there may be a tendency to overdiagnose epilepsy, especially in children. Approximately 20%–30% of individuals referred to specialized epilepsy clinics with a possible diagnosis of epilepsy are found to have nonepileptic conditions (Aicardi, 1994). Several tools are now available to investigate epilepsy, of which the routine EEG is an essential component.

Electroencephalogram   A routine EEG is the most common test for epilepsy. In 1929, Hans Berger demonstrated that the electrical impulses within the human brain can be measured and recorded by electrodes attached to the outside of the skull (Sands & Minters, 1977). The shape, voltage, and frequency of waves from specific sites help determine whether an individual has epilepsy and, if so, which type of epilepsy. Many individuals with epilepsy have abnormal brainwave patterns between seizures. When these exist, they will appear on a single EEG in 40%–50% of cases. A second or third EEG will raise the probability that disturbances will be found to 70% or 90%, respectively (Riley & Massey, 1979). Recording for prolonged periods, during wakefulness and sleep, after sleep deprivation, while flashing lights, and after 3–5 minutes of deep breathing all can help detect abnormal EEG patterns (Devinsky, 1994). Nevertheless, an EEG cannot always conclusively diagnose or rule out epilepsy. A normal EEG procedure takes 45 minutes to 1 hour and requires the individual receiving it to remain reasonably still during this time (MacDougall, 1982). Sedation may be used, if required, but its use sometimes influences the results. It is often difficult to obtain good EEG records from children and from people with severe disabilities who may not cooperate fully with the procedure. Involuntary movements or uncooperative behavior may contaminate the EEG record with artifacts. The interpreter of an EEG should be fully informed of the individual's status during recording. An EEG also may be taken with special electrodes in place for long periods while the individual is mobile (i.e., an ambulatory EEG).

Neuroimaging of the Brain   Computed tomography (CT) scans and magnetic resonance imaging (MRI) of the head are used frequently to get pictures of the brain. The former uses X-rays and the latter uses strong electromagnetic fields. Both procedures produce images of the brain. CT was introduced in the 1970s, whereas MRI revolutionized brain imaging in the 1980s. Although both CT and MRI scans depict anatomy of the brain, MRI scans produce images with much higher resolution and greater detail. Positron emission tomography (PET) scans can be used to study the actual functioning of different regions of the brain by determining the amount of glucose being used. The injection of a low dose of radioactive material is necessary for PET scans. A new MRI technique, fMRI (referred to as either fast MRI or functional MRI) is being used as a noninvasive technique to visualize brain functions with high spatial and temporal resolution without requiring injection of radioactive material (Jackson, 1994; Perrine, 1994). An fMRI is based on the alterations in magnetic fields as a result of the varying oxygen content of blood flow changes during various functional tasks (Perrine, 1994).

Other Investigative Procedures   Brain electrical activity mapping (BEAM), ultrasonography (use of sound waves), and single photon emission computer tomography (SPECT) are some other investigative techniques that are used in the diagnosis of seizure disorders. Simultaneous recording of EEG and video monitoring of individuals for prolonged periods is very useful in determining how activity in the brain is related to specific seizure manifestations.

Types of Seizures

Seizures are typically described by their symptoms. The specific manifestations seen in any individual depend on the area of the brain where the seizure originates (i.e., focus) and how the abnormal activity spreads through the brain. The descriptions in this book follow the 1981 classification of seizures by ILAE. Other common terms used to describe some of these seizures are also given.

Partial Seizures   Partial seizures involve a group of neurons in some part of one cerebral hemisphere. When the epileptic activity remains localized and does not spread to the reticular activating system, consciousness is not impaired. These are called *simple partial seizures*. The clinical manifestations depend on the area of abnormal electrical activity. If the epileptic activity is localized to the motor area of the cerebral cortex, the muscles on the opposite side of the body contract in a rhythmic fashion. For example, if there is an epileptic focus in the hand area of the left brain and the focus slowly spreads toward the area of the brain supplying nerves to the forearm, upper arm, and shoulder, then there will be initial rhythmic contractions of the right hand that spread to the right forearm, upper arm, and shoulder. This kind of progression of epileptic symptoms is referred to as a Jacksonian march, named after Sir Hughlings Jackson, a pioneer in the area of epileptology. Simple partial seizures can also produce sensory symptoms (e.g., pain, tingling, numbness), special sensory symptoms (e.g., strange visual or auditory perceptions, atypical taste, strange smell), autonomic symptoms (e.g., palpitation, sweating, flushing of face, discomfort in abdomen), or psychic symptoms (e.g., loss of speech, dreamy states, distortion of time sense, illusions, hallucinations).

Complex partial seizures (CPS) are associated with additional symptoms. They usually produce loss of consciousness and automatisms (i.e., complex, involuntary movements that occur during loss or impairment of awareness). They can take the form of sucking movements, lip smacking, looking around, searching, grimacing, fumbling with clothes or sheets, or scratching movements. Sometimes the individual may hum a tune or use senseless words (verbal automatisms). Automatisms can also include goal-directed motor behavior (Aicardi, 1994). Temporal lobe epilepsy (TLE) was the term that was once most commonly used for complex partial seizures because it was believed that the manifestations of CPS were the result of damage to an area of the brain in the temporal lobe called the hippocampus. It is now believed that damage to other areas of the brain also can lead to automatisms. However, the spread of epileptic discharge to temporal lobe structures is necessary for the clinical manifestations of CPS to occur (Aicardi, 1994). If the seizure activity spreads to the structures in the midline and the reticular activating system, it triggers generalized seizures, referred to as secondary generalization.

Generalized Seizures   In generalized seizures, disturbances initially occur in subcortical structures. These may be convulsive or nonconvulsive. Convulsive seizures may be tonic (i.e., muscles become rigid), clonic (i.e., rhythmic jerky movements of the limbs), tonic-clonic (i.e., rigidity followed by jerky movements), or myoclonic (i.e., repeated twitching movements). Generalized tonic-clonic seizures (formerly called *grand mal seizures*) are the most common (about 60% of cases) epileptic convulsions (Yousef, 1985). Before these seizures, some individuals experience prodromal symptoms for varying periods of time. These can provide warning of impending seizures. These may include changes in behavior that can help caregivers predict when seizures are likely to occur, even if a child's communication is limited.

Generalized seizures may be primary or secondary. If they are primary, the epileptic discharge starts suddenly throughout the cerebral cortex. If they are secondary, the impulses start in a specific region of the cerebral cortex (epileptic focus), but the seizure activity spreads until it reaches the reticular activating system and triggers generalized seizures. At that point, the individual immediately loses consciousness, becomes rigid, and often falls over. During this tonic (rigid) phase, breathing does not occur and the person may begin to turn blue. The following clonic (shaking) phase is characterized by alternating, involuntary contraction and relaxation of muscles that produces undirected movement throughout the body, usually most noticeable in the arms and legs. The individual remains unconscious during this phase and breathing is very inefficient, which may lead to additional cyanosis (turning blue). Frequently, individuals urinate or defecate involuntarily while unconscious. They sometimes injure themselves while falling or unconsciously flailing their arms and legs. Sometimes they bite their tongues. An entire seizure rarely lasts more than 5 minutes. During the postictal (after seizure) phase, the individual has no recollection of the seizure and may be confused or irritable. People are typically drowsy at this stage and usually require rest (Batshaw & Perret, 1992). Sometimes, the individual may remain unconscious after the seizure and require positioning to maintain an open airway.

In secondary generalized seizures, while the seizure activity spreads from the epileptic focus to the subcortical structures, the person may experience a peculiar sensation called an *aura* (breeze). An aura can be an auditory or visual hallucination (e.g., hearing bells, seeing floating patches of color), a feeling of vertigo, a feeling of unfamiliarity or discomfort, or a wide variety of other unusual sensations. An aura is generally remembered by the individual who experienced the seizure and is generally constant. The nature of the aura can help to localize the probable source of epileptic discharge.

While tonic, clonic, and tonic-clonic seizures are closely related and commonly overlapping categories, myoclonic seizures form a separate group. They are characterized by sudden, jerky movements of the muscles. The movements may be symmetrical, asymmetrical, unilateral, bilateral, confined to a group of muscles, and so forth. Based on the clinical type and age of onset, different syndromes (e.g., infantile spasms, Lennox-Gastaut syndrome, juvenile myoclonic epilepsy) are described. In all of the above-mentioned syndromes, sudden jerky movements of muscles cause the individual to collapse and he or she may sustain injury. Myoclonic epilepsy and mental retardation occur together in Lennox-Gastaut syndrome (Aicardi, 1994). Myoclonic seizures also are encountered frequently in children with Down syndrome, tuberous sclerosis, Tay-Sachs disease, and phenylketonuria. Occasionally, generalized seizures occur repeatedly without the individual regaining consciousness between seizures and result in almost continuous seizures. Such a condition is called status epilepticus (continuous seizures) and requires immediate medical attention.

Absence seizures (commonly called *petit mal epilepsy*) are generalized seizures without convulsions. They occur most frequently in childhood between the ages of 4 and 10. They occur as a series of isolated absence spells. When they occur, the child suddenly loses consciousness for a brief period (usually 5–30 seconds), typically staring into space without moving. The child looks dazed momentarily, stops speaking, becomes immobile, appears pale, and assumes a fixed glazed appearance with dilated pupils. Posture and balance are maintained and the individual may have minor, brief muscular contractions around the eyes. The individual is unaware of having had an absence attack, but sometimes there is a perception of change in environment. Some absence seizures produce clonic movements of the eyelids, head, or (rarely) arms. Others may produce repeated chewing, swallowing, or lip-smacking movements. When the seizure is over, the child typically resumes previous activities unaware of any interruption (Howard, 1980). These seizures may be frequent and, if so, disruptive to learning and other activities. When occurring infrequently, absence seizures generally cause few problems and may go unnoticed much of the time. Absence seizures occurring in rapid succession form a condition called *absence status* (petit mal status). Diagnosis of absence seizures is by characteristic EEG pattern (three per second spike and waves). Sometimes, an absence seizure can be precipitated in a child by rapid breathing (hyperventilation) with eyes closed. When the attack occurs the eyes open automatically (Aicardi, 1994). The frequency of absence attacks diminishes with increase in age. About 32% of children developing absence seizures before the age of 8 years develop generalized tonic-clonic seizures later in life (Loiseau et al., 1983).

Special Forms of Seizures   In addition to partial and generalized seizures, there are other varieties of seizures: febrile convulsions, neonatal convulsions, and reflux epilepsies (stimulus-sensitive epilepsies). *Febrile convulsions* are a feature of childhood and normally occur between 3 months and 5 years of age, in the presence of fever but without evidence of intracranial infection or other definable cause (Consensus Development Panel, 1980). Children with febrile convulsions form a heterogeneous group. In the majority there is a genetic susceptibility to convulse in response to increased body temperature. This could be the result of an unrecognized brain injury associated with fever. In some children, febrile convulsions signal the onset of chronic epilepsy (Aicardi, 1994).

Seizures in the neonatal period are considered separately because the brain is not fully developed in the neonatal period. Hence, features of *neonatal seizures* are different from those experienced by adults. In addition, seizures in the neonatal period often indicate serious neurological disorders, with 15%–30% mortality. About one third of survivors will have serious aftereffects (Aicardi, 1994).

Environmental stimuli have been known to trigger seizures in some individuals (Dreisbach, Ballard, Russo, & Schain, 1982). These individuals are said to have *reflex* or *stimulus-sensitive epilepsy*. Although this phenomenon has been given considerable attention, it is important to note that only 5%–6% of people with epilepsy report that sensory stimulation triggers or exacerbates seizure activity (Newmark, 1983b). In a survey of mothers of children with epilepsy, 2.5% reported sensory-evoked seizures in their children (Verduyn, Stores, & Missen, 1988). Of those sensitive to external stimuli, the majority of individuals are sensitive to various stimuli, but a small subgroup is sensitive only to very specific stimuli. Therefore, people with epilepsy do not need to be generally restricted from any stimulus (e.g., fluorescent lights, television, cold water) unless their personal histories indicate that a specific stimulus affects them. For example, photic-induced seizures (triggered by flickering lights, headlights, helicopter blades, or other visual stimulation) have been reported in some individuals. However, Newmark (1983b) notes that only 25 of 20,000 people with epilepsy have photic-induced seizures, and these were usually susceptible to only one or two (not all) of these stimuli. For the other 99.8% of individuals with epilepsy, restriction from all of these stimuli is an unnecessary intrusion. It is not surprising that the suggested relationship between fluorescent lights and seizures has not been supported by research (Binnie, deKorte, & Wisman, 1979), but it may be important for a few individuals. Similarly, auditory-evoked, movement-evoked, startle-evoked, and even language-evoked epilepsy have been found, but these cases are very rare. Some individuals have even been found to be selectively sensitive to card games or other highly specific stimuli such as music or water running down a tap (Senanayake, 1987). Restrictions on exposure to stimulation should occur only if justified by demonstrable benefits to the specific child. When sensory-evoked seizures do occur, they may be tonic-clonic, complex partial, or any other type of seizure. In some instances, characteristic behavior may be a manifestation of epilepsy.

Pseudoseizures   Sometimes, what appears to be a seizure may be a good imitation. Riley and Massey (1979) found that the behavior problem of pseudoseizures occurred frequently among individuals referred to them for epilepsy, and Lechtenberg (1990) reported that "as many as 36 percent of the patients diagnosed and treated as epileptic have fictitious seizures rather than or in addition to true seizures" (p. 51). Pseudoseizures also may occur among children with severe disabilities. Although pseudoseizures may look very much like the real thing, breathing rarely stops and a tonic phase rarely precedes the convulsive stage. In addition, people with pseudoseizures rarely injure themselves during a seizure attack, pseudoseizures do not occur during sleep, there is rarely wetting or soiling of clothes, the attacks generally occur when people are around, and there is likely to be a secondary gain (e.g., gaining attention, being relieved of a demand) when all the environmental factors are considered. Riley and Massey suggested careful evaluation of anyone able to make a voluntary movement during a seizure. Lechtenberg suggested that grunting, moaning, sobbing, speaking, coughing, intentional or semi-intentional movements, or avoidance behavior during seizures and rapid return to full alertness after seizures may be signs of pseudoseizures. EEG studies and analysis of the context in which the seizure episode occurs may also be useful. It is important to remember that these signs are not conclusive, and atypical seizures may easily be mistaken for counterfeit ones. Evaluation should include diagnostic procedures and behavioral assessment, but this process is far from foolproof. Pseudoseizures may be particularly difficult to detect in a child who also has genuine seizures, and the dangers of misdiagnosis may be just as great (or greater) if real seizures are mistaken for pseudoseizures. A matter-of-fact (nonreinforcing) attitude toward all seizures that minimizes social reaction may make discrimination of pseudoseizures from real seizures unnecessary. Nonaversive behavior management procedures and psychotherapeutic methods may be used if pseudoseizures are causing serious problems.

Seizure Management

Seizure management refers to prevention, protection, and first aid measures applied by the transdisciplinary team. Because every child is an individual, seizure management must be tailored to the specific needs of the child, and none of the management provisions discussed here will be appropriate for every child. Rather, these provisions should be thought of as general recommendations to be considered for each individual.

Prevention　Although complete control over seizures is not possible with every child who has epilepsy, reduction in the frequency and severity of seizures can be accomplished for most through a program of prevention. In most cases, the primary prevention method is the careful maintenance of medical treatment. Unless presented with evidence to the contrary, most physicians will assume that the level of medication prescribed is actually the amount received. Unfortunately, many intervening factors can influence the actual amount of medication that reaches the bloodstream. Failure to take prescribed medication is a major cause of difficulty in controlling epilepsy (Schmidt & Leppik, 1988). Some children with multiple disabilities refuse medications and may conceal them in their mouths for later disposal. This may result in an inadequate dosage. Also, the resulting low blood levels of medication may influence the physician to increase the dosage prescribed; subsequently, if the child begins to accept the medication consistently, an overdose may result. When administering medications, it is essential to be certain that they are accepted by the child. The manner in which drugs are given also affects maintenance levels. For example, some anticonvulsants are given in suspension form. Unless the suspension is thoroughly mixed before each administration, dosage will be unreliable (Gumnit, 1983). Some doses will be too strong, others too weak. Mixing medications in food can also affect dosage, especially if not all of the food is eaten. Some drugs will be absorbed differently if tablets are crushed or chewed or capsules are opened before swallowing (Gumnit, 1983). When these or other factors influence dose maintenance, careful consultation among pharmacist, physician, and individuals administering the medication can develop suitable strategies for ensuring accurate and consistent dosage. The benefits of taking any particular type and amount of medication must be carefully balanced with the negative effects and risks of taking the medication. Freeman (1987) advocates using less medical treatment for seizures, pointing out that the major risks from additional seizures for most children are psychosocial and that anticonvulsants often cause behavior problems and learning difficulties in addition to having negative health effects.

Avoiding factors that may precipitate seizures is another important component of seizure prevention for some children with epilepsy (Svoboda, 1979). As discussed previously, specific environmental stimuli that trigger seizures may be identified for some children through careful observation. When they occur, they may be eliminated or controlled in the child's environment. Other factors can lower the threshold for seizure triggers. These factors may be internal or external to the central nervous system (Shreeve, 1983). External factors can often be identified and sometimes controlled. These factors vary among individuals, but some common ones are stress, fatigue, metabolic changes (e.g., lowering of blood pressure as a result of missing meals), effects of drugs (e.g., tranquilizers), and electrolyte imbalances (e.g., inappropriate fluid or salt intake). Careful recording of events that precede seizures can help identify contributing factors for a specific child. Once identified, these factors can often be eliminated or controlled. Intervention during the prodrome can also help prevent seizures. Zlutnick, Mayville, and Moffat (1975) found that specific behavioral chains could be identified in some individuals prior to seizures and interrupting these chains of behavior could reduce the frequency of seizures. For example, careful observation may reveal that a child frequently stares out the window and hums prior to seizures. Interrupting this behavior prior to a seizure may prevent some seizures. Biofeedback has achieved some success controlling epilepsy that has responded poorly to medication or when the dosage required to control seizures has had undesirable side effects (Lechtenberg, 1990). The application of biofeedback to control seizures in children with multiple disabilities needs further exploration but could prove valuable.

Protection   When seizures do occur, protection against injury is important. Protective measures, like other interventions, need to be individualized to meet the needs of the specific child. For example, absence seizures typically do not require special risk-reduction procedures, but some activities (e.g., riding a bicycle) can be hazardous if periods of unconsciousness are long or frequent. In determining the suitability of any potential measure for a specific child, it is important to recognize that unnecessary restrictions and overprotectiveness can become greater problems than the risks they are intended to reduce (Yousef, 1985). The team must carefully consider the following before placing restrictions on the child: 1) the nature of the risk, 2) the extent of the risk, 3) the extent of risk reduction that can be expected as a result of the proposed measure, and 4) the intrusiveness of the risk-reduction measure.

There are many methods for reducing risks. One method is environmental modification. Architectural decisions made during building design stages may greatly influence environmental hazards. For example, long, steep, straight staircases present much greater hazards than stairs interrupted by large landings. Many simple modifications can be made in existing buildings. Padded carpeting will greatly reduce the risk of brain injury for some children with epilepsy. Furniture with rounded corners also reduces the risk of injury during a fall. These and other modifications can be achieved, when needed, within the standards of typical classroom environments. Another common risk-reduction measure is the use of protective clothing, most commonly helmets (Spooner & Dykes, 1982). For individuals experiencing frequent, injurious falls, helmets can be extremely useful. The potential benefit to the wearer, however, must be weighed against the intrusiveness of the intervention. Wearing a helmet may contribute to the perception of the wearer as unusual, may restrict the child's movements, and/or may be uncomfortable (especially in warm weather) and poorly tolerated. If protective headgear is required, it should be lightweight, well fitting, and as appropriate in the social environment as possible. For example, a hockey helmet is much lighter than a football helmet and is not necessarily unusual apparel for a school-age child at play. A knit hat or other common type of thick hat will provide considerable protection and will appear more common in many environments than a helmet. The thick hair typically found on the human scalp provides significant natural protection. Hairstyles that are thick over frequently injured areas of the scalp can also provide significant protection without creating an unusual appearance. Another strategy for risk reduction involves the restriction of hazardous activities. Again, weighing the potential for risk reduction against the restriction of the activity requires careful judgment on the part of the team, and, regardless of the communication and cognitive skill level, the child's input should be included in the decision-making process. Restricting a child from a favorite or highly prized activity should occur only if great risk is present and restriction substantially reduces the risk. Swimming is a common example of an activity that many children with multiple disabilities (including epilepsy) enjoy. It can be dangerous if the individual has a seizure while in the water. Gumnit (1983) recommends that a person with poorly controlled seizures not swim, but a person with well-controlled seizures may swim providing someone is nearby to assist if necessary. The nature of the seizures, size of the person, and other factors may also need consideration. For example, during a tonic phase, water normally cannot enter the lungs. This provides a brief period for a rescuer to remove a person from the water. A heavy individual may be more difficult to bring out of the water, and, once the clonic phase begins, removing the individual from the water without allowing water to get into the lungs is extremely difficult. Also, chlorinated water and sea water pose special hazards because even small amounts in the lung are potentially fatal.

First Aid Measures When seizures occur, simple first aid measures may be required. These are summarized in Table 5.3. In most cases, little intervention is required, and misguided efforts are potentially harmful. First aid measures are aimed at preventing injury and generally involve simply using common sense. Generalized tonic-clonic and other major motor convulsions often cause injury as a result of falling or from powerful involuntary movements. Often, the onset is too sudden for the individual to be eased to the floor, but sometimes (e.g., usually when the child is sitting in a chair) the person does not fall immediately. Easing the person to the ground can prevent serious injury. Furniture with hard or

Table 5.3. First aid for seizure

Type of seizure	Do	Do not
Generalized tonic-clonic (grand mal)	*During* Ease to floor Remove hazards Cushion vulnerable body parts	Put anything in mouth Move, unless absolutely required Restrain movements
	After Allow rest Position for airway, if required Check for injuries	Give food or fluids until fully conscious
Generalized absence (petit mal)	Protect from environmental hazards	Give foods or fluids until fully conscious
Partial complex with automatisms (psychomotor)	Remove hazards from area or pathway Supervise until fully conscious	Restrain movements Approach, if agitated, unless necessary Give food or fluids, until fully conscious

sharp edges and other hazardous objects should be removed from the area, if possible. Only if a hazard cannot be moved (e.g., stairwell, swimming pool) should the child be moved away from it. Placing a soft object (e.g., cushion, sweater) under the head or other vulnerable body parts can also prevent injury. Never attempt to put anything in a person's mouth during a seizure. Although people can bite their tongues causing injuries during seizures, these injuries are not as frequent or severe as those caused by items placed in the mouth. Items placed in the mouth may 1) force jaws out of joint due to unequal pressure, 2) break teeth, 3) obstruct the airway, or 4) spear oral structures if the person flips over on his or her face. Because the child is unconscious and anything given by mouth may enter the airway, it is essential to refrain from giving food or fluid. During the seizure, it is usually not useful to attempt to open or clear the airway, but it may be necessary after the seizure is over. If the child remains unconscious, it is desirable to position him or her on the right or left side, with the neck in slight extension and the head slightly lower than the midline of the body to encourage saliva or any other secretions to run out of the mouth and not back into the throat. The child should then be examined for signs of injury. Observation should continue until the child is fully conscious, but it is not generally necessary to call for medical help unless one or more of the following occurs: 1) breathing does not resume (in which case mouth-to-mouth resuscitation should be started), 2) one seizure follows another, 3) the person sustains a significant injury (Gumnit, 1983), 4) the seizure lasts more than 5 minutes, 5) the child has no history of epilepsy, or 6) the seizure appears substantially different from previously known seizures. Other types of seizures typically require no first aid procedures. Only general precautions, such as removing dangerous objects, are necessary to protect the child from hazards with which he or she might come into contact. For example, a child experiencing a complex partial seizure might walk off the edge of a porch or a child having an absence seizure might not be conscious of an approaching car. Prolonged or repeated seizures, as previously mentioned, require immediate medical attention. This situation occurs most often when serum levels of medication drop suddenly from failure to take prescribed medication, metabolic changes (e.g., fever), or interactions with other medications (Gumnit, 1983). Other physiological changes (e.g., brain injury, illness) can also contribute to prolonged or repeated seizures. Some individuals routinely have two or more generalized tonic-clonic seizures in a day or have seizures that last as long as 7 or 8 minutes, but, unless the observer is certain that this represents typical behavior for the child, immediate medical assistance should be requested. In a case of uncertainty, it is better to request assistance when it is not required than to fail to request it when it is needed. Whether or not a seizure is reported immediately, it should be carefully observed and recorded for the planning of care and treatment.

Observing and Recording   Because most physicians rarely have the opportunity to observe their patients over extended periods of time and seizures generally are unpredictable, physicians must treat most of their patients with epilepsy without ever observing their seizures. Therefore, they depend on parents, teachers, and others who directly observe seizures for accurate descriptions to guide their diagnoses and treatment.

Reports of seizures should be descriptive, not diagnostic (Sobsey, 1982). Using diagnostic descriptions may mislead the physician and/or fail to provide important details required for appropriate treatment. For example, a seizure reported as generalized may be briefly preceded by focal seizure symptoms (e.g., a shaking right arm). This may be treated more effectively as a partial seizure because its origin is probably localized, but it will likely be considered a generalized seizure if merely described as generalized tonic-clonic or grand mal. The careful observation and recording of the events that precede and follow seizures are also important. A record of antecedent events can help to identify seizure triggers or prodromal symptoms. These events can be useful in providing warning and even preventing seizures. A record of subsequent events can be helpful in determining a recovery pattern, the severity of the seizure, and whether an injury has occurred. No special form is required for reporting seizures, but the use of a form may help ensure uniform reporting and speed the recording process. Figure 5.1 shows an example of a form. Copies of seizure reports should be sent home to parents and kept on file for team consideration, and they should be made available to the physician whenever the child's seizure history is reviewed.

Treatment of Epilepsy

The primary treatment for epilepsy is the administration of anticonvulsant drugs. (Additional information about the use of drugs is included in Chapter 6.) Research continues to produce many new anticonvulsant medications. During 1994, for example, there were at least 27 new antiepileptic drugs in various stages of development throughout the world (Sheilds, 1994), with at least eight being tested on children. Felbamate (FBM), Vigabatrin (VGB), Clobazam (CLB-Friseum), Zonisamide (ZNA), and Lamotrigene (LTG) are some new drugs that seem to show some promise. In addition to medication, three other types of treatments for epilepsy are considered here: 1) surgery, 2) behavioral intervention, and 3) dietary control.

Since the 1950s, when Penfield and the Montreal Neurological Institute popularized it, surgical treatment for uncontrollable cases of epilepsy has continued to increase in use (Dreifuss, 1983). Four major categories of procedure have been identified by Dreifuss (1983). First, prophylactic surgery can prevent epilepsy through removal of bone fragments, prevention of infection, and relief of pressure after brain injury. Second, when seizures can be traced to a specific lesion, the lesion can be removed or inactivated (often by freezing). Third, even when no specific lesion can be identified, seizure foci (areas of origin) can be removed. Commonly, this involves removal of a section of the temporal lobe. This is probably the most frequently used surgical treatment for epilepsy. Fourth,

•• SEIZURE RECORD ••

Student's Name: _____   Date: _____

Time (of occurrence): _____   Classroom: _____

—— ANTECEDENTS

Student's location: _____

Student's activity: _____

Warning signs: ☐ No Yes ☐ *If "Yes," describe:* _____

—— SEIZURE BEHAVIOR

Duration *(If approximate, state it):* _____

Did student's body stiffen?	☐ No	☐ Yes	**Parts of Body Involved :**
Did student's body shake?	☐ No	☐ Yes	Arms ☐ Left Right ☐
Did the student fall?	☐ No	☐ Yes	Legs ☐ Left Right ☐
Any apparent injury?	☐ No	☐ Yes	Other: _____

Describe: _____

Did the student appear to become unaware of the environment?   ☐ No ☐ Yes

Was there a change in color of the student's lips, nailbeds, etc.?   ☐ No ☐ Yes

Describe: _____

Did student wet or soil?   Urine: ☐ No ☐ Yes   Feces: ☐ No ☐ Yes

Did student have difficulty breathing?

  Before: ☐ No ☐ Yes   During: ☐ No ☐ Yes   After: ☐ No ☐ Yes

Other/*Describe:*_____

_____

_____

—— SUBSEQUENCES

Describe first aid given: _____

_____

Describe student's activity after seizure: _____

_____

Notifications: ☐ None required   ☐ Parents   ☐ Physician

                    ☐ Other (Specify): _____

Reported By:_____   Date/ Time Filed:_____

Figure 5.1. A behavioral seizure observation record. (Based on Sobsey, 1982).

surgical procedures can obstruct the spread of abnormal electrical activity in the brain. Frequently, this involves severing part—usually the anterior two thirds—of the corpus callosum, a connecting tissue between the right and left hemispheres. A procedure called multiple subpial transection (series of small cuts in the cerebral cortex) is done in instances where seizures begin in areas of the brain that are vital to functions such as language, movement, or sensation

(Devinsky, 1994). Some of the procedures used are lobectomies (resecting a portion of a lobe of the brain) and hemispherectomies (removal of one half of the brain). Despite the fact that surgical intervention is well tolerated by many patients, it is still considered to be intrusive and risky. Therefore, surgery is performed on only a small percentage of individuals whose seizures do not respond to other treatment but can be traced to specific areas of the brain (Dreifuss, 1983). Developmental disabilities are still generally considered to contraindicate surgical treatment of epilepsy by many physicians, but decisions about the appropriateness of such treatment should be made on the basis of risks and benefits to individuals, not on the basis of diagnostic labels. Because some procedures require patients to remain conscious and to describe their sensations during surgery, patients who cannot participate in this manner may be difficult or impossible to accommodate.

Behavioral intervention has also proven useful in treating some individuals with epilepsy. Parrino (1971) demonstrated that, for some people who have epilepsy with identified seizure triggers, systematic desensitization (gradual exposure) to triggering stimuli reduced seizures. Wright (1973) showed that self-induced seizures could be reduced by punishing the seizure-inducing behavior. Certainly, similar results could be achieved with nonaversive behavior management techniques. Zlutnick et al. (1975), as reported previously, found that seizures could be reduced when prodromal behavior chains were interrupted. Each of these approaches has enormous potential for some individuals. They provide alternatives or supplements to medications, which often have deleterious side effects. Children with epilepsy should be considered good candidates for behavioral intervention if they have one or more of the following: 1) self-induced seizure activity, 2) identifiable preseizure behavior patterns, or 3) identifiable environmental seizure triggers. Careful evaluation and planning by the entire transdisciplinary team is required to determine the appropriateness of behavioral intervention and evaluate its success.

Dietary intervention is also used to treat epilepsy in some individuals. The *ketogenic* diet, which accumulates byproducts of fat metabolism in the blood, was developed in 1921 to control seizures, primarily in children (Ekvall & Iannaccone, 1993). As awareness of problems related to high fat intake increased and better drug therapy became available, ketogenic diets became less frequently used. In the 1970s, however, the medium-chain triglyceride (MCT) ketogenic diet came into use, which reduced some concern over high intake of saturated fats. Dietary intervention should be considered when drugs are ineffective or have serious side effects and when decreased seizure activity can be demonstrated during a trial period. A dietitian or nutritionist should be part of the transdisciplinary team considering and monitoring dietary intervention.

Educational Implications

Many of the topics already discussed greatly affect the provision of education for children with epilepsy (e.g., observing and reporting seizures in the classroom, behavioral intervention), but a few specific educational concerns are addressed here: 1) the effects of epilepsy on learning and behavior, 2) social implications of epilepsy, and 3) some specific roles of the transdisciplinary team.

Learning and Behavior   Although epilepsy is only weakly correlated with intelligence, it may influence learning in a number of ways (Dreisbach et al., 1982). Drugs, intense and frequent seizures, brain damage, related behavior problems, and attention deficits have all been identified as impediments to learning for some children with epilepsy (Yousef, 1985). Postictal (after seizure) effects such as confusion, mental impairment, headache, or fatigue may interfere with learning in some children (Dreisbach et al., 1982). It is important to remember, however, that not all children who experience seizures are affected equally by these factors, and some are not affected by any of these factors. Team decisions must be reached through careful consideration of the effects on specific children. For example, there have been reports of attention deficit as a result of subclinical seizure activity (Dreisbach et al., 1982). Although these deficits may be controlled by medication, the medications may occasionally result in sluggishness, lethargy, depression, irritability, or behavior problems that also interfere with learning. Careful evaluation of both liabilities and benefits of treatment must be undertaken by the team based on clear and complete records of the child's social, learning, and seizure behavior.

The role of epilepsy in violence, aggression, and lack of impulse control remains controversial. Although Solomon, Kutt, and Plum (1983) reported that 25%–35% of individuals with psychomotor epilepsy showed excessive aggressive behavior or episodic dyscontrol (a loss of normal inhibition), Lechtenberg (1984) pointed out that the results of such studies have been inconsistent. Intervening social factors make it extremely difficult to interpret any correlational studies (e.g., Taylor, 1972). The Epilepsy Foundation of America (1985) reported that epilepsy was three times more common among prison inmates, but it also pointed out that the stigma associated with epilepsy and the increased risk of brain injury (as well as other factors) may account for these figures. Regardless of the interpretation of these statistics, however, it is clear that the majority of people with epilepsy exhibit no special behavior problems. Therefore, behavior problems should not be anticipated simply because a child has epilepsy. When behavior problems do occur in children with epilepsy, they should be treated exactly like behavior problems in any other child. In the rare instances in which behavior problems appear to be direct results of seizure activity, medical treatment with anticonvulsants may be considered.

Social Implications of Epilepsy   Epilepsy has a long history of social stigma that continues to be a major problem (Lindsay, 1983). In one study (Dreisbach et al., 1982), parents of 36% of children with epilepsy reported stigma, lack of social acceptance, and negative public opinion as their children's greatest problems. Fortunately, public attitudes toward epilepsy are improving. Caveness and Gallup (1980) found that public attitudes became progressively more favorable over 30 years. For example, in 1949, 57% of respondents indicated that they would not object to their children playing with a child with epilepsy. By 1979, the percentage indicating no objection had grown to 89% (Caveness & Gallup, 1980). Another encouraging finding of the Caveness and Gallup (1980) study was that responses became more favorable as educational level and exposure to individuals with epilepsy increased. This suggests further improvement through public education and integration efforts.

It might be argued that the stigma associated with severe and multiple disabilities is more prevalent and intense than the stigma associated with epilepsy, and therefore, improved attitudes toward children with epilepsy have little benefit for the child with multiple disabilities. If such severe stigma does exist toward people with multiple disabilities, the improved attitudes toward epilepsy provide a hopeful note on how such attitudes may change.

In addition to public opinion, attitudes about epilepsy within the child's family are a special concern. Many parents have serious misconceptions about their child's seizures (e.g., death is likely to occur during a seizure) or epilepsy in general (Ford, Gibson, & Dreifuss, 1983). Parents of children with epilepsy have reported lowered self-esteem and difficulty with communication within the family (Ferrari, Matthews, & Barabas, 1983). Parents' attitudes toward their children's epilepsy became more positive as mothers adjusted to their children's epilepsy (Austin, McBride, & Davis, 1984). These findings suggest that intervention to teach families about epilepsy and to encourage acceptance of their children's condition can be valuable components of the child's program.

It is being increasingly recognized that there are sudden unexplained deaths among people with epilepsy. Kirby and Sadler (1995) reported that 15% of seizures brought to medical attention resulted in injury or death. Incidence of death as a complication of seizure was 2.68 per 100,000 people in a prospective study of patient visits to four emergency departments serving adults. Similar figures in people with multiple disabilities are not yet known. The risk factors for sudden unexplained deaths in people treated for epilepsy, as noted in a cohort study in Saskatchewan, Canada, were low antiepileptic drug levels, age between 20 and 40 years, alcohol use, mental retardation, regular but infrequent seizures, male sex, three or more antiepileptic drugs, and prescription of psychotropic drugs (Tennis et al., 1995).

Specific Transdisciplinary Team Roles   Because control of seizures and learning are closely interrelated, decisions affecting either must consider both. The physician should be part of the decision-making team, along with parents, teachers, and other staff. Unfortunately, direct communication between the teacher and the physician regarding children with epilepsy is extremely rare (Gadow, 1982). It is essential that strategies for communication be put in place. Sending seizure records with a brief summary of educational performance to the physician and providing a form for a brief report back is one method of encouraging communication. Education and training of all team members and other school staff are essential to ensure that they are prepared to handle seizures.

Workshops are effective in imparting information about epilepsy, improving teacher attitudes toward epilepsy, and building teachers' confidence in their ability to cope with seizures (Rassel, Tonelson, & Appolone, 1981). Nurses may play a central role in providing training for other team members as well as administering medications and maintaining health records.

Education of families is also important. MacDougall (1982) suggests six major goals for training: 1) understanding the nature of seizures, 2) understanding the basis for diagnostic procedures, 3) knowing what to do when a seizure occurs, 4) recognizing effects and side effects of medications, 5) knowing how to control seizure triggers (when appropriate), and 6) enhancing self-esteem. Decisions regarding behavioral intervention for seizure control should include the entire team. Even when treatment is solely medical, team members must participate in the evaluation of treatment by carefully recording the effects of treatment. Similarly, decisions regarding restrictions of activity or protective equipment must include the entire team. Daily activity schedules may require modification to take advantage of peak learning times, especially when medication side effects reduce responsiveness during specific parts of the day. Careful planning and scheduling by the team can work around some of these side effects, and, by allowing some flexibility in scheduling, it becomes possible to compensate, at least partially, for unpredictable changes.

DUAL DIAGNOSIS

The term *dual diagnosis* refers to the diagnosis of two conditions in the same person. In the area of mental retardation and developmental disabilities, dual diagnosis typically refers to mental illness and mental retardation. It is recognized that people with mental retardation can manifest the full range of psychopathological conditions and behavior problems seen in people without mental retardation. People with mental retardation are a high-risk group for emotional and behavioral difficulties for several reasons, including 1) the greater likelihood of experiencing violence or institutionalization, 2) inorganic brain damage, 3) inadequate coping strategies, 4) social and emotional stress, and 5) poorly developed defense mechanisms. Prevalence figures vary widely because of differences in diagnostic criteria, diagnostic instruments, sample size, type of study, and location of residence. A conservative estimate would be 20%–30%. Characteristics such as physical or sensory disabilities and limited communication skills often impair performance on tests and contribute to the difficulties of diagnosing mental health problems in people with mental retardation. One of the major problems noted by researchers in this field is that there are no standard diagnostic criteria appropriate for people with mental retardation. Standard classification systems like the *Diagnostic and Statistical Manual of Mental Disorders* (DSM-IV) (American Psychiatric Association, 1994) have been used to classify mental illness among people with mental retardation, but they can result in inappropriate diagnoses. For example, a child without a disability whose speech is irrelevant and who uses many gestures could be diagnosed with schizophrenia, but that diagnosis may not be appropriate for a person with severe mental retardation who uses adaptive communication. Furthermore, psychiatric diagnoses are based on an individual's reporting of his or her subjective experiences and feelings. This may be difficult or impossible for people with severe communication impairments. Therefore, a separate or modified diagnostic and classification system may be needed for people with multiple disabilities. With the development and growth of groups like the National Association on Dual Diagnosis (NADD) and the European Association on Mental Health aspects of Mental Retardation (MHMR), the 1990s are a promising time of emerging interest in dual diagnosis of mental illness and mental retardation.

Several screening and diagnostic instruments have been developed for detecting mental illness in people with mental retardation (Reiss, 1993). The Reiss Screen for Maladaptive Behavior (Reiss, 1988) and Psychopathology Instrument for Mentally Retarded Adults (PIMRA) (Matson, 1988) are two that are demonstrating value. The Reiss Screen can be used effectively by teachers to determine if students with mental retardation need further assessment (Reiss, 1993).

Diagnostic overshadowing (Reiss, 1993) refers to instances in which the presence of mental retardation makes it more difficult to interpret mental health symptoms. In other words, atypical behavior may be attributed to mental retardation rather than to a mental health problem. Sovner (1986) identified four factors that may influence the diagnosis of mental illness in mental retardation: 1) intellectual distortion, 2) psychosocial masking, 3) cognitive disintegration, and 4) baseline exaggeration. Intellectual distortion refers to the increased difficulty that may be experienced in coping with various situations because of limited communication and cognitive skills. Psychosocial masking is the effect of disabilities on the content of psychiatric symptoms. Cognitive disintegration is the tendency of people with mental retardation to become disorganized under emotional stress. Baseline exaggeration refers to the fact that during a period of emotional stress, these behavior problems may significantly increase in severity. In spite of these problems with diagnosis, a clinician may diagnose mental illness in a person with mental retardation if there has been a sudden change in behavior; there is no obvious communicative function for the behavior; there are accompanying biological disturbances such as disturbed sleep, lack of appetite, and lack of interest in activities that the individual usually enjoys; and there is no physical illness detected that would account for the change in behavior.

Studies on clinical symptoms of psychiatric disorders in people with mental retardation show that those with mental retardation requiring intermittent to limited supports have symptoms similar to individuals without mental retardation (Bergman, 1991). Patterns of psychopathology manifested by individuals with mental retardation who require extensive supports appear to be different. Autism and related pervasive developmental disorders appear to be more common in this latter group. Stereotypic behaviors (e.g., hand flapping, toe walking) and self-injurious behaviors may occur as symptoms of underlying major neuropsychiatric disorder, especially in people with mental retardation requiring extensive supports (Bergman, 1991). More research needs to be done, however, before it will be known whether these differences actually represent real differences in mental processes between people with mild disabilities and people with more severe disabilities or whether the apparent differences are the result of limited communication with people with disabilities.

Closely related to the issue of dual diagnosis are concerns about the use of psychoactive medication used with people with mental retardation. In institutions, people with severe behavior problems often have been and sometimes still are given massive doses of tranquilizers in order to reduce behavior problems. Often, the consequence is inhibition of the total functioning of the person, not just the target behavior. In addition, these individuals often experienced long-term side effects such as tardive dyskinesia, which is characterized by involuntary movements and interferes with typical activities. Since the 1970s, there has been a public outcry regarding the unnecessary and inappropriate use of medications on people with mental retardation and developmental disabilities (Arnold, 1993; Baumeister, Todd, & Sevin, 1993). Major tranquilizers are the drugs used and frequently misused most for controlling behavior (Gadow & Poling, 1988).

It is agreed that psychotropic drugs are useful in some cases of aberrant behavior in people with mental retardation, but they must be carefully selected, administered for a limited period of time, and their effects evaluated. When used inappropriately, these drugs may aggravate rather than improve psychiatric symptoms. In addition, other drugs, such as opioid antagonists, lithium, beta adrenergic blocking drugs, and stimulant medications can be helpful in some cases (Baumeister et al., 1993). One must be judicious while considering pharmacotherapy for people with mental retardation. The long history of misuse of drugs to control the behavior of people with mental retardation provides even more reason for caution. The decision should be based on the recommendations of the transdisciplinary team and only after benefits of nonpharmacological methods of management are given to the child.

SELF-INJURIOUS BEHAVIOR

Self-injurious behavior is seen in some students with severe or multiple disabilities. These students harm themselves through their own repetitive, stereotypic, or intense episodic behavior. They may bang their heads, poke their eyes, scratch or tear their skin, bite their arms or fingers, or engage in other self-damaging behavior. The effects of this behavior range from mild irritation to severe and permanent injury. In addition, self-injurious behavior is often very disruptive to activities and demoralizing to parents, staff, and others. It should be noted that self-injury is not restricted to people with mental retardation and autism. Deliberate self-injury can occur in people with typical intelligence and may serve multiple functions within a given individual, and the prerequisite condition can be neurochemical, environmental, or both (Thompson, Axtell, & Schaal, 1993).

Causes

A variety of possible causes and contributing factors for self-injurious behavior have been proposed, and many appear to provide at least a partial explanation (Meyer & Evans, 1989). Some organic conditions appear to predispose individuals to self-injurious behavior. For example, children with Lesch-Nyhan syndrome often exhibit severe and intractable forms of self-injurious behavior. Some hypotheses with organic components suggest that self-inflicted pain may help block other more aversive sensations, may increase the production of natural opiates in the system and thus be reinforced, or may be used by the individual to raise the general level of arousal (much in the way that a tired driver sometimes turns up the car radio, opens the window to let in cold air, or even slaps his or her own cheeks to try to stay alert). Other explanations are more behavioral, suggesting that the behavior is developed, maintained, and strengthened as the individual learns that it is associated with reinforcement or escape from aversive stimuli. For example, individuals may learn that self-injurious behavior quickly attracts the attention of caregivers; distracts caregivers, thereby providing the individual with the opportunity to escape from demands of a task; or both. Behavioral and organic explanations are not mutually exclusive, and it is likely that these and other factors interact in at least some individuals (Meyer & Evans, 1989).

If associated features like progressive lack of interest in surroundings, unresponsiveness to social overtures, and bizarre gesticulations are present, self-injury may be a sign of a schizophrenic illness in a person with mental retardation (Thompson et al., 1993). There is some evidence to show that self-injurious behavior can be a symptom of periodic affective disorder in people with mental retardation. Sovner, Fox, Lowry, and Lowry (1993) noted that self-injurious behavior had a periodicity in the two individuals with mental retardation they observed and suspected they had a depressive illness. Treatment with antidepressants resulted in the reduction of severe self-injurious behavior. There were some efforts at developing certain models of self-injurious behavior. Some of the biological models involve dysfunction of chemical substances like dopamine, serotonin, and endorphin in the brain (Aman, 1993). Self-injurious behavior can also occur as a symptom of physical or sexual abuse. While making decisions on the management plan for a person with self-injury, three factors are recommended to be considered: 1) the temporal pattern and degree of repetitiveness (regularity) of action, 2) the degree to which self-injurious performance is under the control of external environmental consequences, and 3) the degree to which pain maintains self-injury (Thompson et al., 1993).

Intervention

A wide variety of drugs is used to reduce or eliminate self-injurious behavior. Tranquilizers, opiate antagonists, beta blockers, stimulants, and anticonvulsants are sometimes used (Gadow & Poling, 1988). Although many of these drugs have been at least partially successful in achieving some reduction for certain individuals, they often suppress other, more appropriate behavior to a greater or equal extent, interfere with learning, have deleterious side effects, and create chronic dependency because any improvement achieved typically is reversed when use of the drug ceases. Therefore, drugs should not be considered as a primary resource for treating self-injurious behavior. They may be considered a time-limited component of intervention if the behavior puts the individual in immediate danger and their application meets the conditions for their use (see Chapter 6).

Another common approach to managing severe self-injurious behavior is restraint. One may apply restraint by holding the individual in a manner that prevents movement or injury. It can also be applied in the form of elbow or knee splints, camisoles (straight jackets), restraint nets, support belts, or a number of other devices. Occlusive bandages that keep the individual from further damaging the part of the body that is the preferred target for injury is another form of restraint. The advantage of restraint is that if it is applied successfully it can prevent further injury immediately for as long as the restraint remains in place. Like medical intervention for self-injurious behavior, however, restraint cannot cure the problem, which often reappears as soon as restraint is removed. Restraint also can cause injury, and the use of restraint has been shown to reinforce the self-injurious behavior in some individuals (Favell, McGimsey, & Jones, 1978). Therefore, restraint should be used only as a last resort on a time-limited basis to prevent imminent and potentially severe injury. It should never be used to take the place of a more appropriate program. Measures such as removing dangerous objects from the environment or keeping the fingernails of those who scratch themselves well trimmed may be justified in some cases as part of a risk-reduction program.

First aid and other forms of treatment are often important elements in a total program for individuals with self-injurious behavior. Methods for controlling bleeding and other first aid measures are discussed in the "Classroom Emergencies" section of this chapter. Other treatments (e.g., sterile dressings, surgery to repair detached retinas) may be required in some cases. The health care team should work closely with the educational team in determining appropriate treatments. Because the care and attention associated with a treatment may reinforce the self-injurious behavior of some individuals, it is essential that their treatment be provided in a neutral manner that minimizes reinforcement. It is also essential to remember that even the best treatment can be expected only to slow the rate of damage if severe self-injurious behavior continues; therefore, treating the injuries should be considered a necessary component of the individual's care, but primary emphasis should be placed on eliminating the self-injurious behavior.

Elimination of self-injurious behavior has been accomplished through aversive and nonaversive means. *Aversive* treatment typically attempts to eliminate unacceptable behavior through punishment procedures. *Nonaversive* treatment attempts to eliminate unacceptable behavior through teaching more appropriate alternatives or through other methods that do not require punishment. Considerable controversy exists among proponents of aversive and nonaversive intervention for this and other severe behavior problems (Repp & Singh, 1990). Those who favor the use of aversive intervention suggest that it has been proven to be more effective, and it is justified because brief punishment frees the individual from chronic self-injury (Axelrod, 1990; Coe & Matson, 1990). Proponents of nonaversive approaches suggest that research demonstrates that nonaversive intervention is as effective or more effective than aversive alternatives (Donellan & LaVigna, 1990; Sobsey, 1990a). An extensive meta-analysis of the research on methods of intervention for problem behavior suggests that more aversive forms of intervention result in no more improvement than nonaversive intervention (Scotti, Evans, Meyer, & Walker, 1991). Although controversy continues, nonaversive approaches appear to be making headway as more questions are raised regarding the research supporting aversive approaches and more research becomes available demonstrating the effectiveness of nonaversive alternatives. The authors of this chapter strongly recommend the use of nonaversive procedures to address self-injurious behavior. Many sources of help are available; for complete information on assessment and design of these programs, see Carr et al. (1994); LaVigna and Donnellan (1986); and Meyer and Evans (1989).

Nonaversive intervention requires a functional analysis of the behavior along with its temporal, social, and physical contexts. Antecedents and consequences of the behavior are carefully examined to determine the function of the behavior for the individual. For example, two individuals may have episodes of hitting their heads, but one may hit herself when she is left alone, and the other may do so when he is asked to carry out a difficult task. For the former, hitting herself may function as a means of attracting attention from caregivers. For the latter, hitting himself may function as a means of escaping from task demands. Because the behavior of the two students is almost identical, one can make and test hypotheses regarding the function only by considering the specific contexts and effects of each behavior. Once the function of the behavior has been identified, intervention is designed to provide training in a more socially appropriate and less dangerous method of serving the function. It is important to remember that requesting attention or protesting a demand is not the problem. Everyone has a right and a need to carry out these functions at times. It is the method of carrying out these functions that needs to change. Unfortunately, caregivers often ignore appropriate requests for attention and protests but respond to inappropriate behavior that is more difficult to ignore. Effective transfer of the behavioral function to a more appropriate form of behavior requires caregivers to respond to the new form of behavior as quickly and as enthusiastically as they responded to the less appropriate form (Carr et al., 1994). More information on methods of teaching communication functions is presented in Chapter 7.

CLASSROOM EMERGENCIES

Every person who works with children in a child care, school, or other group setting should be prepared to prevent health-related emergencies whenever possible and to treat emergencies when necessary.

General Strategies

A practical course in safety and first aid with periodic refresher classes should be included in the training of all staff. Staff working with students with multiple disabilities also need specific training related to the special needs of these children. For example, staff who serve students with tracheostomies need to be familiar with modifications to the resuscitation procedures required for these children in respiratory emergencies (Holvoet & Helmstetter, 1989). Every classroom needs a plan for handling emergencies, and it is important that all staff be familiar with the plan in advance. For example, staff need to know whether to call the school nurse, the principal, the parent, or an ambulance in case of a serious emergency. They should have all important telephone numbers available. In cities with 911 emergency service coordination numbers, this task is greatly simplified, but in other locations, separate numbers may be required for an ambulance service, the police, a hospital, the poison control center, and other vital services. Staff must be able to reach parents or guardians quickly during the day because medical treatment may be delayed if parents cannot be notified. For some students, particularly those with highly individualized health care needs, there should also be a plan in place (and approved by parents) to contact the child's physician directly. Any health care information that is likely to be relevant in an emergency situation (e.g., current medications, blood type, allergies) should be kept in an easily accessible file that can be taken with the child if he or she needs to be transported to a hospital or other setting for treatment. It may be useful to keep general consent forms for emergency treatment in this file, although the value of this type of consent is questionable. Because these types of consent are given in advance and not after being informed of a current situation and the specific risks and potential benefits of treatment, they cannot substitute for the fully informed consent to permit medical treatment. Because first aid measures that are necessary to prevent the death of or serious harm to a child are permitted if the parent or guardian is unavailable, general consent is not required for these purposes. Nevertheless, there often remains a large area of uncertainty regarding what treatments are essential and how long a delay is justifiable. Some health care team members suggest that general consent forms may be helpful, because knowing the general intentions of the parents helps physicians determine how far to take the limits of justifiable emergency procedures.

Some Specific Emergencies

Airway Obstruction   Preventing and treating airway obstruction are probably the most important emergency health care skills for teachers of students with multiple disabilities. These skills are essential for four important reasons. First, airway obstruction is a major cause of accidental death of children in schools (Torrey, 1983). Second, the risk of airway obstruction is greater for children with disabilities. Third, if complete obstruction of the airway occurs, treatment must be given immediately; there is rarely enough time to obtain outside help to save a child. Fourth, simple prevention and treatment methods could save almost every choking victim. Although the exact extent of the increased risk for children with multiple disabilities is unknown, a number of risk factors have been identified in the general public (Dailey, 1983) that indicate substantially increased risk for children with disabilities: 1) decreased gag reflex, 2) incomplete chewing, 3) use of medication, 4) missing teeth, and 5) altered consciousness.

Food asphyxiation occurs when food enters the airway or when it becomes stuck in the upper part of the throat, preventing the epiglottis from opening. Four specific foods (hot dogs, candy, nuts, and grapes) account for more than 40% of choking deaths in young children (Harris, Baker, Smith, & Harris, 1984). About 15% of deaths are caused by soft, loosely textured foods that become compressed upon swallowing (Dailey, 1983). This is probably more common in older children and adults with multiple disabilities. Bread and similar compressible foods have been found trapping the epiglottis (which closes the airway) at autopsy of a number of victims with disabilities.

Prevention   One simple prevention measure is to eliminate some of the high-risk foods from meals or to alter them to reduce the risk. For young children with small airways, peanuts and hard candies should be eliminated. Hot dogs and sausages, which together constitute the single largest threat category, should be included only if ground. Grapes should be cut in half. Bread and similarly compressible foods should be given in small pieces that do not permit a large bolus to collect in the mouth and be swallowed at once. Bread with sticky spreads (e.g., peanut butter, marshmallow spread) should not be given to children who are at risk. Although the completely puréed food diets have sometimes been used to reduce the risk of choking, they are not typically justifiable because these diets cause other health problems and increase the risk of aspiration, which may also be life threatening.

Several other measures can be taken to decrease the risk of choking. First, children must be properly positioned in an upright position for eating. Second, slight flexion of the neck assists proper swallowing (Logemann, 1983) and helps encourage closure of the epiglottis before food approaches. In addition, because flexion narrows the throat, it allows the throat to widen through extension if obstruction occurs. Third, children must not be allowed to eat too fast or to attempt to swallow large amounts of food that have accumulated in their mouths. Fourth, adequate fluids must be provided with dry foods to lubricate them adequately for swallowing. Fifth, rapid attention should be given to any health problem (e.g., reduced alertness as a side effect of medication) that might increase the risk of choking. Sixth, good dental care and appropriate training to chew will help prevent choking.

Signs and Symptoms   In spite of the best prevention efforts, choking incidents will continue to occur from time to time. Parents, teachers, and other mealtime caregivers must be adequately trained to recognize and treat airway obstruction. Early symptoms of complete airway obstruction are nonspecific. In the first 1–3 minutes, the child is likely to remain conscious but indicate distress through agitated movement and possible clutching of the throat or tears in the eyes. The child attempts to breathe, but no air can be felt entering or leaving the nose or mouth. Because no air can enter or leave, the child cannot vocalize. Pulse and blood pressure increase rapidly. Color gradually begins to change to a deep red or purple; this condition is called *cyanosis* (Dailey, 1983). During the next phase, which lasts approximately 3 minutes, the child loses consciousness. Cyanosis deepens to a mottled blue or purple. Pulse and blood pressure drop rapidly. Attempts at aspiration weaken. About 5 minutes (often less) after the initial obstruction, the child enters a third phase, deep coma. Blood pressure, pulse, and attempts at respiration are absent. Pupils become dilated. Brain damage and death will ensue rapidly unless the airway is cleared and pulse and respiration restarted (Dailey, 1983).

Treatment   The rapidity of these events demands immediate action. Available time is often further restricted by failure to notice a problem until the second stage or by the mistaken belief that an epileptic seizure or other problem is the cause. Attempting mouth-to-mouth resuscitation and finding that air will not go in or come out confirms airway obstruction.

The best training requires direct instructor-to-student contact, which can be obtained in first aid courses or specialized training programs, but some general discussion of these procedures is included below. Although considerable controversy existed during the 1980s over the best choice of treatment for airway obstruction (i.e., back blows versus Heimlich maneuver) (Day, Crelin, & DuBois, 1982), in July of 1985, agreement was reached among all major first aid groups that the Heimlich maneuver, already credited with saving thousands of lives, should be the sole treatment in choking emergencies (American Heart Association, 1986). Heimlich (1982) urged the use of the subdiaphragmatic thrust (Heimlich maneuver) as treatment for choking. He stated that back blows are less effective and may convert a partial obstruction into a complete one or a treatable obstruction into an untreatable one. The following describes the procedure for performing the subdiaphragmatic thrust (see Figure 5.2): 1) place arms around the victim from the rear, 2) grasp one wrist with the other hand, 3) make a fist with the empty hand, 4) press the fist against the victim's upper abdomen just below the tip of the sternum (breastbone), and 5) hug forcefully while pressing the fist upward and into the abdomen (Heimlich & Uhley, 1979). This procedure forces the abdomen upward and compresses the air in the lungs, which pushes out the obstruction. If the mouth is full, it is desirable to clear it *carefully* (so that nothing is pushed further into the throat or airway) before carrying out the subdiaphragmatic thrust. If the rescuer cannot position him- or herself behind the victim, an alternative procedure positions the victim supine on the floor or firm surface and the rescuer kneeling over the victim, facing the victim's head. The rescuer applies the thrust by positioning the hands just below the sternum (as described previously) and leaning rapidly and forcefully forward. Chest thrusts (see Figure 5.2) are similar to the subdiaphragmatic thrusts, except that pressure is applied directly to the middle of the sternum (breast-

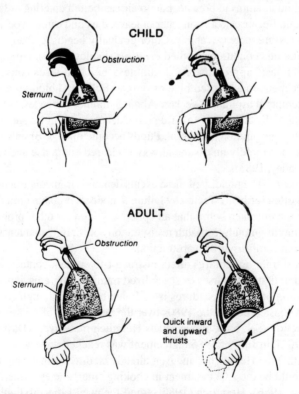

Figure 5.2. Subdiaphramatic thrust and chest thrust. (From Batshaw, M.L., & Perret, Y.M. [1986]. *Children with handicaps: A medical primer* [2nd ed., p. 439]. Baltimore: Paul H. Brookes Publishing Co.; adapted by permission of the author.)

bone). They may be necessary to use if the choking victim is quite obese or in the advanced stages of pregnancy. Chest thrusts may be applied with two fingers and the infant-in-supine position for children younger than 1 year old (St. John Ambulance, 1988).

A finger sweep of the mouth and upper throat also may remove obstructions. This method is sometimes effective when other methods fail, but it cannot be recommended as an initial measure because there is the danger of pushing obstructions farther into the airway or compacting the obstruction, which makes the obstruction more difficult to remove. These difficulties are especially likely to occur with a young child with a small oropharyngeal space in which to work. The finger sweep is recommended while the victim is still conscious (Dailey, 1983) or after the subdiaphragmatic thrust has been attempted repeatedly without success. Performance involves the rescuer positioning the victim supine (on a sloping surface with head lower than feet if possible) with the head extended back. The rescuer inserts an index finger into the mouth with the back of the finger pressed against the obstruction; this can allow removal of all or part of the obstruction. If part of the obstruction is removed, the procedure is repeated only after a check reveals that the airway remains obstructed.

Brain Injury   This section includes some basic information about some common signs of brain injury and the appropriate response when brain injury is suspected. Some of the special considerations related to recognizing and treating brain injury in children with severe disabilities are also discussed. Brain injury is frequently classified as *concussion* (a temporary disturbance in brain function as a result of an impact) or *compression* (pressure on some part of the brain caused by a fracture of the skull, swelling, or the collection of fluid in an area of the brain). Although compression is typically more serious, differentiating between the two is difficult, and first aid measures discussed here are the same. Therefore, the two types of injury are discussed jointly. Table 5.4 lists some of the common signs of concussion and compression along with some special considerations for people with multiple disabilities and basic first aid measures. As shown in this table, signs of concussion and compression overlap, and the distinction between the two is more difficult to make if the individual sustaining the injury has epilepsy, a movement disorder, or communication impairments. Many medications used by people with disabilities can also mask symptoms. Because the rapid diagnosis and treatment of brain injury is essential to the best treatment, and accurate diagnosis may be impossible without careful evaluation by a physician using sophisticated tests and equipment, it is better to err on the side of safety and have the child evaluated if signs of injury are ambiguous.

First aid measures often consist only of keeping the individual safe and calm until help arrives (St. John Ambulance, 1988). No food or fluids should be given because intake may increase swelling in the brain and creates the risk of aspiration because swallowing may be difficult. The danger of vomiting is also increased. This is particularly problematic because vomiting is likely to increase

Table 5.4.   Some common signs of brain injury and first aid treatment

Concussion[a]
  Partial loss of consciousness
  Shallow breathing
  Weak pulse
  Pale appearance
  Headache
  Confusion
  Complete loss of consciousness
  Rapid pulse
  Cool skin
  Vomiting
  Loss of memory (especially for recent events)
  Potentially injurious event (may have been seen)
Compression[b]
  Partial loss of consciousness
  Seizures (mild to severe) may occur
  Slowing of pulse
  Raised body temperature
  Dilated pupils
  Coordination problems
  Confusion
  Complete loss of consciousness
  Irregular breathing
  Flushed face
  Unequal pupils
  Weakness (may affect one side more than the other)
  External injury may or may not be present
  Potentially injurious event (may have been seen)
Special Considerations for Individuals with Multiple Disabilities
  Many of these signs can be masked if they are present prior to injury.
  Seizures are more common in concussion among people with preexisting
    seizure disorders.
  Seizures sometimes produce many of the same signs as head injury.
  Seizures may also result in head injury.
  Medications (e.g., anticonvulsants, tranquilizers) may mask symptoms.
First Aid Treatment and Response
  Assess consciousness, observe for breathing difficulties, and keep under con-
    stant observation.
  Maintain open airway and provide assisted breathing, if required.
  Do not give food or fluids.

(continued)

Table 5.4.   *(continued)*

Protect area of injury from any further trauma (and from contamination, if open wound).

Keep injured person calm and inactive if possible (do not use excessive restraint).

Avoid nose blowing if possible.

Avoid pressure to area of injury.

Unless bleeding is so severe that it must be stopped, do not use direct pressure to skull injuries.

Call for medical assistance.

---

[a]Usually these signs begin immediately or shortly after injury.

[b]These signs may begin immediately or shortly after injury but may be delayed significantly.

pressure on the brain and creates further risk of aspiration. Because people sustaining brain injury are likely to lose consciousness or have a seizure, they should be protected against falls. If bleeding from a head wound is not too severe, it is better to allow bleeding than to apply pressure. One should keep the person calm and comfortable, observing continuously for changes, particularly any difficulty with breathing. If the person will lie down quietly, he or she should be encouraged to do so, but it is important that the person avoid restraint or struggling, which may aggravate the injury.

Poisoning   Children with multiple disabilities sometimes ingest potentially toxic substances. These may include medications, cleaning products, herbicides, pesticides, certain household and garden plants, and a variety of other substances. Often this problem can be prevented, and prevention efforts should be practiced carefully by everyone who works with children who have multiple disabilities. These efforts include 1) keeping all household cleaners, pesticides, drugs, and other dangerous substances safely locked away; 2) being certain that no poisonous plants are kept in areas frequented by children; 3) discarding old or excess medication, pesticides, cleaners, and so forth in a safe manner; 4) keeping all dangerous substances in childproof containers; and 5) never transferring toxic materials to old food containers (St. John Ambulance, 1988).

Fortunately, the development of a network of poison control centers across North America has greatly simplified the basic first aid protocol for ingestion of toxic substances. If a telephone is available, one should contact the poison control center immediately, be prepared to give complete information regarding the substance, and follow the instructions provided. Staff of the poison control center will need to know what substance was ingested, how much, and how long ago. They should also be told the child's age, approximate weight, any available information regarding special medical conditions, and what medications, if any, the child normally takes. Poison control staff may recommend immediate first aid measures and will often suggest that the child be brought in for examination.

When the child goes for examination, the container that held the substance, any labeling material available, and any remaining sample of the substance should be brought. If the toxic substance was a plant, one should bring it or part of it for identification. If the child vomited, one should try to bring the vomitus or at least a sample for examination. It is essential to note the time of the ingestion and bring along any records available regarding health conditions, allergies, and medications. In the rare case that contacting the poison control center is not possible, one should check the label of the substance for directions on how to treat ingestion. Several glasses of water may help to dilute the substance and may induce vomiting. Syrup of ipecac also is commonly used to induce vomiting. Inducing vomiting may be difficult in some children with multiple disabilities because of medications (particularly Thorazine) that they are receiving. Inducing vomiting is not recommended, except under specific medical instructions, if the victim is drowsy or unconscious, under 1 year old, has ingested a petroleum product (because these would be much more dangerous in the lungs than in the stomach), or has ingested a corrosive substance that may do additional damage to the mouth, throat, and esophagus on the way out. Children with motor impairments are at greater risk for aspiration, and inducing vomiting should not be attempted unless the ingested substance poses a serious risk and medical help is unavailable.

Bleeding   External bleeding is easily recognized and easily treated. Almost all bleeding, including bleeding that results from severe injuries, can be controlled by direct pressure. If available, a sterile bandage or clean cloth can be pressed over a wound. When those items are unavailable, pressure applied with the bare hand works quite satisfactorily. Whenever possible, and particularly if the individual applying pressure has any broken skin, the use of gloves is recommended to minimize the risk of transmission of communicable disease.

The person who is injured should be encouraged to rest and stay calm and, if possible, the injured body part should be elevated in relation to the rest of the body. If the injury appears to be severe, medical advice and assistance must be sought. If internal bleeding is suspected, the person who is injured should be at rest. If possible, the individual should lie down with the legs slightly elevated. The person who is injured should be kept warm and medical advice and assistance should be sought as quickly as possible (St. John Ambulance, 1988).

Efforts to prevent classroom emergencies can greatly reduce the frequency and severity of these episodes. Despite even the best prevention efforts, emergencies sometimes occur, and all staff working with children with multiple disabilities must be prepared to respond to them.

ABUSE

Child abuse is a terrible reality for too many children in contemporary society. A significant proportion of children from all segments of society are subjected to physical, sexual, or emotional abuse or neglect (Sobsey, Gray, Wells, Pyper, &

Reimer-Heck, 1991; Sobsey, Wells, Lucardie, & Mansell, 1995). According to the U.S. Advisory Board on Child Abuse and Neglect (1995), there are 1.9 million cases of child abuse and neglect reported each year in the United States. Of these, more than 990,000 are substantiated. At least 2,000 children are killed each year. More children under 4 years old die from child abuse than from motor vehicle accidents, fires, drowning, suffocation, choking, or falls. In addition, 141,000 children are seriously injured, including 18,000 who are left with serious disabilities. These figures suggest that violence is among the leading causes of developmental disabilities. Increasing awareness of the extent of these problems and of the degree of harm suffered by victims of abuse has resulted in the development and implementation of programs to prevent and detect abuse in addition to intervention programs for victims of abuse (e.g., West Contra Costa Rape Crisis Center, 1986).

The connection between disability and abuse is well established, but the precise nature of the relationship remains obscure. Even so, abuse is recognized as a significant cause of disability. As diagnostic techniques improve, the role of abuse in causing disability becomes clearer and appears more extensive than previously believed (Sobsey, 1989). For example, improved brain neuroimaging techniques have helped to identify many cases of whiplash shaken infant syndrome, which likely would have been diagnosed only as "brain damage of undetermined origin" in previous years (Sobsey, 1989). Different factors can contribute to both abuse and disability. For example, excessive use of alcohol within families has been found to be associated with physical and sexual abuse of children within these families and to fetal alcohol syndrome, which causes disability (O'Sullivan, 1989). Even when the cause of disability appears to be unrelated to abuse, children with disabilities are more frequently targets of abuse than are children who do not have disabilities. Furthermore, although children with disabilities suffer the same effects of abuse as other children, they are often excluded from intervention programs that serve other children. Even when programs are accessible to children with disabilities, they are rarely appropriately individualized to meet the needs of children with severe or multiple disabilities.

The Nature and Extent of Abuse

Increased Risk   Children with disabilities are approximately 2 times as likely as children without disabilities to experience abuse. Sobsey and Varnhagen (1989) estimated the risk of being abused for children with disabilities to be at least 1.5 times as great as for other children. A well-controlled prospective study using a nationally representative U.S. sample suggests the risk is 1.67 times as great for children with disabilities than for children without disabilities (Crosse, Kaye, & Ratnofsky, 1993). Sullivan and Knutson (1994) found that children who are abused were 2.2 times as likely to have a disability than children who were not abused. They point out that "children with multiple disabilities are at much higher risk for experiencing the most serious forms of maltreatment than children with a single disability or children without disabilities" (Sullivan & Knutson, 1994, p. 41). They also point out that the average duration of neglect, physical abuse, and sexual abuse is longer for children with multiple disabilities than for children with a single disability or for children without a disability.

An Ecological Model   The traditional explanations for the increased abuse of children with disabilities are inadequate. Much emphasis has been placed on a model that suggests that with increasing severity of disability, the individual becomes more dependent. As dependency increases, family stress also increases, and this increase in family stress precipitates abuse. Although this model appears to have gained some general acceptance, available research strongly contradicts it (Sobsey, 1990b). The level of severity of disability or dependency is a poor predictor of abuse and much of the abuse occurs from sources outside the family. The willingness of researchers and professionals to accept a model that ultimately places the cause of abuse with the victim not only is ethically worrisome, but also shows little potential for producing solutions. However well intentioned, research that attempts to identify characteristics of people with disabilities that supposedly provoke abuse (e.g., Rusch, Hall, & Griffen, 1986) will have limited value for solving problems of abuse and may help to perpetuate the victim-blaming attitudes that encourage abuse. An alternative explanation for the abuse of people with disabilities suggests that "it may not be the disability that contributes to the increased risk, but rather a function of society's explanations and treatment of disabled people" (Sobsey & Varnhagen, 1989, p. 202). Based on this principle and considerable clinical and research evidence, a multifactorial ecological model has been proposed (Sobsey, 1994a). This model includes factors within the victim and offender, but it considers these within the context of the interaction between the two (microsystem), the setting (exosystem), and the social and cultural milieu (macrosystem). For example, excessive compliance has been identified in many victims of abuse who have disabilities, but this may result from the "educational focus" on compliance training for people with disabilities (in a world where people who do not have disabilities receive assertiveness training) and not from any inherent trait in the victims.

The ecological model provides a framework for examining the individual characteristics of abusers and victims along with their interaction patterns within a family or other environmental setting, and the broader social context. It also provides a framework for the identification of prevention and intervention methods.

Prevention and Intervention

Detecting and Reporting Abuse   Most states require educational and health care professionals to report suspected abuse to police or child protection agencies, and some states require any individual to report suspected abuse

(Holvoet & Helmstetter, 1989). Nevertheless, abuse frequently goes undetected, and when detected, it often goes unreported (Sobsey, 1994a).

Several reasons contribute to poor detection (Holvoet & Helmstetter, 1989). First, offenders generally hide their abusive behavior well. They select times and places that provide privacy, and they often select victims who cannot tell what has happened to them. Offenders also may go to great lengths to construct alternative explanations for unexplained injuries or other signs of abuse. Many children with severe disabilities cannot communicate clearly about their mistreatment and may not know that they have a right to better treatment (Sobsey, 1994b). For example, when one mother asked her 5-year-old daughter why she never told about the frequent sexual assaults she had endured, her daughter replied simply, "I thought you knew." Even when they understand that they are being mistreated and are capable of telling about the abuse, many victims are intimidated by the offenders. Most signs of abuse are inconclusive and may easily be attributed to other causes. Symptom masking, the attribution of a particular symptom to a known preexisting condition rather than its real cause, often occurs when the victim of abuse has a disability. For example, behavioral changes, withdrawal, fearfulness, and frequent bruises or even fractures that result from abuse may be attributed to the child's disability rather than mistreatment. Finally, team members may be reluctant to accept evidence that their colleagues and co-workers are abusing the children they serve. In spite of these problems, knowledge of the signs of abuse can be very useful in detecting it. Signs of abuse are listed in Table 5.5. Many of these signs are ambiguous, and it is often an overall pattern or impression that is more powerful than any single sign. Each school or agency should have a protocol in place for reporting *suspected* abuse. Because there is rarely direct or overwhelming evidence at the time of the initial report, it is important that staff understand that they must report suspected abuse, and that many of these reports will prove unfounded or lack sufficient evidence for confirmation. Child abuse is a crime, and reporting suspected abuse to police or a child welfare agency is mandatory in most states. In schools and agencies that have protocols requiring internal reporting, there should also be provisions mandating external reporting. No report should be dismissed arbitrarily; thorough investigation is essential.

Preventing Abuse   Abuse prevention efforts cannot eliminate all risk of abuse, but they can significantly reduce those risks. Effective prevention methods may involve efforts directed toward the child, potential offenders, other program staff and family members, administrative reform, legislative reform, and cultural attitude change (Sobsey & Mansell, 1990). Education is a powerful intervention against abuse. Teaching children that they have a right to be treated decently and how to assert those rights helps to reduce their risk for abuse. Communication skill training is vital to abuse prevention. Children who can express their feelings and indicate when they feel that they are being mistreated are less likely to be abused or exploited. Appropriate social and sex education is also

Table 5.5. Some common signs of abuse

All forms of abuse
Direct observation
Withdrawal
Resistance to touch
Fear of specific caregivers
Poor self-esteem
Victimization of others
Disclosure
Escape behavior
Hypervigilance

Sleep disturbances
Passivity
Reenactment
Fear of specific environments
Self-abuse
Stoical responses to discomfort
Inappropriate behavior
Behavior regression

Physical abuse
Frequent injury
Unexplained coma
Noncompliance
Unexplained injury
Threats
Grab marks

Atypical injury
Aggression
Unreported fractures
Patterned injury
Temporally dispersed injuries

Sexual abuse
Genital irritation
Aggression
Resistance to touch
Noncompliance
Gender-specific fear
Promiscuity

Threats
Sexual precocity
Extreme withdrawal
Inappropriate sexual behavior
Unexplained pregnancy
Sexually transmitted disease

Neglect
Low affect
Dehydration
Indifference to other people
Unusual need for attention

Poor nutritional status
Stoical responses to discomfort
Untreated illness or injuries

Abusive caregiver traits
Authoritarian behavior
Seeks isolated contact
History of violence or coercion
Dehumanizing attitudes
Difficulty relating to authority
Hostility toward reporters
Abusive counterculture in setting
Fearful of victim
Grooming behavior
Competition with child
Rationalization and euphemism

Unusual concern for privacy
Use of alcohol or disinhibiting drugs
Problems with self-control
Negative evaluation of child
Failure to support abuse control measures
Expression of myths of devaluation
Subverts investigation
Blames victim
Tests limits and boundaries
Self-reports of stress

important to prevention of sexual abuse and exploitation (Sobsey, 1994b). Children who do not receive appropriate sex education from parents and teachers are likely to accept inappropriate sex education from an abuser. Program staff, parents, and advocates also need to learn to recognize and report abuse. Early recognition and response to problems is an essential element of abuse prevention because most abuse begins in milder forms and escalates to more severe forms.

Learning to recognize and respond to one's own difficulty in responding to a situation may be among the most difficult things to learn. Family members and caregivers should learn to recognize early signs of difficulty that they are experiencing and know where they can go for advice or counseling. Although stress may play a smaller part in precipitating abuse than previously believed (Sobsey, 1990b), helping individuals through periods of stress may avert some abuse. Even more important, because family homes generally appear safer than institutional care, family support may help to hold families together and keep the child in a safer environment.

Administrative reform is also useful in preventing abuse. Careful screening of staff is essential. Individuals with known histories of perpetrating physical or sexual abuse or other violent crimes should not be hired to provide care to children with disabilities. Administrative reform is also essential to demonstrate an unequivocal commitment to protecting the children served by an agency. Criminal behavior must be treated as such and not as an employee relations problem or, perhaps worse, as a public relations problem. DiLionardi and Kelly's (1989) study of children in group care suggested that "some institutions have a high tolerance for child abuse and need to develop a low threshold culture for child abuse" (p. 253). In another study, Hass and Brown (1989) asked agencies serving people with disabilities if they would report crimes committed against these people by staff; not a single agency indicated that they "would report the sexual assault of a client without fail" (p. 46). Some even admitted that the "impact of reporting on the agency" (p. 46) would be considered in the filing of reports. These findings suggest that much more can and must be done to ensure that agencies place a high priority on protecting the children they serve. Clustering both vulnerable and aggressive people with disabilities together without adequate safeguards to prevent injury to the vulnerable individuals is another form of abuse.

Further inclusion of children with disabilities into general services and reduction of isolated services is also an essential component of abuse prevention. The risk of abuse in institutional settings appears to be 2–4 times as high as in community settings. Serving more children in community settings helps to reduce the risk they experience (Sobsey & Mansell, 1990). Legal reform is also essential. Many states and some Canadian provinces have introduced protection and advocacy programs for children with disabilities (Sobsey & Mansell, 1990). More can be expected to follow. Some specific provisions that may serve as useful deterrents to abuse include 1) allowing victims of abuse to testify in a manner most appropriate to their communication skills, 2) guaranteeing that employees who report abuse will not be administratively harassed, 3) guaranteeing that victims of abuse who have disabilities and their families will not have services disrupted in retaliation for reporting abuse, and 4) ensuring that all reports of abuse go to an impartial advocate outside of the agency involved.

Attitude change is also essential to preventing abuse. The powerful role of attitudes in facilitating abusive behavior cannot be ignored (Shaman, 1986). Perceptions of people with disabilities as less than fully human, "damaged merchandise," incapable of suffering, dangerous, or helpless have all been identified as factors in abuse. In the abuser, these myths become full blown and provide the rationale that abusers may use in disinhibiting aggressive and sexual drives (Sobsey & Mansell, 1990).

Intervention for Victims of Abuse   Children with multiple disabilities suffer the same negative effects of abuse as other children who are victimized. Physical harm can be significant and may add to a child's existing disability. Emotional, behavioral, and social harm may be even more serious (Mansell, Sobsey, & Calder, 1992). The best general intervention is ending the abuse and ensuring a supportive environment that can begin to nurture some positive growth in the child. Medical treatment is required for some children. Teaching self-protection skills may reduce the chances for repeated victimization.

Counseling is typically an important component of the intervention children receive to minimize or reverse the effects of abuse. Counseling will often require significant modification to be appropriate for children with severe communication impairments. Nevertheless, individualized programs developed through consultation between generic abuse counselors and specialists in areas related to the child's disability are probably the most effective approach to providing services to abused children with multiple disabilities. A number of resources are available for those who wish to develop such programs (e.g., Brown & Craft, 1989).

The Transdisciplinary Team and Abuse Issues   All members of the transdisciplinary team should be actively involved in abuse prevention. Signs of physical abuse, sexual abuse, and neglect must be watched for carefully. Protocols must be in place for how to respond to potential incidents of abuse. The health care team should be skilled in recognizing patterns of abuse. Administrators should exercise careful screening procedures in hiring staff. Social workers, child protection workers, and sometimes police can be a part of the team that plans prevention or responds to suspected abuse. Psychologists, counselors, and sex educators may also play valuable roles in prevention programs and in providing services to victims if abuse occurs.

SUMMARY

This chapter has presented some of the common health care problems experienced by children with multiple disabilities and presented some basic information about methods of prevention and intervention. Communicable diseases, seizure disorders, self-injurious behavior, classroom emergencies, and abuse are among the health concerns that have particular implications for children with multiple disabilities. The education and health care teams must work together to determine individual needs in these areas and develop individual prevention and intervention strategies.

REFERENCES

Aicardi, J. (1994). *Epilepsy in children* (2nd ed.). New York: Raven Press.

Aman, M.G. (1993). Efficacy of psychotropic drugs for reducing self-injurious behavior in the developmental disabilities. *Annals of Clinical Psychiatry, 5*, 171–188.

American Heart Association. (1986). *Transcript of National Conference on Standards and Guidelines for CPR and Emergency Care* [Cassette recording]. Dallas, TX: Author.

American Psychiatric Association. (1994). *Diagnostic and statistical manual of mental disorders* (4th ed.). Washington, DC: Author.

Arnold, L.E. (1993). Clinical pharmacological issues in treating psychiatric disorders of patients with mental retardation. *Annals of Clinical Psychiatry, 5*, 189–198.

Austin, J.K., McBride, A.B., & Davis, H.W. (1984). Parental attitude and adjustment to childhood epilepsy. *Nursing Research, 33*(2), 92–96.

Axelrod, S. (1990). Myths that (mis)guide our profession. In A.C. Repp & N.N. Singh (Eds.), *Perspectives on the use of nonaversive and aversive intervention for persons with developmental disabilities* (pp. 59–72). Sycamore, IL: Sycamore Publishing Co.

Batshaw, M.L., & Perret, Y.M. (1986). *Children with handicaps: A medical primer* (2nd ed.). Baltimore: Paul H. Brookes Publishing Co.

Batshaw, M.L., & Perret, Y.M. (1992). *Children with disabilities: A medical primer* (3rd ed.). Baltimore: Paul H. Brookes Publishing Co.

Baumeister, A.A., Todd, M.E., & Sevin, J.A. (1993). Efficacy and specificity of pharmacological therapies for behavioral disorders in persons with mental retardation. *Clinical Neuropharmacology, 16*, 271–294.

Benenson, A.S. (Ed.). (1990). *Control of communicable diseases in man* (15th ed.). Washington, DC: American Public Health Association.

Bergman, J.D. (1991). Current developments in the understanding of mental retardation. Part II: Psychopathology. *Journal of the American Academy of Child and Adolescent Psychiatry, 30*, 861–872.

Binnie, C.D., deKorte, R.A., & Wisman, T. (1979). Fluorescent lighting and epilepsy. *Epilepsia, 20*, 725–727.

Brown, H., & Craft, A. (1989). *Thinking the unthinkable: Papers on sexual abuse and people with learning difficulties.* London: FPA Education Unit.

Caldwell, T.H., Todaro, A.W., & Gates, A.J. (1991). Special health care needs. In J.L. Bigge (Ed.), *Teaching individuals with physical and multiple disabilities* (3rd ed., pp. 50–74). New York: Macmillan.

Carr, E.G., Levin, L., McConnachie, G., Carlson, J.I., Kemp, D.C., & Smith, C.E. (1994). *Communication-based intervention for problem behavior: A user's guide for producing positive change.* Baltimore: Paul H. Brookes Publishing Co.

Caveness, W.F., & Gallup, G.H. (1980). A survey of public attitudes toward epilepsy in 1979 and an indication of trends over the past thirty years. *Epilepsia, 21*, 509–518.

Coe, D.A., & Matson, J.L. (1990). On the empirical basis for using aversive and nonaversive therapy. In A.C. Repp & N.N. Singh (Eds.), *Perspectives on the use of nonaversive and aversive intervention for persons with developmental disabilities* (pp. 465–475). Sycamore, IL: Sycamore Publishing Co.

Consensus Development Panel. (1980). Febrile seizures: Long-term management of children with fever-associated seizures. *Pediatrics, 66,* 1009–1012.

Crosse, S.B., Kaye, E., & Ratnofsky, A.C. (1993). *A report on the maltreatment of children with disabilities* (Contract No. 105-89-1630). Washington, DC: National Center on Child Abuse and Neglect.

Dailey, R.H. (1983). Acute upper airway obstruction. *Emergency Medicine Clinics of North America, 1,* 261–277.

Day, R.L., Crelin, E.S., & DuBois, A.B. (1982). Choking: The Heimlich abdominal thrust vs. backblows: An approach to measurement of enteral and aerodynamic forces. *Pediatrics, 70,* 113–119.

Delgado-Escueta, A.V., Serratosa, J.M., Liu, A., Weissbecker, K., Medina, M.T., Gee, M., Treiman, L.J., & Sparkes, R.S. (1994). Progress in mapping human epilepsy genes. *Epilepsia, 35*(Suppl. 1), S29–S40.

Devinsky, O. (1994), *A guide to understanding and living with epilepsy.* Philadelphia: F.A. Davis.

DiLionardi, J., & Kelly, E. (1989). Preventing and managing child abuse in group care: Report and recommendations of a report on practice. In E.A. Balcerzak (Ed.), *Group care of children: Transitions toward the year 2000* (pp. 239–253). Washington, DC: Child Welfare League of America.

Donnellan, A.M., & LaVigna, G.W. (1990). Myths about punishment. In A.C. Repp & N.N. Singh (Eds.), *Perspectives on the use of nonaversive and aversive intervention for persons with developmental disabilities* (pp. 33–57). Sycamore, IL: Sycamore Publishing Co.

Dreifuss, F.E. (Ed.). (1983). *Pediatric epileptology.* Boston: John Wright—PSG, Inc.

Dreisbach, M., Ballard, M., Russo, D.C., & Schain, R.J. (1982). Educational intervention for children with epilepsy: A challenge for collaborative service delivery. *Journal of Special Education, 16*(1), 111–121.

Ekvall, S.W., & Iannaccone, S. (1993). Epilepsy. In S.W. Ekvall (Ed.), *Pediatric nutrition in chronic diseases and developmental disorders: Prevention, assessment, and treatment* (pp. 99–102). New York: Oxford University Press.

Epilepsy Foundation of America. (1985). *The legal rights of persons with epilepsy* (5th ed.). Landover, MD: Author.

Favell, J., McGimsey, J., & Jones, M. (1978). The use of physical restraint in the treatment of self-injury and as positive reinforcement. *Journal of Applied Behavior Analysis, 11,* 225–241.

Ferrari, M., Matthews, W.S., & Barabas, G. (1983). The family and the child with epilepsy. *Family Process, 22,* 53–59.

Ford, C.A., Gibson, P., & Dreifuss, F.E. (1983). Psychosocial considerations in childhood epilepsy. In F.E. Dreifuss (Ed.), *Pediatric epileptology* (pp. 277–295). Boston: John Wright—PSG, Inc.

Freeman, J.M. (1987). A clinical approach to the child with seizures and epilepsy. *Epilepsia, 28*(Suppl. 1), 103–109.

Gadow, K. (1982). School involvement in treatment of seizure disorders. *Epilepsia, 23,* 215–224.

Gadow, K.D., & Poling, A.G. (1988). *Pharmacotherapy and mental retardation.* Boston: Little, Brown.

Guess, D., Roberts, S., Siegel-Causey, E., Ault, M., Guy, B., Thompson, B., & Rues, J. (1993). Analysis of behavior state conditions and associated environmental variables among students with profound handicaps. *American Journal on Mental Retardation, 97,* 634–653.

Gumnit, R.J. (1983). *The epilepsy handbook: The practical management of seizures.* New York: Raven Press.

Harris, C.S., Baker, S.P., Smith, G.A., & Harris, R.M. (1984). Childhood asphyxiation by food: A national analysis and overview. *Journal of American Medical Association, 251,* 2231–2235.

Hass, C.A., & Brown, L. (1989). *Silent victims: Canada's criminal justice system and persons with mental handicap.* Calgary: The Calgary Sexual Assault Committee.

Heimlich, H.J. (1982). First aid for choking children: Back blows and chest thrusts cause complications and death. *Pediatrics, 70,* 120–125.

Heimlich, H.J., & Uhley, M.H. (1979). The Heimlich maneuver. *Clinical Symposia, 31*(3), 1–32.

Holvoet, J.F., & Helmstetter, E. (1989). *Medical problems of students with special needs: A guide for educators.* Boston: Little, Brown.

Howard, J. (1980). Seizures. In J. Umbreit & P.J. Cardullias (Eds.), *Educating the severely physically handicapped: Treatment and management of medically related disorders* (Vol. II, pp. 8–15). Columbus, OH: Special Press.

Jackson, G.D. (1994). New techniques in magnetic resonance and epilepsy. *Epilepsia, 35*(Suppl. 6), S2–S13.

Keats, S. (1965). *Cerebral palsy.* Springfield, IL: Charles C Thomas.

Kirby, S., & Sadler, R.M. (1995). Injury and death as a result of seizures. *Epilepsia, 36,* 25–28.

LaVigna, G.W., & Donnellan, A.M. (1986). *Alternatives to punishment: Solving behavior problems with non-aversive strategies.* New York: Irvington.

Lechtenberg, R. (1984). *Epilepsy and the family.* Cambridge, MA: Harvard University Press.

Lechtenberg, R. (1990). *Seizure recognition and treatment.* New York: Churchill Livingstone, Inc.

Lindsay, M. (1983, May 11). Never mind the label. *Nursing Mirror, 156,* 18–19.

Lishman, W.A. (1987). *Organic psychiatry: The psychological consequences of cerebral disorder* (2nd ed.). Oxford: Blackwell Scientific.

Logemann, J. (1983). *Evaluation and treatment of swallowing disorders.* San Diego: College-Hill Press.

Loiseau, P., Pestre, M., Dartigues, J.F., Commenges, D., Barberger-Gateau, C., & Cohadon, S. (1983). Long term prognosis in two forms of childhood epilepsy: Typical absence seizures and epilepsy with rolandic (centrotemporal) EEG foci. *Annals of Neurology, 13,* 642–648.

MacDougall, V. (1982, April). Teaching children and families about seizures. *The Canadian Nurse, 78,* 30–36.

MacFaul, R. (1986). Medical care in severe mental handicap [Editorial]. *Archives of disease in childhood, 61,* 533–535.

Mansell, S., Sobsey, D., & Calder, P. (1992). Sexual abuse treatment for persons with developmental disabilities. *Journal of Professional Psychology: Research and Practice, 23,* 404–409.

Matson, J.L. (1988). *The PIMRA manual.* Orland Park, IL: International Diagnostic Systems.

McCormick, K. (1989). *Reducing the risk: A school leader's guide to AIDS education.* Alexandria, VA: National School Boards Association.

McIntosh, K., Avery, M.E., & First, L.R. (1994). Infectious diseases. In M.E. Avery & L.R. First (Eds.), *Pediatric medicine* (2nd ed., pp. 1183–1187). Baltimore: Williams & Wilkins.

Meyer, L.H., & Evans, E.M. (1989). *Nonaversive intervention for behavior problems: A manual for home and community.* Baltimore: Paul H. Brookes Publishing Co.

National Institute of Health. (1990). National Institute of Health consensus conference: Surgery for Epilepsy. *Journal of American Medical Association, 264,* 729–733.
Newmark, M.E. (1983a). Genetics of epilepsies. In F.E. Dreifuss (Ed.), *Pediatric epileptology* (pp. 89–116). Boston: John Wright—PSG, Inc.
Newmark, M.E. (1983b). Sensory evoked seizures. In F.E. Dreifuss (Ed.), *Pediatric epileptology* (pp. 199–219). Boston: John Wright—PSG, Inc.
O'Donohoe, N.V. (1994). *Epilepsies of childhood* (2nd ed.). Oxford: Butterworth-Heinemann.
O'Sullivan, C.M. (1989). Alcoholism and abuse: The twin family secrets. In G.W. Lawson & A.W. Lawson (Eds.), *Alcoholism and substance abuse in special populations* (pp. 273–303). Rockville, MD: Aspen Publishers, Inc.
Parrino, J. (1971). Reduction of seizures by desensitization. *Behavior Therapy and Experimental Psychiatry, 2,* 215–218.
Perrine, K. (1994). Future directions for functional mapping. *Epilepsia, 35*(Suppl. 6), S90–S102.
Rassel, G., Tonelson, S., & Appolone, C. (1981). Epilepsy workshop for public school personnel. *Journal of School Health, 51,* 48–50.
Reiss, S. (1988). *The Reiss Screen for Maladaptive Behavior test manual.* Orland Park, IL: International Diagnostic Systems.
Reiss, S. (1993). Assessment of psychopathology in persons with mental retardation. In J.L. Matson & R.P. Barrett (Eds.), *Psychopathology in the mentally retarded* (2nd ed., pp. 17–40). Boston: Allyn & Bacon.
Repp, A.C., & Singh, N.N. (Eds.). (1990). *Perspectives on the use of nonaversive and aversive intervention for persons with developmental disabilities.* Sycamore, IL: Sycamore Publishing Co.
Richardson, S.A., Koller, H., & Katz, M. (1981). A functional classification of seizures and distribution in the mentally retarded population. *American Journal of Mental Deficiency, 85,* 457–466.
Riley, T.L., & Massey, W. (1979, November 15). Pseudoseizures versus real. *Emergency Medicine, 11,* 122–129.
Rusch, R.G., Hall, J.C., & Griffen, H.C. (1986). Abuse-provoking characteristics of institutionalized mentally retarded individuals. *American Journal of Mental Deficiency, 90,* 618–624.
St. John Ambulance. (1988). *First aid: Safety oriented.* Ottawa, Ontario, Canada: Author.
Sands, H., & Minters, F.C. (1977). *The epilepsy fact book.* Philadelphia: F.A. Davis.
Schmidt, D., & Leppik, I. (Eds.). (1988). *Compliance in epilepsy.* New York: Elsevier.
Scotti, J.R., Evans, I.M., Meyer, L.H., & Walker, P. (1991). A meta-analysis of intervention research with problem behavior: Treatment validity and standards of practice. *American Journal on Mental Retardation, 96*(3), 233–256.
Senanayake, N. (1987). Epileptic seizures evoked by card games, draughts, and similar games. *Epilepsia, 28,* 356–357.
Shaman, E.J. (1986). Prevention for children with disabilities. In M. Nelson & K. Clark (Eds.), *The educator's guide to preventing sexual abuse* (pp. 122–125). Santa Cruz, CA: Network Publications.
Sheilds, W.D. (1994). Investigational antiepileptic drugs for the treatment of childhood seizure disorders: A review of efficacy and safety. *Epilepsia, 35*(Suppl. 2), S24–S29.
Shorvon, S.D. (1990). Epidemiology, classification, natural history and genetics of epilepsy. *Lancet, 336,* 93–96.
Shreeve, C. (1983, May 11). Treating epilepsy. *Nursing Mirror, 156,* 20–21.
Sobsey, D. (1982). Behavioral observation and recording of seizures. *DPH Journal, 6*(1), 14–19.

Sobsey, D. (1989). Whiplash shaking syndrome. *Newsletter of the American Association on Mental Retardation, 2*(6), 2, 8.

Sobsey, D. (1990a). Modifying the behavior of behavior modifiers: Arguments for countercontrol against aversive procedures. In A.C. Repp & N.N. Singh (Eds.), *Perspectives on the use of nonaversive and aversive intervention for persons with developmental disabilities* (pp. 421–433). Sycamore, IL: Sycamore Publishing Co.

Sobsey, D. (1990b). Too much stress on stress? Abuse and the family stress factor. *Quarterly Newsletter of the American Association on Mental Retardation, 3*(1), 2, 8.

Sobsey, D. (1994a). Sexual abuse of individuals with intellectual disabilities. In A. Craft (Ed.), *Practice issues in sexuality and learning disabilities* (pp. 93–115). London: Routledge.

Sobsey, D. (1994b). *Violence and abuse in the lives of people with disabilities: The end of silent acceptance?* Baltimore: Paul H. Brookes Publishing Co.

Sobsey, D., Gray, S., Wells, D., Pyper, D., & Reimer-Heck, B. (1991). *Disability, sexuality, and abuse: An annotated bibliography.* Baltimore: Paul H. Brookes Publishing Co.

Sobsey, D., & Mansell, S. (1990). The prevention of sexual abuse of people with developmental disabilities. *Developmental Disabilities Bulletin, 18*(2), 61–73.

Sobsey, D., & Varnhagen, C. (1989). Sexual abuse of people with disabilities. In M. Csapo & L. Gougen (Eds.), *Special education across Canada: Challenges for the 90's* (pp. 199–218). Vancouver: Centre for Human Development & Research.

Sobsey, D., Wells, D., Lucardie, R., & Mansell, S. (1995). *Violence and disability: An annotated bibliography.* Baltimore: Paul H. Brookes Publishing Co.

Solomon, G.E., Kutt, H., & Plum, F. (1983). *Clinical management of seizures: A guide for the physician* (2nd ed.). Philadelphia: W.B. Saunders.

Sovner, R. (1986). Limiting factors in the use of DSM-III criteria with mentally ill/mentally retarded persons. *Psychopharmacology Bulletin, 22*(4), 1055–1059.

Sovner, R., Fox, C.J., Lowry, M.J., & Lowry, M.A. (1993). Fluoxetine treatment of depression and associated self-injury in two adults with mental retardation. *Journal of Intellectual Disability Research, 37*, 301–311.

Spooner, F., & Dykes, M.K. (1982). Epilepsy: Impact upon severely and profoundly handicapped persons. *Journal of The Association for the Severely Handicapped, 7*(3), 87–96.

Sullivan, P.M., & Knutson, J.F. (1994). *The relationship between child abuse and neglect and disabilities: Implications for research and practice.* (Contract No. 90-CA-1457). Washington, DC: National Center on Child Abuse and Neglect.

Svoboda, W.B. (1979). *Learning about epilepsy.* Baltimore: University Park Press.

Taylor, D.C. (1972). Mental state and temporal lobe epilepsy: A correlative account of 100 patients treated surgically. *Epilepsia, 13*, 727–765.

Tennis, P., Cole, T.B., Annegers, J.F., Leestma, J.E., McNutt, M., & Rajput, A. (1995). Cohort study of incidence of sudden unexplained death in persons with seizure disorder treated with antiepileptic drugs in Saskatchewan, Canada. *Epilepsia, 36*, 29–36.

Thompson, T., Axtell, S., & Schaal, D. (1993). Self-injurious behavior: Mechanisms and intervention. In J.L. Matson & R.P. Barrett (Eds.), *Psychopathology in the mentally retarded* (2nd ed., pp. 179–211). Needham, MA: Allyn & Bacon.

Thuppal, M. (1994). *Health care needs of persons with severe disabilities.* Unpublished master's thesis, University of Alberta, Edmonton, Ontario, Canada.

Tishler, D.M., Weinberg, K.I., Hinton, D.R., Barbaro, N., Annett, G.M., & Raffel, C. (1995). MDR-1 gene expression in brain of patients with medically intractable epilepsy. *Epilepsia, 36*, 1–6.

Torrey, S.B. (1983). The choking child—A life threatening emergency. *Clinical Pediatrics, 22,* 751–754.

United Nations International Children's Emergency Fund (UNICEF). (1991). *The state of the world's children 1991.* New York: Oxford University Press.

U.S. Advisory Board on Child Abuse and Neglect. (1995). *A nation's shame: Fatal child abuse and neglect in the United States.* Washington, DC: National Clearinghouse on Child Abuse and Neglect Information.

Verduyn, C.M., Stores, G., & Missen, A. (1988). A survey of mothers' impressions of seizure precipitants in children with epilepsy. *Epilepsia, 29,* 251–255.

Vining, E.P.G., & Freeman, J.M. (1996). Epilepsy and developmental disabilities. In A.J. Capute & P.J. Accardo (Eds.), *Developmental disabilities in infancy and childhood: Vol. II. The spectrum of developmental disabilities* (2nd ed., pp. 511–520). Baltimore: Paul H. Brookes Publishing Co.

Watkins, B.A., Klotman, M.E., & Gallo, R.C. (1995). Human immunodeficiency viruses. In G.L. Mandell, J.E. Bennett, & R. Dolin (Eds.), *Mandell, Douglas and Bennett's principles and practice of infectious diseases* (4th ed., pp. 1590–1606). New York: Churchill Livingstone.

West Contra Costa Rape Crisis Center. (1986). *Disabled children's prevention program.* San Pablo, CA: Author.

Wright, L. (1973). Aversive conditioning of self-induced seizures. *Behavior Therapy, 4,* 712–713.

Yousef, J.M. (1985). Medical and educational aspects of epilepsy: A review. *DPH Journal, 8*(1), 3–15.

Zlutnick, S., Mayville, W.J., & Moffat, S. (1975). Modification of seizure disorders: The interruption of behavioral chains. *Journal of Applied Behavior Analysis, 8,* 1–12.

6

Integrating Health Care and Educational Programs

Dick Sobsey and Ann W. Cox

AS NOTED IN CHAPTER 1, many students with multiple disabilities have significant health care needs. Intervention that is carefully coordinated with the students' educational programs is the best method for meeting those needs. This chapter includes a discussion of some issues that affect the coordination of health care with educational services and provides some practical strategies for planning and implementing services.

Local and state education agencies have been struggling with the definition of "school health services" as it pertains to the "related services" clause in PL 94-142, the Education for All Handicapped Children Act of 1975 (reauthorized as PL 101-476, the Individuals with Disabilities Education Act [IDEA] of 1990). The distinction between "medical services," which are to be provided for diagnostic and evaluation purposes only, and school health-related services, which are to be provided to students who qualify under the provisions of PL 101-476, has been tested in the courts. It has become clear through litigation and grievance petitions (e.g., *Bevin H. by Michael H. v. Wright,* 1987; *Department of Education, State of Hawaii v. Dorr,* 1983; *Detsel by Detsel v. Board of Education of Auburn,* 1986; *Irving Independent School District v. Tatro,* 1984) that variability exists in the interpretation of the definition of school health services.

CHILDREN WHO NEED SERVICES

In spite of this variability, however, students with special health care needs are entering public school systems in increasing numbers. Lehr and Noonan (1989) suggested that the presence of this new group of students can be attributed to three factors: 1) improvements in medical technology, 2) development of early childhood programs, and 3) application of the principle of normalization.

Advances in medical technology have increased the survival rates for low birth weight infants and children with chronic conditions (Cohen, 1990; Gittler & Colton, 1987; Koop, 1987). The result is often that more children with health care needs survive, including those who depend on technology such as respirators, monitoring equipment, and nutritional support (Moskop & Saldanha, 1986). The U.S. Congress, Office of Technology Assessment (1987), estimates that 27% of babies admitted to neonatal intensive care units will die, 57% will develop normally, and 16% will survive with severe disabilities. This increase in survivors with severe disabilities may be more than offset, however, by the increase in the number of children who avoid disability or experience milder disabilities because of the same or closely related medical advances (Sobsey, 1989a), as illustrated in Figure 6.1. For example, about 6 of every 100 children with paralytic polio actually died, and about 94 were left with varying degrees of disability (Smith, 1990). A vast reduction in polio infection has occurred. As a result, the number of children with disabilities has decreased, not increased. Similarly, advances in trauma care and perinatal care are reducing morbidity (the

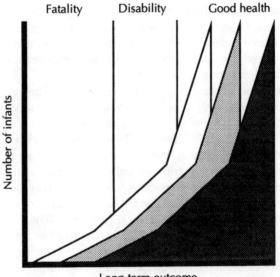

Figure 6.1. The shift in mortality and disability as a result of improved perinatal care. (☐ = no treatment; ▨ = treatment; ■ = improved treatment.)

rate at which illness occurs) more than mortality (the rate at which death occurs). A growing body of research supports the notion that the total number of children with disabilities is *decreasing*, not increasing, because of advances in perinatal care (Anderson, Butland, & Strachan, 1994; Haas, Buchwald-Saal, Leidig, & Mentzel, 1986; Hagberg, Hagberg, & Olow, 1982; Marlow, D'Souza, & Chiswick, 1987; 1987; McCormick, 1993; Robertson & Etches, 1988; Shapiro, McCormick, Starfield, & Crawley, 1983), as well as advances in genetic counseling, control of communicable disease, and other preventive strategies (Menolascino & Stark, 1988).

More research is needed to understand the real effects on distribution of various types and severities of disabilities occurring in infants receiving perinatal care. Whether the number of children with disabilities is increasing or decreasing, the nature of the health-related services they require changes as the relative frequency of occurrence of various disabilities changes. Furthermore, many more of these children, who once would have been cared for in hospitals or special residential care facilities, are receiving health care services from their families and school personnel in the least restrictive environments of their homes and neighborhood schools (Knight & Wadsworth, 1994; Palfrey, Singer, Walker, & Butler, 1986). For example, massive and immobile hospital respirator units of the past have been replaced almost completely by portable and self-contained ventilator units, allowing mobility for individuals dependent on ventilators.

The passage of PL 99-457, the Education of the Handicapped Act Amendments of 1986, heralded an increased commitment to younger children with disabilities by mandating special educational services to children beginning at age 3, with incentives to agencies providing services to infants and toddlers (birth to 3 years). These younger children have been the beneficiaries of technological advancements in medicine and the values of community-based health care. Therefore, there are a growing number of children with special health care needs in this group of preschoolers receiving special education services in the public schools (Lehr & Noonan, 1989).

POLICY, ADMINISTRATIVE
GUIDELINES, AND ROLE DELINEATION

The principle of normalization (Wolfensberger, 1972) provides the rationale from which the least restrictive environment (LRE) requirement of PL 94-142 evolved. The least restrictive, most normalized environment for special education services is in general schools with typical peers. For students with special health care needs who are receiving health care in community-based, family-centered systems, the natural extension of the LRE requirement is that special educational services be provided in community schools with the supports necessary from school health services.

The result is that younger students with new and often different health service needs are entitled to participate in special education in the least restrictive, most inclusive manner. This has particular relevance for students with multiple disabilities, because it is likely that the prevalence of complex health care needs is higher in this student group (Abromowicz & Richardson, 1975).

Many complex issues surround the provision of health-related services in educational settings (Chomicki & Wilgosh, 1994). Most states have either 1) nursing practice acts that restrict the administration of health care procedures to nurses and members of other health-related disciplines, with no provision for delegating responsibilities or training others; or 2) ambiguous laws regarding what nursing functions, if any, can be carried out by others (e.g., New York State Department of Education, 1988; Statutes of Alberta, 1990). Moreover, few states have developed clear guidelines for carrying out health-related procedures in the classroom (Wood, Walker, & Gardner, 1986), and local school divisions frequently are left to determine policies and procedures without guidance (Virginia Departments of Education and Health, 1995). Nevertheless, many local education agencies, with or without state-level involvement, are beginning to develop their own guidelines regarding educational programming, placements, personnel training, and management policies for various school health services that support the education and inclusion of students with special health care needs (e.g., Heller et al., 1990).

In response to requests for assistance from educators, health care providers, and administrators, representatives of five professional organizations in the United States convened a Task Force in 1988 to examine and make recommendations regarding role delineation for personnel who care for children with special health care needs in educational programs (Joint Task Force for the Management of Children with Special Health Needs, 1990). The five organizations were the National Association of School Nurses, National Education Association Caucus for Educators of Exceptional Children, Council for Exceptional Children, American Academy of Pediatrics, and American Federation of Teachers. Although the guidelines recommended are consistent with law in most states, they prohibit many transdisciplinary practices that frequently are carried out in schools. For example, teachers would not be permitted to administer oral medication, feed a child with a gastrostomy or nasogastric tube, or perform clean intermittent catheterization. To conform to these guidelines would require a massive influx of health care personnel into the schools, the clustering of students with disabilities into segregated settings, or both. For example, of 1,424 teachers responding to a survey (about 80% general education classroom teachers and 20% special education teachers), 49.6% had at least one child in their classrooms receiving oral medication, and teachers (30.7%), secretaries (15.2%), and teaching associates (12.3%) were more likely to administer medications than nurses (8.1%) (Orelove & Sobsey, 1990). Most of the remainder of medications taken were self-administered or administered by parents. Furthermore, classroom personnel in Virginia schools were found to perform health care procedures more often than nursing personnel, nonprofessional staff, parents, or therapists, although some variation existed within categories of procedures (Virginia Departments of Education and Health, 1995).

A few states have allowed for more transdisciplinary service delivery in their legislation. Kansas, for example, provides the following specific exemption for school health care:

> (k) performance in the school setting of selected nursing procedures, as specified by rules and regulations of the board, necessary for handicapped students; or
> (l) performance in the school setting of selected nursing procedures, as specified by rules and regulations of the board, necessary to accomplish the activities of daily living and which are routinely performed by the student or student's family in the home setting. (Kansas Nurse Practice Act, 1988, revised)

Other states may follow the lead of this progressive legislation, but as of 1996, most states have significant discrepancies among law, policy, and practice.

A survey of state guidelines regulating the administration of medications and eight common nursing care procedures (Wood et al., 1986) found that only 13 of 50 states had guidelines for the delivery of medication, and only 6 of the 50 states had guidelines for the other health care procedures. Sciarillo, Draper, Green, Burkett, and Demetrides (1988) suggest that "clear and thorough guidelines and regulations are not likely to be forthcoming" (p. 83) because of the complex licensing, liability, administrative, legal, and training issues that remain unresolved.

In this fragmented and changing legislative and administrative climate, it is difficult to recommend universally applicable practices. Therefore, the methods and strategies suggested in this chapter are based on the principles of recommended transdisciplinary practice, individualization, and the overall welfare of the student, and not on any specific legal or administrative framework. Professionals are advised to consult local legislation and policy to determine the best application of these practices to their own students. It is important to remember, when developing or revising law and policy, that legal and administrative decisions regarding the sharing of professional responsibility and the blurring of traditional roles should always be guided by the students' best interests and should never become a rationale for service provision that threatens the quality of services to students with disabilities.

DELIVERY OF HEALTH CARE SERVICES
THROUGH A TRANSDISCIPLINARY MODEL

The transdisciplinary coordination of health care and education has at least three major advantages. First, training and expertise of the direct service providers is tailored more to the individual needs of the student receiving services than to inflexible procedure. Teachers, parents, and other team members become experts in meeting the needs of individual students with the specific care that each student requires. Thus, parents of the students who require these procedures are often recommended as the best people to train school-based personnel to perform them (Schwab, Brown, & Grant, 1990).

Second, decisions regarding the best person to carry out a specific procedure also are based on the individual needs of students rather than general rules. For example, according to the Joint Task Force for the Management of Children with Special Health Care Needs (1990), teachers should be allowed to feed students orally but not by nasogastric or gastrostomy tubes, correctly implying that tube feedings typically require more specialized skills. For some students, however, oral feedings require extremely sophisticated training and skill, and for others, tube feedings are relatively trouble free. Such decisions should be carefully evaluated by the entire team to decide how each procedure can be administered to best meet the needs of the individual.

Third, the administrative arrangements required to ensure that specific health care procedures are performed only by appropriately licensed or certified personnel often result in social, educational, and sometimes even health care disadvantages. Because most schools lack adequate nursing personnel to perform the health care procedures required by students, attempts to restrict administration of these procedures to allied health personnel typically lead to inappropriate clustering of students with physical disabilities, hurried performance of procedures that threatens the quality of care, and procedures that need to be rescheduled to conform to the schedule of busy health care personnel rather than the times ideal for maintaining the health of the student.

Health care services to people with developmental and multiple disabilities are often inadequate, regardless of the setting in which they are provided (Chomicki & Wilgosh, 1994). The need to provide better and more health care services outside hospital environments and the challenges presented in doing so have been recognized through increasing emphasis on home care (Kaufman & Hardy-Ribakow, 1987). Kohrman (1984) suggests that quality will be best ensured if programs "empower the formal and informal caretakers of the child to assess the effectiveness" (p. 103). A narrow focus on home care as opposed to community care, however, would fail to serve the underlying principle of the best quality care in the most natural setting. School-based care providers also should be empowered through training and support to provide health-related services.

Challenges and opportunities exist for those responsible for providing comprehensive services for students with special health care needs and their families. Unique challenges surface regarding the delineation of roles and responsibilities of parents, educators, health care providers, and students in partnerships to achieve the goal of educational services that are inclusive, normalized, and provided in the least restrictive environments. Opportunities exist for collaboration among parents, health care and educational agencies, and various support services within the educational setting. The opportunity to practice a transdisciplinary model for the inclusion of students with multiple disabilities, including those with special health care needs, in the public school system requires appropriate planning that involves the student, parents, physician, teachers, therapists, school administrators, and school nurse. Before addressing a transdisciplinary model related to school health services, however, it is important to discuss the scope of health-related services for students with multiple disabilities.

COMMON MEDICAL CONDITIONS

All children have health care needs. Some of these needs are addressed by school health services. Other students may have health care needs that require a broader range of services. Students with multiple disabilities are at greater risk for developing certain health impairments that may adversely affect their educational program. These students also may have ongoing conditions requiring attention during the school day.

It is important to remember that the need for health-related services in school settings is not unique to children with multiple disabilities or to students in special education programs. In a survey of teachers in North Carolina, for example, 76% had taught at least one child with health care needs for chronic conditions (Johnson, Lubker, & Fowler, 1988). It is important to note that this survey included general and special education teachers in their natural proportions. Only 7% of the North Carolina teachers surveyed believed they had been adequately prepared by their preservice education to meet the health care needs of the students they served. Similarly, only 5% of teachers surveyed in Alberta, Canada, believed they had been adequately prepared to meet the health care needs of their students (Orelove & Sobsey, 1990).

A basic knowledge of common medical conditions is necessary for education professionals, especially those serving students with multiple disabilities. This section briefly addresses some health conditions to which students with multiple disabilities may be more susceptible. It is important for school personnel to be aware of the causes of common health impairments so that measures may be taken to prevent complications and children can be referred for appropriate medical follow-up.

Anemia

Anemia is caused by a combination of factors that contribute to inadequate ingestion of foods high in iron, folic acid, or vitamin B_{12}; poor gastrointestinal absorption; or excessive loss of these nutrients (Healy, 1990). Students receiving anticonvulsants are particularly at risk for folic acid anemia (Truman, 1984). In addition, some syndromes associated with multiple disabilities (e.g., Fanconi anemia) also produce anemia. Because anemia interferes with the oxygen-carrying capacity of the blood, the student with anemia may be less active and more irritable. Mild anemia is not visibly detected. Moderate to severe and prolonged anemia can be visibly detected by pale skin and loss of the pink coloration of the gums, lips, and conjunctiva (mucous lining of the eyelids).

Chewing and swallowing difficulties that may be associated with students with multiple disabilities tend to cause children or those selecting foods for them to avoid foods such as meats, poultry, and dried fruits—foods that are high in iron. A diet that contains other foods rich in iron, such as fortified bread, cereal (e.g., cream of wheat), peanut butter, dark vegetables (e.g., spinach, broccoli), and dried beans may be more easily tolerated. To help the body use folic acid found in foods, the diet also should be rich in vitamin C. Vitamin C sources include oranges, berries, broccoli, cabbage, grapefruits, melons, and citrus juices. School personnel who become concerned that a student is acting unduly lethargic or irritable should speak with the family. Anemia can be diagnosed by a physician, who samples a small amount of blood. If anemia is detected, appropriate intervention at home and school can be planned. More information about diet and nutrition is provided in Chapter 8.

Asthma and Related Respiratory Problems

Although asthma is one of the most common problems experienced by children, experts disagree on how it should be defined (Nolan, 1994). It is characterized by recurrent episodes of the narrowing of the airways that result in wheezing and difficulty in breathing. Typically, such episodes occur as the result of an allergic reaction, but they can also occur in some individuals as a result of stress, exercise, infection, cold temperatures, or a variety of other conditions. Although some researchers and clinicians have tried to separate asthma from "wheezy bronchitis" and other conditions, all of these conditions appear to overlap substantially. Many studies suggest that 2%–10% of children are diagnosed as having asthma and 20% or more experience respiratory problems that involve wheezing (Nolan, 1994). Sometimes asthma attacks triggered by allergic reactions are referred to as *extrinsic* asthma, and asthma attacks triggered by exercise or other internal physiological changes are referred to as *intrinsic* asthma. The lack of a clear definition of asthma makes it difficult to establish reliable prevalence rates, but most researchers agree that the frequency and severity of asthma in children is increasing (Carlson & O'Connell, 1993). In any case, asthma is among the most frequent chronic health conditions experienced by children and is probably the condition most commonly requiring medication and treatment in the schools (Orelove & Sobsey, 1990). In addition, asthma is responsible for more days of school lost through absence than any other chronic health condition (Harvey, 1982).

Chronic aspiration problems experienced by some children with multiple disabilities can produce asthma-like breathing problems, and respiratory distress syndrome, typically found in infants and adults, can occur in children with multiple disabilities as a result of aspiration or secondary to prematurity (Todisco et al., 1993). Some syndromes associated with severe and multiple disabilities also are associated with respiratory problems. For example, children with Down syndrome are often unusually susceptible to lung infections and other respiratory problems (Howenstine, 1992). As a result of these and other factors, children with multiple disabilities are somewhat more likely to have respiratory problems than other children. These children may require aerosol therapy, postural drainage, percussion, or suctioning to help maintain the best possible respiratory function (Morse & Colatarci, 1994). Children whose asthma is triggered by specific allergens also require careful supervision to minimize exposure. Children who have severe attacks also require plans for dealing with respiratory emergencies that can occur.

Otitis Media

Otitis media is an inflammatory disease of the middle ear and is common in children under 6 years of age. There are two types of otitis media. *Acute otitis media* is related to a bacterial or viral infection and is characterized by a red, bulging eardrum, ear pain, and pus in the middle ear. *Serous otitis media*, a more chronic condition, may have similar symptoms but is characterized by an accumulation of fluid in the middle ear. The eustachian tube connects the middle ear space with the nasal cavity and equalizes pressure between the middle ear and the atmosphere. This promotes drainage of secretions. If the tube becomes blocked because the nasal tissues are swollen, fluid may accumulate in the middle ear. This trapped fluid becomes an excellent medium for the growth of bacteria and viruses and results in an infection (acute otitis media). Even after the infection has been treated, the fluid may persist for many weeks (serous otitis media). The recurrence of otitis media can be a major problem because it affects hearing and, therefore, language development and learning. Recurrent otitis media may place great stress on the family, the child, and the educational process (Blackman, 1990).

Students spending a large amount of time in a recumbent position are more susceptible to otitis media. To facilitate drainage of the middle ear, these students should be positioned in a more upright position, particularly during eating. Educators of students with multiple disabilities can note changes in the behavior of students at risk for ear infections. By noting, recording, and bringing changes to the attention of the school nurse and parent, educators may help in the identification of otitis media and prompt early treatment. Students with poor resistance to infection or chronic upper respiratory infections, including many students with Down syndrome, have increased risk of experiencing otitis media. Treatment of otitis media may include antibiotics, decongestants, myringotomy tube insertion, dietary regulation, or a combination of any of the above under the supervision of a physician. It is important to note that because there is an accumulation of fluid in the middle ear, hearing is affected and teaching strategies need to account for this hearing loss (see Chapter 11).

Dehydration

Dehydration occurs when the output of fluids from the body exceeds the intake. *Intake* refers to the amount of fluid taken, usually through feeding (i.e., drinking or eating foods high in liquid). *Output* includes the fluid excreted in urine, through perspiration, vomiting, and defecation, particularly diarrhea. The cells of the body can carry out their normal functions when there is a relative balance between intake and output. When imbalance occurs, however, as in dehydration, the body attempts to compensate in a variety of ways. Dehydration classifications range from mild to severe.

Young students, students with decreased mobility, and students with certain ongoing medical conditions are susceptible to developing dehydration. In these students, simply missing a meal or refusing fluid during the school day may lead to mild dehydration or quickly increase the severity of ongoing dehydration. Fortunately, there are several warning signs of dehydration. The skin will appear pale and may feel cool to cold. The turgor (elasticity) of the skin is reduced. One may test this by slightly pinching the back of the hand. If the child is moderately dehydrated, the skin does not snap back into position quickly. The mucus inside the mouth does not glisten because it is dry. Tearing of the eyes also diminishes. Mild dehydration is best treated with frequent, small amounts of liquid. Parents should be informed of the condition so that they may evaluate the student at home. Moderate to severe dehydration must be evaluated by a physician to determine the cause and appropriate treatment. To help prevent dehydration, fluids should be offered regularly, especially during warm weather or after exertion.

Skin Irritation

Students with multiple disabilities are especially prone to skin irritation because of limited mobility, the need for bracing, and lack of bladder control. In each of these situations, the skin must be inspected regularly for irritated, reddened, and ulcerated areas. Repositioning students who are unable to move their body parts is essential. The exact frequency varies depending on individual needs, but many students require repositioning at least four times per hour (see Chapter 3). Padding around prominent bony areas may be necessary for the child with braces. Light massage to the affected area will stimulate blood supply. For a student in diapers or one who may dribble urine, the groin area should be washed with mild soap and warm water and dried thoroughly each time the student becomes soiled. Some students can be encouraged to do all or part of this cleansing activity independently. To promote home monitoring, parents should be informed about any irritated areas. Skin ulcerations that are not healing will require medical follow-up.

SPECIAL HEALTH-RELATED PROCEDURES

Public school systems are experiencing an increase in the number of students requiring special health-related procedures (Mulligan-Ault, Guess, Struth, & Thompson, 1988). These special health-related procedures may include a variety of tasks ranging from the administration of medications to assistance with mechanical ventilation. The following sections address three health care procedures: clean intermittent catheterization, tube (gavage) feeding, and administering medication. Each section identifies the principles and issues surrounding the inclusion of special health care procedures into the individualized education program (IEP) provided for by IDEA. The sections include a description of each procedure and a discussion of when the procedure is required, the necessary safeguards, the individuals responsible for administering the procedure, and a review of the issues. This is followed by a discussion of planning procedures and the role of the school nurse in the delivery, supervision, and evaluation of the effectiveness of the plan.

Clean Intermittent Catheterization

CIC is required because of either a temporary or permanent inability to empty the bladder. A catheter is a slender, hollow tube that is inserted into a cavity to provide drainage. When the catheter is inserted periodically, it is considered an intermittent process. Intermittent urinary catheterization is performed to provide for the periodic drainage of urine from the bladder for those individuals who, otherwise, are unable to excrete urine efficiently. Intermittent urinary catheterization can be performed by a sterile or a nonsterile, but clean, technique.

When the bladder is not properly emptied, it can become overdistended. An overdistended bladder slows the circulation of blood through the bladder walls and has weakened resistance to infection (Altshuler, Meyer, & Butz, 1977). Residual urine in the bladder provides an excellent medium for the growth of bacteria and can lead to infection. The infection may remain confined to the bladder (cystitis) or may ultimately lead to a kidney infection (nephritis). Thus, the primary medical goal of CIC is to decrease the likelihood of infection within the urinary tract system by providing periodic draining of urine from the bladder for those students unable to do so independently.

Some students with myelomeningocele (a form of spina bifida) or spinal cord injury have little or no control over urination. Some of these students may dribble urine or be unable to empty the bladder completely. In other students, the bladder may overdistend to the point that urine is forced up the ureters back into the kidneys. This ultimately may lead to significant kidney damage. To prevent serious infections, the bladder must be drained by CIC frequently (as often as every 3–4 hours), at prescribed times throughout the day. Therefore, CIC will need to be completed at school according to a time schedule ordered by a physician.

CIC is a procedure that can be safely and effectively carried out independently by some students once they are adequately trained. Skill training can begin as early as 6–7 years of age if the student has sufficient motor and cognitive ability. More than likely, the student already has been involved with helping during the procedure at home. It is important to ask the parent or student about the previous level of involvement. There are many advantages to the student performing CIC, including greater independence, self-esteem, and privacy. If appropriate, training typically involves a process of task analysis of the skill, instruction, demonstration, and return demonstration. However, before embarking upon teaching the skill to the student, the team (school personnel, parents, student, physician) must all agree to the plan and the timing.

It is important to consider several issues as part of the planning process regarding performing CIC at school. One issue involves training providers about the aspects of administering the procedure. The training must include the primary caregiver and alternative caregivers. Areas of content include the purpose of the procedure, risks, safeguards, and emergency measures. Although printed materials are helpful (e.g., Taylor, 1990), skill in performing the technique of CIC is best acquired through demonstration and return demonstration. The parent, if willing, can demonstrate the procedure on the student, and with the supervision of a health professional, the designated caregiver can then demonstrate the skill. The involvement of these individuals sets the tone for subsequent cooperation and collaboration among the parents, health professionals, and teacher. CIC is classified as a skilled nursing procedure under some state laws, regulations, or guidelines. Therefore, determining responsibility for carrying out CIC is among the complex issues discussed previously in this chapter under "Policy, Administrative Guidelines, and Role Delineation."

Another issue is communication, both written and verbal. A record-keeping system for recording the administration of the procedure and the student's response is needed. For instance, it would be important to document and verbally report to the parent that the urine drained by CIC during the school day appeared cloudy or had a foul odor. Both might be indicators of infection. Furthermore, one should record the color and general amount of urine. If the amount significantly decreases, one might become concerned about whether the student is receiving adequate fluids. Typically, the teacher, nurse, and parent work out a system for telephone and written communication that allows each to update the other as needed. Also, it is helpful to identify in advance an effective way to communicate with the physician. Except in an emergency, the student's physician usually is updated by the parent or through written communication from the school. A survey of physicians' involvement with schools indicates direct communication is relatively uncommon. Palfrey et al. (1986), for example, found that parents reported any history of contact between school personnel and the physician for only 13.8% of students with special needs.

Finally, the issue of legal responsibility is addressed during the planning process. Local and state guidelines regarding training about health-related procedures and determining who is qualified to carry out the procedures must be reviewed. Staff should follow these guidelines for their own protection and for the safety of the student. If not in place, guidelines should be developed. A system for initial training, supervision, follow-up support, and retraining will help to diminish apprehension. Adequate training and systematic documentation are important safeguards.

Tube (Gavage) Feeding

The purpose of tube (gavage) feeding is to provide fluid and nutrients for the student who otherwise is unable to take in adequate amounts. In addition, oral medications may be given through a feeding tube. Students with conditions that cause severe central nervous system dysfunction (e.g., cerebral palsy with oral-motor difficulties, brain injury with resultant muscular and nervous system impairment, craniofacial or structural conditions, hypersensitivity of the mouth or throat) are the most likely to require tube feeding for a prolonged period. Because providing adequate nutrition and fluids by tube requires frequent administration in small amounts, especially during warm weather, these procedures must be provided during the school day.

Placement   Feeding tubes may be placed through the nose (nasogastric tube) or, occasionally, through the mouth (orogastric tube) and allowed to descend through the esophagus into the stomach. One must exercise caution to be certain that the tube is placed correctly before feeding begins because improper placement may introduce food or fluids into the airway. Nasogastric (NG) tubes are usually temporary and may either be removed and replaced with each feeding or be allowed to remain in place from several days to a few weeks. The decision will be made by the physician, parents, and student, and it depends on the type, size, and material of the feeding tube and the condition and individual response of the student. As explained in Chapter 8, NG tube feedings should be used only as a short-term method of feeding, typically less than a few weeks. Nevertheless, these tubes may become dislodged during the school day, necessitating reinsertion by a trained caregiver.

Feeding tubes that are inserted through the skin of the abdomen directly into the stomach (gastrostomy tube) or into the small intestine (jejunostomy tube) typically are considered permanent or long-term placements. They, too, may become accidentally dislodged or obstructed and must be replaced. Students with more permanent tube placements may have a gastrostomy button. This device is made of silicon and is put into place by the physician. The button is inserted under the skin through the abdominal cavity. One end is inserted into the stomach or intestine, and the other end comes through the abdominal cavity and appears as an opening on the skin of the abdomen. A dome is inflated around the middle of the button to prevent it from slipping. A feeding tube is attached to the end of the button during feeding. After the feeding, the tube is removed, and a cap is placed on the button. Advantages to this method include 1) less frequent changes of the feeding system, 2) reduced incidence of accidental displacement of the tube and the need to reinsert during the school day, 3) more freedom of movement for the student without fear of dislodging the tube, and 4) more typical appearance of the student during other activities.

Methods   Three basic methods may be followed to meet the nutritional requirements of students requiring tube feedings. The specific method for a given student will be prescribed by the physician. The *tube syringe,* or *gravity,* method is intermittent feeding that is given by a liquid being poured into a receptacle, either a syringe or a funnel, attached to a feeding tube. The rate of flow is regulated as the receptacle is raised or lowered. The higher the receptacle above the level of the stomach, the faster the liquid will flow by gravity from the receptacle through the tube into the stomach. The flow is slowed when the receptacle is lowered. Care must be exercised to avoid too much pressure in the tube or too rapid a flow, because the feeding and other contents of the stomach may be pushed up the esophagus and may enter the airway and cause irritation.

An alternative intermittent feeding method is the *slow-drip* method. A clamp is introduced along the tubing of the feeding system to allow the flow to be regulated by how far one opens or closes the clamp. The advantages to the slow-drip method include decreased 1) vomiting, 2) abdominal cramping, and 3) reflux (contents of the stomach moving back into the airway). The disadvantage is the need for the student to be connected to the feeding apparatus for longer periods of time. Tube feeding may be given continuously throughout the school day. To regulate the slow flow needed for this method, a mechanical infusion pump may be required. The person who spends the most time with the student must become familiar with operating the pump. Issues include how to set and regulate the rate, the capacity of the battery to operate the system, the length of time to recharge the battery, and troubleshooting as problems arise. Like CIC, tube feeding may be classified as a skilled nursing procedure, and the qualifications of a person administering tube feedings may be regulated by law, policy, or guidelines.

Requirements for Administering and Monitoring Tube Feedings   The following requirements apply to all methods of administering and monitoring tube feedings:

1. Tubing should be checked for placement and patency (openness). The parent or health professional (physician or nurse) can provide invaluable information regarding techniques. The tube must be in the proper location and be unobstructed to avoid complications.
2. The student should be fed in an upright (i.e., elevated at least $30°-40°$) or sitting position. If the student is fed in a reclining position, there is increased chance of reflux and aspiration.
3. Generally, the liquid fed should be given at room temperature and should always be refrigerated between feedings to prevent contamination from bacteria. Some students may require slightly warmed liquid. Parents can provide information regarding the temperature best tolerated by the student.
4. Equipment must be clean. Keeping the feeding tube clean requires washing with warm water and soap between feedings or flushing with a small amount of water to remove liquid residue following feeding.
5. Speed of the flow of liquid should be that which has worked well for the student in the past. Parents and health professionals can be helpful with rel-

evant information. This information typically is provided by the physician when tube feeding is first recommended. Generally, one should avoid giving the liquid too fast in order to avoid possible abdominal distension, cramping, reflux, and vomiting.

6. Contamination of the feeding system must be prevented. The end of the feeding tube should be sealed when not in use. A cap usually is available; if one is not, the end may be covered with gauze and held in place with a rubber band.

7. The procedure should be included in the education program for the student in a way that provides opportunities for student decision making, participation, and typical social interaction during eating activities with other students.

8. Appropriate training for all individuals who provide tube feeding is essential. Periodic clinical supervision also must be provided to ensure quality control.

Administering Medication

In general terms, as used here, medication, drug, or medicine is used to describe any substance ingested by (or applied to) an individual intended primarily to influence subsequent behavior, development, or healing. Almost every person in this society uses some of the thousands of available medications at some time, but this chapter emphasizes the few categories of medication and administrations commonly used to treat children with severe or multiple disabilities. These include 1) anticonvulsants, used to control seizures; 2) tranquilizers, used to control undesirable behavior; 3) stimulants, used to control hyperactivity, treat depression, or increase activity level; 4) muscle relaxants, used to decrease excess muscle tone; and 5) nebulizers and inhalers, used to administer bronchodilators, mucolytics, and anti-inflammatory agents. Of course, only a small amount of the information available on these drugs can be included here, so the emphasis will be placed on the purposes for which drugs are prescribed, common side effects of the drugs, and methods of evaluating response to treatment. More detailed information about specific drugs can be found in the *Physicians' Desk Reference* (Barnhart, 1995); the Canadian counterpart, *Compendium of Pharmaceuticals and Specialties* (Canadian Pharmaceutical Association, 1995); or a variety of other reference materials (e.g., Karb, Queener, & Freeman, 1989; Malseed, 1985). Therefore, the information provided here should be considered an overview of selected topics and not a substitute for more specific information or training.

Anticonvulsants   One of the most common uses for anticonvulsant medications with children who have multiple disabilities is for epilepsy. Anticonvulsants do not cure epilepsy, but they can reduce the frequency and severity of seizures (Karb et al., 1989). Although the effectiveness of anticonvulsants varies with the type of epilepsy, environmental factors, and the individual,

Gadow and Poling (1988) reported that medication allows 50% of individuals with epilepsy to be seizure free and another 25% to have significantly fewer and less severe seizures. About 15% are not helped by medication. Unfortunately, the benefits provided must be carefully balanced against undesirable effects of treatment. Often, these include impaired learning and physical and mental performance in addition to changes in behavior and health problems (Santelli, Dodson, & Walter, 1991; Wardell & Bousard, 1985). Since 1968, reliable methods have been available to measure anticonvulsant levels in the blood (Sands & Minters, 1977). Because blood levels may vary independently from dosage levels, these tests have been extremely useful in the regulation of treatment of convulsions.

Although the use of a single drug (monotherapy) is generally recommended and has been associated with a number of advantages, using two or more drugs (polypharmacy) remains a common practice (Gadow & Poling, 1988; Reynolds & Shorvon, 1981). Shreeve (1983) reported that monotherapy provides 1) more rapid establishment of therapeutic blood levels, 2) easier maintenance of those blood levels, 3) better patient compliance (medication is taken more with better regularity), and 4) fewer problems caused by drug interactions. In a related study, Thompson and Trimble (1982) found that reducing polypharmacy and switching some patients to carbamazepine (Tegretol) improved memory, concentration, mental speed, and motor speed with no loss of seizure control. In spite of these findings, however, Gadow and Poling (1988) reported that 50% of children in early childhood special education programs who receive drugs to control seizures receive two or more anticonvulsants. They also reported that 64% of children in self-contained special education classes who receive drugs to control seizures receive two or more anticonvulsants.

Table 6.1 lists some of the anticonvulsant drugs commonly used with children. Drugs are listed by bold generic names, with brand names below in italics. Of course, only the pharmacist, physician, and other appropriately trained health care professional should be directly involved in substitution of equivalent drugs or calculating dosage. Information provided under "Seizures Typically Treated" indicates which types of seizures each type of medication typically is recommended to treat. Typically, anticonvulsants that are not recommended for the specific type of seizure that a child exhibits will not help and often can increase severity or frequency of seizures. "Untoward Reactions/Side Effects" lists some of the more common and more serious undesirable effects of each drug. Many of these can seriously affect behavior, growth, and learning. For example, Gadow (1982) reported that one third of children receiving medication for epilepsy were reported as drowsy by peers and teachers. Hahn and Avioli (1984) reported studies that up to 70% of individuals receiving anticonvulsants have lowered blood calcium levels, which can lead to weakened bones, deformities, and frequent fractures. Therefore, although these drugs are extremely valuable in controlling seizures, they must be used conservatively to minimize undesirable effects. Although anticonvulsants remain the primary treatment for epilepsy, other inter-

Table 6.1.   Some commonly used anticonvulsant drugs

Drug	Seizures typically treated	Untoward reactions/side effects
Carbamazepine *Tegretol*	Complex partial Tonic-clonic	• Confusion, coordination problems, speech disturbances, rash, blood abnormalities, frequent urination, loss of appetite, impaired liver function, changes in blood pressure • Educational impairment often less severe than with other drugs, but blood and liver problems may be serious • Sore throat, loss of appetite, easy bruising may be early signs of serious problems
Dextroamphetamine *Dexedrine*	Absence Sleep	• Dry mouth, diarrhea, loss of appetite, headache, hyperactivity, increased blood pressure, irritability, aggression, psychotic episodes • May increase frequency of some types of seizures
Diazepam Valium	Myoclonic	• Drowsiness, fatigue, lethargy, coordination problems, depression, constipation, weight gain
Ethosuximide *Zarontin*	Absence	• Gastric irritation, drowsiness, coordination problems, dizziness, irritability, hyperactivity, impaired concentration, insomnia, blurred vision, blood abnormalities, rash, hair loss, vaginal bleeding • May increase aggressive behavior
Mephobarbital *Mebaral*	Tonic-clonic	• Lethargy, dizziness, irritability, nausea, diarrhea, blood abnormalities, rash • Often used if phenobarbital causes hyperactivity
Methsuximide *Celontin*	Absence	• Blood abnormalities, liver damage, nausea, diarrhea, vomiting, loss of appetite, drowsiness, coordination and balance problems, confusion, headache, insomnia, rash

(continued)

Table 6.1.   *(continued)*

Drug	Seizures typically treated	Untoward reactions/side effects
Phenobarbital *Luminal*	Tonic-clonic	• Hyperactivity, sedation, impaired learning, dizziness, rash, nausea, diarrhea, blood abnormalities, loss of calcium, bone weakness
Phenytoin *Dilantin*	Tonic-clonic	• Overgrowth of gums, coarsening of facial features, drowsiness, impaired coordination, loss of calcium, bone weakness, slurred speech, nausea, diarrhea, vomiting, difficulty swallowing, rash, increased facial and body hair, joint pain, liver damage, blood abnormalities • May worsen partial seizures
Primidone *Mysoline*	Complex partial	• Folic acid anemia, sedation, impaired learning, dizziness, rash, nausea, drowsiness, hyperactivity, coordination problems
Valproic acid *Depakene*	Myoclonic Tonic-clonic	• Nausea, vomiting, indigestion, lethargy, liver damage, eye damage, dizziness, coordination problems, tremor, loss of hair, hyperactivity, aggression, weakness • Irritation of mouth and throat are likely if capsules are not swallowed whole

ventions also can be useful. Some of these other approaches to controlling epilepsy are discussed in Chapter 5.

Tranquilizers   Gadow and Poling (1988) estimate that 20% of school-age children with mental retardation requiring extensive to pervasive supports receive tranquilizers. These are generally divided into two categories: 1) antipsychotic drugs (major tranquilizers), and 2) antianxiety drugs (minor tranquilizers) (Malseed, 1985). These two groups are compared in Table 6.2. In this table, the "Examples" list drugs by generic names, with brand names in parentheses.

Considerable controversy exists regarding the appropriate use of tranquilizers, especially for children with severe disabilities. For example, the Court of Appeals of Iowa upheld a lower court decision awarding $785,165 to a person who developed chronic movement problems after being treated with antipsychotic drugs in a state institution for individuals with mental retardation (*Clites v. State of Iowa*, 1982). The court found that the use of these drugs was not proper-

Table 6.2.   Tranquilizer categories

	Antianxiety drugs (minor tranquilizers)	Antipsychotic drugs (major tranquilizers)
Examples	Chlordiazepoxide (Librium) Diazepam (Valium) Hydroxyzine (Atarax, Vistaril) Meprobamate (Equanil, Miltown) Oxazepam (Serax)	Chlorpromazine (Thorazine) Chlorprothixene (Taractan) Fluphenazine (Prolixin) Halperidol (Haldol) Mesoridazine (Serentil) Prochlorperazine (Compazine) Perphenazine (Trilafon) Promazine (Sparine) Thioridazine (Mellaril) Trifluoperazine (Stelazine)
Common side effects	(Typically less severe) Drowsiness, fatigue, lethargy, coordination problems, rash, dry mouth, weight gain, impaired learning	(Typically more severe) Drowsiness, low blood pressure, dry mouth, blurry vision, constipation, stuffy nose, palpitations, weight gain, impaired learning
Potentially serious reactions	Confusion, disorientation, slurred speech, hyperactivity, constipation, difficulty swallowing, dizziness, headache, depression, vomiting, increased incidence of tonic-clonic seizures	Lowered seizure threshold, hyperactivity, confusion, insomnia, depression, tremor, movement disorders, blood abnormalities, incontinence

ly monitored, was not part of a therapeutic program, and was not appropriate for the symptoms displayed.

Although some studies suggest clinical improvement in the behavior of children with disabilities treated with tranquilizers, many of these studies have four significant problems (Sobsey, 1989b). First, although some children improve, others do not. There is little information to help predict who will improve, and, often, the absence of an appropriate control group leaves doubt that the number improving is much greater that it would be in the absence of treatment. Second, improvements generally are measured as a simple decrease in undesirable behavior. Because tranquilizers may depress all behavior, however, this so-called improvement may merely reflect the incapacitating effects of the medication. Third, many of these studies have design flaws related to the lack of random assignment of subjects and the use of post hoc analyses instead of true experimental control. Fourth, most published studies compare treatment with tranquilizers to no treatment at all rather than to alternative forms of treatment. When Lennox, Miltenberger, Spengler, and Erfanian (1988) compared drugs to other forms of intervention (e.g., role playing, overcorrection, reinforcement of more appropriate behavior), they found medication to have a very low mean rate of effectiveness. In view of this questionable support for improved function in response to tranquilizers and the severe side effects often associated with long-term use, tranquilizers should be used extremely rarely, if ever, with children who have multiple disabilities. They should be considered only if *all* of the following 10 conditions apply:

1. A specific, observable, measurable behavior problem has been identified.
2. The identified problem presents a risk to the individual's physical health or social adjustment that is more serious than potential drug effects.
3. A thorough, functional analysis of behavior has been completed to determine the function that the undesirable behavior serves for the individual. Some children, for example, develop noncompliant or other inappropriate behavior in response to abuse (Sobsey, 1990). Treating the behavioral system without addressing the abuse is unlikely to succeed.
4. A thorough medical examination has been completed to find any illness or condition that may be contributing to the behavior problem. The pain associated with otitis media (middle ear infection) or toothaches, for example, sometimes precipitates aggressive or self-injurious behavior, particularly in individuals who cannot discuss their problem or seek help in other ways.
5. Less dangerous and intrusive alternatives for controlling the undesirable behavior have been exhausted.
6. Tranquilizers are used as part of—not in place of—a comprehensive program for behavior change.
7. Tranquilizers are used for a limited, prespecified period.
8. The behavior requiring intervention is observed and recorded before and during drug treatment.
9. A specific, minimum criterion for behavioral improvement is specified and achieved (otherwise, use of tranquilizers is discontinued).
10. A plan is implemented to observe, record, and evaluate health, behavior, and learning side effects.

Stimulants   Another category of drugs used to control behavior in children with multiple disabilities is stimulants. A survey of elementary schools in four areas of the United States found that although the mean rate of use of stimulants was less than 2% of all students, usage tended to be significantly higher in some school districts, particularly in urban areas and in those with more students with disabilities (Frankenberger, Lozar, & Dallas, 1990). Although these drugs have been demonstrated as effective in reducing hyperactivity in some children, group studies involving subjects with severe and multiple disabilities have failed to show positive effects (Gadow, 1986). Other studies involving subjects with mental disabilities requiring intermittent and limited supports have shown inconsistent results. When stimulants proved effective, they were combined with other educational and behavioral treatment approaches, which led Mira and Reece (1977) to conclude that "the use of medication alone or as primary treatment, although a common practice, is not warranted on the basis of what we know about the complexity of problems of hyperactivity" (p. 63). Unfortunately, stimulants are rarely used as an adjunctive treatment; when used, they are typically the sole therapy (Bosco & Robin, 1980).

Stimulants also have negative side effects, most frequently insomnia, loss of appetite, and depression or agitation on withdrawal (Cohen, 1980; Karb et al., 1989). Although recovery from growth retardation tends to occur after withdrawal from treatment (Levitsky, 1984), long-term treatment may result in permanent losses. In view of this information, stimulants should be considered rarely and used only as a partial intervention, not the whole treatment. Although these drugs have different effects, the differences usually exist primarily in degree and are, therefore, spoken of here in general terms for convenience.

Muscle Relaxants Children with excess muscle tone are sometimes treated with muscle relaxants, although this treatment remains relatively rare (Gadow & Poling, 1988). Often, minor tranquilizers (e.g., diazepam, meprobamate) are used to reduce tone in muscles affected by cerebral palsy, but their general sedative effects make them undesirable for many children, and, generally, benefits are limited (Gadow & Poling, 1988). Dantrium (dantrolene sodium) continues to be used for some children, especially those in whom spasticity results in discomfort (Karb et al., 1989). Like stimulants, muscle relaxants can have a number of undesired effects. Drowsiness, impaired memory and learning, depression, dizziness, weakness, and vomiting are common side effects. Careful measurement of the drugs' benefits must be considered along with risks to each individual.

Nebulizers and Inhalers Some medication, particularly medication for respiratory problems, is administered by nebulizer or inhaler (California Department of Education, 1990). A nebulizer is a device that converts liquid medication into an aerosol mist. The child breathes the mist with the aid of a mouthpiece or mask for a prespecified period of time (e.g., 10 minutes) or until the medication is used up. An inhaler is a small pressurized container that can deliver short bursts of aerosol medication intended for inhalation in a single breath or a few breaths. A full inhaler can deliver 200–300 brief puffs of aerosol medication. A full inhaler is not suitable to deliver medication over longer periods of time but generally contains more concentrated forms of medication.

Timing is critical with the use of an inhaler. The medication must be sprayed just as the child is about to breathe in deeply (California Department of Education, 1990). If the timing is incorrect, the child may get little or none of the medication into his or her lungs. In addition, it may be difficult for the person who is administering the medication to be certain whether the timing was correct or not, and making the wrong guess can result in too much or too little medication. For this reason, nebulizers are often the preferred mode of administering medication to children with disabilities. Nevertheless, inhalers may be useful because they are much more portable and because they are a very fast way to administer medication in an emergency situation.

Three kinds of medication commonly administered by nebulizer are 1) bronchodilators, to help open the airway; 2) mucolytics, to help break up secretions in the lungs; and 3) anti-inflammatory drugs, to reduce swelling and irritation in the lungs. School personnel often administer these medications under the indirect supervision of nursing staff (California Department of Education, 1990). Staff participating should be well trained by professionals and periodically supervised directly. Specific protocols for administration should be carefully consulted. It is essential that all equipment be washed, allowed to dry fully, and periodically disinfected, because contaminants will be introduced directly into the lungs and soap or disinfectant can be harmful. In some cases, the person who administers the medication may need to monitor pulse and respiration. Because bronchodilators are typically powerful stimulants, careful monitoring of responses can be essential with some children. Children with multiple disabilities often do better with a mask that covers their mouth and nose rather than a mouthpiece that must be kept in the mouth or inserted for each inhalation. Many children remove the mask frequently until they become used to the procedure, but most tolerate it well after they become accustomed to it. Engaging the child in a reinforcing activity or interaction during nebulization generally helps minimize removal of the mask. The individual administering medication must also be careful that the chamber holding the medication does not become grossly contaminated with saliva, mucus, or vomitus during the procedure, because these substances will also be nebulized and introduced into the child's lungs. If the medication chamber becomes grossly contaminated, it will be necessary to stop and restart with clean equipment and new medication. If children drool, it is sometimes helpful to punch a small hole at the lowest point in the inhalation mask to allow drainage of saliva from the mask and decrease the risk of saliva entering the medication chamber.

Team Roles Related to Medication   Although major responsibility for decisions about medication rests with the physician, pharmacists, and other health care professionals, all transdisciplinary team members must be involved in medical treatment. Three major areas require specific consideration: 1) observing treatment effects, 2) observing side effects and adverse reactions, and 3) providing treatment alternatives.

Observing Treatment Effects   Any drug prescribed should be directed toward a specific goal (e.g., to reduce seizures, to improve learning). To evaluate the effectiveness of the drug, the transdisciplinary team should develop a specific criterion and continue careful observation and record keeping. Teachers, therapists, and other team members should help develop goals and criteria. For example, if Dantrium is given to reduce spasticity, the physical therapist should determine an appropriate measure of spasticity and measure it repeatedly before treatment. Once the level and variability of spasticity is known, the therapist, physician, and other team members should decide how much improvement would be required to justify the use of medication. They should then conduct ongoing evaluation during treatment to determine whether the criterion is met.

Observing Side Effects and Adverse Reactions   Because side effects and adverse reactions are difficult to predict, observing them is more complex than observing treatment effects. All team members should be acquainted with potential side effects and be alerted to medication changes to maximize the chance of early recognition of any developing problems. It should be pointed out that side effects may take a long time to develop, so they can occur at any time.

Providing Treatment Alternatives   Possibly, the most valuable thing that the team can do regarding medication is to provide effective programming that does not require the use of medication. Physicians are criticized frequently for using drugs to treat behavior problems, but, if the physician is not communicating adequately with other team members, he or she might assume that all other educational and behavioral approaches were exhausted before a medical referral was made. Careful implementation of well-designed programs will eliminate the need for treatment with medication in most problems with behavior. Many children treated with drugs do as well or better with behavioral therapy (Duckham-Shoor, 1980).

Storing and Dispensing Medication   Many children with multiple disabilities receive medication at school. This creates significant concern about procedures used to store and administer these medications. Although it is not known how many states currently have laws regulating administration of medications in schools, Wood and colleagues (1986) point out that clear guidelines regarding medication administration are unavailable generally. Many drugs used (especially stimulants and many anticonvulsants) are controlled substances (Malseed, 1985). In hospitals, these drugs require tight security (e.g., must be kept in a locked box inside a locked drug cabinet, every pill counted between shifts). This kind of security is not typically provided in schools. Laws and policies require trained nurses to dispense drugs in hospitals; however, teachers, associates, and secretaries dispense them in some schools (Gadow & Kane, 1983).

School personnel who administer medication must be appropriately trained and must follow a set of procedures that has administrative approval and complies with relevant law. These procedures must specify 1) who can dispense medications; 2) an appropriate system for storing medications; 3) labeling requirements (including simple language, without codes or abbreviations); 4) recording procedures; and 5) a method of communication between the person administering medication and the physician.

Many people with developmental disabilities, including some with multiple disabilities, learn to administer their own medications. Although self-administration may not be a reasonable alternative for very young students, many older students can learn to self-administer medication with various degrees of assistance or supervision (Harchik, 1994). When appropriate, teaching children with disabilities to administer their own medication helps prepare them for greater independence as adults.

Communication with the Physician

As suggested previously, lack of communication between the physician and other team members is a common and serious problem. Although there may be many methods for improving communication, one simple method is the use of a concise communication form that shows relevant behavior observations, areas of concern, and the physician's response (Brulle, Barton, & Foskett, 1983).

General Guidelines for Administration of Health-Related Procedures

Specific guidelines for performing a variety of health-related procedures can be found in many excellent manuals. Still, one must exercise caution to avoid assuming that reading alone is adequate preparation for performing these procedures. Most of the procedures are skill based and require, besides reading, opportunities for performance under the supervision of a well-trained parent or health professional.

The more thorough the planning and preparation, the easier it is to integrate the procedure into the daily routine for the student in the classroom. Essential elements of a well-designed program of special, health-related school services include a thorough knowledge of the purpose for which a procedure is to be performed, policies and guidelines for performing the procedure, individualized methods, monitoring student reactions to the procedure and learning how to handle them, and where and how to record performance of the procedure.

Planning for Health-Related Procedures

Upon receiving a request to provide special health-related procedures during the school day, the school administrator must decide whether the resources within the system are sufficient to ensure the safety of the student while providing appropriate educational opportunities. New and different health care procedures may cause fear and apprehension, especially for individuals unfamiliar with them. The tendency in the past has been to meet the student's education needs in home programs or noninclusive schools, yet it is recognized that such action limits the opportunities of these students to have the benefits of educational services within the context of a general education classroom. A systematic, planned approach can alleviate much of the concern. Such an approach should address the following phases.

Initial Planning Phase   The initial planning phase begins with selection of a student coordinator. This individual should be familiar with the implications of the health-related procedure and knowledgeable about the school resources. Where available, the school nurse is an ideal candidate to establish and maintain effective communication among the school, physician, and parents throughout this initial phase and to serve as student coordinator. A few school districts employ physicians to serve this function (Sobsey, Orelove, Sehring, & Todaro, 1989). As the student proceeds through program eligibility, the coordinator is responsible for facilitating the process by ensuring that all the necessary forms are completed, evaluation sessions are attended, consents are received, and issues are addressed.

After student evaluation, the school team, parents, physician, student, and personnel from other relevant community resources hold a planning meeting to identify issues from a variety of perspectives that must be addressed in the individualized education program. Questions regarding the nature and extent of the procedure (e.g., who will be responsible for administration, the safety issues, the responsibilities of the parents, whether other support services are indicated) can and should be addressed during this planning meeting, particularly when a special health-related procedure is required. The result should be the development of an IEP that is reasonable, supportive of the student's education program, inclusive, and nonrestrictive. Another outcome of this planning meeting is the enhancement of collaborative decision making and the clarification of expectations of those involved. Such collaborative decision making will lead to a transdisciplinary service model.

Physicians rarely participate directly in IEP meetings. In a study of five nationally dispersed urban school districts, Palfrey et al. (1986) found that physicians attended only 1.8% of IEP meetings. With or without direct participation, however, it is essential that physicians be aware of and contribute to school-based health care programs, and it is important that they have the opportunity to contribute to other components of the IEP.

The team develops the IEP with parents and appropriate health care professionals as full partners in the decision-making process. Decisions regarding placement are made during the development of the IEP. It is important for educational placement decisions to be made for provision of services in the most appropriate setting and in the LRE for each individual student; decisions should not be based primarily on the need for health care. During the IEP development meetings, the team should define and discuss what must take place during the next phase of planning, the pre-entrance phase. A school health services plan may be developed as a component of the IEP or as a separate document. Because the needs of students with complex health care needs will change frequently, a separate health services plan that can be revised and updated regularly is preferred (Lowman & Rosenkoetter, 1994). The school health services plan should specify the health care procedures required by the student; who will carry out the procedures; any training that is required; who will provide clinical supervision; and any documentation, equipment, or resources that are necessary. Figure 6.2 illustrates a page from a sample school health services plan. Although a separate school health services plan may not be necessary for every child, the categories of information illustrated in the sample plan should be addressed for each procedure required by a student and incorporated in some manner as part of the child's IEP.

Pre-entrance Phase   After the development of the IEP, the second phase, pre-entrance, includes those activities that are necessary for implementing the education program, including providing health-related procedures. The team will need to identify whether there are guidelines or protocols in place within the local or state education agency to provide guidance regarding the health-related procedures required for the student. If not, these guidelines must be developed. Guidelines generally include the purpose of the procedure, safeguards, equipment needs, training, supervision, and a record-keeping system. If adaptation or modification of the procedure is indicated, approval by the physician and parent must be obtained in writing.

Most of what occurs during this phase includes identifying who will administer the procedure and how training will be completed. Five areas of training must be considered: 1) specific procedures, 2) emergency measures, 3) back-up equipment and supply needs, 4) precautions, and 5) record keeping. It is helpful to identify one person to be responsible for all aspects of training. The school nurse, community nurse, physician, and parent may all be involved. The

School Health Care Plan	Name: *John Doe*	Date: *December 20, 1996*	Page: *1/5*

Procedure:	Administer oral antivconvulsants (as ordered by physician)
Goal/Rationale:	Seizure control
Schedule:	Daily/after lunch
Duration:	Allow 10 minutes for set-up, administration, and recording
Staff:	Trained classroom teacher
Backup:	Trained teacher from another classroom
Required training:	18-hour medication course
Clinical supervision:	Direct observation by an R.N. at least once in each 60-day period
Clinical supervision dates:	9/15/1997 Jane Goe, R.N. 11/11/1997 Jane Goe, R.N.
Evaluation:	Physician reviews orders once per month, blood tests as required, school nurse visits at least every 2 weeks
Target date:	Ongoing, consider reduction on reviews if seizure free
Review dates:	Every 30 days
Documentation:	Sign medication record, maintain seizure observation records
Contacts:	Parents' home 555-1234, work 555-4321; Dr. Poe's office 555-9876
Resources:	*Physicians' Desk Reference* in principal's office; drug administration form
Equipment:	Locked medicine cabinet in classroom
Precautions:	Contact school nurse for advice before giving medications if John appears quite drowsy; parents notify school immediately if medication orders are changed
Other:	See drug administration form for additional information

Teacher: *A. Boe*   Principal: *B. Coe*   Parent: *C. Doe*   Nurse: *J. Goe*   Physician: *K. Poe*

Figure 6.2.   A sample page from a school health services plan, a component of an IEP.

important issue is that the person providing training must be competent in the procedure and available for support following training. Collaboration between the parent, who is uniquely qualified in understanding what works best for the student, and a health professional, ideally the school or community nurse, who is licensed, generally works well. For professionals to become familiar with individual students and their unique needs, it is helpful for parents to bring their children to the school for the demonstration and practice of procedures (Schwab et al., 1990).

Other issues to be addressed during the pre-entrance phase include the identification and training of support personnel. A back-up system of qualified personnel is essential for times when the primary caregiver is absent or unable to perform the procedure. Anticipating the training needs of individuals involved in transportation, playground supervision, and emergency services must be addressed before the student enters school.

Finally, some attention must be given to whether the environment supports the completion of the procedure in a manner that is safe and accommodates the right to privacy. The classroom environment must be equipped with hot and cold water for washing hands and equipment. Refrigeration may be required for storing feeding liquids and medications. An area equipped with a cot that is shielded somewhat from other activity in the room may be useful not only during certain procedures but also when a student becomes ill. The school nurse and teacher can discuss what environmental supports will be needed. The time and effort spent during the pre-entrance phase is crucial to ensure the safety of the student, confidence and legal protection of school personnel, and clarification of roles and responsibilities.

Monitoring Procedures   The third phase involves monitoring procedures and begins when the student enters the classroom. The student coordinator will need to evaluate the effectiveness of the planning and training. The monitoring of procedures will be most intensive during the first several weeks. Questions that must be answered during this phase include the following:

1. Is the procedure being provided in a safe and effective manner?
2. Is the record-keeping system sufficient without being cumbersome?
3. Are staffing needs adequate?
4. Is the process supportive of the student's education program?
5. Are the parents comfortable with and supportive of the plan?
6. Is communication between the school and home ongoing and effective?

If the answer to any of these questions is no, then certain modifications may be required. However, with adequate time and appropriate support, some issues may be resolved. It is important to recognize that the integration of certain health-related procedures into the education program is a new and different set of responsibilities for educators and support personnel in public schools.

NURSING ROLE ON TRANSDISCIPLINARY TEAMS

Effective transdisciplinary team members share a common purpose, compatible personal qualities, and a values and belief system that are suitable underpinnings for the decisions regarding student programs (Giangreco, York, & Rainforth, 1989). As members of these teams, nurses recognize that their contribution must extend beyond a competent, purely unidisciplinary perspective. Like all other team members, they must be willing to share and learn information and skills across traditional disciplinary boundaries. This willingness supports the view of one's role from a perspective of reciprocal, collaborative interaction in which the release of traditional roles is valued.

Nurses typically share in the belief that health care practices should be the least restrictive for the student, and they will try to provide services in a manner consistent with maximizing inclusion. For example, a student requiring intermittent tube feeding does not need to be removed from the classroom and taken to an office for the procedure. It may be more appropriate to provide the feeding in the classroom or, even better, in the cafeteria. The more the procedure is treated as a typical experience, the better the student's peers will accept the student and the procedure.

Optimizing the health status of students is an important element in achieving educational progress. Frequent absences from school, distraction resulting from discomfort, and drowsiness associated with illness are several ways in which poor health threatens educational success. Also, health-care service delivery should support the education program in a manner that emphasizes educational outcomes. Additionally, a health care procedure should be included with other instructional methods within the context of the functional activities of the instructional environment. This is particularly relevant for students requiring CIC. The educational goal for these students might be to develop independence in activities of daily living to the greatest extent possible. In addressing this goal, the teacher, parent, and school nurse may use the activities involved in CIC as an opportunity to foster independence. They may begin by assessing the current level of involvement in the procedure and follow by deciding, with the student, how acquisition of the skill must gradually develop for greater independence in performing the procedure. The involvement of the parent in the decision-making process at the outset will provide for consistency in approach between home and school. The participation of the student will encourage motivation and communication.

Provision of services must foster the belief that students with severe and multiple disabilities can be educated in the LRE of classrooms with peers without disabilities. The concept of inclusion has particular relevance for nurses assuming responsibility for planning, providing, and supervising school health-related services and procedures that support the education program.

Nurses may provide direct care to students, conduct pre-intervention and progress evaluations, and provide technical assistance and consultation to other team members. Technical assistance may include 1) health information and referral services, 2) workshops and other forms of in-service training, and 3) on-site consultation and training individualized to the student and setting (Sciarillo et al., 1988). Nurses often provide a primary channel of communication between the education and medical communities (Holvoet & Helmstetter, 1989).

Limitations on Realizing Transdisciplinary Team Nursing Roles

The role of school nursing services as part of a transdisciplinary team service model in planning for and providing health-related services for students may be confounded by restrictions imposed by a given state's Nurse Practice Act. Typically, these acts specify the dependent and independent activities in which the licensed nurse can legally engage. The importance of full knowledge regarding the implications of these acts must be stressed because they provide state policies that may affect whether school nurses are permitted to function with regard to health-related procedures within the school setting. For example, a state Nurse Practice Act may restrict the nurse from training a teacher or any non-nursing personnel in performing tracheal suctioning unless the nurse assumes supervisory responsibility. The nurse may be reluctant to delegate responsibility for the procedure if the nurse can be available only one time a week for supervision, especially during the early weeks of skill monitoring. Clear, written consents from the physician and the student's parents and guidelines and policy at the local level will support the nurse in her or his supervisory role. Likewise, a somewhat flexible schedule that is adaptable to the particular needs in the schools at any given period will support the nurse as he or she addresses particular supervisory functions.

The role of the school nurse may involve actually performing a procedure, training others to perform the procedure, supervising and coordinating the management of a procedure in the classroom, or serving as a consultant and providing support for the classroom teacher. Mulligan-Ault et al. (1988) revealed that teachers of students with severe disabilities in Kansas were willing to assume the responsibility for implementing many health-related procedures. Still, they felt that the school nurse should assume responsibility for implementing others. It is notable that the mix of procedures designated as the responsibility of teachers was as complex as those that teachers believed the school nurse should assume. Complicating the delineation of the roles of teachers and school nurses is the reality that school nurses may be unfamiliar with some health-related procedures and require training themselves. Training others, performing health-related procedures, monitoring outcomes, consulting, and evaluating are new responsibilities for many school nurses. As school systems serve more students with

246 Sobsey and Cox

multiple disabilities who have special health care needs, the role of the school nurse must be more clearly defined and supported.

Collaborative Service Delivery

For students requiring special health care procedures during the day, opportunities to receive transdisciplinary services are enhanced through reciprocal, collaborative teamwork among parents, school nurses, and educators. As those most familiar with the health care needs of their own children, parents have the primary responsibility for providing health care to their children. To the maximum extent possible, health care procedures should be carried out before and after school. However, it is recognized that certain health care procedures will be required during the school day. Families of students with multiple disabilities should be full partners in the decision-making process necessary for the transition into the school environment.

The school nurse brings a traditional, holistic approach to providing health care services to the student within the context of the family and community. The teaching role of the nurse is deeply entrenched within the discipline. The nurse is responsible for teaching the family various interventions, procedures, and monitoring protocols in preparation for a child's discharge from the hospital. Community health nurses have particular knowledge about community resources that may be of assistance to the student and family. The nurse is in the unique position of having an understanding of the interactive nature of the various physiological systems of the body and being able to combine this with sound clinical judgment. Most important, perhaps, the nurse has a strong family orientation and values time spent working with parents. In concert with the primary physician, the nurse can serve as a student coordinator in the education system for students with special health care needs.

Parents and nurses can gain valuable perspectives from the educator through collaborative planning. In particular, the educator's focus on enhancing the functional abilities of the student places the education program within the context appropriate for approaching the student as a learner, not a patient. The educator's knowledge of the student's unique learning characteristics is invaluable. Finally, the educator's emphasis on the ideas and values inherent in integration and normalization shape the direction and intent of activities regarding educational opportunities.

Together, the parent, nurse, and educator can plan, implement, and evaluate the response of the student with special health care needs better than each can individually. With full communication and support of the physician and the school administrator, decisions can be reached collaboratively regarding how to modify and adapt health care techniques in an inclusive school setting; when and how to implement procedures to attain the desired educational outcomes; and how and to whom to provide training, monitoring, and evaluation.

REFERENCES

Abromowicz, H.K., & Richardson, S.A. (1975). Epidemiology of severe mental retardation in children: Community studies. *American Journal of Mental Deficiency, 80,* 18–39.

Altshuler, A., Meyer, J., & Butz, M.K.J. (1977). Even children can learn to do self-catheterization. *American Journal of Nursing, 77*(1), 97–101.

Anderson, H.R., Butland, B.K., & Strachan, D.P. (1994). Trends in prevalence and severity of childhood asthma. *British Medical Journal, 308*(6944), 1600–1604.

Barnhart, E.R. (1995). *Physicians' desk reference* (45th ed.). Oradell, NJ: Medical Economics Company.

Bevin, H. by Michael H. v. Wright, 666 F. Supp. 71 (W.D. Penn. 1987).

Blackman, J.A. (1990). Middle ear disease. In J.A. Blackman (Ed.), *Medical aspects of developmental disabilities in children birth to three* (pp. 191–196). Rockville, MD: Aspen Publishers, Inc.

Bosco, J.J., & Robin, S.S. (1980). *Parent, teacher and physician in the life of the hyperactive child: The coherence of the social environment.* Rockville, MD: National Institute of Mental Health. (ERIC Document No. ED 244 498)

Brulle, A.R., Barton, L.E., & Foskett, J.J. (1983). Educator/physician interchanges: A survey and suggestions. *Education and Training of the Mentally Retarded, 18,* 313–317.

California Department of Education. (1990). *Guidelines and procedures for meeting the specialized physical health care needs of pupils.* Sacramento, CA: Author.

Canadian Pharmaceutical Association. (1995). *Compendium of pharmaceuticals and specialties* (30th ed.). Ottawa, Ontario: Canadian Pharmaceutical Association.

Carlson, C.M., & O'Connell, E.J. (1993). Asthma in childhood: A review. *Minnesota Medicine, 76,*(9), 31–33.

Chomicki, S., & Wilgosh, L. (1994). Obtaining health care for individuals with intellectual impairments: A literature review. *Physical Disabilities: Education and Related Services, 13*(2), 55–69.

Clites v. State of Iowa, 322 N.W.2d 917 (Iowa Court of Appeals, 1982).

Cohen, L. (1990). *Before their time: Fetuses and infants at risk.* Washington, DC: American Association on Mental Retardation.

Cohen, M.W. (1980). Medications. In J. Umbreit & P.J. Cardullias (Eds.), *Educating the severely physically handicapped: Treatment and management of medically related disorders* (Vol. 2, pp. 1–7). Columbus, OH: Special Press.

Department of Education, State of Hawaii v. Dorr. U.S. District Court, 727 F. 2d 809 (D.H. Cir. 1983).

Detsel by Detsel v. Board of Education of Auburn, 637 F. Supp. 1022 (N.D.N.Y. 1986).

Duckham-Shoor, L.A. (1980). *Behavioral alternatives to stimulant medication in treating childhood hyperactivity: Effects on school and home behavior: Final report.* Washington, DC: Office of Special Education and Rehabilitative Services. (ERIC Document No. ED 244 503)

Education for All Handicapped Children Act of 1975, PL 94-142, 20 U.S.C. § 1400 *et seq.*

Education of the Handicapped Act Amendments of 1986, PL 99-457, 20 U.S.C. § 1400 *et seq.*

Frankenberger, W., Lozar, B., & Dallas, P. (1990). The use of stimulant medication to treat attention deficit hyperactive disorder in elementary school children. *Developmental Disabilities Bulletin, 18*(1), 1–13.

Gadow, K.D. (1982). Problems with students on medication. *Exceptional Children, 49,* 20–27.

Gadow, K.D. (1986). *Children on medication: Vol. I. Hyperactivity, learning difficulties and mental retardation.* San Diego, CA: College-Hill Press.

Gadow, K.D., & Kane, K.M. (1983). Administration of medication by school personnel. *Journal of School Health, 53,* 178–183.

Gadow, K.D., & Poling, A.G. (1988). *Pharmacotherapy and mental retardation.* Boston: Little, Brown.

Giangreco, M.F., York, J., & Rainforth, B. (1989). Providing related services to learners with severe handicaps in educational settings: Pursuing the least restrictive option. *Pediatric Physical Therapy, 1*(2), 55–63.

Gittler, J., & Colton, M. (1987). *Alternatives to hospitalization for technology dependent children: Program models.* Iowa City: University of Iowa, National Maternal Child Health Resources Center.

Haas, G., Buchwald-Saal, M., Leidig, E., & Mentzel, H. (1986). Improved outcome in very low birth weight infants from 1977 to 1983. *European Journal of Pediatrics, 145,* 337–340.

Hagberg, B., Hagberg, G., & Olow, I. (1982). Gains and hazards of intensive neonatal care: An analysis from Swedish cerebral palsy epidemiology. *Developmental Medicine and Child Neurology, 24,* 13–19.

Hahn, T.J., & Avioli, L.V. (1984). Anticonvulsant-drug-induced mineral disorders. In D.A. Roe & T.C. Campbell (Eds.), *Drugs and nutrients: The interactive effects* (pp. 409–427). New York: Marcel Dekker.

Harchik, A.E. (1994). Self-medication skills. In M. Agran, N.E. Marchand-Martella, & R.C. Martella (Eds.), *Promoting health and safety: Skills for independent living* (pp. 55–69). Baltimore: Paul H. Brookes Publishing Co.

Harvey, B. (1982). Asthma. In E.E. Bleck & D.A. Nagel (Eds.), *Physically handicapped children: A medical atlas for teachers* (2nd ed., pp. 31–42). New York: Grune & Stratton.

Healy, A. (1990). Anemia. In J.A. Blackman (Ed.), *Medical aspects of developmental disabilities in children birth to three* (pp. 1–7). Rockville, MD: Aspen Publishers, Inc.

Heller, K.W., Alberto, P.A., Schwartzman, M.N., Shiplett, K., Pierce, J., Polokoff, J., Heller, E.J., Andrews, D.G., Briggs, A., & Kana, T.G. (1990). *Suggested physical health procedures for educators of students with special needs.* Atlanta: Georgia State University.

Holvoet, J.F., & Helmstetter, E. (1989). *Medical problems of students with special needs: A guide for educators.* Boston: Little, Brown.

Howenstine, M.S. (1992). Pulmonary concerns. In S.M. Pueschel & J.K. Pueschel (Eds.), *Biomedical concerns in persons with Down syndrome* (pp. 105–118). Baltimore: Paul H. Brookes Publishing Co.

Individuals with Disabilities Education Act (IDEA) of 1990, PL 101-476, 20 U.S.C. § 1400 *et seq.*

Irving Independent School District v. Tatro, 468 U.S. 883, 82 L. Ed. 2d 664, 104 S. Ct. 3371 (1984).

Johnson, M.P., Lubker, B.B., & Fowler, M.G. (1988). Teacher needs assessment for the educational management of children with chronic illnesses. *Journal of School Health, 58,* 232–235.

Joint Task Force for the Management of Children with Special Health Needs. (1990). *Report on the delineation of roles and responsibilities for the safe delivery of specialized health care in the educational setting.* Reston, VA: Council for Exceptional Children.

Kansas Nurse Practice Act, Revisions of 1988, § 65-1124 (1988).

Karb, V.B., Queener, S.F., & Freeman, J.B. (1989). *Handbook of drugs for nursing practice.* St. Louis, MO: C.V. Mosby.

Kaufman, J., & Hardy-Ribakow, D. (1987). Home care: A model of a comprehensive approach for technology-assisted chronically ill children. *Journal of Pediatric Nursing, 4,* 244–249.

Knight, D., & Wadsworth, D.E. (1994). Guidelines for educating students who are technology dependent. *Physical Disabilities: Education and Related Services, 13*(1), 1–8.

Kohrman, A.F. (1984). *Criteria for admission to programs for funding: Home care for children with serious handicapping conditions.* Proceedings of the Association for the Care of Children's Health Conference, Houston, TX.

Koop, C.E. (1987). *Surgeon General's report: Children with special health care needs* (DHHS Publication No. HRS/D/MC 87-2). Rockville, MD: U.S. Department of Health and Human Services.

Lehr, D.H., & Noonan, M.J. (1989). Issues in the education of students with complex health care needs. In F. Brown & D.H. Lehr (Eds.), *Persons with profound disabilities: Issues and practices* (pp. 139–160). Baltimore: Paul H. Brookes Publishing Co.

Lennox, D.B., Miltenberger, R.G., Spengler, P., & Erfanian, N. (1988). Decelerative treatment practices with persons who have mental retardation: A review of five years of literature. *American Journal on Mental Retardation, 92,* 492–501.

Levitsky, D.A. (1984). Drugs, appetite and body weight. In D.A. Roe & T.C. Campbell (Eds.), *Drugs and nutrients: The interactive effects* (pp. 375–408). New York: Marcel Dekker.

Lowman, D.K., & Rosenkoetter, S.E. (1994). Creating successful transitions for children with complex health care needs: New friends on the journey. In S. Rosenkoetter, A. Haines, & S. Fowler, *Bridging early services for children with special needs and their families: A practical guide for transition planning* (pp. 181–196). Baltimore: Paul H. Brookes Publishing Co.

Malseed, R.T. (1985). *Pharmacology: Drug therapy and nursing considerations* (2nd ed.). Philadelphia: J.B. Lippincott.

Marlow, N., D'Souza, S.W., & Chiswick, M.L. (1987). Neurodevelopmental outcome in babies weighing less than 2001 g at birth. *British Medical Journal, 294,* 1582–1586.

McCormick, M.C. (1993). Has the prevalence of handicapped infants increased with improved survival of the very low birth weight infant? *Clinical Perinatology, 20*(1), 263–277.

Menolascino, F.J., & Stark, J.A. (Eds.). (1988). *Preventive and curative intervention in mental retardation.* Baltimore: Paul H. Brookes Publishing Co.

Mira, M., & Reece, C.A. (1977). Medical management of the hyperactive child. In M.J. Fine (Ed.), *Principles and techniques of intervention with hyperactive children* (pp. 47–76). Springfield, IL: Charles C Thomas.

Morse, J.S., & Colatarci, S. (1994). The impact of technology. In S.P. Roth & J.S. Morse (Eds.), *A life-span approach to nursing care for individuals with developmental disabilities* (pp. 351–383). Baltimore: Paul H. Brookes Publishing Co.

Moskop, J.C., & Saldanha, R.L. (1986, April). The Baby Doe rule: Still a threat. *Hastings Center Report, 16*(2), 8–14.

Mulligan-Ault, M., Guess, D., Struth, L., & Thompson, B. (1988). The implementation of health-related procedures in classrooms for students with severe multiple impairments. *Journal of The Association for Persons with Severe Handicaps, 13*(2), 100–109.

New York State Department of Education. (1988, December). *Nursing handbook.* Albany, NY: Author.

Nolan, T. (1994). Asthma. In I.B. Pless (Ed.), *The epidemiology of childhood disorders* (pp. 414–438). New York: Oxford University Press.

Orelove, F.P., & Sobsey, D. (1990, December). *Who should deliver health care services to children with severe disabilities in public schools?* Paper presented at the Sixteenth Annual Conference of The Association for Persons with Severe Handicaps, Chicago.

Palfrey, J.S., Singer, J.D., Walker, D.K., & Butler, J.A. (1986). Health and special education: A study of new developments for handicapped children in five metropolitan communities. *Public Health Reports, 101,* 379–388.

Reynolds, E.H., & Shorvon, S.D. (1981). Monotherapy or polytherapy for epilepsy? *Epilepsia, 22,* 1–10.

Robertson, C.M.T., & Etches, P.C. (1988). Decreased incidence of neurological disability among neonates at high risk born between 1975 and 1984 in Alberta. *Canadian Medical Association Journal, 139,* 225–229.

Sands, H., & Minters, F.C. (1977). *The epilepsy fact book.* Philadelphia: F.A. Davis.

Santelli, N., Dodson, W.E., & Walter, A.V. (1991). *Students with seizures: A manual for school nurses.* Cedar Grove, NJ: HealthScan, Inc.

Schwab, W., Brown, L., & Grant, L. (1990, December). *Parent–professional collaboration in planning services for children with special health care needs.* Paper presented at the Sixteenth Annual Conference of The Association for Persons with Severe Handicaps, Chicago.

Sciarillo, W.G., Draper, S., Green, P., Burkett, K., & Demetrides, S. (1988). Children with specialized health care needs in the special education setting: A statewide technical assistance approach. *Infants and Young Children, 1,* 74–84.

Shapiro, S., McCormick, M.C., Starfield, B.H., & Crawley, B. (1983). Changes in infant morbidity associated with decreases in neonatal mortality. *Pediatrics, 72,* 408–415.

Shreeve, C. (1983, May 11). Treating epilepsy. *Nursing Mirror, 156,* 20–21.

Smith, J.S. (1990). *Patenting the son: Polio and the Salk vaccine.* New York: William Morrow & Co.

Sobsey, D. (1989a). Are we preventing mental retardation? *Newsletter of the American Association on Mental Retardation, 2*(2), 2, 8.

Sobsey, D. (1989b). Issues in the use of medications. *Newsletter of the American Association on Mental Retardation, 2*(4), 2, 8.

Sobsey, D. (1990). Modifying the behavior of behavior modifiers: Arguments for countercontrol against aversive procedures. In A.C. Repp & N.N. Singh (Eds.), *Perspectives on the use of nonaversive and aversive interventions for persons with developmental disabilities* (pp. 421–433). Sycamore, IL: Sycamore Publishing Company.

Sobsey, D., Orelove, F., Sehring, M., & Todaro, A. (1989, December). *Health care and education.* Paper presented at the Fifteenth Annual Conference of The Association for Persons with Severe Handicaps, San Francisco.

Statutes of Alberta. (1990, September 1). *Nursing Profession Act* (Chapter N-14.5). Edmonton.

Taylor, M. (1990). Clean intermittent catheterization. In J.C. Graff, M.M. Ault, D. Guess, M. Taylor, & B. Thompson. *Health care for students with disabilities: An illustrated medical guide for the classroom* (pp. 241–252). Baltimore: Paul H. Brookes Publishing Co.

Thompson, B.J., & Trimble, M.R. (1982). Anticonvulsant drugs and cognitive function. *Epilepsia, 23,* 531–544.

Todisco, T., de Benedictis, F.M., Iannacci, L., Baglioni, S., Eslami A., Todisco, E., & Dottorini, M. (1993). Mild prematurity and respiratory functions. *European Journal of Pediatrics, 152*(1), 55–58.

Truman, J.T. (1984). The blood. In M. Ziai (Ed.), *Pediatrics* (3rd ed., pp. 387–410). Boston: Little, Brown.

U.S. Congress, Office of Technology Assessment. (1987). *Technology-dependent children: Hospital v. home care—A technical memorandum* (OTA-TM-H-38). Washington, DC: U.S. Government Printing Office.

Virginia Departments of Education and Health. (1995). *Report on the needs of medically fragile students*. Richmond: Commonwealth of Virginia.

Wardell, S.C., & Bousard, L.B. (1985). *Nursing pharmacology: A comprehensive approach to drug therapy*. Monterey, CA: Wadsworth Health Sciences Division.

Wolfensberger, W. (1972). *Normalization: The principle of normalization in human services*. Toronto, Ontario, Canada: National Institute on Mental Retardation.

Wood, S.P., Walker, D.K., & Gardner, J. (1986). School health practices for children with complex medical needs. *Journal of School Health, 56*(6), 215–217.

Communication Skills

COMMUNICATION IS THE COMPLEX PROCESS of information transfer that individuals use to influence the behavior of others. It includes writing, speech, gestures, facial expressions, body language, physical contact, and many other modes of behavior. Communication skills are critical for developing and maintaining social relationships, learning, community living, and meeting almost all human needs.

This chapter includes information on assessing communication and teaching communication skills to children with multiple disabilities and their communication partners. It is based on five fundamental principles: 1) maximization, 2) functionality, 3) individualization, 4) mutuality, and 5) normalization. These principles are relevant to each of the topics included in this chapter.

The principle of maximization dictates that intervention should aim toward the greatest possible increase in the frequency of appropriate communication and the utilization of all modes available to the child. This means that initial emphasis should be placed on acquisition and building fluency rather than quality. Because each attempt at communication also provides an opportunity to learn, refinements can be made more easily after frequency is increased.

The principle of functionality, sometimes referred to as pragmatics, requires a focus on social outcomes. Thus, concerns about *how* a person communicates are considered important only to the extent that they contribute to or interfere with the purpose of the communication.

The principle of individualization, a central theme in all areas of education of children with multiple disabilities, requires a unique assessment of each child and his or her environmental requirements, and it requires a consideration of the context in order to determine appropriate intervention and supports. No single approach, mode, or device can be expected to be ideal for all children with multiple disabilities or all children in any other category.

The principle of mutuality recognizes that all communication requires at least two partners. Therefore, all assessment and intervention must be aimed at both partners and the social and physical contexts that surround their interaction. It may be possible to teach individual words or gestures in isolation, but making sounds and handshapes is not communication unless it occurs as a functional part of a dynamic interaction.

The principle of normalization implies that unless a particular modification can be justified by an unequivocal benefit to the individual, the patterns of communication common to other people in the community should be the ones taught to children with multiple disabilities. Although normalization is a principle that should be considered in every aspect of education programming for children with multiple disabilities, there are two reasons it is particularly relevant to communication. First, this principle interacts directly with the principle of mutuality. Unless people with disabilities learn to use forms of communication compatible with those used by other members of the community who are their potential communication partners, communication will be difficult or impossible. Second, intensive study of language and communication, particularly as used by people with disabilities, tends to focus on highly technical approaches to teaching language; these methods sometimes alienate educators from simpler and more natural approaches. This often leads to an artificial and counterproductive emphasis on pathology and the differences between communication for people with disabilities and other communicators. People with disabilities are often viewed as users of augmentative systems and electronic devices, and others are viewed as speech users. Such distinctions are artificial and simplistic. More important, they often lead away from the most productive and most natural approaches to communication.

All five principles have implications for the following example of a mother and daughter. Mandy, the mother, uses alternative communication modes and augmentative systems. She wakes up to the sound of a voice from her clock radio (electronic communication aid) and receives information on the day's weather before deciding what to wear. She hugs her children (tactile mode) before giving them breakfast, and telephones (augmentative device) her neighbor to verify carpool arrangements. On the way to work, she carries on a conversation with her colleagues (vocal mode) riding with her while honking the car horn (augmentative device) and gesturing (gestural mode) to other drivers. On arriving, she shows her new family pictures (graphic mode) to her secretary and starts work. During her workday, she uses pen and paper, computers, fax machines, and a number of other communication aids. She talks, gestures, smiles, rearranges environmental cues (e.g., leaves something on her boss's desk that needs urgent attention), makes and breaks eye contact, and employs a range of communicative behavior. Some of her communication is deliberate; some of it is quite unintentional but equally important and effective. She chooses which mode to use according to the functional requirements of the situation, and she would feel constrained by the loss of any of these modes of communication.

Mandy's daughter, Candi, has an intellectual disability and athetoid cerebral palsy. Because she can make only a few discriminable speech sounds and has poor finger control, the team of experts evaluating her communication prescribed a communication board (graphic mode) system and suggested focusing on the board as a sole mode of communication, because they believed that Candi might be confused by exposure to a mixture of modes and systems. Like most individuals with multiple disabilities, Candi will never communicate as easily or proficiently as Mandy does, but her mental and physical disabilities may not be the greatest obstacle to her success.

The primary challenge that Candi faces in developing improved communication skills may be the rigid and artificial nature of the decisions guiding her training. Restricting her to a single mode of communication will place an unnecessary limitation on the size of her total communication repertoire, and, perhaps more important, it will ensure failure in functional areas that are poorly suited to graphic communication. Furthermore, it will likely reduce her frequency of communication by prohibiting some natural communication alternatives, and this reduction in frequency will reduce natural opportunities for her and her communication partners to learn. It seems absurd to imagine her mother trying to communicate about the physical appearance of her children by honking her car horn or holding up pictures to attract attention of other drivers. Restricting her to any single communication mode, regardless of the communication context and function, would necessitate such obvious and ridiculous mismatches of mode and function. Nevertheless, the devastating effects of placing the same kind of restrictions on her daughter seem less obvious to the team of experts making this decision. Keeping the expectations for Candi's communication close to the expectations for her mother's communication might help avoid such counterproductive approaches to intervention. Before any decisions can be made about how Candi communicates, one must consider her communication partners, the context, and, most important, the potential function of her communication.

COMMUNICATION FUNCTIONS

Pragmatics is the study of communication in a social context, emphasizing the functional nature of communication to achieve goals through social interaction (Donnellan, Mirenda, Mesaros, & Fassbender, 1984; Doss & Reichle, 1991). Thus, it is less concerned about the content (semantics) or form (syntax) of a message than about its effects on other people. The messages "Give me some soup," "That soup smells good," and "Do you have any extra soup?" are all different, but all of them may serve the same function (prompting the listener to give some soup). Some communications, called *performatives,* primarily direct social interactions (e.g., requesting attention or assistance), whereas others, called *propositionals,* primarily make declarative statements (e.g., naming objects), although these also must have some social component in order to be useful (Bates, Camaioni, & Voltera, 1979). Many communication programs for children with severe language impairments concentrate on propositional content (e.g., object labeling); however, the early communications of most children appear to lack propositional content and to be pure performatives (Greenfield & Smith, 1976). A pragmatic focus suggests that more emphasis on communication function (why children communicate) and structure (how children communicate) would result in faster and more relevant progress (MacDonald, 1985).

The discussion of the power of children's communication behavior to control others might seem to imply that they preconceive the desired effects on their audiences and plan their communications to produce these effects. This would require intent prior to communication (illocution). Communication partners may be influenced by the child even before intent develops (perlocution). For example, the crying or smiling of infants may not be intended to make caregivers attend to their needs, but caregivers consistently respond to this behavior as if intent were present. Through these consistent responses, real intent eventually develops (MacDonald, 1985). Such interpretation of communicative intent and its role in developing communication skills suggests the power of the expectations of caregivers. When potential respondents in the child's environment assume intent, they react to communication and help develop language. When potential respondents assume the child lacks intent or the capacity to communicate and subsequently fail to respond, development of language is impeded. This means that caregivers' expectations of communication from children and consistent responses to possible attempts at communicating are critical to the ability of children with severe and multiple disabilities to acquire functional language.

Relatively little information is available regarding the communication functions of children with disabilities, and, to date, the most current information comes from data gathered on the development of infants who do not have disabilities (Leonard, 1984). Experience in other curricular areas with attempting to apply developmental models to individuals with severe or multiple disabilities suggests that great caution should be used when applying such information to these learners. Often developmental sequences 1) fail to correspond to the typical order in children with multiple disabilities, 2) fail to include age-appropriate skills for individuals with severe delays, and 3) lack functional value (Guess & Noonan, 1982). These potential difficulties, however, do not invalidate all developmental tasks. They simply require that developmentally generated goals and objectives be validated as age appropriate and functional in current and potential future environments. Because pragmatic communication acts are defined by their effects rather than by the forms of the behaviors, they typically have functional value and can be acquired in an age-appropriate form. For example, attracting the attention of others is functional for everyone. Crying to receive attention is age appropriate for an infant but not typically appropriate for an adult. In the rare pragmatic assessments of communication among people with severe disabilities that have been published (Cirrin & Rowland, 1985; Owings, McManus, & Scherer, 1981), there is empirical support for the role of similar communication functions (e.g., requesting objects, protesting, asking for information). More research is needed in this area to further validate functions and to help determine the relative importance of specific functions. Although specific functional categories of communication have been proposed by many authors (e.g., Halliday, 1975; Karlan & Lloyd, 1983; McShane, 1980; Waterson & Snow, 1978), many functions identified by specific investigators have no precise equivalents in alternative communication systems, and no universal classification system exists.

An analysis of the communication functions of one 5-year-old child is illustrated in Table 7.1. This analysis is based on careful observation of the child and her communication partners. In addition to the function, information regarding mode (the general response category), form (the specific response), and content (a basic translation) is included. This child already has at least 11 communication functions, and several of these are expressed in more than one mode and form. It is important to note the diversity of modes used; limiting this child to a single mode (e.g., vocal) would severely restrict communication. It is also significant (and typical) that although this child is an active communicator, she can name only three people and one object. Many language programs focus on naming objects; however, this skill may have little functional value to the beginning communicator when compared with more general communication acts (e.g., generalized attention or item requests).

Waterson and Snow (1978) report that the most common communication functions (in order of frequency) in an infant without disabilities (12–16 months old) were 1) requesting items, 2) directing another's attention to objects, 3) calling attention to self, 4) requesting exchanges of objects, and 5) protesting situations. These five functions made up 94% of all communication acts. The only labels used were caregivers' names to attract their attention. Cirrin and Rowland (1985) reported that the most common communication functions (in order of frequency) in a group of 15 youths who are nonverbal (10–18 years old) and live in a facility for people with mental retardation were 1) requesting items, 2) requesting actions, 3) protesting, 4) directing attention to self, and 5) directing attention to communication. Again, these functions were typically produced without the use of object labels.

Further information on pragmatic functions is provided, along with discussions of assessing and teaching communication skills, in the "Assessment, Planning, and Intervention" section of this chapter. Pragmatic functions provide

Table 7.1. Language functions of a 5-year-old with severe communication impairments

Function	Mode	Form	Content
Request attention	1. Proximity	1. Approach	(pay attention to me)
	2. Contact	2. Touch	
	3. Vocal	3. Scream	
Request item or event (general)	1. Gesture	1. Reach toward	(give me)
	2. Gesture	2. American Sign Language (ASL) MORE sign	
	3. Proximity	3. Go to location	
	4. Graphic	4. Point to snapshot	(give me that)
Request item or event (specific)	1. Gesture	1. ASL HELP sign	(help me)
	2. Gesture	2. ASL DRINK sign	(give me a drink)
	3. Gesture	3. Raise arms	(pick me up)
	4. Object + action	4. Present book	(read to me)
	5. Object + action	5. Present cup	(give me a drink)
Initiation/ greeting	1. Gesture	1. Wave	(hello)
Termination	1. Gesture	1. Wave	(goodbye)
Direct attention	1. Gesture	1. Point	(look at that)
	2. Vocal	2. "Kah"	(look at that car)
Name items	1. Speech	1. "Mum"	(mother)
	2. Speech	2. "Dod-dod-dah"	(father)
		3. "Nanh"	(sister)
		4. "Kah"	(car)
Reinforce others	1. Contact	1. Hug	(I love you)
	2. Facial expression	2. Smile	(I liked that)
Affirm	1. Gesture	1. Nod "yes"	(yes)
Deny/reject	1. Gesture	1. Nod "no"	(no)
	2. Vocal	2. Scream	(NO!!)
	3. Gesture	3. Fall down/kick	(NO!!!!)
Fill turn	1. Gesture	1. Imitate action	(my turn; your turn)
	2. Vocal	2. Imitate sounds	(my turn; your turn)
	3. Object action	3. Push toy	(my turn; your turn)

ASL = American Sign Language.

essential guidance for determining what to teach and assist in planning how to teach it. Before covering these areas, however, some consideration of communication modes and systems may be helpful.

COMMUNICATION MODES AND SYSTEMS

Communication modes refer to general categories of behavior used to communicate. Vocal, gestural, and graphic modes have been identified as communication alternatives for children with multiple disabilities (Musselwhite & St. Louis, 1988; Silverman, 1980). Other modes include physical contact with the respondent, environmental modification, augmentative systems (often grouped within graphic systems but with distinct response requirements and output options), simultaneous modes (presenting the same parts of a message in two or more modes), and mixed modes (presenting different parts of a message in two or more modes). *Communication systems* refer to specific sets of responses used to communicate with a mode. For example, American Sign Language (ASL) is a communication system in the gestural mode.

Although modes and systems might be considered for both reception and production of communication, more emphasis has traditionally been placed on production. Although greater consideration probably should be given to reception in communication intervention, data generally support the development of receptive skills that surpass productive skills (e.g., Leonard, 1984; Oviatt, 1980; Terrace, 1979), and direct instruction on production of signs was shown to lead to the emergence of reception of signs in an adult with multiple disabilities (Kleinert & Gast, 1982). In spite of these general assurances that emphasis on production in training is justified, reception must be verified carefully in communication assessment. Intervention that considers both partners and the interactive process avoids the artificial isolation of reception and production in training (MacDonald, 1985).

Combining Modes

Before discussing individual modes, it may be helpful to consider the multimodal options. Vanderheiden and Lloyd (1986) recommended designing communication systems for people with disabilities that utilize a combination of the most accessible and effective graphic symbols. They suggest that dependence on a single communication strategy is limiting, and effective communicators must be able to adjust their communication strategy to the context. Elements from different specific systems within modes may be used in combination (e.g., photographs, PIC symbols, and Rebus symbols from within the graphic mode) as well as in addition to combinations that use elements from different modes (e.g., photographs from the graphic mode, pointing from the gestural mode, words from the local mode). These combined modes can be categorized as simultaneous, mixed, or duplicated.

Simultaneous modes, which concurrently duplicate the same message in two individual modes, have been used with many children. For example, total communication (simultaneous speech and sign) has been used in training (Silverman, 1980). Its potential advantages include 1) providing communication to both signers and listeners concurrently; 2) providing extra cues to interpretation when either speech or signing is not completely intelligible; and 3) providing more easily acquired signs to learners having difficulty with speech, while maintaining their exposure to speech and working toward its acquisition in the longer term. Unfortunately, empirical support for such advantages has been mixed (Mustonen, Locke, Reichle, Solbrack, & Lindgren, 1991). For example, total communication has been shown to have few advantages over signing without speech for children with autism (Carr & Dores, 1981; Remington & Clarke, 1983). The simultaneous mode probably has its greatest utility when used by teachers working with groups that include students who are verbal and nonverbal, and it may also be useful during initial training to help assess which of two modes a student responds to best.

Mixed modes use different modes for different communications or different parts of the same communication (e.g., vocalizing to attract attention and gesturing to obtain an object) (Mustonen et al., 1991). Although the possibility of combining modes is generally recognized, the fact that interventionists are encouraged to make decisions regarding modes before function and content decisions (e.g., Musselwhite & St. Louis, 1988; Shane & Bashir, 1980; Silverman, 1980) discourages the use of mixed modes. Postponing the decision regarding mode until content is selected and making individual modal decisions for each communication objective encourage mixed modes. Bricker (1983) pointed out that early communication of people without disabilities typically has gestural and vocal components. Similarly, the data in Table 7.1 reveal the use of several modes, the students with disabilities studied by Cirrin and Rowland (1985) used mixed modes, and casual observation of most communicators who do not have disabilities will reveal a similar mix. Reichle and Keogh (1986) pointed out the confusing and contradictory nature of decision-making rules for selecting modes, recommended mixed modes as the best alternative for most learners with severe disabilities, and suggested that mixed modes improve intelligibility. Similarly, MacDonald (1985) supported mixed modes because they 1) allow intervention to begin at the current level of function; 2) allow intervention with every child; and 3) allow analysis of all current behavior, permitting access to current semantics and pragmatics. Thus, mixed modes allow the interventionist to take advantage of the full spectrum of behavior in the individual's repertoire. For children who can produce a limited number of discriminably different classes of response within different modes, using as many modes as possible greatly increases the number of items in their general repertoire. For example, if a child can vocalize three distinct words, form four signs, point to five pictures, and communicate two concepts through touch, this child can communicate 14 items by mixing modes.

Mixed modes also allow for fitting the mode to the function and content of communication as well as to learner characteristics. For example, pointing to pictures in a book may be an excellent means of identifying objects for some learners, but it is a poor way of attracting someone's attention from across the room. Even gestures (as anyone who has had difficulty attracting a server's attention in a restaurant can attest) are poorly suited for attracting the attention of another person. Not surprisingly, although Cirrin and Rowland (1985) found that signs and other gestures accounted for most of the communications used by youths with severe disabilities who are nonverbal, signs and other gestures were not used to request attention. Attention was requested almost exclusively by physical contact. Similarly, other functions or specific vocabulary items may be better suited to other modes.

Mixed modes allow the child, family, and educational team to take advantage of the best components of vocal, gestural, and graphic modes (Mustonen et al., 1991). Because the mixed mode is normalized, allows for maximum use of the student's entire behavioral repertoire, and allows matching modes to communicative function, it is strongly recommended. The proportion of the individual modes within the mix, however, will vary for each child based on his or her abilities and communication needs. Therefore, each individual mode requires discussion.

Duplicated modes of communication require the child to learn to represent the same vocabulary or function in more than one mode (Mustonen et al., 1991). Unlike simultaneous modes, however, only a single mode is typically used during a communication interaction, and the mode of expression selected for a particular interaction is chosen according to its appropriateness to the communication partner and context.

Vocal Mode

Speech is the most commonly used individual mode of communication in modern society. In addition to its normalization value (Musselwhite & St. Louis, 1988), it is portable, rapid, and precise when used by a proficient communicator. Unfortunately, speech demands good auditory discrimination, extremely fine motor control of oral and respiratory structures, and considerable cognitive development. These (and probably other) factors account for the fact that many children with multiple disabilities do not develop speech or develop only very limited speech. For example, Morris (1978b) reported that 75%–95% of people with cerebral palsy have speech disturbances. Problems with head control, respiration, phonation, or eating skills typically suggest potential difficulty acquiring speech (Love, Hagerman, & Taimi, 1980). In a mixed-mode system, however, it is not necessary to select or reject vocal expression totally. Thus, potential limitations may influence the extent of vocal communication, but such limitations need not eliminate its use as long as a child can make at least a single vocalization. For example, if a child can cry, this cry typically can be shaped into a reliable (and more socially acceptable) attention signal, first by consistent responses to the cry as a request for attention and second by differential responses to more socially acceptable occurrences of the cry.

Even when children have developed considerable vocal skills, augmenting their vocal skills with gestural and graphic components can enhance the functional communication repertoire. Furthermore, considerable evidence suggests that learning other modes of communication enhances acquisition in the vocal mode rather than competes with vocal communication (Reichle, 1991).

Gestural Mode

Some gestures accompany the words of most speakers, and, for many communicators with hearing impairments, gestural language is the primary communication mode. Although signing has been criticized as a primary mode of communication, because it is not understood by many potential communication partners (Sailor & Guess, 1983), it is a useful component of a mixed mode system and may be an appropriate primary mode when speech and other alternatives are ruled out or when communication occurs in a gestural language environment. Evidence suggests that some learners acquire language more easily through gestures than speech (Carr & Dores, 1981), although which learners will benefit remains somewhat unpredictable (Creekmore, 1982).

Reichle, Williams, and Ryan (1981) suggested that signs should be taught when 1) the age and history of the learner suggest a poor prognosis for speech; 2) there are signing communication partners in the environment; 3) arm, hand, and finger dexterity is adequate (relative to oral-motor skills); 4) adequate cognitive skills are present (Piaget's stage VI); and 5) a portable system is desirable. When initial goals require acquisition of only a few gestures rather than a large repertoire, even these basic requirements may be relaxed. Other discussions of entry-level skills cast significant doubt on the reality of cognitive prerequisites (Reichle, 1991).

Similarly, a number of criteria have been identified for selecting initial signs, including 1) ease of production (Dennis, Reichle, Williams, & Vogelsberg, 1982); 2) iconicity (extent of resemblance between sign and the object or action represented) (Reichle et al., 1981); 3) topographical dissimilarity (ease of distinction from previously or concurrently trained signs) (Musselwhite & St. Louis, 1988); 4) potential frequency of use (Reichle et al., 1981); 5) familiarity of work or object (Reichle et al., 1981); and 6) functionality across settings (Reichle et al., 1981). Without question, it is the last criterion, functionality, that is most important. The pragmatic function of each individual communication act should be considered first, and decisions about modes or systems should be considered only after the purpose of the communication is determined. If the communication serves an important function, some effective means of expressing it to the appropriate communication partners should be found. If the function is unimportant, it may not be worth training simply because of ease of acquisition. Still, once communication functions are targeted, the remaining criteria can be useful in determining whether the gestural mode is suitable to serve this function and, if so, what form the gesture might take.

Gestural Systems   Musselwhite and St. Louis (1988) grouped sign systems into four basic categories: 1) sign languages (e.g., ASL) having their own structure and rules; 2) educational sign systems using standardized gestures to represent spoken English or some other spoken language; 3) gestural language codes using signs to represent letters or sounds of a language; and 4) other unaided gestural systems that include a range of systems that fall outside of the three previous categories. Gestural language codes and sign languages have limited application with children with severe and multiple disabilities because the cognitive and motor requirements are quite demanding and the children require communication partners with considerable signing skills. Although some specific signs or gestures from these systems may be useful as part of a mixed mode system, educational sign systems and other gestural systems are more likely to prove useful than are complete sign languages or gestural codes.

Educational Sign Systems   Educational sign systems, also called pedagogical sign systems (Allaire & Miller, 1983), use signs to substitute for or accompany their English equivalents. They are especially well suited to a simultaneous (speech and sign) mode and also work well in a mixed mode. Some examples include Signing Exact English, Paget-Gorman Systematic Sign, Linguistics of Visual English, and Duffy's System (Musselwhite & St. Louis, 1988). Duffy's System is inherently a mixed mode because it uses some vocalization along with gestures.

These systems differ in their motor requirements, transparency (ease of interpretation by an untrained observer), and the number of signs available. For example, Signing Exact English has enough similarity to ASL to be interpreted fairly well by ASL signers. This might be an advantage if potential communication partners already are familiar with ASL. Duffy's System requires less fine motor skill, but it includes fewer than 500 signs and may require creation of new signs for some learners (Musselwhite & St. Louis, 1988).

Other Gestural Systems   Among other gestural systems, Amer-Ind is not considered a language because the gestures have broader conceptual interpretations rather than single-word equivalents. It has been shown to be more transparent than ASL to observers with and without training (Kirschner, Algozzine, & Abbot, 1979). Although it is unclear if this transparency to observers who do not have disabilities implies transparency to children with multiple disabilities, transparency to potential communication partners may be of equal importance.

Amer-Ind gestures also typically use more gross motor and fewer fine motor skills than ASL, and, as a result, they may be more easily acquired by individuals with motor limitations.

Natural gestures are also included under the general category of other gestural systems, and, although they received relatively little attention from interventionists and researchers until the 1980s, they are an important alternative to other gestural systems. Natural gestures refer to actions that are generally understood by most observers without training. Some researchers believe these gestures are inborn traits (Morris, 1982). They represent an important part of the mainstream of human communication and have several advantages: 1) they are understood by a wide variety of communication partners; 2) they require no special equipment; 3) they appear typical because they are in common usage; 4) they have many models in the natural environment to aid in instruction; 5) they have a high potential for being part of the learner's entry-level repertoire; 6) they typically involve simple gross motor movements; and 7) they often include two or more alternative forms, which increases the probability that one of the alternatives will be suited to the learner (e.g., raising hands palm out and pushing away or horizontal head nod for "no").

Idiosyncratic gestures are actions (which are not shared by the majority of communicators) that a specific individual uses to communicate specific content or functions. In some cases, they are easily interpreted and are therefore also natural gestures. In many other cases, however, they are not easily interpreted. Of course, when a gesture is both easily interpreted and already present in the individual's repertoire, it is ideal, but when a choice must be made between an idiosyncratic or a natural gesture, the alternatives must be considered carefully. For the child with a limited repertoire and infrequent communication, it may be more important to reinforce current (idiosyncratic) communication efforts than to attempt to teach a more widely understood gesture. For the more advanced communicator who already can communicate with a few significant others but lacks the ability to communicate with a larger audience, the natural gesture will be more useful.

Graphic Mode

The graphic mode of communication has also received considerable attention as an alternative to speech (Mustonen et al., 1991). The graphic mode has frequently been labeled the symbolic mode (e.g., Musselwhite & St. Louis, 1988). The term graphic is used here because all modes of communication (e.g., vocal, graphic) are symbolic. Graphic systems may use 1) actual objects, 2) photographs, 3) drawings, 4) iconic graphics (which share at least some characteristics with the item they represent), 5) abstract graphics (which have no resemblance to the items they represent), or 6) combinations of two or more of the others (Beukelman & Mirenda, 1992). Of course, this type of categorization of graphic systems is based on the representation of objects rather than actions, relationships, or conditions, which are typically more difficult to represent directly. The fact that graphic systems are typically classified in this way may reflect a specific suitability for object labels.

Graphic communication systems may be homemade or purchased. Homemade systems typically 1) are less expensive, 2) provide easier control of symbol size, 3) allow a better fit of content to the learner's needs, and 4) are easy to update or expand. However, they may also be time consuming, require special design or construction skills, and cause difficulty when placing unique graphics or pictures (Mirenda, 1985). Drawings, photographs, magazine clippings, and product labels are good sources of visual symbols for homemade systems (Mirenda, 1985).

Some attempts have been made to compare commercial systems. Generally, systems that are more abstract appear to be more difficult for learners with severe and multiple disabilities. For example, Hurlbut, Iwata, and Green (1982) found that Blissymbols (which are more abstract) required four times as many trials for acquisition as a less abstract iconic alternative and that the iconic symbols were retained better. While pointing out these general advantages of the more iconic Rebus System over Blissymbolics, Clark (1984) noted that each system has some advantages and that decisions on suitable systems are best made after consideration of the needs of each individual learner. Mirenda (1985) further stressed this need for matching the system to the communicator on the basis of the multiple dimensions of the task. She pointed out that black-and-white line drawings may require less advanced discrimination skills because they present fewer stimulus dimensions than color photographs, but, even so, they may require more advanced graphic language skills than photographs. Therefore, graphic system selection requires the formulation of a hypothesis (based on the learner's environments and characteristics) regarding which systems might be suitable, and it requires empirical support for those systems based on a limited field test with the learner.

Electronic Systems   Because most electronic communication systems use graphic symbols, they have traditionally been considered part of the graphic mode. As an increasing number of input (e.g., photoelectric, myoelectric) and output (e.g., printing, synthesized speech) options become available with various electronic systems, their relationship to graphic systems weakens; consequently, electronic augmentation systems can be considered a separate mode, or, as Beukelman and Mirenda (1992) suggest, they can be considered "alternative access" (p. 49) to various other modes.

Electronic augmentation systems use movements already in the communicator's repertoire and transform them to more interpretable communication responses. For example, a series of puffs and sucks on a mouth tube may be electronically transformed to a written or spoken word. Some individuals are assisted greatly by these devices, particularly people with very limited motor skills but good sensory, receptive language, and cognitive skills. For many others, particularly those with very limited cognitive skills, these augmentative devices provide few advantages.

Electronic systems have an input mode, an output mode, and a processor that converts the available input into the desired output. For example, many electronic devices use touch symbols for input and speech for output. An electronic processor concerts or translates the touch into speech. In some devices, input, output, and processing are all performed by a single unit. In others, each is performed by a separate component. Two kinds of devices are commonly used: 1) custom-purpose devices and 2) adapted personal computers. Adapted personal computers are increasing in popularity as augmentative communication devices for many reasons. Some examples are included in this section. They are generally less expensive than custom-purpose units with similar capabilities because many more are produced, and repair and replacement is often easier and faster because custom-purpose units often need to be returned to the factory for repair. Because personal computers have become common items in homes, schools, and various other environments, their use as communication devices has become more common than custom-purpose devices. Because there is almost an endless variety of software for personal computers, they can often serve more than one purpose, and a variety of input and output devices can be attached to most personal computers.

In spite of these advantages, custom-purpose devices continue to be the best choice for some children because they meet their individual needs. These devices frequently require less time and expertise to program to suit individual needs than generic personal computers. Often the processor and the output components of generic personal computers are appropriate, but the input device needs to be highly individualized. The processor rarely needs to be individualized because generic computers with the proper software can easily convert the electronic impulses from an input device to the desired output. The output device rarely needs individualization because most of the individual's communication partners will not have significant hearing, language, or vision impairments. Only the input device needs to be highly individualized to make maximum use of the communicator's abilities while overcoming the communicator's limitations.

The IntelliKeys (IntelliTools, 55 Leveroni Court, Suite 9, Novato, CA 94949) is a good example of an adaptive keyboard. This keyboard has a touch-sensitive active input area 8 inches tall and 12 inches wide. The area can be divided into any number from one very large key to 576 very small keys. Each key can easily be programmed to represent a letter, sound, word, or sentence. The inactive space between touch keys and the layout of the board are also easily adjustable. Overlays that use pictures or symbols are created easily and printed on regular computer printers using Overlay Maker software, and various overlays (e.g., a student might have one for home and one for school) can be switched and the appropriate program loaded in the computer in seconds. A set overlay controls how long an area must be touched to activate it, and there are other features that benefit from individualization. Figure 7.1 illustrates an example of an IntelliKey's overlay for one child. Software is available for Macintosh and IBM computers. IntelliKeys overlays can also be used in several scanning modes with the ClickIt program's various switches. Output can be in any form that is desired, usually text (from computer monitor or printer), speech, or both.

For individuals who cannot use a touchboard because of limited movement of their arms and hands, Origin Instruments' HeadMouse (available from Madenta Communications, 9411A 20th Avenue, Edmonton, Alberta, Canada T6N 1E5), bundled with various software programs depending on the child's individual needs, is a possible input alternative. HeadMouse is a sophisticated electronic device that allows the user to control the computer with head movements without requiring an awkward pointer attached to the individual's head. A small, ¼-inch-diameter dot on the user's forehead is all that is needed. When the user moves his or her head, an infrared device on top of the computer tracks the movement and guides the computer based on those movements. Depending on the software used, the HeadMouse can be used to type or scan a communication board displayed on the computer monitor. IntelliKeys and HeadMouse are just two of many input devices that are helping to make computers accessible to children and adults with severe disabilities. Other switches and control devices can be activated by students with multiple disabilities using a variety of body sites. Tanaka and Lian (1995) provide a good description of training and assessment procedures designed to identify the best body site for an individual child.

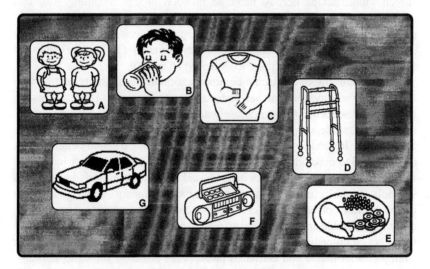

Figure 7.1. Simple, individualized overlay for IntelliKeys Board. Touching the symbols produces computer-synthesized speech. (A = "I want to play with my friends"; B = "May I have a drink, please?"; C = "Please help me put on my sweater"; D= "May I have my walker?"; E = "Can I have something to eat?"; F = "Let's listen to music"; G = "Can we go for a ride in the car?") (Produced with IntelliKeys Overlay Maker Version 2.2 for Macintosh.)

Custom-purpose devices, such as Zygo Industries's Macaw II (available from Post Office Box 1008, Portland, Oregon 97207), are the best choice for some users. The Macaw II is a self-contained communication device with 2–32 membrane keys (depending on the size desired) that can be programmed for a total of 1–2 minutes (depending on output quality) of prerecorded speech and up to 8½ minutes with optional memory modules installed. It can be accessed through direct selection or a number of scanning options.

Speech output has also improved greatly (Edwards, 1991). Two kinds of speech output are available: 1) synthesized speech, which is created electronically; and 2) digitally recorded speech, which uses previous speech input. Because digital speech is reproduced from an original human voice, it sounds very natural, and provided that an appropriate individual is available to record the speech, it is appropriate to the age and gender of the communicator. The chief disadvantages of recorded speech output are that it generally requires more memory in the communication device and each message must be recorded in advance, which limits its flexibility. Alternatively, individual words are sometimes recorded and linked together to form messages, but this detracts from the natural sound and flow of the speech. New and improving methods of compressing audio signals are significantly reducing memory requirements and making digitally recorded speech a more viable option. Synthesized speech is also improving rapidly. Many common computer programs now can read text clearly and a variety of voices are available. In addition to requiring less memory, synthesized speech is more flexible because messages do not require prerecording. Although synthesized speech lacks some of the natural expression of recorded speech, its neutral expression is as much of an advantage as a disadvantage because the emotions represented in recorded speech may or may not be appropriate to the situation that the communicator encounters when using it.

Successful use of electronic communication devices requires students to activate various types of switches. Schweigart and Rowland (1992) suggest an instructional sequence for switch use with students with dual sensory impairments. First, students learned to gain attention with single-switch activation. Second, they learned to request objects and events using a single switch. Third, they learned to make choices using several switches. Finally, they learned to make choices using multiple switches based on discrimination of associated symbols. An objective of early training for some students simply may be to establish cause and effect. The child learns that activating the input device produces a predictable and reinforcing effect. In these early states, it is essential that the effect be immediate, easily perceptible, and reinforcing to the student. For example, brief music and animated pictures are effective for some students. Interactive programs, including games, can be effective means of enhancing general icon selection and activation prior to and during training with computer-based communication programs.

In conclusion, electronic communication devices are suitable for an increasing number of students with severe and multiple disabilities. Personal computers with adaptive input devices, appropriate software, and speech or print output are often reasonably priced and effective, but some students do better with specially designed electronic devices.

Although advances in electronic technology have made high-technology communication boards a good alternative for increasing numbers of children with severe disabilities, low-technology alternatives are still more appropriate for many, perhaps most, students with multiple disabilities. Simple communication boards using photographs, pictures cut from catalogs, or other graphic symbols typically cost less, can be easily individualized and revised, are more durable and easily repaired, and frequently are equally useful in communication. These advantages need to be weighed against the disadvantages of limited input and output requirements. The weight given to these advantages and disadvantages must be considered on the basis of each child's individual needs (Sigafoos & Iacono, 1993).

Graphic Arrays   For graphic communication, an array of graphic symbols must be available to the learner and the communication partner, and the learner must have a reliable method of indicating which symbol is chosen. The physical arrangement of this array must consider the sensory, cognitive, and motor characteristics of the communicator in order to maximize the speed and reliability of communication. The simplest method of indicating the chosen symbol is direct selection, which requires the learner to touch, point to, look at, or otherwise indicate one symbol at a time with each selection.

For children with limited movement, suitable arrays may be determined by 1) range of motion (areas through which they can move in various planes); 2) resolution of motion (smallest movement reliably differentiated); 3) control (reliability, speed, freedom from involuntary movement for a given location); 4) endurance (length of time a movement can be maintained or repeated); and, sometimes, 5) force (amount of pressure that can be exerted) (Capozzi & Mineo, 1984). York and Weiman (1991) recommended eight principles of designing, positioning, and handling to help maximize the performance of children with limited movement. These include 1) using one's own movements as reference models for planning, 2) using dynamic rather than static assistance whenever possible to minimize dependency, 3) controlling position and movements from key points, 4) increasing time and frequency of practice, 5) normalizing muscle tone, 6) providing a stable base of support, 7) working toward symmetrical alignment, and 8) using a variety of positions. (More detailed information on handling and positioning is included in Chapters 3 and 4.) Graphic symbol size must be based on visual acuity as well as motor accuracy. Placement of individual symbols within the array may be based on a number of factors. For example, frequently used symbols are typically placed in the most accessible positions in order to minimize the effort and time required for communication, but frequently used symbols associated with high levels of reinforcement are sometimes placed in peripheral positions to encourage learners to reach farther toward their limits. When the number of selections increases beyond six or so, it typically becomes helpful to group them into categories by content or function (Musselwhite & St. Louis, 1988).

Many factors should be considered in the design of communication boards (Baumgart, Johnson, & Helmstetter, 1990). Figure 7.2 illustrates the top view of a communication board on a young girl's lap tray mounted on her wheelchair. Although some machines and computers move easily across rows and down columns, children do not. Because this child uses one hand for direct selection, one must consider the arc of movement of that arm across the lap tray in planning the location of symbols on the board. The white area represents the area of the board that allows best access and accuracy for this child. As illustrated, some other areas of the board are inaccessible, limit accuracy, cannot be seen, or require maladaptive positioning or movement patterns to reach. Some areas of the board can be reached but require extra effort. If the child is being encouraged to use these areas, symbols associated with highly reinforcing items or events may be placed in these areas. Symbol size is determined primarily by visual abilities and accuracy of selection. It may be desirable to elongate symbols in one dimension, because accuracy may differ from the vertical to the horizontal axis. The size and distance between symbols may also be varied according to accuracy in each particular area of the board. Usually, accuracy is best near the center of the arc of movement and worsens as distance increases from the arc. Placing

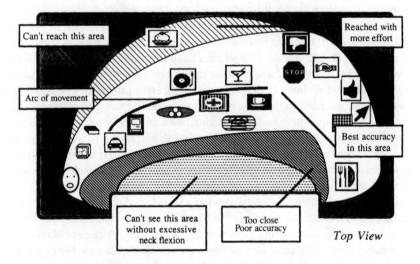

Figure 7.2. A communication board individualized to the movement patterns and visual abilities of one child with multiple disabilities.

conceptual classes of symbols and related pragmatic functions close together is desirable for some students, but placing them farther apart is often better when accuracy is an issue. For example, if "yes" and "no" symbols are close together and the child is asked a "yes/no" question, great accuracy is required to answer. If these symbols are far apart, however, communication partners can more reliably discriminate the intended answer despite some inaccuracy. Physical therapists and occupational therapists can be extremely useful team members in helping to map a child's movement patterns and determining the best placement of symbols.

The space between graphic symbol locations must be wide enough to ensure reliable discrimination between responses. A raised divider between symbols may be useful for eliminating borderline responses. Building a confirmation exchange into each selection may be necessary to ensure reliable selection with some learners, particularly those using gaze (eye pointing) for selection. For example, when the learner appears to be looking at a specific symbol, the partner touches that selection (as if saying, "This one, right?"), and the communicator signals "yes" or "no" with a nod or other reliable movement or vocalization. When eye gaze is the best selection mode, an ETRAN (a clear, vertical, Plexiglas rectangular board with an open center), which is placed between the communicators, improves discriminability of gaze direction (Bigge, 1991). Still, only about 8–10 items can be displayed and reliably selected in this manner.

Scanning and encoding provide alternatives when the number of graphic symbols needed exceeds the number than can be indicated reliably. Scanning presents symbols sequentially to the communicator, who indicates selection by some predetermined response when the appropriate symbol appears (Musselwhite & St. Louis, 1988). Linear scanning presents every item in order, whereas group item scanning first presents categories (e.g., rows on the chart, content areas) for selection and then presents specific items within a category only after that category is selected (Musselwhite & St. Louis, 1988). Directed scanning can be controlled by the communicator proceeding horizontally, vertically, or diagonally in order to shorten the path to a desired item (Silverman, 1980). Because linear scanning is the simplest method, it probably has the greatest potential for most learners with severe and multiple disabilities. Similarly, encoding methods probably will be useful only with communicators with relatively advanced cognitive skills. Encoding uses a series of simpler selections to indicate an item (Bigge, 1991). For example, selecting one of six shapes may indicate a row, and selecting one of six colors may indicate a column. Thus, 36 items may be encoded, but the learner need only reliably select from an array of six.

Piché and Reichle (1991) recommended four major steps for students who are learning scanning: 1) selecting the signaling response, 2) learning to use this response selectively, 3) increasing selectivity to larger arrays of items, and 4) generalizing the response across different types of arrays. Scanning involves an elaboration of a confirmation function because items are presented sequentially until one is confirmed as the correct selection. Therefore, indicating "yes" may be viewed as an essential initial step.

Physical Contact and Environmental Modification

Although vocal, gestural, and graphic modes are the predominant elements of mixed mode systems, other communication modes also can be identified. Two of these modes that play an important role in basic communication are physical contact and environmental modification. Physical contact is often used to attract attention (e.g., tap on shoulder); to display affection (e.g., hug); or to reject another (e.g., push away). Environmental modification (e.g., placing a coat by the door to indicate wanting to leave) may be a similarly useful mode of communication. Although neither of these modes can easily serve as the sole mode of communication, each can be an important element in a mixed modal system.

Facilitated Communication

Undoubtedly, the most controversial mode of communication for children with severe disabilities is facilitated communication (FC), a mode introduced in Australia by Rosemary Crossley in the 1970s. It is a method in which a facilitator provides physical assistance to a communicator while the communicator types out messages or selects symbols from an array. Usually, the assistance begins as support at the communicator's hand or wrist. Once FC is established, the facilitator fades assistance by gradually moving the support to the forearm, elbow, upper arm, and shoulder. The ultimate goal is independence from the facilitator, but most communicators continue with facilitator support indefinitely (Crossley, 1994). In fact, advocates for FC have given variable and conflicting estimates of the number of FC learners who have become independent, and those critical of FC suggest that "none have been verified objectively" (Green & Shane, 1994, p. 155).

Advocates for FC suggest that it opens new worlds for many people diagnosed as having autism or mental retardation (e.g., Biklen, 1993). In many cases, such individuals have demonstrated extraordinary progress and exhibited remarkable abilities to use sophisticated ideas and language. Such remarkable demonstrations of ability have led some to begin to view the very existence of mental retardation as a myth or to question whether the diagnosis is incorrect in a large number of cases (e.g., Biklen, 1993). Some suggest that autism and at least some cases of apparent mental retardation are subtle movement disorders that interfere with communication (Donnellan & Leary, 1995).

Those who criticize FC, however, suggest that apparent progress produced with FC is not what it appears to be. They believe that rather than assisting people to communicate, facilitators are communicating for them. They assert that the messages produced in FC come, in at least most cases, from the facilitator and not the apparent communicator (e.g., Green & Shane, 1994).

The views of these two groups are diametrically opposed. If the advocates for FC are correct, it is essential that there is proof. If FC is what it appears to be, it has enormous value for many people who are otherwise unable to communicate. No individual should be denied that opportunity. People who are unable to communicate their needs and feelings must be allowed to gain expression and greater control of their lives whenever possible. For example, through facilitation, some people have apparently been able to disclose a history of abuse that they were formerly unable to communicate (Sobsey, 1994; Williams, 1994). In addition to the direct obvious benefits, the positive shifts in the social perception of individuals who apparently have made major gains in communication is undeniable. Beyond these essential individual benefits, FC ultimately leads to a drastic reformulation of commonly held previous beliefs about autism and other disabilities (Biklen & Duchan, 1994). The apparently rapid and powerful effects of FC would leave little reason for communication specialists to waste time with traditional alternative and augmentative communication methods that produce much more modest results.

If FC does not really produce the remarkable results that have been commonly attributed to it, however, it has the potential to do great harm. If the communication produced through the process is really the product of the facilitator and not the communicator, it is merely another form of paternalistic oppression legitimized by the illusion of the "communicator's" authorship. Clearly, it would not add to anyone's respect or personal dignity to gain greater social status based on a false perception of that individual or what he or she is communicating. If cognitive impairment is a fiction, we should deny its existence; but if it is real, we should love and respect people for who they are, not create fictional alternative personae for them.

Allegations of abuse that arise through FC only serve to raise the stakes (Sobsey, 1994). If these are legitimate disclosures of abuse and originate from the apparent communicator, it is important they they be heard (Williams, 1994). The individual must be protected from further abuse, and justice must be done whenever possible. If these allegations are false, however, and do not originate with the apparent communicator, the potential harm is immense. Anyone falsely accused may suffer undeserved disgrace or even false conviction and punishment. The individual who supposedly made the allegation may suffer loss of a caring family member or caregiver. In addition, negative publicity about false and unproven allegations may result in failure to properly respond to other real ones.

In one of the first cases, in 1990, a young woman named Carla in Melbourne, Australia, was removed from her home by social services authorities after allegations that she had been raped by her father and brother and that her mother restrained her during the assaults. The sole evidence of the attacks was Carla's disclosure made through FC. Only after she was removed from her home and her parents tried to regain custody did the court order testing to validate the FC. The result showed that Carla was not communicating by FC; her facilitator was the author of her messages (Hudson, Melita, & Arnold, 1993). Carla was returned to her home. Astonishingly, her facilitators later claimed that through facilitation Carla had admitted that *she* lied (Heinrichs, 1992). Hundreds of similar FC allegations have followed, with the vast majority of charges clearly disproven or unconfirmed. In at least one case, however, an individual was convicted.

Evidence for and Against FC   The essential question was well framed by Biklen, Saha, and Kliewer (1995): "Are the words typed those of the people with disabilities or the advertent or inadvertent work of the facilitators?" (p. 45). Traditional, systematic, scientific investigation of FC has failed to produce substantial support for its use (Green & Shane, 1994). Although a few studies seem to suggest validation for some individuals and circumstances, it appears to fail in 98% of controlled tests (Green, 1993). More worrisome is that many studies indicate that the real source of authorship and control in most FC is the facilitator, not the apparent communicator (Green, 1993). For example, one study found that when both the facilitator and the communicator saw the stimulus item, it was correctly identified on 14 of 60 trials; when only the communicator saw the stimulus item, there were no correct responses in 60 trials; when the facilitator and the communicator were shown different items, there were no correct responses, but on 12 of 60 trials, FC produced a response matching the stimulus that only the facilitator had seen. Such responses can only be explained by facilitator influence or telepathy. Surprisingly, a number of advocates for FC suggest that such events demonstrate that people who use FC have telepathy (e.g., Crossley, 1994).

Those who argue in favor of facilitation suggest that traditional scientific tests are inappropriate (Biklen et al., 1995). Many suggest that we rely on phenomenological approaches to assessment (e.g., Biklen et al., 1995). Phenomenology and similar qualitative approaches to research are extremely valuable to study attitudes, beliefs, and subjective experiences, but are rarely, if ever, the most appropriate method to test hypotheses (Marshall & Rossman, 1989). There are also other complications in the application of qualitative research to this question. If FC really works, the best potential informants or co-researchers are the people with disabilities; because they are the ones using FC, it is their experience that is of interest. However, it cannot be expected that people will deny that FC works while using it, and if it is affirmed, there is still the question of whether it was the informant or facilitator who was affirming it.

Advocates suggest that the very notion of questioning the validity of the communication of people with severe disabilities may block their ability to communicate. This may be true, but it cannot explain why test anxiety allows communication when the facilitator knows the answer and not when *only* the communicator knows the answer, and it cannot explain how communicators identify stimuli that only the facilitators see. Even when researchers (Simon, Toll, & Whitehair, 1994) arranged testing under naturalistic conditions (i.e., typical activities and environments), results indicated fewer than 4% correct responses and more than 56% of responses that appeared to be facilitator guided. It is inevitable to conclude that in most cases FC messages come from the facilitator and not the communicator.

Proceed with Caution   Does FC work in some cases? This possibility cannot be ruled out. At this stage it is unclear how many people, if any, really benefit from FC. If FC is valuable for even one individual, it should not be taken away. As Crossley and McDonald (1984) eloquently argued, "crushing the personalities of speechless individuals is very easy; just make it impossible for them to communicate freely" (p. 142). If FC or any other mode of communication is working, it should be validated.

On the basis of the problems with validation in previous studies, initiation of FC training is not recommended if any other alternative is producing functional communication. If an individual is already using FC, controlled validation is recommended. If FC is really working for any child or adult, it will be possible to demonstrate that an individual can answer questions, identify objects, or perform other communication functions when the facilitator is unaware of the question and the desired answer. If FC is objectively validated for any individual, it should be continued with that person. If it cannot be validated in an individual, it should be discontinued.

ASSESSMENT, PLANNING, AND INTERVENTION

Before an effective and functional communication training program can be implemented, four basic decisions must be made. First, there must be a decision as to which communication functions would be most useful to the individual. Second, the specific content or messages to be communicated must be determined. Third, the form of the communication (which includes mode and system decisions) must be selected. Fourth, the way in which each item will be taught must be chosen.

Figure 7.3 illustrates a decision-making process for determining the functions and modes to be taught and the kinds of training that may be required. The process starts with an ecological assessment (Sigafoos & York, 1991) to determine what behaviors are required in the current environment and which will be required potentially in less restrictive and age-appropriate environments in the future. Priority may be placed on skills essential to maintaining a placement in current desirable environments or critical to placement in a future desirable environment. Functions that are already present need not be taught, but they may require fluency training or topographical refinement to improve understanding by communication partners. Functions that are easily understood, fluent, and appropriate should be supported by maintenance and generalization programming that takes advantage of natural reinforcers to the greatest extent possible. If functions are present in socially inappropriate forms, pragmatic functional alter-

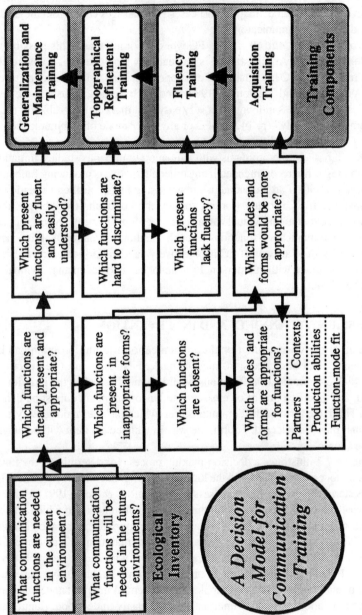

Figure 7.3. A decision-making model for communication training. Ecological inventory is used to determine the functions, modes, and forms to be taught. Analyses of these content components are used to determine instructional program components.

natives should be taught. Any required function that is absent needs to be taught in a mode and form that considers the context, partners, production abilities of the child, and the best fit between mode and function. The new forms and functions taught become the focus of the child's communication acquisition program. Early in the process of acquisition, fluency training should begin. For low-frequency communicators, it is typically desirable to stress fluency rather than topographical refinement because increased use of communication will provide more opportunities for feedback and subsequent refinement.

Assessment

Traditional assessment has emphasized decisions of candidacy for communication training (Musselwhite & St. Louis, 1988). Mirenda and Iacono (1990), however, suggested that the participation model first proposed by Rosenberg and Beukelman (1987) is more appropriate for individuals with severe and multiple disabilities. This model assumes that all individuals are candidates for communication intervention and focuses on the development of opportunity and access rather than candidacy for intervention. Standardized assessments of language and communication skills are typically inappropriate for children with severe and multiple disabilities for at least six reasons (Correia & Sobsey, 1984):

1. They typically emphasize more advanced skills and fail to evaluate adequately very basic skills.
2. They generally assume the child understands that a task is being presented and is motivated to perform as well as possible.
3. They often focus on the individual rather than the communication dyad and environment.
4. They commonly require demonstration of specific skills and fail to allow for functional alternatives.
5. Many depend on a sampling of target behavior that is too small.
6. Most are designed to determine how the child compares with some reference group, which is not useful information (when the individual obviously differs from the norm) for planning and intervention.

Because such standard assessments measure communication responses to test stimuli, they are particularly poor indicators of children's behavior in natural environments and of skills used in initiating communication (Reichle & Yoder, 1979). Although more time consuming, a flexible, natural communication sample provides a more accurate indication of such behavior. This individualized approach to assessment also permits greater consideration of the environmental requirements when determining appropriate program content.

In view of their deficiencies, standard assessments of communication have only limited application to children with multiple disabilities and should only be used to help answer specific program decisions. For example, the Pre-Speech

Assessment Scale (Morris, 1978a) may be very useful for identifying the specific oral-motor skills that need improvement for speech.

Assessment must include consideration of communication partners and
context (Rogers-Warren, 1984). Sigafoos and York (1991) outlined procedures
for ecological inventories of communication behavior. This process considers
communication demands and opportunities along with communication intents,
modes, and vocabulary.

Correia and Sobsey (1984) suggested a flexible evaluation process that
combines 1) identifying information, 2) relevant data from physical and learning histories, 3) information gathered in an interview with significant others,
4) results of a natural communication sample, 5) results of an elicited communication sample, 6) a description of the physical and social environment, 7) a summary, and 8) program recommendations. Although suggested interview
questions are included, evaluators are advised to select those that seem relevant
and to supplement them with their own questions. Both natural and elicited communication samples are potentially useful, because data collected during the natural sample can be used to formulate interventions that can be field tested during
the elicited sample. Similarly, an interview with significant others before the natural sample is collected may help suggest the best times, places, and communication partners for the natural sample. Assessment information can help
interventionists with each of the four decisions (functions, content, form, intervention) they face, but it may be necessary to do additional assessment after each
decision before the next one can be made.

Olswang, Stoel-Gammon, Coggins, and Carpenter (1987) have prepared a
structured, yet flexible, assessment designed to evaluate prelinguistic and early
linguistic communication responses in children who are at early developmental
stages. This comprehensive package evaluates cognitive antecedents, play
behavior, communicative intent, language comprehension, and language production. Even though considerable modification is necessary in most cases,
some components of this assessment instrument can be useful in designing individualized assessments for children with severe and multiple disabilities.

Determining Communication Functions,
Content, Form, and Interventions

The discussion of functional communication that appears previously in this
chapter mentions that no generally agreed-upon, comprehensive list of pragmatic functions is available. Therefore, in generating the list of functions most useful to a specific child, the interventionist must depend on his or her observations
of current communication behavior and the child's current and potential future
environments. Environmental information reveals why and what the child needs
to communicate. Information regarding the child's behavior in the environment
tells what communication functions the child currently fulfills and what skills

the learner may be able to use for additional communication. Parents, other team members, and those who regularly interact with the child can provide a great deal of information about current communication, reducing the amount of time required for direct observation by the interventionist.

Attention   One basic function in all communication is to draw the attention of a potential communication partner to oneself. Without this skill, a communicator is restricted to the role of passive respondent and cannot initiate interaction. Although this function is so basic that it may be taken for granted, Light, Collier, and Parnes (1985) found that, in their study, 15% of initiation attempts by children with physical disabilities failed because the children did not have the attention of their communication partners. Similarly, Reichle, Rogers, and Barrett (1984), in teaching a student with severe, multiple disabilities to make requests, found that requests were often nonfunctional because they were made prior to having another person's attention.

More complex functions may direct the communication partner's attention to an object or event, but the attention must be drawn to the communicator before it can be directed elsewhere. Therefore, if a reliable method for attracting attention is not already in the individual's repertoire, this should probably be one of the first functions taught. The graphic mode is generally poorly suited for attracting attention. The gestural mode can be more effective in some contexts, especially with gross motor gestures (e.g., waving, hand raising). The vocal mode is often the most effective mode for attracting attention because the communication partner need not be looking at the communicator to receive this message. Augmentative devices with auditory output (e.g., ringing telephone, buzzer, bell) are also well suited to this task. Sobsey and Reichle (1989) suggested that the auditory feedback of a buzzer may act as an intermediate conditioned reinforcer and facilitate the acquisition of single-switch activation as an attention signal.

After a basic attention signal is taught, it may be differentiated into various forms with more specific content (e.g., "Look at me," "Listen to me," "Look at that"), but to start with, a single message (e.g., "I need you") is the only content required. If the child has an existing behavioral form for the attention function, its effectiveness and appropriateness should be examined; if it is currently working well, it should be preserved and other functions targeted for training. The behavioral form used for the attention function must be easily discriminable at a distance. If the potential communication partner must already be paying attention in order to receive the message, it has no functional value. Therefore, although some gross motor gestures may be useful, the graphic mode and much of the gestural mode are poorly suited to this communication function. Moving into proximity or touching another may be useful for some learners. If the learner can produce adequate volume, even though articulation may be poor, vocalization is well suited to this function. For individuals without a suitable response in their repertoire, a buzzer system is a simple and typically effective alternative (Sobsey & Reichle, 1989).

Teaching the individual to request attention is generally easy to accomplish. The primary teaching method involves consistently responding to the learner's use of the signal. If initial signaling rates are low, it may be necessary to build high rates by adding instructional reinforcers to the attention response or through prompting and reinforcing signal production during massed trial instruction. Once high rates of signaling have been developed, the artificial reinforcers can be faded, and attention can take over as the reinforcer.

Occasionally, signaling rates may be too high. The learner may request attention so frequently that communication partners consider these repeated requests to be disruptive and stop responding to them. Such situations should be carefully evaluated. Often, the number of requests for attention is not as high as believed. Although potential communication partners may subscribe, in theory, to the importance of encouraging initiation, they may not be prepared to allow the learner to control their interactions. An adjustment in the attitudes of these partners may be required before successful training can take place. It is pointless to attempt to teach requests for attention if they will be ignored when made. In other cases, requests for attention temporarily reach disruptively high levels but return to more acceptable levels as the learner becomes more accustomed to this new power. If signaling levels do not become normalized, raising the signal requirements (e.g., moving buzzer switch to a location demanding more reaching) or adjusting the reinforcement schedule (e.g., to a fixed interval) may help bring the signaling rate to a typical level.

Requesting Items and Events   Requests are an important part of early communication and continue to be important to communicators at every level. Reichle and Keogh (1985) noted that early requests are typically undifferentiated and require the communication partner to use contextual cues (e.g., history of learner's previous requests, presence of possible referents in the environment) to determine what is requested. Only later, when more advanced communication skills develop, does the ability to request specific items or events emerge. Requests also appear to generalize from the training to the natural environment better than naming or question-asking responses (Warren & Rogers-Warren, 1983). At this basic level, communication content might be interpreted as "I want something." This allows one communication form to request many different items and events (Reichle & Sigafoos, 1991). Once generalized requests are taught, item-specific content may be considered.

The form selected for teaching depends mostly on learner characteristics. Graphic, gestural, and vocal modes are equally suited to the task, and many learners have some form of requesting in their natural repertoire. If such a response can be identified, it should be used in current or modified form rather than being discarded for a new form.

Keogh and Reichle (1985) taught generalized requesting in a massed trial format. They presented an array of choices to the learner to reinforce communicating "want." To ensure that the communication did not become bound to a single reinforcer, they suggested rotating the reinforcers in the array or replacing any item that the learner selected three times in a row. This method has led to rapid acquisition of requesting by learners with severe and multiple disabilities. Reichle and Sigafoos (1991) provided detailed procedures for teaching generalized requests for items and events.

Rejection and Protest Just as the ability to request items and events is important for establishing control over the environment, the ability to reject or protest against them may be equally important. Cirrin and Rowland (1985) found this protest function particularly common among infrequent communicators. Often, natural gestures (e.g., moving away, turning one's face away) are already available in the learner's repertoire and require only improvement of reliability through standardization or minimal modification to more acceptable forms. The basis message of these protests might be interpreted as "No" (Sigafoos & Reichle, 1991). As with requests, their form is best determined on the basis of learner characteristics.

As with attention signals, the success of training depends largely on the willingness of communication partners to accept the message and allow learners to refuse the things they attempt to reject. If communication partners refuse to take "No" for an answer, communication of rejection has no functional value. Of course, there may be some instances that require ignoring the learner's protests. For example, most people would feel justified in saving a child from drowning even though the child struggled against (protested) the effort. The rationale for many other things (e.g., eating the last bite of liver) that are imposed on protesting learners with severe and multiple disabilities, however, is much less clear. Any attempt to increase functional communication skills requires empowering the learner with greater control over the social environment and, therefore, requires communication partners to relinquish some of their control. Before overriding the protests of the learners one serves, one must carefully examine the reasons for one's restrictive response. Such an imposition on the freedom of the individual is not justified simply because one judges something to be good for that person. After all, people in general can think of things that would be good for them but that they refuse because they simply do not like them. Such intrusions can be justified only if the consequences of the learner's refusal would be catastrophic. An extremely important by-product of empowering the learner to refuse or protest unwanted items and events is the subsequent need for caregivers and interventionists to ensure that activities are adequately reinforcing to make certain that participation is voluntary.

Confirmation and Negation For some learners, particularly those with relatively advanced receptive skills but limited productive communication, confirmation and negation responses are particularly useful (Bigge, 1991). Because these "yes" and "no" responses may require frequent usage, a set of responses that can be discriminated from each other quickly and reliably is desirable. Vertical and horizontal head nods are often used. The same responses used as request and reject signals may also be generalized to this purpose.

Often, confirmation or negation is used when the communication partner repeats the message received from the learner. Examples of the form that this communication might take include vocal repetition or touching the symbol of an ETRAN on which the learner's gaze seemed to focus. If the message repeated by the respondent is correct, the learner confirms it and proceeds with the conversation. If the message repeated is incorrect, the learner communicates negation and tries again to communicate the original message.

Reference and Description   Many programs designed to train children with severe or multiple disabilities to use language focus on identification or naming of objects or events. Although these references and description functions no doubt are important, they are difficult (Light et al., 1985), and they require relatively large amount of learned behavior for more limited functional value (i.e., learning a generalized requester can be useful in requesting anything, whereas learning an object name is useful for requesting only one thing). Such advanced communication behavior should not be considered for training until most of the basic communication functions described previously have been mastered. Providing training in early forms of establishing joint reference (e.g., touching, pointing, looking at objects) can be accomplished through modeling and prompting methods. The graphic mode can be especially useful for object identification when specific labels are required. Once a general match-to-sample (picture-to-object) strategy is learned, new labels can often be learned with relative ease.

Questions   Another advanced communication function is requesting additional information about an object, event, or previous communication. In speech, questioning is often indicated by changes in pitch and rhythm of the voice (sometimes called prosodic features) rather than by the content or sequence of the utterance. Such an add-on feature also can be devised for graphic, gestural, and mixed modes. For example, a child may add the vocalization "Nuh?" to pointing to something in order to indicate more information is desired about that thing. Although training in questioning behavior should probably be reserved until more basic communication functions are mastered, it is a function that becomes increasingly useful as communication progresses.

The Interactive Process   In considering the various ways that communication functions to control and modify the environment, it is easy to miss one of the most basic. The very process of communication requires interaction between participants. This interaction is the basic medium upon which all other functions and content are overlayed; overlooking the functional significance of the medium would be a grave mistake. As suggested by McLuhan (1964), "the medium is the message" (p. 9). In much of communication, the primary function is to interact. It is the medium that Macdonald (1985) considers to be the primary target of communication intervention. Thus, conversational functions might be viewed as fundamental acts that maintain and regulate communication. They allow communication of specific content, but often "the 'content' of any medium blinds us to the character of the medium" (McLuhan, 1964, p. 9), and we remain unaware of these conversational functions. Nevertheless, these functions are among the most valuable both because of their vital role in transmitting other content and because of the inherent value of interaction. Pragmatic conversational functions have been taught to students with severe disabilities in structured learning contexts and have generalized well to natural communication contexts (Hunt, Allwell, Goetz, & Sailor, 1990).

McLean and Snyder-McLean (1978) identified some basic behaviors that support early language transactions: 1) receiving reinforcement from social attention, 2) enjoying the presence of others, 3) benefiting from others' assistance, 4) showing objects to others, 5) offering objects to others, and 6) participating in reciprocal exchanges. Others might be added to this list (e.g., providing reinforcement to communication partners may be as important as receiving reinforcement from them). The learner who smiles or entertains communication partners is often much more successful in maintaining interaction.

Developing simple turn-taking routines between communicators is one essential interaction behavior required for all communication. Participants must attend to their partners' behavior and then, on cue, fill their turns with related behaviors while their partners attend to them. Traditionally, imitation has been the primary form of turn-taking routine taught in early communication (Sailor et al., 1980). Imitation is believed to help develop the skills required for production of spoken or gestural language and to assist in acquisition (Leonard, 1984); however, empirical evidence has not supported its necessity for either.

Sternberg, Pegnatore, and Hill (1983) described a progression of behaviors that help develop imitation and more general turn-taking routines. The first, *resonance*, uses physical contact and motion to coordinate the behavior of the learner with that of the interventionist. The second, *coactive behavior*, interrupts physical contact but maintains the simultaneous coordination between learner and interventionist. The third, *deferred imitation*, delays the learner's response until the interventionist finishes, which establishes turn taking.

These and other turn-taking routines often can be taught through play. Stacking blocks for the learner to knock over, give-and-take games, and dancing can be simple and effective methods of establishing turn-taking routines. Siegel-Causey and Ernst (1989) emphasized early interactive patterns, stressing five essential instructional strategies for developing interaction: 1) developing nurturance, 2) enhancing sensitivity of communication partners, 3) sequencing experiences, 4) increasing opportunities for communication, and 5) utilizing movement. Similar strategies are recommended by van Dijk (1986) for developing communication with children who are deaf-blind.

There is no question that additional valuable communication functions could be identified, and some of those discussed may be unsuitable for some learners because they are too advanced or because the learners already have the response function in their repertoire. In general, however, determining program content by pragmatic function is a relatively simple and extremely productive process.

Initiation   There has been an increased emphasis on training the learner in initiating communication, rather than solely in responding to the initiations of others. The lack of initiation and control that has been demonstrated by children with physical disabilities during their interaction with caregivers without disabilities is not surprising because caregivers seldom have afforded these children sufficient time to respond or to initiate their own topics (Light et al., 1985). Instructional programs that train students only in responding to teachers or peers, while ignoring initiation, may actually make matters worse. For example, the findings of Kohl, Moses, and Stettner-Eaton (1983) that school children without disabilities assumed more dominant roles over their peers with disabilities after being trained to provide them with instruction suggest the need for the utmost care in training. Efforts to better conceptualize and implement initiation training provide valuable suggestions for all who design programs, but further efforts are needed to determine which methods actually encourage initiation. Kaczmarek (1990) suggested that careful analysis of the communication context is essential. To begin with, spontaneous requests should be developed through delay procedures and faded prompting with the desired object in full view, proximity to the communication partner, and the full attention of the communication partner. Once requests occur under these conditions, one increases task requirements by reducing the visibility of the object and by reducing proximity to or initial attention of the communication partner.

Teaching Methods

Most of the instructional methods described in this chapter are generic and can be applied to a variety of modes or systems of communication. A generic approach has been selected because it is consistent with the mixed-mode approach recommended in this chapter and with the principle of individualization emphasized throughout this book. Despite this generic approach, some specific methods have particular application to specific modes. For example, molding a child's hand around an object to teach the shape of a gesture may be useful, but directly applying this method to the vocal or graphic mode is impossible.

Three basic approaches can be identified easily for teaching communication: 1) intensive, structured programs; 2) planned instruction, included in typical activities throughout the day; and 3) environmental intervention to increase exposure to speech and/or reinforcement for vocalization. These should not be viewed as alternatives, because good teaching often requires the use of all three. These three basic approaches also can be used for training in other communication modes, but they have most often been used in teaching speech.

Intensive Programs   Musselwhite and St. Louis (1988) discussed 20 vocal language programs for use with children with severe and multiple disabilities that share four common stages originally identified by Harris (1975): 1) attention, 2) nonverbal imitation, 3) verbal imitation, and 4) functional language. Establishing the child's attention is essential in training all communication. Evidence suggests that generalized imitation is not required to teach communication functions (Reichle et al., 1984) and its value as an intermediate step is questionable (Sailor et al., 1980). Even the inclusion of verbal imitation might be questioned because imitation, in itself, is not typically a functional skill. There is some evidence, however, that verbal imitation helps develop language production and may facilitate acquisition of spontaneous language (Leonard, 1984). Problems with structured programs typically include 1) requiring steps that are too large for students with very severe disabilities, 2) lacking flexibility to be individualized to each learner, 3) encouraging the learners only to respond and ignoring training in initiation of conversation, 4) failing to generalize outside the lesson, and 5) failing to teach the skills most functional for the individual. Many of these problems are solved partially through the use of integrated instruction and environmental intervention along with intensive programs. Advantages of structured intensive programs include 1) providing a vastly increased number of learning trials, which reduces acquisition time; 2) planning instruction to increase the probability of correct responses; and 3) providing a turn-taking format that teaches a basic interaction pattern required in all communication. These advantages are particularly important for response acquisition (e.g., learning to say words), but they are less valuable for training in the functional use of words in appropriate situations.

Inclusive Instruction   Planned instruction, included in typical activities, includes 1) incidental teaching, 2) delay procedures, 3) the mand-model procedure, and 4) the interrupted behavior-chain procedure. Additional procedures could be identified or devised in this category, but these four are representative.

Incidental Teaching   In incidental teaching, the interventionist selects appropriate occasions within ongoing activities for a prespecified communication behavior. If the learner fails to respond appropriately, natural cues are strengthened (and additional prompts are added only if necessary). Natural reinforcers (items or events that would be likely consequences in the noninstructional environment) are used whenever possible (Halle, 1982). Incidental teaching has been demonstrated to be more effective than a less structured approach during free play (Cavallaro & Bambara, 1982).

Delay Procedures   In the delay procedure, the interventionist creates or selects a situation that calls for communication from the child, then stops for a few seconds to encourage the learner to communicate (Halle, 1982). For example, the teacher or parent might bring the child's plate of food, but delay just before putting it down, hoping to evoke communication of "eat" or "want" from the learner. This technique has been demonstrated to be effective both when the delays between natural cues and prompts have been gradually increased and when these delays have been held constant (Kleinert & Gast, 1982).

Mand-Model Procedure   The mand-model procedure is similar to incidental teaching in selecting appropriate teaching moments. If learners fail to respond, however, they are prompted by a direct question (e.g., "What do you want?"), and, if they still fail to respond, the correct response is modeled for them (Rogers-Warren & Warren, 1980). Like incidental teaching and the delay procedure, the mand-model procedure may be particularly useful in helping to generalize speech learned in structured lessons to functional times and places.

Interrupted Behavior-Chain Procedure   The interrupted behavior-chain procedure goes a step further in actually integrating structured training and the natural environment. The interventionist interrupts a partially completed task and teaches a brief (one trial), but complete, lesson before the task is resumed (Goetz, Gee, & Sailor, 1985). Thus, it is possible to begin training in the natural environment without prior training in a massed trial format (i.e., concentrating a large number of training trials in a block of instructional time). Interrupted behavior chains have been shown to be effective in teaching communication and also in developing generalization to new environments (Alwell, Hunt, Goetz, & Sailor, 1989).

Environmental Intervention   Both intensive programs and inclusive instruction differ from the informal interactions between children and their caregivers that teach communication skills to most people who do not have disabilities. Although structured intervention is desirable and probably necessary to assist many children with multiple disabilities in acquiring communication skills, providing a social environment that fosters communication skill acquisition is probably of equal or greater importance. Inclusive education and structured social interaction with children who have more advanced language skills increase the communication skills and social competence of children with a variety of disabilities (Jenkins, Odom, & Speltz, 1989).

Structuring the environment to maximize opportunities for incidental instruction has been shown to be an effective method for teaching communication skills to individuals with severe disabilities (e.g., Hamilton & Snell, 1993). Such methods reduce the need for separate generalization and maintenance training because the conditions differ little from the natural environment.

General Principles   Many of the environmental interventions described in Chapter 12 contribute substantially toward building communication skills. Although there is inadequate space here for a full discussion of environmental interventions, some general principles follow:

1. Family members and other primary caregivers must have a major role in developing communication skills (Bloom & Lahey, 1978). Isolated intervention is unlikely to produce changes in functional communication without this participation.

2. The interaction between the learner and primary caregivers, rather than the behavior of the individual, should be seen as the target of intervention (MacDonald, 1985). The interventionist's failure to recognize or respond to initial efforts and expectations that are too low or too high often teaches children with multiple disabilities not to communicate.

3. Siblings, peers, and others should be considered and included along with parents and caregivers in enhancing the communication environment (Allaire & Miller, 1983; Sobsey & Bieniek, 1983). The nature as well as quality and number of interactions should be considered. Children with severe disabilities sometimes interact primarily with caregivers and less frequently with peers (Hill & Whitely, 1985), but attempts to increase peer interaction by training peers as caregivers or instructors may not increase true peer interactions (Kohl et al., 1983).

4. Care must be taken not to anticipate all of the children's needs. If all their needs are met before being communicated, there will be little motivation for them to communicate (Silverman, 1980).

5. Adequate time must be provided by communication partners for the individual to respond. Memory and processing are often slower among people with disabilities (Merrill, 1985).

6. Intervention (e.g., suggestions, demonstrations, guided practice) during play has been shown to facilitate communication interactions between mothers and their children (Rosenberg & Robinson, 1985). Play in which the child and caregiver actively participate and enjoy interaction may be an important medium for building communication skills.

7. Both the child and the communication partner must use feedback mechanisms to let the other know that the message is understood (Snyder & McLean, 1976). This feedback may be simple confirmation or reinforcement. Reinforcement should be functional rather than instructional. For example, if a child says "Look," and points toward a dog, the respondent should look and comment on the dog rather than failing to look and telling the child, "Nice talking" (Bottorf & De Pape, 1982).

8. A rich communication environment should be provided (Allaire & Miller, 1983). Often potential communication partners fail to talk to minimally responsive children. The result is reduced opportunity for language learning. Selecting topics of potential or known interest and using simple vocabulary and construction are also important.

9. Any structured language programs must be integrated with events in the natural language environment (Nietupski, Scheutz, & Ockwood, 1980).

This means that information from the natural environment (e.g., what and how the learner currently communicates, what the learner needs or wants to communicate) must be considered in the design and implementation of the structured program and that information from the program (e.g., functions and forms of communication) must be communicated to and considered by communication partners in the natural environment.

10. Children must be encouraged to actively initiate communication, not only passively respond (Kaczmarek, 1990). This requires allowing the learner to exercise as much control and make as many decisions as possible (Shevin & Klein, 1984) during daily activities.

Educational and Social Inclusion   The decreased use of noninclusive living and learning environments by children with multiple disabilities means greater participation in society. As these children enter general education classrooms and inclusive activities, their opportunities for interaction change in character and frequency. These changes facilitate learning age-appropriate, functional communication skills (Stremel-Campbell, Campbell, & Johnson-Dorn, 1985). Research suggests that peer interactions occur more frequently and that more advanced patterns of communication are used by children with disabilities in inclusive settings (Guralnick & Groom, 1988). Brinker (1985) studied the interactions between students with severe disabilities in noninclusive and inclusive settings. Students with disabilities made significantly more social bids to their peers and received more social bids from their peers in inclusive settings. Students who did not have disabilities also responded more frequently to the social bids from students with severe disabilities. Inclusion by itself, however, is not usually adequate to produce major effects on interaction (Guralnick, 1984). It is most useful when used in conjunction with good instructional programs and, when required, with intervention to encourage peer interaction.

A communication program that combines structured language programs, inclusive instruction, and environmental modification is ideal for teaching vocal language, but it is also suited for teaching communication in other modes or mixed modes, as previously suggested. For this reason, discussion of these modes will not duplicate the previous information; instead, it will add other information and issues relevant to the mode discussed.

Teaching Gestural Communication   The training interventions discussed for the vocal mode are also useful for gestural communication, but there are some important differences. First, gestural systems frequently require more special training of families, interventionists, peers, and other potential respondents who are more likely to use the vocal mode for most of their communication. Coordinated efforts of all involved are essential to generalizing gestures to new communication contexts (Kollinzas, 1983). Second, because there likely will be fewer natural models in the learner's environment (especially if gestures are being used exclusively as the learner's output mode and communication partners use speech for the learner's reception), more instructional models may be necessary. Third, unlike the vocal mode, gestures are often taught through the use of physical prompts.

Two physical prompting methods are commonly used (Musselwhite & St. Louis, 1988). *Handshaping* uses physical contact, with the trainer positioning the learner's hands appropriately. *Molding* positions the learner's hands by placing them around an object and is useful when the gesture being taught resembles the shape of the hand formed by grasping the object (e.g., cup).

Teaching Graphic Communication   Many of the same methods used to teach speech or gestures can be adapted to teach graphic communication. Most often, learners who use graphic symbols for production, use speech for receptive communication. Keogh and Reichle (1985) suggested a basic training sequence for labeling photographs. First, the learner is taught to touch the object when its name is spoken. Second, the learner is taught to touch a photograph of the object when the object's name is spoken. Third, the learner is taught to select the photograph from an array when its name is spoken. Fourth, the learner is taught to touch the photograph from the array to request the item. Fifth, the learner is taught to touch the photograph from the array when the object is presented along with the question, "What is this?" (Keogh & Reichle, 1985). Empirical evidence suggests that teaching only one object at a time produces faster acquisition but that concurrent teaching of items produces better discrimination among these items (Waldo, Guess, & Flanagan, 1985). Graphic symbol systems can provide the primary mode of communication for learners with severe disabilities and play an important part in many mixed mode approaches.

Generalization and Maintenance

Closely associated with the concern for developing initiation are the generalization and maintenance of communication behaviors. Warren, Baxter, Anderson, Marshall, and Baer (1981) observed that, although the need to address generalization and maintenance in training has been acknowledged, the manner of addressing them often has questionable application to the natural environment. This implies, for example, that even though multiple trainers may be used, there is no certainty that the behavior will generalize to the natural environment. This is part of the reason that structured programs often fail to produce generalization. Reichle and Keogh (1985) recommended the integration of structured and incidental approaches to overcome this problem.

In considering generalization, it is important also to consider its limits. The effective use of communication in the natural environment requires the learner not only to generalize across appropriate partners and situations, but also to discriminate inappropriate ones. For example, it may be appropriate to request help in toileting from family members and caregivers but not from bus drivers or cashiers in the grocery store. The ability to use communication discriminatively is as important as the ability to generalize it.

Communication training not only must generalize across settings and cues, it should also generalize to new variations of communication behavior. Such spontaneous use of communication is the ultimate goal of structured training and requires that incidental teaching and exposure to a rich communication environment accompany structured lessons (Sigafoos & Reichle, 1993).

It is often true that communication behavior is not maintained over time because it is not functional for the learner. It is important to remember that no attempt to communicate is functional unless communication partners respond to it appropriately. For example, requesting foods or beverages would generally be considered a functional communication skill, but, in fact, it is functional only if, at least to some degree, it can be used to control access to food or beverages. If the learner requests something, but the responses to the request are "Not now, I'm busy," "You just ate," "It's almost lunchtime," and so forth, the communication will not be maintained because it is not functional. Before attempting to teach any communication act, the communication partner must be prepared to respond to it.

Communication Functions and Problem Behavior

One of the most rapidly growing subjects in educating children with multiple disabilities is the emerging model of problem behavior as a form of communication (Donnellan et al., 1984). In this model, bizarre, disruptive, or destructive behavior is analyzed in terms of its pragmatic function (i.e., control over environmental events). It may serve as a request for attention, assistance, a desired item, or relief from an unpleasant situation. Using this paradigm, interventionists have provided training in more appropriate methods of communicating the same function and thereby reduced the inappropriate behavior (e.g., Carr & Durand, 1985). Many issues still need to be resolved before the full impact of such findings can be known. The percentage of behavior problems that can be successfully treated through communication training has not yet been determined, but this training does work in many cases. It is usually ethically more appropriate to provide the above-mentioned behavior because it provides the opportunity to intervene positively by reinforcing adaptive behavior, rather than merely suppressing inappropriate behavior. In addition, treating behavior through functional communication training appears to produce more permanent reductions in inappropriate behavior (Durand & Carr, 1992).

From a communication perspective, viewing behavior problems as communication difficulties has another interesting implication. When problem behavior serves an identifiable pragmatic function, it is likely that the learner has been unable to master a more appropriate form for that function (Doss & Reichle, 1991). Therefore, behavior problems may help to identify communication functions for which the child needs training. For example, if it is determined that a learner bangs his or her head on the floor in order to obtain the attention of caregivers, it is likely that no appropriate attention-requesting response is available in the learner's repertoire or that caregivers ignore more appropriate requests and respond to the inappropriate behavior. In either case, the learner's investment of energy and pain reveal that this function is important to him or her. If the learner has no more appropriate requesting form in his or her repertoire, he or she should be taught one. If the learner already has one, he or she must be prompted to use it, and caregivers must be trained to respond to it. Doing so will improve both communication and behavior.

Basic steps in application of pragmatics to improving inappropriate behavior include the following:

1. Conducting a functional analysis of the behavior to determine the contexts in which it occurs and the environmental responses to the behavior
2. Hypothesizing the pragmatic function that the behavior may serve
3. Determining an appropriate mode and form for an alternative behavior to serve the same function
4. Prompting and functionally reinforcing the new behavior
5. Differentially reinforcing the appropriate behavior over the inappropriate behavior
6. Maintaining data on both the appropriate and the inappropriate behavior (and modifying the program if progress is not apparent)
7. Providing for generalization and maintenance of the new behavior to prevent regression

Transdisciplinary Teamwork

The need for an environment that is responsive to the child's communication is just one important reason for close cooperation among parents, teachers, therapists, and all other members of the transdisciplinary team. Isolated communication therapy is unlikely to 1) provide adequate training time, 2) provide consistent responses from communication partners, 3) generalize to the natural environment, or 4) provide an appropriate communication context (Nietupski et al., 1980). Integrated assessment, program development, and intervention efforts contribute toward elimination of all of these problems.

The communication therapist may act as a consultant sharing his or her expertise with all other team members (Musselwhite & St. Louis, 1988), in addition to providing some specific training to the learner, locating resources (e.g., assessment instruments, training programs, adaptive communication equipment), and maintaining progress records (Silverman, 1980) within integrated systems. Occupational therapists and physical therapists can be extremely helpful in evaluating motor function for gestural and augmentative systems of communication. Often, they are helpful in designing or modifying equipment to suit the child's capabilities or in helping the child develop the motor control required for a specific communication system (Silverman, 1980).

Increasingly, biomedical and electrical engineers are participating on the team when specialized electronic equipment is required (Beukelman & Mirenda,

1992). Their expertise allows for design and construction of equipment that meets the requirements identified by other team members.

Family members and other caregivers play a vital role on this team, helping to identify the functions and content for training. Their interactions with the learner are critical to the development of functional communication. They are the primary communication partners with the child. Their responses can make the child's communication meaningful or futile in the child's current environments, and their interactions provide a model for potential future environments.

The teacher's role overlaps that of many other team members. He or she is often caregiver, evaluator, and interventionist, and typically has the additional role of coordinator. In discussing the need for integrated services, it is important to point out that, although the integration process need not be a struggle, it does require active and ongoing efforts to facilitate communication and ensure smooth transdisciplinary coordination. Most often, the teacher plays a major role in this.

This list of team members is far from complete. Teacher's associates may provide much of the instruction in structured and natural environments. Audiologists, physicians, and others may provide important assessment of sensory abilities or limitations. The communication team must not be a fixed entity with prespecified members. It must be flexible enough to alter its membership based on the current decisions to be addressed for the individual child.

SUMMARY

This chapter provides information related to training in communication functions for children with severe and multiple disabilities. In doing so, it concentrates on very basic communication. A pragmatic focus, in which the purpose (social effectiveness) of communication is emphasized, provides the major framework for program content. Eclectic training methods that are not restricted to a single communication mode are strongly recommended because they place the fewest restrictions on the child and most closely approximate typical communication. Finally, the need to consider the interaction between communication partners, rather than only the behavior of the individual in isolation, is stressed.

REFERENCES

Allaire, J.H., & Miller, J.M. (1983). Nonspeech communication. In M.E. Snell (Ed.), *Systematic instruction of the moderately and severely handicapped* (2nd ed., pp. 289–311). Columbus, OH: Charles E. Merrill.

Alwell, M., Hunt, P., Goetz, L., & Sailor, W. (1989). Teaching generalized communicative behaviors within interrupted behavior chain contexts. *Journal of The Association for Persons with Severe Disabilities, 14*, 91–100.

Bates, E., Camaioni, L., & Voltera, V. (1979). The acquisition of performatives prior to speech. In E. Ochs & B.B. Schieffelin (Eds.), *Developmental pragmatics* (pp. 111–130). New York: Academic Press.

Baumgart, D., Johnson, J., & Helmstetter, E. (1990). *Augmentative and alternative communication systems for persons with moderate and severe disabilities*. Baltimore: Paul H. Brookes Publishing Co.

Beukelman, D.R., & Mirenda, P. (1992). *Augmentative and alternative communication: Management of severe communication disorders in children and adults*. Baltimore: Paul H. Brookes Publishing Co.

Bigge, J.L. (1991). *Teaching individuals with physical and multiple disabilities* (3rd ed.). Columbus, OH: Charles E. Merrill.

Biklen, D. (1993). *Communication unbound: How facilitated communication is challenging traditional views of autism and developmental disability*. New York: Teachers College Press.

Biklen, D., & Duchan, J.F. (1994). "I am intelligent": The social construction of mental retardation. *Journal of The Association for Persons with Severe Handicaps, 19*(3), 173–184.

Biklen, D., Saha, N., & Kliewer, C. (1995). How teachers confirm the authorship of facilitated communication. *Journal of The Association for Persons with Severe Handicaps, 20*(1), 45–56.

Bloom, L., & Lahey, M. (1978). *Language development and language disorders*. New York: John Wiley & Sons.

Bottorf, L., & De Pape, D. (1982). Initiating communication systems for severely speech impaired persons. *Topics in Language Disorders, 2*, 55–71.

Bricker, D.D. (1983). Early communication: Development and training. In M.E. Snell (Ed.), *Systematic instruction of the moderately and severely handicapped* (2nd ed., pp. 269–288). Columbus, OH: Charles E. Merrill.

Brinker, R.P. (1985). Interactions between severely mentally retarded students and other students in integrated and segregated public school settings. *American Journal of Mental Deficiency, 89*, 587–594.

Capozzi, M., & Mineo, B. (1984). Nonspeech language and communication systems. In A.L. Holland (Ed.), *Language disorders in children: Recent advances* (pp. 173–209). San Diego, CA: College-Hill.

Carr, E.G., & Dores, P.A. (1981). Patterns of language acquisition following simultaneous communication with autistic children. *Analysis and Intervention in Developmental Disabilities, 1*, 347–361.

Carr, E.G., & Durand, V.M. (1985). Reducing behavior problems through functional communication training. *Journal of Applied Behavior Analysis, 18*, 111–126.

Cavallaro, C.C., & Bambara, L.M. (1982). Two strategies for teaching language during free play. *Journal of The Association for the Severely Handicapped, 7*(2), 90–92.

Cirrin, F.M., & Rowland, C.M. (1985). Communicative assessment of nonverbal youths with severe/profound mental retardation. *Mental Retardation, 23*, 52–62.

Clark, C.R. (1984). A close look at the standard Rebus System and Blissymbolics. *Journal of The Association for Persons with Severe Handicaps, 9*, 37–48.

Correia, L.M., & Sobsey, D. (1984, May). *Assessing communication and precommunication skills in clients with severe multiple handicaps*. Paper presented at the Annual Meeting of the American Association on Mental Deficiency, Minneapolis, MN. (ERIC Document Reproduction Service No. ED 252 032)

Creekmore, N. (1982). Use of sign alone and sign plus speech in language training of autistic children. *Journal of The Association for the Severely Handicapped, 6*(4), 45–55.

Crossley, R. (1994). *Facilitated communication training*. New York: Teachers College Press.

Crossley, R., & McDonald, A. (1984). *Annie's coming out*. New York: Viking Press.

Dennis, R., Reichle, J., Williams, W., & Vogelsberg, R.T. (1982). Motoric factors influencing the selection of vocabulary for sign production programs. *Journal of The Association for the Severely Handicapped, 7*(1), 20–32.

Donnellan, A.M., & Leary, M.R. (1995). *Movement differences and diversity in autism/mental retardation: Appreciating and accommodating people with communication and behavior challenges*. Madison, WI: DRI Press.

Donnellan, A.M., Mirenda, P.L., Mesaros, R.A., & Fassbender, L.L. (1984). Analyzing the communicative functions of aberrant behavior. *Journal of The Association for Persons with Severe Handicaps, 9*, 201–212.

Doss, L.S., & Reichle, J. (1991). Replacing excess behavior with an initial communicative repertoire. In J. Reichle, J. York, & J. Sigafoos, *Implementing augmentative and alternative communication: Strategies for learners with severe disabilities* (pp. 215–237). Baltimore: Paul H. Brookes Publishing Co.

Durand, V.M., & Carr, E.G. (1992). An analysis of maintenance following functional communication training. *Journal of Applied Behavior Analysis, 25*, 777–794.

Edwards, A.D.N. (1991). *Speech synthesis: Technology for disabled people*. London: Paul Chapman Publishing Co.

Goetz, L., Gee, K., & Sailor, W. (1985). Using a behavior chain interruption strategy to teach communication skills to students with severe disabilities. *Journal of The Association for Persons with Severe Handicaps, 10,* 21–30.

Green, G. (1993). Controlled evaluation of facilitated communication. *Autism Research Review, 7*(1), 2.

Green, G., & Shane, H. (1994). Science, reasons, and facilitated communication. *Journal of The Association for Persons with Severe Handicaps, 19*(3), 151–172.

Greenfield, P., & Smith, J. (1976). *The structure of communication in early language development*. New York: Academic Press.

Guess, D., & Noonan, M.J. (1982). Curricula and instructional procedures for severely handicapped students. *Focus on Exceptional Children, 5*, 1–12.

Guralnick, M.J. (1984). The peer interactions of young developmentally delayed children in specialized and in integrated settings. In T. Field, J. Roopnarine, & M. Segal (Eds.), *Friendships in normal and handicapped children* (pp. 139–152). Norwood, NJ: Ablex.

Guralnick, M.J., & Groom, J.M. (1988). Peer interactions in mainstreamed and specialized classrooms: A comparative analysis. *Exceptional Children, 54*, 415–425.

Halle, J.W. (1982). Teaching functional language to the handicapped: An integrative model of natural environment teaching techniques. *Journal of The Association for the Severely Handicapped, 7*(4), 29–37.

Halliday, M. (1975). *Learning how to mean: Explorations in the development of language*. New York: Elsevier.

Hamilton, B.L., & Snell, M.E. (1993). Using the milieu approach to increase spontaneous communication book use across environments by adolescents with autism. *Augmentative and Alternative Communication, 9*, 259–271.

Harris, S.L. (1975). Teaching language to non-verbal children—with emphasis on problems of generalization. *Psychological Bulletin, 82*, 565–580.

Heinrichs, P. (1992, February 23). Tortured family may call for probe on facilitated evidence. *The Sunday Age*, p. 8.

Hill, C.A., & Whitely, J.H. (1985). Social interactions and on-task behavior of severely multihandicapped and non-handicapped children in mainstreamed classrooms. *Canadian Journal of Exceptional Children, 1*, 136–140.

Hudson, A., Melita, B., & Arnold, N. (1993). Brief report: A case study assessing the validity of facilitated communication. *Journal of Autism and Developmental Disorders, 23*(1), 165–173.

Hunt, P., Alwell, M., Goetz, L., & Sailor, W. (1990). Generalized effects of conversation skill training. *Journal of The Association for Persons with Severe Handicaps, 15,* 250–260.

Hurlbut, B.I., Iwata, B.A., & Green, J.D. (1982). Non-vocal language acquisition in adolescents with severe physical disabilities: Blissymbols versus iconic stimulus formats. *Journal of Applied Behavior Analysis, 15,* 241–258.

Jenkins, J.R., Odom, S.L., & Speltz, M.L. (1989). Effects of social integration on preschool children with handicaps. *Exceptional Children, 55*(5), 420–428.

Kaczmarek, L.A. (1990). Teaching spontaneous language to individuals with severe handicaps. *Journal of The Association for Persons with Severe Handicaps, 15,* 160–169.

Karlan, G., & Lloyd, L.L. (1983). Considerations in the planning of communication intervention: Selecting a lexicon. *Journal of The Association for the Severely Handicapped, 8*(2), 13–25.

Keogh, W.J., & Reichle, J. (1985). Communication intervention for the "difficult-to-teach" severely handicapped. In S.F. Warren & A.K. Rogers-Warren (Eds.), *Teaching functional language: Generalization and maintenance of language skills* (pp. 157–194). Baltimore: University Park Press.

Kirschner, A., Algozzine, B., & Abbott, T.B. (1979). Manual communication systems: A comparison and its implications. *Education and Training of the Mentally Retarded, 14,* 5–10.

Kleinert, H.L., & Gast, D.L. (1982). Teaching a multihandicapped adult manual signs using a constant delay procedure. *Journal of The Association for the Severely Handicapped, 6*(4), 25–37.

Kohl, F.L., Moses, L.G., & Stettner-Eaton, B.A. (1983). The results of teaching fifth and sixth graders to be instructional trainers with students who are severely handicapped. *Journal of The Association for Persons with Severe Handicaps, 8*(4), 32–40.

Kollinzas, G. (1983). The communication record: Sharing information to promote sign language generalization. *Journal of The Association for the Severely Handicapped, 8*(3), 49–55.

Leonard, L.B. (1984). Normal language acquisition: Some recent findings and clinical implications. In A.L. Holland (Ed.), *Language disorders in children: Recent advances* (pp. 1–36). San Diego, CA: College-Hill.

Light, J., Collier, B., & Parnes, P. (1985). Communicative interaction between young nonspeaking physically disabled children and their primary caregivers. *Augmentative and Alternative Communication, 1,* 74–83.

Love, R.J., Hagerman, E.L., & Taimi, E.G. (1980). Speech performance, dysphagia, and oral reflexes in cerebral palsy. *Journal of Speech and Hearing Disorders, 45,* 59–75.

MacDonald, J.D. (1985). Language through conversation: A model for intervention with language-delayed persons. In S.F. Warren & A.K. Rogers-Warren (Eds.), *Teaching functional language: Generalization and maintenance of language skills* (pp. 89–122). Baltimore: University Park Press.

Marshall, C., & Rossman, G.B. (1989). *Designing qualitative research.* Beverly Hills, CA: Sage Publications.

McLean, J., & Snyder-McLean, L. (1978). *A transactional approach to early language training.* Columbus, OH: Charles E. Merrill.

McLuhan, M. (1964). *Understanding the media: The extensions of man.* New York: McGraw-Hill.

McShane, J. (1980). *Learning to talk*. London: Cambridge University Press.

Merrill, E.C. (1985). Differences in semantic processing speed of mentally retarded and nonretarded persons. *American Journal of Mental Deficiency, 90,* 71–80.

Mirenda, P. (1985). Designing pictorial communication systems for physically able-bodied students with severe handicaps. *Augmentative and Alternative Communication, 1,* 58–64.

Mirenda, P., & Iacono, T. (1990). Communication options for persons with severe and profound disabilities: State of the art and future directions. *Journal of The Association for Persons with Severe Disabilities, 15,* 13–21.

Morris, D. (1982). *A pocket guide to manwatching*. London: Triad/Panther Books.

Morris, S.E. (1978a). Pre-Speech Assessment Scale. In J.M. Wilson (Ed.), *Oral-motor function and dysfunction in children* (pp. 133–148). Chapel Hill: University of North Carolina, Division of Physical Therapy.

Morris, S.E. (1978b). Sensorimotor prerequisites for speech and the influence of cerebral palsy. In J.M. Wilson (Ed.), *Oral-motor function and dysfunction in children* (pp. 123–128). Chapel Hill: University of North Carolina, Division of Physical Therapy.

Musselwhite, C.R., & St. Louis, K.W. (1988). *Communication programming for persons with severe handicaps* (2nd ed.). Boston: Little, Brown.

Mustonen, T., Locke, P., Reichle, J., Solbrack, M., & Lindgren, A. (1991). An overview of augmentative and alternative communication systems. In J. Reichle, J. York, & J. Sigafoos, *Implementing augmentative and alternative communication: Strategies for learners with severe disabilities* (pp. 1–37). Baltimore: Paul H. Brookes Publishing Co.

Nietupski, J., Scheutz, G., & Ockwood, L. (1980). The delivery of communication therapy services to severely handicapped students: A plan for change. *Journal of The Association for the Severely Handicapped, 5,* 13–23.

Olswang, L.B., Stoel-Gammon C., Coggins, T.E., & Carpenter, R.L. (1987). *Assessing prelinguistic and early linguistic behaviors in developmentally young children*. Seattle: University of Washington Press.

Oviatt, S. (1980). The emerging ability to comprehend language: An experimental approach. *Child Development, 51,* 97–106.

Owings, N., McManus, M., & Scherer, N. (1981). A deinstitutionalized retarded adult's use of communication functions in the natural setting. *British Journal of Disorders of Communication, 16,* 119–128.

Piché, L., & Reichle, J. (1991). Teaching scanning and selection techniques. In J. Reichle, J. York, & J. Sigafoos, *Implementing augmentative and alternative communication: Strategies for learners with severe disabilities* (pp. 257–274). Baltimore: Paul H. Brookes Publishing Co.

Reichle, J. (1991). Defining the decisions involved in designing and implementing augmentative and alternative communication systems. In J. Reichle, J. York, & J. Sigafoos, *Implementing augmentative and alternative communication: Strategies for learners with severe disabilities* (pp. 39–60). Baltimore: Paul H. Brookes Publishing Co.

Reichle, J., & Keogh, W.J. (1985). Communication intervention: A selective review of what, when, and how to teach. In S.F. Warren & A.K. Rogers-Warren (Eds.), *Teaching functional language: Generalization and maintenance of language skills* (pp. 25–59). Baltimore: University Park Press.

Reichle, J., & Keogh, W.J. (1986). Communication instruction for learners with severe handicaps: Some unresolved issues. In R.H. Horner, L.H. Meyer, & H.D.B. Fredericks (Eds.), *Education for learners with severe handicaps: Exemplary service strategies* (pp. 189–220). Baltimore: Paul H. Brookes Publishing Co.

Reichle, J., Rogers, N., & Barrett, C. (1984). Establishing pragmatic discriminations among communicative functions of requesting, rejecting and commenting in an adolescent. *Journal of The Association for Persons with Severe Handicaps, 9*, 31–36.

Reichle, J., & Sigafoos, J. (1991). Establishing an initial repertoire of requesting. In J. Reichle, J. York, & J. Sigafoos, *Implementing augmentative and alternative communication: Strategies for learners with severe disabilities* (pp. 89–114). Baltimore: Paul H. Brookes Publishing Co.

Reichle, J., Williams, W., & Ryan, S. (1981). Selecting signs for the formulations of an augmentative communicative modality. *Journal of The Association for the Severely Handicapped, 6*(1), 48–56.

Reichle, J.E., & Yoder, D.E. (1979). Assessment and early stimulation of communication in the severely and profoundly mentally retarded. In R. York & G. Edgar (Eds.), *Teaching the severely handicapped* (Vol. IV, pp. 180–218). Columbus, OH: Special Press.

Remington, B., & Clarke, S. (1983). Acquisition of expressive signing by autistic children: An evaluation of relative effects of simultaneous communication and sign-alone training. *Journal of Applied Behavior Analysis, 16*, 315–328.

Rogers-Warren, A., & Warren, S. (1980). Mands for verbalization: Facilitating the display of newly trained language in children. *Behavior Modification, 4*, 361–382.

Rogers-Warren, A.K. (1984). Ecobehavioral analysis. *Education and Treatment of Children, 7*, 283–303.

Rosenberg, S., & Beukelman, D. (1987). The participation model. In C.A. Coston (Ed.), *Proceedings of the National Planners Conference on Assistive Device Service Delivery* (pp. 159–161). Washington, DC: RESNA, The Association for the Advancement of Rehabilitation Technology.

Rosenberg, S.A., & Robinson, C.C. (1985). Enhancement of mothers' interactional skills in an infant education program. *Education and Training of the Mentally Retarded, 20*, 163–169.

Sailor, W., & Guess, D. (1983). *Severely handicapped students: An instructional design.* Boston: Houghton-Mifflin.

Sailor, W., Guess, D., Goetz, L., Schuler, A., Utley, B., & Baldwn, M. (1980). Language and severely handicapped persons: Deciding what to teach to whom. In W. Sailor, B. Wilcox, & L. Brown (Eds.), *Methods of instruction for severely handicapped students* (pp. 71–108). Baltimore: Paul H. Brookes Publishing Co.

Schweigart, P., & Rowland, C. (1992). Early communication and microtechnology: Instructional sequence and case studies of children with severe multiple disabilities. *Augmentative and Alternative Communication, 8*, 273–286.

Shane, H.C., & Bashir, A.S. (1980). Election criteria for adoption of an augmentative communications system: Preliminary considerations. *Journal of Speech and Hearing Disorders, 45*, 408–414.

Shevin, M., & Klein, N.K. (1984). The importance of choice-making skills for students with severe disabilities. *Journal of The Association for Persons with Severe Handicaps, 9*, 159–166.

Siegel-Causey, E., & Ernst, B. (1989). Theoretical orientation and research in nonsymbolic development. In E. Siegel-Causey & D. Guess, *Enhancing nonsymbolic communication interactions among learners with severe disabilities* (pp. 15–51). Baltimore: Paul H. Brookes Publishing Co.

Sigafoos, J., & Iacono, T. (1993). Selecting augmentative communication devices for persons with severe disabilities: Some factors for educational teams to consider. *Australia and New Zealand Journal of Developmental Disabilities, 18*(3), 133–146.

Sigafoos, J., & Reichle, J. (1991). Establishing an initial repertoire of rejecting. In J. Reichle, J. York, & J. Sigafoos, *Implementing augmentative and alternative com-

munication: Strategies for learners with severe disabilities (pp. 115–132). Baltimore: Paul H. Brookes Publishing Co.

Sigafoos, J., & Reichle, J. (1993). Establishing spontaneous verbal behavior. In R.A. Gable & S.F. Warren (Eds.), *Strategies for teaching students with mild to severe mental retardation* (pp. 191–230). Baltimore: Paul H. Brookes Publishing Co.

Sigafoos, J., & York, J. (1991). Using ecological inventories to promote functional communication. In J. Reichle, J. York, & J. Sigafoos, *Implementing augmentative and alternative communication: Strategies for learners with severe disabilities* (pp. 61–70). Baltimore: Paul H. Brookes Publishing Co.

Silverman, F.H. (1980). *Communication for the speechless.* Englewood Cliffs, NJ: Prentice-Hall.

Simon, E.I., Toll, D.M., & Whitehair, P.M. (1994). A naturalistic approach to the validation of facilitated communication. *Journal of Autism and Developmental Disorders, 24*(5), 647–657.

Snyder, L.K., & McLean, J.E. (1976). Deficient acquisition strategies: A conceptual framework for analyzing severe language deficiency. *American Journal of Mental Deficiency, 81,* 338–349.

Sobsey, D. (1994). *Violence and abuse in the lives of people with disabilities: The end of silent acceptance?* Baltimore: Paul H. Brookes Publishing Co.

Sobsey, D., & Reichle, J. (1989). Components of reinforcement for attention signal switch activation. *The Mental Retardation and Learning Disability Bulletin, 17*(2), 46–60.

Sobsey, R., & Bieniek, B. (1983). A family approach to functional sign language. *Behavior Modification, 7,* 488–502.

Sternberg, L., Pegnatore, L., & Hill, C. (1983). Establishing interactive communication behavior with profoundly mentally handicapped students. *Journal of The Association for the Severely Handicapped, 8*(2), 39–46.

Stremel-Campbell, K., Campbell, R., & Johnson-Dorn, N. (1985). Utilization of integrated settings and activities to develop and expand communication skills. In M.P. Brady & P. Gunter (Eds.), *Integrating moderately and severely handicapped learners: Strategies that work* (pp. 185–213). Springfield, IL: Charles C Thomas.

Tanaka, N.K., & Lian, M.J. (1995). The operation of a computer adaptive switch by a child with cerebral palsy using two body sites. *Physical Disabilities: Education and Related Services, 13*(2), 31–42.

Terrace, H.S. (1979). *Nim.* New York: Alfred A. Knopf.

van Dijk, J. (1986). An educational curriculum for deaf-blind multihandicapped persons. In D. Ellis (Ed.), *Sensory impairments in mentally handicapped people* (pp. 374–382). San Diego, CA: College-Hill.

Vanderheiden, G.C., & Lloyd, L.L. (1986). Communication systems and their components. In S.W. Blackstone (Ed.), *Augmentative communication: An introduction* (pp. 49–161). Rockville, MD: American Speech-Language-Hearing Association.

Waldo, L., Guess, D., & Flanagan, B. (1985). Effects of concurrent and serial training on receptive labeling by severely retarded individuals. *Journal of The Association for the Severely Handicapped, 6*(4), 56–65.

Warren, S.F., Baxter, D.K., Anderson, S.R., Marshall, A., & Baer, D.M. (1981). Generalization of question-asking by severely retarded individuals. *Journal of The Association for the Severely Handicapped, 6*(3), 15–22.

Warren, S.F., & Rogers-Warren, A.K. (1983). A longitudinal analysis of language generalization among adolescents with severely handicapping conditions. *Journal of The Association for the Severely Handicapped, 8*(4), 18–31.

Waterson, N., & Snow, C. (1978). *Development of communication.* New York: John Wiley & Sons.

Williams, D. (1994). In the real word. *Journal of The Association for Persons with Severe Handicaps, 19*(3), 196–199.

York, J., & Weiman, G. (1991). Accommodating severe physical disabilities. In J. Reichle, J. York, & J. Sigafoos, *Implementing augmentative and alternative communication: Strategies for learners with severe disabilities* (pp. 239–255). Baltimore: Paul H. Brookes Publishing Co.

Mealtime Skills

PROBABLY NO SINGLE ACTIVITY CLUSTER is as critical to the health, education, and happiness of children with multiple disabilities as mealtimes. People with disabilities often spend several hours each day in mealtime activities, and more than one third of caregiving time is typically spent in these activities (Ohwaki & Zingarelli, 1988). Taking food by mouth is one of the best predictors of increased life expectancy in people with severe disabilities (Eyman, Grossman, Chaney, & Call, 1990), but mealtimes also help determine quality of life. In the best instances, meals combine the nutrition needed for growth and survival; the pleasure of enjoyable tastes, aromas, and textures; the opportunity for positive social interaction; and the chance to increase independence in eating and feeding skills. Such mealtimes are undoubtedly among the most pleasant times spent by children and their caregivers. For others, however, mealtimes can be stressful and unpleasant. Some children struggle through seemingly endless meals with little opportunity for positive social interaction or learning, desperately trying to obtain adequate foods and fluids without choking or gagging. Caregivers struggle to overcome the children's atypical movement and behavior problems. For many children, the mealtime experience falls somewhere between these two extremes; but what are the factors that determine whether meals will be more like the positive or negative extreme? Can caregivers alter some of these factors, and if so, how?

Although complete answers to all of these questions will probably never be known, research and clinical experience in a number of disciplines have provided at least partial answers. Some factors that influence mealtime performance are related to the characteristics of the child who is eating (e.g., muscle tone, reflex patterns). Other factors are related to the physical environment (e.g., food texture, types of utensils provided). Still others are related to the social environment (e.g., pace of feeding, noise and disruption in the dining area). Although some factors may be easier to control than others, intervention can produce significant improvements in performance regardless of whether internal or external factors must be addressed.

This chapter describes common mealtime concerns and discusses methods for intervening to achieve specific objectives. Both eating and feeding skills are included. Although these two closely related skills are often grouped together, they are treated separately here to ensure that each receives adequate coverage. *Eating* refers to accepting and processing food in the mouth and to swallowing food. *Feeding* refers to bringing food to the mouth. Two other topics, nutrition and dentistry, are also considered here because of their close relationship with eating and feeding skills. Finally, this chapter discusses the roles of various members of the transdisciplinary team in assessing performance and planning programs. Prevention and treatment of airway obstruction is an essential topic for all staff involved in eating and feeding activities, and information on this topic is included in Chapter 5.

EATING AND DRINKING SKILLS

Many children with multiple disabilities have difficulty eating their food. Disorders of muscle tone may make lip closure difficult, interfering with the child's ability to take food from a spoon or hold liquids in the mouth. Primitive reflexes (e.g., tonic bite reflex) may make chewing difficult or impossible. Inappropriate selection of food textures and utensils, poor positioning, improper presentation of foods, or stress factors in the mealtime environment can aggravate these problems or cause additional problems. Structural abnormalities (e.g., cleft lip, cleft palate) can further complicate eating, and oral-motor patterns that develop to help compensate for these impairments (e.g., excessive neck extension to keep food from falling out of mouth) may create secondary problems. Compounding all of these problems, dysfunctional eating patterns are inadvertently taught to some children by their caregivers in well-intentioned attempts to improve eating (e.g., feeding the child in a supine position). Often, many of these factors interact in the same child, and it is difficult to determine which factor is primarily responsible for a given problem.

Of course, each child is an individual, and it is impossible to describe a general pattern of eating and drinking for all children with disabilities or even for all children with any specific category of disability. Similarly, typical eating and drinking includes a range of behavior. Notwithstanding this variability, some general patterns of eating and drinking behavior are described here along with intervention methods.

Oral-Motor Patterns

Typical Development   Eating and drinking are complex physiological processes (Morris & Klein, 1987). Three major body systems make major contributions to the process:

1. The skeletal system provides underlying structural support, anchors muscles, and provides the cutting and grinding surfaces on the teeth required to chew food.
2. The muscular system provides additional structure as well as movement required to accept, retain, chew, and mix food with saliva, which lubricates and begins to digest food in the mouth. The muscular system also moves food into the esophagus and closes off the airway to allow its safe passage.
3. The nervous system directs and coordinates these activities.

Although eating and drinking are generally considered to be under voluntary control, experimental evidence indicates that much of oral-motor behavior is primarily reflexive or patterned by neural circuits. Biting, chewing, licking, and sucking all follow the same rhythmic pattern for each individual (Campbell, 1978). Each movement in the cycle results in sensory stimulation that influences the next response in the cycle. For example, the closing of the jaws during chewing stimulates pressure receptors. The pressure receptors signal the jaws to open, and so forth. A central neural pattern generator controls the pace and coordination of movements. Voluntary control can modify activity of this generator but cannot replace its function. So, the responses involved in eating behavior are a combination of reflexes, more complex (reflex-like) patterns, and voluntary movements.

Newborns who do not have related impairments obtain nourishment through sucking or suckling patterns. *Sucking* refers to obtaining liquid as a result of the suction created by raising and lowering the tongue after sealing the oral cavity by pressing the lips against the nipple. *Suckling* refers to obtaining liquid as a result of rhythmic licking of the nipple and does not require lip seal for suction (Morris, 1978a). Although some investigators have reported observing early sucking patterns, suckling is generally considered the predominant pattern in young infants. Swallowing is integrated with both of these patterns.

For most children, the next stage of eating occurs when semisolid foods are introduced at about 6 months of age. The exact age varies greatly because it depends more on the caregivers' decision to introduce semisolids than on the child's ability to handle them. In fact, the handling of semisolid food as a developmental stage is highly questionable because children in many parts of the world routinely progress directly from liquids to solids with no apparent difficulty (R.J. Sobsey, 1983). Initially, babies respond to semisolids with the same suckling pattern used for liquids. Much of the food is pushed back out of the mouth by the tongue at this stage. Gradually, babies learn to keep their tongues in their mouths and to use their lips to take food from the spoon.

As more solid foods are introduced, children learn to bite and chew. At about age 5 months, *munching* is exhibited by most infants. Munching combines vertical jaw movements with a flattening and spreading of the tongue. *Rotary chewing*, which combines lateral tongue and rotary jaw movements, replaces munching as increasingly more solid foods are presented over time (Morris, 1978a). The emergence of teeth makes chewing more effective, but the chewing pattern is typically fully or nearly fully developed by the age of 6–9 months, well before the molars emerge. Drinking from a cup is also commonly introduced at this time. Again, the child typically responds with a suckling pattern, but, gradually, he or she learns to control excess tongue movements and to accept and hold liquids in the mouth before swallowing them.

Although sucking, suckling, munching, rotary chewing, and drinking are all distinct patterns, common components can be seen in all of these actions, and each subsequent pattern integrates elements of the previous patterns. The rhythmic signature of each individual's neural pattern generator leaves little doubt that all of these behaviors are under the control of the same mechanism.

The basic facts about typical oral-motor development have important implications for understanding the atypical oral-motor patterns encountered among children with multiple disabilities, and this knowledge may help to suggest appropriate intervention strategies (Morris & Klein, 1987). Because many basic patterns are not under voluntary complex control, intervention that can evoke or facilitate more typical reflexive patterns is desirable. Similarly, intervention that inhibits or blocks atypical patterns could be equally useful. Because the mechanisms that generate these patterns are not directly accessible (or even clearly identified), intervention must influence these patterns indirectly by altering their environment (e.g., positioning, food texture). Voluntary responses play some role and all responses are influenced to some degree by learning experiences, and, therefore, traditional teaching methods may also play an important role. Finally, because it is known that typical eating patterns usually emerge in the first few months of life, intervention should begin as soon as possible.

Common Difficulties   Most children with multiple disabilities have problems eating (Gallender, 1979). As the number and severity of disabilities increase, so does the likelihood of eating problems. These problems fall into five general categories, depending on their origin: 1) disorders of muscle tone, 2) abnormal reflexes or dysfunctional primitive reflexes, 3) problems associated with structural abnormalities, 4) learning problems, and 5) combinations of these four. Each category is briefly discussed here.

Disorders of Muscle Tone   As discussed in Chapter 3, inadequate muscle tone (hypotonicity) or excessive muscle tone (hypertonicity) are frequent problems among children with multiple disabilities. These problems often affect the oral musculature as well as many other parts of the body and result in significant eating problems.

Generalized hypotonicity may result in drooping of the head, jaw, and lips, as well as weak and futile attempts at chewing. Inadequate tone is likely to lead to secondary problems because inability to maintain stability of the trunk, neck, and head makes control of fine oral-motor movements impossible (Morris & Weber, 1978).

Generalized hypertonicity, however, may result in extreme rigidity that severely limits any movement of the oral structures and may deform some of these structures as a result of constant pressure. Because increased tone may be present in the muscles controlling movement in opposing directions, great effort may be required for any movement.

Making matters more complicated, abnormalities of muscle tone do not typically affect all muscles in the same manner or to the same extent. Most children with disorders of muscle tone exhibit uneven tone across muscle groups. Typically, patterns of extension or of flexion predominate as a result of uneven tone. This may result in the chronic retraction of lips, protrusion of the tongue, limited voluntary control, or a number of other problems. Unfortunately, the dominant muscles grow stronger as a result of continual contraction, and their antagonists grow weaker as a result of disuse. This leads to further restriction of movement and more difficulty with voluntary control.

Some children have fluctuating muscle tone that may result in involuntary movements of oral structures or make precise coordinated movements of lips, tongue, and jaw impossible (Morris & Weber, 1978). All of these disorders of muscle tone have adverse effects on eating skills, and intervention to normalize tone is an important component of an eating skills program. Some of the positioning and stimulation procedures described under the "Intervention Techniques" section of this chapter are useful in normalizing muscle tone, but, before intervention is considered, other problems that affect eating skills are presented.

Abnormal Reflexes or Dysfunctional Primitive Reflexes   Several types of involuntary motor patterns (discussed in Chapter 3) can create eating problems for children with multiple disabilities. *Abnormal reflexes* are involuntary responses to stimuli that do not occur in children without disabilities of any age. *Primitive reflexes* are involuntary responses to stimuli that are normal (and appear to be functional) in very young children, but that may persist in children with multiple disabilities well beyond the time of typical integration or disappearance. *Hyposensitive reflexes* are involuntary responses to stimuli that are normal in all children, but that may require much higher levels of stimulation (or are totally absent) in children with disabilities. *Hypersensitive reflexes* are responses to stimuli that occur in all children but are triggered by much lower levels of stimulation in children with disabilities. A hyposensitive cough reflex, for example, may allow fluids to enter the airway; a hypersensitive cough reflex may protect the airway but interfere with normal swallowing by producing unnecessary coughing. Although not all authors and clinicians agree on which reflexes are normal, abnormal, primitive, or hypersensitive, or even on whether some response patterns should be considered reflexes, all of them agree that the control of these patterns is important for improving eating skills.

The following are descriptions of several specific reflexes:

- *Rooting reflex*   The rooting reflex begins soon after birth and helps the infant orient his or her mouth toward a food source. The head turns toward any stimulus that lightly touches either cheek (Gallender, 1979). When this persists beyond the first few months of life, it interferes with voluntary head control, especially during meals.
- *Tonic bite*   The tonic bite reflex is exhibited when stimulation in the mouth produces a forceful, involuntary, and generally prolonged clamping of the jaws (Palmer & Horn, 1978). This response pattern obviously interferes with spoon feeding and also often makes chewing extremely difficult.
- *Tongue thrust/tongue protrusion*   Tongue thrust, or tongue protrusion, may not be a true reflex (Morris & Weber, 1978), but it still occurs involuntarily in some children. Each attempt to chew or swallow results in the tongue pushing forward against or between the teeth. Often, this pushes food or fluids back out of the mouth, and over time, this may also push the teeth out of position.
- *Generalized infantile suck–swallow pattern*   Similar movements are also described in a generalized infantile suck–swallow pattern (Gallender, 1979; Morris & Weber, 1978). Although the tongue does not typically protrude for as long as it does with tongue thrust, each swallow is followed by an infant sucking or suckling pattern. Although it is often most evident during drinking, it may also occur during the eating of solids.
- *Asymmetrical tonic neck reflex*   Although an asymmetrical tonic neck reflex (ATNR) affects the whole body, it creates specific problems for eating and feeding (Gallender, 1979). As the head rotates to one side, the arm on that side involuntarily extends, and the other arm flexes in a "fencing pose." The legs may be similarly affected when the reflex is strong (Fraser & Hensinger, 1983). Not only does the turning head make it difficult to put food into the mouth, but muscle contractions generalize to the tongue and jaw, interfering with normal oral-motor control.

In addition to the problems caused by abnormal or dysfunctional primitive reflexes, problems may be associated with normal, age-appropriate reflexes that are hyperreactive or hyporeactive (Morris & Klein, 1987). A *gag reflex* is normal in children and adults, and it protects against the inadvertent swallowing of things that might obstruct the windpipe. When hypersensitive, it causes difficulties because chewing and swallowing become difficult. Hyporeactive gag reflexes are also problematic because they do not protect against the swallowing of large pieces of food or foreign objects (Palmer & Horn, 1978). Hypersensitivity of the *startle reflex* may also create problems. Any loud noise, change in position, or sudden movement may result in total flexion or extension patterns (Gallender, 1979). These patterns interfere with voluntary movements, and they may also contribute to excessive muscle tone. Generally, hypersensitivity of oral and facial areas may exaggerate these and other reflexes. Such hypersensitivity is frequent among children with multiple disabilities, especially in children with excessive muscle tone or severe visual impairment. These children are often reluctant to accept new textures, tastes, or temperatures in food, and, often, they resist any feeding or eating intervention that results in even minimal facial contact.

Structural Abnormalities Abnormal function of the oral structures may cause or complicate eating problems. Some of the more common problems are cleft lip, cleft palate, high-arched palate, and missing or displaced teeth. Uncorrected cleft lip and cleft palate make sucking and swallowing difficult. This may require the infant to develop abnormal patterns (e.g., increased use of the tongue to obtain milk from the nipple) that lead to secondary eating problems (e.g., tongue thrust) later in life. Tongue thrust, as well as sucking and swallowing abnormalities, occur frequently (Kalisz & Ekvall, 1978; Springer, 1982). Surgical correction, as early as possible, is frequently the best treatment for these conditions.

High-arched palates are also common. Food may collect on the roof of the mouth and be impossible for the child to reach. Some problems may result from a lack of appropriate oral stimulation or from abnormal muscle tone during infancy and childhood rather than from genetic factors (Goose & Appleton, 1982), and, therefore, they are partially if not entirely preventable. Similarly, missing and/or displaced teeth are largely preventable and contribute significantly to eating problems. Methods of preventing or treating dental conditions are discussed in the "Dental Care" section of this chapter.

Learning Problems Many eating problems experienced by children with severe disabilities are not the result of anatomical or physiological defects; instead, they result from not learning to perform eating skills properly or from learning inappropriate eating behaviors. Often, these learning problems are mistaken for physical problems. Some examples include 1) refusing to accept solid foods, 2) swallowing with little or no chewing, 3) eating too rapidly or too slowly, 4) not closing the lips completely, and 5) allowing food to fall back out of the mouth. Of course, any of these examples may have a physiological basis in some children, and, conversely, many other eating problems with physiological causes may also have significant behavioral components.

Combinations In fact, although discussed as separate factors, disorders of muscle tone, abnormal reflexes, dysfunctional primitive reflexes, structural abnormalities, and learning problems most commonly interact to produce eating difficulties encountered by children with multiple disabilities and their caregivers. To be successful, intervention need not be based on a precise diagnosis of the cause; rather, it needs to focus on determining how to bring about desired changes.

Intervention Techniques

A large number of intervention techniques have been proposed to improve eating skills. Some of these techniques have been demonstrated to be effective in clinical practice or structured research. Entire books (e.g., Campbell, 1982; Gallender, 1979) have focused on this topic, and the limited length of this chapter does not permit the same comprehensive treatment of these techniques. Therefore, 10 major categories of intervention are discussed below, with some specific examples included in each: 1) modifying positioning, 2) modifying foods, 3) modifying utensils, 4) modifying feeding schedules, 5) modifying food presentation, 6) modifying the mealtime environment, 7) providing physical assistance, 8) providing sensory stimulation, 9) providing specific training, and 10) preventing aspiration.

Modifying Positioning   The importance of positioning for performance of eating skills cannot be overemphasized. The optimal position for eating varies from student to student (Mueller, 1975; Utley, Holvoet, & Barnes, 1977), but certain principles remain constant. First, one should provide as much support as required to ensure stability (Utley et al., 1977). This may require lateral supports in the chair, a firm table or tray surface to rest the elbows on, and/or foot supports at the appropriate height. The finer muscle coordination required for eating and feeding is impossible unless larger muscle groups provide a stable base (Campbell, 1987). Second, the child should be kept as near to upright as possible (Palmer & Horn, 1978). Recumbent or semirecumbent positions encourage infantile feeding patterns. Third, positioning should be normalized as much as possible (Stainback, Stainback, Healy, & Healy, 1980). Providing more support than is needed can be restrictive, discourage independence, and actually weaken muscles that the student would otherwise use for support. Dynamic or temporary support is often adequate and makes more restrictive, static support unnecessary. Most children will do best if their necks are slightly flexed, but the degree of flexion required must be determined individually through careful observation. It is important to position many children, especially those with excess tone, a short time (often 10 or 15 minutes) before the meal begins in order to allow time to relax and adjust to the new position. For some children, it will be important not to position them too far ahead of time, so that they will not become fatigued. The great majority of children will eat best if positioned in a manner as nearly symmetrical as possible (Cautner & Penrose, 1983). For some children with unilateral reflex patterns, slightly asymmetrical postures may work better. The key to determining the best position for each student is careful transdisciplinary assessment and planning.

Modifying Foods   Changes in food selection and preparation also influence performance of eating skills. Often, students with multiple disabilities are given diets that consist wholly or primarily of puréed foods. Although some of the literature suggests using soft or puréed foods with students at early developmental levels (e.g., Blockley & Miller, 1971), later empirical studies suggest that many children given puréed foods would do as well or better with whole or coarser textured foods (Jones, 1983; D. Sobsey, 1983). A study of adults with swallowing disorders found that those receiving puréed diets were significantly more likely to experience episodes of aspiration pneumonia than those fed a soft diet with thickened liquids (Groher, 1987). The rate of aspiration problems in the group receiving puréed foods was more than five times as high as that of the group receiving a soft diet. Alexander (1991) recommended avoiding thin purées whenever possible and using more coarsely ground table foods if the child cannot chew solids. Because many normal eating skills (e.g., chewing) require the stimulation of having solid food in the mouth, puréed foods do not allow the development of some skills. Puréed foods also contribute to constipation, dental caries, weakened and deformed oral structures, and vitamin deficiencies (D. Sobsey, 1983). Unfortunately, many children who are not exposed to whole foods in infancy may resist them later in life.

Although gradual increments in introducing more solid foods are most typically recommended (Morris, 1978b; Stainback et al., 1980), Jones (1983) found more rapid adjustment with rapid transitions to whole foods. The time required to consume the same quantity of food increases when whole rather than puréed foods are eaten, but the number of chewing cycles also increases, providing more opportunities to learn and to strengthen muscles (Gisel, 1991). A few children may never learn to eat whole foods and transitions must be carefully supervised and evaluated, but most students will eat whole foods better than purée, and the transition to coarser textures is generally accomplished with little difficulty (Jones, 1983; D. Sobsey, 1983).

Similarly, consideration needs to be given to the choice of foods. Because not all solid foods have the same consistency, careful matching of the food to the current abilities of the child is essential (Alexander, 1991). Foods that combine liquid and solid components (e.g., soup, fruit cup) may cause particular problems. Some children may exhibit better performance if hot or cold foods are avoided. Careful selections must be made, and the caregiver should consider nutritional concerns and child preferences.

Modifying Utensils   Most often, utensils are modified to assist with self-feeding, but some modified utensils also help with the performance of eating skills. The cutaway cup is used to allow drinking without hyperextension of the neck (Morris, 1978b). Regular glasses and cups require hyperextension of the neck because when they are tipped up far enough for the contents to pour into the mouth, the rim hits the drinker's nose unless the head is tipped back. Unfortunately, many children with multiple disabilities choke, gag, exhibit infantile suck–swallow patterns, or have other difficulties when they tip their heads back to drink. Cutting away part of the rim of a cup or glass allows it to be tipped up farther without hitting the child's nose or requiring the head to be tipped back. For children who are being fed, clear, plastic cups are best. These allow the person doing the feeding to observe the fluid in the cup and the child's mouth without having to move to an inappropriate position for presentation.

Some children with hypersensitive bite or gag reflexes may do better with modified spoons. Trefler, Westmoreland, and Burlingame (1977) suggest a spatula-spoon to minimize stimulation within the mouth for individuals with extreme intraoral hypersensitivity. Nylon, plastic, or rubber-coated spoons may work well for children with hypersensitivity, especially those who react strongly to hot or cold stimuli, because metal utensils conduct heat to or from the oral structures very rapidly. Nonmetal spoons are also useful for children who bite down on utensils because they are generally softer and are less likely to cause injury. Although small, disposable, plastic spoons are excellent for some children because they minimize stimulation, they are not suitable for a child who may bite down on them because they break, often leaving sharp splinters of plastic in the mouth.

Modified utensils can be extremely useful for many children with disabilities when used in combination with other interventions. Other children, however, eat as well or better with regular utensils. It is important to remember the normalization principle and to use specialized eating utensils only when a clear benefit over the more common alternative can be demonstrated. Careful, ongoing assessment is the best method for determining whether modified utensils have value for a specific student, and it allows planning for their introduction and use as well as planning for a return to more common alternatives.

Modifying Feeding Schedules   Considerable controversy exists regarding the best times and places to teach eating skills (Snell & Farlow, 1993). Some researchers suggest that frequent small meals provide faster acquisition of skills than just three meals per day (Azrin & Armstrong, 1973). Others suggest that quiet times and places may produce better acquisition than busy lunchrooms at mealtimes (Wilson, 1978). It also may be argued that skills taught in a natural setting, under typical conditions, are most likely to be generalized and maintained over time. In view of the apparent disagreement, it is difficult to see how all of these points of view could be correct unless the individual nature of each child is taken into account. Again, if no clear benefit can be demonstrated as a result of using modified times or places, the normalization principle dictates that meals be provided at regular times in the typical environment. Several reasons can be identified, however, for providing at least part of a child's eating skills training at specialized times and sometimes in specialized places. In general, when specialized training times and places are used, they should supplement rather than substitute for regular mealtime training.

One important reason for supplementing regular mealtimes with specialized training sessions is to allow for a temporary reduction in function that may occur during acquisition of a new behavior. For example, a child with cerebral palsy may exhibit an infantile suck–swallow pattern when drinking from a cup. Although he or she uses an inefficient pattern and has difficulty obtaining adequate fluids, it is the most efficient drinking pattern currently in his or her repertoire. Teaching the child a more efficient and more mature drinking pattern will be extremely useful, but during the initial acquisition phase, it will be much less efficient than his or her current pattern. Requiring the child to use the new pattern at his or her regular meal and drink times has two major disadvantages. First, it will reduce fluid intake and may threaten his or her health. Second, the child will almost certainly resist because the new pattern at first will lessen fluid intake. By teaching initial acquisition outside regular meal and drink times, more fluids are provided instead of less, and the additional fluids provided at these special times reinforce the newly acquired pattern. When the new pattern becomes as efficient as the old one, it can be introduced (and reasonably required) at regular meal and drink times. Acquisition of new eating and drinking patterns typically leads to such temporary reductions in efficiency. The addition of specialized training times can be useful to overcome the problems associated with these temporary reductions.

Another reason for providing training in eating and drinking skills outside regular mealtimes is to overcome resistance by the child. Many parents report that their children will not accept new tastes and textures at home, but quickly accept them in a new environment. Therefore, it is not surprising that researchers have found a similar increase in willingness to accept new foods among children with developmental disabilities when the children are in a new environment (Linschied, Oliver, Blyer, & Palmer, 1978).

Providing small meals for training purposes in addition to regular mealtimes may also be useful for training in eating skills because this provides distributed rather than massed practice (Snell & Farlow, 1993). Although providing small meals has advantages for all learners, it may be particularly useful for children who tire quickly or become distracted or disruptive during longer meals. Other children may benefit from additional or alternative eating and drinking times because they take advantage of their peak learning times. Peak learning times are easily identified for many students who may be active, alert, and attentive at some times during the day and may be lethargic, unresponsive, or irritable at other times. Finally, it should be noted that snacks are common in the United States, and few people restrict their eating to only three meals a day. Using snacks for either structured or incidental learning is consistent with typical patterns of everyday life.

Modifying Food Presentation   The manner in which food is presented to the child is extremely important, especially when the child is being fed by another individual. If food or drink is presented from above, it will encourage extension patterns. If it is presented from below, it will encourage flexion patterns. If it is presented from either side, it will encourage the child to turn to that side. The pace and cues provided with presentation can enhance relaxation or increase tension in the child. As with other interventions, presentation must be individualized for each child, but some general strategies will be useful for most children with eating problems.

The person feeding the child should be seated on a low chair so that the food is well below the child's face and the feeder's face is at or below eye level when the child is properly positioned (Stainback et al., 1980). This encourages a slightly flexed neck, which makes swallowing without aspiration easier and minimizes abnormal reflexes. Exceptions may be when the child has excess flexion and encouraging extension is desirable or when the feeder must be positioned behind or beside the child to provide physical assistance.

The person feeding the child and the food itself should be positioned as closely as possible to directly in front of the child (Stainback et al., 1980). This encourages symmetrical positioning and discourages asymmetrical reflex patterns (e.g., asymmetrical tonic neck reflex). Exceptions may occur when the need to provide physical assistance requires that the feeder be positioned behind or alongside the child and when the child's posture and reactions are so strongly oriented toward one side that food presented from the opposite side brings the child's position closer to midline and reduces asymmetrical patterns.

Similar attention must be given to the way in which the spoon or cup comes into contact with the child's mouth. The bowl of the spoon should be inserted only partially into the mouth. If the entire bowl of the spoon is inserted, it may cause gagging, and it will be difficult to tip the spoon up to transfer its contents without scraping the spoon against the upper teeth. For the great majority of children, food should be placed in the middle of the mouth on the tongue, but a few children with very limited tongue movement may require food to be placed directly between the teeth.

The rim of the glass or cup should be placed on the child's lower lip, encouraging good lip seal and avoiding stimulation of the bite reflex, which often occurs if the rim is placed between the teeth. Cups and glasses must be tipped up just far enough to allow a controlled flow from the vessel to the mouth. If the cup or glass is tipped up too far, it will encourage the child to use an extension pattern to compensate or to assume a sudden and extreme flexion posture. Either of these extremes will interfere with drinking.

The timing of presentation also is extremely important. Individuals must coordinate eating and drinking behavior with their breathing patterns. Failure to do so will result, at least, in increased difficulty eating or, at most, in life-threatening aspiration or airway obstruction.

Modifying the Mealtime Environment   For most children, especially those with excess tone or hypersensitive reflexes, providing a relaxing mealtime environment can help greatly with the performance of eating skills (Stainback et al., 1980). Similarly, providing a training environment that is as close as possible to the child's natural environment (or the environment to which the child will progress) is consistent with the normalization principle and provides the best possibility for maintenance and generalization. This means that sources of stress should be identified and eliminated from both the natural and the training environments. This requires careful attention to the attributes of both the child and the environment. Sources of excessive noise and other disruption in the environment must be controlled. Children who may be aggressive or steal food must be controlled or separated from children with severely limited movement. Of course, some children are more sensitive to specific environmental stimuli than others. These stimuli must be identified for each individual and modifications made where necessary.

Not all environmental modifications require the elimination of problem stimuli. Perhaps even more emphasis should be placed on developing a supportive and relaxing environment. Lighting should be adequate but not harsh. Neither child nor feeder should be backlighted because each must carefully observe the details of the other's movements in order to coordinate the feeding and eating processes. Acoustical dampening will soften the sounds of large dining areas, and the addition of soft music is sometimes helpful. Maintaining a comfortable air temperature is also important. Uncomfortable temperatures (especially cold) increase muscle tone and may increase abnormal reflex activity. Attention to these and other environmental factors will improve the performance of eating skills by most children with multiple disabilities.

Providing Physical Assistance   Although physical assistance, especially head and jaw control, is an important component of many eating skill programs (e.g., Alexander, 1991; Morris, 1978b; Stainback et al., 1980; Utley et al., 1977), it should be used as sparingly as possible. Overusing physical assistance is unnecessarily intrusive and interferes with independent mastery of skills. It can also create dependency on external stimuli rather than on stimuli that are typically part of the behavior that is being learned.

The feeder may provide head control by placing his or her hand on top of the child's head or on the neck area. Pushing the head forward at the occipital area (back of the head) is not recommended because it frequently stimulates an increased extension reaction (Stainback et al., 1980). Static positioning of the head is best accomplished through positioning aids (e.g., cushions) rather than physical assistance; however, intermittent positioning is a more desirable alternative for children who need positioning help only part of the time because it allows for greater independence. For example, many children with cerebral palsy have particular difficulty swallowing liquids (Logemann, 1983). These children may need help keeping their heads in a flexed position when drinking but have adequate head control for the rest of the meal. The feeder may physically assist with head flexion by placing a hand on top of the child's head during drinking but still allowing the child to exercise independent head control at other times during a meal.

Direct control of the jaw, lips, and tongue may be accomplished through manual guidance, but it should be considered only when minimally adequate performance is unattainable through other means (Alexander, 1991). Applying jaw control from the front is typically suitable only for minimal assistance; it is usually better applied from the back or side of a child. Usually, the feeder uses the nondominant hand to control the jaw and the dominant hand to feed. Depending on the amount of control required and the position the feeder finds most comfortable and effective, however, this may change. Although opinion still differs, most authors agree that jaw control should not involve control of the upper lip because pulling down the upper lip will stimulate more lip retraction. Morris (1978b) suggests that the feeder place the middle finger under the child's chin just behind the bony part, placing the index finger between the tip of the chin and the lips, and placing the thumb on the side of the face near the eye. This allows the feeder to assist and control the opening and closing of the jaw.

These procedures can be very helpful with some students, but extreme caution should be exercised in their use. One must remember that muscle strength and tone are developed by working against resistance. External control may produce the movements required, but it will not contribute to movements developing by themselves. Worse yet, it may strengthen and increase tone in overdeveloped and hypertonic muscles, while further weakening the underdeveloped muscles that work in opposition to them. This may be a particular problem for the hypertonic child, because considerable force may be required to produce the desired movements. Therefore, external jaw control is not recommended if it is possible to use other methods that allow the child to produce the desired movements for him- or herself. When jaw control must be used, it is essential that the minimum effective force be used and that other procedures (e.g., exercises outside mealtime) be used to develop the independent responses in the child.

Similarly, tongue protrusion is sometimes controlled by the feeder pushing the tongue back in the mouth with the spoon or fingers. This external control may also strengthen the muscles that produce the inappropriate movement (protrusion) and weaken the muscles that produce the desired movement (retraction). Again, this procedure is not recommended if alternatives that require the child to exert his or her own efforts to retract the tongue are available.

One alternative to using external control is to stimulate the child to produce the desired response. Although these elicitation procedures are much more effective with some students than others, the appropriateness of these procedures for a specific child can be assessed rapidly. Generally, these procedures exert pressure or apply resistance *against* the direction of the desired movement. For example, upward pressure briefly applied against the bony part of the chin will stimulate some children to open their jaw. Upward pressure briefly applied to the soft area beneath the chin at the root of the tongue will stimulate some children to retract a protruding tongue. This type of stimulation acts to elicit desired responses with the child's own muscles rather than through external control. When using these procedures, it is also important to use the minimum effective level of stimulation. This will make it easier to transfer control of the desired behaviors from the training stimuli to typical stimuli, leading to complete voluntary control. Such eventual transfer to voluntary control by the child should be considered and planned for in the use of any physical assistance techniques.

Providing Sensory Stimulation   Various stimulation procedures have been used by many therapists and teachers to reduce oral-facial hypersensitivity (e.g., Alexander, 1991; Campbell, 1982), facilitate appropriate movement patterns (e.g., Utley et al., 1977), or inhibit dysfunctional movement patterns (e.g., Gallender, 1979). Empirical evidence supports the use of these procedures for improving eating skills (Sobsey & Orelove, 1984). Such procedures may include general relaxation procedures, such as stroking the lips, face, and cheeks; rubbing the gums and hard palate; brushing the skin over muscles involved in chewing, swallowing, and lip closure; applying ice to these areas (lips, cheeks, gums, and so forth); applying "stretch pressure" to the areas around the lips and cheeks; vibrating oral and facial muscles; and "walking" a tongue blade back on the tongue. The specific procedures appropriate for a particular child must be determined by the service team, including a therapist who is appropriately trained. Ongoing evaluation is required to determine whether the treatment is producing the desired results for the child, especially because results appear to be inconsistent among different children.

At least two theories have been used to explain the effects of stimulation procedures. One theory suggests that increased sensory input increases motor output and control by lowering the threshold for motor neuron firing. Another theory suggests that the threshold for hypersensitive oral and facial reflexes that interfere with desired behavior can be raised through increased sensory input. In any case, exteroceptive (through superficial skin receptors) and proprioceptive (through deeper muscle receptors) stimulation have been shown to be useful for improving lip closure and chewing in some children (Sobsey & Orelove, 1984) and may also prove useful for training in other eating skills.

Alexander (1991) suggested that when a child has extreme hypersensitivity, desensitization must begin with less sensitive areas of the body before proceeding to the mouth and other sensitive surrounding areas. She also points out that oral stimulation can be provided in a variety of ways (e.g., using a soft toy, the child's fingers, a toothbrush) and that careful attention to the child's preferences is helpful in increasing tolerance.

Providing Specific Training   Most of the methods for improving eating skills discussed so far have been highly specialized, but many of the most useful procedures for teaching eating skills are basically the same procedures as those used to teach any other skill. Campbell (1982) stresses the need for performing careful assessment, establishing reasonable and measurable objectives, and collecting regular progress data. These three elements should be included as parts of any eating skills training program, regardless of the intervention techniques used. Other specific training components that should be considered in planning eating skills programs include reinforcement, shaping, chaining, prompting, modeling, and response-cost procedures.

Reinforcement   Reinforcement procedures that reward target behaviors are a natural way of teaching eating skills for children. Food and drink, which are integral parts of these programs, are powerful reinforcers for most children. Programs should be structured so that children obtain food more efficiently when they use the desired eating behaviors. Care must be taken to ensure that the specific food or drink used is an effective reinforcer for the particular child involved. Using social reinforcers in addition to edible reinforcers may be desirable or even necessary with some children, especially if these children do not respond positively to edibles. The combination of reinforcers may also be useful during acquisition and early fluency-building stages, when the target behaviors may be less efficient than current inappropriate eating patterns. The natural reinforcement power of food and drink is a valuable component of almost any mealtime program. In addition to its effectiveness with most children, it has the additional advantage of providing for excellent maintenance and generalization because it is common to the natural mealtime environment as well as to the training situation.

Shaping   Shaping, a specific reinforcement method, is extremely useful in eating and drinking programs. When a child cannot perform a target behavior exactly as it should be performed, the child's best approximation of that behavior can be reinforced. As performance improves, the criterion for reinforcement becomes stricter. Shaping must be used to make reinforcement an effective part of almost any eating and drinking training because the amount of food and drink used must remain fairly constant throughout training. If this were not so, children would be undernourished during early stages of the program and overfed during later stages. Shaping the criterion to the child's current level of performance allows contingent delivery of food without resulting in significant changes in total intake. It also allows the child to experience success no matter how low his or her current skill level may be.

Chaining   Chaining, the assembling of separately taught discrete responses into a more complex behavior, may also have a part in training in eating and drinking skills. Although eating and drinking skills typically require whole-task presentation, task analysis can be extremely useful in pinpointing which step or steps need work and focusing training on a single step or only a few steps often provides the best results.

Prompting   Prompting, which involves providing extra cues or assistance to the child, is also useful for training in eating skills. Although physical prompts are often too disruptive or impossible for eating or drinking skills (e.g., reaching into a child's mouth to help position his or her tongue properly), many of the physical assistance procedures described above might be considered physical prompts. Verbal and gestural prompts are also commonly useful.

Modeling   Modeling, which involves demonstrating the appropriate behavior, is also extremely useful for training in eating and drinking skills. Most commonly, the trainer models the behavior for the child to imitate, but peers also can be powerful models. Inclusive settings provide some of the best opportunities for peer modeling.

Response-Cost Procedures   Response-cost procedures, which penalize the child for inappropriate behavior, may occasionally be needed if reinforcement of the correct responses is not adequate to eliminate the less desirable alternative. Because deprivation of food and drink would rarely be ethically justified, most response-cost procedures in eating skills training programs are delay procedures. If the child responds inappropriately, the opportunity to obtain food or drink is withheld for a brief period (e.g., 15 seconds). For example, after a child has acquired a mature drinking pattern, he or she may occasionally revert to a primitive suck–swallow pattern. The trainer may immediately withdraw the cup for 15 seconds each time the primitive behavior is demonstrated. This delay in reinforcement will often discourage the inappropriate behavior.

All of the *specific* training strategies discussed above and other basic teaching techniques can be used as part of a training program in eating and drinking skills. The other training techniques described above, which focus on physiological responses, can be used in conjunction with these specific behavioral methods. Together, they provide a wide range of alternatives that can be employed by the service team in designing effective programs.

Preventing Aspiration   Two health care concerns need special consideration at mealtimes. First, all those involved in mealtime routines need to be prepared to prevent, recognize, and treat airway obstruction. Total airway obstruction (discussed in Chapter 5) typically occurs without warning and requires immediate action. Aspiration of fluids or particles of food into the lungs also can cause serious health problems with or without immediate distress.

Second, aspiration, the inhalation of fluids or food particles into the lungs, is one of the major risks for children and adults with multiple disabilities (Chaney, 1987; Chaney, Eyman, & Miller, 1979; Sheppard, 1991). Aspiration can also occur during such activities as swimming or bathing. Water that contains soap, bath oils, chlorine, or other chemicals is particularly dangerous because these chemicals are likely to damage the lungs. At mealtimes, aspiration can occur when food or fluids are on their way down to the stomach or when the contents of the stomach reflux up the esophagus. Reflux aspiration is likely to occur when the individual is in a supine or semirecumbent position and is associated with nasogastric tube or gastrostomy feedings. Reflux occurs when the contents of the stomach flow up the esophagus. Vomiting involves active pushing of these contents of the stomach up the esophagus by the muscles of the gastrointestinal tract and normally a protective closing of the airway. Unlike vomiting, reflux usually involves the passive flow of these contents, often without the airway being closed off, and therefore creates greater risk for the individual.

In aspiration, small particles or drops of liquid enter the lower airway and lungs. In some cases, there is severe coughing, wheezing, or gurgling sounds, but in other cases, sometimes referred to as "silent aspiration," there may be no immediate signs of difficulty, particularly if the individual is not fully conscious or has hyposensitive reflexes. In severe cases of aspiration or when the individual already has some difficulty receiving adequate oxygen into circulation, lips, nailbeds, and the face may turn blue. In other cases, however, especially if protective reflexes are inadequate, silent aspiration occurs without any of these signs (Groher, 1988).

Health care professionals may be required to evaluate and treat chronic aspiration problems. Videofluoroscopy is a procedure that is used to visualize the swallowing process in action to help determine if anatomical or functional problems exist. Sometimes the procedure can help identify the safest and the most risky positions for feeding an individual (Rasley et al., 1993). In many other cases, simple clinical observation (Sheppard, 1991) at meals and other times when aspiration may occur will be of greater value. Medication and surgery (Eisele, 1991) can also be useful in some cases.

Incidents of suspected aspiration should be recorded and reported to the health care team. The report should include the signs of aspiration that were observed and how long they lasted, and information should be included regarding conditions before and during the incident. If the aspiration incident occurs during eating or drinking, the report should include 1) positioning; 2) feeding procedures; 3) foods and fluids involved; 4) texture of foods and fluids involved; 5) when during the meal aspiration seemed to occur (e.g., the beginning, middle, near the end, several minutes after); 6) any treatment that was given; and 7) any other factors that might be useful for future prevention. If only a few drops are aspirated and the individual is alert, the body's natural defenses (e.g., constriction of the airway, increased mucus production, coughing) often will resolve the problem in a few minutes. For an individual who is unconscious, positioning in the seizure recovery position described in Chapter 5 will facilitate drainage and reduce the risk of aspiration. If gurgling or wet breathing sounds are present, if the individual has significant difficulty breathing, or if signs of oxygen deficit appear (e.g., blue tint of nailbeds or lips), health care professionals should be notified immediately. In some cases, suctioning or other procedures can be useful, and the administration of oxygen is useful in severe cases. If the airway is completely obstructed, the Heimlich maneuver (described in Chapter 5) can open the airway and save the person's life, but most cases of aspiration do not result in complete airway obstruction.

Most episodes of aspiration produce discomfort, and severe episodes result in immediate danger of insufficient oxygen. The worst effects of aspiration, however, are often delayed. Aspiration pneumonia usually occurs a day or more after the incident, and, frequently, it is aggravated by secondary infection. Chronic aspiration results in scarring of the lungs, which impairs breathing and makes the individual more vulnerable to future aspiration episodes. These effects are life threatening and treatment is limited; consequently, prevention is essential.

Fortunately, many aspiration problems are preventable, and aspiration prevention should be a major goal for every child with increased risk for aspiration or a history of aspiration problems. Evaluation of the success of prevention programs may be based on the reduction in the number of incidents, normalization of breathing sounds and rate, or other objective data (Sobsey, 1988).

Some drugs that are commonly taken by people with disabilities increase the risk of aspiration by relaxing the muscles that keep the stomach contents from entering the esophagus or inhibiting reflexes that protect the airway. These drugs include phenobarbital, Valium, Dantrium, Cogentin, and other tranquilizers and anticonvulsants (Karb, Queener, & Freeman, 1989). Reducing these medications, if possible, will reduce the risk of aspiration. If the medication is necessary, the effects may be counteracted through the use of other drugs that stimulate the depressed gastrointestinal function (e.g., Duvoid, Clopra, Reglan), which can reduce reflux in some individuals. Unfortunately, children with epilepsy often cannot take these drugs because they increase seizure activity (Karb et al., 1989).

Aspiration problems occur more frequently with tube feedings than with oral feedings. Whenever possible, one should use oral feedings and avoid nasogastric or gastric tube feedings. If tube feeding is a temporary measure, work to restore oral feedings as quickly as possible. If tube feeding will be used for an extended period of time, fundoplication, a surgical procedure that alters the connection between stomach and esophagus, may be needed to reduce the risk of aspiration (Groher, 1988).

Rapid or forced entry of food into the stomach may result in pressure that pushes food up the esophagus and into the lungs. Tube feedings should use small portions every few hours and be given slowly over 30 minutes to an hour to prevent overfilling the stomach and the subsequent pressure, which may result in reflux aspiration (Groher, 1988).

Normal peristalsis keeps food moving down the esophagus. It prevents reflux and helps maintain muscle tone in the upper gastrointestinal system. Because people being tube fed do not regularly swallow food, they lack peristalsis and are more likely to aspirate. Maintaining some oral feedings of solid foods may decrease reflux from tube feedings by stimulating normal peristalsis. If no food can be taken by mouth, oral stimulation before or during tube feeding may help to stimulate peristalsis and muscle tone (Sobsey, 1988).

Whether feeding occurs orally or by tube, positioning is an essential prevention strategy. When one is in an upright position, gravity helps prevent reflux of food out of the stomach; but when one is in a reclining position, the contents of the stomach flow easily into the esophagus. Tube feeding the individual in an upright position or with the head elevated 45° helps prevent reflux. Those receiving their meals by mouth should be fed in an upright position with their heads flexed slightly forward, which encourages active swallowing and prevents food from passively running down their throats. Because reflux may occur after the meal is finished, the individual should remain in an upright to semi-reclining position for at least 45 minutes after finishing a meal (Groher, 1988).

Other factors may contribute to aspiration problems. Constipation may block the intestinal system. As a result, the contents of the stomach cannot move down and are more likely to be pushed up. Taking precautions to prevent constipation, watching carefully for signs, and treating it quickly help ensure that food in the stomach is free to move into the intestines, which helps reduce the risk of aspiration (Sobsey, 1988). Puréed foods and thin liquids increase the risk of aspiration because they can easily run down the throat without stimulating a true swallow response, which closes the airway and protects against aspiration. Using solids, soft solids, or coarsely ground foods and thickened liquids may provide better stimulation for swallowing and reduce the risk of aspiration (Sobsey, 1988). Children should be relaxed but alert when they eat. Feeding someone who is stuporous is very risky. Waiting until children recover fully from seizures before giving anything by mouth and stimulating children with activities before meals can help ensure alertness and decrease the risk of aspiration (Sobsey, 1988). Children sometimes aspirate their own secretions while unconscious. Placing them in the seizure recovery position described in Chapter 5 until they are fully conscious helps to reduce this risk (Sobsey, 1988). The best combination of prevention and treatment procedures for each individual should be identified by the health care and educational teams. No prevention program can totally eliminate risk, but a well-designed program can reduce substantially the risks associated with feeding.

FEEDING SKILLS

Every child who eats and drinks must feed him- or herself or be fed by caregivers. The ability to feed oneself is an important step toward independence. For the individual who seems far from total independence, partial participation may be an important intermediate goal. Even for the child who continues to require feeding by a caregiver, the way in which feeding is carried out will have a major effect on the quality of the child's life. Some methods of feeding and of providing training in self-feeding are discussed in this section. These include passive feeding alternatives, cooperative feeding skills and development of communication, and self-feeding skills.

Passive Feeding Alternatives

Passive feeding alternatives are methods of providing nutrition without any active participation on the part of the child being fed. Methods of passive feeding include intravenous feeding, enteral feeding (e.g., nasogastric tube, gastrostomy), and bird feeding (a term used for pouring liquified food into the child's throat).

Intravenous Feeding   Intravenous feeding does not provide total nutrition, and, therefore, it can be considered only as an extremely short-term alternative. It should not be considered for children with multiple disabilities, except under the same conditions that it would be used for individuals who do not have disabilities (e.g., to maintain blood volume, electrolyte balance, and glucose levels following surgery).

Enteral Feeding Enteral feeding—nasogastric tube feeding (through a tube inserted into the stomach via the nose and throat) and gastrostomy feeding (through a direct opening in the stomach)—has been used frequently for a number of reasons. Often, the reasons for using any of these procedures with a child with multiple disabilities are not clearly identified, but the procedures may be started during a specific illness or simply because less intrusive feeding methods are of little effectiveness.

Nasogastric tube feeding should not be used for long-term treatment. Bastian and Driscoll (1984) suggested a maximum of 4–8 weeks. At least 28 negative effects of nasogastric tube feeding have been identified, including pulmonary aspiration, depressed cough and gag reflexes, dysphagia, otitis media, diarrhea, vitamin deficiencies, and chronic vomiting (Silberman & Eisenberg, 1982). Infants who are not given solid foods by mouth by the age of 6 or 7 months are at risk for chronic rumination, have more difficulty learning to chew, may refuse solids, and may be at increased risk for choking as a result of a permanently depressed gag reflex (Kennedy-Caldwell & Caldwell, 1984). Recognizing these problems, the team should make every effort to avoid using nasogastric tube feeding. If nasogastric tube feeding must be used, several measures can be taken to minimize their negative effects. First, the period for which they will be used should be kept as short as possible. Second, nasogastric tubes should not be left in place between feedings. Third, any feeders must be adequately trained by a nurse specialist or another individual with appropriate training. Fourth, each time the tube is passed, its location must be checked carefully by x-ray or other adequate method before feeding begins (Silberman & Eisenberg, 1982). Fifth, nasogastric tube feeding should not be used for unconscious, sleeping, or stuporous individuals. Sixth, if possible, some oral feedings should be given between tube feedings to help normalize oral responses. Seventh, intraoral stimulation (e.g., pacifiers for infants) should be provided if no oral feedings are possible. Eighth, even before starting the first nasogastric tube feeding, a plan should be developed by the team for transition to oral feeding.

Gastrostomy and jejunostomy (tube directly enters the small intestine) may initially seem more intrusive than nasogastric tube feeding because they require surgery, but for many children with multiple disabilities, these procedures have several advantages. First, they greatly reduce the risk of aspiration. Second, they do not irritate the throat or depress the gag or cough reflexes. Third, they may typically be used concurrently with oral feedings and therefore allow eating and feeding skill training along with their use. The gastrostomy button is easily inserted into the abdominal stoma (surgical opening) (Gauderer, Picha, & Izant, 1984). This device means that tubes do not have to be reinserted, and no dangling feeding tube needs to be left in place, which makes gastrostomy more compatible with everyday activities. Since 1980, many gastrostomies have been done with a punch procedure that does not involve major surgery (Gauderer, Ponsky, & Izant, 1980). These procedural changes make gastrostomy less intrusive and available to some children who might have been excluded from the older procedures.

Although oral feedings are preferred whenever possible, the nutritional status is greatly improved with tube feedings in some children. Families and other caregivers, as well as the children involved, sometimes also benefit from stress reduction because unsuccessful attempts at oral feedings can produce great frustration (Campbell, 1988). It is important that parents and others involved in decisions about feeding alternatives have full information about the potential benefits, costs, and risks of all possible alternatives.

Those administering tube feedings should carefully follow procedures. General procedures for administering these feedings are available from a number of sources (e.g., Graff, Ault, Guess, Taylor, & Thompson, 1990), but it is important to individualize the procedures (e.g., positioning, rate of flow) to each child.

One of the most challenging aspects of tube feeding is the transition back to oral feeding. These transitions are often difficult for six reasons. First, the problems that led to the initial decision to use tube feeding are often still present. Second, the initial problem is often aggravated by a weakening of the oral structures as a result of disuse. Third, because the oral structures lack stimulation typically provided by feeding, they may be hypersensitive. Fourth, although some oral reflexes become hypersensitive, others may become hyposensitive. For example, children who frequently have a nasogastric tube in place may have hyposensitive swallow reflexes because they are desensitized to feeling something in the back of their throats. Fifth, children who become accustomed to tube feeding sometimes resist the reintroduction of oral feedings. Sixth, the motivation of family and team members may be reduced because the availability of tube feeding makes oral feeding less vital.

Programs to reinstitute oral feedings must be individually developed. Usually, the best time to begin the program is as soon as the child starts tube feedings or even before tube feedings are started. Blackman and Nelson (1985) described a program designed to reduce resistance to feeding, tasting, and swallowing food that is often present in children without oral feeding experiences. Some children were served on an outpatient basis, but those with more intensive medical needs were hospitalized for the transition. Praise and other reinforcement procedures for accepting food orally were used, and initial protest behavior was ignored. Of 10 children, 9 made successful transitions to oral feedings, and the 10th had aspiration problems associated with swallowing and was returned to tube feedings. Blackman and Nelson (1987) subsequently reported data from another 11 children placed in a rapid transition program. In this study, 10 of the 11 children made a transition from tube feeding to total oral feeding in 2–3 weeks.

Morris and Klein (1987) described many stimulation procedures designed to ease the transition to oral feedings. Often, the mouth, tongue, lips, and other oral structures are hypersensitive as a result of deprivation of the stimulation typically involved in eating. They suggested encouraging or assisting the child to explore the environment with the tongue and lips. Voice and sound play are also useful components of a transition program. Stimulating the child with smells and tastes throughout the tube-feeding phase may also be useful, even if the child cannot be allowed to actually swallow food during this time. If it is possible to allow some oral feedings concurrently with the tube-feeding phase, this should be done with an emphasis on making the experience as pleasant as possible for the child.

Bird Feeding   Bird feeding merits little discussion here. This method of pouring food into the throat of a person whose head is extended back and who is lying in a semirecumbent position can only serve to interfere with the acquisition of appropriate eating and feeding skills. Children who have been fed in this way may have difficulty adapting to more common methods, but almost all of them will attain more functional eating skills as they begin to adapt.

Cooperative Feeding Skills and Development of Communication

Cooperative feeding skills are needed by individuals being fed and by their caregivers. These skills allow the coordination of movements and the smooth transition of food or drink from the feeder to the person being fed. Both members of this dyad must work together to develop these skills. In addition to their obvious help in the feeding process, these basic turn-taking and coordinated movement skills may be useful in many other activities of daily living.

Coactive movement refers to the coordination of movements between two individuals who are not in direct physical contact. It has been recognized and trained as an early communication skill (Sternberg, Pegnatore, & Hill, 1983). If the ability to coordinate movements at the coactive level is not present, it may be necessary to start resonance, which develops coordination through physical contact as well as movement, at an even earlier level. In addition to use at mealtime, coordinated movement is developed through affectionate contact, play, and physical prompting procedures.

Other measures can also facilitate coordination. First, the feeder should watch and listen carefully to the child and coordinate presentation of food with the child's natural breathing and movement patterns. Second, lighting and positioning should ensure a clear view of food or drink as it approaches the mouth. Third, the feeder should establish a smooth and predictable pace. Fourth, for many children, a verbal (or tactile) ready signal from the feeder is helpful. It should be pointed out that many children will not require this signal and some hypertonic children may respond with a countertherapeutic increase in tone (Campbell, 1982). Fifth, some children may be able to signal (e.g., look up, grunt) when they want the next bit of food or drink. One should encourage this by attending carefully to these signals and responding to them. Sixth, distractions and interruptions (to feeder and child) need to be minimized. Most feeders will find it impossible to coordinate their movements with the children they are feeding and carry on a conversation with a third party because each activity involves coordination with a different person.

The turn-taking behavior developed in feeding builds an essential foundation for more advanced communication skills. Feeding is also one of the important interactive contexts for the development of attachment between children and their caregivers, and attachment is also a powerful force in the development of communication (Alexander, 1991). The oral-motor skills that are refined in eating are fundamental to the development of speech (Alexander, 1991). These influences on the development of communication skills make mealtimes an important context for teaching early communication. Teaching more advanced communication and social skill objectives is also easily integrated into mealtime activities because these behaviors are natural elements of mealtime routines.

Self-Feeding Skills

Probably much more has been written about training in feeding skills than training in eating skills. Basic self-feeding skills may include handling finger foods, drinking from a self-held cup, and eating with a spoon. More advanced skill training may include using other utensils, table manners, serving foods, food preparation, and food-purchasing skills.

Finger Foods   Generally, teaching children to feed themselves with their fingers is best accomplished at the beginning of a meal when they are hungry (Snell & Farlow, 1993). Some children, however, may become easily frustrated at this time and tolerate training better after having something to eat. The trainer must be certain that the child knows and likes the foods (in the forms provided) to ensure reinforcement value. Many children need little more than this opportunity to begin self-feeding, and their training may focus primarily on improving dexterity or establishing a suitable pace. For other children, movement difficulties or skill deficits may make acquisition more difficult. Modeling the desired behavior may be helpful, but graduated guidance is the most common training method. Generally, the trainer will find it easier to work from behind the child. The child is guided through the required movements with as little assistance as needed. Assistance is gradually withdrawn over time as independence increases.

Drinking from a Self-Held Cup   Learning to drink from a cup is a messy but rewarding experience for almost any child. For many children, only the willingness of caregivers to provide ample learning opportunities is required. For others, the coordination of arm, hand, head, and mouth movements is extremely challenging. Good, stable positioning will help. For some individuals, this may mean having a solid place to rest their feet. For others, it may mean having their elbows on the table while drinking. For some, thickened liquids may be easier to control at first. Selecting a cup or glass with the best shape and weight for the specific child will often be helpful. Although spout cups reduce spilling, they are not generally recommended because they may encourage dysfunctional drinking patterns. For many children, the goal may be limited to partial participation until they develop adequate oral skills to handle their first imprecise independent attempts to transfer fluids into their own mouths.

Eating with a Spoon Graduated guidance is also a common method of teaching children with disabilities to eat with a spoon. Because spoon-feeding involves a fairly long chain of discrete responses, task analysis may be useful in determining exactly which steps need work. Adaptive spoons will be helpful for some children who have difficulty gripping, bringing the spoon into the mouth at the appropriate angle, or keeping food balanced on the spoon while bringing it to the mouth. For many children, spoon-feeding is possible but less efficient than eating with their fingers. For children who revert to finger feeding, a delay or interruption procedure may be useful (Snell & Farlow, 1993). Interruption to attempts at finger feeding causes spoon-feeding to become more efficient and differentially reinforcing.

Advanced Mealtime Skills For children who master basic self-feeding skills, training in more advanced mealtime skills will increase their level of independence and allow them to function in a wide array of environments. The selection and order of skills taught will not be the same for all students. They should be selected on the basis of the needs and skills of the child and requirements of his or her current and potential future environments. For example, tray-carrying skills may not be relevant for children who eat only family-style meals at home and in their classrooms, but these same tray-carrying skills may be extremely important for children who eat in a school cafeteria. Some advanced skills include table manners, mealtime social skills, food serving, table setting, food preparation, selecting nutritious foods, requesting desired foods, ordering in restaurants, and food shopping. Many more skills could be added to this list. Few children with multiple disabilities can be expected to master all of these skill areas, but many of them can be expected to master at least some basic goals in several of these areas. Because advanced mealtime skills include so many areas and this chapter focuses on more basic skills, only a brief discussion of mealtime social skills is included here.

Mealtime social skills programs are often viewed as fitting into two categories: 1) building desirable behaviors, and 2) eliminating undesirable behaviors. In practice, the development of desirable social behavior at mealtime is often adequate to control or eliminate inappropriate behavior, which, in turn, eliminates the need to institute direct intervention to reduce inappropriate behavior. This focus on building appropriate behavior is consistent with the increasing awareness that behavior that is inappropriate (in the eyes of caregivers) is typically extremely functional for the child and that teaching a more appropriate functional alternative may be the best means of behavioral control (Evans & Meyer, 1985; Meyer & Evans, 1989). For example, if a child finishes his or her food and then grabs food off other children's plates, this behavior may function to satisfy the child's continuing hunger. The intervention team might try to use punishment procedures to eliminate food stealing, but such procedures probably have little chance for success if the child has no more acceptable way of asking for a second helping. If the child is taught to obtain food through an acceptable requesting behavior (e.g., hand raising, standing in line), the unacceptable behavior may be eliminated with no other intervention or with less intrusive intervention than otherwise might be required.

Of course, the success of this type of training procedure depends on correctly identifying the function of the undesired behavior. Certainly, attaining food is the most obvious function one might ascribe to food grabbing. If the child does not really want the food and instead grabs food to attract the caregiver's attention, teaching the child more appropriate requesting behavior may do little to control food grabbing. Therefore, the success of these programs depends on careful analysis of behaviors, consequences, and antecedents and on careful ongoing evaluation of behavioral changes, all of which will confirm or rule out the hypothesis developed regarding behavioral function.

Eliminating problem behaviors is only one aspect of mealtime social skills. Perske, Clifton, McLean, and Stein (1986) estimate that "better than eighty percent of . . . severely handicapped persons do not experience relaxed, human-communion types of meals" (p. xix). Programs that focus on the mechanical process of efficient eating and feeding fail to meet emotional human needs. A physical and social environment must be created that meets these needs.

No single recipe will work for every child in every environment, but a number of measures are worth consideration. Caregivers should make the dining room environment as typical as possible. Communication between caregivers and the children they feed is desirable, but communication among caregivers that excludes the children they feed is undesirable and potentially dehumanizing. Such communication may include verbal, touch, and/or visual components. Whenever possible, children should be allowed to make choices for themselves. Mealtimes should be long enough to avoid the need for rushing. The room should be fairly quiet and relaxed. These and other simple measures can do much to provide a positive mealtime social environment.

NUTRITIONAL CONCERNS

Any discussion of eating and feeding skills training for children with multiple disabilities should consider nutrition. After all, one of the major goals of teaching eating and feeding skills is to help ensure adequate nutrition, and any intervention that affects what or how children eat also affects their nutrition.

Of course, for the most part, children with multiple disabilities have the same nutritional needs as other children, and normalization suggests that the same methods be used to maintain good diet and nutrition. Unfortunately, children with multiple disabilities appear to be at far greater risk for nutritional deficits than their peers without disabilities, and a number of factors can be identified that demand special consideration (McCamman & Rues, 1990; R.J. Sobsey, 1983). Comprehensive discussion has been devoted to these special considerations elsewhere (e.g., Palmer & Ekvall, 1978; Springer, 1982), and they merit some discussion here.

Signs and Symptoms

One of the difficulties of providing better recognition of nutritional deficits in children with multiple disabilities is that signs and symptoms of these deficits are often ascribed to other causes. Lethargy and poor resistance to infection, major signs of anemia, and other nutritional deficiency diseases are often considered to be a result of the child's primary diagnosis or to the medication given to the child. Retarded growth and scoliosis, which may be signs of inadequate calcium or vitamin D, are often seen as resulting from some genetic syndrome or disorders of muscle tone and posture. Thus, nutritional problems may be masked by other risk factors. Of course, this does not mean that the non-nutritional factors never play a role in these problems. Rather, it means that maintaining adequate nutrition is even more important, because any nutritional risk factor is likely to interact with a number of other risk factors to produce potentially devastating results. It also means that nutritional assessment must be particularly thorough to avoid the masking of signs and symptoms by other risk factors in children with multiple disabilities.

Some Nutritional Risk Factors

Some nutritional risk factors are associated with the specific disability (McCamman & Rues, 1990). Children with increased tone and limited movement typically require fewer calories than their peers. Because their needs for protein and vitamins do not decrease proportionally, their diets may require more of these (R.J. Sobsey, 1983). Children with phenylketonuria (PKU) cannot eat foods with phenylalanine, including foods with the artificial sweetener aspartame, which is being used with increasing frequency. When specific foods are eliminated from the diet, it is important to assess the effects of the restriction on the entire diet to ensure balance. Children with Prader-Willi syndrome typically eat to excess and often become obese, causing secondary health problems (Lupi & Porcella, 1987; McCamman & Rues, 1990). Frequently, the diet consumed is high in caloric value but low in other essential nutrients. Even with average caloric intake, these children gain weight, and a diet very low in calories is needed to maintain an ideal weight (Lupi & Porcella, 1987). In order to maintain adequate nutrition with reduced caloric intake, the diet must include a higher ratio of vitamins, minerals, and protein to calories.

Oral-motor problems that affect eating directly affect nutritional status. Children with cerebral palsy and oral-motor involvement have been shown to be shorter in stature and weigh less for their height when compared with children with cerebral palsy who do not have oral-motor involvement (Krick & Van Duyn, 1984).

Other risk factors may be related to problems that affect all children, but they may be less frequently noticed in children with multiple disabilities. Although congenital lactose intolerance (lactase deficiency) is usually detected in infancy, late-onset lactose intolerance may begin gradually as the child approaches adulthood (Springer, 1982). Gradual onset makes detection more difficult, and the child's inability to communicate discomfort will further complicate detection. Inability to communicate and dependence on others to meet one's needs can also lead to serious problems with maintaining adequate hydration, another nutritional concern. Although people generally require about 1 milliliter of water for each calorie consumed (Batshaw & Perret, 1992), differences in air temperature, electrolyte intake, and other factors can greatly influence these requirements. For most people, adjustment to these altered requirements occurs spontaneously through increased intake, but for the child who lacks the mobility to obtain fluids without assistance and lacks the communication skills to request fluids, caregivers must carefully monitor signs of hydration status.

Other nutritional problems may be related to the methods used to feed children. Puréed diets tend to be high in carbohydrates and low in protein, vitamin C, and fiber, and, as discussed under the "Modifying Foods" section of this chapter, they should be replaced whenever possible by diets more typical in texture. Similarly, nasogastric tube feedings are often nutritionally inferior, and children maintained on enteral feedings for extended periods may lose interest in resuming regular diets, which can cause additional nutritional problems (Hargrave, 1979).

Nutritional problems can also develop as a result of medication side effects (McCamman & Rues, 1990). Many drugs have nutritional side effects, but the significance of these side effects may be small with short-term usage. For example, the effects of an occasional aspirin in depressing vitamin C and folic acid (Crump, 1987) are probably unimportant, but individuals receiving daily doses of aspirin may be significantly affected. Because children with multiple disabilities often take medications with known nutritional side effects for extended periods, they are more likely to be affected. Crump (1987) pointed out that drugs may affect nutrition in six ways: 1) increasing or decreasing intake, 2) inhibiting synthesis of nutrients, 3) interfering with absorption, 4) altering transport of metabolites, 5) blocking storage or utilization of metabolites, and 6) increasing excretion of nutrients.

In regard to specific drugs, many anticonvulsants irritate the stomach lining and may interfere with the general absorption of nutrients (Hargrave, 1979). Some anticonvulsants also interfere with vitamin D and calcium metabolism and cause depletion of folic acid (R.J. Sobsey, 1983). Careful consultation with a physician, nutritionist, and other team members is required to eliminate or at least minimize these potential problems, especially because attempts to supplement folic acid can precipitate seizures if not properly carried out. Tranquilizers tend to reduce caloric requirements and increase caloric intake, which leads to weight gain. Stimulants, conversely, decrease intake and increase activity, which may result in growth retardation as well as weight loss (Lucas, 1981). Laxatives, another category of medications used frequently with children with multiple disabilities, also have nutritional side effects. They decrease absorption of most nutrients and some specifically interfere with particular nutrients. For example, mineral oil decreases absorption of fat-soluble vitamins (R.J. Sobsey, 1983). Whenever possible, reducing or eliminating the use of medications is the simplest method of eliminating nutritional side effects. When medication is essential, however, carefully assessing and controlling diet and nutrition helps to minimize these drug side effects.

The lack of mobility associated with many disabilities also contributes to nutritional concerns in several ways. First, decreased mobility reduces caloric requirements. This means less food with higher proportions of protein and vitamins is needed. Second, decreased mobility often leads to constipation, which can impair absorption of nutrients. Third, decreased mobility leads to decalcification of bones and atrophy of muscle, which requires nutritional intervention (Hargrave, 1979). Finally, lack of mobility often results in less time outdoors and, therefore, less exposure to the sun, the major source of vitamin D for most children (Batshaw & Perret, 1992).

Maintaining weight within the normal range is difficult for many children with disabilities. Obesity is a problem for many children with developmental disabilities (Steadham, 1994) and tends to increase with age. Other children are chronically underweight. Maintaining normal weight promotes general health and often makes the development of gross motor skills easier. For example, children who are obese typically have more difficulty walking independently.

All of the risk factors described in this section contribute to nutritional problems for a large percentage of children with multiple disabilities. Awareness of these concerns by all team members and careful periodic evaluation by a professional in dietetics and nutrition are important components of total service delivery to each child. Improved nutrition can make a major contribution to health, learning, and quality of life for children with multiple disabilities. Children with disabilities should be encouraged to learn to participate in choosing their own food (Smith, 1994). Pairing choices between reasonably nutritious foods allows them to make choices and to learn to enjoy nutritious foods.

Diet and Behavior

Much has been written about specific dietary interventions that aim to produce substantive changes in behavior and learning potential. These include participating in megavitamin or orthomolecular therapy to reduce hyperactivity and improve learning, reducing sugar intake to eliminate hyperactivity, eliminating common food allergens to eliminate hyperactivity, and the Feingold diet (eliminating natural salicylates, artificial colors and flavors, and certain preservatives). Some published research has supported these kinds of intervention, but the great majority of carefully controlled research has demonstrated that they have little or no effect (Lucas, 1981). Such conflicting results suggest that some small subgroup of children may be helped by these interventions, but only a small number. Therefore, whenever such therapy is considered for a child, it must include careful, systematic, criterion-based evaluation. If it helps the child, it should be continued as one element of the child's program but not as a substitute for other intervention. If clear benefits for an individual are not demonstrated, the intervention should be abandoned.

DENTAL CARE

Dental care is another area of concern closely related to feeding, eating, and nutrition. Like many services for children with multiple disabilities, dental care has evolved through fairly distinct stages. Lange, Entwistle, and Lipson (1983) described the first stage as supervised neglect. Few services were available, and, often, the services that were available were of poor quality. Restraints and sedation characterized the next phase. During the early 1970s, increasing concern was demonstrated through the development of specialized dental techniques and equipment. Later in the 1970s and during the 1980s, the trend toward normalization and increased training efforts resulted in fewer specialized and more generic services. The traditional reluctance of many dentists to treat individuals with disabilities has been eliminated or greatly reduced as a result of efforts to shape more positive attitudes in dental schools (Gurney & Alcorn, 1979) and through public education. These changes in attitude have resulted partly from the efforts of specific organizations. The Academy of Dentistry for the Handicapped and the National Foundation of Dentistry for the Handicapped, along with the American Academy of Pediatric Dentistry, have promoted high-quality dental care for children with disabilities, preparation of dentists to work with individuals with disabilities, and research relevant to these goals. They also serve as useful resources to the public, assisting in locating dentists with appropriate skills in individuals' geographical areas. With funding from the Robert Wood Johnson Foundation, the American Fund for Dental Health coordinated development of dental school program components during the 1970s to prepare graduating dentists to work with people with a range of disabilities (Walker, 1979). In the 1980s and 1990s, as more people with disabilities moved out of institutions and into the community, more dentists who possessed the skills and attitudes necessary for serving these individuals were needed (Ferguson, Kamen, Ratner, & Rosenthal, 1992). In order to meet these needs, special training programs and, in some cases, special dental fellowships (e.g., those offered by the New York State Office of Mental Retardation and Developmental Disabilities) have been offered.

Although there has been significant progress in dental care for children and adults with developmental disabilities, challenging legal, ethical, and economic issues have also arisen (Shuman & Bebeau, 1994). For example, a dental procedure that could easily be done in the dentist's office with most patients may require general anesthesia and hospitalization for an individual who does not understand the need to keep still during the procedure. Most health care and dental insurance will not cover the additional costs of anesthesia and hospital care, however. A dentist may have to choose among performing a needed procedure under less than ideal conditions in his or her office, insisting on hospitalization even when the family has difficulty meeting the expense, or neglecting work that is necessary.

Special Dental Concerns

Although dental care for children with multiple disabilities is not much different from dental care for other children, some particular concerns exist. Children with cerebral palsy often have more cavities, more periodontal disease, poor occlusion, and damaged teeth due to bruxism (grinding of the teeth). Children with Down syndrome appear to have fewer cavities than other children, but they often have increased periodontal disease and poor occlusion (McIver & Machen, 1979). Children with epilepsy are at risk for damaging teeth in a fall, may have gingival hyperplasia (abnormal overgrowth of the gums), and may have poorly developed teeth due to calcium and vitamin D metabolism disturbances caused by medication. Difficulty in communicating the reason for dental procedures may make some children fearful and difficult to manage during dental treatment (Burkhart, 1984). Children with mobility problems have difficulty cleaning their own teeth and gums thoroughly. Many children are not taught to brush their teeth adequately. Soft, sticky diets provided to some children are cariogenic (promote cavities) and increase the need for brushing (Albertson, 1974). Abnormal reflexes and limited ranges of motion may make dental treatment more difficult for some children with multiple disabilities. All of these factors contribute to the need for ongoing, high-quality dental services. These services can best be provided through close cooperation between dental specialists and other service team members.

Dental Care and Prevention

Good dental care requires the teamwork of dentists, dental assistants, dental hygienists, parents, teachers, and other caregivers. Introducing solid foods as early as possible and avoiding soft and puréed foods can reduce cavities (Coffee, 1986) and encourage normal development of oral structures (Goose & Appleton, 1982). Avoiding the use of sweets as reinforcers and snacks will reduce cavities (R.J. Sobsey, 1983). Perhaps most important, regular brushing and flossing are major preventers of both cavities and periodontal disease (Coffee, 1986). Whenever possible, children should be taught to brush their own teeth, but there may

332 Orelove and Sobsey

be a need to supplement this with cleaning by caregivers until proficiency is developed. Oral irrigators, disclosing solution, and electric toothbrushes may help ensure the quality of cleaning for many children. The introduction of mouthwashes that contain ingredients (e.g., chlorhexidine) that inhibit formation of plaque has been a significant advantage in oral hygiene. Applications of the mouthwashes directly to the teeth and gums with swabs has proven effective to decrease plaque and gingivitis among people with disabilities who are unable to use an oral rinse properly (Stiefel, Truelove, Chin, & Mandel, 1992).

Regular dental care is also essential. Visits to the dentist three or four times per year may be required for some children. In addition to allowing for early treatment of cavities and preventive care, regular visits to the dentist provide opportunities to build a history of positive interactions without the stress of a toothache or invasive procedures. Fluoride treatments are a valuable part of preventive care. Since the widespread introduction of fluoride treatments, dental health for most citizens has improved markedly. Careful observation for signs of cavities can help to ensure early treatment. This is particularly important because early treatment of cavities can typically be accomplished through single-surface fillings. More advanced decay often requires treatment of two or more tooth surfaces. These reconstructions of multiple surfaces are extremely difficult to accomplish if the individual cannot or will not hold extremely still in the position required. This may require general anesthesia and hospitalization for some children with multiple disabilities.

Specific dental problems can often be ameliorated through team intervention. For example, approximately 50% of children who receive Dilantin (phenytoin) have significant gum overgrowth (Lange et al., 1983). If tolerated, a reduction in phenytoin can reduce this overgrowth. If phenytoin cannot be reduced, ascorbic acid may be prescribed to reduce some of the negative effects (Lange et al., 1983). Such intervention will require careful consultation with the physician, who must assess the potential effects on seizure activity. If overgrowth of gums cannot be prevented, careful and frequent cleaning of teeth and gums will reduce the infection and irritation that can lead to serious dental disease, and periodic surgical removal of excess tissue can keep the overgrowth in check.

Modern dental procedures allow for the elimination of almost all pain and discomfort. Every effort should be made to minimize discomfort and the need for restraint. This is not only important for ethical reasons, but it is crucial for encouraging patient cooperation. Every effort should be made to let the child know what will be done and why. Efforts to communicate must also include making every attempt to understand and respond to the child's concerns and desires.

This list of measures to enhance dental care for children with disabilities is not comprehensive, but their application can make a significant difference in dental health. Improved dental health, in turn, can contribute significantly to better eating skills, nutrition, and feeding procedures. Together, these components can improve quality of life throughout the day, including during mealtimes.

ASSESSMENT AND PROGRAM PLANNING

This chapter has presented a discussion of many of the factors and concerns related to the mealtime skills of children with severe disabilities. Developing and implementing mealtime programs that consider these factors require transdisciplinary assessment and planning. This process is described briefly in the following section.

The Mealtime Program Team

Many people have expertise that should be considered in mealtime planning. Some disciplines will be more important to include on the team for some children than for others, depending on the child's individual needs. Some team members may contribute to assessment and planning in only a few specific areas, based on their expertise in their disciplines. Other team members may contribute to more decisions because of their knowledge of the child.

One person, commonly the teacher, must take overall responsibility for integrating input from the entire team. This science coordinator (or educational synthesizer) organizes the assessment and planning processes as well as program implementation. The teacher also brings expertise in training methods to the team. The physical therapist can contribute valuable information about motor skills, reflexes, and therapeutic interventions. The occupational therapist's skills may partially overlap with the physical therapist's skills, but they are typically applied more to functional activities. The occupational therapist is often also an excellent resource for adaptive utensils and furniture. The speech-language therapist can contribute expertise that will help with potential speech, as well as eating skills, because motor patterns developed in eating will influence those used in speech (Alexander, 1991). The nurse may help train staff to prevent choking and recognize signs of discomfort. Parents and other primary caregivers must be included for two reasons. First, they typically know the child and history of interventions better than any other team member. Second, they generally participate in feeding the child most of his or her meals. Aides and any other caregivers involved in feeding also should be included. The nutritionist or dietitian has important expertise that should be included in planning. Failure to consider nutritional planning can have disastrous consequences. Similarly, the dentist should be part of mealtime planning. Many decisions made by these professionals and other members of the feeding team interact with the physician's treatment decisions. Therefore, the physician should also be included. When it is not possible to have all of these professionals attend team meetings, input should be gathered from them prior to team planning, and programs should be circulated to them for approval prior to implementation.

The Assessment Process

Assessment of eating and feeding skills requires both a determination of what the child can and cannot do and a determination of which skills are critical to improving the child's functioning in current and potential future environments. Assessment of nutritional concerns requires careful recording of daily intake, measures of physical characteristics, and measures of physiological functions. Assessment of dental status requires a physical examination and a review of risk factors. Each child's evaluation must be individualized. Although some may prove useful, no specific assessment protocol is required. Ekvall (1978) included two assessment protocols that evaluate both eating skills and nutritional status in her thorough discussion of assessing nutritional status. Schmidt (1976) provided a concise format for evaluating feeding and eating skills. Several curricula (e.g., Tawney, 1979) provide skill sequences for eating and feeding that are appropriate for assessment. Munk and Repp (1994) provided an assessment for evaluating food refusal and determining the most appropriate intervention. Elements that seem most relevant to the child being evaluated can be selected from these and other assessment instruments, or evaluation can proceed without the use of any specific instrument as long as the assessment collects and organizes the information required to set measurable and realistic objectives.

Setting objectives is an important step in program planning (Campbell, 1982). Vague goals such as "to improve nutritional status" or "will chew better" defy evaluation and make training extremely difficult. Typically, objectives should have criteria that reflect a level of performance sufficient for independent function in a typical environment. Occasionally, setting intermediate objectives with criteria at lower levels may be desired, especially if intervention techniques will be modified after the intermediate objective is mastered.

SUMMARY

This chapter presents information and discusses issues concerning mealtime skills and related concerns for children with multiple disabilities. Mealtime skills are essential for survival, health, and good quality of life. Interventionists can do much to promote these by providing training in eating and feeding skills, creating a typical and relaxed mealtime environment, protecting against the dangers of airway obstruction and aspiration, and ensuring good nutrition and dental care. Transdisciplinary teamwork is required to assess the child's level of functioning and the demands of the environment and to implement effective mealtime programming.

REFERENCES

Albertson, D. (1974). Prevention and the handicapped child. *Dental Clinics of North America, 18*, 595–608.
Alexander, R. (1991). Prespeech and feeding. In J.L. Bigge, *Teaching individuals with physical and multiple disabilities* (3rd ed., pp. 175–198). New York: Macmillan.
Azrin, N.H., & Armstrong, P.M. (1973). The "Mini-Meal"—A method of teaching feeding skills to the profoundly retarded. *Mental Retardation, 11*, 9–13.

Bastian, C.H., & Driscoll, R.H. (1984). Enteral tube feeding at home. In J.L. Rombeau & M.D. Caldwell (Eds.), *Enteral and tube feeding* (pp. 494–512). Philadelphia: W.B. Saunders.

Batshaw, M.L., & Perret, Y.M. (1992). *Children with disabilities: A medical primer* (3rd ed.). Baltimore: Paul H. Brookes Publishing Co.

Blackman, J.A., & Nelson, C.L.A. (1985). Reinstituting oral feedings in children fed by gastrostomy tube. *Clinical Pediatrics, 24,* 434–438.

Blackman, J.A., & Nelson, C.L.A. (1987). Rapid introduction of oral feedings to tubefed patients. *Developmental and Behavioral Pediatrics, 8*(2), 63–67.

Blockley, J., & Miller, G. (1971) Feeding techniques with cerebral palsied children. *Physiotherapy, 57,* 300–308.

Burkhart, N. (1984). Understanding and managing the autistic child in the dental office. *Dental Hygiene, 58,* 60–63.

Campbell, A.L. (1988, April). Tube feeding: Parental perspective. *Exceptional Parent,* 36–40.

Campbell, P. (1982). *Problem-oriented approaches to feeding the handicapped child* (Rev. ed.). Akron, OH: Children's Hospital Medical Center. (ERIC Document Reproduction No. ED 231 127)

Campbell, P.H. (1987). Physical management and handling procedures with students with movement dysfunction. In M.E. Snell (Ed.), *Systematic instruction of persons with severe handicaps* (3rd ed., pp. 174–187). Columbus, OH: Charles E. Merrill.

Campbell, S.K. (1978). Oral sensori-motor physiology. In J.M. Wilson (Ed.), *Oralmotor function and dysfunction in children* (pp. 1–11). Chapel Hill: University of North Carolina, Division of Physical Therapy.

Cautner, M., & Penrose, J. (1983, December 21). Solving feeding problems. *Nursing Times, 51,* 24–26.

Chaney, R.H. (1987). Risk of pulmonary edema in mentally retarded persons. *American Journal on Mental Deficiency, 91,* 555–558.

Chaney, R.H., Eyman, R.K., & Miller, C.R. (1979). Comparison of respiratory mortality in the profoundly mentally retarded and the less retarded. *Journal of Mental Deficiency Research, 23,* 1–7.

Coffee, L. (1986). Planning daily care for healthy teeth. In R. Perske, A. Clifton, B.M. McLean, & J.I. Stein (Eds.), *Mealtimes for persons with severe handicaps* (pp. 119–122). Baltimore: Paul H. Brookes Publishing Co.

Crump, I.M. (1987). Interactions and influences on nutrient function. In I.M. Crump (Ed.), *Nutrition and feeding of the handicapped child* (pp. 19–28). Boston: Little, Brown.

Eisele, D.W. (1991). Surgical approaches to aspiration. *Dysphagia, 6*(2), 71–78.

Ekvall, S. (1978). Assessment of nutritional status. In S. Palmer & S. Ekvall (Eds.), *Pediatric nutrition in developmental disorders* (pp. 502–550). Springfield, IL: Charles C Thomas.

Evans, I.M., & Meyer, L.H. (1985). *An educative approach to behavior problems: A practical decision model for interventions with severely handicapped learners.* Baltimore: Paul H. Brookes Publishing Co.

Eyman, R.K., Grossman, H.J., Chaney, R.H., & Call, T.L. (1990). The life expectancy of profoundly handicapped people with mental retardation. *New England Journal of Medicine, 323*(9), 584–589.

Ferguson, F.S., Kamen, P., Ratner, S., & Rosenthal, R.L. (1992). Dental fellowships in developmental disabilities help broaden care of the disabled. *New York State Dental Journal, 59*(1), 55–58.

Fraser, B.A., & Hensinger, R.H. (1983). *Managing physical handicaps: A practical guide for parents, care providers, and educators.* Baltimore: Paul H. Brookes Publishing Co.

Gallender, D. (1979). *Eating handicaps.* Springfield, IL: Charles C Thomas.

Gauderer, M.W.L., Picha, G.J., & Izant, R.J. (1984). The gastrostomy "button": A simple, skin-level, non-refluxing device for long-term enteral feedings. *Journal of Pediatric Surgery, 19,* 803–805.

Gauderer, M.W.L., Ponsky, J.L., & Izant, R.J. (1980). Gastrostomy without laparotomy: A percutaneous endoscopic technique. *Journal of Pediatric Surgery, 15,* 872–875.

Gisel, E.G. (1991). Effect of food texture on the development of chewing of children between six months and two years of age. *Developmental Medicine and Child Neurology, 33,* 69–79.

Goose, D.H., & Appleton, J. (1982). *Human dentofacial growth.* Oxford, England: Pergamon.

Graff, J.C., Ault, M.M., Guess, D., Taylor, M., & Thompson, B. (1990). *Health care for students with disabilities: An illustrated medical guide for the classroom.* Baltimore: Paul H. Brookes Publishing Co.

Groher, M. (1987). Bolus management and aspiration pneumonia in patients with pseudobulbar dysphagia. *Dysphagia, 1,* 215–216.

Groher, M. (1988, January). *Approaches in the evaluation of swallowing disorders.* Paper presented at the Current Concepts in Mealtime Management for Neurologically Impaired and Mentally Retarded Clients: Special Topics Symposium, Dallas, TX.

Gurney, N.L., & Alcorn, J. (1979). The concept of attitudes. In K.E. Wessels (Ed.), *Dentistry and the handicapped patient* (Postgraduate Dental Handbook Series, Vol. 5, pp. 1–19). Littleton, MA: PSG Publishing.

Hargrave, M. (1979). *Nutritional care of the physically disabled.* (Publication No. 719). Minneapolis, MN: Sister Kenny Institute.

Jones, T.W. (1983). Remediation of behavior-related eating problems: A preliminary investigation. *Journal of The Association for Persons with Severe Handicaps, 8*(4), 62–71.

Kalisz, K., & Ekvall, S. (1978). Cleft palate. In S. Palmer & S. Ekvall (Eds.), *Pediatric nutrition in developmental disorders* (pp. 36–41). Springfield, IL: Charles C Thomas.

Karb, V.B., Queener, S.F., & Freeman, J.B. (1989). *Handbook of drugs for nursing practice.* St. Louis, MO: C.V. Mosby.

Kennedy-Caldwell, C., & Caldwell, M. (1984). Pediatric enteral nutrition. In J.L. Rombeau & M.D. Caldwell (Eds.), *Enteral and tube feedings* (pp. 434–479). Philadelphia: W.B. Saunders.

Krick, J., & Van Duyn, M.A. (1984). The relationship between oral-motor involvement and growth: A pilot study in a pediatric population with cerebral palsy. *Journal of the American Dietetic Association, 84,* 555–559.

Lange, B.M., Entwistle, B.M., & Lipson, L.F. (1983). *Dental management of the handicapped: Approaches for dental auxiliaries.* Philadelphia: Lea & Febiger.

Linschied, T.R., Oliver, J., Blyer, E., & Palmer, S. (1978). Brief hospitalization for behavioral treatment of feeding problems in the developmentally disabled. *Journal of Pediatric Psychology, 3,* 72–76.

Logemann, J. (1983). *Evaluation and treatment of swallowing disorders.* San Diego, CA: College-Hill.

Lucas, B. (1981). Diet and hyperactivity. In P.L. Pipes (Ed.), *Nutrition in infancy and childhood* (2nd ed., pp. 236–248). St. Louis, MO: C.V. Mosby.

Lupi, M.H., & Porcella, J.E. (1987). Some considerations in the education and management of the child with Prader-Willi syndrome in the special education classroom. *Techniques: A Journal for Remedial Education and Counseling, 2,* 230–235.

McCamman, S., & Rues, J. (1990). Nutrition monitoring and supplementation. In J.C. Graff, M.M. Ault, D. Guess, M. Taylor, & B. Thompson, *Health care for students with disabilities: An illustrated medical guide for the classroom* (pp. 79–117). Baltimore: Paul H. Brookes Publishing Co.

McIver, F.J., & Machen, J.B. (1979). Prevention of dental disease in handicapped people. In K.E. Wessels (Ed.), *Dentistry and the handicapped patient* (Postgraduate Dental Handbook Series, Vol. 5, pp. 77–115). Littleton, MA: PSG Publishing.

Meyer, L.H., & Evans, I.M. (1989). *Nonaversive intervention for behavior problems: A manual for home and community.* Baltimore: Paul H. Brookes Publishing Co.

Morris, S.E. (1978a). Oral-motor development: Normal and abnormal. In J.M. Wilson (Ed.), *Oral-motorfunction and dysfunction in children* (pp. 114–122). Chapel Hill: University of North Carolina, Division of Physical Therapy.

Morris, S.E. (1978b). *Program guidelines for children with feeding problems.* Edison, NJ: Childcraft.

Morris, S.E., & Klein, M.D. (1987). *Pre-feeding skills.* Tucson, AZ: Therapy Skill Builders.

Morris, S.E., & Weber, S.S. (1978). Problems of cerebral palsy and oral-motor function. In J.M. Wilson (Ed.), *Oral-motorfunction and dysfunction in children* (pp. 163–166). Chapel Hill: University of North Carolina, Division of Physical Therapy.

Mueller, H. (1975). Feeding. In N.R. Finnie (Ed.), *Handling the young cerebral palsied child at home* (2nd ed., pp. 113–132). New York: E.P. Dutton.

Munk, D.D., & Repp, A.C. (1994). Behavioral assessment of feeding problems of individuals with severe disabilities. *Journal of Applied Behavioral Analysis, 27,* 241–250.

Ohwaki, S, & Zingarelli, G. (1988). Feeding clients with severe multiple handicaps in a skilled nursing care facility. *Mental Retardation, 26*(1), 21–24.

Palmer, S., & Ekvall, S. (Eds.). (1978). *Pediatric nutrition in developmental disabilities.* Springfield, IL: Charles C Thomas.

Palmer, S., & Horn, S. (1978). Feeding problems in children. In S. Palmer & S. Ekvall (Eds.), *Pediatric nutrition in developmental disorders* (pp. 107–129). Springfield, IL: Charles C Thomas.

Perske, R., Clifton, A., McLean, B.M., & Stein, J.I. (Eds.). (1986). *Mealtimes for persons with severe handicaps.* Baltimore: Paul H. Brookes Publishing Co.

Rasley, A., Logemann, J.A., Kahrilas, P.J., Rademaker, A.W., Pauloski, B.R., & Dodds, W.J. (1993). Prevention of barium aspiration during videofluoroscopic swallowing studies: Value of change in posture. *American Journal of Roentgenology, 160*(5), 1005–1009.

Schmidt, P. (1976). Feeding assessment and therapy for the neurologically impaired. *AAESPH Review, 1,* 19–27.

Sheppard, J.J. (1991). Managing dysphagia in mentally retarded adults. *Dysphagia, 6,* 83–87.

Shuman, S.K., & Bebeau, M.J. (1994). Ethical and legal issues in special patient care. *Dental Clinics of North America, 38*(3), 553–575.

Silberman, H., & Eisenberg, D. (1982). *Parenteral and enteral nutrition for the hospitalized patient.* Norwalk, CT: Appleton-Century-Crofts.

Smith, M.A.H. (1994). Nutrition and diet. In M. Agran, N.E. Marchand-Martella, & R.C. Martella (Eds.), *Promoting health and safety: Skills for independent living* (pp. 33–53). Baltimore: Paul H. Brookes Publishing Co.

Snell, M.E., & Farlow, L.J. (1993). Self-care skills. In M.E. Snell (Ed.), *Instruction of students with severe disabilities* (4th ed., pp. 380–441). Columbus, OH: Charles E. Merrill.

Sobsey, D. (1983). A comparison of feeding pureed and whole foods to a multihandicapped adolescent. *Mental Retardation and Learning Disabilities Bulletin, 11,* 85–91.

Sobsey, D. (1988, January). *Mealtime skills cluster: Bringing it all together.* Paper presented at the Current Concepts in Mealtime Management for Neurologically Impaired and Mentally Retarded Clients: Special Topics Symposium, Dallas, TX.

Sobsey, R.J. (1983). Nutrition of children with severely handicapping conditions. *Journal of The Association for Persons with Severe Handicaps, 8*(4), 14–17.

Sobsey, R., & Orelove, F.P. (1984). Neurophysiological facilitation of eating skills in children with severe handicaps. *Journal of The Association for Persons with Severe Handicaps, 9*, 98–110.

Springer, N.S. (1982). *Nutrition casebook on developmental disabilities.* Syracuse, NY: Syracuse University Press.

Stainback, S., Stainback, W., Healy, H., & Healy, J. (1980). Basic eating skills. In J. Umbreit & P.J. Cardullias (Eds.), *Educating the severely physically handicapped: Basic principles and techniques* (Vol. I, pp. 16–30). Reston, VA: Council for Exceptional Children, Division on Physically Handicapped.

Steadham, C.I. (1994). Health maintenance and promotion. In S.P. Roth & J.S. Morse (Eds.), *A life-span approach to nursing care for individuals with developmental disabilities* (pp. 147–169). Baltimore: Paul H. Brookes Publishing Co.

Sternberg, L., Pegnatore, L., & Hill, C. (1983). Establishing interactive communication behaviors with profoundly mentally handicapped students. *Journal of The Association for the Severely Handicapped, 8*(2), 39–46.

Stiefel, D.J., Truelove, E.L., Chin, M.M., & Mandel, L.S. (1992). Efficacy of chlorhexidine swabbing in oral health care for people with severe disabilities. *Special Care in Dentistry, 12*(2), 57–62.

Tawney, J.W. (1979). *Programmed environments curriculum.* Columbus, OH: Charles E. Merrill.

Trefler, E., Westmoreland, D., & Burlingame, D. (1977). A feeding spatula for cerebral palsied children. *American Journal of Occupational Therapy, 31*, 260–261.

Utley, B.L., Holvoet, J.F., & Barnes, K. (1977). Handling, positioning and feeding the physically handicapped. In E. Sontag, J. Smith, & N. Certo (Eds.), *Educational programming for the severely and profoundly handicapped* (pp. 279–299). Reston, VA: Council for Exceptional Children.

Walker, P.O. (1979, January–March). The patient with a handicap—Are we adding insult to injury? *Dental Dimensions*, pp. 9–12.

Wilson, J.M. (1978). Helpful hints for feeding children with oral-motor dysfunction. In J.M. Wilson (Ed.), *Oral-motor function and dysfunction in children* (pp. 198–202). Chapel Hill: University of North Carolina, Division of Physical Therapy.

9

Self-Care Skills

ONE AREA OF THE CURRICULUM for students with multiple disabilities that everyone agrees is important is self-care skills. In fact, many educational programs focus almost solely on teaching students to become more proficient in taking care of their own hygiene and appearance. In addition to mealtime skills (discussed in Chapter 8), toileting, dressing, grooming, and personal hygiene are viewed as particularly important self-care skills for several reasons. First, individuals use toileting, dressing, and grooming skills every day, and these skills are used for a lifetime. Second, helping these children to dress, undress, use the toilet, and tend to the rest of their personal care requires much time and energy from parents, teachers, and other caregivers. Teaching students to perform even parts of these skill sequences is helpful to caregivers. Third, the ability to dress, groom, and, especially, handle self-toileting is a badge of independence. The performance of these tasks not only serves to make individuals feel better about themselves but often creates a perception in others that the students are more competent and capable of learning. Fourth, in the case of toileting and personal hygiene, learning appropriate techniques can improve students' health by preventing rashes, sores, and, in some cases, bladder and kidney infections (Gallender, 1980; Stauffer, 1983).

This chapter discusses approaches to teaching students with multiple disabilities to become more independent in toileting, dressing, grooming, and personal hygiene. Suggestions are provided for assessing students' behaviors and for adapting materials and instructional approaches to accommodate children with severe physical involvement. Emphasis is given to a team approach in all of these important skill areas.

TOILETING SKILLS

Typical Development of Voiding and Toileting Skills

Urinary System and Urination   The urinary system consists of two kidneys, two ureters, one bladder, and one urethra (Gallender, 1980) (see Figure 9.1). These organs excrete, store, and eliminate urine as waste, thus maintaining the body's fluid and electrolyte balance. Their functions are as follows:

- Kidneys: Extract urea and other substances from the blood
- Ureters: Tubes that transport urine from kidneys to bladder
- Bladder: Stores urine until it is voided
- Urethra: Tube that carries urine from bladder to the exterior to be expelled

The process of urination is basically a reflex act under voluntary control. When the bladder fills to a certain extent, the reflex is initiated, and the person has a desire to urinate. The restraint or inhibition is voluntarily removed, and urination follows automatically (Gallender, 1980; Yeates, 1973). This voluntary control, of course, does not develop in the typically developing child until between 2 and 3 years of age.

Gastrointestinal Tract and Defecation   The gastrointestinal tract consists mainly of the stomach, small intestine, and large intestine (see Figure 9.2). The food in the stomach mixes with gastric juices and enters the duodenum, or the first part of the small intestine (Schaefer, 1979). Much of the food mixture, now in a semiliquid state, is absorbed by the large intestine (colon). The remainder is formed into feces or stools. The colon pushes the stool to the lower part of the intestine and into the rectum to be evacuated.

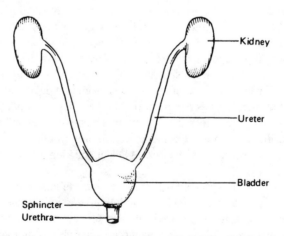

Kidney

Ureter

Bladder

Sphincter

Urethra

Figure 9.1.   The urinary system. (From Schaefer, C.E. [1979]. *Childhood encopresis and enuresis: Causes and therapy,* p. 99. New York: Van Nostrand Reinhold; reprinted by permission.)

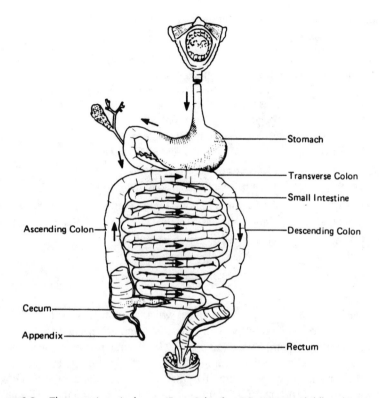

Figure 9.2.   The gastrointestinal tract. (From Schaefer, C.E. [1979]. *Childhood encopresis and enuresis: Causes and therapy,* p. 12. New York: Van Nostrand Reinhold; reprinted by permission.)

The ability to control bowel movements is related to tightening and relaxing two circular muscles (sphincters) that circle the anus. The muscle near the outside, the external sphincter, comes under voluntary control around age 2 or 3 years (Myers, Cerone, & Olson, 1981). The internal sphincter usually opens automatically when a stool fills the rectum.

Toileting Skills   The ability to urinate or defecate at appropriate times and places involves more than voluntarily constricting or relaxing certain muscles. Children without disabilities follow a predictable developmental sequence, as depicted in Table 9.1. Two points, however, should be noted. First, several of the more advanced toileting skills, such as managing clothes and seating oneself on the toilet, may never be possible for many students with multiple disabilities because of their pronounced motor impairments. Even more basic skills (e.g., signaling the need to go) may be difficult for some children. It is important to avoid requiring of the child too many nonphysiological, developmental prerequisites before initiating a training program.

Table 9.1.   Typical developmental sequence of toileting skills

Approximate age	Toileting skill
10 months	Child indicates when wet or soiled
12 months	Regularity of bowel movements
15 months	Child will sit on toilet when placed there and supervised (short time)
18–21 months	Regularity of urination
20 months	Toileting becomes regulated
22 months	Child indicates need to go to toilet
24 months	Daytime control with occasional accidents Must be reminded to go to bathroom
30 months	Child tells someone he or she needs to go to bathroom
34 months	Child seats self on toilet
3–4 years	Goes to bathroom independently May need help with clothing
4–5 years	Completely independent

The second point concerns the age at which an individual with disabilities is ready for toilet training. Surprisingly, there is no empirical evidence to answer this question. Lohmann, Eyman, and Lask (1967), in a review of institutional records, concluded that residents around 6 years old with an IQ of 20 or greater had a better chance of being toilet trained than older residents with lower (between 10 and 20) IQ scores. Smith and Smith (1977) found that residents in institutions under age 20 progressed faster than adults over 25 and that children with mental disabilities requiring intermittent support did better than residents with mental disabilities requiring more extensive support. In addition, Foxx and Azrin (1973a) suggested that their procedures might work best for individuals with mental disabilities requiring extensive support who are over 5 years old. No study, however, reports an attempt to train younger (2½–5 years) children with multiple disabilities, so an answer is not available for them. A prudent course would be to follow the advice of Snell (1980) and Snell and Farlow (1993) to provide training regardless of level of disability, assuming the child is medically sound and physiologically mature.

Assessing Toileting Skills

Assessment in toileting encompasses three areas: assessing readiness, assessing elimination patterns, and assessing related skills.

Assessing Readiness   It was intimated in the previous section that children who are candidates for toilet training should exhibit certain essential prerequisites. In addition to a suggested minimum chronological age of 2½ years, Snell and Farlow (1993) listed two other prerequisites: 1) a stable pattern of elimination, such that voiding occurs within certain daily time periods; and

2) daily periods of dryness. Campbell (1977) also included 1) freedom from medical problems that preclude training, 2) adequate liquid intake, and 3) ability to be properly positioned on a potty chair. Once the student has a thorough medical examination to rule out any obvious organic problems, his or her patterns of elimination and dryness are easily determined by using a simple chart.

Assessing Elimination Patterns A chart of the child's toileting behavior proves helpful to detect when the child 1) is wet or dry, 2) has urinated or defecated, and 3) has voided in a toilet rather than elsewhere. (Because many students with multiple disabilities are nonambulatory, they will be unable to take themselves to a toilet facility.) A sample chart, constructed for one child for 1 week, is presented in Figure 9.3. The child should be checked at half-hour intervals and the appropriate notation marked. This particular chart covers a 24-hour period and can be marked by both parents and school staff. A small period that includes only the school day can be used instead. Daytime regulation and training typically precede nighttime training, although it is possible for a child to be dry at night but not during the day (MacKeith, Meadow, & Turner, 1973). How long the charting of elimination patterns should continue will vary depending on the student's regularity and the type of training to be done. It is important to take enough data upon which to base a training program (usually between 7 and 15 days). It is also essential to change students' clothing after detecting accidents to avoid confusing new accidents with earlier ones (Snell & Farlow, 1993).

Figure 9.3. Chart for assessing toilet training.

Assessing Related Skills   It is helpful to the toilet-training process if the student can perform parts or all of such related skills as adjusting clothing, flushing, wiping, and washing hands. As indicated previously, however, students unable to perform these skills should not be kept from a toilet-training program. More specific information on dressing is covered later in this chapter. Other skills can be assessed through a task-analytic format, in which the skills are broken down into steps, and the student's performance on those steps is recorded. The child with limited use of motor or sensory systems can be taught to do parts of related skills or alternatives to traditional methods of performing those skills through individualized adaptations and the use of partial participation (see Chapters 4 and 10).

Positioning for Toileting

Prior to beginning training, it is important to establish a comfortable position for the student on the toilet. Ideally, the head and shoulders should be slightly forward and in midline, the arms relaxed and close to the body, the hips at approximately a 90° angle, the knees bent, and the feet supported (Finnie, 1975; Gibson, 1980) (see Chapter 3). Many children with multiple disabilities are unable to assume this exact sitting posture, but approximations to it should be attempted because it is important for the student's own sense of comfort and well-being and for the success of the program that the student be relaxed and secure. Voiding requires voluntary relaxation of muscles, which is difficult when the body is struggling to maintain balance.

Toileting adaptations for young children with cerebral palsy are depicted by Finnie (1975). The student with severe impairment might benefit from the box-type potty chair shown in Figure 9.4. This chair provides support at the front, back, and sides as well as at the head and feet. (Bergen, 1974, provides procedures for constructing this chair.)

Several other possible adaptations for the training area include 1) a stepping stool to help a small child get on the toilet, with rubber matting on the stool and underneath it to prevent slipping; 2) nonslippery floor, with either well-fastened carpeting or a rubber mat around the toilet; and 3) removing the bathroom door to allow the child using a wheelchair, walker, or crutches to enter more easily (Calkin, Grant, & Bowman, 1978). School-based occupational therapists or physical therapists can provide much help in determining and fashioning specific adaptations.

Because toileting success is facilitated by consistent use across settings, the family may desire help in adapting the bathroom in their home. If the child uses a wheelchair, the doorway into the room should be 36 inches wide, with enough clearance to allow the child to move the wheelchair up to the side of the toilet (Palmer & Toms, 1992). Other environmental considerations are the location and type of grab bars and the location of the toilet paper dispenser, sink, mirror, and towel rack. In short, modifications should aim toward accommodating the child's functional movement and providing for maximum independence.

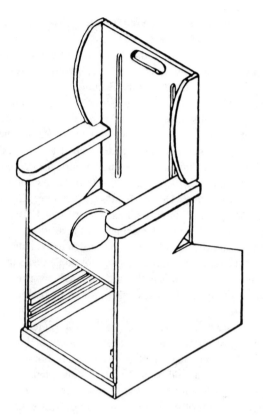

Figure 9.4.   Box-type potty chair.

Transferring the child to and from a wheelchair to the toilet should be carefully planned and executed. The small space in many bathrooms makes manipulation of the wheelchair difficult (Palmer & Toms, 1992). Readers are urged to review the general guidelines for transfers presented in Chapter 3.

Methods of Toilet Training Students

The zero-reject principle, put into practice by PL 99-457, the Education of the Handicapped Act Amendments of 1986, terminated the common practice of refusing to accept children with enuresis or encopresis (involuntary urination or defecation) into public school programs. Unfortunately, some community-based vocational and residential programs still refuse to accept individuals who are not toilet trained. Numerous studies since the 1970s have demonstrated that most people with severe or profound disabilities can be taught to regulate their toileting behaviors and to decrease their rate of accidents (e.g., Foxx & Azrin, 1973b; Lancioni, 1980).

Several cautions are in order, however. First, although individuals with severe disabilities were studied in much of the research, experimenters frequently excluded people who were nonambulatory (e.g., Baumeister & Klosowski, 1965; Hundziak, Maurer, & Watson, 1965). Because many students with multiple disabilities are nonambulatory and have additional sensory, behavior, and medical problems, it is not always possible to apply procedures in their entirety from one group of individuals to another. Second, the great majority of studies were performed in institutional settings, where the environment, staffing, and motivation to train typically differ from those in public school programs. This is especially true of the studies in the 1960s and early 1970s, when educational programs in residential facilities were not required. Third, the exact procedures for toilet training are not detailed in many studies, and the degree of experimental control is often slight. It is therefore hard to tell what part of a package of procedures made the difference. One early study (Bensberg, Colwell, & Cassel, 1965) even speculated that all or part of their success may have been the result of the increased amount of personal attention given the resident.

Despite these caveats, however, there is sufficient evidence, including hundreds of successful cases, that individuals with multiple disabilities can be toilet trained with thoughtfully designed and executed programs. This section describes several of the techniques that have been included in successful programs.

Early Research on Toilet Training   Ellis (1963) presented a 15-step plan for a toilet-training program that detailed who should be included, what they should be given to eat, on what schedule the program should be conducted, and even what the attendants should wear. The model and plan, although theoretical in nature, stimulated research with individuals with mental retardation in institutions with varying degrees of success (Baumeister & Klosowski, 1965; Bensberg et al., 1965; Dayan, 1964; Giles & Wolf, 1966; Hundziak, Maurer, & Watson, 1965; Kimbrell, Luckey, Barbuto, & Love, 1967; Levine & Elliott, 1970; Lohmann et al., 1967; Roos & Oliver, 1969). None of these studies, however, included individuals with severe physical disabilities. Many of them were designed to reduce administrative costs and attendant care. The major measure of success in two of the studies, in fact, was a decrease in the amount of soiled laundry (Dayan, 1964; Levine & Elliott, 1970). Even studies that were relatively well designed (e.g., Giles & Wolf, 1966) suffered from ethically questionable procedures, including restraining residents in jackets and tethering them with ropes.

Foxx and Azrin Procedures   Azrin and Foxx (1971) toilet trained nine adults with mental retardation requiring pervasive support and 34 children without disabilities (Foxx & Azrin, 1973b). Their procedures, detailed in an often-cited book (Foxx & Azrin, 1973b), ushered in the more modern era of toilet training research and practice. This section describes the main components of the Foxx and Azrin program.

Increased Fluid Consumption   Toilet training requires that individuals have numerous opportunities to practice and to be reinforced. As a way of increasing elimination, Foxx and Azrin (1973b) gave residents extra fluids (e.g., coffee, tea, soft drinks, water) to induce more frequent urination, a technique referred to as *rapid toilet training*. It should be noted that the Foxx and Azrin procedures were developed with adult residents in a state school for people with mental retardation. School staff contemplating using a rapid technique for children with multiple disabilities should consult with a nurse or physician to determine an appropriate liquid to use. It is best to avoid giving children large amounts of caffeine and sugar or other fluids (e.g., apple juice) that might cause or aggravate constipation or other health problems. Perhaps more important, forcing liquids over an extended period may lead to a condition called *hyponatremia*. Marked by nausea, vomiting, seizures, and even coma, hyponatremia requires emergency medical care (Thompson & Hanson, 1983). No staff should begin a toilet-training program that uses hydration without first having the student medically evaluated.

Bladder Training   The first phase of the toilet-training program, bladder training, is designed for the person to gain control over his or her bladder and bowel muscles so that elimination occurs only on the toilet. The sequence for this phase is presented in Table 9.2. A prompting–fading procedure is used throughout bladder training. Prompts appropriate to the learner's skill level (ver-

Table 9.2.   Sequence of steps in bladder-training procedure

(Step one is begun exactly on the half-hour)
1. Give as much fluid to the resident as he [or she] will drink while seated in his [or her] chair.
   a. Wait about 1 minute.
2. Direct resident to sit on toilet seat using the minimal possible prompt.
3. Direct resident to pull his [or her] pants down using the minimal possible prompt.
4. a. When resident voids, give edible and praise while seated, then direct him [or her] to stand.
   b. If resident does not void within 20 minutes after drinking the fluids, direct him [or her] to stand.
5. Direct resident to pull up his [or her] pants using the minimal possible prompt.
   a. If resident voided, direct him [or her] to flush the toilet using the minimal possible prompt.
6. Direct resident to his [or her] chair using the minimal possible prompt.
7. After resident has been sitting for 5 minutes, inspect him [or her] for dry pants.
   a. If pants are dry, give edible and praise.
   b. If pants are wet, only show him [or her] the edible and admonish him [or her].
8. Check resident for dry pants every 5 minutes.
9. At the end of 30 minutes, begin the sequence of steps again.

From *Toilet Training Persons with Developmental Disabilities* (p. 45) by R.M. Foxx and N.H. Azrin, 1973, Champaign, IL: Research Press. Copyright 1973 by the authors. Reprinted by permission.

bal, gestural, and/or physical) are provided to teach approaching the toilet, pulling down pants, and so forth and are faded as soon as possible. Obviously, many students with severe physical disabilities may require help with some or all of the steps, even after bladder control has been achieved.

Dry-Pants Inspection   As Table 9.2 indicates, individuals are checked every 5 minutes to detect whether they are wet or dry. This procedure includes 1) asking the person, "Are you dry?", using gestures if appropriate; 2) prompting the person to feel his or her crotch area; and 3) reinforcing the person for dry pants or admonishing for wet pants and withholding reinforcement. Dry-pants inspection can be used as part of any toilet-training program and should be performed less frequently in programs that did not increase fluids. Step 2 (feeling the crotch area) could also be modified for students lacking the necessary arm movements.

Accident Treatment   During bladder training, Foxx and Azrin (1973b) used a "brief cleanliness training procedure" when an individual had an accident. The procedure consists of grasping the person and stating, "No, you wet your pants," and requiring him or her to wash the chair and floor. During self-initiation training (see the following section), accidents are followed by the "full cleanliness" procedure. The individual must secure a mop and bucket, wipe up the area, clean and return the materials, change his or her clothes, and wash the wet clothes. Following this procedure, the individual is made to practice the toileting procedure (walk to toilet, lower pants, sit, arise, raise pants, and so forth) six times. Most children with multiple disabilities are physically unable to perform such a procedure, and the time it takes the staff member to complete it renders it impractical in school settings. Smith (1979) discovered that a reprimand and a 10-minute time-out from reinforcement worked equally as well as the cleanliness training for children with severe disabilities.

A 10-year follow-up of the 10 individuals in the Smith (1979) study revealed that the original reduction in incontinent episodes following intensive toilet training was well maintained (Hyams, McCoull, Smith, & Tyrer, 1992). In contrast, independence was not maintained. Hyams et al. suggest that "inappropriate prompting by staff was the most important factor in failure to maintain complete independence at toilet" (p. 557).

Self-Initiation Training   Once the learner initiates toileting without prompting, self-initiation training begins. Table 9.3 presents this procedure. Note that many individuals with multiple disabilities will be unable to initiate ambulating to the toilet. Others may ambulate to the proper location, but find it difficult to move themselves onto the commode. Gibson (1980) described several types of techniques children can use to transfer to and from a toilet, both with and without assistance. As with all physical care procedures, proper body mechanics and handling techniques are essential (see Chapter 3).

Moisture-Signaling Devices   Foxx and Azrin (1973b) used two special devices that detect moisture and emit an auditory signal (Azrin, Bugle, &

Table 9.3. Self-initiation training procedure

1. Give fluids immediately following an elimination.
2. No further toilet-approach prompts are given.
3. Continue to provide guidance and prompts for dressing and undressing and for flushing the toilet, if necessary, but never at a level greater than that needed on previous toiletings.
4. Move resident's chair farther from the toilet after each successful self-initiation.
5. Gradually lengthen the time between dry-pants inspections.
6. Intermittently reward correct toileting.
7. When resident is self-initiating from the area where he [or she] spends most of his [or her] time, remove urine alert from the toilet bowl, pants alarm from resident's briefs, and the chair.
8. Require resident to show you that he [or she] can find the toilet from various areas on the ward.
9. Include resident on the Maintenance Program after 9 self-initiations.

From *Toilet Training Persons with Developmental Disabilities* (p. 54) by R.M. Foxx and N.H. Azrin, 1973, Champaign, IL: Research Press. Copyright 1973 by the authors. Reprinted by permission.

O'Brien, 1971). The function of these devices is to alert the trainer at the moment of voiding, thus facilitating implementation of reinforcement and cleanliness-training procedures. One such device is a pants alarm (depicted in Figure 9.5), which signals the presence of wetness. The other device is a urine alert (Figure 9.6), which fits into a toilet bowl and signals urination or defecation.

Other researchers have used similar signaling devices. Van Wagenen and associates (Van Wagenen, Meyerson, Kerr, & Mahoney, 1969; Van Wagenen & Murdock, 1966) fitted children with auditory signal generators that sounded a tone while the child was urinating. A later study (Mahoney, Van Wagenen, &

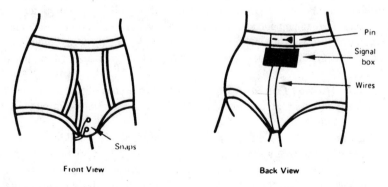

Figure 9.5. Pants alarm. (From *Toilet Training Persons with Developmental Disabilities* [p. 32] by R.M. Foxx & N.H. Azrin, 1973, Champaign, IL: Research Press. Copyright 1973 by the authors. Reprinted by permission.)

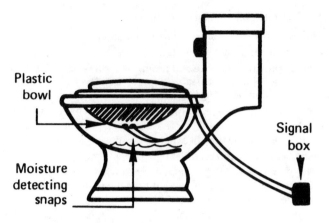

Figure 9.6. Urine alert. (From *Toilet Training Persons with Developmental Disabilities* [p. 30] by R.M. Foxx & N.H. Azrin, 1973, Champaign, IL: Research Press. Copyright 1973 by the authors. Reprinted by permission.)

Meyerson, 1971) used a modified device by 1) adding a miniature transistor radio receiver through which an audio alert was triggered by an FM transmitter, and 2) replacing speakers with earphones. These devices were used to prompt correct responding toward the toilet, rather than to signal the trainer when reinforcement or punishment was needed. Herreshoff (1973) provided schematics for constructing electronic devices that operate a relay switch to activate a light or any electric appliance, rather than sounding a tone. A list of commercially available antienuretic devices has been compiled by Mountjoy, Ruben, and Bradford (1984).

The use of electronic devices may facilitate toilet training but cannot be viewed as an essential part of a training procedure. They certainly should never be used to replace techniques of systematic prompting and reinforcement. Moreover, Snell and Farlow (1993) criticize moisture-signaling equipment as being potentially stigmatizing and simply infeasible in general education classes and in the community. It is extremely unlikely that technology in the form of automated elimination-signaling devices (Watson, 1968) will ever replace a caring teacher or parent.

Other Training Procedures   This section examines other training procedures, many based on Foxx and Azrin (1973b), and their applications to other individuals and settings.

Variations of Foxx and Azrin   Many individuals have children or adults (who are toilet trained) with mental retardation requiring limited to extensive support who use procedures based largely on those used by Foxx and Azrin (1973b). Williams and Sloop (1978) trained six individuals using all of these procedures except for moisture-signaling devices. Smith, Britton, Johnson, and Thomas (1975) taught five adults with mental retardation requiring pervasive support using shorter time-out periods and less intense cleanliness-training procedures. Full cleanliness procedures were used to treat encopresis in an 8-year-old boy with mental retardation requiring limited support (Doleys & Arnold, 1975). Finally, Trott (1977) reported successful application of the Foxx and Azrin procedures with an 11-year-old boy in a public school setting.

Mahoney et al. (1971) Procedure   Mahoney et al.'s technique is distinctly different from the Foxx and Azrin procedure. The learner is taught to approach the toilet in response to an auditory signal (see the previous section, "Moisture-Signaling Devices"). Training proceeds through six phases:

1. The student walks to the toilet in response to an auditory signal.
2. The student lowers his or her pants after a signal.
3. The student sits on or stands at the toilet.
4. The student drinks liquids. (The student voids in the toilet.)
5. The student pulls up his or her pants.
6. The student practices the preceding steps without a signal.

Although Mahoney et al. (1971) found their technique successful, it is somewhat limited for children with multiple disabilities, who often lack the ability to walk independently or to manipulate their clothing. A study that compared these procedures to the Foxx and Azrin procedures, however, revealed that the transistorized equipment used with the latter was difficult for staff to maintain and use, in addition to being expensive (Smith, 1979).

Training with Individuals with Other Disabilities   Two studies reported attempts to toilet train children with autism. The earlier study (Marshall, 1966) used salt to reinforce initial toileting plus punishment (slap on the buttocks) for accidents after 2 weeks. Five children with autism in Japan were given similar reinforcement and punishment, with varying degrees of success (Ando, 1977).

Finally, nine students who are deaf-blind were toilet trained with a variation of the Foxx and Azrin procedures (Lancioni, 1980). Treatment was conducted for only 4 hours daily. To accommodate the students' sensory impairments 1) they were taught to touch the toilet stall door on their way to the commode, 2) edible reinforcers were brought into contact with their lips, and 3) tactile reinforcement (rubbing students' backs) was used. The researchers found that cleanliness training was not feasible because the total physical guidance necessary to help students clean the urine was reinforcing to them.

Ethical Issues in Toilet Training   Some of the procedures used in standard toilet training, including those described in this chapter, must be viewed as ethically and/or educationally questionable. First, no study has demonstrated the effectiveness of aversive techniques; indeed, there is reason to believe that eliminating those techniques is at least equally effective. Second, such techniques are likely to lose their effectiveness over time; students will retaliate by withholding voiding and thus preventing being punished. Third, the techniques are difficult on everyone, including the staff, family, and, of course, student. One parent

(Dunklee, 1989) described the torture on her and her family of being required to withhold food from their 9-year-old son after he had accidents. Fourth, treating children with aversive techniques is morally wrong. We concur with Snell and Farlow (1993), who conclude that

> *It is better to use carefully designed and socially valid teaching methods based on what is known about toileting but that are not precisely data-based approaches than to use procedures based solely on published data but that are socially invalid...or that use educationally questionable practices.* (p. 394, emphasis in original)

Irregular Enuresis   Irregular enuresis, or wetting on a sporadic basis, was treated in three boys with mental retardation requiring limited to extensive support (Barmann, Katz, O'Brien, & Beauchamp, 1981). Procedures included a shortened version of the Foxx and Azrin procedure, with verbal praise for staying dry and cleanliness training for having accidents. A unique feature of this study was its implementation in the boys' homes, with parents as trainers, and with data recorded concurrently at school. The children reduced their accidents to zero, even when teachers only performed dry-pants checks and praised the children for staying dry.

Nighttime Toilet Training   The preceding material concentrated on daytime toilet-training programs. A common problem among people with multiple disabilities (and in children who do not have disabilities) is nocturnal enuresis, or bed-wetting. This section briefly examines procedures that have proved successful in nighttime toilet training.

Traditional Procedures   Snell (1980) summarized the following components of traditional nighttime procedures:

1. Reducing fluids 1½–2 hours before bedtime
2. Toileting just before bedtime
3. Giving simple instructions to the child about receiving a reward for a dry bed in the morning
4. Performing regular awakenings and recording accidents and successes every 1–1½ hours during the parents' or caregivers' working hours
5. Guiding the child to the toilet for 5 minutes without allowing sleeping
6. Praising on-toilet eliminations and recording them
7. Changing wet linens, with awakening of child at an earlier time the next night

Bed-Wetting Equipment   The use of signaling devices to awaken the person who wets the bed goes back to the 1930s. Much of the research of the 1970s and 1980s on nocturnal enuresis has examined procedures that include using a bed pad that sets off a buzzer when wet (Azrin, Sneed, & Foxx, 1974; Baller, 1975; Bollard, 1982; Bollard & Nettelbeck, 1982; Bollard, Nettlebeck, & Roxbee, 1982; Bollard & Woodroffe, 1977; Lovibond, 1963). Sloop and Kennedy (1973) used such a device for night training of residents with mental retardation in a state training facility. Slightly over half of the individuals were successfully trained, with a relapse rate of 36%. Data on typical children show the alarm to be the most effective treatment for control of nocturnal enuresis (Maizels, Gandhi, Keating, & Rosenbaum, 1993).

Rapid Training Procedures   As with rapid training procedures for daytime toilet training, rapid nighttime-training procedures include increased fluid consumption. One specific rapid procedure designed by Azrin, Sneed, and Foxx (1973) also includes components similar to those used by Foxx and Azrin (1973a, 1973b) in their daytime-training protocol. Figure 9.7 outlines their dry-bed procedure as used in the home with enuretic children who do not have disabilities (Azrin et al., 1974). This procedure (in a slightly different format, to accommodate staff in institutions) significantly reduced nighttime accidents in 12 individuals with mental retardation requiring pervasive support (Azrin et al., 1973).

Smith (1981) used a modified version of the Azrin et al. (1973, 1974) program to train successfully five residents in England with severe or profound disabilities. Given that many early toilet-training studies purposely excluded people with such disabilities, it is notable that three of these individuals had behavior problems described as fairly major. Although Smith used the alarm, reinforcement, and increased fluids, she reduced the degree of punishment for accidents, using only a verbal reprimand and requiring the person to feel the "nasty wet bed." Day staff also expressed disapproval to the residents the day after an accident. No cleanliness training was used, as opposed to the procedure used by Azrin et al. (1973). It is clear that reinforcement for a dry bed was designed for the individual, including "tea and biscuits; long lie in bed; new trendy clothing to wear that day; and access to the juke box" (p. 69). Smith's (1981) nighttime procedure is important for individuals with multiple disabilities because it demonstrates, as did the Smith (1979) study of daytime training, that complicated, aversive punishment techniques may not be essential to the success of a program.

Alternative Toileting Techniques

Some children with multiple disabilities are physically unable to control the muscles that contribute to the normal processes of urination and defecation. These individuals cannot be toilet trained in the ways described in the previous sections of this chapter. Their bladder and bowel care are important for cleanliness, comfort, and overall health, however (Bigge, 1982). This section describes several of the alternative techniques for managing bladder and bowel functions. It should be stressed that general descriptions of procedures should never be substituted for individualized physical care protocols developed by medical personnel and implemented by trained practitioners in the educational setting.

Bladder Management   Often because of injuries to or maldevelopment of the spinal cord or because of other medical reasons, children are left with partial or total loss of bladder control. One of the most common causes in children with multiple disabilities is a condition in which the nervous system fails to form properly in the developing embryo. The infant is born with the spinal cord sev-

I.   Interview training (one night)
   (A) One hour before bedtime
      1. Child informed of all phases of training procedure
      2. Alarm placed on bed
      3. Positive practice in toileting (20 practice trials)
         (a) child lies down in bed
         (b) child counts to 50
         (c) child arises and attempts to urinate in toilet
         (d) child returns to bed
         (e) steps (a), (b), (c), and (d) repeated 20 times
   (B) At bedtime
      1. Child drinks fluids
      2. Child repeats training instructions to trainer
      3. Child retires for the night
   (C) Hourly awakenings
      1. Minimal prompt used to awaken child
      2. Child walks to bathroom
      3. At bathroom door (before urination), child is asked to inhibit urination for 1 hour (omit for children under 6)
         (a) if child could not inhibit urination
            (i)   child urinates in toilet
            (ii) trainer praises child for correct toileting
            (iii) child returns to bed
         (b) if child indicated that he could inhibit urination for one hour
            (i)   trainer praises child for his urinary control
            (ii) child returns to bed
      4. At bedside, the child feels the bed sheets and comments on their dryness
      5. Trainer praises child for having a dry bed
      6. Child is given fluids to drink
      7. Child returns to sleep
   (D) When an accident occurred
      1. Trainer disconnects alarm
      2. Trainer awakens child and reprimands him for wetting
      3. Trainer directs child to bathroom to finish urinating
      4. Child is given Cleanliness Training
         (a) child is required to change night clothes
         (b) child is required to remove wet bed sheet and place it with dirty laundry
         (c) trainer reactivates alarm
         (d) child obtains clean sheets and remakes bed
      5. Positive Practice in correct toileting (20 practice trials) performed immediately after the Cleanliness Training
      6. Positive Practice in correct toileting (20 practice trials) performed the following evening before bedtime

(continued)

Figure 9.7. Dry-bed procedure. (Reprinted from Azrin, N.H., Sneed, T.J., & Foxx, R.M. [1974]. Dry-bed training: Rapid elimination of childhood enuresis. *Behaviour Research and Therapy, 12*, 150–151, Copyright 1974, with kind permission from Elsevier Science Ltd., The Boulevard, Langford Lane, Kidlington OX5 1GB, UK.)

Figure 9.7.   *(continued)*

II. Post training supervision (begins the night after training)
  (A) Before bedtime
    1. Alarm is placed on bed
    2. Positive practice given (if an accident the previous night)
    3. Child is reminded of need to remain dry and of the need for Cleanliness Training and Positive Practice if wetting occured
    4. Child is asked to repeat the parent's instructions
  (B) Night-time toileting
    1. At parents' bedtime, they awaken child and send him to toilet
    2. After each dry night, parent awakens child 30 minutes earlier than on previous night
    3. Awakening discontinued when they are scheduled to occur within one hour of child's bedtime
  (C) When accidents occurred, child receives Cleanliness Training and Positive Practice immediately on wetting and at bedtime the next day
  (D) After a dry night
    1. Both parents praise child for not wetting his bed
    2. Parents praise child at least 5 times during the day
    3. Child's favorite relatives are encouraged to praise him

---

ered and partially enclosed in a sac along the back. This condition, known as myelomeningocele (a form of spina bifida or open spine), causes a neurogenic bladder because of the loss of connections of nerves to it (Myers et al., 1981). There are two types of neurogenic bladders—flaccid and spastic. Flaccid (limp or relaxed) bladder muscles cannot be tightened completely to force out all of the urine, which often results in continual leakage. Spastic (tight) bladders cannot store urine because even small amounts cause the bladder to tighten, causing leakage. The child with myelomeningocele needs a permanent alternative means of voiding. Three different bladder management strategies are 1) external catheters, 2) clean intermittent catheterization, and 3) surgical intervention.

External Catheters   Used with males, an external catheter is a urinary collection device (condom catheter) that is placed over the penis. A tube drains into a collection bag that is fastened to the child's leg with Velcro straps. It is important that the device fit well to avoid leakage or backflow of urine into the condom (Jones, 1985). Staff and parents can consult local surgical supply stores for help.

Clean Intermittent Catheterization (CIC)   This technique for emptying the bladder has gained wide acceptance since the mid-1970s. Children with neurogenic bladders can be tested to determine their eligibility for CIC. The purposes of CIC are 1) to prevent bladder distention through regular voiding, 2) to prevent kidney infection by controlling bladder infection, and 3) to reduce the social distress caused by wet clothes and odor (Stauffer, 1983). The technique involves inserting a catheter into the urethra to the bladder in order to drain off urine and collect it in a basin. The key to preventing infection is not the sterility, but the frequency, of catheterization (Altshuler, Meyer, & Butz, 1977). The procedure typically is performed every 3–4 hours during the day (Ault, Graff, & Rues, 1993). Children who are capable of performing CIC themselves are encouraged to do so (see Robertson, Alper, Schloss, & Wisniewski, 1992), although few individuals for whom this book is intended are able to be completely independent. Fortunately, school staff and parents can be taught CIC quite successfully (Wolraich, Hawtrey, Mapel, & Henderson, 1983). Children are sometimes given medications in conjunction with catheterization to prevent infections, relax the bladder, minimize irregular bladder contractions, or tighten the bladder sphincter (Taylor, 1990). Consultation with a urologist before and during CIC training is essential.

Surgical Intervention   Occasionally surgery is required to redirect the normal course of urine flow. One such intervention, designed to prevent progressive kidney disease, is the ileal conduit. The ureters are disconnected from the bladder and implanted in a segment of the small bowel, which is brought out to the surface of the abdomen. The segment is sutured there to form a hole, or stoma, through which urine passes. The child is fitted with a pouch to collect the urine. Medical personnel who specialize in this, called enterostomal therapists, can provide information and support on physical care and diet before and after the operation.

Bowel Management   In a way similar to having a neurogenic bladder, children may also possess a neurogenic bowel. Individuals with myelomeningocele often experience an absence of tone in their sphincter muscles, a loss of the sensation of fullness or need to evacuate, and sluggish bowel contractions. They may also have constipation, diarrhea, and impaction (each of which is discussed later in this section). Other people require surgery to facilitate removal of wastes. Any bowel-management program should be designed for regular emptying of the bowels with no leakage of stool in between (Myers et al., 1981). It should be noted that many children with multiple disabilities have bowel movements less frequently and less regularly than the typical individual. It is common for students with multiple disabilities, in fact, not to have bowel movements during the school day. Bowel-management programs in the school, therefore, should be coordinated carefully with home interventions.

Bowel Evacuation   One of the keys to helping students regulate their bowel movements is to help ensure a stool consistency that is fairly firm without being too hard. Two important factors that contribute to stool consistency are food and water intake. High-fiber foods should be included in the diet daily; these include whole grain products and edible skins of fruits and vegetables. Consultation with a dietitian can prove very helpful. Water is also essential to prevent stools from becoming too hard. If stools become loose, adjusting the diet should involve a change in foods rather than reduction of fluids.

Bowel evacuation also can be facilitated by proper positioning. Although a squatting or flexed position usually is best, some students may find it easier to assume a left sidelying position, with hips and knees flexed and shoulders forward (Ault et al., 1993).

Bowel evacuation can take advantage of the peristaltic action of the stomach occurring after meals. This action can be triggered by digital stimulation (i.e., the stimulation of the anal sphincter with one's finger) (Jones, 1985). It is possible to check for the presence of a stool inside the rectum by using a gloved lubricated finger. (This should be done only by a parent, nurse, or other qualified professional.)

Occasionally a large mass of hard stool will collect in the rectum, creating an impaction (Myers et al., 1981). The child with this impaction often has frequent soft stools in small amounts, because the mass holds the sphincters open and allows the liquid stool to slip around and pass through. Impactions must be removed, often with an enema to help soften the stool. Sometimes glycerin suppositories are used to help evacuate a normal stool that does not move (Jones, 1985).

Finally, laxatives often are administered to facilitate bowel evacuation. There are four basic types: 1) a stool softener with a substance designed to break surface tension and keep the stool moist; 2) a bulk former, which absorbs water and keeps the stool soft; 3) an irritant to stimulate peristalsis; and 4) a purgative, usually used to empty the bowel before testing or surgery. Many laxatives are combinations of any of these four types. Physicians and pharmacists should be consulted for the correct type and form for a given child (Jones, 1985). Laxatives should not be a substitute for a regular bowel-management program, including exercise when possible (Cheever & Elmer, 1975).

Constipation and Diarrhea   Constipation is a common problem in children with multiple disabilities because they are inactive, eat inadequate amounts of fiber, do not drink enough fluids, and often are in poor health. Preventing constipation through a sensible and individualized bowel-management program is the best approach to this problem (Klauser & Muller-Lissner, 1993). Otherwise, removing stools can be done through the techniques described in the preceding section. Prolonged constipation can lead to urinary tract infections, especially in girls (Graff, Ault, Guess, Taylor, & Thompson, 1990).

Diarrhea, an intestinal disorder characterized by soft or watery bowel movements, is often a symptom of an illness or food intolerance (Jones, 1985). Because the stools are watery, diarrhea can be confused with impactions. The most serious consequence of diarrhea is the loss of water, which usually is reabsorbed into the body during the passage of feces through the colon. Water loss can lead to dehydration, a serious condition needing prompt medical care (Graff et al., 1990). Mild diarrhea can be controlled by a diet of clear liquids such as apple juice, with the gradual addition of foods like bananas, rice, applesauce, and toast (Jones, 1985). A child unable to eat these foods should be taken to a doctor for possible medications. Very young children and infants with diarrhea should see a physician.

Surgical Intervention   Because of certain diseases or conditions that involve the small or large intestine or the rectum, some individuals require surgery to create an alternative method of removing bowel contents. When the end of the small intestine (ileum) is brought out through the abdominal wall, the procedure is termed an *ileostomy*. When a portion of the large intestine (colon) is involved, the procedure is called a *colostomy*. In both cases, the patient discharges fecal matter through a hole, or stoma, in the abdominal wall.

School personnel who work with a student with an ileostomy or colostomy need to understand how to handle the external collecting appliances. Although the collection pouches are usually changed at home, a bag may become loose or leak at school (Ault et al., 1993). In addition, the student will be placed on a specific diet that needs to be followed carefully. Typically, this involves a progression from a clear liquid to a low-fiber diet, in small quantities (Graff et al., 1990). Finally, the ostomy equipment needs to be reevaluated over time; the child's growth may affect the size and location of the stoma (Morse & Colatarci, 1994). Teachers, therapists, school nurses, and others are encouraged to consult *These Special Children* (Geter, 1982), a book written for parents of children who have had ostomies.

DRESSING SKILLS

This section focuses on strategies for selecting, assessing, and teaching dressing skills. The final section discusses selecting and adapting clothing, both closely linked to success in dressing.

Typical Development of Dressing Skills

It is helpful to remember that dressing skills require relatively sophisticated and coordinated movements of almost every body part. A child who does not have disabilities is about 12 months old before he or she cooperates in even a simple way with dressing and is age 5 years or older before becoming completely independent (Finnie, 1975). Table 9.4 presents the order in which children without disabilities usually acquire dressing and undressing skills. This information should not suggest that children with multiple disabilities will or should learn these skills in the same sequence or in the same fashion. Nor should the chronological ages listed in the table be used to exclude children at given "functioning levels" or "mental ages" from participating in dressing programs. It is apparent from a typical developmental sequence, however, that certain skills (e.g., undressing, using gross motor actions) tend to be easier and learned faster than others (e.g., dressing, fastening buttons). This information can be useful in developing general guidelines for selecting target skills for instruction.

Table 9.4. Typical developmental sequence of dressing skills

Approximate age	Dressing skill
12 months	Begins to cooperate by holding out foot for shoe, arm for sleeve
12–18 months	Begins to remove hat, socks, mittens
2 years	Removes unlaced shoes, socks, and pants
2½ years	Removes all clothing Can put on socks, shirt, coat
3 years	Undresses rapidly and well Dresses, except for heavy outer clothing
4 years	Dresses and undresses with little assistance

Selecting Dressing Skills for Instruction

A glance at early curricula for students with severe disabilities (e.g., Tawney, Knapp, O'Reilly, & Pratt, 1979; Williams & Fox, 1979) quickly reveals a range of dressing and undressing skills from which to choose. It becomes clear that no child with multiple disabilities can learn all of the possible skills at one time. Moreover, most curricula fail to organize the various skills in a sequence designed for the individual with severe disabilities. Table 9.5 presents a sequence based on the complexity of motor acts required for dressing, from easier to more difficult (Campbell, 1977). This progression, as with others, serves as a rough guide only; the physical and cognitive abilities of individual students

Table 9.5. Sequence of dressing based on motor complexity

Removing clothing
  Removes hat, mittens
  Removes socks from toes
  Takes arms from sleeves of garment with front opening
  Takes legs from pants when pants have been pulled to knees
  Takes arms from sleeves of pullover garment
  Removes shoes (laces untied)
  Removes socks
  Removes pants
  Removes pullover garment
Putting on clothing
  Puts arms through large armholes on garment with front opening
  Puts head into pullover garment
  Pulls on pants
  Puts on shoes
  Puts on socks

Adapted from Campbell (1977).

must be assessed to help determine individualized teaching targets. Furthermore, the complexity of a specific dressing skill can be reduced by modifying the materials.

Decisions on selecting dressing skills should reflect the following considerations:

1. The wishes of the parents or caregivers for the student to learn specific skills
2. The frequency with which the student needs to use the skill during the day
3. The importance of learning the skill for moving into a less restrictive vocational or residential setting
4. An analysis of the features of the student's clothing
5. The degree to which learning the skill would facilitate acquisition of other important skills (e.g., toileting)

In short, the student should be taught simpler undressing and dressing skills first, but not at the expense of learning *meaningful* skills.

Assessing Dressing Skills

Assessment is done for two purposes. First, an overall evaluation of the student's dressing abilities can be used to help determine a starting point for instruction and to gain information on how the student moves to perform various tasks. Second, ongoing assessment of performance on specific dressing tasks is used to monitor progress and to make decisions about possible changes in instructional procedures.

The first type of assessment, the overall evaluation, is best achieved through criterion-referenced checklists. Figure 9.8 presents an example (Copeland, Ford, & Solon, 1976). Space is provided for recording information on how the child attempts each item. A physical or occupational therapist, working with a teacher, can gain valuable information on the *quality* of a student's movements, which is equally important as knowing whether a student performed a particular action. It is important to remember that commercially published checklists typically fail to yield specific information on individual students that can be readily translated into instructional objectives. Moreover, tasks often need to be divided into smaller parts to accommodate the learning and physical needs of a particular child.

The second type of assessment, ongoing assessment, is used to determine the performance of a student on a particular skill both before and throughout instruction. Figure 9.9 depicts a data sheet used to assess a child's ability to remove a jacket. This format reflects a task-analytic approach to data collection. Performance on each of the steps is recorded with a simple plus or minus. The data sheet depicts the cues given to the student, the materials, the response latency (the time allowed between the initial cue and the beginning of the student's response), and the criterion for success. The student whose data sheet appears in Figure 9.9 has just completed her fifth instructional session on this task.

Child's name: Date: Pretest of dressing skills	Independent	Verbal assistance	Physical assistance	Description of method child uses to complete the task
Undressing trousers, skirt 1. Pushes garment from waist to ankles 2. Pushes garment off one leg 3. Pushes garment off other leg				
Dressing trousers, skirt 1. Lays trousers in front of self with front side up 2. Inserts one foot into waist opening 3. Inserts other foot into waist opening 4. Pulls garment up to waist				
Undressing socks 1. Pushes sock down off heel 2. Pulls toe of sock pulling sock off foot				
Dressing socks 1. Positions sock correctly with heel-side down 2. Holds sock open at top 3. Inserts toes into sock 4. Pulls sock over heel 5. Pulls sock up				
Undressing cardigan 1. Takes dominant arm out of sleeve 2. Gets coat off back 3. Pulls other arm from sleeve				
Dressing cardigan flip-over method 1. Lays garment on table or floor in front of self 2. Gets dominant arm into sleeve 3. Other arm into sleeve 4. Positions coat on back				
Undressing polo shirt 1. Takes dominant arm out of sleeve 2. Pulls garment over head 3. Pulls other arm from sleeve				
Dressing polo shirt 1. Lays garment in front of self 2. Opens bottom of garment and puts arms into sleeves 3. Pulls garment over head 4. Pulls garment down to waist				
Undressing shoes 1. Loosens laces 2. Pulls shoe off heel 3. Pulls front of shoe to pull shoe off of toes				
Dressing shoes 1. Prepares shoe by loosening laces and pulling tongue of shoe out of the way 2. Inserts toes into shoe 3. Pushes shoe on over heel				

Figure 9.8.   Checklist of dressing skills. (From Copeland, M., Ford, L., & Solon, N. [1976]. *Occupational therapy for mentally retarded children*, p. 95. Baltimore: University Park Press; reprinted by permission of author.)

Strategies for Teaching Dressing Skills

Positioning   As with all other activities, dressing is facilitated when the student has been properly positioned. The choice of position is largely determined by the individual's postural tone and movement patterns and by the actions required in the specific dressing task. Thus, consultation with a therapist is strongly encouraged. Parents also can provide helpful information because they have more practice than anyone else and often develop useful tricks.

Teacher: Lesley Bain   Instructional Cue: "Take off your jacket and hang it up."
Target Behavior: Remove the jacket and hang it up   Setting: Near coat hooks   Times: After all trips outside
Student: Christina   Assessment Procedure: Single opportunity

	DATE	9-10	9-11	9-12	9-13	9-14
1	Grab the jacket (both zipper edges at waist)	+	-	+	+	-
2	Pull up and back	-	-	+	+	-
3	Let go	-	-	-	-	-
4	Straighten arms (at sides)	-	-	-	-	-
5	Grab the cuff (behind back, opposite hand)	-	-	-	-	-
6	Pull your arm out (straighten both arms)	-	-	-	-	-
7	Let go (of cuff)	-	-	-	-	-
8	Grab the other cuff (with other hand)	-	-	-	-	-
9	Pull your arm out (don't drop jacket)	-	-	-	-	-
10	Grab the collar (other hand)	-	-	-	-	-
11	Let go (of cuff)	-	-	-	-	-
12	Grab the collar (turn inside away, then grab collar)	-	-	-	-	-
13	Hang it on the hook (no falling)	-	-	-	-	-
	Total %	8%	0%	8%	8%	0%

Materials: Jacket (unbuttoned, unzipped) on student   Recording Key: + correct   - incorrect

Response Latency: 3 seconds   Criterion: 3 consecutive days 100% performance

Figure 9.9. Data sheet used to assess a child's ability to remove a jacket, which reflects a task-analytic approach to data collection. Performance on each of the steps is recorded with a single plus or minus. (From Snell, M.E. [1990]. Basic self-care instruction for students without motor impairments. In M. Snell [Ed.], *Systematic instruction of people with severe handicaps* [3rd ed., p. 378]; reprinted by permission of Prentice Hall, Upper Saddle River, NJ.)

Guidelines for positioning children with neuromotor involvement for dressing activities (Connor, Williamson, & Siepp, 1978; Copeland & Kimmel, 1989; Finnie, 1975) follow:

1. Dressing children when they are supine (on their backs) should be avoided. Most children in this position have a tendency to push their head and shoulders back and to straighten and stiffen their hips and legs. Children on their backs also are unable to see and are likely to become uninterested in the activity. (It is, however, sometimes necessary to dress older, heavier children in this position. In these cases, a hard pillow should be placed under the child's head and his or her shoulders should be raised slightly.)
2. Children should be dressed while they are sitting, if possible. They should be made to feel secure in this position. Children who cannot sit and maintain their balance unsupported are easier to dress if they sit with their backs to you and lean forward. Children who can maintain their balance unsupported can use hard surfaces, such as walls, for stability.
3. Children should be dressed on their sides when sitting is not possible. Side-lying often relaxes children, makes bringing their shoulders and head forward easier, facilitates bending their legs and feet, and enables them to see.
4. Infants should be dressed in prone (on their stomachs) across one's lap. Sometimes diapering can be performed in this position, as well, especially if the infant tends to push his or her head back or his or her body backward with the feet.

General Teaching Strategies   Dressing skills can be taught in the same general manner as any other skill. One breaks down the specific task (e.g., putting on a hat, fastening snaps) into its component parts; decides on a teaching approach (e.g., backward chaining, whole task); selects a system of prompts; reinforces correct responses; and remediates errors.

In light of the importance of dressing skills in the curriculum, surprisingly few studies have examined the effects specific techniques have on individuals with severe disabilities. Two relatively early studies (Martin, Kehoe, Bird, Jensen, & Darbyshire 1971; Minge & Ball, 1967) failed to describe their teaching methods in sufficient detail for replication of the procedures. Later studies (Azrin, Schaeffer, & Wesolowski, 1976; Diorio & Konarski, 1984) employed a broad package of techniques to teach people with mental retardation requiring pervasive support how to dress, making it impossible to determine specific aspects of the package that may have contributed to success. Moreover, Diorio and Konarski (1984) failed to replicate the success of the Azrin et al. (1976) study. Finally, all of these studies were conducted in institutional settings and purposely excluded individuals with severe motor impairments. Thus, their applicability to students with multiple disabilities in public schools is questionable.

Fortunately, a more recent study (Reese & Snell, 1991) resolves many of the flaws of earlier research. The authors successfully used graduated guidance (see Chapter 10) to teach three children with multiple disabilities in an inclusive elementary school to put on and remove their jackets and coats. The teaching techniques also involved using clothing initially that was one or two sizes too big for the child and subsequently reducing the size to the one typically worn by the child. Similarly, Young, West, Howard, and Whitney (1986) used a whole-task approach to teach two preschoolers with developmental disabilities to put on and remove a pullover shirt and to put on pants. The authors did not describe whether the children had physical disabilities.

Despite the scarcity of applied research data, it is clear that many students who experience significant physical restrictions in movements will be unable to complete most dressing tasks with total independence. It is also clear that these students usually can perform at least part of most tasks. The principle of partial participation (see Chapters 4 and 10) can be especially useful in dressing and undressing tasks. For example, an adult (e.g., teacher, therapist, parent) might have to position the shirt sleeve for a child and let the child lift his or her arm. Later in the session, the adult may insert the child's arm halfway through the sleeve and encourage the child to extend his or her arm the rest of the way. Partial participation in dressing often refers to personal assistance, as in the preceding example.

Another form of assistance is the use of specialized adaptive devices or dressing aids. Many of these devices require sufficient upper extremity strength or dexterity to use, but can be modified by a clever therapist or teacher to suit an individual child's needs. Some common dressing aids include dressing sticks to help people pick up, pull up, and push off clothes; stocking aids to help pull up stockings; adapted shoe horns; and buttonhooks (Hale, 1979; Kohlmeyer, 1993; Kreisler & Kreisler, 1982; Melvin, 1994; Ruston, 1977). Sokaler (1981) described a simple-to-make buttoning aid in which a small button is attached to a crocheted loop of elastic thread that enables the person to slip a hand through the sleeve without unbuttoning the cuff. Specialized companies, including Fred Sammons (in Western Springs, IL), Concepts ADL, Inc. (in Benton, IL), and Smith and Nephew Rolyon (in Germantown, WI), offer many aids through their catalogs. One more type of partial participation, adapting clothing, is discussed later in this chapter under "Specific Guidelines for Selecting and Adapting Clothing."

Campbell (1993), Finnie (1975), and Ruston (1977) offered the following general strategies for dressing a child with cerebral palsy:

1. Dress the more disabled arm or leg first and undress it last.
2. Straighten the arm before putting on the sleeve.
3. Do not pull on the child's fingers.
4. Bend the child forward at the hips to enable the caregiver to bring the child's arms forward.
5. Bend the child's leg before putting on socks and shoes.
6. Guide the extremities *slowly* through the clothing.

7. Place seams on a garment correctly before putting on the garment to prevent having to pull them into position later.

Specific Teaching Techniques   A variety of strategies for putting on and removing specific articles of clothing has been developed. Often there are three or four methods of accomplishing the same task, depending on the abilities and disabilities of the student. Several particularly good sources that describe these techniques are Case-Smith (1994); Klein (1988); Orelove and Gibbons (1981); and Shepherd, Proctor, and Coley (1996). Each reference includes diagrams or photographs that accompany the narrative. It is interesting to note that the authors of these books or articles come from various backgrounds, including education, occupational therapy, and nursing.

Before considering any teaching strategy, one must give thought to the article of clothing to be used in the program. Although the goal of dressing programs is to teach students to put on and remove their own clothing, it may prove helpful to use oversize shirts, sweaters, and so forth to allow easier movement and greater success in early phases of training. Similarly, the size, shape, and location of fasteners may facilitate speed of learning. Kramer and Whitehurst (1981), for example, found that children with mental retardation did better with larger buttons at the top of the garment (that were not visually accessible) than with smaller buttons situated lower. Special, permanent modifications of clothing and fasteners may be required (e.g., Velcro fasteners for buttons). It is easier to justify altering the task or materials to speed up learning than it is to spend months or years teaching a minute step of a dressing skill. When use of permanent adaptations is not anticipated, however, materials that resemble the student's own clothing in size and orientation are best used whenever possible. Thus, a button vest that fits over the student's clothes, with temporarily oversize buttons, is preferable to a buttoning board or doll (Adelson-Bernstein & Sandow, 1978).

Selecting and Adapting Clothing

As the preceding material suggests, the ease with which children learn to dress (or to be dressed) is linked to the type of clothing they wear. The garment design features (e.g., cut, sleeve style, fabric) are of particular importance (Levitan-Rheingold, Hotte, & Mandel, 1980). The choice of clothing not only can facilitate dressing but also can make the student feel and look better. This section presents both general and specific guidelines for selecting clothing.

General Guidelines for Selecting Clothing   The following guidelines can be used as general rules of thumb in selecting clothing (Bigge, 1991; "Convenience Clothing and Closures," n.d.; Finnie, 1975; Hale, 1979; Hoffman, 1979; Jones, 1985; Reich, 1976; Ruston, 1977).

Fabric   The choice of fabric influences comfort, durability, and ease of care. Comfort is affected by what fibers the material is made of and how they are woven into fabric. Loosely woven natural fibers (e.g., cotton, wool) or blends that breathe can help with regulation of body temperature. Synthetic insulators (e.g., Thinsulate) can provide warmth without weight and bulk. Slippery fabrics (e.g., nylon) may make it harder for students to maintain balance or for staff to pick up and carry students. Some stretch fabrics, which expand somewhat, may increase comfort by not binding the student.

Durability is greater in more tightly woven or knit fabrics. Many synthetic fibers are stronger than natural fibers. Ease of care is enhanced with synthetics that can be machine washed and dried. Print, textured, and dark fabrics show stains less than light, solid color fabrics. This is especially important for parents and other caregivers of children with multiple disabilities, because these children often drool, have food on their clothes, and are incontinent.

Construction   How a garment is constructed helps determine the student's comfort and the garment's durability. Several desirable design features include the following:

1.   Double-stitched seams
2.   Adequate seam allowance with small, even stitches
3.   Reinforcement of all openings (e.g., pockets, fly)
4.   Reinforcement with double fabric on areas of heavy wear

Fastenings   Buttons are manipulated more easily if they are medium size and sewn onto a shank; flat and concave buttons slip through holes more easily, although rims may make the buttons easier to hold. Zippers are easier than buttons for children with the strength and coordination to pull them up. Larger-tooth zippers and zipper pulls facilitate zippering. Most hooks, clasps, and buckles are difficult to close for people with multiple disabilities. Velcro is an ideal solution to most fastening problems. It is sold by the foot in various widths and also comes as precut fasteners in specific sizes and strengths. Velcro should be fastened before laundering to prolong its life.

Specific Guidelines for Selecting and Adapting Clothing   The abilities of children with multiple disabilities vary markedly. This variability demands that clothing be chosen and adapted to meet the needs of the individual. Sometimes the student's use of mobility aids (e.g., crutches) and orthoses (e.g., braces) also requires special clothing accommodations. Table 9.6 presents some specific suggestions for selecting or modifying garments based on students' physical needs. Jones (1985) also offers practical suggestions to parents and caregivers for buying specific articles of clothing for their children with disabilities. In general, parents should buy clothes that offer a good fit. Rather than buy clothes in larger sizes, which can make the garment simply look too big or create a safety hazard, it is better to buy clothes that are cut with added room for movement or clothes that can be adapted to give added room only where it is needed (Goldsberry, 1987).

Occasionally a child will present a unique challenge to the designer of specialized clothing. For example, White and Dallas (1977), an occupational therapist and a university instructor in textiles and clothing, respectively, designed

Table 9.6. Specific suggestions for modifying clothing

Problem or disability	Suggested solutions
Difficulty with pullover shirts or sweaters	Use garments of stretchable knits.
	Use elasticized necklines.
	Open seams under arms and at sides.
	Use Velcro/dots along seam lines.
	Use large sleeve openings.
Difficulty with cardigans, jackets, or front-opening shirts	Use garments of stretchable knits.
	Select styles with fullness in back (add gathers, action pleats, gussets).
	Use large sleeve openings.
	Use smooth, nonslippery fabrics.
Difficulty with pants or pull-on skirts	Sew loops at waistband.
	Use elasticized waistbands.
Difficulty with socks	Use tube socks.
	Sew loop tabs at top sides of socks.
Crutches	Add fabric patches to underside.
	Line garment.
	Choose knit or stretch fabric.
	Select longer shirt tails.
	Use overblouses or sweaters.
Long leg braces or cast	Choose pant legs loose enough to fit over braces/cast.
	Apply long zipper to inside seam.

Adapted from "Convenience Clothing and Closures" (n.d.) and Orelove and Gibbons (1981).

attractive, practical clothing for a 7-year-old girl who was a congenital, quadruple amputee. School personnel confronting similar situations might consult university clothing and textiles departments, home economics teachers, or state Cooperative Extension programs. In addition, many home dressmakers are skilled at altering patterns or ready-to-wear clothing (Ahrbeck & Friend, 1976). Finally, a variety of mail order businesses produce and sell adapted clothing. Fraser, Hensinger, and Phelps (1990) provide a partial list of those companies.

GROOMING AND PERSONAL HYGIENE SKILLS

Many individuals may consider grooming skills as less critical instructional targets than toileting and dressing. Part of the reason may be that many grooming skills—especially showering and bathing—are viewed traditionally as the responsibility of the parents or primary caregiver and lend themselves less easily to school instruction. There is also a limit on the degree to which individuals with multiple disabilities can participate in grooming activities, and, therefore, learners often become passive recipients of caregiving.

Although both of these points may have merit, there are at least three reasons why it is valuable to work on grooming and personal hygiene skills. First, being and feeling clean makes most people feel better about themselves generally. Second, a well-groomed appearance makes individuals more approachable by others, which is vitally important for establishing and maintaining friendships. Third, cleanliness and good personal hygiene help prevent illness and infection, already a concern among individuals with multiple disabilities.

This section of the chapter briefly explores the instruction of grooming and personal hygiene skills. It focuses on assistive devices that can be used in school and at home to help the teacher and caregiver.

Grooming Skills

Grooming skills consist of basic routines such as hand and face washing, showering and bathing, and hair washing and hair care. (Dental care, a vital grooming area, is discussed in Chapter 10.) Some adolescent boys, of course, may also need to add shaving to their daily grooming routine. For the most part, grooming skills can be taught through the basic principles of systematic instruction that are described in Chapter 10. (Snell and Farlow [1993] also do a nice job of detailing instructional strategies and applying them to teaching selected grooming skills.) The concept of partial participation becomes especially salient, because the average child with multiple disabilities lacks the motor skills necessary to complete most grooming tasks independently.

The most common application of partial participation in daily practice no doubt is personal assistance, whereby the instructor or parent performs major parts of the grooming tasks for the child. For many children, this is quite appropriate, and these individuals may always require some form of personal assistance. Instruction can be provided in accomplishing tasks that the child is able to learn to perform. As noted in Chapter 3, however, even a relatively simple task, such as face washing, requires sophisticated coordination of positioning and movement skills. Before beginning instruction on any grooming task, the reader is cautioned to take into consideration the principles relevant to the sensorimotor systems and handling and positioning, described in Chapters 2 and 3, respectively.

Decisions on which grooming skills to teach and how to teach them can be based on the following general guidelines (Snell & Farlow, 1993):

1. Select skills to make students as independent as possible.
2. Select skills that reflect practices typical for the student's age.
3. Choose settings for instruction that are the most natural for the activity.
4. Teach simplest skills first, moving later to more complex skills.
5. Use peers as models and teachers for some grooming skills (e.g., hair styling).

In addition to these guidelines, the use of assistive devices and equipment in the completion of grooming routines cannot be overemphasized. Some of these, such as liquid soap in a pump dispenser substituted for bar soap and a self-soaping, long-handled bath sponge, are being used increasingly by people in general. The soap dispenser, however, may require further modification, such as extension of the handle and more secure mounting to the sink or wall (see Chapter 4 for additional ideas). Other assistive devices require more individualization, such as creating special splints and cuffs to allow someone to use a hairbrush or razor.

Special devices and equipment for bathing and showering may be less familiar to school personnel. However, children who participate in physical education classes, especially at the secondary level, should be allowed the opportunity to shower after exercising. Some of the following items may prove useful (Hale, 1979; Jones, 1985):

1. Safety stripping for the bottom of the tub or shower
2. Permanent safety guard or grab rails
3. Bath mats made from the foam pads that are used for backpacks
4. Hand-held shower head
5. Bath seats, usually constructed of tubular metal with plastic seat
6. Wooden ramp built up to the shower stall
7. Shower caddy to hold soap, shampoo, and other items

A variety of companies manufacture and sell, through catalogs, adaptive devices that facilitate grooming skills. Professionals might also wish to consult local specialty stores and pharmacies that sell items to older individuals or individuals recovering from illness. Naturally, nothing can replace the work of a transdisciplinary team that coordinates efforts to devise effective and common strategies for accomplishing tasks.

Personal Hygiene Skills and Menstrual Care

An important area of personal hygiene is menstrual care. The benefits of teaching menstrual hygiene to girls and young women are obvious. Unfortunately, few individuals have published in this area. In one of the few data-based studies available, Richman, Reiss, Bauman, and Bailey (1984) taught menstrual skills to four women with mental retardation requiring extensive support. The study has limited direct relevance to individuals with multiple disabilities, however, because the authors selected participants who were ambulatory and proficient in toilet training. Many of the steps in the menstrual training package, in fact, involved gross and fine motor skills akin to those involved in toileting and would be too difficult for the typical female with multiple disabilities. As with grooming skills, instruction on menstrual hygiene should not be avoided simply because a particular person has motor and sensory impairments. Rather, an attempt should be made to involve the learner in as many aspects of the routine as practical.

SUMMARY

This chapter has presented strategies for assessing and teaching toileting, dressing, grooming, and personal hygiene skills to students with multiple disabilities. It is undoubtedly apparent that the specialized skills of many people are needed to provide these students with a full range of services. Occupational therapists and physical therapists play major roles in ensuring proper positioning, adapting materials, and so forth. Other specialists, including urologists, nurses, dietitians, and home economics teachers, among many others, can provide important consultation and direct services. Clearly, in self-care skills, as in all other parts of the curriculum, team efforts are essential.

REFERENCES

Adelson-Bernstein, N., & Sandow, L. (1978). Teaching buttoning to severely/profoundly retarded multihandicapped children. *Education and Training of the Mentally Retarded, 13,* 178–183.

Ahrbeck, E.H., & Friend, S.E. (1976). Clothing—An asset or liability? Designing for specialized needs. *Rehabilitation Literature, 37*(10), 295–296.

Altshuler, A., Meyer, J., & Butz, M.K.J. (1977). Even children can learn to do clean self-catheterization. *American Journal of Nursing, 77,* 97–101.

Ando, H. (1977). Training autistic children to urinate in the toilet using operant conditioning techniques. *Journal of Autism and Childhood Schizophrenia, 7*(2), 151–163.

Ault, M.M., Graff, J.C., & Rues, J.P. (1993). Special health care procedures. In M.E. Snell (Ed.), *Instruction of students with severe disabilities* (4th ed., pp. 215–247). Columbus, OH: Charles E. Merrill.

Azrin, N.H., Bugle, C., & O'Brien, F. (1971). Behavioral engineering: Two apparatuses for toilet training retarded children. *Journal of Applied Behavior Analysis, 4,* 292–253.

Azrin, N.H., & Foxx, R.M. (1971). A rapid method of toilet training the institutionalized retarded. *Journal of Applied Behavior Analysis, 4,* 89–99.

Azrin, N.H., Schaeffer, R.M., & Wesolowski, M.D. (1976). A rapid method of teaching profoundly retarded persons to dress by reinforcement–guidance method. *Mental Retardation, 14,* 29–33.

Azrin, N.H., Sneed, T.J., & Foxx, R.M. (1973). Dry-bed: A rapid method of eliminating bed-wetting (enuresis) of the retarded. *Behaviour Research and Therapy, 11,* 427–434.

Azrin, N.H., Sneed, T.J., & Foxx, R.M. (1974). Dry-bed training: Rapid elimination of childhood enuresis. *Behaviour Research and Therapy, 12,* 147–156.

Baller, W.R. (1975). *Bed-wetting: Origins and treatment.* Elmsford, NY: Pergamon.

Barmann, B.C., Katz, R.C., O'Brien, F., & Beauchamp, K.L. (1981). Treating irregular enuresis in developmentally disabled persons. *Behavior Modification, 5*(3), 336–346.

Baumeister, A.A., & Klosowski, R. (1965). An attempt to group toilet train severely retarded patients. *Mental Retardation, 3,* 24–26.

Bensberg, G.J., Colwell, C.N., & Cassel, R.H. (1965). Teaching the profoundly retarded self-help activities by behavior shaping techniques. *American Journal of Mental Deficiency, 69,* 674–679.

Bergen, A. (1974) *Selected equipment for pediatric rehabilitation.* Valhalla, NY: Blythedale Children's Hospital.

Bigge, J. (1982). Self-care. In J.L. Bigge, *Teaching individuals with physical and multiple disabilities* (2nd ed., pp. 290–313). Columbus, OH: Charles E. Merrill.

Bigge, J.L. (1991). *Teaching individuals with physical and multiple disabilities* (3rd ed.). Columbus, OH: Charles E. Merrill.

Bollard, J. (1982). A 2-year follow-up of bed-wetters treated by dry-bed training and standard conditioning. *Behaviour Research and Therapy, 20,* 571–580.

Bollard, J., & Nettelbeck, T. (1982). A component analysis of dry-bed training for treatment of bed-wetting. *Behaviour Research and Therapy, 20,* 383–390.

Bollard, J., Nettelbeck, T., & Roxbee, L. (1982). Dry-bed training for childhood bedwetting: A comparison of group with individually administered parent instruction. *Behaviour Research and Therapy, 20,* 209–217.

Bollard, R.J., & Woodroffe, P. (1977). The effect of parent-administered dry-bed training on nocturnal enuresis in children. *Behaviour Research and Therapy, 15,* 159–165.

Calkin, A.B., Grant, P.A., & Bowman, M.M. (1978). *Toilet training: Help for the delayed learner.* New York: McGraw-Hill.

Campbell, P.H. (1977). Daily living skills. In N.G. Haring (Ed.), *Developing effective individualized education programs for severely handicapped children and youth* (pp. 115–138). Washington, DC: Department of Health, Education, and Welfare, Office of Education, Bureau of Education for the Handicapped.

Campbell, P.H. (1993). Physical management and handling procedures. In M.E. Snell (Ed.), *Instruction of students with severe disabilities* (4th ed., pp. 248–263). Columbus, OH: Charles E. Merrill.

Case-Smith, J. (1994). Self-care strategies for children with developmental deficits. In C. Christiansen (Ed.), *Ways of living: Self-care strategies for special needs* (pp. 101–156). Rockville, MD: American Occupational Therapy Association.

Cheever, R.C., & Elmer, C.D. (1975). *Bowel management programs.* Bloomington, IL: Accent Press.

Connor, F.P., Williamson, G.G., & Siepp, J.M. (Eds.). (1978). *Program guide for infants and toddlers with neuromotor and other developmental disabilities.* New York: Teachers College Press.

Convenience clothing and closures. (n.d.). New York: Talon/Velcro Consumer Education.

Copeland, M., Ford, L., & Solon, N. (1976). *Occupational therapy for mentally retarded children.* Baltimore: University Park Press.

Copeland, M.E., & Kimmel, J.R. (1989). *Evaluation and management of infants and young children with developmental disabilities.* Baltimore: Paul H. Brookes Publishing Co.

Dayan, M. (1964). Toilet training retarded children in a state residential institution. *Mental Retardation, 2,* 116–117.

Diorio, M.S., & Konarski, E.A. (1984). Evaluation of a method for teaching dressing skills to profoundly mentally retarded persons. *American Journal of Mental Deficiency, 89*(3), 307–309.

Doleys, D.M., & Arnold, S. (1975). Treatment of childhood encopresis: Full cleanliness training. *Mental Retardation, 13*(6), 14–16.

Dunklee, N.R. (1989, July/August). Toilet training Carl. *Exceptional Parent,* 36–40.

Education of the Handicapped Act Amendments of 1986, PL 99-457, 20 U.S.C. §1400 *et seq.*

Ellis, N.R. (1963). Toilet training the severely defective patient: An S-R reinforcement analysis. *American Journal of Mental Deficiency, 68,* 98–103.

Finnie, N.R. (1975). *Handling the young cerebral palsied child at home.* New York: E.P. Dutton.

Foxx, R.M., & Azrin, N.H. (1973a). Dry pants: A rapid method of toilet training children. *Behaviour Research and Therapy, 11,* 435–442.

Foxx, R.M., & Azrin, N.H. (1973b). *Toilet training the retarded: A rapid program for day and nighttime independent toileting.* Champaign, IL: Research Press.

Fraser, B.A., Hensinger, R.N., & Phelps, J.A. (1990). *Physical management of multiple handicaps: A professional's guide* (2nd ed.). Baltimore: Paul H. Brookes Publishing Co.

Gallender, D. (1980). *Teaching eating and toileting skills to the multihandicapped.* Springfield, IL: Charles C Thomas.

Geter, K. (1982). *These special children.* Palo Alto, CA: Bull Publishing.

Gibson, B.D. (1980). Adaptive toilet training. In J. Umbreit & P.J. Cardullias (Eds.), *Educating the severely physically handicapped: Basic principles and techniques* (Vol. I, pp. 31–47). Reston, VA: Division on Physically Handicapped, Council for Exceptional Children.

Giles, D.K., & Wolf, M.M. (1966). Toilet training institutionalized, severe retardates: An application of operant behavior modification techniques. *American Journal of Mental Deficiency, 70,* 766–780.

Goldsberry, E. (1987, April). Choosing clothes for your child. *The Exceptional Parent,* 28–33.

Graff, J.C., Ault, M.M., Guess, D., Taylor, M., & Thompson, B. (1990). *Health care for students with disabilities: An illustrated medical guide for the classroom.* Baltimore: Paul H. Brookes Publishing Co.

Hale, G. (Ed.). (1979). *The source book for the disabled.* New York: Paddington Press.

Herreshoff, J.K. (1973). Two electronic devices for toilet training. *Mental Retardation, 11*(6), 54–55.

Hoffman, A.M. (1979). *Clothing for the handicapped, the aged, and other people with special needs.* Springfield, IL: Charles C Thomas.

Hundziak, M., Maurer, R.A., & Watson, L.S. (1965). *American Journal of Mental Deficiency, 70,* 120–124.

Hyams, G., McCoull, K., Smith, P.S., & Tyrer, S.P. (1992). Behavioural continence training in mental handicap: A 10-year follow-up study. *Journal of Intellectual Disability Research, 36,* 551–558.

Jones, M.L. (1985). *Home care for the chronically ill or disabled child.* New York: Harper & Row.

Kimbrell, D.L., Luckey, R.E., Barbuto, P.F.P., & Love, J.G. (1967). Operation dry pants: An intensive habit-training program for severely and profoundly retarded. *Mental Retardation, 5,* 32–36.

Klauser, A.G., & Muller-Lissner, S.A. (1993). How effective is nonlaxative treatment of constipation? *Pharmacology, 47*(Suppl. 1), 256–260.

Klein, M.D. (1988). *Predressing skills.* Tucson, AZ: Therapy Skill Builders.

Kohlmeyer, K.M. (1993). Assistive and adaptive equipment. In H.L. Hopkins & H.D. Smith (Eds.), *Occupational therapy* (8th ed., pp. 316–320). Philadelphia: J.B. Lippincott.

Kramer, L., & Whitehurst, C. (1981). Effects of button features on self-dressing in young retarded children. *Education and Training of the Mentally Retarded, 16,* 277–283.

Kreisler, N., & Kreisler, J. (1982). *Catalog of aids for the disabled.* New York: McGraw-Hill.

Lancioni, G.E. (1980). Teaching independent toileting to profoundly retarded deaf-blind children. *Behavior Therapy, 11,* 234–244.

Levine, M.N., & Elliott, C.B. (1970). Toilet training for profoundly retarded with a limited staff. *Mental Retardation, 8,* 48–50.

Levitan-Rheingold, N., Hotte, E.B., & Mandel, D.R. (1980). Learning to dress: A fundamental skill toward independence for the disabled. *Rehabilitation Literature, 41*(34), 72–75.

Lohmann, W., Eyman, R.K., & Lask, E. (1967). Toilet training. *American Journal of Mental Deficiency, 71,* 551–557.

Lovibond, S.H. (1963). The mechanism of conditioning treatment of enuresis. *Behaviour Research and Therapy, 1,* 17–21.

MacKeith, R., Meadow, R., & Turner, R.K. (1973). How children become dry. In I. Kolvin, R.C. MacKeith, & S.R. Meadow (Eds.), *Bladder control and enuresis* (pp. 3–21). London: William Heinemann.

Mahoney, K., Van Wagenen, K., & Meyerson, L. (1971). Toilet training of normal and retarded children. *Journal of Applied Behavior Analysis, 4,* 173–181.

Maizels, M., Gandhi, K., Keating, B., & Rosenbaum, D. (1993). Diagnosis and treatment for children who cannot control urination. *Current Problems in Pediatrics, 23*(10), 402–450.

Marshall, G.R. (1966). Toilet training of an autistic eight-year-old through conditioning therapy: A case report. *Behaviour Research and Therapy, 4,* 242–245.

Martin, G.L., Kehoe, B., Bird, E., Jensen, V., & Darbyshire, M. (1971). Operant conditioning in dressing behavior of severely retarded girls. *Mental Retardation, 9,* 27–31.

Melvin, J.L. (1994). Self-care strategies for persons with arthritis and connective tissue disease. In C. Christiansen (Ed.), *Ways of living: Self-care strategies for special needs* (pp. 157–187). Rockville, MD: American Occupational Therapy Association.

Minge, M.R., & Ball, T.S. (1967). Teaching of self-help skills to severely retarded patients. *American Journal of Mental Deficiency, 71,* 864–868.

Morse, J.S., & Colatarci, S.L. (1994). The impact of technology. In S.P. Roth & J.S. Morse (Eds.), *A life-span approach to nursing care for individuals with developmental disabilities* (pp. 351–383). Baltimore: Paul H. Brookes Publishing Co.

Mountjoy, P.T., Ruben, D.H., & Bradford, T.S. (1984). Recent technological advancements in the treatment of enuresis. *Behavior Modification, 8*(3), 291–315.

Myers, G.J., Cerone, S.B., & Olson, A.L. (Eds.). (1981). *A guide for helping the child with spina bifida.* Springfield, IL: Charles C Thomas.

Orelove, F.P., & Gibbons, S.J. (1981). A guide to independent dressing. *Exceptional Parent, 11,* 50–53, 55–56.

Palmer, M.L., & Toms, J.E. (1992). *Manual for functional training* (3rd ed.). Philadelphia: F.A. Davis Co.

Reese, G.M., & Snell, M.E. (1991). Putting on and removing coats and jackets: The acquisition and maintenance of skills by children with severe multiple disabilities. *Education and Training in Mental Retardation, 26,* 398–410.

Reich, N. (1976). Clothing for the handicapped and disabled. *Rehabilitation Literature, 37*(10), 290–294.

Richman, G.S., Reiss, M.L., Bauman, K.E., & Bailey, J.S. (1984). Teaching menstrual care to mentally retarded women: Acquisition, generalization, and maintenance. *Journal of Applied Behavior Analysis, 17,* 441–451.

Robertson, J., Alper, S., Schloss, P.J., & Wisniewski, L. (1992). Teaching self-catheterization skills to a child with myelomeningocele in a preschool setting. *Journal of Early Intervention, 16*(1), 20–30.

Roos, P., & Oliver, M. (1969). Evaluation of operant conditioning with institutionalized retarded children. *American Journal of Mental Deficiency, 74,* 325–330.

Ruston, R. (1977). *Dressing for disabled people.* London: The Disabled Living Foundation.

Schaefer, C.E. (1979). *Childhood encopresis and enuresis: Causes and therapy.* New York: Van Nostrand Reinhold.

Shepherd, J., Procter, S.A., & Coley, I.L. (1996). Self care and adaptations for independent living. In J. Case-Smith, A.S. Allen, & P.N. Pratt (Eds.), *Occupational therapy for children* (3rd ed., pp. 461–503). St. Louis, MO: C.V. Mosby.

Sloop, E.W., & Kennedy, W.A. (1973). Institutionalized retarded nocturnal enuretics treated by a conditioning technique. *American Journal of Mental Deficiency, 77*(6), 717–721.

Smith, L.J. (1981). Training severely and profoundly mentally handicapped nocturnal enuretics. *Behaviour Research and Therapy, 19,* 67–74.

Smith, P.S. (1979). A comparison of different methods of toilet training the mentally handicapped. *Behaviour Research and Therapy, 17,* 33–43.

Smith, P.S., Britton, P.G., Johnson, M., & Thomas, D.A. (1975). Problems involved in toilet training profoundly mentally handicapped adults. *Behaviour Research and Therapy, 13,* 301–307.

Smith, P.S., & Smith, L.J. (1977). Chronological age and social age as factors in intensive daytime toilet training of institutionalized mentally retarded individuals. *Journal of Behavior Therapy and Experimental Psychiatry, 8,* 269–273.

Snell, M.E. (1980). Does toilet training belong in the public schools? A review of toilet training research. *Education Unlimited, 2*(3), 53–58.

Snell, M.E. (1990). Basic self-care instruction for students without motor impairments. In M. Snell (Ed.), *Systematic instruction of people with severe handicaps* (3rd. ed., p. 378). Columbus, OH: Charles E. Merrill.

Snell, M.E., & Farlow, L.J. (1993). Self-care skills. In M.E. Snell (Ed.), *Instruction of students with severe disabilities* (4th ed., pp. 380–441). Columbus, OH: Charles E. Merrill.

Sokaler, R.A. (1981). A buttoning aid. *American Journal of Occupational Therapy, 35,* 737.

Stauffer, D.T. (1983). A spina bifida student? You may have to catheterize! *DPH Journal, 7*(1), 14–21.

Tawney, J.W., Knapp, D.S., O'Reilly, C.D., & Pratt, S.S. (1979). *Programmed environments curriculum.* Columbus, OH: Charles E. Merrill.

Taylor, M. (1990). Clean intermittent catheterization. In J.C. Graff, M.M. Ault, D. Guess, M. Taylor, & B. Thompson (Eds.), *Health care for students with disabilities: An illustrated medical guide for the classroom* (pp. 241-252). Baltimore: Paul H. Brookes Publishing Co.

Thompson, T., & Hanson, R. (1983). Overhydration: Precautions when treating urinary incontinence. *Mental Retardation, 21,* 139–143.

Trott, M.C. (1977). Application of Foxx and Azrin toilet training for the retarded in a school program. *Education and Training of the Mentally Retarded, 12,* 336–338.

Van Wagenen, R.K., Meyerson, L., Kerr, N.J., & Mahoney, K. (1969). Field trials of a new procedure for toilet training. *Journal of Experimental Child Psychology, 8,* 147–159.

Van Wagenen, R.K., & Murdock, E.E. (1966). A transistorized signal-package for toilet training of infants. *Journal of Experimental Child Psychology, 3,* 312–314.

Watson, L.S. (1968). Applications of behavior shaping devices to training severely and profoundly mentally retarded children in an institutional setting. *Mental Retardation, 6,* 21–23.

White, L.W., & Dallas, M.J. (1977). Clothing adaptations: The occupational therapist and the clothing designer collaborate. *American Journal of Occupational Therapy, 31*(2), 90–94.

Williams, F.E., & Sloop, E.W. (1978). Success with a shortened Foxx-Azrin toilet training program. *Education and Training of the Mentally Retarded, 13,* 399–402.

Williams, W., & Fox, T. (Eds.). (1979). *Minimum objective system for learners with severe handicaps.* Burlington: University of Vermont.

Wolraich, M.L., Hawtrey, C., Mapel, J., & Henderson, M. (1983). Results of clean intermittent catheterization for children with neurogenic bladders. *Urology, 22*(5), 479–482.

Yeates, W.K. (1973). Bladder function in normal micturition. In I. Kolvin, R.C. Mac-Keith, & S.R. Meadown (Eds.), *Bladder control and enuresis* (pp. 28–36). London: William Heinemann.

Young, K.R., West, R.P., Howard, V.F., & Whitney, R. (1986). Acquisition, fluency training, generalization, and maintenance of dressing skills of two developmentally disabled children. *Education and Treatment of Children, 9*(1), 16–29.

10

Curriculum and Instruction

Fred P. Orelove and Anne Malatchi

DECIDING WHAT TO TEACH STUDENTS with multiple disabilities and how to teach them may seem to be insurmountable tasks. Most children have so many things to learn that team members may find it difficult to determine which goals are most important for a given school year. Other children have limited response repertoires and multiple sensory and motor impairments, which challenge the creativity of instructional staff to design teaching strategies.

Fortunately, the rapid maturation of the field of educating learners with severe disabilities since the 1980s has resulted in a variety of models and practical solutions to the challenges described above. Federal and state grants and other incentives fueled an explosion of demonstration initiatives and research studies that gave rise to a host of effective practices. At the same time, the field was undergoing a sea change in philosophy and values about the worth and role of individuals with multiple disabilities (cf., Meyer, Peck, & Brown, 1991).

It is safe to say that the single biggest driving force behind these changes has been the promotion of the philosophy and practice of inclusive education (i.e., serving children with disabilities in general education classes with their same-age peers). The effect has been obvious, dramatic, and wide reaching. Hundreds of children who formerly were placed in noninclusive classrooms or schools and often had few expectations placed on them have been active members of general education classes and have shown academic and social gains (cf., Downing, 1996; Haring & Romer, 1995).

Although the authors of this chapter recognize that many educators and some parents have not embraced inclusion, the multitude of success stories and research data suggest that inclusion has had, and will continue to have, a profound influence on our thinking and practices. Thus, this chapter is based on an assumption that readers either serve children with multiple disabilities, or are interested in serving them, in general education classrooms. The ideas and information should be useful, however, in other service delivery models.

This chapter is based on several other assumptions, as well:

1. **Every child can learn.**   While this statement may appear trivial, it is not. Some educators have developed individualized education programs (IEPs) for certain children as if those children had little or nothing to gain from education. Each child, in spite of possible significant motor, sensory, cognitive, and health care needs, should be assumed to be capable of learning (Orelove, 1991).

2. **A transdisciplinary team is necessary.**   This, of course, is a theme running through the entire book (see Chapter 1). The team becomes especially critical in the design and implementation of the student's educational program, particularly when one considers the range of challenges in the learner with multiple disabilities. Implicit in the transdisciplinary approach is the belief that program planning is *collaborative*.

3. **Families are vital.**   Families have an obvious keen interest in the welfare of their family member with a disability, and they should be given every opportunity to be actively involved in decisions about what and how to teach the child. Moreover, families typically know the child better than anyone else and are a rich source of ideas that should be tapped. This is especially important given the large percentage of children who have not been taught a reliable means of communicating. Parents typically develop a finely tuned ability to "read" their child's needs and feelings.

There is no one correct way to perform educational program planning, and many excellent models are available that describe such processes in detail (e.g., Ferguson, Meyer, & Willis, 1990; Giangreco, Cloninger, & Iverson, 1993; Rainforth, York, & Macdonald, 1992; Snell, 1993). Although every model differs in its sequence, level of detail, and so forth, they all share common components:

• The belief that program planning must be *individualized*, taking into account the needs, strengths, and dreams of each child, rather than determining content on the basis of categorical labels or test scores

• The understanding that the *IEP is the core planning document* and that it must reflect the input of the entire team working together and incorporating the ideas and desires of the student's family and other people significant in the student's life

- The recognition that each student (and staff member) needs *individually determined supports and resources* for maximum educational gains
- The belief that instruction should focus on attaining *important outcomes* for the learner and that teaching strategies should be effective, inclusive, and humane

The process proposed in this chapter incorporates these elements. It emphasizes, in particular, "up-front" planning to ensure that the child's IEP is not only clear and effective, but that it results from careful and thoughtful planning. Figure 10.1 presents a flowchart of the process. The remainder of the chapter is devoted to describing each step; Figure 10.2 provides a brief summary of the steps involved. Although curriculum and instruction in reality are interrelated, for convenience this chapter is organized into two sections, treating each area separately.

Finally, although this chapter provides examples whenever possible, it does not attempt to deal with the full range of content issues specific to learners with multiple disabilities. Readers are invited to consult the three preceding chapters for more detailed information on communication skills (Chapter 7), mealtime skills (Chapter 8), and self-care skills (Chapter 9). In addition, Chapter 4 should be viewed as an adjunct to this chapter.

CURRICULUM

Curriculum is, strictly speaking, the *content* to be taught. Although it would be relatively easy to agree on the broad areas needed by most learners with multiple disabilities, decisions on particular skills and activities must be made individually for each child.

Those decisions should be based on a thorough understanding of the needs, strengths, and abilities of the child, and of the dreams, hopes, and nightmares of the family. Determining what to teach, however, must also be based on a set of values concerning the role of education. For what is the learner being prepared? What vision do we have of the student's life after graduation? On one hand, if educators envision a life in which the individual is totally dependent, with no meaningful employment and no friends, then what the student is taught is not particularly important. On the other hand, if educators envision a life in which the individual is a part of his or her community, with friends and a reasonable job, then what and how the student is taught becomes of vital importance.

Determine Strengths, Interests, Dreams, and Nightmares

The first step in the process of determining what to teach is to determine the child's special qualities and to discover his or her interests and dreams and those of the family and others close to the child. One effective way of doing this is through developing action plans, or MAPs (Forest & Pearpoint, 1992; Vandercook, York, & Forest, 1989).

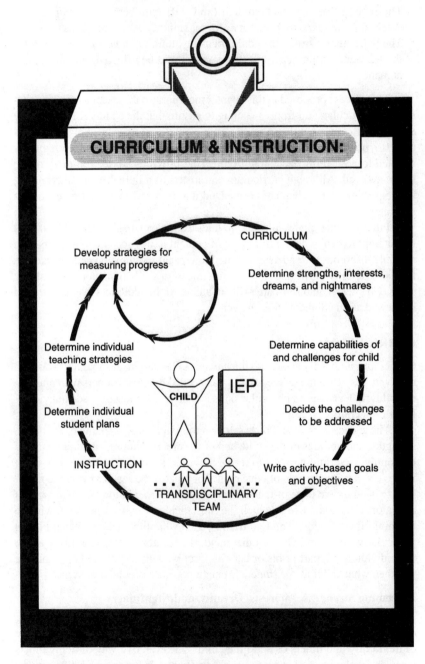

Figure 10.1.   Flowchart of instructional planning process.

What?	Why?	How?	Who?	Where?	When?
Step 1: Determine strengths, interests, dreams, and nightmares	• It is the child's life • The family knows/understands child best • Most efficient way of getting information	• Talk to child • Do MAPs • Conduct other inventories	• Child • Family • Friends • Current and future teachers • Other team members	• Home, school, and other comfortable settings	• As soon as possible, before developing IEP
Step 2: Determine capabilities of and challenges for child	• To develop best education for child • To verify what child can do in real-life contexts	• Formal assessment (e.g., environmental assessments, discipline-specific assessment) • Informal assessment (e.g., observation, checklists)	• Transdisciplinary team, including child and family	• Where skills needed (natural settings)	• After MAPs, before IEP development
Step 3: Decide the challenges to be addressed	• To focus on priorities • To focus on most relevant, functional skills	• Use "decision rules" from Ferguson and Wilcox (1988) • Examine child, family, team priorities	• Transdisciplinary team, led by child and family	• Any place	• After assessment information is compiled

(continued)

Figure 10.2. Summary of the components of instructional planning process.

Figure 10.2. *(continued)*

What?	Why?	How?	Who?	Where?	When?
Step 4: Write activity-based goals and objectives	• To ensure meaningful outcomes in natural settings	• Criteria from Ferguson and Wilcox (1988) • Examine priority environments, activities	• Transdisciplinary team	• At meetings that include all team members, including family	• After Steps 1–3 are completed
Step 5: Determine individual student plans	• To provide daily opportunities to learn and practice skills	• Use matrix	• Transdisciplinary team, including general education teacher	• General education classroom, other natural environments within and outside school	• Following IEP development, before school year begins
Step 6: Determine individual teaching strategies	• To ensure child will meet objectives	• Prepare student • Determine learning styles • Teach skills directly (antecedent and consequent events) • Handle challenging behaviors	• Transdisciplinary team	• Natural environments, general education classroom	• As soon as possible following prior step
Step 7: Develop strategies for measuring progress	• To ensure progress • To know when goals are met • To improve instruction	• Formal data collection • Informal data, including portfolio assessment	• Transdisciplinary team	• Environments where goals and objectives are being addressed	• Ongoing

MAPs is a "group, problem-solving, cooperative collaborative team approach to planning" (Forest & Pearpoint, 1992, p. 53). The process results in a personalized plan of action that assists in bringing the person closer to the daily life of the school (Forest & Pearpoint, 1992). Figure 10.3 provides a description of each step (questions to answer) in the process, and Figure 10.4 provides a completed MAP for a 7-year-old boy, Harry, who has cerebral palsy. Although Harry's MAP was developed by a group of 16 individuals, 2–24 people can be involved. "The key ingredients for participants are Intimate and Personal Contact with the individual being mapped" (Forest & Pearpoint, 1992, p. 54).

It should be noted that developing a MAP is not a part of or a substitute for the IEP, but rather precedes the IEP. The MAP not only provides the transdisciplinary team with important information that is helpful to writing the IEP, but it also helps paint a positive portrait of the learner, thereby focusing the group on the child's capacity, rather than deficiencies. Emphasizing the child's strengths

---

The following MAPs questions are addressed by all the participants. Questions #2, #3, and #4 are usually answered first by family members (Forest & Pearpoint, 1992):

1. **What is a MAP?**   Describe how a road map is used for travel (e.g., for directions, places to stop). The information gathered during this MAPs session will help determine direction for [child's name] life. It is very important to answer all the questions.

2. **What is [child's name] history?**   Describe the highlights of the child's life. Include information regarding medical, educational, social, and communication issues. Review in advance to avoid spending too much time on this question.

3. **What is your dream for [child's name]?**   Describe your dreams for the next 5 years, 10 years, and as an adult. Include dreams for where [child's name] will live and work and about the relationships in his or her life.

4. **What is your nightmare for [child's name]?**   Nightmares (i.e., institutions, isolation, dependency) cannot be avoided if they are not discussed.

(Questions #5, #6, and #7 should be lists of words or phrases.)

5. **Who is the child?**   Brainstorm to give words and phrases that describe the child.

6. **What are the child's strengths, gifts, and talents?**   Include likes, dislikes, preferences, what works, successes, and so forth.

7. **What are the child's needs and challenges?**   Include supports necessary for success.

8. **a) What action plans are needed to meet these dreams and avoid the nightmares?**   Be specific with follow-up plans (i.e., when IEP meetings will be held, when circle of friends activities will begin); **b) What would an ideal day at school look like?**   Using the information just generated, a matrix might be developed (see Figure 10.6) for use in the general education classroom.

Figure 10.3.   Steps in the MAPs process.

WHAT IS HARRY'S HISTORY?

- He is 7 years old, lives with mom, dad, younger sister
- Both his parents are doctors

- **Medical:** Normal delivery, parents soon noticed delays, took 6 months to convince doctors
- Parents (doctors themselves) very angry at nightmare treatment from doctors
- Eventual diagnosis of cerebral palsy
- Parents were told to have no expectations, would never walk or talk
- Began therapies (occupational, physical) when he was 1 years old, currently walking and running!
- Overall now very healthy, on medications for seizures

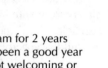

- **Educational:** Early intervention programs for 2 years
- Excellent general education preschool from 2–4 years old
- Big improvement in motor skills, independence
- Moved to another state and into a special education program for 2 years
- Attends kindergarten at his neighborhood school, has not been a good year
- Parents believe proper supports are not in place, school not welcoming or understanding Harry
- Pull out inconsistent; some days more 'out' than 'in' class
- School and parents very frustrated

- **Communication:** Used pictures at 2 years of age, began signing at 3 years of age and using Intro-Talker, now on Dynavox (augmentative communication systems)
- Entire family, including younger sister, uses sign language with Harry

- **Social:** Friends at preschool, but no school friends from kindergarten
- Friends from the neighborhood are older

WHAT ARE YOUR DREAMS FOR HARRY?

- Will be accepted, not made fun of
- Keep friends from now and make new ones
- His friends, family, and educators will support him to meet his dreams
- Will have a job helping others with similar challenges
- Able to make choices
- Success at communicating
- Work in a zoo because he loves animals
- Will read and write
- Live independently, loved, happy
- Accepting of himself
- Healthy, safe
- Married with a family
- Contributing member of society

(continued)

Figure 10.4. Harry's MAP held in the spring of his kindergarten year with his family, relatives, family friends, babysitters, neighbors, current and future teachers, principal, and assistant principal.

Figure 10.4. *(continued)*

WHAT ARE YOUR NIGHTMARES FOR HARRY?

- Will not find the keys to make his dreams happen
- Will not develop to fullest potential
- Safety issues
- People will not take the time to learn how special Harry is
- Still in kindergarten at 21
- Will be institutionalized
- No family
- No circle of friends
- Noninclusive classes because people do not understand his actions
- Will be judged by his DISabilities, not abilities
- Will become frustrated and give up
- No support for his progress
- Will not learn skills needed for life by 21
- No communication skills

WHO IS HARRY? WHAT DOES HE LIKE?

- Loves animals (especially horses and dogs), people, tractors
- Likes mechanical things, music, water
- Likes blowing bubbles
- He has a beautiful smile
- He is affectionate, exuberant, curious, expressive, intuitive, loving
- He is determined, helpful, and joyful
- Likes colors, reading, being read to, running
- Loves sports
- He is a son, brother, grandson, and nephew
- He is wonderful and much loved!

WHAT ARE HARRY'S STRENGTHS, GIFTS, AND TALENTS?

- Strong desire to communicate and lots to say
- Easy to motivate, knows what he wants
- Visual learner and 'do-er,' learns by imitation, from other kids, and with singing games
- Excellent big brother
- Motivated by praise, acceptance, satisfaction
- Sign language, memory, mobility, following directions
- Personality, his family, neighbors
- With assistance, can participate fully in everything

(continued)

Figure 10.4. *(continued)*

WHAT ARE HARRY'S NEEDS AND CHALLENGES?

- Communication with friends, communication between home and school
- Facilitation in developing a circle of friends
- For people who work with Harry to realize that all behavior is a communicative intent
- For his teachers to have some training in positive behavior supports, positive behavior support plans
- Decrease in verbal directions, repetition; use 'wait' time, pair verbal prompt with visual or tactile cue
- Help for Harry in understanding limits, choices, and consequences
- Loving family, friends, neighbors
- Diversity awareness for his school
- Curriculum accommodations and adaptations
- Self-help skills, encouragement, patience
- Help with daily transitions, longer attention span, consistency
- Experience in large group participation
- Sign language for his classmates
- Daily schedule with functional, realistic goals and activities
- To feel a sense of acceptance, belonging, and community

ACTION PLANS FOR HARRY

- Support team (including parents) will meet within 1 month to begin planning for first grade
- This team will have several meetings to develop IEP
- IEP will be functional, goals stated in proactive language, include interactions with friends
- Positive behavioral supports (PBS) workshop for teachers will be end of June; teachers paid to attend
- After PBS training, team will meet to determine support plans to include in IEP
- His first-grade teacher will be chosen and begin observing Harry now, transition plans developed
- Circle of friends and awareness activities will begin now in kindergarten, once a week, continue next year
- Daily schedule developed now, using a matrix, and will include times for Harry to get a drink
- Harry will not be pulled from class for "punishment"
- PTA program regarding diversity and inclusion for next year
- Harry will invite classmates to his birthday party

(continued)

Figure 10.4. *(continued)*

Harry's MAPs session was the catalyst for significant changes in his and his family's life, including major changes at his school. A training in positive behavioral supports was offered at the end of June and was attended by Harry's first-grade teacher, assistant principal, special education coordinator for the district, and others from Harry's school. Friends began going to Harry's house over the summer, he was invited to many parties, and his entire class attended his birthday party. During his first-grade year, his parents have become active participants in monthly team meetings. His service coordinator and classroom teacher conduct class meetings weekly, and his first-grade teacher designs weekly lesson plans addressing his IEP goals and objectives. The former assistant principal is now the principal and she works hard to assure the staff and community that their school welcomes *all* children. Last, but not least, Harry has begun to make a concerted effort to talk.

---

from the very beginning has important benefits throughout the program planning and implementation process.

Determine Capabilities of and Challenges for Child

As suggested in the preceding section, the learner with multiple disabilities has both numerous capabilities and needs. In order for the team to develop realistic instructional goals that move the student toward greater control over his or her environment, at school, and in the home and community, these capabilities and needs must be determined through a strategy that should also take into account a child's inability to move and/or take in and transmit information in a manner available to typical children. These various needs suggest a broad-based assessment process that builds on the strengths of the transdisciplinary team and recognizes that the learner will be acquiring, and relying on, skills in many different settings and possibly through different modalities.

One assessment strategy that has been used widely is based on the development of children who do not have disabilities. In this *developmental approach,* curriculum content is determined through administering informal checklists or developmental scales (e.g., Bayley Scales of Infant Development [Bayley, 1993], Learning Accomplishment Profile [LeMay, Griffin, & Sanford, 1981]). The items missed by the child thus become instructional targets.

Unfortunately, a developmental approach has serious disadvantages for learners with multiple disabilities (Brown & Snell, 1993). Children with multiple disabilities, for example, do not necessarily develop or acquire skills in a "normal" sequence; some of the skills, of course, are physically impossible. Moreover, the focus on developmental assessment instruments is on the *form* of the behavior (e.g., "grasps pellet"), rather than its *function* (e.g., getting an item from one place to another, which can be done in a variety of ways) (White, 1985). In addition, checklist items tend to be irrelevant to the skills and materials needed by learners with multiple disabilities, particularly as they move beyond the early childhood years. Finally, items on checklists often are viewed (and taught) in isolation, an approach that tends to be less effective, efficient, and enjoyable than teaching in the context of meaningful activities.

An alternative to a developmental model is an environmental or ecological approach to assessment (Brown et al., 1979). In an environmental approach, the settings (or environments) are examined for a particular student. The team learns what activities are useful for the specific learner in his or her current and anticipated future environments (at school, home, community, and sometimes work) and then determines which of those activities, and the necessary skills, the child can and cannot perform and at what level of independence.

In the context of an ecological model, Rainforth, Macdonald, York, and Dunn (1992) described a four-step process of assessment:

1. **Planning the assessment**   This includes establishing the assessment team and designating an assessment coordinator, who organizes and documents the process. This is essential to ensure that assessment is truly coordinated and not merely a compilation of reports from several different professionals. The assessment planning chart denotes which team members will conduct which parts of the assessment in which settings. "At school, students are usually assessed first in environments and activities that comprise typical routines....When students reach middle and high school age, community environments assume increasing importance" (Rainforth, Macdonald, et al., 1992, p. 109). For students new to a program, it is particularly important to start the observation process with familiar environments.

2. **Assessing student performance in natural environments**   Before the assessment, the team conducts inventories of priority environments and activities. These inventories describe the performance expected of a person without a disability who is approximately the same age as the student with a disability. Then, the student is observed during naturally occurring activities to determine how he or she performs with and without assistance, with special note being taken of the kind of assistance that elicits the best performance. A complete assessment usually takes several sessions, with team members assuming varying roles of facilitator, observer, and recorder.

3. **Analyzing performance discrepancies and generating hypotheses**   The team meets to identify discrepancies between the student's performance and the way the skills are performed by individuals without disabilities. Members then hypothesize about factors that may have contributed to specific performance difficulties (e.g., sensory overload, fear or discomfort, inability to communicate).

4. **Conducting diagnostic assessment**   This final step has two main purposes. First, it is designed to help answer questions raised in the previous step. Second, it is used to gather additional important information that was not available or feasible to obtain earlier in the process. Diagnostic assessment consists of both informal and formal techniques. Rainforth, Macdonald, et al. (1992) describe a variety of formal assessment tools for several areas of sensorimotor performance.

Following the completion of all four steps, the team develops a comprehensive assessment report in one of two styles. In the first, the team describes each area of skill development (e.g., gross motor, fine motor, play, communication) and relates it to performance in activity routines. In the second approach, the team describes the student's overall performance in activity routines, with corresponding discussions of embedded sensorimotor, communication, and other skills.

Certainly, the process for assessing skills that Rainforth, Macdonald, et al. (1992) describe is one of many possible methods for determining the needs of learners with multiple disabilities. Readers may wish to consult the following sources for additional approaches to assessment and curriculum development: Brown, Evans, Weed, and Owens (1987); Ford et al. (1989); Guess and Helmstetter (1986); Neel and Billingsley (1989); Wilcox and Bellamy (1987); and, in particular, Browder (1991). Whatever technique one uses, it is essential that it is individualized to the needs and situation of each learner.

Decide on the Challenges to Be Addressed

The first two steps typically yield more desires and needs than can be addressed in a given school year. It is therefore essential to focus on those concerns of greatest importance to the student and family, while simultaneously building on the child's strengths.

In making decisions about establishing priorities, it is useful to work from a set of guidelines. A variety of individuals have articulated such guidelines. Ferguson and Wilcox (1988), for example, stipulated nine "decision rules" for selecting IEP goals and objectives. They wrote that activity goals and supporting activities should be selected to do the following:

1. Increase participation in activities and use of materials typically engaged in and used by peers without disabilities.
2. Increase participation across a variety of activities and environments, including the domains of personal management, leisure, and jobs and chores across classroom, school/community, and home environments.
3. Maximize the repertoire of each student, increasing the variety of activities while also facilitating longitudinal development.
4. Contribute to the outcome of the activities. Parts of activities targeted for either acquisition or participation should make a difference to the completion of the entire activity.
5. Enhance image and appeal, resulting in the student being perceived by others as a more valuable, less different, contributing, striving, and productive member of society.
6. Increase opportunities for interaction with peers without disabilities.
7. Focus on establishing a functional communication system that is maximally accessible to any person without a disability, not just people who are familiar to the student. If not yet achieved, communication objectives should be developed for all possible activity goals.

8.   Increase efficient mobility and movement across all activities and domains and include a range of mobility alternatives as well as movement goals that contribute to improved body mechanics. If not yet achieved, motor/ mobility objectives should be developed for all possible activity goals.
9.   Increase ease in providing for a student's basic needs including eating, dressing, and hygiene. Goals might target direct skill building and/or improving the assistance the student can provide to a caregiver.

The decision rules by themselves, of course, are of little practical value in generating potential IEP goals. In their activity-based approach, therefore, Ferguson and Wilcox (1988) have developed a clear process for determining content, based on the needs and interests of the child and his or her family. A modified version of an ecological inventory, termed a "Home Activities Interview," is used to determine current home and community activities and the level of the child's current and desired participation.

Giangreco et al. (1993) proposed a "cross-prioritization" process. After the family ranks a minimum of their top eight overall priorities, the person who is facilitating the process verifies the intent of the priorities and clarifies how they are referenced to the "valued life outcomes." For example, the facilitator might say,

> I want to make sure I understand your priorities. Please tell me if I am accurately summarizing your views that led you to select [them]. Drinking and eating by mouth was your top priority for Tommy. I understand that this is because you are concerned that he does not eat and drink enough to maintain his health and that he aspirates food into his lungs which causes chest infections. Is that correct? (p. 46)

Following this step, the family makes a final decision and reaches agreement with the interviewer about how each priority should be addressed. The choices are 1) "Included in the IEP," which means the priority should be translated to annual goals and short-term objectives; or 2) "Breadth of Curriculum," which involves keeping the activity as a potential learning outcome, but not giving it IEP goal status; or 3) "Home," which means the family takes primary responsibility for the activity (Giangreco et al., 1993, p. 46).

Write Activity-Based Goals and Objectives

Those behaviors, skills, or needs selected as priorities to be included in the IEP need to be restated as annual goals and short-term objectives. There are many reasonable formats for writing goals. Ferguson and Wilcox (1988) suggested that well-written goals meet the following criteria:

1.   The goal is *measurable*; that is, it describes an observable, measurable behavior that the student (not the staff) will perform.
2.   The goal is an *activity*; that is, it describes three phases: initiation or preparation, execution or doing, and resolution or ending. The activity must result in an outcome that is functional for the student.

3. The goal is *age appropriate*; that is, it represents an activity that is typically performed by individuals of the same age who do not have disabilities.
4. The goal is *generalizable*; that is, it describes the range of natural settings in which the behavior is to be exhibited.

It is critical to appreciate that the process the team follows to develop instructional goals will have a profound influence on not only the quality of the goals, but ultimately on how instruction is organized and delivered. In particular, this book emphasizes the desirability of a transdisciplinary approach, in which instructional teams organize themselves to conduct assessment, develop goals, and deliver instruction in a coordinated fashion wherein traditional disciplinary borders are easily crossed. Traditionally written IEPs (i.e., those that have separate sections for instructional goals and "therapy" goals) will invariably result in fragmented educational programs. In contrast, IEP goals and objectives that incorporate qualitative aspects of the student's performance are typically more successful. The following objective offers an example of this approach: "After 1 minute of tone reduction and while given physical guidance at the elbow and wrist, Sonja will reach to her communication board five times without pulling back, for 3 consecutive days" (Rainforth, York, et al., 1992, p. 165).

In general, goals and objectives should conform to the ecological approach described previously in this chapter. That implies that they should explicitly include the priority environments and activities in which the skills will be used. In this vein, Rainforth, York, et al. (1992) suggested two broad approaches to writing goals and objectives: 1) the goals specify priority skills and the objectives specify contexts for performance, and 2) the goals specify priority environments and activities and the objectives specify component skills. An example of each type is provided in Figure 10.5.

Goals (and, by extension, objectives) should be written to reflect the learner's active performance. Unfortunately, sometimes the opposite is done, and the student becomes a passive receiver of stimuli, or, worse, a mere presence. To avoid this situation, Ford (1994) suggested applying a criterion to instructional goals: the "potato test." Simply, if a goal is one that a potato could do, then the goal fails the potato test. For instance, the goal "Latisha will lie quietly for 20 minutes in a sidelyer" does not pass the potato test because it addresses the *absence* of performance and, hence, a potato could perform the goal (Orelove, 1995). By the same measure, it is inadequate to write a goal that requires that a student "not scream," yet not offer an alternative, desirable behavior that makes it unnecessary for the student to scream to gain attention.

Other health management objectives for children may be valuable but should not be confused with active, instructional goals. Examples include "David will receive a high-calorie dietary supplement" and "Michelle's position will be changed every half hour" (Rainforth, York, et al., 1992, p. 161). Such service objectives would be appropriate to include as part of the Health Services Plan, described in Chapter 6.

Goals specify priority skills; objectives specify contexts for performance

GOAL

Missy will improve visual scanning and focusing to make and convey choices in daily routines.

OBJECTIVE

When positioned in her chair with her head stabilized and presented with two objects at eye level, Missy will look at each object for 1 second and focus on her preference for 5 seconds, in 3 out of 4 trials, on 3 consecutive days, in each of the following situations:

1. Mealtime (choose between food and drink)
2. Free time (choose between toys for microswitch)
3. Grooming (choose sequence from washcloth, toothbrush, hairbrush)

Goals specify priority environments and activities; objectives specify component skills

GOAL

Tess will participate in a sixth-grade science class.

OBJECTIVES

1. Tess will read "science" from her schedule and print "science" next to the model, without overlapping letters, for 1 week.
2. When given a verbal reminder, Tess will tell other students in her science group, "I can do this, thanks," or "I need help, please" on 80% of opportunities for 1 week.
3. At the end of class, Tess will converse with a friend in a turn-taking routine by answering the friend's question and then asking a question about the preceding science activity, daily for 1 week.

Figure 10.5.   Examples of instructional goals and objectives. (From Rainforth, B., York, J., & Macdonald, C. [1992]. *Collaborative teams for students with severe disabilities: Integrating therapy and educational services* (pp. 166–167). Baltimore: Paul H. Brookes Publishing Co.; reprinted by permission.)

INSTRUCTION

Having determined *what* to teach the learner, the team must then turn to devising practical, effective strategies for ensuring that the goals and objectives are achieved. Doing this requires staff to develop a specific plan for each student across the school day, determine teaching strategies that work for a particular child and a particular activity, and determine and apply methods for measuring progress toward meeting the instructional goals. At the same time, the team must consider 1) each student's need for adaptations and special supports (including assistive technology and any directly provided related services); 2) the relationship of the child's physical, sensory, and health status to organizing and delivering instruction; and 3) the need to develop specialized strategies for reducing any challenging behaviors (see Figure 10.1). This portion of the chapter explores each of these components.

It is necessary first, however, to remind the reader of the assumption within this chapter that instruction will be conducted in the context of the general education classroom. There are many elements that are crucial to the success of inclusive educational programs that are simply beyond the scope of this chapter. For instance, certain service delivery issues (e.g., the organization and roles of teaching and support staff, school policies and procedures; student ratios) must be considered (Halvorsen, 1992; Sailor, Gee, & Karasoff, 1993). At the building level, supports and strategies must be put in place, such as staff development and collaborative team structures (Kronberg, 1992). Finally, specific classroom strategies (e.g., multilevel instruction, team teaching, peer support) are important in enhancing the success of inclusive education for learners with disabilities (Neary, 1992). Readers seeking specific strategies for developing inclusive school and classroom environments, which are necessary for the success of the child-specific strategies described in this chapter, are encouraged to consult Goodman (1994); Putnam (1993); Thousand, Villa, and Nevin (1994); and Vandercook et al. (1993).

Determine Individual Student Plans

Once IEP goals and objectives have been developed, the team must decide how to set up the school day so that each learner has the opportunity to learn and to practice the necessary skills for those objectives. Fortunately, an inclusive classroom complements perfectly the activity-based approach to instructional goal setting described previously in the chapter.

One of the simplest and most effective ways to ensure that the child's objectives are being addressed is to develop a matrix. Although several formats have been promoted (see, e.g., Downing, 1996; Giangreco et al., 1993; Neary, 1992; Rainforth, York, et al., 1992), they are all based on the same simple process: One lists the activities or periods of the school day across the top and the specific IEP objectives down the side (or vice versa). Figures 10.6 and 10.7 provide examples of matrices for students in inclusive elementary and secondary school programs.

A matrix offers several advantages. First, it ensures that each student is included in a meaningful way in as many regularly scheduled activities as possible during the day. Second, a matrix provides opportunities for the child to learn skills at naturally occurring times and in response to natural cues, both of which facilitate acquisition. Third, a matrix provides many opportunities for students to practice skills in different situations, a critical condition for promoting generalization. Finally, a matrix offers the transdisciplinary team a simple method of organizing the day and of seeing at a glance what the student should be doing at any given moment.

One may question how a child with a multiple disability can participate in typical educational activities. The answer, simply, is adaptations. Readers are encouraged to review Chapter 4, which addresses strategies for designing indi-

Anna   Classroom schedule   *First grade 1990-1991*

IEP Objective	8:30 A.M.–9:50 A.M. Opening; salute the flag; attendance; calendar	8:50 A.M.–9:45 A.M. Language; reading; phonics; choice	9:45 A.M.–10:00 A.M. Recess; snack	10:00 A.M.–10:15 A.M. Sharing	10:15 A.M.–10:50 A.M. Math; manipulatives; sorting; classifying	10:50 A.M.–11:30 A.M. Music; gym; social studies	11:30 A.M.–12:15 P.M. Lunch	12:15 P.M.–12:35 P.M. Story	12:35 P.M.–1:20 P.M. Language; journal; math; brainstorming; choice	1:20 P.M.–1:30 P.M. Recess	1:30 P.M.–2:15 P.M. Art; gym; social studies
Walk independently	✓	✓	✓	✓	✓	✓	✓	✓	✓	✓	✓
Clap hands			✓		✓	✓				✓	✓
Participate with peers in gym games		✓				✓	✓			✓	✓
Use name stamp independently		✓			✓	✓			✓		✓
Use crayon or paint appropriately		✓			✓	✓			✓		✓
Complete three-piece puzzle		✓			✓	✓			✓		✓
Follow multistep routine	✓	✓	✓			✓	✓			✓	
Get in and out of a wheelchair	✓		✓				✓			✓	✓
Get up from/down on the floor	✓	✓		✓	✓			✓	✓		
Use five new signs to communicate	✓	✓	✓	✓	✓	✓	✓	✓	✓	✓	✓
Say "Mom" to photo or mother	✓	✓			✓	✓			✓		✓
Choose using communication board		✓	✓		✓	✓			✓	✓	
Turn taking with peers		✓	✓		✓				✓	✓	✓
Circle of friends; initiate interaction		✓	✓		✓		✓		✓	✓	✓
Computer use-games; communication		✓			✓				✓		✓

Figure 10.6.   An IEP objectives/classroom schedule matrix for a student in an inclusive elementary program. (From Neary, T. [1992, December]. Student-specific strategies. In T. Neary, A. Halvorsen, R. Kronberg, & D. Kelly, *Curriculum adaptations for inclusive classrooms,* pp. 56–125. San Francisco, CA: San Francisco State University; adapted by permission.)

vidual adaptations. In addition to individual adaptations, there are ways of adapting the curriculum to meet the needs of the learner who requires special assistance. The codes (S, ML, and CO) in the cells in Figure 10.7, which depicts the matrix for a secondary school student, refer to specific curriculum adaptation strategies.

Name: Rob		Period 1	Period 2	Period 3	Period 4	Period 5	Lunch	Period 6
		Science	Gym	Work experience	Work experience	Library	Library	Computers
IEP objectives	1. Use Intro-Talker to initiate conversations with peers without disabilities	S	S	S	S	S	S	S
	2. Use self-monitor checklist	ML		ML	ML			ML
	3. Order from snack bar						S	
	4. Make transition independently to next class/activity	S	S	S	S	S	S	S
	5. Use watch to be on time	S	S	S	S	S	S	S
	6. Recognize correct bus stop and route			S	S			
	7. Model voice level of peers	CO	CO	ML	ML	CO	S	CO
	8. Use Apple II printer							ML
Management needs	1. Written behavior plan	✓	✓	✓	✓	✓	✓	✓
	2. Peer assistants in classes	✓	✓	✓	✓	✓	✓	✓
	3. Intro-Talker (updates overlay)	✓	✓	✓	✓	✓	✓	✓

Figure 10.7. A matrix for a student in an inclusive secondary program. (✓ = opportunity to work on student's IEP objectives.) (From Neary, T. [1992, December]. Student-specific strategies. In T. Neary, A. Halvorsen, R. Kronberg, & D. Kelly, *Curriculum adaptations for inclusive classrooms*, pp. 56–125. San Francisco, CA: San Francisco State University; adapted by permission.)

The codes and strategies are as follows (Neary, 1992):

S refers to *same*; that is, the student is involved in the same lesson as other students (i.e., without disabilities) with the same objectives and using the same materials. For instance, Sam takes photographs to help put together the candid photograph pages for the school yearbook.

ML refers to *multilevel curriculum*. Students work in the same subject area, but at different levels of curriculum. For example, while other students write book reports, Emma draws a picture about the story.

CO refers to *curriculum overlapping*. In this adaptation, students are involved in the same activity with other students, but may have a goal from a different curriculum area. For instance, during math enrichment time, Irene works on her range-of-motion skills to activate an audiotape recorder.

Determine Individual Teaching Strategies

Once team members have matched a student's IEP objectives to instructional activities and times, they must then develop specific strategies for helping the student meet those objectives. This is one of the points at which transdisciplinary teaming becomes most critical. Effective teaching for students with multiple disabilities demands the pooled knowledge and skills of families, teachers, therapists, nurses, and other professionals and the creativity of all of them working in concert.

At a minimum, individual teaching strategies must incorporate the components that follow (Downing, 1996; Rainforth, York, et al., 1992) (see Table 10.1).

Preparing Student for Instruction   Getting the student ready to learn is as important as the direct instruction that follows. As noted in Chapter 3, the position in which a child with a multiple disability is placed should accommodate not only the child's physical needs, but the specific instructional activity on which he or she is working. Position is integrally related to movement, as well as vision and comfort, all of which play major roles in the ability to see and interact with materials and people and to be motivated to learn. It is also important to remember that many children will require extra time to move from one activity to another. These transitions should be thought of as useful, natural opportunities for practicing important mobility skills. Teams are encouraged to write specific positions and transition times directly on the student's schedule. (See Rainforth, York, et al., 1992, p. 187, for an example.)

Another way that students can be prepared for instruction is by normalizing their muscle tone (Rainforth, York, et al., 1992; see Chapter 3). Slow, rhythmic movement can "relax" children with spasticity and give them more freedom of movement for the activity to follow.

Finally, although not related to the lesson or task itself, students might be prepared for an activity through knowing about or anticipating what will be the next activity. Students who are unable to read or comprehend a daily schedule

Table 10.1.   Questions for the educational team to ask to accommodate inclusive learning

---

1. What is the best position for the student?
   • Where are the other students? On the floor? At desks? Standing at tables?
   • What allows the student the greatest movement needed for the activity? The best vision? The best hearing?
   • Is the student physically isolated or right with the others?

2. Is the student able to obtain information from the teacher?
   • What is the learning style of the student?
   • Does the student learn in an auditory, visual, tactile, and/or kinesthetic way? Is the necessary information available in the activity?
   • Can additional information be added to an activity to make it more understandable to a given student?

3. How can the student participate?
   • Can the student raise his or her hand to gain attention? Is another way possible (e.g., switch-activated voice output mode)?
   • Can the student respond verbally to questions? If not, can he or she be given choices of objects and/or pictures as responses?
   • Can the student engage in movement related to the activity (e.g., act out a skit, pass items, get out and put away materials)?
   • How does participation in each activity support the student's IEP objectives?

4. Who can assist in the learning process?
   • Can other students help? Teachers? Support staff? Volunteers? Older students?

From Downing, J.E., & Demchak, M.A. (1996). First steps: Determining individual abilities and deciding how best to support students. In J.E. Downing, *Including students with severe and multiple disabilities in typical classrooms: Practical strategies for teachers* (p. 44). Baltimore: Paul H. Brookes Publishing Co.; reprinted by permission.

may be confused or may feel they are being randomly moved from one place to another and from one activity to the next. One practical solution is through the use of a *calendar box*. The calendar box is a series of containers (e.g., shoe boxes, margarine tubs) that are taped or glued together (see Figure 10.8). Within each box is placed a representational object, a part of an actual object, or a picture—depending on the learner's communication level—in the sequence in

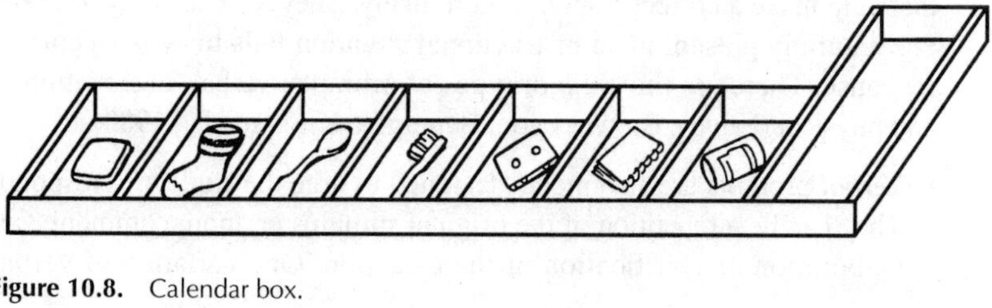

Figure 10.8.   Calendar box.

which the activity occurs, from left to right. The learner takes an object from the box to understand what activity comes next. When the activity has been completed, the object is placed in the "finished" container. Calendar boxes can help the student develop a variety of skills, including left to right order, beginnings and endings, choice making, and anticipation (Beukelman & Mirenda, 1992).

Determining Individual Learning Styles   It is an axiom that each person learns best in his or her own particular way. This is especially true for children with multiple disabilities, many of whom have additional sensory losses (see Chapter 11) or impairments of one or more of the sensorimotor systems (see Chapter 2). Despite these characteristics, however, one must be careful not to assume that a particular reduction in sensory function will make teaching through that modality fruitless. As Downing and Demchak (1996) observed, "Some children, for instance, will acquire considerable information via the auditory mode even though they have a moderate hearing loss" (p. 44). The same is true for learners with severe visual impairments.

There is no one method of determining which mode will best help a student learn. Often, the specific activity itself influences the teaching method (Downing & Demchak, 1996). Knowledge of the child's sensorimotor systems can be quite useful in understanding the difficulties the child may be having in performing a particular activity. Readers are encouraged to consult Table 2.5 in Chapter 2.

Teaching Skills Directly   "Simply including a student with severe sensory and multiple disabilities in a typical classroom does not mean that instruction of that student no longer needs to occur. If an activity is important enough to target in the IEP as an objective, it is important enough to teach systematically." (Downing & Demchak, 1996, p. 46). An instructional technology for teaching skills to students with severe disabilities is well developed and documented (see Snell & Brown, 1993). This section describes several of the essential components of direct instruction, subdivided into two broad categories. It should be noted that much of the information in the following sections can appear intimidating to general education teachers who are not familiar with the jargon.

Antecedent Events   Antecedent events include cues or directions, the materials used in instruction, and the instructional arrangement itself, all of which exert a tremendous influence on a student's responses.

1. *Types of prompts*   Prompts are stimuli added before or during a response that help make a correct response more likely. They are used only after the cue naturally present in an instructional situation fails to evoke a correct response. There are three major types of prompts: verbal, observational, and physical (Falvey, Brown, Lyon, Baumgart, & Schroeder, 1980).

   • *Verbal* prompts are statements designed to urge the student to respond. They can be a repetition of the original stimulus or, more commonly, an elaboration or clarification of the direction. One variation of verbal prompts is the auditory prompt, involving the use of supplemental speech or other sound cues different from the initial verbal cue. Verbal prompts are particularly useful in working with students with significant visual loss.

- *Observational* prompts can be either models of the behavior itself (i.e., "Do this") that the student imitates, or gestures (e.g., pointing, leaning) that cue the student to the form or location of a response. One might also include in this category augmentative visual cues (e.g., shining flashlight on an item) that help call attention to an item for a learner with a visual impairment.
- *Physical* prompts, usually considered to be the most intrusive (i.e., they interfere with the natural sequence), are commonly used with individuals with multiple disabilities. They can be partial (i.e., helping with part of the task or providing part of the total movement) or total (i.e., actually guiding the student through the task). They can also provide tactile input for students with visual impairments by providing manual assistance, for example, to a child trying to turn his or her head to track.

2. *Prompting systems* Typically, prompts are used in combinations to evoke correct responses while preventing continued dependence on the instructor. Two common systems are briefly described here.

- *Least intrusive prompts* involve giving the student an opportunity to respond to the naturally occurring stimulus. If the student does not respond in a reasonable amount of time, the instructor adds a verbal prompt (assuming the student has adequate hearing, of course). This process is repeated, as necessary, with a verbal and observational prompt combination and, finally, a verbal and physical prompt combination. The concept is to allow the student to perform the behavior at the least intrusive/most natural level of prompt possible.
- *Graduated guidance* uses a most-to-least prompt hierarchy. The instructor applies partial to full physical assistance and gradually reduces, or fades, the location or degree of assistance to allow the student to take over.

More information on these and other prompting strategies can be found in Demchak (1990), Schoen (1986), and Snell and Brown (1993). It should be noted that the necessity for adding prompt hierarchies and artificial prompts should be reduced through instruction on natural routines within natural environments.

3. *Task presentation* Research shows that the way instructional trials or tasks are organized makes a difference in skill acquisition (e.g., Holvoet, Mulligan, Schussler, Lacy, & Guess, 1982; Kayser, Billingsley, & Neel, 1986). One relevant variable is the spacing of trials. Mulligan, Lacy, and Guess (1982) differentiated among three types of trial sequencing:

- *Massed* trials are those presented so closely together that no other behavior can be expected to occur between them.
- *Distributed* trial sequences have separated trials or periods of time between two trials from the same program, in which trials from one or more other programs are inserted.
- *Spaced* trial sequences also have spaces between trials, but there is a rest or pause in those spaces instead of trials from other programs.

Although massed or spaced trial presentations have been commonly used with children with multiple disabilities, the research clearly demonstrates the superiority of distributed trial learning. One of the obvious practical advantages of this approach is that it most closely mirrors what happens in group instruction. Table 10.2 offers several suggestions for teachers who are teaching a group in the same content area.

Consequent Events   Students with multiple disabilities, like other people, learn from the consequences of their behaviors. When students are correct, they typically are rewarded, either as a natural consequence of their actions or by a reinforcer given by an adult or peer. Incorrect responses are corrected and desired behaviors taught in their place.

1. *Delivering reinforcement*   The idea that a behavior needs to be reinforced (or to generate reinforcers) to strengthen the chances that it will occur again

Table 10.2.   Suggestions for teaching students in same content area

- Encourage students to listen and watch other group members as they take their turns. Then praise them when they do.
- Keep the group instruction interesting by keeping turns short, giving all members turns, giving turns contingent on attending (or on being prompted to attend if need be), and using demonstrations and a variety of materials that can be handled.
- Involve all members by using multilevel instruction to individualize to a student's targeted skills and mode of response. Use partial participation and material adaptation to enable all students to respond. Involve students in the process of praising other group members and in assisting or prompting group members. Let students participate in demonstrations (or give demonstrations themselves). Let students handle materials related to the skill of concept being taught.
- Keep waiting time to a minimum by controlling the group size, the amount of teacher talk and presentation, and the amount of student response in a single turn.
- Promote cooperation among group members over competition between members so that all students experience success.
- Above all, individualize instruction through multilevel instruction, adapted materials, peer assistance, and cooperative learning methods, so that all group members are challenged and learn.

From Snell, M.E., & Brown, F. (1993). Instructional planning and implementation. In M.E. Snell (Ed.), *Instruction of students with severe disabilities* (4th ed., p. 141); reprinted by permission of Prentice Hall, Upper Saddle River, NJ.

is fundamental to all learning. It is also recognized that reinforcing stimuli have individualized effectiveness and are situation specific; what works with one student in one situation may not work with a different student or even with the same student in a different situation. Despite the almost endless possibilities for reinforcers (e.g., food, drink, praise, activities, toys, special time), it is not uncommon for team members to report finding it impossible to discover a reinforcer that "works."

The only true way to discover whether a stimulus works as a reinforcer is to deliver the stimulus immediately following, and contingent on, the behavior and see if the behavior then strengthens (e.g., becomes faster, more proficient). The mere delivery of a stimulus after a response does not ensure that the stimulus will have a positive effect on learning. Stimuli may, in fact, have the opposite effect in certain situations. Nevertheless, it can be frustrating to identify a true reinforcer for the student with multiple disabilities. One can ask the child who is verbal what he or she would like or give the student free rein over the classroom to point out a preference. The learner who cannot communicate or move about freely, however, usually has more limited—or at least different—means of expressing preferences. There are several strategies for determining potential reinforcers:

- Surveys of people who know the child well, in addition to the information from the MAPs process (see Figure 10.3) can be used to discover what items or events the child seems to enjoy.
- The environment can be structured for trying out possible items. In reinforcer sampling, the student briefly samples small groups of similar items and is then allowed to choose freely.
- Several studies (e.g., Pace, Ivancic, Edwards, Iwata, & Page, 1985; Wacker, Wiggins, Fowler, & Berg, 1988) have described procedures for systematically assessing the reinforcement value of items for individuals with mental retardation requiring pervasive supports who have restricted movement. This research clearly reveals how individualized and consistent the choice of reinforcers truly is.
- The *Comprehensive Communication Curriculum Guide* (Klein et al., 1981) describes an excellent process for establishing potential reinforcers for children with very limited motor and communication repertoires. The techniques involve noting changes in facial expression, vocalization, and body movement upon presentation and withdrawal of stimuli. In a particularly interesting variation, the parent or professional repeatedly presents an item to the child over several days and then withholds it, looking for an anticipatory response from the child.
- Shevin (1982) has described guidelines for selecting reinforcers, particularly food and drink, for students with severe disabilities.

2. *Correcting errors*   Although instruction is often arranged to prevent errors, they are an inevitable—and often constructive—part of learning. It

is difficult to separate the correction aspect of a task (i.e., consequences) from the cues before the task (i.e., antecedents), particularly when a system of least prompts is used. Nevertheless, a few general guidelines may be helpful:

- Errors should be corrected either immediately following the incorrect response or by interrupting the incorrect response. The student should be provided with another chance to respond correctly, with additional help if necessary.
- Correction procedures that are as close as possible to those in the student's natural environments should be used.
- Only the least assistance necessary to help the student to respond correctly the next time should be provided; *one should avoid doing everything for the student.* If total physical assistance is needed initially, it should be removed gradually to prevent the student's overdependence on staff or peers.
- Partial participation should be considered if the task appears to be too difficult. Numerous errors may also suggest that the task needs to be reanalyzed or that antecedents or materials need to be modified.

Handling Challenging Behaviors   Many students engage in extra behaviors that get in the way of learning and that frustrate teachers and other team members. These behaviors range from annoying (e.g., humming, rocking) to disruptive (e.g., shouting, throwing materials) to harmful (e.g., biting oneself, hitting others).

It is essential to understand that all behaviors serve a particular function for the individual in that particular situation (Carr et al., 1994; Durand, 1990). Students may engage in challenging behaviors because they are bored, frustrated, or in some way reacting to an aspect of their daily routine or instructional program. Other students may be in discomfort from improper positioning, poorly designed equipment, illness, or medications. Some behaviors (e.g., drooling, tongue thrusting) may result from students' physical conditions and may not be entirely under their control.

The only way to determine why a child is engaging in a particular behavior is to conduct a thorough functional assessment (Horner, O'Neill, & Flannery, 1993). This can be done through interviews, rating scales, direct observations, and functional analyses. An assessment should yield four major outcomes:

1. A clearly written operational description of the behavior(s) so anyone can read and understand it. The definition should also specify how often the behavior occurs, how long a typical episode lasts, and how intense the behavior is.
2. An identification of the variables (e.g., times, settings, activities) that predict when the behavior(s) will and will not occur.

3. An identification of, or hypotheses about, the consequences that maintain the behavior(s) (e.g., Does the behavior help the student obtain a desired event or object? Does it enable the student to avoid or escape an activity?).
4. A verification of the predictors and consequences through direct observation.

Once the behavior has been appropriately assessed, the team can meet and determine strategies for dealing with it. In some cases, a relatively simple change can be made in scheduling, environment, or expectations. For other situations, however, a student may benefit from a behavioral support plan. There are comprehensive (but not necessarily lengthy) plans to decrease the challenging behavior by supporting the student. Behavioral support plans have six major elements (Horner et al., 1993):

1. *A clear description of the problem behavior(s)*   It is helpful to put the behavior in context (i.e., in what situation does it typically occur?).
2. *Hypotheses* about what is maintaining the behavior, based on the outcomes of the functional assessment   These can be both specific to the behavior (e.g., he hits others when interrupted in the middle of his seat work) and general (e.g., she has very little control over the activities she is given during the day).
3. A description of both *broad and specific environmental procedures* to address the problem behavior   These procedures typically fall into one or more of the following categories: changes in physical settings, changes in social context, changes in medical and health supports, sleep and diet patterns, activity patterns and daily schedules, and curriculum changes.
4. A plan for implementing changes in *immediate antecedents* to the behavior   Antecedent changes include increasing predictability for the student, increasing the student's choices and preferences, changing pacing and voice intonation, and interspersing requests and maintenance tasks.
5. Description of *consequences* for selected behaviors   These should be aimed at maximizing reinforcement for appropriate, alternative behaviors, redirecting the student, and minimizing the reinforcement for problem behaviors.
6. Delineation of *monitoring and evaluation* procedures   Teams should formally examine and summarize progress at least weekly.

Develop Strategies for Measuring Progress

The final step in instruction is to determine how to measure each student's progress toward meeting goals and objectives. Although there are a myriad of specific methods of collecting information, the decision of what method to use for a particular time and place comes down to two basic questions: 1) Will it reveal useful or meaningful information? and 2) Is it practical?

The first question has to do partly with the degree to which the data being collected are accurate; that is, do they reflect what is really happening? More important, however, is that measurement is meaningful if the information can be used to make intelligent decisions about how well the student is meeting the objectives. (This presupposes that the objectives, themselves, are relevant to the student and his or her world.) One can measure tiny, incremental gains on a task that add up to nothing significant, and thereby miss the forest for the trees. For instance, one may observe that a child has increased the intensity (i.e., loudness) of vocalizing, yet fail to determine that he or she has made no real gains in getting his or her needs known to others.

The second question concerns practicality. Since the 1960s, professionals in psychology and special education have developed many sophisticated and increasingly sensitive techniques for measuring behavior change. Many of them, however, were designed to be used in self-contained classrooms for learners with disabilities. Moreover, many of these techniques required a fair amount of specialized training and time. If measurement is going to be useful, it must be *used* (i.e., strategies that can be incorporated easily into the flow of the general education classroom and other areas in and around the school).

The goal, of course, is to maximize both meaningfulness and practicality. Efficient measurement strategies do not necessarily yield useful information and, conversely, a highly sensitive technique will not be used if it is overly time consuming or cumbersome. Fortunately, some situations lead naturally to simple solutions. If the goal is to clean one's face, for example, then an obvious measure is to look and see if the face looks clean. Other paper and pencil and manipulation tasks also lend themselves to inspecting the products or results left behind. Brown and Snell (1993) suggest other creative strategies, such as keeping notes on small index cards or Post-its.

Sometimes the solution to measuring performance is to think more broadly about the outcomes of interest. For instance, an instructional team that wishes to foster an expanded social network for a child may include an IEP objective for that child to demonstrate increased participation in school activities and play with peers. The measurement strategies might include keeping activity records and conducting informal observations at lunch and on the playground (Meyer & Janney, 1989).

It must be remembered that the major purpose of measuring performance is to obtain valid information that can be used to improve instruction. A challenge for transdisciplinary teams is for members to share useful information with each other efficiently. One such strategy is depicted in Figure 10.9 (Rainforth, York, et al., 1992).

One technique for keeping track of student performance that has broad application to all learners in all settings is *portfolio assessment*. Portfolios are "systematic, purposeful, and meaningful collections of students' works in one or more subject areas" (De Fina, 1992, p. 13). They may include input from all members of the team, plus parents, peers, and administrators. Portfolios can also include work in a variety of media.

PROGRAM CHANGE NEEDED	PROGRAM CHANGE MADE
Date: 10-12-92	Date:
To: Lisa W. (OT)	To:
From: Jake S. (Teaching Assistant)	From:
Student: Jamal W.	Student:
Program: Driving wheelchair	Program:
Reason change is needed: ____ criterion met _X_ no progress ____ other (specify)	Reason change was met: ____ criterion met ____ no progress ____ other (specify)
Comments/suggestions: He's not doing as well as during baseline. He seems interested but he gets real stiff and seems to resist my prompts.	Comments/suggestions:

PROGRAM CHANGE NEEDED	PROGRAM CHANGE MADE
Date: 10-12-92	Date: 10-16-92
To: Lisa W. (OT)	To: Jamal W.'s team
From: Jake S. (Teaching Assistant)	From: Lisa W.
Student: Jamal W.	Student: Jamal W.
Program: Driving wheelchair	Program: Stamping mail, driving wheelchair, turning on tape recorder
Reason change is needed: ____ criterion met _X_ no progress ____ other (specify)	Reason change was met: ____ criterion met _X_ no progress ____ other (specify)
Comments/suggestions: He's not doing as well as during baseline. He seems interested but he gets real stiff and seems to resist my prompts.	Comments/suggestions: Jamal does much better when relaxed and stretched before asked to use his hands. I'll work with each of you to use warm-up procedure (attached)

Figure 10.9. Program change notes. (From Rainforth, B., York, J., & Macdonald, C. [1992]. *Collaborative teams for students with severe disabilities: Integrating therapy and educational services* [p. 200]. Baltimore: Paul H. Brookes Publishing Co.; reprinted by permission.)

Assessing portfolios can be useful in examining a learner's growth over time. The process can also be used to help students gain a sense of ownership of their work and to facilitate discussion among staff and between family and school. Moreover, portfolios (especially those including videotaped footage) are valuable in facilitating a smooth transition for the student from one year to the next. Perhaps most important, portfolio assessment can help teams learn which instructional practices work well and which are not particularly effective.

CONCLUSION

This chapter briefly discusses a variety of key elements in developing curriculum and teaching students with multiple disabilities. No chapter, no book, and no manual, no matter how detailed, can ever convey all the subtleties needed to teach. But it is also true that a professional may be an excellent technician without possessing the value base for making important decisions. It is hoped that this chapter provides enough of a flavor of some of the essential values and whets the reader's appetite for learning more and trying out some new ideas.

REFERENCES

Bayley, N. (1993). *Bayley Scales of Infant Development—Second edition manual*. San Antonio, TX: The Psychological Corporation.

Beukelman, D.R., & Mirenda, P. (1992). *Augmentative and alternative communication: Management of severe communication disorders in children and adults*. Baltimore: Paul H. Brookes Publishing Co.

Browder, D.M. (1991). *Assessment of individuals with severe disabilities: An applied behavior approach to life skills assessment* (2nd ed.). Baltimore: Paul H. Brookes Publishing Co.

Brown, F., Evans, I.M., Weed, K.A., & Owens, V. (1987). Delineating functional competencies: A component model. *Journal of The Association for Persons with Severe Handicaps, 12*, 117–124.

Brown, F., & Snell, M.E. (1993). Measurement, analysis, and evaluation. In M.E. Snell (Ed.), *Instruction of students with severe disabilities* (4th ed., pp. 152–183). New York: Macmillan.

Brown, L., Branston, M.B., Hamre-Nietupski, S., Pumpian, J., Certo, N., & Gruenewald, L. (1979). A strategy for developing chronological age appropriate and functional curricular content for severely handicapped adolescents and young adults. *Journal of Special Education, 13*, 81–90.

Carr, E.G., Levin, L., McConnachie, G., Carlson, J.I., Kemp, D.C., & Smith, C.E. (1994). *Communication-based intervention for problem behavior: A user's guide for producing positive change*. Baltimore: Paul H. Brookes Publishing Co.

De Fina, A.A. (1992). *Portfolio assessment*. New York: Scholastic Professional Books.

Demchak, M. (1990). Response prompting and fading methods: A review. *American Journal on Mental Retardation, 94(6)*, 603–615.

Downing, J.E. (1996). *Including students with severe multiple disabilities in typical classrooms: Practical strategies for teachers*. Baltimore: Paul H. Brookes Publishing Co.

Downing, J.E., & Demchak, M.A. (1996). First steps: Determining individual abilities and how best to support students. In J.E. Downing, *Including students with severe and multiple disabilities in typical classrooms: Practical strategies for teachers* (pp. 35–62). Baltimore: Paul H. Brookes Publishing Co.

Durand, V.M. (1990). *Severe behavior problems: A functional communication training approach*. New York: Guilford Press.

Falvey, M., Brown, L., Lyon, S., Baumgart, D., & Schroeder, J. (1980). Strategies for using cues and correction procedures. In W. Sailor, B. Wilcox, & L. Brown (Eds.), *Methods of instruction for severely handicapped students* (pp. 109–133). Baltimore: Paul H. Brookes Publishing Co.

Ferguson, D., Meyer, G., & Willis, C. (Eds.). (1990). *The elementary/secondary system: Supportive education for students with severe handicaps: Module 4a. Regular class participation system.* Eugene: University of Oregon, Specialized Training Program.

Ferguson, D.L., & Wilcox, B.L. (Eds.). (1988). *The elementary/secondary system: Supportive education for students with severe handicaps: Module I. The activity-based IEP.* Eugene: University of Oregon, Specialized Training Program.

Ford, A., Schnorr, R., Meyer, L., Davern, L., Black, J., & Dempsey, P. (Eds.). (1989). *The Syracuse community-referenced curriculum guide for students with moderate and severe disabilities.* Baltimore: Paul H. Brookes Publishing Co.

Ford, J. (1994, June). Keynote address presented at the First Annual Together We Can Summer Institute, Virginia Institute for Developmental Disabilities, Richmond.

Forest, M., & Pearpoint, J. (1992). MAPS: Action planning. In J. Pearpoint, M. Forest, & J. Snow, *The inclusion papers: Strategies to make inclusion work* (pp. 52–56). Toronto, Ontario, Canada: Inclusion Press.

Giangreco, M.F., Cloninger, C.J., & Iverson, V.S. (1993). *Choosing options and accommodations for children (COACH): A guide to planning inclusive education.* Baltimore: Paul H. Brookes Publishing Co.

Goodman, G. (1994). *Inclusive classrooms from A to Z: A handbook for educators.* Columbus, OH: Teachers' Publishing Group.

Guess, D., & Helmstetter, E. (1986). Skill cluster instruction and the individualized curriculum sequencing model. In R.H. Horner, L.H. Meyer, & H.D.B. Fredericks (Eds.), *Education of learners with severe handicaps: Exemplary service strategies* (pp. 221–248). Baltimore: Paul H. Brookes Publishing Co.

Halvorsen, A. (1992, December). Classroom-based strategies. In T. Neary, A. Halvorsen, R. Kronberg, & D. Kelly, *Curriculum adaptation for inclusive classrooms* (pp. 38–55). San Francisco: San Francisco State University, California Research Institute.

Haring, N.G., & Romer, L.T. (Eds.). (1995). *Welcoming students who are deaf-blind into typical classrooms: Facilitating school participation, learning, and friendships.* Baltimore: Paul H. Brookes Publishing Co.

Holvoet, J., Mulligan, M., Schussler, N., Lacy, L., & Guess, P.D. (1982). *The KICS model: Sequencing learning experiences for severely handicapped children and youth.* Lawrence: University of Kansas, The Kansas Individualized Curriculum Sequencing Project.

Horner, R.H., O'Neill, R.E., & Flannery, K.B. (1993). Effective behavior support plans. In M.E. Snell (Ed.), *Instruction of students with severe disabilities* (4th ed., pp. 184–214). New York: Macmillan.

Kayser, J.E., Billingsley, F.F., & Neel, R.S. (1986). A comparison of in-context and traditional instructional approaches: Total task, single trial versus backward chaining, multiple trials. *Journal of The Association for Persons with Severe Handicaps, 11*(1), 28–38.

Klein, M.D., Wulz, S.V., Hall, M.K., Waldo, L.J., Carpenter, S.A., Lathan, D.A., Myers, S.P., Fox, T., & Marshall, A.M. (1981). *Comprehensive communication curriculum guide.* Lawrence: Kansas Early Childhood Institute.

Kronberg, R. (1992, December). Building level support and strategies. In T. Neary, A. Halvorsen, R. Kronberg, & D. Kelly. *Curriculum adaptation for inclusive classrooms* (pp. 21–37). San Francisco: San Francisco State University, California Research Institute.

LeMay, D.W., Griffin, P.M., & Sanford, A.R. (1981). *Learning Accomplishment Profile—Diagnostic edition* (Rev. ed.). Chapel Hill, NC: Chapel Hill—Outreach Training Project.

Meyer, L., & Janney, R. (1989). User-friendly measures of meaningful outcomes: Evaluating behavioral interventions. *Journal of The Association for Persons with Severe Handicaps, 14*(4), 263–270.

Meyer, L.H., Peck, C.A., & Brown, L. (Eds.). (1991). *Critical issues in the lives of people with severe disabilities.* Baltimore: Paul H. Brookes Publishing Co.

Mulligan, M., Lacy, L., & Guess, D. (1982). Effects of massed, distributed, and spaced trial sequencing on severely handicapped students' performance. *Journal of The Association for the Severely Handicapped, 7*(2), 48–61.

Neary, T. (1992, December). Student-specific strategies. In T. Neary, A. Halvorsen, R. Kronberg, & D. Kelly, *Curriculum adaptation for inclusive classrooms* (pp. 56–125). San Francisco: San Francisco State University, California Research Institute.

Neel, R.S., & Billingsley, F.F. (1989). *Impact: A functional curriculum handbook for students with moderate to severe disabilities.* Baltimore: Paul H. Brookes Publishing Co.

Orelove, F.P. (1991). Educating all students: The future is now. In L.H. Meyer, C.A. Peck, & L. Brown (Eds.), *Critical issues in the lives of people with severe disabilities* (pp. 67–87). Baltimore: Paul H. Brookes Publishing Co.

Orelove, F.P. (1995, February). Consider the potato. *FourRunner: Newsletter of the Severe Disabilities Technical Assistance Center, 1.* Richmond: Virginia Commonwealth University, Virginia Institute for Developmental Disabilities.

Pace, G.M., Ivancic, M.T., Edwards, G.L., Iwata, B.A., & Page, T.J. (1985). Assessment of stimulus preference and reinforcer value with profoundly retarded individuals. *Journal of Applied Behavior Analysis, 18*, 249–255.

Putnam, J.W. (Ed.). (1993). *Cooperative learning and strategies for inclusion: Celebrating diversity in the classroom.* Baltimore: Paul H. Brookes Publishing Co.

Rainforth, B., Macdonald, C., York, J., & Dunn, W. (1992). Collaborative assessment. In B. Rainforth, J. York, & C. Macdonald, *Collaborative teams for students with severe disabilities: Integrating therapy and educational services* (pp. 105–155). Baltimore: Paul H. Brookes Publishing Co.

Rainforth, B., York, J., & Macdonald, C. (1992). *Collaborative teams for students with severe disabilities: Integrating therapy and educational services.* Baltimore: Paul H. Brookes Publishing Co.

Sailor, W., Gee, K., & Karasoff, P. (1993). Full inclusion and school restructuring. In M.E. Snell (Ed.), *Instruction of students with severe disabilities* (4th ed., pp. 1–30). New York: Macmillan.

Schoen, S.F. (1986). Assistance procedures to facilitate the transfer of stimulus control: Review and analysis. *Education and Training of the Mentally Retarded, 21*(1), 62–74.

Shevin, M. (1982). The use of food and drink in classroom management programs for severely handicapped children. *Journal of The Association for the Severely Handicapped, 7*(1), 40–46.

Snell, M.E. (1993). *Instruction of people with severe handicaps* (4th ed.). Columbus, OH: Charles E. Merrill.

Snell, M.E., & Brown, F. (1993). Instructional planning and implementation. (1993). *Instruction of people with severe handicaps* (4th ed., pp. 99–151). Columbus, OH: Charles E. Merrill.

Thousand, J.S., Villa, R.A., & Nevin, A.I. (Eds.). (1994). *Creativity and collaborative learning: A practical guide to empowering students and teachers.* Baltimore: Paul H. Brookes Publishing Co.

Vandercook, T., Tetlie, R.R., Montie, J., Downing, J., Levin, J., Glanville, M., Solberg, B., Branham, S., Ellson, L., & McNear, D. (1993). *Lessons for inclusion.* Toronto, Ontario, Canada: Inclusion Press.

Vandercook, T., York, J., & Forest, M..(1989). The McGill action planning system (MAPS): A strategy for building the vision. *Journal of The Association for Persons with Severe Handicaps, 14*, 205–215.

Wacker, D.P., Wiggins, B., Fowler, M., & Berg, W.K. (1988). Training students with profound or multiple handicaps to make requests via microswitches. *Journal of Applied Behavior Analysis, 21*, 331–343.

White, O.R. (1985). The evaluation of severely mentally retarded populations. In D. Bricker & J. Filler (Eds.), *Severe mental retardation: From theory to practice* (pp. 161–184). Reston, VA: Council for Exceptional Children, Division on Mental Retardation.

Wilcox, B., & Bellamy, G.T. (1987). *A comprehensive guide to The Activities Catalog: An alternative curriculum for youth and adults with severe disabilities.* Baltimore: Paul H. Brookes Publishing Co.

11

Children with Sensory Impairments

Dick Sobsey and Enid Wolf-Schein

MOST PEOPLE SEE AND HEAR WITHOUT significant difficulty and would find it difficult to imagine life without these abilities. With the loss of only one of these senses, mobility, communication, and learning become much more difficult. When both senses are impaired or additional disabilities are present and one is unable to use functional alternatives, all aspects of life are affected.

Sensory impairments require substantial accommodation and creativity in assessment, curriculum, task presentation, and reinforcement strategies. For example, music has been shown to be a particularly useful reinforcer with some individuals who have visual impairments (Hill, Brantner, & Spreat, 1989), and tactile adaptations are usually necessary for individuals who are deaf-blind. It may be necessary to employ structured presentations of possible reinforcers to determine a useful array of items and events for a particular student (Green, Reid, Canipe, & Gardner, 1991), but informal observation and suggestions from individuals who know the student can also be very helpful.

This chapter 1) presents basic information about hearing and vision disorders as they affect children with multiple disabilities, 2) reviews available prevalence data, 3) identifies suitable assessment procedures that can provide the intervention team with a clear picture of the nature and extent of sensory impairments, 4) describes methods of prevention and treatment, 5) discusses the educational implications of sensory impairment for children with multiple disabilities, and 6) explores the roles of transdisciplinary team members in maximizing the child's performance.

SENSORY IMPAIRMENT AMONG CHILDREN WITH MULTIPLE DISABILITIES

Estimates of the number of children with multiple disabilities who also have hearing or vision impairments are notoriously inconsistent and inaccurate.

Prevalence

Inconsistencies in the estimates of sensory impairment among children with multiple disabilities result from differences in the definitions used for various disabilities and from differences in sampling procedures. The Annual Survey of Deaf and Hard of Hearing Children and Youth (Schildroth & Hotto, in press) obtains reports of "additional educationally significant handicaps." This definition has the virtue of limiting the number of "multiply disabled deaf and hard of hearing students" to those who have one or more additional disabilities that affect their education. Some evidence of the validity of this approach can be found in the relative consistency of the rates reported over the years. Approximately 3 in 10 of the students included in the survey are said to have one or more additional disabilities. Over the years, this rate has varied from 33.4% in 1972 (Schein, 1979), to 30.2% in 1985 (Wolff & Harkins, 1986), to 32.6% in 1994 (Schildroth & Hotto, in press). In considering the Annual Survey's data, readers should realize that two groups are probably underrepresented by it: 1) children with significant disabilities *and* hearing impairments who are not in schools and 2) children with mild hearing impairments who attend general education classes with children who do not have hearing impairments. For example, a high rate of hearing impairment has frequently been observed in institutions for people with developmental disabilities (Moores, 1987), but because most of these institutions do not participate in the Annual Survey, these children are not counted. Looking within the category of additional educationally significant impairments, one finds that 5% of the students in the 1994–1995 survey have visual impairments, 1.4% of the students are blind, and 3.6% have uncorrected visual disabilities. That rate—1 in 20 students who are deaf or hard of hearing also have significant visual impairments—has also been consistently noted over the Annual Survey's nearly 25 years of data.

Kirchner (1985) examined data collected in the 1977 Health Interview Survey conducted by the U.S. National Center for Health Statistics, which defined "severe visual impairment" as being "unable to read ordinary newspaper print even with the aid of corrective lenses" (p. 5). Kirchner noted that 59% of respondents with visual impairments also had other disabilities, sometimes two or more. Other surveys conducted in Scandinavia and the United States suggest that children who are blind with mental retardation outnumber those without cognitive impairments (Brett, 1983). Some research suggests that as many as

75%–90% of people with severe or profound disabilities also have visual impairments (Cress et al.,1981). The New York State study of the "frail/severely handicapped" found that 43% of the children in the community and 42% of the children in institutions had visual impairments (Jacobson & Janicki, 1985). It also has been suggested that the number of children with visual impairments may be increasing because of medical advances that have made survival possible for many infants who are premature and/or have low birth weight and health problems (Leung & Hollins, 1989). Children with conditions, including cerebral palsy, myelomeningocele, and chromosomal or metabolic disorders, such as Down syndrome or Hurler syndrome, are also at risk for both hearing and visual impairments.

Experts disagree about the number of children with both hearing and visual impairments in the United States. In 1986, Dantona reported a total of 6,117 children who were deaf-blind in the United States. A projection of data from the Jacobson and Janicki (1985) study suggests that 12,000 or more children with visual and hearing impairments also have developmental disabilities. This discrepancy arises, in part, because Dantona reported a *count* of children who were deaf-blind, whereas Jacobson and Janicki's figure was an *estimate* that guessed at those likely to have been missed by the enumeration.

The definition of deaf-blind introduces another element leading to confusion about the number of people with this condition. Determining when a person is deaf and when a person is blind is somewhat arbitrary because impairments of these senses fall along a continuum from typical to profound. A study of the size and characteristics of individuals of all ages in the United States who are deaf-blind divides the definition into four groups based on the relative severities of the two impairments: 1) deaf and blind, 2) deaf and severe visual impairments, 3) blind and severe auditory impairments, and 4) severe auditory and visual impairments (Wolf-Schein, 1989). The prevalence for all four groups was 747,457. Another factor to be considered is residence. People who live in institutions have higher rates of disabilities than those living in the community. Combining people who live in institutions and people who do not live in institutions who are deaf-blind, the survey showed a prevalence of 45,310. This provides a strong indication that the number varies depending on the way the group is defined and that even when the most stringent definition was used, the numbers were greater than generally assumed. Other findings indicate that females were represented in each group at a higher rate than males, that the highest prevalence rate in each of the categories was for individuals 65 years old and over, and that there were considerable differences in prevalence rates among the nation's geographical regions.

Data from Statistics Canada also help to put the joint occurrence of hearing and vision impairments in perspective (Schein, 1989). The Health and Activity Limitation Survey (HALS) reported that 7 of 10 adults with hearing impairments have one or more additional disabling conditions. With respect to the kind of additional disability, HALS found that one in five Canadian adults with hearing impairments also have vision impairments (Schein, 1992). HALS did not gather information about additional disabilities among Canadian children.

From the preceding studies, it appears justified to conclude that vision and hearing impairments occur more frequently among children with multiple disabilities than among other children. In the United States, approximately one child in five with multiple disabilities appears to have hearing impairments, and about two in five appear to have vision impairments. Teachers of children with severe and multiple disabilities can expect, therefore, to encounter students with either or both of these disabilities, and they should be prepared to meet these children's special needs. Program planners need to be aware that prevalence rates for any disability vary by location and period of time (Schein, 1992; Wolf-Schein, 1989), and, therefore, they should seek data as close as possible to the planning period and location as they can find.

The Nature of Sensory Impairments

Vision   There are degrees of blindness; some people who are blind are unable to see at all, others can see a little, whereas still others can see enough to recognize another person using nonvisual cues. The definition of legal blindness involves measures of acuity, the visual system's ability to perceive detail, and visual field. Visual acuity is typically measured with an eyechart placed 20 feet away from the person being tested and is typically described as a fraction. The top number or numerator represents the actual distance (20 feet) of the chart from the person, and the bottom number or denominator represents the distance that the smallest letters that the individual can read at 20 feet should be readable by a person with typical vision. For example, if an individual has 20/40 vision, he or she can read letters (from 20 feet away) that an individual with typical vision should be able to read from a distance of 40 feet. The person without vision impairments can read letters a certain size at 20 feet and is said to have 20/20 vision. The worse the person's visual acuity, the larger the denominator. Individuals are considered *legally blind* when, with the best visual correction for their better eye, their visual acuity is 20/200 or worse. They need to be 10 times closer than a person without vision impairments to see the same thing.

A person may also be legally blind because of a restricted visual field. Anyone whose visual field is less than 20° in diameter qualifies as being legally blind, regardless of acuity in the region of the field that remains (Hollins, 1989). Being *partially sighted* is defined as having vision of 20/70–20/200 after correction (Batshaw & Perret, 1992). The term *low vision* is now sometimes used to describe the vision of individuals who have a serious visual impairment but still have some functional vision.

Visual impairment is much more complex than indicated by these simple numbers or categories of acuity. The visual system is highly sophisticated with many components, as illustrated in Figure 11.1. Defects in any of these compo-

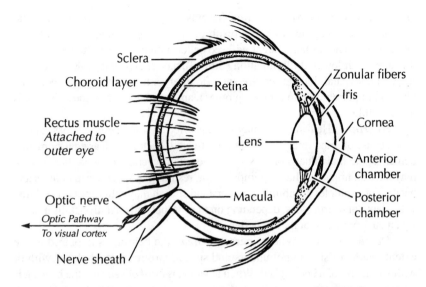

Figure 11.1. Some of the structures of the eye frequently involved in visual impairment.

nents may result in visual impairment. The muscles that control the eye may lack mobility or coordination. The *cornea*, which covers the pupil, may be misshapen, distorting the light that enters the eye. The *iris*, which opens and closes to control the amount of light entering the eye, may be damaged and let in too much or too little light. The *lens*, which focuses light as it enters the eye, may become opaque, preventing light from entering. All or part of the *retina*, which transforms the pattern of light to chemical-electrical impulses, may be damaged in ways that create blind spots or limit the field of vision. Weak receptors in the retina may require extra light for vision. *Optic pathways*, which carry visual impulses to the brain, may be damaged, limiting vision severely. The *visual cortex*, an area at the back of the brain that translates visual images, may be damaged, restricting or eliminating vision (Bach-y-Rita, 1972). Even when all of these visual components are working properly, higher brain centers may have difficulty using visual information. This may be due to a problem with neurological function or simply a learning impairment. Instances of sudden restoration of sight to people who have been blind since birth or from a very early age provide powerful examples of the essential role of learning in vision (Sacks, 1995). For example, even though an individual may be completely capable of identifying circular, triangular, and square shapes, these shapes cannot be identified visually until the individual specifically learns to associate the visual image with the tactile experience. This suggests that learning to integrate sensory information can be useful in some forms of cortical blindness. It is important that all transdisciplinary team members understand the specific nature of a child's impairment and its implications for intervention. For example, two students may have 20/180 vision, but one may have vision impairments as a result of *aniridia* (congenital lack of the iris) and the other as a result of *optic atrophy* (degeneration of the optic nerve). The former student will see better with increased illumination and the latter with lowered illumination (Sims-Tucker & Jensema, 1984). Because the various visual defects require specific interventions, the vision specialist plays an important role in preparing other team members to best meet the needs of each child.

Hearing   Hearing loss may be classified by the degree of loss, age at onset, cause of impairment, or structures affected. Factors such as environmental demands, the individual's other senses, and often several additional factors also may have an impact on hearing impairment, resulting in specific capabilities and needs. For example, the ability to understand speech may differ for two children with identical hearing loss, depending on their visual and cognitive skills and the social environment that they experience.

Degree of Loss   When a person is *deaf*, the hearing is impaired to the extent that he or she cannot understand speech through the ear alone, with or without the use of a hearing aid. When a person is *hard of hearing*, the hearing is impaired to an extent that makes difficult but does not preclude the understanding of speech through the ear alone, with or without a hearing aid (Moores, 1987). Degree of loss may be classified according to sound frequency (cycles per second or hertz [Hz]) and intensity levels (decibels [dB]) that the individual requires to hear speech and other sounds (Moores, 1987). The degree of hearing loss may differ across frequencies, but particular attention is usually paid to losses in the 500-Hz to 2,000-Hz range because this range is critical for discrimination of speech.

Individuals with *mild hearing loss* (Level I, 35 dB–54 dB) can hear most speech and many other sounds in their environment, but generally benefit from classroom modifications, including amplification in many cases. Speech-language therapy and auditory training will also be helpful for these students. Although some will benefit from nonspeech language alternatives, partially depending on the nature and extent of other concurrent disabilities, for many speech is a viable receptive and productive language alternative. Students with *moderate hearing loss* (Level II, 55 dB–69 dB) require special speech, hearing, and language assistance and amplification, unless the nature of the hearing loss precludes benefit (e.g., some types of neural hearing loss are not helped with amplification). Speech can still be an important part of communication for these students. Individuals with *severe hearing loss* (Level III, 70 dB–89 dB) and other disabilities will require special speech, hearing, language, and educational assistance. Some will benefit from amplification, but many will not. Most will benefit from the use of nonspeech language alternatives. Individuals with *profound hearing loss* (Level IV, 90 dB or greater) require intensive language and educational assistance. With this level of impairment, nonspeech language alternatives are almost always necessary, but careful assessment of individuals by speech and hearing professionals is important to determine the most appropriate intervention.

Age at Onset   Individuals are considered to have prelingual deafness when their deafness was present at birth or occurred prior to the development of speech and language. People with postlingual deafness are those whose deafness occurred after they had acquired speech and language. Students with multiple disabilities who have been exposed to speech and learned some basic receptive and productive speech skills will have a better chance of acquiring useful speech with any given degree of loss than students with prelingual deafness.

Cause   Deafness can result from many causes. For example, it may be the result of environmental factors such as infections or injury before, during, or after birth or exposure to loud noise over a period of time. It may also be of genetic origin. Often when deafness is genetic in origin, parents and siblings are also deaf. Children who are deaf who grow up in homes where sign language is used often learn this language alternative with greater ease, so this may be a factor in selecting a language alternative. The full extent of the hearing loss may be present from birth or it may be progressive. The frequency with which deafness occurs is also influenced by sickness, disease, and the quality of health care. A dramatic example is the rubella (German measles) epidemic of 1963–1965, which tripled the number of children born deaf in the United States during that period. Since then there have been several epidemics in North America, resulting in increased numbers of individuals with hearing loss in specific years.

Structures Affected   Hearing losses are usually categorized as either *conductive, sensorineural, mixed,* or *central auditory disorders*. Conductive impairments result from interference in the pathway from the ear canal to the inner ear. They may be caused by wax, a hole in the eardrum, middle ear infection (otitis media), bony growth of the small bones (ossicles) in the middle ear, or a birth abnormality. Sensorineural (nerve damage) hearing loss occurs in the inner ear or along the eighth cranial (vestibulocochlear) nerve, which is the auditory pathway. This may result from such maternal infection as rubella or from inherited conditions, early childhood problems (e.g., anoxia, meningitis), ototoxic (harmful to hearing) drugs, or other causes, some of which may be unknown. Mixed impairments are those in which both the conductive and sensorineural systems are impaired. Conductive loss is often medically or surgically correctable, while a sensorineural loss is not. Figure 11.2 depicts some of the structures that may be involved in hearing loss.

Individuals are considered to have central auditory disorders when they cannot respond meaningfully to sound due to central organic dysfunctions. Remediation is accomplished through language therapy and educational intervention. Often this diagnosis is made as a result of the elimination of other possible causes rather than clear identification of damage to the central auditory system, and it is particularly difficult to make this diagnosis with certainty in students with multiple disabilities.

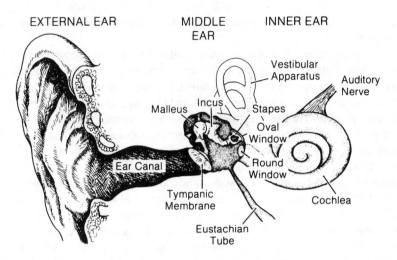

Figure 11.2. Components of the auditory system. (From Batshaw, M.L., & Perret, Y.M. [1992]. *Children with disabilities: A medical primer* [3rd ed., p. 323] Baltimore: Paul H. Brookes Publishing Co.; reprinted by permission of the author.)

There is no such thing as a "typical" student with a hearing impairment who has additional disabilities. Service providers face a challenge in dealing with the diversity of characteristics found among students with hearing impairments who have developmental disabilities (Karchmer, 1985). Even when two individuals have identical degrees of hearing impairment, the effects may differ (Schein, 1989). One student may benefit from a hearing aid, whereas another student will not. The audiologist and communication therapist can play important roles in helping all transdisciplinary team members understand the nature of the child's hearing loss and how best to provide intervention.

Vision and Hearing   Children with both vision and hearing impairments have unique support needs including specialized communication and mobility instruction (Huebner, Welch, & Prickett, 1993). For the individual with only one of these sensory impairments, the ability to compensate often depends on increased dependence on the unimpaired sense; if the other sense is also impaired, alternatives are greatly reduced. This problem is compounded when children also have motor and cognitive disabilities. Depending on the nature and degree of the impairments, students with this dual disability have often attended a hierarchy of programs:

1. A general education classroom with special devices, attention, and support
2. A classroom for children with either hearing impairments or visual impairments
3. A noncategorical special education program with specialized educational procedures provided for the student with visual and hearing impairments

4. A self-contained program for students who are deaf-blind, with all activities geared toward their special needs

5. A highly protective environment with the focus primarily on adaptive skills

Any educational setting should be monitored so that the student will have opportunities for movement to a more typical setting. As with students who have other types of disabilities, the setting may not always be as important as the skill of the teacher, the specialized support that is available, and the technical aids that can be provided. The degree of the visual or hearing impairment may not be as important in determining an educational setting as the motivation of the student to learn, the nature and extent of socially unacceptable behavior, and the motivation of others to accept and meaningfully include the child. The individualized education programs of students who are deaf-blind highlight an ongoing theme woven throughout the national discussion on inclusive schooling; that is, balancing the "academic" outcomes of schooling by learning the skills and concepts associated with mastery of a discrete content area (e.g., algebra, braille) with the "social participation" outcomes of schooling (Goetz, 1995). Ideally, students should receive intensive, specialized training in typical environments. No student or family should be forced to choose between a good educational program and a typical environment. Whatever the setting, students who are deaf-blind must have available a variety of specialized services ranging from braille to sign language to interpreters with skills specific to deaf-blindness (Curry, 1989).

Children who are deaf-blind frequently exhibit stereotypic, self-stimulating behaviors that can be disruptive or even harmful (Billingsley, Huven, & Romer, 1995). The function of some of the self-stimulation (e.g., eye gouging, screaming) appears to be either an attempt to intensify visual and auditory input to their impaired senses or to provide a general tactile-kinesthetic stimulation. These behaviors are often socially unacceptable and sometimes self-injurious, which makes it difficult for these children to be in typical social and educational environments where more socially acceptable behavior is likely to be learned. Typically, the best approach to elimination of these behaviors is not to suppress them but to provide less harmful and more socially acceptable substitute activities. These substitute activities must be incorporated in the educational process, because many of these students do not have the ability to determine what is acceptable or the skills to develop an alternative behavior. For example, body rocking may be viewed as deviant behavior, but an exercise program providing similar stimulation may be socially valued.

Etiology   The high correlation between sensory impairments and other disabling conditions is probably due to six factors. First, any of the same factors that cause sensory impairments can also cause other defects. For example, *Haemophilus influenzae B* can cause otitis media (middle ear infection), which may lead to hearing impairments, and also can cause meningitis, which may lead to cognitive and motor impairments.

Second, the same syndromes that cause other developmental disabilities may be associated with sensory impairments (Efron, 1981). For example, children with Down syndrome often have *keratoconus* (a malformation of the cornea that distorts vision); decreased resistance to middle ear infections; and narrow, easily blocked ear canals. In fragile X syndrome, which is now considered second only to Down syndrome as a genetic cause of mental retardation, a connective tissue disorder may facilitate a tendency toward ocular problems (e.g., myopia, strabismus), as well as malfunction of the eustachian tube, which can result in an increased number of middle ear infections (Wolf-Schein, 1990).

Third, attempts to treat another disability may result in a sensory impairment. For example, high oxygen levels given to premature infants may cause retinopathy of prematurity (previously referred to as retrolental fibroplasia [a term now used only to refer to the most severe forms]) producing severe visual impairment. Toxic reactions to some antibiotics may also produce hearing impairment.

Fourth, failure to recognize early signs of illness or disability among children with multiple disabilities may result in permanent sensory impairment. For example, middle ear infections may go untreated when children are unable to communicate that they are experiencing discomfort, and the resulting delay can cause permanent hearing loss.

Fifth, although it should never occur, treatment has sometimes been withheld from children with severe or multiple disabilities. For example, Cress et al. (1981) point out that corrective lenses may not be prescribed because it is believed that vision is "adequate for the learner's needs." They urge that no such discriminatory criterion be applied and that corrective intervention be considered according to the same criteria as for children without disabilities.

Sixth, there can be decreased expectations for performance of individuals with mental disabilities. Negative expectations sometimes result in reduced stimulation during the developmental period, and the lack of adequate stimulation may lead to functional impairment of vision, hearing, and related functional skills. For example, lack of sensitivity to nonintentional communicative behavior may hinder emergence of intentional communication (Siegel-Causey & Downing, 1987).

ASSESSMENT OF SENSORY IMPAIRMENTS

Professionals or caregivers who need sensory assessment data on children with multiple disabilities often meet with obstacles. In some cases, they may be told that because of the severity of the disability the child's hearing or vision cannot be tested. In other cases, after inadequate assessment, they may be told that the child is totally and irrevocably deaf or blind and no remediation will be of value. Fortunately, neither of these situations needs to occur. Adequate assessment of both hearing and vision can be carried out for every child. There is no longer any justification for placing loosely applied labels (e.g., cortical blindness) on a child without clear and objective evidence of pathology (Harden, 1983). Furthermore, increasing evidence suggests that even children who lack hearing or vision at a given point may develop or recover it in time. For example, some children who have been blind for several months after birth have shown the first signs of vision at 6–8 months and developed normal vision by 2 or 3 years of age (Harel, Holtz-man, & Feinshod, 1985). This means that no diagnosis should be viewed as a "life sentence" for the young child.

Typically, evaluation procedures are categorized as *screening*, which is used to identify increased risk of sensory impairment, and *clinical assessment*, which is used to determine the nature and extent of sensory abilities and impair-ments. Because children with multiple disabilities are already identified as being at risk for sensory impairments and typically require individualized testing pro-cedures rather than the standard screening procedures, all children with multiple disabilities should have a complete clinical assessment of vision and hearing (Cress et al., 1981).

Assessing Vision

Assessing the vision of children with multiple disabilities requires two main areas of evaluation: 1) tests of physiological function and 2) evaluation of func-tional use of vision. Each type of evaluation supplies valuable information, and neither can substitute completely for the other.

Tests of Physiological Function   The testing of vision can be a highly technical process, employing a large number of tests and sophisticated equip-ment. Only a few of these tests are discussed here. Those selected for discussion are tests that are often well suited to assessing children who cannot or will not actively participate in more traditional tests.

Modified Subjective Acuity Tests   Students who do not have disabilities usually take subjective acuity tests in which they are typically shown a Snellen eye chart and asked to read letters of various sizes. The smaller the letter the stu-dent can read, the better his or her vision. Of course, most children with multiple disabilities will not be able to read letters at any distance, making these charts inappropriate for them.

One approach to solving this problem is to replace the letters with various objects or pictures. From 20 feet away, a child with 20/20 vision should be able to recognize an item ⅜-inch long and with details as small as ¹⁄₁₆ inch. A child with 20/200 vision should be able to recognize an item 3½ inches long with details as small as ³⁄₁₆ inch, and so forth. For children capable of recognizing and labeling familiar items, a chart replacing the standard letters with items of simi-lar size provides a good alternative, but for many others, such a task goes far beyond their current skills (Cress et al., 1981).

Forced-Choice Preferential Looking   Forced-choice preferential looking (FPL) requires a simpler response. In the FPL procedure, two screens lit with the same average illumination intensity are projected. As illustrated in Figure 11.3, one has no pattern and the other is striped, checkered, or has lines that wiggle.

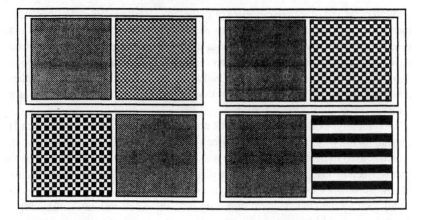

Figure 11.3.   Four stimulus pairs used in a forced-choice preferential looking test. All are 50% black and 50% white.

Most children will consistently look at the patterned screen. If the child demonstrates a preference for the patterned screen, repeated pairings are presented, with the patterned side alternated and with increasingly finer patterns. When the individual units in the pattern become too small to be discriminated by the individual, the square appears gray and cannot be discriminated from the other item in the pair. Therefore, no pattern preference occurs. The smallest pattern size for which the child demonstrates consistent preference indicates visual acuity (Atkinson, 1985). Such tests of visual acuity are extremely important because they test the function of the entire visual system rather than its individual parts; even so, the FPL procedure may be extremely difficult for some students.

Optokinetic Nystagmus   Another test that can be useful in estimating visual acuity, but with further reduced response requirements, is the optokinetic nystagmus (OKN) test (Hall & Jolly, 1984). OKN refers to the natural reflex response in which the eyes follow a moving stimulus. Repetitive stimuli are projected on a moving drum so that they move across the child's entire visual field at a rate of 20–30/second (Atkinson, 1985). Figure 11.4 is an example of an OKN test. If the child tracks the stimuli, the eyes, visual pathways, and some basic cortical processing must be functioning (Taylor, 1983). When line size is too small to be seen, the observer no longer perceives rotation and the eyes cease to follow. Although more work is needed to determine the accuracy and reliability of these estimates, the smallest size component in the moving patterns tracked by the student allows the examiner to estimate visual acuity (Taylor, 1983). An OKN test is also useful for assessing movement patterns of the eyes and how well the right and left eyes are coordinated (Atkinson, 1985).

Orthoptic Tests   Tests of alignment of the eyes are known as orthoptic tests. Severe *strabismus* (misalignment of the eyes, which makes it difficult or

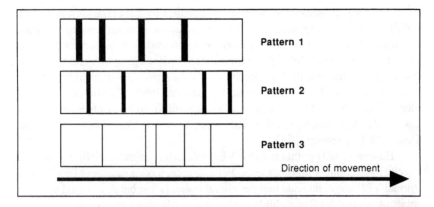

Figure 11.4. Optokinetic Nystagmus (OKN) Test. Lines move on rotating drum and eyes follow direction of rotation. When line size is too small to be seen, the observer no longer perceives rotation and the eyes cease to follow.

impossible to point them toward the same target) can typically be detected by casual observation, but milder or transient forms of misalignment may require examination. Often, these misalignments are given a diagnostic label that indicates the type of deviation. *Esotropia* (an eye pointing inward), *exotropia* (an eye pointing outward), *hypertropia* (an eye pointing upward), and *hypotropia* (an eye pointing downward) all result in difficulty integrating visual images from the two eyes and are generally correctable through simple surgical procedures.

Tests to detect alignment problems examine eye alignment during a variety of visual tasks and when covered eyes are suddenly uncovered (Atkinson, 1985). Symmetrical or asymmetrical reflections of a lighted stimulus in the child's eyes also provide valuable data.

Retinoscope An objective method of assessing refractive error of an eye, called *retinoscopy* or *skiascopy*, allows for diagnosis of *myopia* (nearsightedness), *hyperopia* (farsightedness), or *astigmatism* (irregular refractive error), all of which can be corrected with the appropriate corrective lenses (Atkinson, 1985). Because the lenses of the eyes permit light to travel in either direction, their refractive power can be measured by the examiner looking in and focusing the retina. The amount of correction required to attain focus indicates the type and degree of refractive error without requiring any response from the child (Cress et al., 1981).

Isotropic Photorefraction Using the same principle, isotropic photorefraction uses a series of at least three flash photographs with the camera focused in front of, on, and behind the child's eyes. White blur circles over the child's pupils indicate where the child's eyes were focused. Misshapen reflections indicate astigmatism (Atkinson, 1985).

Electrical Discharge Tests In *electroretinography* (ERG), electrodes attached near the eyes allow measurement of the retina's general ability to produce electrical charges in response to stimulation by light (Batshaw & Perret, 1992). *Visual evoked potentials* (VEP), also known as *visual evoked response* (VER), measure electrical activity from the visual cortex at the back of the brain in response to flashes of light (Baine, 1985). Although much remains to be learned regarding exactly how much this test can reveal, patterns responded to can provide a rough estimate of acuity (Atkinson, 1985). Careful placement of electrodes is essential because poor data that result from badly placed electrodes can easily be misinterpreted as indicating visual defects (Longo, Rotatori, Heinze, & Kapperman, 1982).

Harden (1983) points out that VEP and ERG are most useful when used together and along with other tests. For example, a poor or absent ERG with a normal VEP might indicate that peripheral vision is lost but that central vision is intact. A normal VEP in a child who has a severely abnormal electroencephalogram (EEG) may indicate that vision is unimpaired but that the child has difficulty processing visual information, a condition that may be reversible, especially with training.

VEP procedures also have been used to assess orientation-selective cortical function. Because subcortical visual mechanisms do not react to orientation, VEP responses to sequenced changes in orientation of line edges superimposed on circular patterns specifically indicate cortical function (Atkinson, 1989).

Other Visual Assessment   The tests discussed previously represent only a few of the many evaluation procedures appropriate for use with children with multiple disabilities. Ultrasound, X ray, reflexes, eye preference, pupillary response, and many more can provide additional, useful information (Jose, Smith, & Shane, 1980). The vision specialist plays an important role in planning and conducting evaluation suited to the child and in helping the other transdisciplinary team members understand the assessment results and their implications for intervention. Tests of physiological function play an important role in this process, but much more information is required to understand the child's functional use of vision.

Evaluation of Functional Use of Vision   In order to evaluate functional use of vision, the team can 1) obtain information about the child's history from existing records; 2) request information from parents, caregivers, or others who have spent significant time with the child; 3) observe the child in natural environments; or 4) attempt to elicit responses related to visual skills. Functional assessment must be individualized on the basis of the child's abilities and disabilities; degree of cooperation given; reaction to reinforcers available; previous learning history; past, current, and future environments; and objectives for learning. Some of the information that might be important to review from the four sources includes the following:

1.   Age at onset and type and degree of problem
2.   Whether the visual problem has been improving or worsening
3.   Effect of environment or activity on the child's ability to see

4. Visual skills required for current objectives
5. Signs of any other condition that could affect vision either temporarily or permanently
6. Use of medication that is known to have visual side effects

For example, phenobarbital may cause double vision, impaired visual pursuit, and many other visual problems; other anticonvulsants and tranquilizers also can have very significant visual effects (Fraunfelder, 1989). Another potential problem is the interaction effects of medications. A child who is using medications is also susceptible to childhood diseases, and many common medications for these illnesses affect other medications (Kelley & Wedding, 1995).

Parents and other informants can also provide information based on their daily experiences. Although their reports may lack precision, they are based on a variety of experiences over a period of time and may be more sensitive than a limited observation by a professional, particularly if the child is not very cooperative. They also contain a perspective based on greater intimacy and acceptance (Goode, 1994). Individuals more familiar with the child are able to report behavior that occurs only occasionally, and obtaining information from these knowledgeable sources may be much more efficient than other methods. The most effective evaluation process usually combines all four methods. Reviewing records and interviewing family and significant others first may provide information about the best times and places for natural observation. Information from natural observation may suggest important stimuli to present or responses to look for in an elicited behavior sample.

The child's history, interviews with significant others, natural observation, and elicited observation together can help provide answers to many important questions (Cote & Smith, 1983; Jose et al., 1980). Does the child orient him- or herself toward light? Does the child move easily around the environment without bumping into things? Does the child exhibit visual discrimination? Does the child recognize faces? Does the child look directly at things? Do the child's eyes track moving objects with smooth and coordinated movements? Does the child demonstrate interest in visual stimuli? Does the child walk with a shuffling gait, arms extended in front, or head shifted back? The answers to these questions must be considered, along with data on the child's physiological functioning, when planning and intervention are carried out by the transdisciplinary team.

Functional evaluation of vision should be part of an overall functional-ecological assessment. Rather than simply determining if the child can see, the team must determine how a child uses vision as part of a larger repertoire of abilities during typical activities in natural environments (Downing & Perino, 1992; Wolf-Schein, 1995; Wolf-Schein & Schein, 1995).

Assessing Hearing

A variety of procedures can be used to assess the hearing of people with severe disabilities who have been characterized as difficult to test. These procedures may be divided into two groups: 1) behavioral test procedures and objective hearing tests, and 2) evaluation of functional use of hearing.

Behavioral Test Procedures   Behavioral test procedures are tests of physiological function that determine whether all of a specific part of the auditory system is functioning properly.

Behavioral Observation Audiometry   Behavioral observation audiometry (BOA) depends on the observation of changes in a child's behavior and activity when test stimuli are presented. Behavioral responses can take several forms and are often subtle, requiring the observations of experienced examiners.

Visual Reinforcement Audiometry   Visual reinforcement audiometry (VRA) is a test procedure that, in its most commonly employed form, involves the presentation of an auditory signal from a loudspeaker, a head-turn response toward the sound source, and the presentation of an attractive visual stimulus (e.g., an animated toy) as reinforcement for appropriate responses (Thompson, Thompson, & Vethivelu, 1989). This procedure has limitations when children have visual impairments, are uninterested in the toys, are unable to turn their heads from side to side, or are able to hear but not able to localize sounds.

Conditioned Play Audiometry   Conditioned play audiometry (CPA) is a procedure in which a child is taught, using instruction or demonstration, to complete a specific play activity (e.g., dropping blocks into a bucket) in response to presentation of an auditory signal (Friedrich, 1985).

Tangible Reinforcement Operant Conditioning Audiometry   Tangible reinforcement operant conditioning audiometry (TROCA) is a procedure that uses a tangible reinforcer (e.g., food, drink, toy) to reinforce a child's response to an auditory stimulus. It was originally developed by Lloyd, Spradlin, and Reid (1968) for use with children with developmental disabilities, but it has since been adapted for many children who are difficult to test. The technique requires the use of specially designed equipment that will dispense the reinforcer to the child after he or she presses a lighted bar or button. Once the child is able to respond to the auditory stimulus and lighted button without assistance, the light is faded until only the auditory stimulus cues the response. Both CPA and TROCA require voluntary motor responses, which may be difficult to teach in some people with severe or multiple disabilities.

Northern and Downs (1991) provide more detailed descriptions of these and other methods of behavioral audiometry, including methods using conditioned avoidance rather than reinforcement. If initial testing reveals a problem, audiometry procedures can also be used with bone conduction, which helps discriminate middle ear from inner ear dysfunction.

Objective Hearing Tests   Like behavioral test procedures, objective hearing tests are tests of physiological function that determine if all or a specific part of the auditory system is functioning properly.

Modified Pure Tone Audiometry   Pure tone audiometry typically identifies the threshold at which the lowest intensity of sound can be heard at various frequencies. A threshold is defined as the level at which the response occurs 50% of the time. Performance at 500 Hz, 1,000 Hz, and 2,000 Hz is particularly important because most sounds critical to understanding speech occur at these frequencies. A range of −10 dB to +25 dB is considered within normal limits (Baine, 1985). Usually, the person being tested is asked to push a button or otherwise signify when a tone is heard; however, as noted previously, many children with multiple disabilities cannot or will not perform tasks requiring voluntary responses. One solution has been to develop objective tests of auditory function. Following are brief descriptions of some of the more commonly used procedures.

Auditory Brainstem Response   Auditory brainstem response (ABR) is appropriate when one desires a benign approach for testing auditory function in infants and very young children, or individuals with severe or multiple disabilities who cannot participate in voluntary audiometry (Berlin & Hood, 1987). This procedure measures changes in electrical brain wave activity that occur when auditory stimuli (i.e., a series of clicks) are presented. This testing requires an individual to sit or lie motionless for 30–45 minutes with electrodes attached to the scalp. For children who are difficult to test, sedation is frequently required. Sleep is commonly induced with chloral hydrate or other short acting medication. This is a medical procedure and must be done with proper safeguards and supervision. In applying this procedure to people with multiple disabilities, the presence or absence of central nervous system pathology can affect the outcome of the evaluation. Some results can be ambiguous and difficult to interpret. Once this limitation is considered, the ABR remains the best measure available to date for objectively evaluating the auditory status of individuals who cannot be tested with traditional audiometry (Worthington & Peters, 1984), because the threshold for electrical discharge is typically very close to the threshold identified by traditional audiometry (Sohmer, 1989). When ABR detects hearing problems, the level of the auditory pathway that is failing to transmit the message can often be identified.

Impedance Audiometry   By measuring changes in air pressure in the ear canal that occur in response to a tone, impedance or immittance audiometry provides information about the condition of the eardrum, mobility, and continuity of bones in the middle ear; acoustic reflexes; and eustachian tube function. It can be used to estimate hearing sensitivity when audiometry cannot be performed satisfactorily (Northern & Downs, 1991). It cannot identify many sensorineural hearing problems and is difficult to carry out with an actively uncooperative or continuously vocal child. Sedation can be used if necessary, but it may influence acoustic reflex (Northern & Downs, 1991).

Heart Rate Response Audiometry   Changes occur in electrocardiograms as an unconditioned response to auditory stimuli. These changes are related to sound intensity and have been used to determine auditory thresholds (Schulman & Wade, 1970). Some disagreement still remains regarding the accuracy of this procedure and what physical conditions may influence responses (Northern & Downs, 1991).

These and other tests of physiological functioning can provide valuable information, especially when interpreted by the audiologist (Bess & Humes, 1995). Assessment of functional hearing also provides essential information to the transdisciplinary team.

Evaluation of Functional Use of Hearing   The audiological tests described previously typically require carefully controlled testing conditions and cannot provide direct information about children's hearing in the educational, domestic, leisure, and community environments where they typically spend time (Kenworthy, 1982). As with vision, the child's history, interviews with significant others, natural observation, and elicited responses can provide this valuable information. Children's responses to speech and other naturally occurring sounds in the environment are particularly significant. It is important to remember that even when hearing acuity in speech frequencies is known to be present, it is only a rough predictor of the child's ability to understand speech, which depends on many additional factors.

There are informal observations that can be made about the hearing responses of most children. A checklist can sometimes be useful in drawing a teacher's or parent's attention to behaviors that might indicate a problem with hearing. The following list of indicators of an individual's problems with hearing is adapted from the "Teacher Orientation Cluster" (Wolf-Schein, 1995):

- Often seems inattentive to what is said
- Shows little interest in auditory stimuli (e.g., music)
- Not alerted by noise when sleeping or concentrating (e.g., on eating, on a task)
- Does not respond to nearby sounds when source is not visible
- Does not respond when name is called from behind
- Does not respond to loud noises (e.g., bells, alarms, sirens)
- Responds only to very loud noises (e.g., bells, alarms, sirens)
- Confuses similar sounding words (e.g., bat/pat, sand/hand, score/snore)
- Turns up volume very high on sound equipment
- Speech and language are not age appropriate
- Voice is too loud or too soft or has other unusual quality
- Obtains more satisfaction from seeing than hearing
- Stares intently at people when they speak to him or her
- Appears to comprehend better when looking directly at person speaking
- Depends on "following" others rather than listening to instructions
- Frequent colds or ear infections

Of course, none of these indicators are conclusive and they must be considered with caution. For example, children with weak muscle tone may appear to show little interest in sounds because they lack head control to orient toward sound. A lack of attentiveness to what is said may indicate a symptom of not understanding rather than not hearing the words. However, it may be a mistake to assume that the difficulty is with understanding, when the problem may be one of not hearing.

Instruments that provide a standard set of items and attempt to grade responses, such as the Auditory Behavior Index for Infants discussed by Northern and Downs (1991), are also available. Unlike the less formal observations suggested previously, these assessments may specify that sounds be a certain loudness and that testing be done in a sound-controlled room. Although these instruments may need to be modified for children with multiple disabilities, they can be extremely useful in suggesting possible items and providing a framework for interpreting responses.

Often, there will be considerable overlap between functional assessment of hearing and of communication skills. The entire team may play a role in the assessment process, with the audiologist and communication therapist having major roles in developing, implementing, and interpreting results.

It is important to remember that hearing function changes over time; consequently, a single evaluation has limited value. In order to reflect changes in learning and physiological function, assessment must be an ongoing process (Stromer & Miller, 1982).

INTERVENTION

Educational experiences and expectations for children with sensory disabilities should provide the same opportunities as those available for children without vision and hearing impairments. The use of environmental modifications or sensory enhancements that allow a child equal access to information should always be available. The number and extent of modifications and enhancements required for any child depends not only on the nature and extent of the sensory impairment, but also on the child's other abilities and disabilities and on environmental conditions. With this in mind, a number of possible interventions are presented here.

Intervention for Children with Vision Impairments

Intervention for children with vision impairments may occur in at least seven areas:

1. Restoration of vision to the greatest extent possible
2. Use of adaptive equipment to help compensate for problems with visual acuity
3. Modification of environmental conditions and training to help children make maximum use of any residual vision
4. Training to enhance use of other senses to compensate for visual loss
5. Modification of tasks to reduce visual requirements

6.   Orientation and mobility training
7.   Behavioral and social intervention to aid children's integration into social settings

Visual Restoration   Children should never be denied access to corrective treatment for visual disorders simply because they have multiple disabilities (Cress et al., 1981). Of course, not every visual impairment can be corrected, but medical treatment, surgery, and corrective lenses can help many individuals. A few examples are discussed here.

Misalignment of the eyes often can be treated with surgery (Harcourt, 1983). Although surgical procedures vary in complexity depending on the type and severity of strabismus, they typically involve simple reattachment or shortening of ocular muscles. This surgery is not always merely cosmetic—in some cases, it allows for properly functioning binocular vision.

Lens implants can replace lenses that are missing or damaged. Although not typically recommended for young children because the implanted lens will not grow with them, the procedure has been used with great success with many individuals with severe and multiple disabilities. Vision often can be restored to near normal, and implanted lenses cannot be lost or broken as can eyeglasses or contact lenses. Implants are frequently used as treatment for cataracts. Old lenses may be frozen for easy removal (*cryoextraction*) or liquified with an ultrasonic probe (*phacoemulsification*) before the fluid that fills the eye is replaced with new, clear fluid. Lenses are then easily inserted through a small incision (Clayman, Jaffe, & Galin, 1983). Although an implanted lens is not adjustable and will not focus on very close objects (just as a fixed-focus camera is more limited than an adjustable focus camera), this procedure has restored near-normal vision to many who were previously blind.

These surgical procedures are only two of many. Often, misshapen corneas can be reshaped, and detached retinas can be reattached. Excessive pressure in the eye can sometimes be relieved. Medical treatment is also useful particularly in prevention of visual impairments. Early detection and prompt medical treatment of infections, injuries, pressure, and other eye problems greatly reduce the chances of permanent damage. In addition to the student having regular checkups, changes in appearance of the eyes, signs of changes in vision, drainage or tearing, pain or itching, or any other sign of possible eye disease should be assessed immediately by an ophthalmologist.

Eyeglasses can be used to help compensate for a variety of visual impairments. Contact lenses are inappropriate for most children with multiple disabilities because they are tolerated poorly and because these children have difficulty caring for the lenses and coping with displaced, poorly hydrated, or irritating lenses. An extra pair (or two) of eyeglasses is often advisable to ensure continuity of use for children who lose or break them frequently. In some cases, it is recommended that an extra set be kept in school. Many children with disabilities require specific reinforcement to aid in adjustment to glasses during the first days or weeks of use. The transdisciplinary team should develop a reinforcement plan *before* introducing the glasses. The best reinforcement plan allows the child to participate in a highly reinforcing, visually directed task (e.g., find the food) while he or she has on the glasses. Sessions begin with fairly short periods and gradually increase as tolerance increases. In time, the ability to see better and consequently have better control over the environment becomes a natural reward.

Some young children benefit from covering or patching one eye. This typically occurs when the child's vision is better in one eye, which results in the child relying too much on the better eye. As a result, the weaker eye is used less and is further weakened. Patching the better eye for several hours per day for a period of a few months sometimes strengthens the weaker eye and helps restore a balance between vision in each eye. The decision to use this method should be made by the entire team considering the potential benefits, how well the child tolerates the procedure, and the extent of visual function lost during patching.

Adaptive Equipment   An increasing variety of highly sophisticated equipment is available to people with visual impairments. High-powered screen-magnification software systems allow for greater use of residual vision (Uslan & Shragai, 1995). Sound and vibration patterns have been used to provide "visual" information in alternative formats (Bach-y-Rita, 1972). However, in the case of students with multiple disabilities, special attention must be paid to readiness levels. A student cannot perform with a low vision device beyond his or her functional ability to manipulate and care for devices (Watson, 1989). As with all augmentative communication devices, the individual's cognitive, social, emotional, and physical needs and abilities must be considered along with communication needs and language abilities (Healy, 1994). More research is needed to determine exactly who might benefit from which aids. In the meantime, teams should carefully consider potential benefits and functional requirements for use on an individual basis, and they should *require* sales representatives to provide a sample for use in evaluating the appropriateness for the child prior to purchase.

Maximizing Use of Residual Vision   Making the best possible use of any residual vision can include modifying environmental conditions to suit the child's individual needs and training the child to use existing vision most effectively. It is recommended that a team that is familiar with the individual determine the most effective interventions, but some examples are provided here for consideration.

Lighting is a major environmental factor. As noted previously, depending on the visual impairment, particularly high or particularly low illumination may be required. Tasks may require additional illumination, but they should not be excessively brighter than their background. Backlighting generally should be avoided except when used to show the outline of an object that the child is expected to discriminate. Print, symbols, pictures, and other critical visual features often can be enlarged. Desks and tabletops with adjustable heights and angles assist optimal viewing. Highly reflective surfaces should be avoided in the classroom. In implementing these and other general guidelines, it is important to evaluate the response of each individual and to identify the optimal working conditions for each child (Wolf-Schein, 1995).

Visually directed skills are typically acquired by children without disabilities with little formal instruction, but children with multiple disabilities, including visual impairments, usually require carefully structured training to learn these skills. Many of the sensorimotor skills outlined by Robinson and Robinson (1983) are visually directed, and methods for teaching these skills are clearly described by these authors. Very basic objectives may be as simple as teaching the child to indicate whether a light source is present and to track visually the light source. One caution is that the light source should not be distressing to the child. For example, it is better to ask the student to follow a light spot moving across a wall than to shine the light directly in his or her face.

Three principles should be considered in providing visual training to individual children. First, mere visual stimulation is not adequate. Contingent control of the visual stimulation or an associated reinforcer is critical for learning (Utley, Duncan, Strain, & Scanlon, 1983). Second, specific visual skills must serve a meaningful function for the child and, whenever possible, training should occur during functional activities. Third, to the maximum extent possible, these activities should be appropriate to the child's chronological age.

Using Other Senses   Training should also encourage children to use their other senses to compensate for lost visual abilities. Although it is *not* true that people who are blind have more sensitive hearing or extra senses, they can learn to use hearing, touch, and smell to *substitute* for some functions that vision normally serves. Tactile and auditory skills should be taught in specific training sessions and then generalized to use in functional activities. Similarly, the sense of smell can be developed through a series of identification and discrimination exercises; following these, the use of olfactory cues may be introduced to identify various significant others by such features as distinctive perfume or aftershave.

Modifying Task Requirements   Task requirements may be altered to take advantage of other senses or to require less visual acuity. Some functional modifications may include the following:

1. Enlarging materials
2. Making outlines bolder
3. Reducing irrelevant stimulus characters
4. Covering that part of the stimulus not currently relevant
5. Putting heavy lines between task stimuli
6. Giving the student more time to examine the material
7. Supplementing visual information with auditory or tactile information
8. Providing alternative materials that require less visual skill

These modifications work well with a variety of appropriate stimulus materials, including paper and pencil or materials used in teacher-developed assessments. However, in standardized testing, if the number and extent of modifications required for students with multiple disabilities is so great that tests bear little resemblance to their original form, interpretation of results becomes less valid. For this reason, use of standardized tests should be minimized, and comprehensive individualization of educational programming in accordance with the principles presented in Chapter 10 is suggested for all children with multiple disabilities.

Orientation and Mobility Training   Although orientation and mobility (O&M) training has long been recognized as critical for children who are blind, children with severe, multiple disabilities often were excluded because they were considered unable to benefit or they failed to meet the entrance criteria (Brady, 1985). Without modification of training methods and content, traditional O&M training probably requires skills beyond the current functioning level of most children with multiple disabilities (Uslan, 1979), but when O&M programs are tailored to the individual needs of children with multiple disabilities, meaningful gains can be achieved. Gee, Harrell, and Rosenberg (1987) developed a model of O&M training specifically for individuals with multiple disabilities that stresses training in natural environments; interspersed training trials; functional, contextual cues; and operant training procedures.

Geruschat (1980) stresses the importance of 1) conducting appropriate initial evaluation of vision, medications, and restrictions; mode of communication; and body and environmental awareness; 2) establishing rapport; 3) establishing a consistent routine to help the student feel comfortable and secure; 4) setting relevant and realistic goals; 5) providing instruction in the use of senses, body awareness, spatial concepts, and route travel; and 6) collecting data to show progress. The Peabody Mobility Scale (Folio & DuBose, 1983) is a criterion-referenced evaluation instrument and program of instruction in O&M designed for children who are blind and have multiple disabilities, with subscales in the areas of motor, sensory, conceptual, and O&M skills. It has been tailored for use with children with low vision who have multiple disabilities, with some revisions and a new area for developmental vision and visual integration (Harley & Merbler, 1980). Some children with multiple disabilities have been successfully taught to use a cane as a navigational aid (Morse, 1980). In addition to acting as a simple walking aid, the cane helps the child keep his or her balance, provides advance warning of danger, and samples the path of travel for changes in terrain (Uslan, 1979).

Electronically controlled auditory cues at key locations have been useful in some environments (Uslan, Malone, & De l'Aune, 1983), but care should be taken not to overuse such external, instructional cues because they may encourage dependency and interfere with generalization to natural environments where these prompts are not available. An ecological approach that identifies landmarks (dominant environmental features), techniques (methods of traveling across or between landmarks), and orientations (methods of maintaining direction) in the natural environment is extremely useful (Geruschat, 1980).

Because motor skills play an important role in O&M (McDade, 1969), occupational therapy, physical therapy, and physical education are important disciplines to involve in O&M programs. Although the entire transdisciplinary team should participate in these programs, the O&M specialist is an extremely important resource for the team. On a practical level, keeping in mind that their students are less able and inclined to engage in even ordinary day-to-day activities involving movement in space (e.g., walking, running, riding a bicycle), caregivers must ensure that the classroom routine includes time for gross motor activity and that special attempts are made to take the children outside for walks and play, even if they are in wheelchairs.

Behavioral and Social Intervention   Another important area of intervention for many children with severe visual impairments is behavioral and social intervention. Poor mobility skills sometimes lead to social withdrawal. Lack of vision may restrict available reinforcing activities. Habitual self-stimulation involving visual or ocular sensation (sometimes called "blindisms") may increase the deviancy of these children's images (Sims-Tucker & Jensema, 1984). Most of these concerns are best approached through reinforcement of more appropriate forms of behavior. Mobility and communication skills should be emphasized to minimize isolation. Reinforcing physical contact can be very helpful. Rather than merely trying to suppress "inappropriate" self-stimulation, caregivers should provide appropriate activities that allow learners to use their other senses and residual vision.

Providing services in the most typical, age-appropriate environment in the individual's natural community is a major concern. Service provision has sometimes involved clustering individuals with visual impairments in residential settings or self-contained classrooms in an attempt to make special resources and modified programs more accessible (Sacks & Reardon, 1989). Unfortunately, such noninclusive alternatives often interfere with social adjustment and make returning to the natural environment more difficult. Because children with multiple disabilities who have visual impairments require highly individualized programs, the advantages of clustering are minimized. In addition, because these same students typically have more difficulty generalizing skills from the training environment to the setting in which those skills are naturally functional, the disadvantages of noninclusion will likely be greater. Therefore, general educational, residential, recreational, and social environments should be considered the top priority environments for training.

Nevertheless, inclusion by itself is not a substitute for carefully planned and structured programs tailored to the unique abilities and needs of individual students and implemented by competent professional staff. Having students with complex educational needs in general education classrooms without adequate planning and support to ensure optimal learning is a form of educational neglect and can never be justified in the name of inclusion. In an ideal world, no one should be forced to choose between powerful interventions applied in isolated, inappropriate settings and inadequate education in fully inclusive settings. Unfortunately, this ideal is achieved rarely in contemporary schools. Even though some compromise may be unavoidable, the goals of educational planners must include *both* the best available educational methods *and* the most typical educational environment appropriate.

The interventions discussed here are only a small representation of the available alternatives for children with multiple disabilities who have visual impairments. The transdisciplinary team must review alternatives, considering every aspect of the child and the requirements of current and future environments.

Intervention for Children with Hearing Impairments

Intervention for children with hearing impairments attempts to do the following:

1. Restore hearing to the greatest degree possible
2. Improve residual hearing using equipment
3. Develop oral and manual communication skills
4. Adapt assessment and training in all content areas
5. Maximize use of residual hearing
6. Maximize social and behavioral adjustment

The manner of application of any or all of these goals to any individual child requires careful consideration by the entire transdisciplinary team.

Hearing Restoration   In some cases, surgical treatment can restore or improve hearing. Broken eardrums often can be repaired. Delicate bones in the middle ear cavity can sometimes be repaired or replaced. Most hearing losses, however, cannot be corrected by middle ear surgery.

For sensorineural hearing losses, the cochlear implant holds much promise. However, its use with individuals with multiple disabilities may be limited. It is important to note that implanting this device is limited to individuals with profound deafness. Even among such cases, its application can be undertaken only when strict anatomical, physiological, and psychological criteria are met. The nature and extent of functional improvement varies enormously (Shea, Domico, & Lupfer, 1994). After the device is installed, considerable calibration is necessary, which usually requires patient participation although some attempt has been made to achieve this passively in young children.

Some of the disputes about using cochlear implants stem from a misunderstanding of the underlying physiology. As has been noted, direct electrical stimulation of the eighth nerve provides atypical stimuli that individuals with the implant must *learn* to use (Schein, 1984). Media exaggerations that refer to cochlear implants in terms such as "a bionic ear" or "a miracle that restores hearing" create unrealistic expectations and do a disservice to parents seeking assistance for their children who are deaf. Nonetheless, evidence shows that many children who are deaf do benefit from cochlear implants (Cohen, Waltzman, &

Fisher, 1993), and refinement in procedures and technology have improved the outcomes substantially since the early implants in the 1970s. Progress is expected to continue and may result in better application to children with severe and multiple disabilities.

Improved Residual Hearing Using Equipment   The use of suitable hearing aids should always be considered when developing comprehensive habilitation programs for children with hearing impairments. Both parents and teachers need to understand that use of amplification not only may accelerate the development of receptive and expressive communication skills, but also may minimize academic difficulties (Matkin, 1984). Despite wide acceptance of this concept, some problems exist. First, many children who would benefit from wearable amplification, particularly those with mild and profound hearing losses, are not aided or are not aided early enough to prevent delays in the development of language. Second, some children do not receive optimal amplification because they need more powerful or more appropriate aids. Third, many children are wearing hearing aids that are in poor condition. Reichman and Healey (1989), examining the status of monitoring and maintenance of amplification systems used in schools, found that 54.1% of American classrooms serving students who required amplification had not achieved the level that would ensure that hearing aids were consistently functioning properly. Fourth, not all children are introduced to their aids with a period of auditory training that enables them to adjust to and use their aids properly and at all appropriate times.

Some audiologists fear that the introduction of wearable amplification may result in either temporary or permanent threshold shifts in cases of mild hearing loss. The probability of further damaging a child's sensorineural auditory mechanism can be substantially minimized by first limiting the maximum output of the hearing aid and then by ongoing monitoring of auditory status (Matkin, 1984). In the case of children with profound hearing losses, even when discrimination of words is not possible, an aid can help the individual respond to and localize environmental sounds and also to perceive other elements of speech, such as tempo and intonation. In the fitting of hearing aids for children, audiologists now recommend a hearing aid for each ear (Northern & Downs, 1991). This is based on findings that improved localization assists the child in locating the speaker quickly and accurately—a prerequisite to adequate speechreading— and that binaural-aided hearing improves speech recognition in adverse listening situations because one aided ear is always favorably placed with respect to the person who is talking. This concept should also be kept in mind when the child has a monaural loss. Often, it is felt that the one unimpaired ear is sufficient. It is not. If hearing in the impaired ear can be improved, then the child should be given the advantage of binaural hearing. In any case, there needs to be a realistic understanding that the use of personal amplification is to enable the child to communicate better (Northern & Downs, 1991).

Care must be taken in selecting, fitting, and maintaining the aid, as well as training the child in its use. The audiologist should not only participate in the initial selection and fitting of the aid, but also in the ongoing monitoring of its function and the child's response to it and in the training of other team members to participate in this monitoring. A daily check of the aid is especially important for children who may not recognize or inform others of problems. A check-up routine can be learned easily by the teacher, and many simple problems can be corrected immediately. A lack of amplification, fluctuating sound levels, whistling, squealing, or other noises may signal damaged equipment, a poor fit, run down batteries, or a number of other problems. Wax should be removed from the earmold or hearing aid itself. A child with problems that are not easily corrected should be referred immediately to a specialist (Holvoet & Helmstetter, 1989).

Children often require specific training to use aids. Reinforcing activities using auditory stimuli are often useful. Short initial periods of use should be gradually lengthened. Excessive prompting and attempting to stop the child from removing the aid should be avoided because this often reinforces attempts to remove it. Because static, overamplification, or an otherwise malfunctioning aid can be aversive to the student, ensuring that the aid is working properly and is adjusted correctly also help improve tolerance for the hearing aid.

There are three major classifications of personal hearing aids: body-worn (BW), behind-the-ear (BTE), and in-the-ear (ITE) or canal hearing aids. BTE aids are the choice for most children, because the instrument's microphones are located at each ear and clothing noise as well as other common problems encountered with body aids (e.g., food in microphones, broken cords) are eliminated (Northern & Downs, 1991). ITE aids are seldom prescribed for children, as their cosmetic advantages are overbalanced by their disadvantages, which include difficulty in manipulating the controls and higher cost. BW aids are typically reserved for use with infants and toddlers whose small external ears do not provide sufficient stability to keep BTE aids in place, children with malformations of the outer ear or ear canal or with recurrent ear disease requiring bone conduction amplification, and for older children with motor impairments and limited manual dexterity who can more easily use and care for a body aid. However, BW aids can provide a higher level of amplification without feedback than BTE and ITE aids and would be recommended in cases requiring very high intensity inputs (Katz, 1985). One further word about hearing aids, as with other technological advances: The rapid pace of improvements in these prostheses demands that practitioners keep up with them, because today's recommendations may be radically altered by tomorrow's developments.

The most common equipment used to enhance the signal-to-noise ratio or the ratio between the teacher's voice and background sounds in classrooms is the FM system. The teacher wears a microphone that broadcasts a signal directly to the child's ear, eliminating a significant amount of background noise. This also allows for child-to-child communication. A promising new type of FM technology, soundfield amplification, amplifies the teacher's voice for all children in the classroom (Flexer, 1990). Another type of technology, infrared systems, offers the transmission of signals by means of infrared light. Although currently used primarily in public facilities, they have potential for use in schools.

Developing Communication Skills   The three primary variables of the overall process of communication for students with hearing impairments are degree of hearing loss, level of speech intelligibility, and mode of expressive communication. The relationships among these three variables are highly significant. A student's degree of hearing loss is the strongest and most consistent correlate to intelligibility of the student's speech. The greater the intelligibility, the more likely the student is to rely on speech for communication (Wolk & Schildroth, 1986). A student's use of manual communication is closely related to whether that student attends an educational program where signing is used for instruction. In the 1982–1983 Annual Survey of Hearing Impaired Children and Youth, 98% of the students who signed were also in education programs in which signing was used (Jordan & Karchmer, 1986).

Because of the major hindrance that lack of hearing presents to language learning, any educational system should recognize the need of a child who is deaf for early natural language competence and for communicative access to curricular material. Fewer than 10% of children with prelingual deafness come from families in which there are parents, siblings, or other relatives who are deaf. This means that those closest to most children who are deaf have had no experience with deafness (Schein, 1989). Thus, it is difficult for these children to acquire a natural language such as American Sign Language (ASL) and thereby to acquire the information that is critical for those aspects of typical socioemotional development founding in family interaction. Typically, a child who is deaf is the first person who is deaf that other members of the family have ever encountered. In addition to the trauma this creates, family members seldom have the communication skills or the knowledge and experience required to provide these children with an optimal context for the acquisition of either a natural language or the cultural understandings and experiences available to children who can hear (Johnson, Liddell, & Erting, 1989). A major goal should be to provide educational and emotional support for the families of children who are deaf so they can provide the environment their children need for enhanced linguistic and developmental experiences. This would include the use of early auditory stimulation, vocal practice, amplification as required, and constant exposure to language, whether signed or spoken.

Adapting Assessment and Training   Most assessment and training relies heavily on verbal instructions and cues. When doing so is not possible, alternatives must be used. These alternatives may require considerable learning on the part of parents, caregivers, and all other team members. If alternative languages (e.g., a gestural language) are used, communication partners must become sufficiently proficient in these languages to provide a rich language environment. Use of standardized tests of cognitive and developmental skills may produce *poor* results strongly influenced by lack of auditory skills. Although selecting the most appropriate test to compensate for the hearing loss may overcome some of this problem (Gill & Dihoff, 1982), the presence of other specific disabilities must also be taken into account. Criterion-based assessment directly related to training objectives is typically more valuable.

Maximizing Use of Residual Hearing   Most children with hearing impairments have some remaining auditory sensation. Training can help them use residual hearing to their advantage. Simple exercises to teach sound awareness, sound discrimination, and sound localization are valuable (Sims-Tucker & Jensema, 1984; Wolf-Schein, 1995). Information about the child's current auditory skills can help suggest which stimuli and tasks might be appropriate. Whenever possible, these exercises should be taught during functional activities in the child's natural environment.

Maximizing Social and Behavioral Adjustment   Social adjustment is an important overall goal for all children with multiple disabilities. Concerns about social adjustment have become particularly complex and intermingled with controversy over *oral* versus *manual* approaches for children with hearing impairments. Maximizing speech reception and production is sometimes considered a key to entering the mainstream of society. Some people believe that individuals with significant hearing impairments will always be at a disadvantage in a "vocal society," but they can become fully functioning members of a "signing society" and so should be encouraged to develop the skills for which they have the greatest potential. Because children with multiple disabilities typically encounter difficulty with acceptance among either group, regardless of their predominant communication mode, this controversy may seem moot, but it does point out the general importance of communication skills for acceptance in either group. Undoubtedly, functional communication skill training in realistically available environments is a major factor in social adjustment.

Self-stimulating behaviors producing auditory feedback (sometimes called "deafisms") are common among children with multiple disabilities including hearing impairments. Rather than attempting to suppress this behavior, intervention should be aimed at developing more suitable behavior and replacing inappropriate stimulation with more fitting auditory input.

No aspect of educational inclusion has been as controversial as the education of students with severe hearing impairments. Although inclusion with students who can hear typically improves social adjustment in the general community (e.g., Esposito & Koorland, 1989), difficulty with speech as the primary method of communication typically leaves individuals with hearing impairments at a disadvantage. Within the deaf community, however, the relevance of speech is vastly diminished, and the individual who is deaf can be a fully functioning member of this vital community. Thus, some individuals view inclusion as pushing children toward adult roles as second-class members of the hearing community and depriving them of the opportunity to develop into first-class members of the deaf community. Ideally, individuals who are deaf should develop the skills that allow them to fully adjust to both communities and permit free choice and easily movement between the deaf community and the hearing community. Unfortunately, only a few individuals seem to achieve this and difficult choices are often necessary in educational planning. This issue may be less relevant to children with multiple disabilities who are deaf because their other disabilities often interfere with the acquisition of a common alternative language (e.g., ASL) and make their inclusion in the deaf community as complex as their inclusion in the hearing community. An assessment of social adjustment and communication development may provide useful data for guiding decisions regarding integration for these individuals. As a rule, the community, age-appropriate, natural environment should be considered the best educational environment. Nevertheless, contact with other individuals who are deaf should be encouraged, and ASL or an appropriate, commonly used alternative should be taught whenever possible through bilingual and bicultural education (Reiman & Bullis, 1989). If social adjustment to the deaf community and nonspeech communication skills are developing at a rate that suggests the individual may adjust better to the deaf community, this choice should be encouraged.

Intervention for Children Who Are Deaf-Blind

Although the principles of intervention for both children with hearing impairments and children with visual impairments generally can be applied to children who are deaf-blind, the unique nature and needs of these children require special consideration (Orlansky, 1980). Children who are deaf-blind with additional disabilities require further program modification, particularly in the area of communication.

Most alternatives to vocal communication depend on vision as a functional alternative to hearing. For children who are both deaf and blind, the visual alternative is unavailable. Van Dijk (1986) suggests that the establishment of communication and rapport is a prelude to progress in all educational and social areas. This might begin at a very basic level, using physical contact to develop an attachment to others and to begin interaction routines. Van Dijk's program to stimulate attachment and develop interaction patterns that serve as a foundation for communication includes the following:

1. *Coactive movement and responsiveness*—Coactive movement means that the teacher joins in with the activity of the child. This has been described as a hands-on method because often one has to lead the child's hands through the activity.

2. *Structuring the child's daily routine*—The most fruitful approach is to build the day around some important activities to build up a chain of expectancies.

3. *Characterization*—Helping the bonding process can involve having the person assigned to the child come to be recognized by a special characteristic, such as a teacher's earring. When the child has residual vision, as many children who are deaf-blind do, one can use drawings or photographs of the favorite person as an object of reference.

Sternberg, Pegnatore, and Hill (1983) also have recommended slightly modified versions of these procedures for developing skills prerequisite to communication in students with profound disabilities who are not deaf and blind.

Tactile, object, picture, and gestural cues can be used to teach a variety of skills to students who are deaf-blind (e.g., Berg & Wacker, 1989; Stremel & Schutz, 1995). Some children who are deaf-blind have enough residual hearing or vision to use speech, symbols, or gestures without special modification; others may require amplification or enlargement. For those with severely limited vision and hearing, it may be necessary to use more specialized materials, such as object or texture boards, or some other tactile modality. These materials include various forms of an alphabet code or adaptations of lipreading and sign language. Criteria for sign selection (including iconicity) appear to be similar for children who are deaf-blind and their peers who can see (Griffith, Robinson, & Panagos, 1983). However, size and speed of signs and gestures need to be adapted to the individual student. Among the more common techniques used are the American one-hand alphabet; the British two-hand alphabet; alphabet gloves; the Lorm alphabet; block printing (on the palm or other part of the body); visual or tactile one-to-one signing; and Tadoma, a method in which the person who is deaf-blind places his or her thumb on the speakers lip with his or her palm and remaining fingers touching the speaker's throat. Alphabet methods, which also include braille, are useful only when the individual has sufficient cognitive level and sensitivity of touch to comprehend abstract symbols (Wolf, 1986). Teaching students who are deaf-blind to initiate requests is important to reduce potential dependency. Interrupted behavior chain procedures have been used to encourage requests from students who are deaf-blind (Romer & Schoenberg, 1991).

Awareness of self and self-concept development are areas of significant delay for children with severe disabilities, and, in particular, body awareness develops very gradually in the absence of visual exploration and observation (Jones, 1988). Tactile stimulation and sensory exploration using other senses (e.g., smell, residual hearing) must be substituted. Adults must make the child aware that they are paying attention and provide some cue as to whether the attention is negative or positive. Leisure, recreational, and physical activities, which are so readily available for other children, require special consideration when children who are deaf-blind are involved. Play skills are very slow in developing and must be specifically taught, often with the adult providing a great deal of physical guidance. Physical education can help develop exteroceptive (touch), proprioceptive (muscle position), and vestibular (equilibrium) senses (Silberman & Tripodi, 1979), all of which are valuable for functional motor behavior. Adults can adapt these and other recreation and leisure programs for individuals who are deaf-blind by enhancing sensory input, matching motor and speed requirements to the child's skills, increasing tactile cues, and stabilizing materials to limit changes in their position (Hamre-Nietupski, Nietupski, Sandvig, Sandvig, & Ayres, 1984).

The development of appropriate social behavior also requires special consideration for children with dual sensory impairments. Stereotypic, self-abusive, autoerotic, and ritualistic-perseverative behaviors are common. With the possible exception of behavior that is severely and immediately damaging to the child or others, efforts should be geared toward developing more acceptable forms of behavior, rather than suppressing current behavior. Some forms of self-stimulation are acceptable at appropriate times and places, and training may be aimed at teaching the child to discriminate these times and places, rather than at eliminating the behavior. Such decisions must be made by the transdisciplinary team, considering each child and the child's environment.

Educational programs for individuals who are deaf-blind may afford little opportunity for students to develop self-sufficiency and autonomy and to learn necessary skills that range from home management to work skills. At some point, it is important to increase independent learning skills if students are to make transitions from school to adult life (Ven & Wadler, 1990). Teaching functional skills, such as food preparation (Horsfall & Maggs, 1986), may be an effective way to build self-esteem in addition to developing greater independence. This factor is critical for all children with multiple disabilities because at some point they will leave the relatively sheltered school and home environment, and the better prepared they are, the better their chances are for a fulfilling life.

THE TRANSDISCIPLINARY TEAM

A well-coordinated transdisciplinary team is essential for providing optimal service to all children with multiple disabilities, particularly those with sensory impairments. Two levels of team professionals need to be considered. The first level includes teachers, school administrators, and other permanent school staff (e.g., social workers, counselors, therapists), who are involved not only in assessment and planning, but also in the ongoing teaching and monitoring of progress. The second level involves team members who are available on an as-needed basis. These include specialists with particular professional competence who also believe that positive changes can occur as a result of their intervention (Murphy, 1983).

An *ophthalmologist* is a physician specializing in detection and treatment of eye diseases. An *optometrist* is a nonmedical professional trained to measure refractive errors and fit lenses to the individual's eyes. An *optician* grinds lenses and fits frames according to prescription by the ophthalmologist or optometrist. All three of these professionals can participate in the delivery of transdisciplinary services, but it is essential to select the appropriate person for the services required. Every child with multiple disabilities and known or potential visual impairment should be evaluated by an ophthalmologist to determine if eye disease exists. Once eye disease has been ruled out, regular visual examinations and prescription of corrective lenses can be carried out by an optometrist. The specialized nature of assessing the vision of children with multiple disabilities requires more than basic professional competence in ophthalmologists and optometrists. They must be willing, interested, and knowledgeable about specialized procedures and resourceful in applying them. They often will require specialized equipment. As professional training expands to consider the special needs of individuals with disabilities and as specialized equipment becomes more readily available, appropriate services become easier to find. In locating vision professionals to examine and treat children with multiple disabilities, it is important to discuss the child's special needs and ask if the professional is prepared to meet them. If the professional is not prepared, he or she may be able to refer the child to a colleague who is better prepared to serve children with multiple disabilities.

The *orientation and mobility specialist* can be very important in teaching O&M skills to children with multiple disabilities. Unfortunately, few specialists trained in O&M are available, and only very few of those are trained to work with individuals with multiple disabilities (Uslan, 1979). Although a specialist in O&M with training and experience relevant to children with multiple disabilities is most desirable, even a specialist in O&M without this specific background will be a valuable consultant to the team, advising them on the principles of O&M, while learning more about the population from other team members.

The *otologist* and *audiologist* play important roles on teams serving children with known or suspected hearing impairments. The role of an otologist is to determine the medical cause of the problem and provide any treatment that would alleviate or improve the condition. Even an acute middle ear infection that creates a temporary hearing loss can have a permanent effect on the child's language development, and chronic problems, including such easily cured conditions as impacted wax, can have major consequences. Children with Down syndrome are particularly vulnerable to middle ear problems that, if left untreated, can result in permanent hearing loss. It is also important to involve an otologist when surgery is an option. The role of the audiologist is to provide an ongoing measure of the individual's hearing acuity. An isolated test producing an audiogram in the child's record is not adequate (Kenworthy, 1982). The audiologist should serve as a consultant to team members, interpreting the implications of test findings for training as well as suggesting and monitoring amplification equipment both for classroom and individual use (Bess & Humes, 1995). It is important to modify hearing aids as changes in hearing occur over time or as more useful modes of amplification become available. Speech-language pathologists or hearing therapists can also provide expertise in interpreting test results and have specialized knowledge about communication systems and adaptive equipment. Their input is extremely valuable for team decisions about communication systems and programs. In addition, these therapists should be available for ongoing assessment and training in their specialized areas. Unlike eyeglasses, hearing aids require a significant amount of auditory training and training in care and use if they are to be optimally used.

These specialists must work closely with teachers, parents, and all other transdisciplinary team members. The specialists depend on other team members to provide vital assessment information, determine appropriate objectives, and integrate sensory-related program components with all other areas of training.

Teachers working with students with multiple disabilities that include visual or hearing impairments need specialized training and materials to do the best job possible. A survey of teachers serving children with visual impairments who have multiple disabilities (Erin, Daugherty, Dignan, & Pearson, 1990) indicated that a substantial number believed they were inadequately prepared. These researchers conclude that there is a need to improve teacher preparation at the preservice and in-service levels, a need that has also been identified by others (Wolf, 1986). Resources are available to assist in training teachers of students with both sensory impairments and multiple disabilities (e.g., Hamre-Nietupski, Swatta, Veerhusen, & Olsen, 1986; Haring & Romer, 1995; Helmstetter, Murphy-Herd, Roberts, & Guess, 1984; Roberts, Helmstetter, Guess, Murphy-Herd, & Mulligan, 1984). Specialized training makes it possible for teachers to apply their instructional skills more effectively as members of transdisciplinary teams.

SUMMARY

This chapter has presented some of the special concerns in educating children with multiple disabilities that include sensory impairment. It was stressed that every child's vision and hearing can be meaningfully assessed. Some interventions designed to maximize residual vision and hearing and to compensate for lost vision and hearing through the use of other senses were suggested. The involvement of specialized professionals who play major roles in assessment and intervention of these children was also discussed.

REFERENCES

Atkinson, J. (1985). Assessment of vision in infants and young children. In S. Harel & N.J. Anastasiow (Eds.), *The at-risk infant: Psycho/socio/medical aspects* (pp. 341–352). Baltimore: Paul H. Brookes Publishing Co.

Atkinson, J. (1989). New tests of vision screening and assessments in infants and young children. In J.H. French, S. Harel, & B. Casaer (Eds.), *Child neurology and developmental disabilities* (pp. 219–227). Baltimore: Paul H. Brookes Publishing Co.

Bach-y-Rita, P. (1972). *Brain mechanisms in sensory substitution.* New York: Academic Press.

Baine, D. (1985). *Selected topics in special education.* Delhi, India: Allied Publishers and Utkal University.

Batshaw, M.L., & Perret, Y.M. (1992). *Children with disabilities: A medical primer* (3rd ed.). Baltimore: Paul H. Brookes Publishing Co.

Berg, W.K., & Wacker, D.P. (1989). Evaluation of tactile prompts with a student who is deaf, blind, and mentally retarded. *Journal of Applied Behavior Analysis, 22*(1), 93–99.

Berlin, C.I., & Hood L.J. (1987). Auditory brainstem response and middle ear assessment in children. In F.N. Martin (Ed.), *Hearing disorders in children* (pp. 151–167). Austin, TX: PRO-ED.

Bess, F.H., & Humes, L.E. (1995). *Audiology: The fundamentals.* Baltimore: Williams & Wilkins.

Billingsley, F.F., Huven, R., & Romer, L.T. (1995). Behavioral support in inclusive school settings. In N.G. Haring & L.T. Romer (Eds.), *Welcoming students who are deaf-blind into typical classrooms: Facilitating school participation, learning, and friendships* (pp. 251–275). Baltimore: Paul H. Brookes Publishing Co.

Brady, M.P. (1985). Orientation and mobility for severely multiple handicapped individuals: A developing technology. *DPH Journal, 8*(1), 32–41.

Brett, E.M. (1983). The blind retarded child. In K. Wybar & D. Taylor (Eds.), *Pediatric ophthalmology: Current aspects* (pp. 113–122). New York: Marcel Dekker.

Clayman, H.M., Jaffe, N.S., & Galin, M.A. (1983). *Intraocular lens implantation: Techniques and complications.* St. Louis: C.V. Mosby.

Cohen, N.L., Waltzman, S.B., & Fisher, S.G. (1993). A prospective randomized study of cochlear implants. *New England Journal of Medicine, 328,* 233–237.

Cote, K.S., & Smith, A. (1983). Assessment of the multiply handicapped. In R.T. Jose (Ed.), *Understanding low vision* (pp. 379–401). New York: American Foundation for the Blind.

Cress, P.J., Spellman, C.R., DeBriere, T.J., Sizemore, A.C., Northam, J.K., & Johnson, J.L. (1981). Vision screening for persons with severe handicaps. *Journal of The Association for the Severely Handicapped, 6*(3), 41–50.

Curry, S. (1989). *Low incidence disability program quality study.* Sacramento: California State Department of Education.

Dantona, R. (1986). Implications of demographic data for planning of services for deaf-blind children and adults. In D. Ellis (Ed.), *Sensory impairments in mentally handicapped people* (pp. 69–82). San Diego: College-Hill.

Downing, J.E., & Perino, D.M. (1992). Functional versus standardized assessment procedures: Implications for educational programming. *Mental Retardation, 30*(5), 289–295.

Efron, M. (1981). Vision assessment and implications. In S.R. Walsh & R. Holzberg (Eds.), *Understanding and educating the deaf-blind/severely and profoundly handicapped* (pp. 73–84). Springfield, IL: Charles C Thomas.

Erin, J., Daugherty, W., Dignan, K., & Pearson, N. (1990). Teachers of visually handicapped students with multiple disabilities: Perceptions of adequacy. *Journal of Visual Impairment and Blindness, 84*(1), 16–21.

Esposito, B.G., & Koorland, M.A. (1989). Play behavior of hearing impaired children: Integrated and segregated settings. *Exceptional Children, 55,* 412–419.

Flexer, C. (1990). Audiological rehabilitation in the schools. *Asha, 32,* 44–45.

Folio, M., & DuBose, R.F. (1983). *Peabody Developmental Motor Scales.* Hingham, MA: Teaching Resources.

Fraunfelder, F.T. (1989). *Drug-induced ocular side effects and drug interactions* (3rd ed.). Philadelphia: Lea & Febiger.

Friedrich, B. (1985). The state of the art in audiologic evaluation. In E. Cherow (Ed.), *Hearing impaired children and youth with developmental disabilities* (pp. 122–153). Washington, DC: Gallaudet University Press.

Gee, K., Harrell, R., & Rosenberg, R. (1987). Teaching orientation and mobility skills within and across natural opportunities for travel: A model designed for learners with multiple severe disabilities. In L. Goetz, D. Guess, & K. Stremel-Campbell (Eds.), *Innovative program design for individuals with dual sensory impairments* (pp. 127–157). Baltimore: Paul H. Brookes Publishing Co.

Geruschat, D.R. (1980). Orientation and mobility for the low functioning deaf-blind child. *Journal of Visual Impairment and Blindness, 74*, 29–33.

Gill, G., & Dihoff, R. (1982). Nonverbal assessment of cognitive behavior. In B. Campbell & V. Baldwin (Eds.), *Severely handicapped/hearing impaired students: Strengthening service delivery* (pp. 77–113). Baltimore: Paul H. Brookes Publishing Co.

Goetz, L. (1995). Inclusion of students who are deaf-blind: What does the future hold? In N.G. Haring & L.T. Romer (Eds.), *Welcoming students who are deaf-blind into typical classrooms* (pp. 3–17). Baltimore: Paul H. Brookes Publishing Co.

Goode, D. (1994). *A world without words: The social construction of children born deaf and blind*. Philadelphia: Temple University Press.

Green, C.W., Reid, D.H., Canipe, V.S., & Gardner, S.M. (1991). A comprehensive evaluation of reinforcer identification processes for persons with profound multiple handicaps. *Journal of Applied Behavior Analysis, 24*(3), 537–552.

Griffith, P.L., Robinson, J.H., & Panagos, J.H. (1983). Tactile iconicity: Signs rated for use with deaf-blind children. *Journal of The Association for the Severely Handicapped, 8*(2), 26–38.

Hall, D.M.B., & Jolly, H. (1984). *The child with a handicap*. Oxford: Blackwell Scientific Publications.

Hamre-Nietupski, S., Nietupski, J., Sandvig, R., Sandvig, M.B., & Ayres, B. (1984). Leisure skills instruction in a community residential setting with young adults who are deaf/blind severely handicapped. *Journal of The Association for the Severely Handicapped, 9*(1), 49–54.

Hamre-Nietupski, S., Swatta, P., Veerhusen, K., & Olsen, M. (1986). *Teacher training modules related to teaching students with sensory impairments*. Cedar Falls: University of Northern Iowa.

Harcourt, B. (1983). Guidelines for the management of incominant strabismus in children. In K. Wybar & D. Taylor (Eds.), *Pediatric ophthalmology: Current aspects* (pp. 341–354). New York: Marcel Dekker.

Harden, A. (1983). Electrodiagnostic assessment in infancy. In K. Wybar & D. Taylor (Eds.), *Pediatric ophthalmology: Current aspects* (pp. 11–18). New York: Marcel Dekker.

Harel, S., Holtzman, M., & Feinshod, M. (1985). The late visual bloomer. In S. Harel & N.J. Anastasiow (Eds.), *The at-risk infant: Psycho/socio/medical aspects* (pp. 359–362). Baltimore: Paul H. Brookes Publishing Co.

Haring, N.G., & Romer, L.T. (Eds.). (1995). *Welcoming students who are deaf-blind into typical classrooms: Facilitating school participation, learning, and friendships*. Baltimore: Paul H. Brookes Publishing Co.

Harley, R.K., & Merbler, J.B. (1980). Development of an orientation and mobility program for multiply impaired low vision children. *Journal of Visual Impairment and Blindness, 74*, 9–14.

Healy, S. (1994). The use of a synthetic speech output communication aid by a youth with severe developmental disability. In K. Linfoot (Ed.), *Communication strate-*

gies for people with developmental disabilities: Issues from theory and practice (pp. 156–176). Baltimore: Paul H. Brookes Publishing Co.

Helmstetter, E., Murphy-Herd, M.C., Roberts, S., & Guess, D. (1984). *Individualized curriculum sequence and extended classroom models for learners who are deaf and blind.* Lawrence: University of Kansas.

Hill, J., Brantner, J., & Spreat, S. (1989). The effect of contingent music on the in-seat behavior of a blind young woman with profound mental retardation. *Education and Treatment for Children, 12*(2), 165–173.

Hollins, M. (1989). *Understanding blindness.* Hillsdale, NJ: Lawrence Erlbaum Associates.

Holvoet, J.F., & Helmstetter, E. (1989). *Medical problems of students with specific needs: A guide for educators.* Boston: College-Hill.

Horsfall, D., & Maggs, A. (1986). Cooking skills instruction with severely multiply handicapped adolescents. *Australia and New Zealand Journal of Developmental Disabilities, 12*(3), 177–186.

Huebner, K., Welch, T., & Prickett, J. (1993). *Deaf-blind learners: A self-study curriculum in communication and mobility.* New York: American Foundation for the Blind Consortium.

Jacobson, J.W., & Janicki, M.P. (1985). Functional and health status characteristics of persons with severe handicaps in New York State. *Journal of The Association for Persons with Severe Handicaps, 10*(1), 51–60.

Johnson, R.E., Liddell, S.K., & Erting, C.J. (1989). *Unlocking the curriculum: Principles for achieving access in deaf education.* (Gallaudet Research Institute Working Paper 89-3). Washington, DC: Gallaudet University.

Jones, C.J. (1988). *Evaluation and educational programming of deaf-blind/severely multihandicapped students: Sensorimotor stage.* Springfield, IL: Charles C Thomas.

Jordan, I.K., & Karchmer, M.A. (1986). Patterns of sign use among hearing impaired students. In A.N. Schildroth & M.A. Karchmer (Eds.), *Deaf children in America* (pp. 125–139). San Diego: College-Hill.

Jose, R.T., Smith, A.J., & Shane, K.G. (1980). Evaluating and stimulating vision in the multiply impaired. *Journal of Visual Impairment and Blindness, 74,* 2–8.

Karchmer, M. (1985). A demographic perspective. In E. Cherow (Ed.), *Hearing impaired children and youth with developmental disabilities* (pp. 36–59). Washington, DC: Gallaudet University Press.

Katz, J. (Ed.). (1985). *Handbook of clinical audiology* (3rd ed.). Baltimore: Williams & Wilkins.

Kelley, P., & Wedding, J.A. (1995). Medications used by students with visual and multiple impairments: Implications for teachers. *Journal of Visual Impairment and Blindness, 89*(1), 38–46.

Kenworthy, O.T. (1982). Integration of assessment and management processes: Audiology as an educational program. In B. Campbell & V. Baldwin (Eds.), *Severely handicapped/hearing impaired students: Strengthening service delivery* (pp. 49–76). Baltimore: Paul H. Brookes Publishing Co.

Kirchner, C. (1985). *Data on blindness and visual impairment in the U.S.* New York: American Foundation for the Blind.

Leung, E.H.L., & Hollins, M. (1989). The blind child. In M. Hollins (Ed.), *Understanding blindness* (pp. 139–170). Hillsdale, NJ: Lawrence Erlbaum Associates.

Lloyd, L.T., Spradlin, J.E., & Reid, M.J. (1968). An operant audiometric procedure for difficult-to-test patients. *Journal of Speech and Hearing Disorders, 33,* 236–245.

Longo, J., Rotatori, A.F., Heinze, T., & Kapperman, G. (1982). Technology as an aid in assessing visual acuity in severely/profoundly retarded children. *Education of the Visually Handicapped, 14,* 21–27.

Matkin, N. (1984). Wearable amplification: A litany of persisting problems. In J. Jerger (Ed.), *Pediatric audiology* (pp. 123–145). San Diego: College-Hill.

McDade, P.R. (1969). The importance of motor development and mobility skills for the institutionalized blind mentally retarded. *New Outlook for the Blind, 63*, 312–317.

Moores, D.F. (1987). *Educating the deaf: Psychology, principles, and practices* (3rd ed.). Boston: Houghton Mifflin.

Morse, K.E. (1980). Modifications of long cane for use by multiply impaired children. *Journal of Visual Impairment and Blindness, 74*, 15–18.

Murphy, K. (1983). The educator-therapist and deaf, multiply disabled children: Some essential criteria. In G.T. Mencher & S.E. Gerber (Eds.), *The multiply handicapped hearing impaired child* (pp. 13–26). New York: Grune & Stratton.

Northern, J.L., & Downs, M.P. (1991). *Hearing in children* (4th ed.). Baltimore: Williams & Wilkins.

Orlansky, M. (1980). Appropriate educational services for deaf-blind students. *Education of the Visually Handicapped, 12*, 122–128.

Reichman, J., & Healey, W.C. (1989). Amplification monitoring and maintenance in schools. *Asha, 31*, 43–47.

Reiman, J.W., & Bullis, M. (1989). Integrating students with deafness into mainstream public education. In R. Gaylord-Ross (Ed.), *Integration strategies for students with handicaps* (pp. 105–128). Baltimore: Paul H. Brookes Publishing Co.

Roberts, S., Helmstetter, E., Guess, D., Murphy-Herd, M.C., & Mulligan, M. (1984). *Programming for students who are deaf and blind.* Lawrence: University of Kansas.

Robinson, C.C., & Robinson, J.H. (1983). Sensorimotor functions and cognitive development. In M.E. Snell (Ed.), *Systematic instruction of the moderately and severely handicapped* (2nd ed., pp. 237–268). Columbus, OH: Charles E. Merrill.

Romer, L.T., & Schoenberg, B. (1991). Increasing requests made by people with developmental disabilities and deaf-blindness through the use of behavior interruption strategies. *Education and Training in Mental Retardation, 26*(1), 70–78.

Sacks, O.W. (1995). *An anthropologist on Mars: Seven paradoxical tales.* New York: Alfred A. Knopf.

Sacks, S.Z., & Reardon, M.P. (1989). Maximizing social integration for students with visual handicaps. In R. Gaylord-Ross (Ed.), *Integration strategies for students with handicaps* (pp. 77–104). Baltimore: Paul H. Brookes Publishing Co.

Schein, J.D. (1979). Multiply handicapped hearing-impaired children. In L.J. Bradford & W.G. Hardy (Eds.), *Hearing and hearing impairment* (pp. 356–364). New York: Grune & Stratton.

Schein, J.D. (1984). Cochlear implants and the education of deaf children. *American Annals of the Deaf, 129*, 324–332.

Schein, J.D. (1989). *At home among strangers.* Washington, DC: Gallaudet University Press.

Schein, J.D. (1992). *Canadians with impaired hearing.* Ottawa, Ontario: Statistics Canada.

Schildroth, A.N., & Hotto, S.A. (in press). Annual survey of deaf and hard-of-hearing children and youth: Changes in student and program characteristics. 1984–1985 and 1994–1995. *American Annals of the Deaf.*

Schulman, C.A., & Wade, G. (1970). The use of heart rate in the audiological evaluation of non-verbal children: II. Clinical trials of an infant population. *Neuropaeditricia, 2*, 197–205.

Shea, J.J., Domico, E.H., & Lupfer, M. (1994). Speech perception after multichannel cochlear implantation in the pediatric patient. *American Journal of Otology, 15*, 66–70.

Siegel-Causey, E., & Downing, J. (1987). Nonsymbolic communication development: Theoretical concepts and educational strategies. In L. Goetz, D. Guess, & K. Stremel-Campbell (Eds.), *Innovative program design for individuals with dual sensory impairments* (pp. 15–48). Baltimore: Paul H. Brookes Publishing Co.

Silberman, R.K., & Tripodi, V. (1979). Adaptation of project "I CAN": Primary skills physical education program for deaf-blind children. *Journal of Visual Impairment and Blindness, 73,* 270–276.

Sims-Tucker, B.M., & Jensema, C.K. (1984). Severely and profoundly auditorially/visually impaired students: The deaf-blind population. In P.J. Valletutti & B.M. Sims-Tucker (Eds.), *Severely and profoundly handicapped students: Their nature and needs* (pp. 269–317). Baltimore: Paul H. Brookes Publishing Co.

Sohmer, H. (1989). Contributions of auditory nerve–brain stem evoked responses to the diagnosis of pediatric neurological and auditory disorders. In J.H. French, S. Harel, & P. Casaer (Eds.), *Child neurology and developmental disabilities: Selected proceedings of the fourth international child neurology congress* (pp. 229–232). Baltimore: Paul H. Brookes Publishing Co.

Sternberg, L., Pegnatore, L., & Hill, C. (1983). Establishing interactive communication behaviors with profoundly mentally handicapped students. *Journal of The Association for the Severely Handicapped, 8*(2), 39–46.

Stremel, K., & Schultz, R. (1995). Functional communication in inclusive settings for students who are deaf-blind. In N.G. Haring & L.T. Romer (Eds.), *Welcoming students who are deaf-blind into typical classrooms: Facilitating school participation, learning, and friendships* (pp. 197–229). Baltimore: Paul H. Brookes Publishing Co.

Stromer, R., & Miller, J. (1982). Training parents of multiply handicapped/hearing impaired children. In B. Campbell & V. Baldwin (Eds.), *Severely handicapped/hearing impaired students: Strengthening service delivery* (pp. 199–218). Baltimore: Paul H. Brookes Publishing Co.

Taylor, D. (1983). Clinical visual assessment in infancy. In K. Wybar & D. Taylor (Eds.), *Pediatric ophthalmology: Current aspects* (pp. 5–9). New York: Marcel Dekker.

Thompson, M., Thompson, G., & Vethivelu, E. (1989). A comparison of audiometric test methods for 2-year-old children. *Journal of Speech and Hearing Disorders, 54*(2), 174–180.

Uslan, M.M. (1979). Orientation and mobility for severely and profoundly retarded blind persons. *Journal of Visual Impairment and Blindness, 73,* 53–58.

Uslan, M.M., Malone, S., & De l'Aune, W. (1983). Teaching route travel to multiply handicapped blind adults: An auditory approach. *Journal of Visual Impairment and Blindness, 77,* 213–215.

Uslan, M.M., & Shragai, Y. (1995). A review of high-powered screen-magnification software for IBM-compatible computers. *JVIB News Service, 89*(2), 14–19.

Utley, B., Duncan, D., Strain, P., & Scanlon, K. (1983). Effects of contingent and noncontingent vision stimulation on visual fixation in multiply handicapped children. *Journal of The Association for the Severely Handicapped, 8*(3), 29–42.

van Dijk, J. (1986). An educational curriculum for deaf-blind multi-handicapped persons. In D. Ellis (Ed.), *Sensory impairments in mentally handicapped people* (pp. 374–382). San Diego: College-Hill.

Ven, J.J., & Wadler, F. (1990). Maximizing the independence of deaf-blind teenagers. *Journal of Visual Impairment and Blindness, 84*(3), 103–108.

Watson, G. (1989). Competencies and a bibliography addressing students' use of low vision devices. *Journal of Visual Impairment and Blindness, 83*(3), 160–163.

Wolf, E. (1986). Deaf-blind. In J. VanCleve (Ed.), *Gallaudet encyclopedia of deaf people and deafness* (pp. 226–252). New York: McGraw-Hill.

Wolff, A.B., & Harkins, J.E. (1986). Multihandicapped students. In A.N. Schildroth & M.A. Karchmer (Eds.), *Deaf children in America* (pp. 55–83). San Diego: College-Hill.

Wolf-Schein, E.G. (1989). A review of the size, characteristics, and needs of the deaf-blind population of North America. *The ACEHI Journal 15*(3), 85–100.

Wolf-Schein, E.G. (1990, May). *Fragile X syndrome: Association with autism and other severe disabilities.* Paper presented at Shaping Alternative Futures: Strategies for Effective Integration, Edmonton, Alberta, Canada.

Wolf-Schein, E.G. (1995). *Pupil attribute study system* (PASS). Edmonton, AB: Psychometrics Canada.

Wolf-Schein, E.G., & Schein, J.D. (1995). *Behavioral assessment system for individual clients.* Coconut Creek, FL: Three Bridge Publishers.

Wolk, S., & Schildroth, A.N. (1986). Deaf children and speech intelligibility: A national study. In A.N. Schildroth & M.A. Karchmer (Eds.), *Deaf children in America* (pp. 139–160). San Diego: College-Hill.

Worthington, D.W., & Peters, J.F. (1984). Electrophysiological audiometry. In J. Jerger (Ed.), *Pediatric audiology* (pp. 95–125). San Diego: College-Hill.

12

Working with Families

Irene H. Carney
and Michael Gamel-McCormick

THE TRANSDISCIPLINARY MODEL ENJOYS ACCEPTANCE and support within a variety of human services fields (Demchak, 1995; McGonigel, Woodruff, & Roszmann-Millican, 1994). The preceding chapters cite such support within the literature in early childhood education, medicine, nursing, occupational therapy, physical therapy, and special education.

Parent participation in team decision making is also generally accepted among service providers (Buckner, 1992; Goldstein, 1993; Slovic, 1982). With the Education for All Handicapped Children Act of 1975 (PL 94-142), parents gained the right to help shape the nature of their children's education. PL 94-142 has allowed parents to contribute to, or at least to review and agree or disagree with, their children's individualized education program (IEP). The law also provides procedural safeguards so that children and families are guaranteed due process of law. The Education of the Handicapped Act Amendments of 1986 (PL 99-457) (since reauthorized as the Individuals with Disabilities Education Act Amendments of 1991 [PL 102-119]) expanded parents' roles even further. Part H, the section of the bill pertaining to infants and toddlers, dictates that services be delivered according to an individualized family service plan (IFSP). In this radical departure from many professionals' established practices, multidisciplinary decision-making teams must consider not only the concerns and preferences, but also the service and support needs, of parents and other family members as well as those of the infant or toddler receiving services. Through the regulations for Part H of the Individuals with Disabilities Education Act (IDEA) of 1990 (PL 101-476) and the individual states' implementation of these regulations, families have been provided with the option to control significant aspects of service delivery to their infants or toddlers with disabilities and their other family members, such as who will constitute the team providing services, who will be the service coordinator for early intervention programming, and what role, if any, the family will play in the delivery of services (Apter, 1994; Colorado State Department of Education, 1993; Office of Special Education and Rehabilitative Services, 1993). In spite of these legislative landmarks, however, and, in contrast to a wealth of arguments in support of parent involvement, few parents experience full membership on the teams with which they are involved. In an excellent review and discussion of parent participation in IEP development, Turnbull and Turnbull (1990) noted that, although some parents are active participants, the majority are not. They based this conclusion on their review of research on parent involvement in IEP planning. They cited, for example, Lynch and Stein's (1982) finding that, of 400 parents of students with disabilities, only 71 (18%) reported participating in the development of their child's IEP. This study reported differences among parents in terms of their racial or ethnic group, their children's age, and the nature of their child's disability. It is worth noting that parents of students with physical disabilities reported significantly less participation than parents of children with other disabling conditions. Research since 1990 tends to support the above-mentioned findings (Baumgartner, 1993; Harry, 1995; Katsiyannis & Ward, 1992; Michael, 1992).

Turnbull and Turnbull (1990) listed several barriers to parent participation, including logistical problems, communication problems, lack of understanding of the school system and parents' rights within that system, feelings of inferiority, and uncertainty about their child's disability. The authors also examined barriers that teachers have identified, including parental apathy, professional time constraints, and lack of professional training for collaboration with parents. Research and practice in the 1990s points to the need for training for teachers and other professionals in the area of equal collaboration with parents (Lewis, Marine, & Van Horn, 1992).

This chapter proposes an alternative explanation for the discrepancy between the *ideal* of parent involvement and the *reality* of parent participation in the team process. This chapter also describes a model for team decision making based on the practices of principled negotiation (Fisher & Ury, 1983). This discussion includes a consideration of the interests that parents bring to the team process in general and at different stages of family life.

AN ALTERNATIVE HYPOTHESIS
REGARDING PARENTAL NONINVOLVEMENT

Chapter 1 notes that it is difficult to organize a truly effective team. Among the factors that contribute to team effectiveness are team size (relatively small teams being preferable), the degree to which team members adhere to group norms, clear and frequent communication, leadership, and a shared framework for making decisions and resolving conflicts.

This chapter suggests that discomfort with disagreement and the lack of a constructive means for resolving differences detract from the functioning of many transdisciplinary teams and, in particular, inhibit parent involvement in team development and team process. Discomfort with conflict, for example, may keep a parent or professional team members from acknowledging and exploring their differences of perspective or opinion.

Other possible reasons for transdisciplinary teams not functioning at full efficiency may be attributable to the lack of full participation of family members. Other team members' contacts with parents may be infrequent and primarily relegated to formal meetings such as triennials, IEP team meetings, assessment sessions, or meetings to address a concern with the parent's child. This level of contact does not promote the parent as a full member of the team.

Disagreements and differences are natural and inevitable features of interdisciplinary or transdisciplinary team discussions. Even more marked than the expected differences among professional team members is the difference between professionals and parents. Ruppman (1990) explained, from a parent's point of view, why this is true:

> I don't get paid for what I do and I didn't choose to do what I do. I didn't choose to go to IEP meetings. I didn't choose to become a physical therapist. I didn't choose to become a behavior management expert. I didn't choose to become a language therapist.... Most of you chose what you do, and this is a very big difference. I am the reluctant, uneasy...IEP team member. I'm the one who doesn't get paid for my time, and I'm the one who doesn't want to be there.... That's a very essential difference between us. (not paginated)

Ruppman has pointed out what researchers have indicated about the participation of parents and school personnel on a transdisciplinary team, namely, that parents are inherently different from all other team members. Parents' status on the team is different, their training is often different, and their goals for their children are sometimes different (Cooper & Rascon, 1994; Giangreco, 1994).

Ruppman further explained tensions between parents and professionals by noting that teams seldom can deliver all the services and experiences that parents would like their children to have: "What do parents want? They want everything! They want every service their child needs. They want people to be competent. They want people to be sensitive....We want everything, and you can't give it to us" (not paginated).

Ruppman is emphatic, however, in her assertion that inevitable tensions between parents and professionals can be helpful by keeping all parties attentive to what they do and why they do it. She maintains that properly directed tension can "improve what I do as a parent and improve what you do as a professional" (not paginated).

Supporting Ruppman's view from a professional perspective is Garland, who, in a discussion of transdisciplinary assessment, states

> When conflict is avoided you negate the whole premise of the transdisciplinary approach, which is that we bring together a team because of the diversity of the teams' perspectives.... We don't need to bring together people who will always agree. We need to bring together our team that will bring different perspectives. When they fail to air those differences, when they fail to air conflicts and use productive strategies for conflict resolution, they haven't done their job on the team. (Child Development Resources, 1989)

In contrast to Garland's and Ruppman's perspectives, however, many people see conflict as necessarily negative. More important, perhaps, relatively few people have information about or experience with confronting conflict and dealing with it in a constructive way.

Team decision making is one of many areas to which a conflict resolution framework can be and has been applied (Brennan & Lynch, 1993; Elliott & Sheridan, 1992; Mitchell, 1992; Stremel, 1992). Variously referred to as conflict resolution, mediation, and negotiation, constructive approaches to resolving differences are now practiced in labor relations, divorce proceedings, child custody decisions, family violence interventions, and parent–child disputes (Ahearn, 1994; Girdner & Eheart, 1984; Symington, 1995). A number of specific paradigms have been developed and demonstrated. One of those most widely used is principled negotiation.

PRINCIPLED NEGOTIATION

Principled negotiation is the term that Fisher and Ury (1983) have used to describe one approach to conflict resolution. Through their work with the Harvard Negotiation Project, these authors have applied this approach to diverse disagreements such as tenant–landlord disputes, conflicts between local governments and their citizenry, and international tensions such as the Middle East Crisis of the 1970s. Fisher and Ury's approach addresses actions or decisions that are stalemated by conflict. Their approach also could be adopted in a proactive way, however, as a general approach to decision making.

The basic elements of principled negotiation include the following:

1. Separating the people from the problem
2. Focusing on interests, not on positions
3. Creating options for mutual gain
4. Using objective criteria to evaluate outcomes

Separating the People from the Problem

Bailey (1984) suggested that in an ideal team conflict is not necessarily absent, but stems from substantive issues. Conflict rooted in personality differences, however, threatens the team's effectiveness. Fisher and Ury (1983) substantiated this observation and asserted that decision makers will be unable to generate effective decisions if they blame problems on individual participation in decision making.

As noted previously, one of the explanations teachers give for lack of parental involvement on IEP teams is parental apathy (Turnbull & Turnbull, 1990). If a teacher were to apply the "separate the people from the problem" approach in this case, the problem might be stated not as the parents' lack of concern, but as the teacher's frustration with the difficulty of obtaining information from parents that might aid in planning. With the problem restated in this way, the potential for solving the problem is improved greatly. The teacher is unlikely to change a parent or the parents' investment in the team. However, the teacher could very well find a means of obtaining needed information from parents such as removing logistical barriers to parents' attending meetings or securing information by means other than the team meeting.

Fisher and Ury (1983) suggested several ways out of the trap of blaming another person for difficulties in the decision-making process. They highlighted the need for clear and consistent communication. They also advocated the practice of recognizing and acknowledging the emotional by-products of conflict (e.g., anger, distress, frustration, confusion). Finally, they emphasized the importance of checking perceptions rather than making assumptions about why people behave as they do or believe what they profess. Fisher and Ury proposed that by transcending personality differences, parties involved in conflict can begin to view one another as allies in the effort to solve a difficult problem.

Focusing on Interests, Not on Positions

One of the most logical yet novel features of principled negotiation is the emphasis on *interests* rather than on positions. Fisher and Ury (1983) provided a succinct description of the difference between the two when they noted, "Your position is something you have decided upon. Your interests are what caused you to decide" (p. 42). A parent team member, for example, may advocate for direct occupational therapy for his son, arguing that the indirect or integrated therapy model that the rest of the team supports does not provide sufficient structure or intensity. Upon exploration, it may become apparent that the father has taken this position because his child, at age 9, does not yet demonstrate the strength and dexterity necessary to manage snaps and zippers and is, therefore, still dependent on others for dressing. The father took a position on a model for service delivery. His real interest, however, had to do with his concern that his son needed to become more independent. With this additional information on the table, the team has the opportunity to construct a plan in which the team's service delivery preference is adopted, but the father's priorities for instructional goals are respected and addressed.

Fisher and Ury (1983) observed that this approach is very effective in resolving disagreements for two reasons. First, focusing on interests helps parties in conflict to find a common ground. In the example above, the parent and professional team members upheld opposing positions regarding the appropriate and desirable model for occupational therapy services. All team members, however, could agree that independent dressing was an appropriate goal. They all shared an interest in seeing this student develop the skills he needed to dress himself.

Second, focusing on interests helps team members to identify different paths to the desired end. In the example above, the team could elect to find or create more frequent opportunities for the student to practice snapping and zipping throughout the school day. They could also choose to modify the child's clothing, for example, with Velcro closures, so that the elusive snapping and zipping skills would no longer be necessary.

On the subject of how to identify interests, Fisher and Ury (1983) suggested taking the others' perspectives and trying to imagine or understand why they take the positions they do. They recommended making a list of interests that might be influencing all parties. They also emphasized that the most powerful and influential interests reflect basic human needs, such as security, recognition, and control over one's life. (The interests that parents have identified as determinants of their preferences and priorities for their children's education are discussed in subsequent sections of this chapter.) Once team members are aware of the interests at work in their decision making, they are able to generate options from among which they ultimately will choose.

Creating Options for Mutual Gain

"The key to wise decision making," Fisher and Ury (1983) asserted, "lies in selecting from a great number and variety of options" (p. 68). A team can best generate a large menu of options through the process of *brainstorming*. Brainstorming is an approach with which most team members are likely to have experience; it is a seven-step process, including the brainstorming itself. The steps in the process are as follows:

1. Defining your purpose
2. Choosing participants and a facilitator
3. Creating an informal and relaxed atmosphere
4. Seating participants side by side, facing a flipchart or chalkboard
5. Clarifying ground rules including the rule that no idea is to be criticized
6. Brainstorming
7. Selecting the most promising ideas and then inventing improvements on them

In the context of transdisciplinary teamwork, these activities would most likely take place in preparation for a program planning meeting such as an IEP meeting. A more formal meeting, however, could be the setting in which the final decision is discussed and agreed upon. Fisher and Ury (1983) listed several considerations that can enhance the effectiveness of brainstorming. Three of their suggestions may be particularly useful for transdisciplinary teams.

First is the idea of making sure that parties who hold different positions, particularly parties who disagree with one another, participate in brainstorming together. In the case of parent and professional team members, this implies that both groups should create the list of options that the team will finally consider. Program planning, as it is most frequently practiced, is characterized by professionals determining what recommendations they will make to parents. Parents are, in fact, often unaware of any options other than those that are preselected and presented to them. The process of reviewing all options together gives all participants equal access to information in addition to ownership of the problem.

A second and related consideration is that brainstorming groups look through the eyes of different experts. A transdisciplinary team has the resources, in the form of its members, to consider possibilities from the perspectives of several professional fields as well as through the parents' expertise.

Third, Fisher and Ury (1983) caution that there may not be one best answer. Teams may find their best and most creative plans by selecting combinations or parts of several different options. Once the team has reached consensus on how they will proceed, they can complete the process of principled negotiation by identifying what objective criteria they will use to evaluate their decision.

Using Objective Criteria to Evaluate Outcomes

Transdisciplinary teams traditionally have been concerned with criteria that indicate whether a student is achieving or progressing toward specific goals and objectives. These criteria can also be the means by which team members choose to evaluate their plans.

When plans have been constructed through principled negotiation, however, teams might also wish to evaluate their plans in terms of whether the interests of team members have been met. This approach is illustrated in the case example that follows.

Principled Negotiation: A Case Example

How can principled negotiation work in the instance in which a decision cannot be made or implemented because of disagreement between a parent and the professional members of the team? This example will apply the components of principled negotiation to such a scenario.

Caitlin is a 6-year-old student with spastic quadriplegic cerebral palsy. Her standardized tests scores indicate mental retardation in the moderate range. She attends elementary school where she receives services from a first-grade teacher, a special education teacher, and a teaching assistant. The classroom staff members receive consultation from a language and communication specialist, an occupational therapist, and a physical therapist. Caitlin lives with her parents, an 8-year-old brother, and an 18-month-old sister. Her mother does not work outside the home. Caitlin's IEP includes a goal that she will self-initiate toileting by the end of the school year. All team members, including Caitlin's parents, agreed to this goal.

During the mid-year parent–teacher conference, the teachers suggest that it is time to begin toilet training and they review a Foxx and Azrin procedure (Foxx & Azrin, 1973; see Chapter 9). The teachers and teaching assistant suggest that training should start at school and then schedule a home visit to help Caitlin's family begin the highly structured intervention there. Once training is underway, Caitlin's parents have a difficult time making a commitment regarding a date for a home visit. The teachers begin to feel frustrated, confused, and a bit angry. Caitlin's parents feel harassed.

Separating the People from the Problem   It would be easy and not unusual for this type of situation to become bogged down at this point with each party blaming the other for the stalemate. The teachers, for example, might make assumptions about Caitlin's parents' behavior and label them, for example, overprotective, apathetic, or uncooperative. The parents might see the school staff as being unrealistic about Caitlin's abilities and insensitive to the demands of their home life.

In order to move beyond this impasse, it will be important for all participants to attribute the problem to something other than the other people involved. If the teachers were to explore why Caitlin's parents are unavailable, they might learn that they are ambivalent about starting training. If the team accepts that position, training will not proceed as planned. Team members adhering to the elements of principled negotiation, however, will try to discern the interests that contribute to the parents' ambivalence.

Focusing on Interests, Not Positions   In shifting their focus from differing positions to interests, the teachers can acknowledge their frustrations and explore the parents' perspectives on the situation. Thereby, teachers might discover that a number of interests, some of them competing with others, influence Caitlin's parents feelings about toilet training. These hypothetical interests are listed in Table 12.1

Once the professionals understand the interests at work, they have many more options to explore in order to reach agreement about whether and when

Table 12.1.   An example of one family's interests that influence parents' position on toilet training

Interests that support training

Ceasing Caitlin's use of diapers in order to save on expense

Completing Caitlin's toilet training before her younger sister is ready to be trained

Interests that interfere with training

Concern that training will take time away from the other children

Interest in not having to do a great deal of additional laundry

Concern about inconvenience of traveling around community if Caitlin is not in diapers training will begin at home. They also have a way to restate the problem: the difficulty of finding a training method and a schedule that are equally appropriate for the home and the school settings.

Creating Options for Mutual Gain Creating options for mutual gain requires that all parties engage in brainstorming to identify all possible paths to a solution. A list of options that could be included in reaching a mutually satisfactory decision for Caitlin and her parents follows:

1. Identify school staff who can help conduct training at home so the mother will be available to her other children.
2. Start training at home during the school day when at least one child is away from home at school.
3. Dress Caitlin in skirts and dresses so only underwear will have to be changed in case of accidents, and put waterproof clothes under her on upholstered furniture.
4. Allow Caitlin to wear diapers when not at home or at school.
5. Start training during a vacation when both parents are home.
6. Identify a neighbor, relative, or babysitter who can help with the other children until the father comes home so the mother can attend to toilet training.

Using Objective Criteria to Evaluate Outcomes Even decisions that result from careful and creative discussion can yield disappointing results. For this reason, it is important to have a means by which participants can evaluate their decision. Agreeing upon objective evaluation criteria and the time at which the decision will be evaluated acknowledges that the decision can be renegotiated. The more fundamental the conflict, the more important this assurance may be.

For this step in the example, the concern is not whether Caitlin has achieved the toilet-training goal, but whether the agreed-upon approach to training satisfies the interests of the team members. Say, for example, the team agreed upon options 3, 4, and 6. The criteria could include 1) no more than one additional load of wash every 2 days, 2) Caitlin making as many trips outside home as she did before training, and 3) the mother consistently having a second adult at home during training.

Summary

Principled negotiation provides a framework that confronts and makes constructive use of differences among team members. In groups that adopt this approach, individual members

1. View one another as allies in the challenge of fashioning a mutually agreeable and effective plan.
2. Explore one another's perspectives in order to better understand differences and to find shared interests.
3. Map several different paths to a solution.
4. Use objective criteria to ensure the effectiveness of the plan.

Fisher and Ury's process of principled negotiation, with the emphasis on identifying each party's interests, has been adopted by many localities and states (Ahearn, 1994; Florida State Department of Education, 1992; New York State Education Department, 1992). The procedures have increased efficacy of services to students with disabilities, have reduced time and costs spent on due process hearing and litigation, and have provided a collaborative alternative to what is sometimes a highly adversarial process of negotiating program plans.

The following section provides perspectives on interests that parents bring into the team process.

CONSIDERING PARENTS' PERSPECTIVES IN TEAM DECISION MAKING

In order for principled negotiation to succeed in the transdisciplinary team context, participants must develop a curiosity about a sincere interest in the perspectives of other team members. Particularly in regard to the steps of separating the people from the problem and focusing on interests rather than positions, team members must attempt to stand in each other's shoes in order to understand the behavior and the opinions of individual participants. This section describes parental interests and perspectives that may influence team decision making.

This discussion of parental perspectives should not be construed to say that families of children with multiple disabilities have a uniform set of beliefs, options, experiences, and needs. Quite to the contrary, families differ from one another on several dimensions. Ethnicity, religion, economic resources, family size, and coping styles all combine to distinguish families from one another (Turnbull & Turnbull, 1990). These characteristics influence a family's values, beliefs, and needs. Families are further influenced by the changes they experience over the course of their family life. These changes have been studied and described as a series of events and stages that constitute a family life cycle.

The Family Life Cycle

Sociological writings on the individual life cycle (Erikson, 1959) established the logic of the family life cycle concept (Carter & McGoldrick, 1980; Duvall, 1957). These theories assert that individuals or families progress through a series of predictable stages and that each stage introduces new developmental tasks. Where the family life cycle is concerned, stages are determined by the changing constitution of the family (e.g., the birth of a child, an adult child's departure from home); by the family's changing relationship to social institutions (e.g., entering the school system, retiring from the work force); and by family members' experiences of important individual stages (e.g., adolescence).

Several authors have theorized about the nature of the family life cycle in typical families (Carter & McGoldrick, 1980; Duvall, 1957; Solomon, 1973). Others have mapped the course of change in families of children with disabilities

(Hanline, 1991; Suelzle & Keenan, 1981; Turnbull, Summers, & Brotherson, 1986; Turnbull & Turnbull, 1990).

Turnbull and Turnbull (1990) cautioned that the family life cycle is a theoretical structure based on broad generalizations. The generalizations that follow are organized by three life cycle stages that appear salient in a discussion of educational teams: birth and early childhood, childhood, and adolescence and young adulthood.

Family Life Cycle Stages

Birth and Early Childhood   The general picture of a family into which a new child has come is one of intense involvement with the simultaneous tasks of establishing a new relationship while adjusting and balancing the patterns and relationships of the family as a whole.

Stage Characteristics   A baby's birth and infancy generally is portrayed as an emotionally warm and happy time in parents' lives and relationships. Magazine pictures and television advertisements portray visions of quietly joyous adults caring for an attractive and responsive newborn. Warmth and happiness may accurately characterize parents' experiences, in part. Parents of a newborn, however, also face several subtle but critical challenges. A new baby's inclusion in the family, whether the child is the firstborn or has one or more siblings, forces change in all other family relationships. The time and attention involved in an infant's care necessarily shift energy away from other children or from the parents' relationships with one another.

Regaining Balance in Family Life   For new parents, one of the central dilemmas of this period involves establishing a balance between their absorption in their child and the energy and attention still required by the other parent; their own personal needs; and by other members of the family, particularly if the family includes older children. This balance clearly is elusive. It is essential, however, if families are to preserve their integrity and carry on the work of family life. This is a critical adjustment that each family confronts during a child's infancy and early childhood. The challenges may be particularly great, however, if the new baby has a health condition or disability that necessitates the family's involvement with extraordinary caregiving routines and specialized professionals and services. In other words, parents of children with special needs not only must reestablish the equilibrium in family life that a new baby disturbs, but must achieve this with a number of additional weights on one side of the balance.

Developing a Relationship with the New Family Member   The presence of a disability may also complicate what is, perhaps, the most important task of infancy—the development of a positive, reciprocal relationship between the parents and the child. Trout and Foley (1989) described this process and the potential impact of a child's delayed development:

> Successful and supportive interactions between infant and caregiver occur when both parent and infant are maximally available, emotionally and physically, and

when a pattern of contingent, attuned responsiveness is developed that helps them to "fit" together. Infants with disabilities may not be available in these ways, and the fit does not come easily. (p. 39)

Likewise, the parents of an infant with a disability may not be completely available to care for the child. Adjusting to the child they have may take away their ability to be emotionally and physically accessible in order to create those essential links between the caregiver and newborn. As Simons (1987) describes, "parents spend much of the child's early life learning to accept that the child they have is not the child they wanted" (p. 5). This need to adjust to a child whose disability and additional needs were not expected by the family is in addition to the adjustments that all families make when a new child enters the household.

In describing her first year as the mother of a premature baby with complex health care needs, Ann Oster (1984) related the pain and confusion of adjusting to her son's birth:

During much of Nick's early life the successes in coping with his problems belonged to professionals. Only the failures were mine. I hadn't had a healthy baby, couldn't seem to get him healthy, couldn't comfort him, and most painful, I didn't feel connected to him. I believed that I wasn't capable of doing him any good. (p. 30)

Oster acknowledges that, after a year, a positive parent–child relationship began to take root.

Sometime after Nicholas had started nursery school, I saw a videotape that demonstrated what Dr. [T. Berry] Brazelton calls the irresistible responsiveness of a premature baby. I almost cried while I watched as a 3 lb. preemie slowly followed a ball with his eyes, looked for the sound of his mother's voice, and with heroic effort, finally turned his head and reached for her. A nurse practitioner had taught that mother to read the subtle clues that would have drawn me to my son so much earlier. It was a piece of information, a teachable skill, that might have changed the course of our lives. (p. 31)

This experience identifies a skill that enabled a parent to become more responsive to her baby. With the following example, Trout and Foley (1989) emphasized that sensitivity to the parent–child relationship should guide team members in identifying goals for the child:

When a blind child fails to develop language because he or she lacks the object constancy necessary to suggest the existence of objects "out there" that might be labeled, it may well be that the child is not saying "Mama." To go about the job of language development with such a child without attending to how it feels to the mother not to be named may well invite failure, not only in the area of language work, but also with respect to establishing the bonds that are essential to both the child's and mother's development. (pp. 61–62)

Greenspan (1988) also emphasized the need to design therapeutic interventions so that they support positive parent–child interactions. This author suggested that educators and therapists must understand the emotional milestones of infancy and early childhood and promote emotional growth by integrating motor, sensory, and cognitive goals with age-appropriate social behaviors. Greenspan suggested, for example, that an 8-month-old infant who needs practice on reaching can be taught to reach out to touch her father's face or reach up to signal to her mother that she wants to be picked up. Such an approach emphasizes the interdependence of transdisciplinary team members in understanding the child and parent in relationship to one another and in designing and implementing activities that maximize the child's own development as well as his or her fit within the family.

This is an area in which it is particularly important for team members to be aware of and responsive to cultural values and patterns of interaction. As Trout and Foley (1989) noted, the family's cultural context will influence parents' concerns and preferences regarding such patterns as involvement of the extended family, the appropriateness of contact comfort, the duration of breast feeding, and promotion of the child's independence. Team members will need to consider patterns of social and emotional behavior through the filter of the family's racial, ethnic, and religious culture and promote developments that support and respect these characteristics.

Implications/Summary   In addition to adjusting and balancing the patterns and relationships of the family, the family with an infant who has a disability is also working to make the adjustments from the child who was expected to the child with a disability. Olson and his colleagues (1983) described the early childhood years as a time of intense absorption with the inner workings of the family. If children have special needs, however, children and parents are thrust from the privacy of the family environment into a world of professionals, services, and bureaucracies. Parent involvement on early intervention teams requires parents to confront other tasks and challenges in addition to the stage-specific tasks described previously. As team members, parents must come to terms with the diagnosis of their child's disability. This process involves understanding the practical implication for the child's behavior and development and experiencing the emotional aftermath of the diagnosis. It is a process that requires the understanding, respect, and support of the professional members of the team.

It is also a process, as several parents have noted, that is facilitated by accurate information and honest communication. Ruppman (1990) described those situations in which professionals have to communicate information that may be difficult for parents to hear. She recalled the following:

> The first tough love I ever received was from my son's first principal who [stopped] me in the hall one day...and he just quite simply said, "[Y]ou haven't asked me this, but I'm going to tell you—you and [your husband] need to gird yourself[ves] for the long haul here. This boy's doing real well. They could call him autistic...they could call him mentally retarded...what they call him doesn't matter.... What you and [your husband] need to know is that physically, emotionally, financially you

need to gird yourselves for the long haul with this young man—it's not going away." And I cried, but it was love. (not paginated)

In summary, the professional members of transdisciplinary teams can promote involvement of parent team members by doing the following:

1. Appreciating and valuing parents' involvement in the team at the level they desire to be involved
2. Remembering that the family is in the midst of a typical process of change and adjustment and at the same time are experiencing an event that is very different from other families
3. Recognizing that the child's fit within the family might be a priority concern
4. Respecting the family's cultural patterns and beliefs and the impact they will have on whether and how the family participates on a program planning team
5. Communicating accurately and honestly with parents

Childhood   As Turnbull and Turnbull (1990) noted, the childhood stage of the family life cycle is the stage when parents begin the process of letting go.

Adjusting to the Child's Involvement in the School System   At some point early in childhood, each child becomes part of a system other than, and in addition to, his or her family. The most universal example of this transition is the child's entry into elementary school. Many children with and without disabilities also attend preschool programs, and thereby experience dual system membership at an earlier age. At either point of entry, a child's introduction to the system of education presents novel challenges and tasks for the family. A subtle but important challenge, for example, is the parents' adjustment to sharing their authority with professional educators. Once in school, a child's teacher exerts a major influence over the child's routine activities, behavior, peer relationships, learning experiences, and development of beliefs and values. Teachers also contribute to students' assessment of their own competence as individuals. For parents, many of whom hold strong personal beliefs about teaching and child rearing, their children's school years require a balance of entrusting their children's care to the schools and monitoring that trust to ensure their children's well-being and appropriate development. Maintaining this balance requires vigilance and energy.

An additional challenge relates to the fact that a child entering the school system enters, along with the family, the public eye. Preschool and school programs, even when they emphasize individualized education, have as their basis a set of norms and ideals for students' behaviors and achievements. Whether the norm relates to a grade level, developmental status, personal appearance, or a standard of independence and normalization, parents and teachers use comparisons to place an individual child on the continuum of strengths and weaknesses. Concern about how their children measure up and represent the family to the outside world is characteristic of parents' reactions to the transition to school-based services, whether on the preschool or early elementary level.

Also, mothers and fathers are subject to comparison with other parents. Parents are judged on the basis of how well they uphold social and cultural mores, determined by, for example, the degree to which they teach their children manners, whether they send their children to school when sick, and whether they pack a nutritious lunch. Professionals also evaluate parents by appraising the extent to which they are interested in, and involved with, their children's education.

Professionals' tendency to evaluate parents may be particularly evident with regard to parents whose children have disabilities because the professionals' involvement is specified and mandated by federal law. Furthermore, parents of children with disabilities have long been seen as critical contributors to their children's ability to learn and change.

The relationship between parent involvement and teacher attitude is reflected in a study by Fuqua, Hegland, and Karas (1985). These authors surveyed teachers of preschool students with disabilities regarding their ideals for, and assessment of, parents' involvement with the school. Respondents reported that their satisfaction with parents increased as a function of 1) teachers visiting the home, 2) parents attending parent group meetings, and 3) parents showing they could teach their children at home.

Home visits, parent group meetings, and home-based teaching do not, however, appear in reports on parents' preferences for involvement. Winton and Turnbull (1981) conducted one of the earliest investigations of parents' preferred means of working with school personnel. Their sample consisted of 31 mothers whose children had mild or moderate disabilities. The mothers, during structured interviews, identified all of the involvement opportunities to which they had access and specified which among those they preferred. The medium for involvement that these parents clearly preferred was informal contact with their child's teacher. Other available activities (listed in decreasing order of importance) included parent training opportunities, opportunities to help others understand their child, and volunteering inside or outside of class.

Carney, Snell, and Gressard (1986) also assessed parents' actual means of involvement, as well as preferences, in various parent–professional activities. Thirty-seven parents of students of various age and disability groups participated in a structured telephone interview. Frequency data indicated that informal communication with the teacher and participation in the IEP meeting were considered the most heavily used and preferred forums for parent–teacher interaction. Activities in which parents expressed less interest included those related to observing or volunteering in the classroom, having the teacher come to their home for information or skill exchange, and participating in parent group activities.

The degree and nature of parents' involvement may vary in relation to a number of influences. Sloper, Cunningham, and Arnljotsdottir (1983), for example, found an inverse relationship between the number of children in the family and the extent to which parents participated in one child's special education program. Other authors have noted that parents from low-income groups with children who have disabilities are less likely to take an active part in their children's schooling (Cone, DeLawyer, & Wolfe, 1985; Leyser & Cole, 1984). Lynch and Stein (1982) concluded that parents whose children had physical disabilities were less actively involved than parents of students with mental retardation or other mental disabilities.

Vincent and Salisbury (1989) and the U.S. Census Bureau (1992) referred to changes in the American family that are likely to influence parents' participation in their children's education. These authors noted the following:

- By 2010, nearly 25% of all children in the United States will be children of ethnic origin other than European American.
- Of the approximately 3 million Americans who are homeless, families with children are the fastest growing segment of the homeless.
- Over 3 million children are reported to be abused or neglected each year. Approximately 1 million cases are confirmed. Roughly 150,000 of those cases involve children with disabilities.
- Everyday, more than 3,000 girls become pregnant and 1,300 babies are born to adolescents.
- Of families with children under 18 years old, 20% are headed by a single parent (90% of whom are women); among African American families, 57% of families with children under 18 are headed by one parent.
- In the United States, 1.5 million children are affected by family divorce each year.
- Over 50% of female-headed families with dependent children and over 65% of female-headed families with preschool children have annual incomes below the poverty level (75% below the mean annual family income of $33,000 for a family of four).
- Preschool children are America's poorest age group. Over 23% of children age 3 and under are poor (i.e., have annual family incomes below the federal poverty level); during the preschool years almost one fourth of all American children lack medical, nutritional, and early learning resources.
- The children's poverty rate for African American families is twice that for Caucasian American families.
- Projections (1990) suggest that 75% of children in the United States under the age of 6 years will receive nonparent care on a daily basis.

Whatever the reason for individual differences among parents, the differences should inform professionals' expectations for parent involvement in team meetings and other school-related activities. As Kaiser and Hayden (1984) admonished their constituents,

Special educators must appreciate that parenting can be every bit as important and helpful a thing to do as teaching or therapy. The parent role must not be inadvertently disparaged on the basis of its departure from standard professional trappings. A parent's effectiveness must not only be judged through criteria measuring his or her successive approximations to the professional therapists and teachers providing treatment. (p. 311)

Stage Characteristics   By the time a child with multiple disabilities enters school, his or her parents are usually veterans of assessments, planning meetings, progress reports, and parent training activities. When the child and family enter the educational system, however, they enter a model that is fundamentally different from the early intervention program they leave behind. Turnbull and Turnbull (1990) listed some of the features of this model to which parents must adjust when the child enters school. These include a lessened commitment to family support activities and a shift to a categorical model within which their child will receive a classification and, too often, an accompanying label. Other factors that parents encounter anew at this point are the reactions to disability from the child's peer group and the parents' need to clarify preferences regarding self-contained, inclusive schools (Turnbull et al., 1986).

The roles of occupational, physical, and speech-language therapy in the child's IEP can also change radically with the transition made to school-based services. In the early intervention program, the family's primary contact and service provider might be, for example, an occupational therapist. Under the provisions of PL 102-119, this therapist might be not only the conduit through whom other members of the team funnel their recommendations but also the service coordinator who links the family with other agencies and assists them with their transition to public school. Once in school, however, occupational therapy provides a related service for which the child is eligible *only* if it relates to the child's attainment of other educational goals. If delivered through a transdisciplinary or integrative therapy model, moreover, occupational therapy may involve little or no direct contact between the child and the occupational therapist. Given this scenario, parents might well believe that the school is failing to provide a needed service and is falling short of its commitment to meeting their child's needs.

Implications/Summary   During the process of letting go, parents begin to share responsibility and control with the professionals with whom their child interacts every day. Turnbull and Turnbull also described this stage as an era during which parents may become concerned for the first time about their child's interactions and relationships with other children.

These adjustments do not generally entail the emotional turbulence of the infancy and early childhood period. Parents are, however, accommodating a variety of changes as the child becomes increasingly involved with a system outside of the family and as parents become familiar with all of the implications of the educational model.

As parents experience this transition, they will need to come to terms with an educational classification, clarify their attitudes and preferences regarding their child's involvement with peers who do not have disabilities, and, perhaps, revise their understanding of the need for and delivery of therapy services. Parents' positions on program placement, inclusion, and related services needs may well differ from those of other team members. In this case, it is particularly important for the professional members of the team to seek out and understand the interests that underlie parents' stated preferences. Such exploration may be the only way in which the team will be able to identify common interests and create a mutually agreed-upon plan.

Differences such as those described above sometimes lead to professionals labeling parents as overprotective, apathetic, hostile, or uncooperative. Such explanations for parents' behaviors are, at best, nonconstructive. Under these circumstances, the practice of separating the people from the problem will be necessary in order to direct the team's problem solving in a productive way.

The differences that parents and professionals encounter during the childhood years provide the opportunity for both groups to assess why they believe what they do and whether their approaches are serving the best interests of the child in question. In this way, teams can follow Ruppman's (1990) advice to make constructive and creative use of the natural tensions between parents and professionals.

Adolescence/Young Adulthood   Adolescence and young adulthood is widely regarded as a troublesome period for both teenagers and their families.

Stage Characteristics   The third stage is characterized by a struggle between the adolescent's competing needs for personal autonomy and continued dependence on the family. As they respond to this struggle, parents are challenged by their child's need for sensitivity and flexibility. Mothers and fathers may be further challenged by issues related to their individual lives, such as diminished energy, career developments and disappointments, and satisfaction with their own relationships (Kraft, 1985).

These same parental issues are likely to accompany a child's transition to young adulthood. The challenges implicit in the child's development are quite different, however, from those that characterize adolescence. At this point, the move toward independence typically acquires more momentum. Parents are called upon to help their sons and daughters establish a life, and perhaps a family, of their own. The transition to young adulthood requires both parents and children to adjust to new roles relative to one another.

The changes implicit in adolescence and young adulthood are difficult for many families. These stages appear to be particularly stressful for parents of young men and women with disabilities. Kraft (1985), for example, reported a direct relationship between stress measured by the Questionnaire on Resources and Stress–Revised (QRS–R) (Holroyd, 1974) and the age of a family member with a moderate or severe disability. Other authors suggested that parents experience the most sadness in response to a disability soon after a disability is identified, during early childhood, and during early adulthood (Wikler, Wasow, & Hatfield, 1981). There are several plausible explanations for the relative difficulty of adolescence and young adulthood. Among these are the chronic or recurrent sense of loss parents feel related to having a child with a disability as is emphasized in the discrepancies between the experiences of families with a member who has a disability and typical families, changing physical characteristics of the adolescent child, and differences between parents' and professionals' attitudes regarding appropriate services for adults.

Discrepancies Between Typical Families and Families with a Member Who Has a Disability In some families, the onset of adolescence prompts parents to revisit the loss they experienced when their child was first diagnosed with a disability. Those milestones that are typically achieved at this time in their lives are often elusive. A child who turns 16 years old may not be able to drive; a child who is 18 years old may not be attending a senior prom; and a child who is 21 years old may not be leaving the house for his or her own living quarters. The expected, predictable life course in which parents and children revise their relationships to accommodate the child's decreasing dependence may not occur in the fashion the parents envisioned it. For example, sons and daughters become self-sufficient in functions once served by their parents. Young adults assume some measure of financial responsibility, and their needs for affection, guidance, and recreation are likely to be met, in large part, by individuals outside of the family. Young men and women may demonstrate further independence by living on their own or by starting a new family, thereby maintaining their domestic routine outside of their parents' home.

For the young adult with multiple disabilities, however, the family is not likely to experience any such relief from responsibility. Once the son or daughter has graduated from high school, in fact, the parents may have to adjust in the direction of satisfying more, rather than fewer, of their child's needs. Particularly in cases in which employment or day activity options are limited, parents face a substantial increase in the amount of time during which they must offer supervision, activity, or company for their adult child.

It is often the case, unfortunately, that as demands on parents increase, their resources diminish. It may be that other children who have helped with social and caregiving routines, for example, no longer live in the parents' home. Brothers and sisters who do not have disabilities may take with them an important source of assistance and support when they leave home. Retirement, too, may imply diminished financial flexibility.

It is important to note that families of adults with disabilities have varied, but often effective, means of coping (Brotherson, 1984). The circumstances with which they cope, however, are undeniably different from the trials experienced by families who are not affected by members with disabilities.

Changing Physical Characteristics of the Child The physical changes that accompany adolescence and young adulthood introduce an unfortunate paradox. As parents become older and usually less strong and healthy, their children become taller and heavier and generally more difficult to lift, carry, and position. Some of the accompanying strains can be alleviated with building modifications and special equipment. On a very basic level, however, strong arms, legs, and back muscles are irreplaceable machines.

Puberty may entail hormonally induced seizures or changes in behavior (DeMyer & Goldberg, 1983). These new characteristics can be confusing and difficult to manage. Puberty also introduces the issues of sexuality, reproduction, and menstrual hygiene.

Differences with Professionals   Trends in the field of disability promote inclusion of people with disabilities with people without disabilities. Furthermore, the emphasis on normalization suggests that all adults be permitted and encouraged to experience the privileges of adulthood. This logic implies independence and self-determination in as many respects as possible, including choices regarding sexual expression.

Parents may not, however, be aware of or agree with such philosophical and practical trends. Research with parents of individuals with mental retardation, in fact, indicates that parents of adults with mental retardation are more conservative regarding normalization than parents of their younger counterparts (Suelzle & Keenan, 1981). Respondents in this study reported concerns about their child's isolation and vulnerability as reasons for preferring more sheltered options for adult services.

Ferrara (1979) found that even parents who agreed theoretically with the principle of normalization were conservative about the extent to which the principle should be applied to their own son or daughter. Hill, Seyfarth, Orelove, Wehman, and Banks (1985) documented similar conservatism among parents of children enrolled in sheltered workshops. The parents in their sample asserted that they were not particularly interested in having their child work alongside peers without disabilities. Moreover, they were not dismayed by their children's low rate of pay or lack of fringe benefits.

These differences may stem, in part, from what Turnbull et al. (1986) termed *transitional resistance.* These authors coined this term to describe families they had studied who appeared to resist their young adult child's potential independence. Turnbull and her colleagues concluded that the continued presence of their adult child in their home might contribute to parents' socialization and self-definition. This conclusion is supported by Seltzer's (1989) finding that mothers caring for an adult child with mental retardation compared favorably to their counterparts without such responsibilities. Caregiving mothers fared better on measures of health and depression than women who did not have an ongoing mothering role.

Implications   In short, the situation that many parents encounter during their child's adolescence and young adulthood is one of increasing demands and diminishing resources. As parents become older, they may become less strong, energetic, and financially flexible. At the same time, however, they face the challenge of providing care for an older, heavier individual. Furthermore, in the absence of jobs or other opportunities for their adult children, parents may find themselves in the position of being the only caregivers. And in the midst of coping with such daily demands, parents may realize the need to make important and difficult decisions about their child's future. The most important work of transdisciplinary teams serving adolescents and young adults relates to this need for future planning and decision making. Team members can best support and collaborate with parents by recognizing parents' concerns regarding their children's futures.

Model programs of the 1980s and 1990s have demonstrated the feasibility of training students with multiple disabilities on competitive jobs and of securing employment for those students following their graduation from high school. This kind of demonstration points the way to a future in which competitive or supported employment might constitute a realistic option for people with multiple disabilities.

In most areas, however, students with multiple disabilities presently make transitions to sheltered work or day activity programs. And in many areas, unfortunately, students with multiple disabilities are barred from even those opportunities because of architectural barriers, motoric requirements of jobs or training for other programs, entry criteria such as independent toileting, and inadequate client–staff ratios. For many families, then, the only certainty they feel about the future is its absolute uncertainty. In response to this dilemma, families may, at one or more points during adolescence and adulthood, desire assistance with the task of future planning.

The need for assistance should be easy to understand. Making decisions about future circumstances requires gathering information about available resources, identifying those agencies and individuals who should be included in the search, assessing the match among students' skills and preferences and availability of local programs, articulating the family's priority concerns, and reaching consensus between the family and relevant professionals. Each of these steps calls for an investment of time, energy, and skill. Together, the components constitute a major commitment of personal, professional, and family resources.

Families and professionals can now refer to a number of resources developed specifically to facilitate parent access to, and progress through, future planning activities. One such resource is a family guide compiled by Goldfarb, Brotherson, Summers, and Turnbull (1986). This volume provides information and strategies pertaining to practices including, but not limited to, planning for the future. The guide covers such topics as coping, sources of formal and informal support, family communication, brainstorming, and taking action. Through reading and structured exercises, the authors invite family members to assess their needs and resources and to apply a problem-solving approach to their own situation and concerns.

Turnbull, Turnbull, Bronicki, Summers, and Roeder-Gordon (1989) compiled a guide to decisions specific to adulthood. Their comprehensive volume covers such issues as the participation of adults with disabilities in making decisions (including mental competence and consent), guardianship, financial planning, relevant government benefits, advocacy, and planning for life in the community. These authors emphasized the importance of long-range planning but acknowledged the difficulty this process can involve for parents. They observed, for example, that future planning activities might elicit painful memories or issues such as parents' fears regarding their children's loneliness and vulnerability. Looking toward the future also requires parents to face their own mortality—a specter that can invite anxiety or depression.

Several authors have developed programs for involving parents in planning for postschool employment (Halvorsen, Doering, Farron-Davis, Usilton, & Sailor, 1989; Morton, Everson, & Moon, 1987; Sowers, 1989). Their collective suggestions include providing in-service training to parents; using examples or videotapes of people working to illustrate models; visiting prospective jobsites; and inviting veteran employers, workers, and parents to describe their experiences. Most important, perhaps, is the assertion that professional team members must listen more carefully to parents' needs and desires regarding employment (Morton et al., 1987; Sowers, 1989). Morton et al. (1987) quoted a parent as follows, "Professionals need to let parents get through the 'feeling part' of transition instead of getting bogged down in solving problems. If professionals let parents express their feelings and talk it out, then they'll be able to work together" (pp. 130-131).

SUMMARY

This chapter has suggested that parents and professionals bring fundamental differences to the transdisciplinary team process and that those differences, if properly explored and directed, can result in more appropriate and effective plans for students with multiple disabilities. The first section presented a framework for team decision making and problem solving. The second section summarized experiences that may influence parents' interests and preferences at three different life stages.

This discussion presented the possibility that an alliance of parents and professional team members will yield more creative and meaningful plans; services; and, ultimately, lives. Wiegle's (1990) comments provide a closing reflection:

> What I ask for from professionals is that you stand next to me, that you believe that those kids that you work with are O.K. Too often I feel that the professionals who are working with me pity me, they pity my child. I do not want to have to fight against the people who are here to help my children. I want you to know that they were born with the same rights and responsibilities as every child born within our country. I want you to help me help them lead the best lives they possibly can. I want you to value them. I want you to value me. (not paginated)

REFERENCES

Ahearn, E. (1994). *Mediation and due process procedures in special education: An analysis of state policies. Final report. Project FORUM* (Report No. Contract No. HS

92015001). Alexandria, VA: National Association of State Directors of Special Education. (ERIC Document Reproduction Service No. ED 378 714)

Apter, D.S. (1994). From dream to reality: A participant's view of the implementation of Part H of PL 99-457. *Journal of Early Intervention, 18*(2), 131–140.

Bailey, D.B. (1984). A triaxial model of the interdisciplinary team and group process. *Exceptional Children, 5*(1), 17–25.

Baumgartner, D. (1993). Thanks for asking: Parent comments about homework, tests, and grades. *Exceptionality, 4*(3), 177–186.

Brennan, J., & Lynch, S. (1993). *Breaking new ground: Carving new forms for resolving conflict. Project SEED* (Report No. CG 025 025). Portland: Maine Center for Educational Services. (ERIC Document Reproduction Service No. ED 361 630)

Brotherson, M.J. (1984, October). *Future planning in families of adolescents with severe disabilities.* Paper presented at the meeting of The Association for Persons with Severe Handicaps, Chicago.

Buckner, A.E. (1992). *Empowering parents of junior high school resource students with specific learning disabilities during the individual education plan process. Practicum report* (Report No. EC 301 664). Ft. Lauderdale, FL: Nova University. (ERIC Document Reproduction Service No. 351 837)

Carney, I.H., Snell, M.E., & Gressard, C.F. (1986). *Parent involvement in IEPs: The relationship between student age and parent preferences.* Unpublished manuscript, University of Virginia, Charlottesville.

Carter, E.A., & McGoldrick, M. (Eds.). (1980). *The family life cycle: A framework for family therapy.* New York: Gardner Press.

Child Development Resources. (1989). *The transdisciplinary arena assessment process.* [Videotape]. Lightfoot, VA: Child Development Resources.

Colorado State Department of Education. (1993). *Part H of the Individuals with Disabilities Education Act (IDEA) for infants, toddlers, and their families annual performance report, year V (1991–1993).* Denver, CO: Division of Special Education Services.

Cone, J.D., DeLawyer, D.D., & Wolfe, V.V. (1985). Assessing parent participation: The parent/family involvement index. *Exceptional Parent, 51*(5), 417–424.

Cooper, K.L., & Rascon, L. (1994, March). *Building positive relationships on the border with parents of special students: Effective practices for the IEP* (Report No. RC 019 597). Austin, TX: 14th Annual American Council on Rural Special Education Conference. (ERIC Document Reproduction Service No. ED 369 627)

Demchak, M.A. (1995). Evaluating transdisciplinary teaming for students with disabilities. *Rural Special Education Quarterly, 14*(1), 24–32.

DeMyer, M.K., & Goldberg, P. (1983). Family needs of the autistic adolescent. In E. Schopler & G.B. Mesibov (Eds.), *Autism in adolescents and adults* (pp. 225–250). New York: Plenum.

Duvall, E. (1957). *Family development.* Philadelphia: J.B. Lippincott.

Education for All Handicapped Children Act of 1975, PL 94-142. 20, U.S.C. §1400 *et seq.*

Education of the Handicapped Act Amendments of 1986, PL 99-457. 20 U.S.C. §1400 *et seq.*

Elliott, S.N., & Sheridan, S.M. (1992). Consultation and teaming: Problem-solving among educators, parents, and support personnel. *Elementary School Journal, 92*(3), 315–338.

Erikson, E. (1959). *Identity and the life cycle.* New York: International Universities Press.

Ferrara, D.M. (1979). Attitudes of parents of mentally retarded children toward normalization activities. *American Journal of Mental Deficiency, 84*(2), 145–151.

Fisher, R., & Ury, W. (1983). *Getting to yes.* New York: Penguin Books.

Florida State Department of Special Education. (1992). *Mediation in special education: Technical assistance paper* (Report No. EC 301 852). Tallahassee: Bureau of Education for Exceptional Students. (ERIC Document Reproduction Service No. ED 354 675)

Foxx, R.M., & Azrin, N.H. (1973). *Toilet training the retarded: A rapid approach for daytime and nighttime independent toileting.* Champaign, IL: Research Press.

Fuqua, R.W., Hegland, S.M., & Karas, S.C. (1985). Processes influencing linkages between preschool handicap classrooms and homes. *Exceptional Children, 51*(4), 307–314.

Giangreco, M.F. (1994). Dressing your IEPs for the general education climate: Analysis of IEP goals and objectives for students with multiple disabilities. *Remedial and Special Education, 15*(5) 288–296.

Girdner, L.K., & Eheart, B.K. (1984). Mediation with families having a handicapped child. *Family Relations, 33*(1), 187–194.

Goldfarb, L.A., Brotherson, M.J., Summers, J.A., & Turnbull, A.P. (1986). *Meeting the challenge of disability and chronic illness: A family guide.* Baltimore: Paul H. Brookes Publishing Co.

Goldstein, S. (1993). The IEP conference: Little things mean a lot. *Teaching Exceptional Children, 26*(1), 60–61.

Greenspan, S.I. (1988). Fostering emotional development in infants with disabilities. *Zero to Three, 9*(1), 8–18.

Halvorsen, A.T., Doering, K., Farron-Davis, F., Usilton, R., & Sailor, W. (1989). The role of parents and family members in planning severely disabled students' transitions from school. In G.H.S. Singer & L.K. Irvin (Eds.), *Support for caregiving families: Enabling positive adaptation to disability* (pp. 253–267). Baltimore: Paul H. Brookes Publishing Co.

Hanline, M.F. (1991). Transitions and critical events in the family life cycle: Implications for providing support to families of children with disabilities. *Psychology in the Schools, 28*(1), 53–59.

Harry, B. (1995). Communication versus compliance: African-American parents' involvement in special education. *Exceptional Children, 61*(4), 364–377.

Hill, J., Seyfarth, J., Orelove, F., Wehman, P., & Banks, D. (1985). Factors influencing parents' vocational aspirations for their mentally retarded children. In P. Wehman & J.W. Hill (Eds.), *Competitive employment for persons with mental retardation* (pp. 315–331). Richmond: Virginia Commonwealth University, Rehabilitation Research and Training Center.

Holroyd, J. (1974). The questionnaire on resources and stress: An instrument to measure family responses to a handicapped member. *Journal of Community Psychology, 2,* 92–94.

Individuals with Disabilities Education Act (IDEA) of 1990, PL 101-476, 20 U.S.C. §1400 *et seq.*

Individuals with Disabilities Education Act Amendments of 1991, PL 102-119, 20 U.S.C. § 1400 *et seq.*

Kaiser, C.E., & Hayden, A.H. (1984). Clinical research and policy issues in parenting severely handicapped infants. In J. Blacher (Ed.), *Severely handicapped young children and their families* (pp. 275–318). New York: Academic Press.

Katsiyannis, A., & Ward, T.J. (1992). Parent participation in special education: Compliance issues as reported by parent surveys and state compliance reports. *Remedial and Special Education (RASE), 13*(5), 50–55.

Kraft, S.P. (1985, November). *Family adaptation to severely handicapping conditions.* Paper presented at the meeting of The Association for Persons with Severe Handicaps, Boston.

Lewis, M., Marine, L., & Van Horn, G. (1992). *Parent involvement in the special education process: A synopsis of exemplary models. CASE information dissemination packet* (Report No. EC 302 211). Bloomington: Indiana University, Department of Special Education. (ERIC Document Reproduction Service No. ED 358 647)

Leyser, Y., & Cole, K.B. (1984). Perceptions of parents of handicapped children about school and parent–teacher partnership. *The Exceptional Child, 31*(3), 193–201.

Lynch, E.W., & Stein, P. (1982). Perspectives on parent participation in special education. *Exceptional Education Quarterly, 3*(2), 56–63.

McGonigel, M.J., Woodruff, G., & Roszmann-Millican, M. (1994). The transdisciplinary team: A model for family-centered early intervention. In L.J. Johnson, R.J. Gallagher, M.J. LaMontagne, J.B. Jordan, J.J. Gallagher, P.L. Hutinger, & M.B. Karnes (Eds.), *Meeting early intervention challenges: Issues from birth to three* (2nd ed., pp. 95–131). Baltimore: Paul H. Brookes Publishing Co.

Michael, M.G. (1992). Influences on teachers' attitudes of the parents' role as collaborator. *Remedial and Special Education (RASE), 13*(2), 24–30.

Mitchell, V. (1992). *A qualitative study of training in conflict resolution and cooperative learning in an alternative high school* (Report No. UD 028 808). New York: Columbia University Teachers College. (ERIC Document Reproduction Service No. ED 359 273)

Morton, M.V., Everson, J.M., & Moon, M.S. (1987). Guidelines for training parents as part of interagency transition planning teams. In J.M. Everson, M. Barcus, M.S. Moon, & M.V. Morton (Eds.), *Achieving outcomes: A guide to interagency training in transition and supported employment* (pp. 125–142). Richmond: Rehabilitation Research and Training Center, Virginia Commonwealth University.

New York State Education Department. (1992). *Special education mediation: Real solutions where everyone wins* (Report No. EC 301 510). Albany: New York State Education Department, Office of Special Education Services. (ERIC Document Reproduction Services No. ED 349 764)

Office of Special Education and Rehabilitative Services. (1993). *Implementation of the Individuals with Disabilities Education Act: Fifteenth annual report to Congress.* Washington, DC: U.S. Department of Education.

Olson, D.H., McCubbin, H.I., Barnes, H., Larsen, A., Muxen, M., & Wilson, M. (1983). *Families: What makes them work.* Beverly Hills, CA: Sage Publications.

Oster, A. (1984). Keynote address. In *Equals in this partnerships: Parents of disabled and at-risk infants and toddlers speak to professionals* (pp. 26–32). Washington, DC: National Center for Clinical Infant Programs.

Ruppman, J. (1990, June). *What parents have to teach professionals.* Paper presented at the conference "Where the Heart Is: Home, Family, and People with Disabilities," Virginia Institute for Developmental Disabilities, Virginia Commonwealth University, Richmond.

Seltzer, M.M. (1989, Spring). Lifelong care, aging family study yields new data. *Newsletter of the University Affiliated Program for Persons with Developmental Disabilities.* (Available from the University of Georgia University Affiliated Program, Athens).

Simons, R. (1987). *After the tears: Parents talk about raising a child with a disability.* San Diego, CA: Harcourt Brace Jovanovich.

Sloper, P., Cunningham, C.C., & Arnljotsdottir, M. (1983). Parental reactions to early intervention with their Down syndrome infants. *Child: Care, Health, and Development, 9*(6), 357–376.

Slovic, R. (Ed.). (1982). *Parent primer: Secondary programs for students with severe disabilities* (Report No. EC 230 587). Eugene: Oregon University. (ERIC Document Reproduction Service No. 318 182)

Solomon, M. (1973). A developmental, conceptual premise for family therapy. *Family Process, 12*, 179–188.

Sowers, J. (1989). Critical parent roles in supported employment. In G.H.S. Singer & L.K. Irvin (Eds.), *Support for caregiving families: Enabling positive adaptation to disability* (pp. 269–282). Baltimore: Paul H. Brookes Publishing Co.

Stremel, K. (1992). *An integrated parent–teacher-related service team approach to communication intervention. Final report* (Report No. EC 301 769). Hattiesburg: University of Southern Mississippi, Department of Special Education. (ERIC Document Reproduction Service No. ED 354 637)

Suelzle, M.J., & Keenan, V. (1981). Changes in family support networks over the life cycle of mentally retarded persons. *American Journal of Mental Deficiency, 86*, 267–274.

Symington, G.T. (1995). *Mediation as an option in special education. Final report* (Report No. EC 303 667). Alexandria, VA: National Association of State Directors of Special Education. (ERIC Document Reproduction Service No. ED 378 768)

Trout, M., & Foley, G. (1989). Working with families of handicapped infants and toddlers. *Topics in Language Disorders, 10*(1), 57–67.

Turnbull, A.P., Summers, J.A., & Brotherson, M.J. (1986). Family life cycle: Theoretical and empirical implications and future directions for families with mentally retarded members. In J.J. Gallagher & P.M. Vietze (Eds.), *Families of handicapped persons: Research, programs, and policy issues* (pp. 45–65). Baltimore: Paul H. Brookes Publishing Co.

Turnbull, A.P., & Turnbull, H.R., III (1990). *Families, professionals, and exceptionality: A special partnership* (2nd ed.). Columbus, OH: Charles E. Merrill.

Turnbull, H.R., Turnbull, A.P., Bronicki, G.J., Summers, J.A., & Roeder-Gordon, C. (1989). *Disability and the family: A guide to decisions for adulthood.* Baltimore: Paul H. Brookes Publishing Co.

U.S. Bureau of the Census. (1992). *1990 U.S. census and projections.* Washington, DC: U.S. Government Printing Office.

Vincent, L.J., & Salisbury, C.L. (1989). Changing economic and social influences on family involvement. *Topics in Early Childhood Special Education, 8*(1), 48–59.

Wiegle, L. (1990, June). *What parents have to teach professionals.* Paper presented at the conference "Where the Heart Is: Home, Family, and People with Disabilities," Virginia Institute for Developmental Disabilities, Virginia Commonwealth University, Richmond.

Wikler, L., Wasow, M., & Hatfield, E. (1981). Chronic sorrow revisited: Parents' vs. professionals' depiction of the adjustment of parents of mentally retarded children. *American Journal of Orthopsychiatry, 51*(1), 63–70.

Winton, P., & Turnbull, A.P. (1981). Parent involvement as viewed by parents of preschool handicapped children. *Topics in Early Childhood Special Education, 1*, 11–19.

Index

Page numbers followed by "f" indicate figures; those followed by "t" indicate tables.

Behavioral seizure observation records, 186, 187*f*
Behavioral support plans, 403
Behavioral test procedures, 426
Behind-the-ear (BTE) hearing aids, 437
Big Red Switch, 130*f*, 130–132
BIGmack Single Message Communication Aid, 130*f*, 130–132
Biobehavioral state, 39–42
Bird feeding, 323
Birth and early childhood
 family life cycle stage, 461–464
 stage characteristics, 461
Bite, tonic, 306
Bladder management, 353–356
Bladder training, 347–348
 accident treatment during, 348
 sequence for, 347*t*
Bleeding, 204
Blindisms, 434
Blindness, 414
 legal, 414
 partial, 414
BOA, *see* Behavioral observation audiometry
Body mechanics, 110–113
 for lifting, 111–113, 112*f*, 113*f*
Body scheme, 35
Body-worn (BW) hearing aids, 437
Book holders, 128, 128*f*, 140
Bowel evacuation, 356–357
Bowel management, 356–358
Box-type potty chair, 344, 345*f*
Braces, 108–110
Brain electrical activity mapping (BEAM), 177
Brain injury, 201–203
 signs and first aid treatment for, 201, 202*t*–203*t*
Brain neuroimaging, 176
Brainstorming, 456
Breathing control, 2–3
Brief cleanliness training procedure, 348
BTE hearing aids, *see* Behind-the-ear hearing aids
BW hearing aids, *see* Body-worn hearing aids

Calendar box, 397*f*, 397–398
Canal hearing aids, 437
Capabilities, determining, 387–389
Carbamazepine (Tegretol), 233*t*
Card holders, 140, 142*f*
Caregivers, 6
Casts, 108–110
Catheterization, clean intermittent, 227–229, 355–356
Catheters
 condom, 355
 external, 355
Celontin (methsuximide), 233*t*

Central auditory disorders, 417
Cerebral palsy
 children with
  face washing, 80, 82*f*
  handling, 83–95
  matching therapeutic positions with daily living activities for, 104–105, 105*f*–107*f*
  positioning, 95–110
  strategies for dressing, 364–365
  teaching protective reactions to, 90–91, 91*f*
 classification, 48–49
 diagnostic terms, 48–49, 49*t*
Chaining, 316
Chairs, adapted
 positioning in, 96–104
 sitting in, 98, 99*f*
Challenges, 25–28
 deciding on, 389–390
 determining, 387–389
Challenging behaviors, handling, 402–403
Change, resistance to, 28
Characterization, 441
Checklists
 of dressing skills, 360, 361*f*
 on group dynamics related to teams, 25, 26*f*
 on personal dynamics related to teams, 25, 25*f*
 for seated positioning, 97*f*, 98
Chest thrust, 200*f*, 200–201
Chewing, rotary, 304
Child abuse, 204–210
 detecting and reporting, 206–207
 deterrents, 209–210
 ecological model of, 206
 increased risk of, 205–206
 nature and extent of, 205–206
 prevention and intervention of, 206–210
 signs of, 207, 208*t*
 transdisciplinary team issues on, 210
Childhood
 early, family life cycle stage, 461–464
 family life cycle stage, 464–468
 stage characteristics of, 467
Children with multiple disabilities
 classification systems for, 48–51
 communicable diseases among, 164, 166*t*–167*t*
 determining capabilities and challenges for, 387–389
 discrepancies between typical families and families with, 469
 educational teaming models for people who serve, 8–11
 involvement in school system, adjusting to, 464–467
 needs of, 1–4, 51–61
 physical characteristics of, 469–470